D0833376

THE ROUGH GUIDE TO

Wales

written and researched by

Paul Whitfield, Mike Parker and Catherine Le Nevez

with additional contributions by

Tim Burford and Norm Longley

roughguides.com

Contents

OPPOSITE HILL WALKER IN SNOWDONIA **PREVIOUS PAGE** SURFING ON A WELSH BEACH

Introduction to
Wales

Perched on the rocky fringe of western Europe, Wales packs a lot of physical beauty into its small mass of land: its mountain ranges, lush valleys, ragged coastline, old-fashioned market towns and ancient castles all invite long and repeated visits. The culture, too, is compelling, whether in its Welsh- or English-language manifestations, its Celtic or its industrial traditions, its ancient cornerstones of belief or its contemporary chutzpah. Wales often gets short shrift in comparison to its Celtic cousins of Ireland and Scotland. Neither so internationally renowned nor so romantically perceived, the country is usually defined by its male voice choirs and tightly packed pit villages. But there's far more to the place than the hackneyed stereotypes and, at its best, Wales is the most beguiling part of the British Isles. Even its comparative anonymity serves it well: where the tourist pound has swept away some of the more gritty aspects of local life in parts of Ireland and Scotland, reducing ancient cultures to misty Celtic pastiche, Wales remains brittle and brutal enough to be real, and diverse enough to remain endlessly fascinating.

Recent years have seen a huge and dizzying upsurge in Welsh self-confidence, a commodity no longer so dependent upon comparison with its big and powerful neighbour of England. Popular culture – especially music and film – has contributed much to this revival, as has the arrival of a **National Assembly** in 1999, the first all-Wales tier of government for six hundred years. After centuries of enforced subjugation, the national spirit is undergoing a remarkable renaissance. The ancient symbol of the country, *y ddraig goch* or the **red dragon**, seen fluttering on flags everywhere in Wales, is waking up from what seems like a very long slumber.

As soon as you cross the border from England into Wales, the differences in appearance, attitude and culture between the two countries are immediately obvious. Wales shares many physical and emotional similarities with the other Celtic lands – Scotland, Ireland,

FACT FILE

• With an **area** of 8000 square miles (20,800 square km), Wales is less than a sixth the size of England and a little larger than New Jersey.

• While Wales is part of the United Kingdom and a member state of the European Union, it also has its own devolved **Welsh Government**, responsible for certain local affairs.

• The **population** of Wales is around three million, sixty percent of whom live in the southeastern corner of the country. One quarter of the population of Wales was born out of the country, the vast majority being migrants from England. Cardiff, the capital city, has a population of 300,000.

• Wales is officially a **bilingual** nation. Everyone speaks English and almost a quarter of the population also speak Welsh, the strongest survivor of the Celtic languages. The vast majority of Welsh-speakers are concentrated in the north and west of the country.

• Wales was a largely **Anglican** nation (attending the Church in Wales) until Nonconformism swept Wales between the seventeenth and nineteenth centuries. This spawned many different divisions of Methodists, Baptists and Calvinists, as can be seen in the legacy of chapels everywhere in the country.

Cornwall, Brittany, and even Asturias and Galicia in northwest Spain. A rocky and mountainous landscape, whose colours are predominantly grey and green, a thinly scattered, largely rural population, a culture rooted deeply in folklore and legend and the survival of a distinct, ancient language are all hallmarks of Wales and its sister countries. To visitors, it is the **Welsh language**, the strongest survivor of the Celtic tongues, that most obviously marks out the country with tongue-twisting village names and vast bilingual signposts. Everyone in Wales speaks English, but a quarter of the population also speaks Welsh: TV and radio stations broadcast in it, all children learn it at school, restaurant menus are increasingly bilingual and visitors too are encouraged to try speaking at least a fragment of the rich, earthy tones of one of Europe's oldest living languages.

After Wales' seven-hundred-year subjugation at the hands of its far larger and more powerful neighbour, many Welsh nationalists call for, if not outright divorce from England, at least a trial separation. The mutual antipathy is almost all good-natured, but often the greatest offence to Welsh people is when those very obvious differences are blatantly disregarded or patronized. Avoid referring to England when you really mean Britain or the United Kingdom, and **don't say English when you mean Welsh**: it is like calling a Kiwi an Aussie or a Canadian an American (probably worse).

Although it is the wealth of prehistoric sites, crumbling castles and wild landscapes that brings visitors here in the first place, they often leave championing **contemporary Wales**. The cities and university towns throughout the country are buzzing with an understated youthful confidence and sense of cultural optimism, while a generation or two of "New Age" migrants has brought a curious cosmopolitanism to the small market towns of mid-Wales and the west. Although conservative and traditional forces still sporadically clash with these more liberal and anarchic strands of thought, there's an unquestionable feeling that Wales is big enough, both physically and emotionally, to embrace such diverse influences. Perhaps most importantly of all, Welsh

culture is underpinned by an iconoclastic democracy that contrasts starkly with the establishment-obsessed class divisions of England. The Welsh character is famously endowed with a **musicality**, lyricism, introspection and sentimentality that produces far better bards and singers than it does lords and masters. And Welsh culture is undeniably inclusive: anything from a sing-song in the pub to the grandiose theatricality of an **eisteddfod** involves everyone – including any visitor eager to learn and join in.

Where to go

Only 160 miles from north to south and 50 miles from east to west, Wales is smaller than Massachusetts and only half the size of the Netherlands. Most of its inhabitants are packed into the southern quarter of the country, a fact which will largely dictate where you travel and what you do. Like all capital cities, **Cardiff** is atypical of the rest of the country. Most

PREHISTORIC AND LEGENDARY WALES

Whether trudging through a dew-soaked field to some mysteriously inscribed **standing stone**, or catching the afternoon sun as it illumines the entrance to a cliff-top **burial chamber**, exploring Wales' prehistoric sites is thoroughly rewarding. At all but a few of the most popular, the bleating of sheep will be the only sound to break the contemplative silence of these spiritual places.

Prehistoric sites litter Wales. **Hut circles** defensively set atop windswept hills attest to a rugged hand-to-mouth pre-Celtic existence dating back four or five thousand years, while stone circles, intricately carved **monoliths** and finely balanced capstones set at crucial points on **ancient pathways** suggest the more spiritual life led by the priestly druids. Britain's greatest **druidic** centre was Anglesey, and the island is still home to many of Wales' best prehistoric sites, including the splendid chambers of Barclodiad y Gawres and Bryn Celli Ddu. Elsewhere, numerous standing stones and circles can be found on the mysterious slopes of the Mynydd Preseli in Pembrokeshire and in the area around Harlech in north Wales. Many sites take their names from great figures in Celtic history and folklore, such as Arthur and Merlin (Myrddin in Welsh); legends abound to connect much of the landscape with ancient tales.

national institutions are based here, not least the infant National Assembly, housed in brand-new splendour amid the massive regeneration projects of **Cardiff Bay**. The city is also home to the National Museum and St Fagans National History Museum – both excellent introductions to the character of the rest of Wales – and the superb Millennium Stadium, the home of huge sporting events and blockbuster gigs. The only other centres of appreciable size are loud-and-lairy **Newport** and breezy, resurgent **Swansea**, lying respectively to the east and west of the capital. All three cities grew as ports, mainly exporting millions of tons of coal and iron from the **Valleys**, where fiercely proud industrial communities were built up in the thin strips of land between the mountains.

Much of Wales' appeal lies outside the larger towns, where there is ample evidence of the warmongering which has shaped the country's development. Castles are everywhere, from the hard little stone keeps of the early Welsh princes to Edward I's incomparable series of thirteenth-century fortresses at **Flint**, **Rhuddlan**, **Conwy**, **Beaumaris**, **Caernarfon** and **Harlech**, and grandiose Victorian piles where grouse were the only enemy. Fortified residences served as the foundation for a number of the stately homes that dot the country, but many castles were deserted and remain dramatically isolated on rocky knolls, most likely on spots previously occupied by prehistoric communities. Passage graves and **stone circles** offer a more tangible link to the pre-Roman era when the priestly order of Druids ruled over early Celtic peoples, and later religious monuments such as the great ruined abbeys of **Valle Crucis**, **Tintern** and **Strata Florida** lend a gaunt grandeur to their surroundings.

Whether you're admiring castles, megaliths or Dylan Thomas' home at **Laugharne**, almost everything in Wales is enhanced by the beauty of the countryside, from the lowland greenery of meadows and river valleys to the inhospitable heights of the moors and mountains. The rigid backbone of the **Cambrian Mountains** terminates in the soaring peaks of **Snowdonia** and the angular ridges of the **Brecon Beacons**, both superb walking country and both national parks. A third national park follows the

LAND OF SONG

"Praise the Lord! We are a musical nation," intones the Rev. Eli Jenkins in Dylan Thomas' masterpiece, *Under Milk Wood*. It's a reputation of which the Welsh feel deservedly proud. Although plucky miners singing their way to the pithead was the dewy-eyed fabrication of Hollywood (*How Green Was My Valley*), Wales does make a great deal more noise, and make it a great deal more tunefully, than most other small countries.

The country's male voice choirs, many struggling to survive in the aftermath of the decimation of the coal industry that spawned them, are the best-known exemplars of Welsh singing, but traditions go much further back, to the bards and minstrels of the Celtic age. Wales continues to nurture big voices and big talent: from the hip-swivelling Sir Tom Jones and show-stopping Dame Shirley Bassey to anarchistic rockers the Manic Street Preachers and young divas like Charlotte Church, Katherine Jenkins and Duffy.

Pembrokeshire Coast, where golden strands are separated by rocky bluffs overlooking offshore bird colonies. Much of the rest of the coast remains unspoilt, though seldom visited, with long sweeps of sand often backed by traditional British seaside resorts: the **north Wales coast**, the **Cambrian coast** and the **Gower peninsula** have a notable abundance. The entire coast is now linked by the 860-mile **All-Wales Coast Path**: be sure to spend some time along its length.

When to go

The English preoccupation with the weather holds equally for the Welsh. The **climate** (see p.49) here is temperate, with Welsh summers rarely getting hot and nowhere but the tops of mountain ranges ever getting very cold, even in midwinter. Temperatures vary little, but proximity to the mountains is a different matter: Llanberis, at the foot of Snowdon, gets doused with more than twice as much rainfall as Caernarfon, seven miles away, and is always a few degrees cooler. For much of the summer, Wales – particularly the coast – can be bathed in sun. Between June and September, the Pembrokeshire coast, washed by the Gulf Stream, can be as warm as anywhere in Britain. The bottom line is that it's impossible to say with any degree of certainty that the weather will be pleasant in any given month. May might be wet and grey one year and gloriously sunny the next, and the same goes for the autumnal months – November stands an equal chance of being crisp and clear or foggy and grim. If you're planning to lie on a beach, or camp in the dry, you'll want to go in **summer** – between June and September – a period when you should book your accommodation as far in advance as possible. For reasonably good weather with less dense **crowds** go in April, May, September or October. For **outdoor pursuits** you'll find June to October the warmest and driest for walking and climbing.

LEFT DAME SHIRLEY BASSEY

Author picks

During our authors' travels throughout the country, they have discovered their own personal favourites among places, pubs, walks, nature reserves, beaches, railway journeys and much more.

Snowdonia's finest scramble The north ridge of Tryfan gives wonderful exposure and great views; bordering on rock-climbing territory. **p.348**

The grimmest beauty A dinky steam railway runs past Blaenau Ffestiniog's hard grey terraces nestled below great slopes of slate waste. **p.368**

Sublime views Admire the Menai Strait and its historic bridges with the Snowdonia mountains as backdrop. **p.422**

Skeletal grandeur Ride Newport's Transporter Bridge, "A giant with the might of Hercules and the grace of Apollo", as it was described when it opened in 1906. **p.73**

Birds flocking together Watch red kites swoop for their daily feed at Gigrin Farm near Rhayader. **p.234**

Buy a pint from Bessie Spend an evening at the quirky *Dyffryn Arms* in bucolic Cwm Gwaun. **p.197**

Stay in a medieval manor Spend the night at Gwydir Castle, really an ancestral manor house with just two baronial bedrooms. **p.346**

Coastal wonder Savour the glorious views of Worms Head and Rhossili Bay from the head of the Gower peninsula. **p.135**

Our author recommendations don't end here. We've flagged up our favourite places – a perfectly sited hotel, an atmospheric café, a special restaurant – throughout the Guide, highlighted with the ★ symbol.

FROM TOP TRAFFIC CONDITIONS IN BLAENAU FFESTINIOG; HIKER DESCENDING GLYDER FACH TOWARDS TRYFAN; DYFFRYN ARMS ("BESSIE'S")

28

things not to miss

It's not possible to see everything that Wales has to offer in one trip – and we don't suggest you try. What follows, in no particular order, is a selective taste of the country's highlights, including beautiful beaches, outstanding national parks, fascinating wildlife encounters and unforgettable urban experiences. All highlights have a page reference to take you straight into the Guide, where you can find out more.

1

1 CONWY
Page 408

One of north Wales' finest walled medieval towns, Conwy contains over two hundred listed buildings within its tight grid.

2 CADAIR IDRIS
Page 282

The dominant mountain of southern Snowdonia, Cadair Idris is a magnificent beast chock-full of classic glacial features.

3 GREEN MAN FESTIVAL
Page 217

Three wonderful days of new folk, American and indie music plus a range of workshops, performance art and comedy in green fields near Crickhowell.

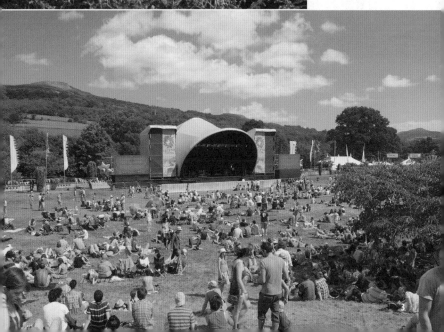

4 ABERYSTWYTH
Page 271
The capital of sparsely populated mid-Wales, Aberystwyth is a breezy and bright university and seaside town surrounded by luscious countryside.

5 MOUNTAIN BIKING AT COED Y BRENIN
Page 295
Some of Wales' finest singletrack and adrenalin-pumping descents through the forest combine with family trails, high-ropes adventures and even geocaching.

6 FFESTINIOG RAILWAY
Page 372
Of Wales' many "great little trains", the Ffestiniog Railway, winding down through the Snowdonia mountains, is one of the best.

7 ST DAVIDS CATHEDRAL
Page 183
The heart of Welsh spirituality, St Davids Cathedral is at Wales' westerly extremity and has drawn pilgrims for a millennium and a half.

8 MAWDDACH TRAIL
Page 295
Ride or walk this easy trail beside Wales' finest estuary, the Mawddach, crossed by the 2253ft rail and foot bridge into Barmouth.

9 CARREG CENNEN CASTLE
Page 152
The most romantic ruin in Wales, Carreg Cennen Castle sits in glorious isolation amid pastures grazed by Welsh longhorns.

10 PEMBROKESHIRE COAST PATH
Page 164

Break up this path around some of Wales' wildest coastal scenery into a series of day walks, or tackle the full 187 miles in one big push.

11 ST FAGANS NATIONAL HISTORY MUSEUM
Page 98

An unmissable chronicle of Welsh life, featuring period buildings from all over the country.

12 SNOWDON
Page 357

Hike one of half a dozen demanding tracks to the top of Wales' highest mountain – or take the train and sup a beer at the summit café.

13 TRYFAN
Page 348

Fabulous views along the Ogwen Valley in the wilds of Snowdonia are just one of the rewards for making the arduous ascent of Tryfan.

14 EDWARD I'S IRON RING
Page 410

The might of the thirteenth-century English monarchy found its fullest expression in this chain of virtually impregnable fortresses, now evocative hollow shells.

15 CARDIFF BAY ARCHITECTURE
Page 86

The wonderful Wales Millennium Centre and National Assembly Building are just two of many striking modern structures around the rejuvenated Cardiff Bay.

16 PORTMEIRION
Page 375

The grandest folly of them all, Portmeirion is a gorgeous visual poem that will melt the hardest heart.

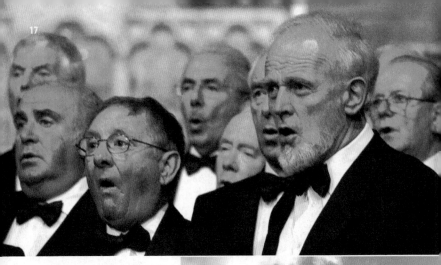

17 MALE VOICE CHOIRS
Page 119

Burly miners singing their hearts out at eisteddfodau may be a thing of the past, but Welsh male voice choirs still survive and thrive.

18 THE WYE VALLEY
Page 60

Soak up the pastoral beauty of this wonderful valley and sense why Wordsworth was so moved as you wander past Tintern Abbey.

19 THE VALLEYS
Page 106

Colourful terraces of housing, hunkered down under the hills, are the hallmark of Wales' world-famous Valleys, the old mining area in the south.

20 A WELSH OAK WOOD
Page 454

Once the sacred place of the druids, the twisty oak woods of Wales, often with lively streams burbling through, clear the mind and soul.

21 ABERGAVENNY'S FOOD
Page 221

Sample some of the best morsels Wales has to offer in this gastronomic hotspot or, better still, time your visit to coincide with September's food festival, among the best in Britain.

22 BIG PIT
Page 109

Plunge into the depths of coal-bearing earth in this superb evocation of what life was like for vast numbers of Valleys miners.

20

21

22

27

28

HARDBACKS 50ᵖ
PAPERBACKS 30ᵖ

Itineraries

Our Grand Tour is ideal for a first visit to Wales, taking in a sampling of the best cities and towns, the country's industrial heritage and its superb mountain and coastal scenery. Fans of Neolithic cromlechs, ruined abbeys and stately homes should follow our Historic Buildings itinerary, while the more energetic will want to sample items on our Active Wales menu.

GRAND TOUR OF WALES

If you've only got ten days and want to tick off Wales' acknowledged highlights, hit these.

① Blaenafon South Wales' industrial heritage: the powerful Big Pit mining museum and the evocative ruins of the Ironworks. **See p.108**

② Cardiff Ground-breaking architecture, top-notch culture and blistering nightlife in the cool Welsh capital. **See p.78**

③ Gower Welsh natural heritage at its most stunning, the Gower peninsula boasts wide-open beaches, rocky bays and steep cliffs. **See p.130**

④ St Davids peninsula Sample some of the finest sections of the Pembrokeshire Coast Path, and stay in delightful St Davids. **See p.183**

⑤ Cadair Idris The folds of this fine mountain harbour old castles, churches and a steam railway, the Centre for Alternative Technology and the sublime Mawddach Estuary. **See p.282**

⑥ Snowdonia Hard-working narrow-gauge railways, slate-mining heritage and nuggety villages in inspiring mountain scenery. **See p.336**

⑦ Portmeirion The whimsical Italianate beauty of Clough Williams-Ellis' "home for fallen buildings". **See p.375**

⑧ Conwy and Llandudno A domineering castle and ancient houses within an intact ring of walls make Conwy an essential stop, best

visited from Llandudno, with its grand seaside architecture, and blustery walks on the Great Orme. **See p.403**

⑨ Llangollen A canal aqueduct, a heritage railway, a hilltop castle, an abbey ruin and the home of the Ladies of Llangollen all wedged into a bucolic valley. **See p.312**

HISTORIC BUILDINGS

Edward I's massive castles across north Wales and the wonderful St Davids Cathedral are well known and covered elsewhere: here are a few equally fascinating monuments which can be inspected in a week or so.

① Tintern Abbey Admire the wonderful roofless ruin that inspired Wordsworth's lines, by the placid River Wye. **See p.64**

② Soar-y-Mynydd chapel Wales' most remote chapel, in the wild countryside of Mynydd Eppynt. **See p.229**

③ Carreg Cennen The most wonderfully sited of all the native Welsh castles, high on a cliff. **See p.152**

④ Pentre Ifan Wales' largest burial stone with its 16ft-long top-stone precariously balanced on stone legs. **See p.195**

⑤ Penrhyn Castle, Bangor Old masters in a grandiose Victorian mansion that loves to show off its slate-mining wealth. **See p.417**

ABOVE FROM LEFT MAWDDACH RAIL BRIDGE; SOAR-Y-MYNYDD CHAPEL, NEAR LLANDOVERY

6 Plas Mawr, Conwy A superb example of an Elizabethan town house. **See p.411**

7 Plas Newydd, Llangollen Fascinating mock-Tudor bolt hole of two aristocratic Anglo-Irish ladies. **See p.316**

8 Erddig, Wrexham A *Downton Abbey* feel to the relationship between servants and masters at this stately home. **See p.311**

ACTIVE WALES

You'll enjoy that slice of bara brith or pint of Purple Moose all the more if you've earned it hiking, biking or surfing. Set aside a week or more.

1 Whitewater rafting: Cardiff Abundant thrills and spills on these superb man-made rapids. **See p.90**

2 Surfing: Gower Suit up and surf some of the UK's finest waves among the bays and beaches of the glorious peninsula. **See p.136**

3 Coasteering: St Davids peninsula Jump off rocks into the sea, swim across bays and explore caves. **See p.185**

4 Walking: Pembrokeshire Coast Path Spend a few hours or a few weeks exploring the gorgeous coves, windswept headlands and long beaches of this magical coastal walk. **See p.164**

5 Mine exploring: Corris Get kitted out with harness and headlamp and listen to arcane tales of mining life in an abandoned slate mine. **See p.286**

6 Mountain biking: Coed y Brenin Among the very best of many fine places to ride off-road in Wales. **See p.295**

7 Rock climbing: Llanberis Pass The ultimate mountain challenge in the home of Welsh rock climbing; some climbers engage the guiding services of nearby Plas y Brenin. **See p.348 & p.358**

8 Walking: Offa's Dyke Path Set aside a couple of weeks if you want to tackle the whole of this classic 177-mile long-distance walk which largely follows the ancient earthwork along the English border. **See p.240**

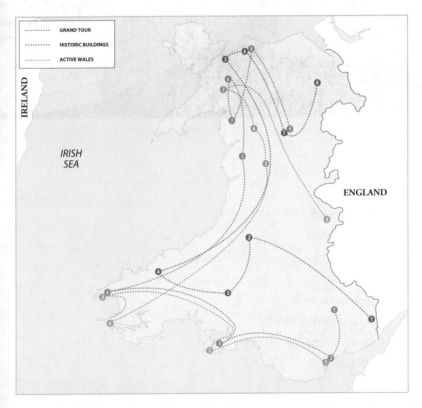

STRAW BOATER AT BRECON JAZZ FESTIVAL

Basics

Getting there

Wales is easily reached from the rest of the UK, Ireland and continental Europe with flights into Cardiff Airport. There are no direct flights to Wales from outside Europe, so you're best off flying to England and continuing overland from there. The widest choice is into London (Heathrow or Gatwick), though Manchester is better placed for north Wales and you might consider Birmingham for direct access to mid-Wales. Airfares are highest from May to August, when the weather is best; fares drop during the "shoulder" seasons (Sept and April) and drop further during the low season (Oct–March, excluding Christmas and New Year, when prices jump and seats are at a premium).

Crossing the border from England into Wales is straightforward, with train and bus services forming part of the British national network. The two roads providing the quickest access into the heart of the country are the **M4 motorway** in the south, and the **A55 expressway** in the north. Both are fast and busy; minor routes are more appealing if you aren't in too much of a hurry.

From Ireland, ferries are by far the cheapest and easiest way of getting to Wales. **From the rest of Europe**, alternatives to air travel are the traditional cross-Channel ferry services or the Channel Tunnel.

Flights from Europe

The only airport of any size in Wales is **Cardiff Airport** (Wwww.tbicardiffairport.com), 12 miles southwest of the capital, which has lots of flights to Mediterranean holiday destinations plus scheduled flights from selected British, Irish and European cities. The main international carriers are KLM (Wklm.com), which flies into Cardiff from Amsterdam; Aer Arann (Waerarann.com) from Cork, Dublin and Shannon; Eastern Airways (Weastern airways.com) from Aberdeen and Newcastle; and Air Southwest (Wairsouthwest.com) from Newquay in Cornwall, England. Many of the most useful routes run mostly business flights, timed and priced accordingly, and often not operating at weekends.

Flights from the US and Canada

Numerous airlines fly from the **eastern seaboard** and the **Midwest** to London, the principal British gateway for visitors to Wales. You'll also come across useful direct flights to Manchester and Birmingham, and lower airport taxes often mean cheaper fares. Several airlines – American, British Airways, United, Virgin and others – fly nonstop from **Los Angeles**. British Airways also fly direct to London from **San Diego**, **San Francisco** and **Seattle**, while other airlines offer easy connections.

Low-season round-trip **fares** from New York, Boston and Washington to London start at around US$650, though US$800 is more normal, and through the summer you can expect to pay over US$1000. Add US$100–200 from other eastern cities. Low-season fares from the West Coast start at a little under US$950, though expect more like US$1400 in peak summer and around Christmas.

In **Canada**, you'll get the best deal flying to London from the big gateway cities of Toronto and Montreal, where fares are Can$1000–1200 round-trip. British Airways fly direct to Heathrow from both Vancouver and Calgary while Air Canada have nonstop links from Vancouver, Calgary, Edmonton and Ottawa. From the west, fares range from Can$1100 to Can$1600.

Flights from Australia, New Zealand and South Africa

To get to Wales from Australia, New Zealand or South Africa you'll need to fly through London, or possibly Manchester in northern England.

The routes from **Australia** are a highly competitive, with flights via Southeast Asia or the Middle East generally being the cheapest options. Fares vary little from between major Australian cities, with Perth only a few dollars cheaper. The cheapest **scheduled return flights** are around Aus$1300 with Royal Brunei (though it takes a convoluted route via Brunei and Dubai). More direct routes cost Aus$2000–2400; good options include Etihad (via Abu Dhabi), Emirates (via Dubai) and Malaysian (via Kuala Lumpur). Korean Airlines are cheap but this involves a 20 hour stopover in Seoul. Singapore Airlines, Qantas/ British Airways, Thai (via Bangkok) and Cathay are usually a little pricier but not always.

If travelling from **New Zealand** via Asia, you can choose between most of the carriers listed above, plus Air New Zealand who fly to London via Shanghai. Prices via Asia are usually comparable with flights via North America. Air New Zealand fly to Heathrow via Los Angeles and do codeshares with United, Continental and others.

Air Canada operate a route via Vancouver. Fares with Brunei, Malaysian and Korean typically run around $2200–2500, with Air NZ usually NZ$2400–2700.

There are direct flights from **South Africa** to London Heathrow with South African Airways (Jo'burg and Cape Town), British Airways (Jo'burg and Cape Town) and Virgin Atlantic (Jo'burg). There are sometimes cheaper deals on indirect routes with Emirates (from Cape Town, Durban and Jo'burg via Dubai); Ethiopian (from Jo'burg via Addis Ababa); KLM (from Jo'burg via Amsterdam); and Lufthansa (from Jo'burg via Frankfurt). Return fares are generally in the ZAR7000–8000 bracket.

Agents and operators

Although you may want to see Wales at your own speed, you shouldn't dismiss the idea of a **package deal**. Many agents and airlines put together very flexible deals, sometimes amounting to nothing more restrictive than a flight plus accommodation and car or rail pass, and these can actually work out cheaper than making the same arrangements yourself on arrival. A package can also be great for your peace of mind, if only to ensure a worry-free first week while you're finding your feet for a longer tour.

There are hundreds of tour operators specializing in travel to the British Isles. Most can do packages of the standard highlights, but of greater interest are the outfits that help you explore Britain's unique points: many organize walking or cycling trips through the countryside, boat trips along canals, and any number of theme tours based around Britain's literary heritage, history, pubs, gardens, theatre, golf – you name it. A few of the possibilities are listed below, and a travel agent will be able to point out others. For a full listing, contact **Visit Wales** directly (see p.54).

Be sure to examine the fine print of any deal, and bear in mind that everything in brochures always sounds great. Choose only an operator that is a member of the United States Tour Operator Association (USTOA) or has been approved by the American Society of Travel Agents (ASTA).

WORLDWIDE

Contiki Tours ⓦ contiki.com. Organized tours with a party-like atmosphere geared toward 18–35-year-olds. Book through a travel agent.

Home at First ☎ 1 800 523 5842, ⓦ homeatfirst.com. Independent travel packages including airfare, ground transportation and cottage, house or apartment rental.

Select Travel Service ☎ 1 800 752 6787, ⓦ selecttravel.com. Customized history, literature, theatre, horticulture and other specialized tours.

IRELAND

Trailfinders Ireland ☎ 01/677 7888, ⓦ www.trailfinders.ie. One of the best-informed and most efficient agents for independent travellers.
USIT Ireland ☎ 01/602 1906, ⓦ www.usit.ie. Ireland's main student and youth travel specialists.

US AND CANADA

STA Travel ☎ 1 800 781 4040, ⓦ statravel.com. Worldwide specialist in independent travel; also student IDs, travel insurance, car rental, rail passes, etc.
TFI Tours ☎ 1 800 745 8000 or 212 736 1140, ⓦ tfitours.com. Consolidator with discount flights.
Travelers Advantage ☎ 1 800 835 8747, ⓦ travelersadvantage.com. Discount travel club; annual membership fee required (currently US$1 for a month-long trial).
Travel Cuts US ☎ 1 800 592 2887, Canada ☎ 1 800 667 2887; ⓦ travelcuts.com. Canadian student-travel organization.

AUSTRALIA, NZ AND SOUTH AFRICA

Adventure World ⓦ adventureworld.com.au and adventureworld.co.nz. Various tours around Wales and the rest of Britain including a Wye Valley cycling tour. Book through major travel agents.
Flight Centre Australia ☎ 133 133, ⓦ flightcentre.com.au; New Zealand ☎ 800 243 544, ⓦ flightcentre.co.nz; South Africa ☎ 0860 400727, ⓦ flightcentre.co.za. High-street agency frequently offering some of the lowest fares around.
STA Travel Australia ☎ 13 4782, ⓦ statravel.com.au; New Zealand ☎ 0800 474 400, ⓦ statravel.co.nz. A major player in student, youth and budget travel with branches in many universities.
Trailfinders Australia ☎ 1300 780 212, ⓦ trailfinders.com.au. Knowledgeable staff skilled at turning up odd itineraries and good prices.
Travel.com.au Australia ☎ 1300 130 483, ⓦ www.travel.com.au. Efficient, online and retail (in Sydney) travel agency offering good fares, hotels and car rental.

By train

We've covered details of train travel within the UK under "Getting around". What follows is a summary of services from Europe.

England has direct, high-speed passenger trains from France and Belgium via the 20-mile-long Channel Tunnel with **Eurostar** (☎ 08432 186186, ⓦ eurostar.com), which runs hourly between London (St Pancras), Stratford (east London),

---

A BETTER KIND OF TRAVEL

At Rough Guides we are passionately committed to travel. We feel that travelling is the best way to understand the world we live in and the people we share it with – plus tourism has brought a great deal of benefit to developing economies around the world over the last few decades. But the growth in tourism has also damaged some places irreparably, and climate change is exacerbated by most forms of transport, especially flying. All Rough Guides' trips are carbon-offset, and every year we donate money to a variety of charities devoted to combating the effects of climate change.

Ebbsfleet (Dartford, near the M25) and Paris, Lille and Brussels. The least expensive return fares to London, which are nonexchangeable and nonre-fundable, are €55 from Paris or Lille and €60 from Brussels. Semi-flexible return fares are €305 from Paris, €388 from Brussels and €285 from Lille. Nonexchangeable, nonrefundable youth tickets (for under-26s) cost from €70 from Paris, Brussels or Lille. Eurostar also offers frequent promotional fares, particularly for advance bookings, so it's always worth checking the website.

Drivers travelling between Calais and Folkestone can use **Le Shuttle** (from the UK ☎ 08443 353535, from other countries ☎ +33 (0)321002061, ⓦ euro tunnel.com), a vehicle-carrying train which whisks through the Channel Tunnel in 35 minutes. You can just turn up on the day you want to travel, but booking is advised and usually cheaper, especially at weekends. The one-way fare for a car and all its passengers starts from £53, with various flexi and short-stay discount return fares available.

By ferry

Ferries from Europe arrive at **ports in England**, usually with lower fares than using the Channel Tunnel. There are regular crossings with SeaFrance and P&O from Calais to Dover, the shortest route, for which the lowest return fare for a car and driver

is around £75, though you'll pay a lot more at busy times. For ferry routes and prices, contact the ferry companies direct or visit the excellent websites Seaview Ferries (ⓦ seaview.co.uk/ferries) and Direct Ferries (ⓦ directferries.co.uk).

There are four **Welsh ferry ports** all serving Ireland with large, spacious vessels: check-in is generally forty minutes before departure. Passenger fares are very competitive, with diverse special deals and midweek and advance purchase offers.

The busiest port is **Holyhead**, on the northwest tip of Wales, with ferries and fast catamarans from both Dublin and Dun Laoghaire (6 miles south of Dublin), though the fast cats often only run in the busiest summer months. Irish Ferries are usually a few pounds cheaper. Typically, the catamarans cost £30 each way for adults in high summer, and the ferries £5 less.

Fishguard has ferries from Rosslare (just outside Wexford), supplemented by fast catamarans in July and August.

The least busy ports are **Pembroke Dock**, with ferry connections from Rosslare, and **Swansea** with sailings from Cork.

Fastnet Line ☎ 0844 576 8831, ⓦ fastnetline.com.
Irish Ferries ☎ 08717 300 400, ⓦ irishferries.com.
P&O Ferries ☎ 08716 642121, ⓦ poferries.com.
Sea France ☎ 0871 423 7119, ⓦ seafrance.com.
Stena Line ☎ 08447 707070, ⓦ stenaline.com.

FERRY CONNECTIONS FROM IRELAND

Route	Company	Frequency	Duration
Cork–Swansea (ferry)	Fastnet	3–4 weekly	11hr 30min
Dublin–Holyhead (ferry)	Stena	4 daily	3hr 15min
Dublin–Holyhead (ferry)	Irish	2–3 daily	3hr 15min
Dublin–Holyhead (cat)	Irish	1 daily	1hr 50min
Dun Laoghaire–Holyhead (cat)	Stena	1 daily	2hr
Dun Laoghaire–Holyhead (ferry)	Stena	3–4 daily	3hr 15min
Dublin–Liverpool (ferry)	P&O	1–2 daily	8hr
Rosslare–Fishguard (ferry)	Stena	2 daily	3hr 30min
Rosslare–Fishguard (cat)	Stena	1 daily	2hr
Rosslare–Pembroke Dock (ferry)	Irish	2 daily	4hr

Getting around

The large cities and densely populated valleys of south Wales support comprehensive train and bus networks, but the more thinly populated areas of mid- and north Wales have to make do with skeletal services. Getting about by car is easy and, outside the cities, sheep and agricultural equipment are likely to be a more persistent problem than other road users. Take the more scenic backroads unless you're in a real hurry. Information for cyclists is listed in the outdoor activities section.

Trains

The train is one of the best ways to get to and around Wales; the views are superb and the engineering often impressive. In addition to the main-line network, there are over a dozen **narrow-gauge trains** (see box, p.29). Britain's trains are run by at least twenty **operators**, but all are required to work as a single network with integrated ticketing.

Travelling to Wales, most use the fast, frequent service from London Paddington to **Newport**, **Cardiff** and **Swansea**, operated by First Great Western. Very few direct trains from England go beyond Swansea, although connections at Newport, Cardiff or Swansea link up with services to Carmarthen and stations in Pembrokeshire. The **north coast service** from London Euston to Chester, Llandudno Junction, Bangor and Holyhead is operated by Virgin Trains. Arriva also runs a direct Manchester–Holyhead service along the north coast line. From other cities in England and Scotland, you'll probably need to change en route –

at Bristol for the south coast line, at Crewe for the north coast.

Journey times between main centres are short: London–Cardiff takes around two hours and London–Swansea around three hours. Heading for the north coast, the London–Holyhead service takes about four hours.

Within Wales, services cover all the main cities and a seemingly random selection of rural towns and wayside halts. As well as the two major lines discussed above (which also have several slower services) there is the **Cambrian Coast line** from Birmingham and Shrewsbury through Welshpool, Newtown and Machynlleth, beyond which it divides at Dyfi Junction. The southern spur goes a few miles to Borth and Aberystwyth, the northern one crawls up the coast through Tywyn, Barmouth, Harlech and Porthmadog to Pwllheli. Even slower (but very picturesque) is the second route from Shrewsbury, the **Heart of Wales line**, which runs through Knighton, Llandrindod Wells, Llanwrtyd Wells, Llandovery, Llandeilo and a host of tiny halts on the way to Llanelli and Swansea.

Apart from the major inter-city services from England, all services are run by **Arriva Trains Wales** with timetables covered in detail on **Traveline Cymru** (see p.29) and on the useful **See Wales by Bus and Train** map, free from tourist offices.

Services on all but the main north and south coast train lines are infrequent, and are occasionally replaced by buses on Sunday. At many smaller stations, ticket offices close at weekends, and in a lot of minor towns they've shut for good. In these instances, there's sometimes a vending machine on the platform. If there isn't a machine, you can buy your ticket on board – but if you've boarded at a station with a machine or ticket office and haven't bought a ticket, you're liable for an on-the-spot fine.

WALES' BEST DRIVES

You can't go far in Wales without experiencing great views, but if you're set on seeking out some of the very finest scenery, try these drives.
Wye Valley Savour the wooded gorge of the River Wye on a journey from Monmouth past Tintern Abbey to Chepstow.
Gospel Pass Take the narrow road over the roof of the Black Mountains from Abergavenny past Llanthony Priory to Hay-on-Wye.
Elan Valley and Cwmystwyth From Rhayader take the mountain road up past the reservoirs of the Elan Valley up to the blasted landscapes around Cwmystwyth and down past Devil's Bridge into the Vale of Rheidol.
Abergwesyn Pass Follow the ancient drovers' road over the spectacularly remote moorland of the Cambrian Mountains from Llanwrtyd Wells to Tregaron.
Marine Drive A short but wonderfully scenic loop around the Great Orme.

WALES' STEAM RAILWAYS: SIX OF THE BEST

With the rising demand for quarried stone in the nineteenth century, quarry and mine owners had to find more economical ways than packhorses to get their products to market, but in the steep, tortuous valleys of Snowdonia, standard-gauge train tracks proved too unwieldy. The solution was rails, usually about 2ft apart, plied by steam engines and dinky rolling stock. The charm of these railways was recognized by train enthusiasts, and long after the decline of the quarries, they banded together to restore abandoned lines and locos. Most lines are still largely run by volunteers, who have also started up new services along unused sections of standard-gauge bed.

Tickets are generally sold separately, but ten railways (including all those listed here) operate as **The Great Little Trains of Wales** (GLT: W greatlittletrainsofwales.co.uk) and offer a Discount Card (£10; valid 1 year), giving you 20 percent off the cost of the return journey on each of the GLT railways.

The railways below are listed north to south:

Snowdon Mountain Railway Llanberis. See p.352.
Welsh Highland Railway Porthmadog. See p.374.
Ffestiniog Railway Porthmadog. See p.372.
Llangollen Railway Llangollen. See p.316.
Talyllyn Railway Tywyn. See p.290.
Vale of Rheidol Railway Aberystwyth. See p.277.

USEFUL CONTACTS FOR RAIL TRAVEL

Arriva Trains Wales info ☎ 08457 484950, bookings ☎ 0870 900 0773, W arrivatrainswales.co.uk. Runs most local train services in Wales.

First Great Western tickets ☎ 08457 000125, W firstgreatwestern.co.uk. Inter-city journeys into south Wales.

The Man in Seat Sixty-One W seat61.com. Superb site covering all aspects of British train travel.

National Rail Enquiries ☎ 08457 484950, from outside the UK ☎ +44 20 7278 5240; W nationalrail.co.uk. Primary contact for all train timetables and booking.

The Train Line W thetrainline.com. Independent UK-wide online ticket retailer with a Best Fare Finder.

Traveline Cymru ☎ 01871 200 2233, W traveline-cymru.org.uk. Integrated train and bus info, particularly useful for planning integrated journeys.

Virgin Trains tickets ☎ 08719 774222, W virgintrains.co.uk. Inter-city journeys to north Wales.

Buses and coaches

Inter-town bus services duplicate a few of the major rail routes, often at half the price of the train or less, but taking considerably longer. Buses are reasonably comfortable and on longer journeys there are refreshment stops.

Throughout Britain, long-distance bus (aka coach) services are almost all run by **National Express**, whose network sends half a dozen tendrils into Wales. The chief routes are from London to Milford Haven via Cardiff, Swansea and Pembroke Dock; London to Wrexham via Birmingham and Llangollen; London to Aberystwyth; London along the north Welsh coast to Holyhead and Pwllheli, both via Birmingham; Birmingham to Cardiff and Swansea; Birmingham to Haverfordwest; Chester along the north coast to Llandudno, Bangor, Caernarfon and Pwllheli and Holyhead; and Chester direct to Holyhead. For a guaranteed seat, book ahead during weekends and holidays.

Fares vary enormously with the cheapest tickets sold early. One-way London–Cardiff fares can be as little as £5.50 (£23.40 for an amendable ticket). Children under 3 travel free; those over 60 get half fare on most services. Those travelling extensively throughout Britain by bus and train should check out the **discount cards and passes** (see box, p.30).

It is also worth considering the limited range of low-cost inter-city services operated by **Megabus** (W megabus.com). They run from UK cities to Cwmbran, Newport and Cardiff with fares as low as £1 (if you're very lucky and book well in advance).

TRAVELLING ON SUNDAYS

Throughout the guide we've given frequencies for trains and buses from Monday to Saturday. Sunday tends to have around 1–3 services, though the main routes are more frequent and some routes have no Sunday service at all.

TRAIN AND BUS PASSES AND DISCOUNTS

Ordinary standard-class fares on UK trains are high, and **first-class** costs an extra 33 percent, but there are various ways to save money. Off-peak and **advance-purchase** fares are much cheaper, **railcards** can save you a third off the price, and there's a huge array of **rail passes** that cover all of Britain, just Wales or smaller regions.

TRAIN TICKET TYPES

Up to two children under 5 travel free with each adult-fare-paying passenger, while those aged 5–15 inclusive pay half the adult fare on most journeys. Bicycles are generally carried free with restrictions (see p.43).

As a guide to **prices**, a standard-class one-way ticket on the London–Cardiff route might cost £15 (Advance), £44 (Off-Peak) or £95 (Anytime).

Anytime Fully flexible ticket allowing travel on any train at any time within a month after purchase. Expensive.

Off-peak Return off-peak fares cost about a third the price of Anytime fares, though single (one-way) fares are seldom much cheaper than returns (round-trips). If you're doing a lot of travelling on one-way journeys, rail and bus passes (see below) make a lot of sense. You generally cannot travel during weekday peak hours (these vary by route and company) and must complete outbound travel on the date shown on the ticket: the return portion is more flexible with the possibility of breaking the journey. At any station outside the morning rush hour, you'll routinely be sold an off-peak ticket.

Advance Advance-purchase tickets are the cheapest available, with no refunds and generally only valid on the train(s) you've booked. They must be bought at least the day before you travel and they're generally cheaper the further in advance you book. These are usually sold as single tickets, making planning a series of one-way journeys realistic if you are prepared to book ahead.

RAILCARDS

You can save 33 percent on fares with one of several **railcards** (Ⓦ railcard.co.uk): either the 16–25 Railcard (£24 a year); the Senior Railcard (£24) for British residents over 60; or the Family Railcard (£24) giving discounts for up to four adults travelling with up to four children (aged 5–15), who get sixty percent off. Children aged under 5 travel free at all times. Railcards also give 33 percent discounts on Explore Wales passes.

NATIONAL EXPRESS DISCOUNTS

16–26 Coachcard Thirty percent off many National Express fares for one year. Must be aged 16–26. £10.

Brit Xplorer Pass available to foreign nationals, offering unlimited travel on consecutive days on the National Express network for

7 days (£79), 14 days (£139) or 28 days (£219). You can buy these passes online or in Britain from major travel agents and at major National Express offices.

Much bus travel **within Wales** is provided by local bus services run by a bewildering array of companies: consult Traveline Cymru (see p.31) for details or visit Ⓦ timetables.showbus.co.uk/wales. htm, which has links to all the major bus companies. Though services are more expensive and less frequent in rural areas, there are very few places without any service, even if it's only a private minibus on market day.

For occasional bus journeys, just pay as you get on, but good savings can be made with one of the various **bus passes** and combined bus and rail passes.

In the **northern** half of Wales, Llandudno-based Arriva Cymru runs the majority of local services, but further south the system is far less unified, though

most services west of Cardiff and south of Carmarthen are run by the Swansea-based First Cymru. Cardiff Bus is the major company serving Cardiff and the Vale of Glamorgan. Various day, weekly and monthly passes are available, all of which can be bought aboard the bus.

Medium-range bus services operate under the TrawsCambria umbrella, which from early 2012 will become TrawsCymru (Ⓦ trawscymru.info). Useful services include: X32 Bangor–Aberystwyth; X40 Aberystwyth–Cardiff; and X94 Wrexham–Barmouth.

All regions have their own detailed local **timetables**, easily obtained from tourist offices, libraries and bus and/or train stations.

RAIL PASSES: BRITAIN AND WALES

All-Line Rail Rover ⓦ nationalrail.co.uk. Unlimited travel on almost the entire network throughout England, Scotland and Wales (including the Ffestiniog Railway) for 7 (£430) or 14 (£650) consecutive days. Available within Britain from larger train stations.

BritRail Pass ⓦ britrail.com. Foreign visitors planning on several long-distance trips through other parts of Britain might consider purchasing online a BritRail Pass, which must be bought before you enter the country. A range of passes is available for unlimited travel in England, Scotland and Wales over various combinations of consecutive days or a certain number of days over 2

months, plus discounts for Child (aged 5–15; half-price) and Youth (under 26; 20 percent). One child can travel free on each adult pass (other children travel at half-price).

Explore Wales Pass tickets ☎ 0870 900 0773, ⓦ www .explorewalespass.co.uk. Eight consecutive days' bus travel and four days' rail travel within the same period (£84). Covers all Wales and extends to Crewe, Shrewsbury and Hereford in England. Includes a 50 percent discount on the Welsh Highland and Ffestiniog narrow-gauge railways, twenty percent discounts on many other narrow-gauge railways, and reduced entry to CADW and National Trust properties. Tickets can be bought at most staffed train stations.

RAIL PASSES: NORTH AND MID-WALES

Explore North & Mid Wales Pass Same deal as the Explore Wales Pass (see above) but only covers the northern half of Wales (£57).

North Wales Rover All-day pass on all trains and most buses in north Wales and down the Cambrian Coast to Aberystwyth. The area is divided into seven zones and you can choose to travel within two

zones (£8), three zones (£13) or all zones (£23). Buy at the station.

Red Rover All-day bus travel throughout northwest Wales for £5.40. Buy on the bus.

Snowdon Sherpa Day Ticket All-day travel on the routes immediately surrounding Snowdon for £4. Buy on the bus.

RAIL PASSES: WEST AND MID-WALES

Cambrian Coaster Day Ranger One day's train travel between Aberystwyth and Pwllheli (£9), valid after 9.15am and all weekend. There's also an Evening Ranger (£5.50; valid after 6.30pm). Buy at any station.

Heart of Wales Line Circular Day Ranger One day's unlimited train travel on the route Shrewsbury–Llandrindod

Wells–Swansea–Cardiff–Hereford–Shrewsbury with as many breaks as the timetable will allow (£31).

West Wales Day Ranger All-day train travel in Pembrokeshire, west of Carmarthen (£8.80). Valid after 8.45 weekdays and all weekend. Buy at the station.

RAIL PASSES: SOUTH WALES

Explore South Wales Pass Same deal as the Explore Wales Pass (see above) but only covers the southern half of Wales (£57).

First Day Ticket A range of all-day bus passes using the First company buses. eg Swansea Bay area (£4.40) or Pembrokeshire (£5.25). Visit ⓦ firstgroup.com/ukbus/wales/swwales for details.

Valley Lines Explorer One day's Cardiff and Valleys bus and train travel. The Day Explorer (£9.10) is valid after 9.15am weekdays and all weekend; the Night Rider (£4.30) is only available after 6.30pm.

USEFUL CONTACTS FOR BUS TRAVEL

Arriva Cymru ⓦ arrivabus.co.uk/wales.

Cardiff Bus ⓦ cardiffbus.com.

First Cymru ⓦ firstcymru.co.uk.

National Express ☎ 08717 818178, ⓦ nationalexpress.com. Inter-city bus travel throughout Britain.

Traveline Cymru ☎ 01871 200 2233, ⓦ traveline-cymru.org.uk. First stop for train and bus info, particularly useful for planning integrated journeys.

Driving

If you want to cover a lot of the countryside in a short time, or just want more flexibility, you'll need your own transport. The **M4 motorway** (from London to Cardiff and Swansea) makes the most

dramatic entry into Wales, across the graceful Second Severn Crossing bridge (£5.70 toll westbound only; no footpath or cycle lane). A few miles north, the M48 links England and Wales over the original Severn Bridge (same toll; footpath and cycle lane available). Neither bridge accepts credit cards; check conditions and closures at ⓦ severn bridge.co.uk. The only other fast road into Wales is the **A55 expressway** running along the north Wales coast to the Ireland-bound ferries at Holyhead. An extensive network of dual carriageways and good-quality "A" roads links all major centres, including the **A5** through Llangollen into Snowdonia and the **A40** into the Brecon Beacons. In rural areas you'll often find yourself on winding, sometimes hair-raisingly narrow single-track lanes with slightly broader **passing places** where two vehicles can squeeze by – with this in mind, you might want to select a compact rental car. In very remote areas, you may still occasionally have to open gates designed to keep sheep from straying (make sure you close them again afterwards).

Most foreign nationals can get by with their **driving licence** from home, but if you're in any doubt, obtain an **international driving permit** from a national motoring organization. All foreign vehicles should carry vehicle registration, ownership documents and **insurance**, so be sure to check your existing policy.

As in the rest of the UK, you **drive on the left** in Wales. **Speed limits** are 30–40mph (50–65km/h) in built-up areas, 70mph (110km/h) on motorways (freeways) and dual carriageways, and 60mph (97km/h) on most other roads. Be alert to posted signs as **speed cameras** are everywhere.

Road signs are pretty much international ("Give Way" means "Yield"), and road rules are largely common sense. You are not permitted to make a kerbside turn against a red light; and must always give way to traffic (circulating clockwise) on a **roundabout**. This applies even for mini-roundabouts, which may be no more than a white circle painted on the road.

Petrol (gas) is sold in litres (a UK gallon = 4.56 litres, a US gallon = 3.8 litres), and is expensive – £1.40 per litre at the time of writing. Diesel costs slightly more.

Motoring organizations including the Automobile Association (AA; breakdowns ☎0800 887766, ⓦtheaa.co.uk), the Royal Automobile Club (RAC; breakdowns ☎0800 828282, ⓦrac.co.uk) and Green Flag (breakdowns ☎0800 400600, ⓦgreenflag .com) all operate 24-hour emergency **breakdown** services. The AA and RAC also provide many other motoring services, as well as a reciprocal arrangement for free assistance through many overseas motoring organizations – check the situation with yours before setting out. You can call the breakdown numbers even if you are not a member, although you'll be charged a substantial fee.

Hitching and lift-sharing

You might get lucky **hitching**, though it's rarely done nowadays, and a safer and more reliable alternative is **lift-sharing**, whereby you share the travel costs with someone already going in your direction. One of the best ways is through web-based agencies such as Rideshare (ⓦrideshare.co.uk) and Freewheelers (ⓦfreewheelers.co.uk), where you register (free) and enter your desired route so that the database can come up with suitable matches. You then contact the resulting matches by email and make arrangements. It's also worth checking noticeboards in hostels, health-food shops and other like-minded establishments to see if anyone's going your way.

Car rental

Car rental is best booked online; phone reservations are usually charged at 5–10p a minute, more from mobiles. You can expect to pay around £110 a week for a small hatchback. **Automatic transmissions** are rare at the lower end of the price scale – if you want one, you should book well ahead and

---

FUN TOURS AND ADVENTURE TRIPS

If you're short on time or want to see the sights in the company of like-minded travellers, join a guided tour. Some of the best include:

Bus Wales ☎0800 328 0284, ⓦbuswales.co.uk. Wide range of backpacker and smarter tours, from day-trips (£50) to six- and ten-day trips (from £400 staying in hostel dorms to £1850 using five-star hotels).

Dragon Tours ☎01878 658124, ⓦdragon-tours.com. Custom tours for individuals, couples and small groups plus a couple of more fixed routes covering the country in six days (£299 including hostel accommodation) or ten days (£499 including hostel accommodation). There's also a wide range of accommodation upgrades.

The Legendary Welsh Adventure Co ☎07861 679205, ⓦlegendarywelshadventure.com. Cardigan-based, hassle-free, multi-day guided adventures mostly in the Brecon Beacons, Pembrokeshire and Snowdonia. Tours include hiking, mountain biking, surfing and even bog snorkelling.

Road Trip ☎020 8133 8375, ⓦroadtrip.co.uk. London-based outfit running all-inclusive minibus trips: the weekend "Wales Coast & Mountains" tour (£169) visits the north Wales coast, Conwy Castle, Snowdonia and the Ffestiniog Railway, while the five-day "Welsh Explorer" (£182) heads to South Wales and includes trekking in the Brecon Beacons.

Shaggy Sheep Tours ☎017919 244549, ⓦshaggy sheep.com. Great fun and hugely enthusiastic, the booziest backpacker tours around leave twice-weekly from London. Choose between a weekend (£118) or a four-day (£148) trip. For independent travellers, there's also a handy jump-on, jump-off return bus service from London (£79) stopping at key destinations in Wales.

PAY-AND-DISPLAY

You often have to pay for parking in towns and at popular beaches, many of which are tucked into folds in the mountains or wedged below cliffs, giving little space for parking on the road.

At most pay-and-display car parks, tickets are issued by machine (you may have to type in your car registration number, a system designed to prevent people passing on their partially used tickets to other drivers). Even shopping centres sometimes require you to pay for parking, though you can sometimes get your parking costs redeemed at the check-out if you make a purchase.

Parking prices can be as little as 20p for 4hr in less popular areas, but 50p to £1 an hour is more common, and some places charge a flat fee of up to £5. It's definitely an incentive to use public transport – some eco-oriented attractions even give discounted entry to those arriving without a car.

expect to pay at least £170 a week for a slightly bigger model. Damage Liability Waiver (aka Collision Damage Waiver) is often included but still leaves you liable for the first several hundred pounds. This can be eliminated by paying roughly £10 a day. Most agencies offer vehicles with **diesel** engines, which give better overall economy despite the slightly more expensive fuel.

You'll also need to show your driving licence: few companies will rent to drivers with less than one year's experience, and most will only rent to people between 21 and 70 years of age. Some charge an additional fee for under-25s.

North Americans might want to contact the independently owned Europe by Car (US ☎1 800 223 1516, Ⓦeuropebycar.com), which has good deals on short and longer-term rentals.

Motorbike rental

A motorbike is a pleasurable way to see the Welsh countryside, but ludicrous insurance premiums mean the few **motorbike rental** outlets in the UK charge at least £350 a week for powerful tourers. Try London-based Raceways (☎020 8749 8181 Ⓦraceways.net), or Manchester-based New Horizons (☎0771 987 6212, Ⓦnewhorizonsbikehire .co.uk).

Accommodation

Tourist accommodation in Wales is constantly improving, with top-rank international hotels, farmhouse accommodation, hostels, restaurants-with-rooms, and the ubiquitous B&Bs. The growing array of farmhouse B&Bs and country houses typically offer a genuinely warm welcome, informal hospitality and quality home cooking. If you want to ensure you're staying in places where Welsh is spoken, check out Ⓦgwyliaucymraeg.co.uk, covering accommodation, pubs, cafés and restaurants.

Hotels and B&Bs

Bed & Breakfasts (B&Bs; in Welsh Gwely a Brecwast) may be anything from a private house with a couple of bedrooms set aside for paying guests to a small, stylish boutique establishment. Guesthouses tend to be larger, usually with around half a dozen rooms plus a guests' lounge, and can also vary from homely to very flash. In both places you'll get a room with TV, tea- and coffee-making facilities and, usually, your own en-suite bathroom, for £25–45 per person, sometimes a little less out of season or in less popular areas. We always mention if a place has rooms without a private bathroom (though usually with a sink in the room) for which you'll pay slightly less. Many places have free wi-fi.

In the countryside you're more likely to find places described as a **farm** (essentially a B&B on a working farm) or an **inn** (usually village pub with rooms above). As visitor expectations and the demand for weekend breaks increase, some places in all the above categories are ramping up the standards, with sumptuous furnishings, better food and those little touches which make your stay special. Of course, you pay considerably more for such pampering. Increasingly, places accept credit cards, but at lower-end B&Bs you should expect to **pay in cash**.

In town centres, B&Bs and guesthouses are supplemented by **hotels**, often just rooms above a noisy bar, but also larger places that can be the grandest in town.

Wherever you stay, **breakfast** will almost certainly be included in the price. This may just be continental (orange juice, cereal, toast and tea or coffee) but

---

TOP 5 COUNTRY HOTELS

Llangoed Hall Bronllys. See p.217
The Grove Narberth. See p.159
Tyddyn Llan Llandrillo. See p.323
Ynyshir Hall Machynlleth. See p.286
Neuadd Lwyd Anglesey. See p.422

more often will also include a full cooked breakfast of eggs, bacon, sausage, fried tomato, etc. In fancier places there'll be a choice of juices, preserved fruit, yogurt, smoked fish and perhaps Welsh dishes like Glamorgan sausages and laver bread.

A couple of free **publications** are well worth looking out for: the *Great Little Places* booklet (available online at Ⓦ little-places.co.uk) which features around fifty of the best small hotels, country inns and farmhouse B&Bs in Wales; and *Welsh Rarebits* (Ⓦ rarebits.co.uk), a similarly select listing of more substantial hotels and country mansions. Both websites give full coverage of all listed establishments, and you can pick up the booklets at bigger tourist offices. There are also Visit Wales' comprehensive *Where to Stay* and *Farm Stay Wales* brochures, which can be ordered through its website Ⓦ visitwales.co.uk.

Reservations can be made direct or through the local **tourist office** (£2 booking fee) though they will only provide information on "verified" accommodation (see box, p.36), and can sometimes be reluctant to divulge details of places that don't advertise in the official local guide: if you don't see something suitable in the guide itself, don't be afraid to ask if there's anywhere else that matches your requirements for price and location.

Hostels

Wales has 35 hostels operated by the **YHA** (reservations Ⓣ 0800 0191700, Ⓦ yha.org.uk), offering bunk-bed accommodation in single-sex dormitories or smaller rooms. A few of these places are spartan establishments of the sort traditionally associated with the wholesome, fresh-air ethos of the first hostels, but many have moved well away from this institutional ambience. Welsh hostels range from some remote, simple barns in the wilds of mid-Wales and Snowdonia to relatively swanky centres in places such as Cardiff and Conwy. The greatest concentration of hostels is in Snowdonia, with smaller clusters around the Pembrokeshire coast and in the Brecon Beacons.

Prices vary according to demand but in summer range from £14 to £23 per night per person, with the majority around £15–18. All hostels have self-catering facilities, and many also serve breakfast (around £5) and a three-course dinner (around £12), as well as offering packed lunches (around £6). Most hostels close from 10am to 5pm and have an 11pm curfew.

Bed prices quoted in this book are for members: non-members are welcome but you'll be charged an extra £3 a night (£1.50 for under-18s). One year's membership of the England and Wales YHA, which is open only to residents of the EU, costs £15.95 per year (£9.95 for under-26s; £22.95 for two adults living at the same address), and can be obtained online or in person at any YHA hostel. Members gain automatic membership of the hostelling associations of the ninety countries affiliated to Hostelling International (HI). Visitors who are not members of the HI organization in their own country can join for £10 a year at any hostel.

At any time of year (particularly at Easter, Christmas and from May to August), it's best to **book ahead** either online or by phone. If you're tempted to turn up on the spur of the moment, bear in mind that few hostels are open year-round, and several have periods during which they take only group bookings.

ACCOMMODATION PRICES

Throughout this guide, hotel and B&B accommodation prices have been quoted based on the lowest price you would expect to pay per night in that establishment for a **double room in high season**, but not absolute peak rates (such as at certain bank holidays). For backpacker hostels and camping barns we've listed the price of a **dorm bed**, plus the price for any double or twin rooms. **Campsite** prices are either listed per person, or per pitch based on two people in one tent. **Single occupancy** rates vary widely. Though typically around three-quarters of the price of a double, some places charge almost the full double rate and others charge only a little over half that.

Almost everywhere will offer **discounts** for multiple-night stays, and many places drop their rates considerably (or offer special deals) outside the late May to early September summer season.

YHA hostels still outnumber **independent hostels**, though there are a growing number of non-affiliated places offering similar facilities to YHAs, though often with a less regimented regime and no curfews or lockouts. We've mentioned the best of the independent hostels in this book but it is worth consulting ⓦindependenthostelguide.co.uk or buying *The Independent Hostel Guide* (£4.95).

These resources also list **bunkhouses**, typically more primitive affairs close to the mountains designed for hikers, climbers, mountain bikers and the like. The flashest are up to hostel standards, but many are little more than barns with toilet, shower and basic cooking facilities, starting from around £10. Bunkhouses may give preference to group bookings, and some purely cater to groups. See also ⓦbunkhousesinwales.co.uk.

Camping, caravanning and self-catering

Wales has hundreds of **campsites**, charging from around £3 per person per night for a spot in a field with a tap and a toilet to upwards of £20 for a two-person tent at the plushest sites, where you'll find amenities such as laundries, shops and sports facilities. Such places are used both by campers and **caravans**.

Some hostels have small campsites on their property, for which you'll pay half the indoor fee. Farmers without a reserved camping area may let you pitch in a field if you ask first, and may charge you nothing for the privilege; setting up a tent without asking is an act of trespass and won't be well received. Note that wild camping is illegal in national parks and nature reserves.

As a hangover from the days when thousands of holiday-makers from northern England and the Midlands decamped to the Welsh coast for a fortnight, many of the traditional seaside resorts are enveloped by camp upon camp of **permanently sited caravans**, rented out for self-catering holidays. Although these can certainly be cost-effective, with facilities such as bars, shops and discos thrown in, many people prefer self-catering holidays in self-contained **cottages**, **farms**, **town houses**, or **apartments**. The usual minimum rental period is a week, though long-weekend breaks can often be arranged out of season. In midsummer or over Christmas and New Year, **prices** start at around £400 for a place sleeping four, although in winter, spring or autumn they can dip towards £250 for the same property. Some companies specializing in Welsh

TOP 5 CAMPSITES

Three Cliffs Caravan Park Gower.
  See p.134
Caerfai Farm St Davids. See p.186
Cae Du Llangelynin. See p.292
Rynys Farm Betws-y-Coed. See p.344
Gwern Gôf Uchaf Ogwen Valley.
  See p.351

holiday cottages are listed below; tourist offices throughout Wales also have lists of self-catering holiday options.

The best of the detailed annual **directories** of Wales' camping and caravan sites are: the AA's *Caravan & Camping: Britain & Ireland*, which lists their inspected and graded sites, and *Cade's Camping, Touring and Motor Caravan Site Guide* (ⓦcades .co.uk). More niche alternatives include Rough Guides' *Camping in Britain* and the independent *Cool Camping: Wales* (ⓦcoolcamping.co.uk), both with in-depth reviews of some superbly situated tent-oriented campsites.

SELF-CATERING AND FAMILY ACCOMMODATION

Asheton Eco Barns ☎ 01348 831781, ⓦeco-barns.co.uk. Five very comfortable, low-impact units (each sleeping 4–7) fashioned from a traditional stone barn in Pembrokeshire.

Brecon Beacons Holiday Cottages ☎ 01874 676446, ⓦbreconcottages.com. Over 300 cottages and other buildings, some decidedly quirky, in the Brecon Beacons National Park and Wye Valley.

Coastal Cottages of Pembrokeshire ☎ 01437 765765, ⓦcoastalcottages.co.uk. Dozens of cottages, chalets, flats and houses – some with impressive leisure and activity facilities – around or near the Pembrokeshire coast.

Landmark Trust ☎ 01628 825925, ⓦlandmarktrust.org.uk. Over a dozen self-catering properties around Wales from a seventeenth-century rural farmhouse sleeping two to a tower in Caernarfon's town walls (sleeps 5).

National Trust Holiday Cottages ☎ 0844 8002070, ⓦnationaltrustcottages.co.uk. Around 50 beautiful cottages all over Wales usually with a three-night minimum. Prices vary widely through the year.

North Wales Holiday Cottages & Farmhouses ☎ 01492 582492, ⓦnorthwalesholidaycottages.co.uk. Extensive array of cottages in the Snowdonia National Park and throughout the northern half of Wales, both on the coast and in the countryside.

Powell's Cottage Holidays ☎ 01834 812791, ⓦpowells.co.uk. Concentrates on properties in Pembrokeshire and the Gower.

Quality Cottages ☎ 0800 007 5299, ⓦqualitycottages.co.uk. Over 300 cottages throughout Wales, mostly coastal.

Under the Thatch ☎ 0844 500 5101, ⓦunderthethatch.co.uk. A select choice of atmospheric cottages and cabins often beautifully

THE ACCOMMODATION GRADING SYSTEM

Visit Wales operates a grading system for accommodation, assigning them a minimum of one star (seldom used) to a maximum of five stars, largely based on amenities rather than subjective impressions such as the general atmosphere of the place or the friendliness of its owners.

Hotels are subdivided into five categories: country house hotel, small hotel, town house hotel, metro hotel and budget hotel. The term "Guest Accommodation" covers B&Bs, guesthouses, farmhouses, inns and restaurants-with-rooms.

To achieve a star rating, an establishment must be "verified" by Visit Wales inspectors, which ensures that you shouldn't be short-changed. For various reasons, some wonderful establishments choose to remain outside the official verification system, so the absence of a rating alone needn't be a deterrent.

restored. As the name suggests, some are traditional Ceredigion thatched cottages, but there are also Romany caravans and yurts. Rates fluctuate widely with the seasons and there are often great last-minute deals; lets are generally weekly or half-weekly and most are in Pembrokeshire or the southern part of the Cambrian coast.
Wales Holidays ☎ 01686 628200, Ⓦ wales-holidays.co.uk. A varied selection of over 500 properties all over Wales.

Food and drink

Wales is now home to some truly world-class food festivals, restaurants, farmers' markets and producers – part of the general renaissance of British cuisine combined with an increasing focus on fresh local produce. The country's natural larder includes freshly caught fish, tender local lamb and a smorgasbord of cheeses. These staple ingredients are used in everything from traditional dishes to fusion creations in some of the cities' most cosmopolitan restaurants.

Eating

Wales still has thousands of cafés, restaurants and pubs where you get chips with everything and a salad means a bit of wilted lettuce and a few segments of fridge-cold tomato, but it is increasingly rare to find a town where you can't find good food. Native **Welsh cuisine** is frequently rooted in economical ingredients, but an increasing number of menus make superb use of traditional fare, such as salt-marsh lamb (best served minted or with thyme or rosemary), wonderful Welsh black beef, fresh salmon and sewin (sea trout), frequently combined with the national vegetable, the leek. Specialities include **laver bread** (*bara lawr*), edible seaweed often mixed with oats then fried with a

traditional breakfast of pork sausages, egg and bacon. Other dishes well worth investigating include **Glamorgan sausages** (a spiced vegetarian combination of Caerphilly cheese, breadcrumbs and leeks), cawl (a chunky mutton broth), and cockles, trawled from the estuary north of the Gower.

The best-known of Wales' famed **cheeses** is Caerphilly, a soft, crumbly, white cheese that forms the basis of a true Welsh rarebit when mixed with beer and toasted on bread. Creamy goat's cheeses can be found all over the country, such as the superb Cothi Valley goat's cheese, as well as delicacies like organic Per Las blue cheese, and Collier's mature cheddar.

Other dairy products include ice cream, which, despite the climate, is exceptionally popular, with numerous companies creating home-made ices such as the Swansea area's Joe's Ice Cream or north Wales' Cadwaladr's.

Two traditional **cakes** are almost universal. *Welsh cakes* are flat, crumbling pancakes of sugared dough (a little like a flattened scone), while *bara brith*, a popular accompaniment to afternoon tea, literally translates as "speckled (with dried fruit) bread".

Menus featuring Welsh dishes can be found in numerous restaurants, hotels and pubs, many of which are part of **Wales the True Taste** (Cymru y Gwir Flas; Ⓦ walesthetruetaste.com), a government scheme to encourage local cuisine. Such establishments generally display a sticker in their windows.

Where to eat

If you're staying in a hotel, guesthouse or B&B, a hearty cooked breakfast (generally served 8–9am) will usually be offered as part of the deal, and may see you through the day. Evening meals are served from 6 to 10pm, though in rural areas, especially early in the week, you may find it difficult to get served after 8.30pm.

Cafés and tearooms (the terms are used pretty much interchangeably) can be found absolutely everywhere, and are generally the cheapest places to eat, providing hearty, cholesterol-laden breakfasts, a solid range of snacks and full meals for lunch (and occasionally, evening meals). Wales' steady influx of New Agers has seen the cheap and usually vegetarian wholefood café become a standard feature of many mid- and west Welsh towns. Throughout the land, cafés and restaurants are also increasingly equipped with espresso machines, though barista competence levels are low.

Food in pubs varies as much as the establishments themselves. Competition has seen mediocre places sharpen up their act, and many pubs now offer more imaginative dishes than microwaved lasagne and chips. Most serve food at lunchtime and in the evening (usually until 8.30 or 9pm), and in many towns, the local pub is the most economical place (and, in smaller towns, sometimes the only place) to grab a filling evening meal. Relatively few Welsh hostelries have done the full gastropub conversion, but the standards in some pubs can now be very high.

Such places, along with bistros and restaurants, sport menus which rely extensively on fresh local produce. They can often tell you which farm the beef came from, and in coastal areas the chef may even know the fisherman.

The Cardiff brewery Brains has recently been buying up pubs around the country and smartening them up (cheap food, good beer and comfortable surroundings), but often robbing them of much individuality in the process.

People of all nationalities call Wales home and few towns of any size are without Indian or Chinese restaurants, though the likes of Japanese, French, Thai, American, Mexican and Belgian are limited to the more cosmopolitan centres.

Our restaurant listings include a mix of high-quality and good-value establishments, but if you're intent on a culinary pilgrimage, you'd do well to arm yourself with a copy of the annual

---

TOP 5 FARMERS' MARKETS AND FOOD SHOPS

Riverside Market Cardiff. See p.95
Swansea Indoor Market Swansea. See p.124
Ultracomida Narberth. See p.160
Machynlleth Market Machynlleth. See p.284
Leonardo's Deli Ruthin. See p.330

TOP 5 RESTAURANTS

The Hardwick Abergavenny. See p.221
Slice Swansea. See p.129
Cwtch St David's. See p.187
Tyddyn Llan Llandrillo. See p.323
Ynyshir Hall Machynlleth. See p.287

Good Food Guide (Which? Publications), which includes detailed recommendations. Throughout this guide, we've supplied the phone number for all restaurants where you may need to book a table. In pubs and cafés you can expect to pay £6–10 for a main course, closer to £15 in good restaurants and around £20 in the very best places.

Drinking

As elsewhere in Britain, daytime cafés are not usually licensed to sell alcohol, and though restaurants invariably are, pubs remain the centre of social activity. The legal drinking age is 18, though an adult can order alcohol for someone aged 16 or 17 who is dining. Some places offer special family rooms for people with children, and beer gardens where younger kids can run free.

Pubs

Welsh pubs vary as much as the landscape, from opulent Edwardian palaces of smoked glass, gleaming brass and polished mahogany in the larger towns and cities, to thick-set stone barns in wild, remote countryside. Where the church has faltered as a community focal point, the pub often still holds sway, with those in smaller towns and villages, in particular, functioning as community centres as much as places in which to drink alcohol. Live music – and, this being Wales, singing – frequently round off an evening. As a rule of thumb, if a pub has both a bar and a lounge, the bar will be more basic and frequently very male-dominated, while the lounge will tend to be plusher, more mixed and probably a better bet for a passing visitor.

Opening times vary but typically are Monday to Saturday 11am to 11pm, Sunday noon to 10.30pm (with many quieter places closed between 3 and 6pm, particularly throughout the week), with "last orders" called by the bar staff about fifteen minutes before closing time. Liberalization of licensing laws has allowed pubs to stay open later, but with the exception of city centres most places stick close to the standard hours.

What to drink

Beer, sold by the pint (generally £2.60–3.20) and half pint (half the price), is the staple drink in Wales, as it is throughout the British Isles. Traditionalists drink **real ale**, an uncarbonated beer, usually hand-pumped from the cellar but sometimes served straight from the cask; it comes in many varieties (some seasonal), including the almost ubiquitous deep-flavoured **bitter**, but sometimes mild, or **dark** as it is often known in Wales. **Lager**, which corresponds with European and American ideas of beer, is also stocked everywhere. Also quite common Is the sweeter and darker **porter**. Irish **stout** (Guinness, Murphy's or Beamish) is widely available.

Among beers worth looking out for are the heady brews produced by Cardiff-based **Brains**, mainly found in the southeastern corner of Wales. Llanelli-based **Felinfoel** covers the whole southern half of Wales, with Double Dragon Premium bitter the aromatic ace in their pack. **Crown Buckley**, also based in Llanelli but owned by Brains, produces three excellent bitters and a distinctive mild.

Newer brews, such as Otley from Pontypridd, Evan Evans from Llandeilo and Purple Moose from Porthmadog, have won numerous awards.

Many pubs are owned by large, UK-wide breweries who sell only their own products, so if you are interested in seeking out distinctive brews, choose your pub carefully. The best resource for any serious hophead is the annual *Good Beer Guide* produced by **CAMRA** (the Campaign for Real Ale; ⓦcamra.org.uk): if you see a recent CAMRA sticker in a pub window, chances are the beer will be well worth sampling.

As in other Celtic regions, **cider** has a huge following; look out for Orchard Gold (a traditional farmhouse apple cider) and Perry Vale (pear cider), both made by the Welsh Cider and Perry Company (Gwynt y Ddraig).

Pubs and off-licences (liquor stores) increasingly stock a growing range of Welsh **spirits**, such as Merlyn (cream liquor, similar to Baileys), Taffoc (toffee spirit), Five (vodka) and Penderyn (single malt whisky). There are also a number of Welsh

TOP 5 FOOD PUBS

Bunch of Grapes Pontypridd. See p.114
Felin Fach Griffin Brecon. See p.212
Y Polyn Nantgaredig. See p.149
The White Eagle Rhoscolyn. See p.430
Tŷ Gwyn Betws-y-Coed. See p.345

wines, though you rarely see these offered on restaurant wine lists. Wines sold in pubs have improved considerably in recent years, although the best world selections tend to be found in the places serving good food.

Few restaurants have a good selection of wines by the glass, generally offering little more than a house white and a house red.

The media

The media that you will encounter in Wales is a hybrid of Welsh and Britain-wide information. Although the London-based UK media attempts to cover life in the other corners of Britain, few people would agree that Wales receives a fair share of coverage in any medium. Of all the solely Welsh media, newspapers are probably the weakest area, and periodicals and TV coverage the strongest and most interesting.

Newspapers and magazines

The **British daily newspapers** are all available in Wales, but news of Wales is not terribly well covered – even the goings-on at Welsh Assembly in Cardiff are rarely analyzed, let alone any other area of Welsh life. The only quality **Welsh daily** is the *Western Mail* (ⓦwalesonline.co.uk), a sometimes uneasy mix of Welsh Assembly, wider Welsh and British news and a token smattering of international affairs coupled with populist lifestyle pap and features on celebrities. With a few honourable exceptions, the quality of writing and analysis is lightweight. What the *Western Mail* is to south Wales, the *Daily Post* (ⓦdailypost.co.uk) is to the north of the country, with a fairly decent spectrum of news and features that marks it out from other local dailies. All areas have their own long-standing **weekly papers**, generally an entertaining mix of local news, parish gossip and events listings. Wales' national **Sunday paper**, *Wales on Sunday*, from the same family as the *Western Mail*, has descended somewhat into tabloid trivia, but it's still worth buying for its bright, colourful take on Welsh life and occasional hard-hitting exposés and campaigning journalism. It's also very good on Welsh sport.

Go into any bookshop in Wales, and you'll be surprised by the profusion of Welsh **magazines**, in both English and Welsh. For a broad overview of the arts, history and politics, it's hard to beat *Planet*

(ⓦ planetmagazine.org.uk), an English-language bimonthly that takes a politically irreverent line, combining Welsh interest with a wider cultural and international outlook. The more serious English-language quarterly *New Welsh Review* (ⓦ newwelshreview.com) is steeped in Wales' political, literary and economic developments, while *Poetry Wales* is an excellent publication of new writing. The bimonthly glossy *Cambria* (ⓦ cambriamagazine.com) subtitles itself as "Wales's Magazine", an epithet that it's doing its best to fulfil with sparky writing on all matters Cymric, together with superb photography. For a wider view of Welsh social issues, with insights into "alternative" culture and news, pick up the weekly *Big Issue Cymru*, sold by homeless vendors on the streets of major towns and cities. If you're half-proficient in Welsh, the weekly news digest *Y Cymro* is an essential read, although younger, funkier features can be found in the weekly glossy *Golwg*, and more political topics are chewed over in the monthly *Barn*. If you're attempting to master the language, try *Lingo Newydd* magazine, aimed at learners at all levels.

Television and radio

In marked contrast to the London-centric print media, **TV and radio** are wholeheartedly moving out of southeast England. Cardiff is home to the Welsh branches of devolved broadcasting organizations including the mighty BBC, ITV, and indigenous Welsh operators such as S4C.

The state-funded BBC (ⓦ bbc.co.uk/wales) operates two **TV** channels in Wales – the mainstream **BBC One Wales** and the more esoteric **BBC Two Wales**. They may sound avowedly Welsh, but the vast majority of programming is UK-wide, with Welsh programmes, principally news and sport, but also features, political and education programmes, slotted into the regular schedules. This is even more the case with the determinedly populist **ITV Wales** (ⓦ itv.com/wales).

The principal **Welsh channel** is **S4C** (*Sianel Pedwar Cymru*, verbally "*ess pedwar eck*"; ⓦ s4c .co.uk), which has grown from shaky beginnings (see box, p.451) to become a major player, sponsoring diverse projects including Welsh animation and feature films. These include the Oscar-nominated films *Hedd Wyn* and *Solomon a Gaenor* and the terrifically tasteless prehistoric cartoon *Gogs*. It now broadcasts solely in Welsh and each weeknight includes a dose of the BBC's longest-running TV soap, *Pobol y Cwm* (*People of the Valley*). The sister English-language Channel 4 is also available throughout Wales.

The BBC is also a major player in **radio**, with five UK networks, all broadcasting in Wales: Radio One combines pop with a slick interpretation of youth and dance culture; Two is pop and rock skewed to those in their 30s and 40s; Three is classical and jazz; Four offers a passionately loved ragbag of magazine shows, current affairs, drama, arts and highbrow quizzes; and Five Live broadcasts a constant, entertaining mix of news and sport. The BBC also operates two stations in Wales alone: **BBC Radio Wales**, a competent, if gentle, English-language service of news, features and music, with occasional dashes of élan, and **BBC Radio Cymru**, a similarly easy-going mix in the Welsh language. Both can often be more entertaining in the evening and at weekends, away from the daytime tyranny of rolling news, sport, weather and traffic congestion.

Of the commercial stations, the brashest is Radio One soundalike **Capital FM**, serving Cardiff, Newport and around, together with **Capital Gold**, its twin for news, features and greatest hits and oldies music. Also in the capital and along the south coast are **Real Radio**, for music, sport and phone-ins, and **Kiss 101** for dance, hip hop and drum n' bass. **Swansea Sound**, whose reception extends west towards Pembrokeshire, is solid and frequently interesting; its local twin **The Wave 96.4** isn't. There are bilingual services from **Radio Ceredigion** and **Radio Pembrokeshire** on the west coast, **Radio Carmarthenshire** inland and **Champion FM** around Caernarfon and Bangor.

Festivals and events

Ranging from the epic to the absurd, Wales' wealth of festivals sees all walks of life partying in muddy fields across the country. Many of the events on the nation's annual calendar are uniquely Welsh with an ancient pedigree, notably eisteddfodau – age-old competitions in poetry and music – that still form the backbone of national culture.

Many towns and cities now have annual **arts festivals** of some kind, mentioned throughout the Guide and, in the case of the major events, in the list below. There are numerous other events with a distinctly surreal edge – from the Cilgerran **coracle races** (see p.266) to bizarre happenings like peat-bog snorkelling competitions and parading around Llangynwyd village with a horse's skull to welcome in the new year (the Mari Lwyd). **Rock festivals**, **DJ-led events** and New Age **fairs** and **festivals** are another common feature of summer throughout Wales; these are usually publicized by handbills, posters in wholefood shops and cafés, and by word of mouth.

Events calendar

Visit Wales maintains a fairly comprehensive events list at Ⓦ visitwales.com, and we've covered folk festivals on p.459.

JANUARY–APRIL

Mari Lwyd (Jan 1; Ⓦ www.folkwales.org.uk/mari.html) At Llangynwyd, near Maesteg, the most authentic survivor of the ancient Welsh custom of parading a horse's skull through the village streets.

Six Nations rugby championship. (Feb–March) Last won by Wales with a tremendous Grand Slam in 2008.

St David's Day (March 1) Wales' national day, with *hwyrnos* (late nights) and celebrations nationwide.

Wonderwool Wales (Mid-April; Ⓦ wonderwoolwales.co.uk) Two-day showcase at Builth Wells, Powys, of Welsh wool and wool products, from raw materials to designer fashion, with plenty of sheep. Held concurrently with the Mid-Wales Mouthful Food Festival, with over 60 stalls.

MAY

Hay Festival (Late May to early June) One of the most feted literary festivals in the world (see p.226).

St Davids Cathedral Festival (End of May to first week in June; Ⓦ stdavidscathedral.org.uk) Superb setting for classical concerts and recitals over ten days.

Urdd National Eisteddfod (End of May to first week in June; Ⓦ urdd.org) Vast and enjoyable youth eisteddfod – one of the largest youth festivals in Europe – alternating between north (Caernarfon in 2012) and south Wales (Pembrokeshire in 2013).

JUNE

Cardiff Singer of the World competition (Mid-June; Ⓦ bbc.co.uk/cardiffsinger) Huge, televised week-long festival of music and song held in odd-numbered years, with a star-studded list of international competitors.

Criccieth Festival (Mid-June; Ⓦ cricciethfestival.co.uk) Music, theatre and art around the Llŷn town.

Escape Into the Park (early to mid-June; Ⓦ escapefestival .com). Fifty top dance and urban artists perform for up to 20,000 fans on one day in Swansea's Singleton Park. The biggest such event in Wales.

Great Welsh Beer & Cider Festival (Mid-June; Ⓦ gwbcf .org.uk) Three days to sample from almost two hundred brews (many of them Welsh) in the Cardiff International Arena.

Gregynog Festival (Last half of June; Ⓦ gwylgregynogfestival .org) Classical music festival in the superb country-house surroundings of Gregynog Hall near Newtown, Powys.

Gŵyl Ifan (Mid-June; Ⓦ gwylifan.org) A weekend of folk-dancing workshops, displays and processions in various locations in and around Cardiff.

Man Versus Horse Marathon (Mid-June; Ⓦ green-events .co.uk) A 22-mile race at Llanwrtyd Wells, Powys, between runners and horses with both equine and human winners in its time.

Tredegar House Folk Festival (Early June; Ⓦ tredegarhousefestival.org.uk) A weekend of international dance, music and song at this grand seventeenth-century mansion.

JULY

Beyond the Border (Early July; Ⓦ beyondtheborder.com) Three-day international storytelling festival at St Donat's Castle, Vale of Glamorgan, in a fairy-tale castle setting, held every even-numbered year.

Cardiff Festival (July & Aug; Ⓦ cardiff-festival.com) Broad-brush festival throughout July and August encompassing theatre, the Cardiff Food and Drink Festival, the LGBT Mardi Gras, a multicultural mela and lots more.

Cardigan Bay Seafood Festival Early July; Ⓦ aberaeron.info /seafood) At Aberaeron, Dyfed, some of Wales' best chefs whip up delicious morsels.

Fancy Dress Night (First Friday in July; Ⓦ llanidloes.org.uk) Llanidloes, Powys. Pubs open late, streets are cordoned off and virtually the whole town dresses up.

Gower Festival (Last half of July; Ⓦ gowerfestival.org) Two weeks of mostly classical music in churches around the Gower.

Llangollen International Eisteddfod (First or second week in July; Ⓦ international-eisteddfod.co.uk) Over twelve thousand participants from all over the world, including choirs, dancers, folk singers, groups and instrumentalists. See box, p.315.

Really Wild Food & Countryside Festival (late July; Ⓦ reallywildfestival.co.uk) St Davids comes alive for a weekend of rural traditions, music, storytelling and great food.

Royal Welsh Show (Late July; Ⓦ rwas.co.uk) Europe's largest agricultural show and sales fair at Builth Wells; an absolute Welsh institution and a top day out. You can watch the ultra-serious judging of prize farm animals, competitive sheep-shearing or wood chopping, displays of falconry and craftsmanship, or simply feast on farm-fresh produce. Hundreds of stallholders sell everything from artisan products to agricultural equipment (see p.230).

Snowdon Race (Late July; Ⓦ snowdonrace.co.uk) A one-day race from Llanberis up Snowdon, attracting masochists from across the world, the best runners recording times of only a little over an hour for the combined ascent and descent.

The Big Cheese (Late July; Ⓦ caerphilly.gov.uk/bigcheese) Massive town festival and fun fair in Caerphilly, with a Big Cheese Race, tasting and more (see p.112).

Wakestock (Mid-July; Ⓦ wakestock.co.uk) Big, bold three-day wakeboarding and music festival in north Wales, attracting up to ten thousand bleached-haired punters for cutting-edge headline acts, top DJs and spectacular wakeboarding.

AUGUST

Brecon Jazz Festival (Mid-Aug; W breconjazz.co.uk) Widely regarded as one of the best jazz festivals in Britain; run over three days.

Croissant Neuf Summer Party (Mid-Aug; W partyneuf .co.uk). Small, friendly and green weekend festival near Usk that's always fun and especially good for families.

Green Man Festival (Late Aug) Wonderful mid-sized, three-day music festival (see p.217).

Gŵyl Machynlleth (Last week in Aug; W tourism.powys.gov.uk) Wide-ranging arts festival, with a solid programme of chamber music at its core.

Llandrindod Wells Victorian Festival (Late Aug; W victorianfestival.co.uk) A week of family fun, street entertainment and Victorian costumes rounded off with a fireworks display.

Royal National Eisteddfod (First week in Aug; W eisteddfod .org.uk) The centrepiece of Welsh culture (originally meaning "a meeting of bards"), this is very much a Welsh festival (largely conducted in Cymraeg) and is Wales' biggest single annual event. The vast maes (field) hosts art, craft, literature, rock music, Welsh-language lessons, theatre and major music and poetry competitions. It alternates between south (Vale of Glamorgan in 2012) and north Wales (Denbigh in 2013), is lots of fun and is worth seeing if only for the overblown pageantry.

World Bog Snorkelling Championships (Aug Bank Holiday Sun; W green-events.co.uk) Muddy swim-off along a 60yd long bog course at Llanwrtyd Wells, Powys.

SEPTEMBER

Abergavenny Food Festival (Mid-Sept; W abergavennyfood festival.com) This weekend chow-down is Wales' premier gastronomic event with a smorgasbord of fresh food showcased by celebrity chefs.

Cardiff Mardi Gras (First Sat in Sept; W cardiffmardigras.co.uk) Cardiff's lesbian and gay festival takes over Coopers Field with live music, market stalls and bars.

Tenby Arts Festival (Late Sept; W tenbyartsfest.co.uk) Well-established week-long arts romp in Tenby, with a lively fringe too.

OCTOBER

Swansea Festival of Music and the Arts (Oct; W swanseafestival.org) Three weeks of concerts, jazz, drama, opera, ballet and art events throughout the city.

Sŵn (Mid- to late Oct; W swnfest.com) This four-day showcase of the best in new music in Wales takes place at venues around Cardiff.

NOVEMBER–DECEMBER

Bonfire Night and Lantern Parade (Early Nov) Superb procession in Machynlleth, culminating in fireworks and performance.

Dylan Thomas Festival (Early Nov; W dylanthomas.com) In Swansea: talks, performances, exhibitions, readings and music with a DT theme.

New Year's Eve celebrations (Dec 31) New Quay in Dyfed is *the* place to party on New Year's Eve.

Real Ale Wobble (Mid-Nov; W green-events.co.uk) Non-competitive mountain biking and real-ale drinking over 15, 25 or 35 miles at Llanwrtyd Wells, Powys.

Sport and outdoor activities

With craggy mountains, large areas of moorland, a deeply indented coastline, wide beaches and fast-flowing rivers, Wales makes a fabulous outdoor playground – you're never far from a stretch of countryside where you can lose the crowds on a brief walk or cycle ride. The short day-hikes are some of the best anywhere, while keen walkers can hike a skyline ridge or tackle a long-distance path over a couple of visits or in one epic tramp. Mountain bikers whizz around the popular forest bike parks, while road options include many wonderfully scenic, little-frequented back roads. Elsewhere, the mountains and cliffs provide scope for fabulous rock climbing and thrilling coasteering trips. Along gentler coasts, watersports prevail, particularly the growing sports of kiteboarding and wakeboarding. And there are plenty of fine beaches for less structured fresh-air activities.

Walking

There isn't a built-up area in Wales that's more than half an hour away from some decent walking country, but three areas are so outstanding they have been designated **national parks**. Most of Wales' northwestern corner is taken up with the **Snowdonia National Park**, comprising a dozen of the country's highest peaks separated by dramatic glaciated valleys and laced with hundreds of miles of ridge and moorland paths. From Snowdonia, the Cambrian Mountains stretch south to the **Brecon Beacons National Park**, with its striking sandstone scarp at the head of the south Wales coalfield and lush, cave-riddled limestone valleys to the south. One hundred and seventy miles of Wales' south-western peninsula make up the third park, the **Pembrokeshire Coast National Park**, best explored along the **Pembrokeshire Coast Path**, one of Wales' increasing number of designated **long-distance paths** (see below).

Unless you're doing your walking on out-of-season weekdays, don't expect to have the major trails in the national parks to yourself. Many of the best one-day walks in the country are detailed in this Guide, but for more arduous mountain treks,

TOP 5 WALKS
Port Eynon to Rhossili via Worms Head
Gower. See p.134
Dinas Head Newport. See p.193
Precipice Walk Dolgellau. See p.295
Cwm Idwal Ogwen Valley. See p.350
Aberglaslyn Gorge Beddgelert.
See p.367

you'll benefit from bringing a specialist walking guidebook, which are widely available. The best are listed on p.468, and you can get more information from The Ramblers' Association (☎020 7339 8500, ⓦramblers.org.uk/wales), Britain's main countryside campaigning organization and self-appointed guardian of the nation's footpaths and rights of way.

Rights of access

Although they are managed by committees of local and state officials, all three Welsh national parks are predominantly privately owned. Until recently it was the goodwill of landowners that gave access to much of the land, but the 2005 **Countryside and Rights of Way Act** (CRoW) gives open access on foot (but not generally by bike or horse) to "all land that is predominantly mountain, moor, heath or down" across Wales. Such areas (almost a fifth of the country) are marked on all new Ordnance Survey maps, and at boundaries you'll see a brown "walking man" sign. Landowners are, however, allowed to restrict access for a number of reasons, and signs are posted locally.

Access to other land is restricted to **public rights of way**: **footpaths** (pedestrians only; yellow waymarkers), **bridleways** (pedestrians, horses and bicycles; blue waymarkers) and **byways** (open to all traffic, but generally unsurfaced; red waymarkers) that have seen continued use over the centuries. Historically, these are often over narrow mountain passes between two hamlets, or linking villages to mines or summer pastureland. Rights of way are marked on Ordnance Survey maps and are indicated from roads with signposts, and intermittently waymarked across the countryside; any stiles and gates on the path have to be maintained by the landowner. Some less scrupulous owners have been known to block rights of way by destroying stiles – and with some walkers wilfully straying from official rights of way, some resentment is perhaps understandable. Disputes are uncommon, but your surest way of avoiding trouble is to meticulously follow the right of way on an up-to-date map.

Ordnance Survey maps also indicate routes with **concessionary path** or **courtesy path** status, where access is given over private land at the goodwill of the owner; though these are usually open for public use they can be closed at any time.

Some places to stay that are particularly geared to walkers display a "Walkers Welcome" sticker in their window and on their website.

WALKING HOLIDAYS
Celtic Trails ⓦ walkingwales.co.uk
Contours Walking Holidays ⓦ contours.co.uk
Drover Holidays ⓦ droverholidays.co.uk
Footpath Holidays ⓦ footpath-holidays.com
Walkabout Wales ⓦ walkabout-wales.com
Walk or Bike Wales ⓦ walkorbikewales.com

Rock climbing and scrambling

As well as being superb walking country, Snowdonia offers some of Britain's best **rock climbing** and several challenging **scrambles** – ascents that fall somewhere between walks and climbs, requiring the use of your hands. One or two of the tougher walks included in the text have sections of scrambling, but for the most part this is a specialist discipline, well covered in books available locally.

The scale may not be huge (the highest route only takes you up 800ft) but the quality is excellent, and there's an astonishing variety of routes in a small area. In fact, the term "cragging" comes from craig, Welsh for cliff. Llanberis, at the foot of Snowdon, is the home of Welsh climbing, with routes ranging from easy hands-on scrambles up mountain ridges to impossibly difficult climbs only achievable by a few dozen people in the world.

In the south of the country, the pick of the crags are the limestone sea cliffs along the Pembrokeshire coast. The bulk of the action happens near Bosherston. The military ordnance testing areas of Range East and Range West here mean that parts of the coast are off limits (permits for some places require climbers to attend a bomb recognition course), but there are plenty of areas with much freer access. Further east, the Gower peninsula is also ringed by tempting sea cliffs.

Beginners should contact Plas y Brenin: The National Mountain Centre, or the British Mountaineering Council (ⓦthebmc.co.uk), which can put you in touch with climbing guides and people running courses.

TOP 5 MOUNTAIN HIKES

Pen y Fan/Corn Du Brecon Beacons.
  See p.208
Pony Path Cadair Idris. See p.295
North Ridge Tryfan. See p.348
Glyder Traverse Ogwen Valley. See p.349
Snowdon Horseshoe Snowdon.
  See p.358

Cycling

Over the last decade or so, Wales has positioned itself as one of Britain's premier **cycling** destinations, with a complex web of traffic-free bike paths, off-road tracks and low-traffic cycle routes, plus some excellent mountain bike parks. Backroad routes along river valleys and over mountain passes have a sufficient density of pubs and B&Bs to keep the days manageable, and while steep gradients can be a problem, ascents are never long, with Wales' highest pass barely reaching 1500ft. The picture isn't so rosy in most towns and cities, where cyclists are still treated with notorious disrespect by many motorized road users and by the people who plan the country's traffic systems. If you plan to ride in built-up areas, get a **helmet** and a secure **lock** – cycle theft is an organized racket.

Transporting your bike by **train** is a good way of getting to the interesting parts of Wales without a lot of stressful pedalling. Bikes are generally carried free on suburban trains outside the weekday rush hours of 7.30 to 9.30am and 4 to 6pm. On most routes in Wales there is only space for two bikes and you are expected to make a reservation (free), though they'll accept unreserved bikes if there is space. On inter-city routes, say from England into Wales, space is still very limited but free reservations are accepted. Arriva's free *Cycling by Train* brochure (downloadable from Ⓦ arrivatrainswales.co.uk), and the *National Rail Cycling by Train* (from Ⓦ nationalrail. co.uk) are both useful resources.

Bike rental is available at bike shops in some large towns (outlined throughout the Guide) and many resorts, but the specimens are seldom top-quality machines – alright for a brief spin, but not for any serious touring. Expect to pay in the region of £25 per day, more for specialist off-road machines with suspension.

Places to stay that are particularly geared to cyclists often have a "Cyclists Welcome" sticker in their window and on their website.

Cycle touring routes

The best of Wales' narrow lanes, disused railway lines and forest paths have been linked together to form **cycle routes** as part of the National Cycle Network created by **Sustrans** (☏ 0845 113 0065, Ⓦ sustrans.org.uk). Set up in 1977, this charity promotes sustainable transport, principally by developing cycling routes – over 10,000 miles have

HEROIC HIKES AND LENGTHY RAMBLES

Wales is traced by a spider's web of over a dozen wonderful long-distance paths (LDPs). Three of these – the Pembrokeshire Coast Path, Offa's Dyke Path and Glyndŵr's Way – are additionally designated National Trails, waymarked at frequent intervals by an acorn symbol. The following is a brief rundown of the most popular LDPs.

All Wales Coastal Path (861 miles) By early summer 2012 existing and new coastal trails will be joined to form a continuous whole. Some of the best bits are covered by the Pembrokeshire Coast Path, the Llŷn Coastal Path (Ⓦ gwynedd .gov.uk) and the Anglesey Coastal Path (Ⓦ anglesey coastalpath.com).

Cambrian Way (275 miles; Ⓦ cambrianway.org.uk) The longest, wildest and most arduous of the Welsh LDPs, cutting north–south over the remote Cambrian Mountains.

Glyndŵr's Way (135 miles; Ⓦ nationaltrail.co.uk/ glyndwrsway) A lengthy meander among the remote mountains and lakes of mid-Wales, visiting sites associated with the great fifteenth-century Welsh hero. See p.238.

Landsker Borderlands Trail (60 miles; Ⓦ ldwa.org.uk) Gentle waterways, quiet villages and easy trails characterize this slightly contrived circular walk around the Landsker region in Pembrokeshire.

Offa's Dyke Path (177 miles) The classic Welsh LDP, running from Prestatyn in the north to Chepstow in south Wales, tracing the line of the eighth-century earthwork along the English border for a third of the way. A blend of wooded lowland walking and higher hilltops, with exhilarating open territory through the Black Mountains. See p.240.

Pembrokeshire Coast Path (186 miles) This hugely rewarding coastal trail dips into quiet coves and climbs over headlands, with sweeping ocean views and plenty of birdlife on the cliffs and offshore islands. See p.164.

Wye Valley Walk (136 miles; Ⓦ wyevalleywalk.org) A lovely, sylvan, sea-to-source trek following the River Wye from Chepstow to Plynlimon, beginning with a long section through a dramatic wooded gorge. See p.63.

SAFETY IN THE WELSH HILLS

Welsh mountains are not high by world standards, but they should still be treated with respect. The fickle weather makes them more dangerous than you might expect, and you can easily find yourself disoriented in the low cloud and soaked by unexpected rain. If the weather looks like it's closing in, get down fast. It is essential that you are properly equipped – even for what appears to be an easy expedition in apparently settled weather – with proper warm and waterproof layered clothing, supportive footwear, adequate maps, a compass and food. Always tell someone your route and expected time of return – and call when you get back so they know you're safe.

been created, 1200 of them in Wales, of which a quarter are traffic-free. The entire network is covered in the official *Cycling in the UK* handbook (£20).

Three major cycling routes cross Wales. The main north–south **Lôn Las Cymru** (the Welsh National Route; Route 8) was opened in 1996 and covers 250 hilly miles from Anglesey, through Snowdonia, the Brecon Beacons and the industrial valleys of the south, to the Severn Bridge. Sustrans publishes two maps of the route (£7 each), one covering Holyhead to Builth Wells and the other from Builth Wells to Chepstow and Cardiff. **Lôn Geltaidd** (Celtic Trail East; Route 4; map £7) traverses 186 miles across the south of the country (70 percent of it traffic-free) from Fishguard to the Severn Bridge. Along the north coast the busy roads are avoided on the **North Wales Coast Route** (Route 5). In addition there are numerous other local routes, sometimes on dedicated traffic-free paths but often directed along quiet lanes: free leaflets available locally are easy to follow. Areas worth considering are the Gower peninsula, Pembrokeshire, Anglesey, the Llŷn and the supremely unspoilt and fairly challenging, three-day **Radnor Ring**, near Llandrindod Wells.

Mountain biking

Since the 1990s, the forests of Wales have gained an enviable reputation for top-class **mountain biking**. Every weekend mud-bespattered bikers weave along miles of single-track at the thirteen dedicated **bike parks** dotted along the mountainous spine of the country – from the Gŵydyr Forest just outside Betws-y-Coed to Cwm Carn in the Valleys northwest of Newport. There's something to suit everyone, from beginners to hardened speed freaks. There's no charge for using them (though there may be a small parking fee), but bike-rental facilities are rare and you are usually better off bringing your own machine or renting one from a nearby town.

Elsewhere, off-road cycling is allowed along designated bridleways (waymarked with blue arrows), including the Snowdon Ranger, Rhyd Ddu and Llanberis paths up Snowdon (detailed on p.359), but conflict between hikers and bikers has led to the creation of the **Snowdon Voluntary Cycling Agreement**, which limits the hours riders can use them. Anytime in winter (Oct–April) is OK and you can ride before 10am and after 5pm throughout the summer: slog up in the pre-dawn cool for that summit sunrise, or head up for sunset and a nerve-wracking dusk descent.

If you really fancy a challenge, make for **Sarn Helen**, an epic route across the country through Snowdonia and the Brecon Beacons loosely following an old Roman route. At 270 miles long – running from Conwy to Gower – it's reckoned to be the most ambitious off-road ride in Britain and is likely to take over a week.

Footpaths, unless otherwise marked, are for pedestrian use only, and even on bridleways you should as a cyclist always pass walkers at a considerate speed and with a courteous warning of your presence.

For more **information** check out: ⓦmbwales .com, a Visit Wales site concentrating on the main bike parks, or ⓦmtb-wales.com, which has excellent articles on routes along with groups where you can hook up with other riders. Local bookshops and bike stores stock relevant guides, but some of the best trails the country has to offer are covered by *Bikefax: The best mountain bike trails in Snowdonia* (£17) and *The Good Mountain Biking Guide* (£20).

The CTC and holidays

Britain's biggest **cycling organization**, the Cyclists' Touring Club (CTC: ☎0844 736 8450, ⓦctc.org.uk), supplies members with touring and technical advice as well as insurance. Its website is a wealth of information, including dozens of routes through Wales.

If you want a guaranteed hassle-free **cycling holiday**, various companies offer easy-going tours where you ride from hotel to hotel, and a van carries your bags. Some give you an arranged itinerary, while others guide you.

CYCLE TOURS

Bicycle Beano ☎01981 560471, ⓦbicycle-beano.co.uk. Book well ahead to join Bicycle Beano on week-long cycling holidays (£540–720) through the Wye Valley, the Cambrian coast and Snowdonia. They pedal along with you and rides include accommodation and all meals (except lunch). They're a lot of fun, good value for money and the cooking is vegetarian (and often organic).

Crwydro Môn ⓦ angleseywalkingholidays.com/cycling.html. Tailored, week-long, self-guided packages around Anglesey with bike, B&B and luggage transfer included.

Drover Holidays ⓦdroverholidays.co.uk. Over a dozen guided and self-guided bike tours all over Wales with everything organized and even the option of an electrically assisted bike to help with the nastier hills.

PedalAway ☎01989 770357, ⓦpedalaway.co.uk. Based over the border in Ross-on-Wye, PedalAway offer bike rental along with two-, four- and six-day self-guide touring itineraries into the Black Mountains, and along the Wye Valley, plus off-road tours.

Wheely Wonderful Cycling ⓦwheelywonderfulcycling.co.uk. Several self-guided tours around wonderfully rural sections of mid-Wales and the borders from a weekend to a week.

Beaches, surfing, kiteboarding and coasteering

Wales is ringed by fine **beaches** and **bays**, many of which are readily accessible by public transport – though some tend to get very busy in high summer. With most of the Welsh coast influenced by the currents of the North Atlantic Drift, water temperatures are higher than you might expect for this latitude, but only the truly hardy should consider swimming outside summer. For swimming and sunbathing, the best areas to head for are the Gower peninsula, the Pembrokeshire coast, the Llŷn and the southwest coast of Anglesey. Though it has more resorts than any other section of Wales' coastline, the north coast certainly hasn't got the most attractive beaches, nor is it a particularly alluring place to swim.

Wales' southwest-facing beaches offer the best conditions for **surfing**, **windsurfing** and **kiteboarding**. The water may not be that warm, but great sweeping beaches lashed by strong, steady winds off the Atlantic make for some excellent spots. Key centres are Rhosneigr on Anglesey, Aberdyfi along the Cambrian coast, Whitesands Bay (Porth-mawr) near St Davids, and Rhossili on the Gower peninsula near Swansea. All these places have shops selling gear and offering lessons. Kiteboarding isn't exactly an easy sport to learn, but a class can get you body-dragging (more fun than it sounds) inside a day, and actually riding a board in a couple of days.

For surfing information, contact the Welsh Surfing Federation Surf School (☎01792 386426, ⓦwsfsurfschool.co.uk) on the Gower peninsula.

If you'd rather surf indoors, the waterpark at Swansea's new state-of-the-art LC leisure complex (☎01792 466500, ⓦthelcswansea.com) features the "Board Rider", the UK's only standing surfing wave machine, with beginner, intermediate and advanced surfing lessons available.

Wales may not be at the cutting edge of adventure sports, but it led the way with **coasteering**, an exhilarating combination of hiking, coastal scrambling, swimming and cliff-jumping. Clad in a wetsuit, helmet and buoyancy aid, you aim to make your way as a group along the rugged, wave-lashed coastline. It was pioneered by St Davids-based TYF Adventure, who run a range of trips, from the relatively tame to full-on blasts along the coast and even eco-trips suited to families.

Kayaking and rafting

Board riders constantly have to compete for waves with the surf ski riders and **kayakers** who frequent the same beaches. Paddlers, however, have the additional run of miles of superb coastline, particularly around Anglesey, the Llŷn and the Pembrokeshire coast. The best general guide is the encyclopaedic *Welsh Sea Kayaking* (£20) by Jim Krawiecki and Andy Biggs.

Inland, short, steep bedrock rivers come alive after rain. As equipment improves, paddlers have become more daring, and Victorian tourist attractions such as Swallow and Conwy falls, both near Betws-y-Coed, are now fair game for a descent. Most of the kayaking is non-competitive, but on summer weekends you might catch a slalom or freestyle kayaking event at the National Whitewater Centre, outside Bala, or at the artificial Cardiff International White Water. In both places you can ride the rapids in rafts. The best whitewater resource is ⓦcanoewales.com.

TOP 5 BEACHES

Rhossili Bay Gower. See p.135
Barafundle Bay Pembrokeshire. See p.173
Tresaith near New Quay. See p.260
Ynyslas near Borth. See p.280
Porth Dinllaen The Llŷn. See p.388

Pony trekking

Wales' scattered population and large tracts of open land are ideal for **pony trekking**. Don't expect too much cantering over unfenced land: rides tend to be geared towards unhurried appreciation of the scenery from horseback, and are often combined with accommodation on farms. Rates are typically around £20 for the first hour and £10–15 for each subsequent hour.

Mid-Wales has the greatest concentration of stables, but there are places all over the country, amply detailed in the brochures supplied by the Wales Trekking and Riding Association (☎01497 847464, ⊛ridingwales.com).

Rugby

Rugby (the "Union" variety) is a passion with the Welsh, and their national game. Support is strongest in the working-class valleys of south Wales, where the fanaticism has traditionally been fuelled by the national side's success. Welsh rugby saw its glory days in the 1970s, when Wales turned out some of the best sides ever seen. The scarlet jerseys struck fear into their opponents in the **Five Nations Championship** – an annual tournament where Wales, England, Scotland, Ireland and France all played each other (now superseded by the Six Nations Championship, with the addition of Italy). That 1970s side won six out of the ten championships – three of them **Grand Slams**, where all the opponents were beaten. The players that made Wales so formidable included fearless fullback J.P.R. Williams, the elusive and magical outside-halves Barry John and Phil Bennett, and the dynamic scrum-half Gareth Edwards.

Victories were harder to come by in the 1980s, and by 1991, the national side reached its nadir with its worst-ever international loss of 63–6 at the hands of Australia. When rugby turned professional in 1995 it was able to coax back players who had defected to the rival code, rugby league, but Wales generally struggled to keep up with the standards of arch adversary England throughout the 1990s, let alone match the power and attacking panache of the all-conquering southern hemisphere sides. Recognizing this dominance of Australia, New Zealand and South Africa, the Welsh Rugby Union (⊛wru.co.uk) enlisted the coaching help of New Zealander, Graham Henry, in 1998. He oversaw an astonishing string of victories including one over South Africa in the first game to be played at the brand-new 72,500-seater **Millennium Stadium**, built on the site of the

legendary Cardiff Arms Park. All this raised hopes of success in the 1999 Rugby World Cup, hosted by Wales. They stumbled at the quarter-final stage, but in the process, Neil Jenkins overtook Australian Michael Lynagh's record for the greatest number of international points scored. An embarrassing loss to Argentina and a drubbing by Ireland put an end to Henry's reign. Wales only managed to get to the quarter-finals of the 2003 Rugby World Cup in Australia, but in 2005 Wales saw a massive turna-round and the national team lifted the Six Nations trophy with a Grand Slam. The next couple of years saw poor results culminating in an abominable 2007 Rugby World Cup when the national team failed to progress to the quarter-finals. Under another Kiwi coach, Warren Gatland, the national side rebounded in 2008 with a massive Grand Slam, conceding just two tries in the process. Results have been poorer since, until Wales pulled one out of the bag during the 2011 Rugby World Cup being robbed of a place in the final after a dubious sending off of captain Sam Worthington against France.

To see an international game, you'll have to be affiliated to one of the Rugby Union clubs or be prepared to pay well over the odds at one of the ticket agencies. Most tickets are allocated months before a match, and touts will often be found selling tickets for hundreds of pounds outside the gates on the day. Away from the international arena, a thriving rugby scene exists at club level, with upwards of a hundred clubs and 40,000 players taking to the field most Saturdays throughout the season (from September to just after Easter). The upper tier is known as the Magners League, with four Welsh teams – Cardiff Blues, Scarlets (formerly the Llanelli Scarlets), Newport Gwent Dragons and (Swansea) Ospreys – playing against the top teams from Ireland, Scotland and (from 2010–11) Italy. Welsh teams have won the competition four of the ten years it has run.

It's often worth going to a match purely for the light-hearted crowd banter – if you can understand the accents. Check with individual clubs for fixtures and ticket prices, which start at under £15 (though £20–25 is typical).

Football

Though **Welsh football** (soccer) is seen as a minority sport, it has just as many participants as rugby. The three top sides in the country – Cardiff City, Swansea City and Wrexham – all play within the English Football League system, though Wrexham were relegated from the fourth division in 2008. At the end of the 2010/11 season both Cardiff and Swansea made the playoffs for promotion from the second tier Championship, with Swansea achieving promotion to the Premier League. Three years earlier, Cardiff reached the final of the FA Cup for the first time since 1927.

The rest of the clubs play in the lacklustre (but improving) **Welsh Premier League** (Ⓦwelsh premier.com). For more on the Welsh game, check the website of the Football Association of Wales (Ⓦfaw.org.uk).

Under the stewardship of former player Mark Hughes, the national side experienced a brief spell of success between 2002 and 2004. Wales remained unbeaten during Hughes' first eight games in charge, often thanks to the mercurial brilliance of Ryan Giggs, with a morale-boosting win over Finland in Helsinki followed by a shock 2–1 victory over Italy.

In the end, Wales narrowly missed out on reaching the finals of Euro 2004, which would have been their first major finals since the 1958 World Cup, when they lost to eventual winners Brazil in the quarter-finals.

Recent results haven't been great, with few wins in the team's unsuccessful campaigns to reach any of the major competitions, including Euro 2012. They are currently ranked around 100th in the world. Maybe Gareth Bale, the Professional Footballers' Association's 2011 Player of the Year, can help galvanize national performances.

Alternative, New Age and green Wales

Possibly more than any other part of Britain, Wales – the mid and west in particular – has become something of a haven for those searching for alternative lifestyles. Permanent testimonials to this include the Centre for Alternative Technology (CAT), near Machynlleth, now one of the area's most visited attractions, and Tipi Valley, near Talley, a permanent community living in Native American tepees who run a regular public sweat lodge. Both institutions were founded in the idealistic mid-1970s and have prospered through less happy times. For the most part, it's been a fairly smooth process, although antagonism

between New Agers and local, established families does break out on occasion, usually stoked by the sometimes liberal smugness of some incomers.

For visitors, the legacy of this "green" influx is evident throughout Wales. Even in some of the smallest rural towns, you'll often find a health-food shop, wholefood café, somewhere flogging esoteric ephemera or an alternative resource centre. Any of these will give you further ideas and contacts for local happenings, places, groups and individuals.

There's also a plethora of good **festivals** from spring to autumn, ranging from big folk and blues bashes to smaller gatherings in remote fields, with little more than a couple of banging sound systems. Information travels best by word of mouth, so keep your eyes and ears peeled for information and don't hesitate to ask around. For more organized and larger events, you'll see adverts and fliers months in advance.

For ecologically minded tourists, there are now numerous package deals that include walking, cycling, dancing and healing holidays and retreats in remote centres, usually with vegetarian and vegan food as part of the deal. Some of these are static, many are in temporary sites, while others keep you on the move.

RETREATS AND HOLIDAYS

Buckland Hall Bwlch, near Brecon ☎ 01874 730330, Ⓦ bucklandhall.co.uk. Beautiful hall and gardens hosting holistic lifestyle courses and workshops.

Cae Mabon near Llanberis, Gwynedd ☎ 01286 871542, Ⓦ caemabon.co.uk. Stunning Snowdonia setting for residential courses, storytelling and arts events, with accommodation in roundhouses, a hogan and benders.

Centre for Alternative Technology Llwyngwern, near Machynlleth, Powys ☎ 01654 705950, Ⓦ cat.org.uk. Residential courses on green themes such as self-build homes and organic gardening.

Dance Camp Wales Pembrokeshire Ⓦ dancecampwales.org. Ten-day participatory dance festival held in July or August in a beautiful location, with about 500 participants.

Healing Tao Britain Conwy ☎ 01492 515776, Ⓦ healingtaobritain.com. Residential weekend workshops on meditation and Chi Kung.

Heartspring Llansteffan, Carmarthenshire ☎ 0845 652 2536, Ⓦ heartspring.co.uk. Three- or five-day retreats in a beautiful house, with holistic therapies and great veggie food.

Spirit Horse Camp Powys Ⓦ spirithorse.co.uk. Camps to celebrate ancient ceremonial and cultural traditions in a stunning, secluded setting.

Vajraloka Buddhist Meditation Centre Corwen, Denbighshire ☎ 01490 460406, Ⓦ vajraloka.org. Regular retreats, either men-only or mixed.

Travel essentials

Costs

Wales is certainly not a cheap destination, but prices are generally lower than in many parts of England, particularly London. With the current weakness of the pound, many foreign visitors should find prices quite reasonable.

The **minimum expenditure**, if you're camping and preparing most of your own food, would be £20–25 per day, rising to £35–40 per day if you're using the hostelling network, some public transport and grabbing the odd takeaway or meal out. Couples staying at budget B&Bs, eating at unpretentious restaurants and visiting a fair number of tourist attractions are looking at £60 each per day – if you're renting a car, staying in comfortable B&Bs or hotels and eating well, you should reckon on at least £80 a day. Single travellers should budget on spending around sixty percent of what a couple would spend, mainly because single rooms cost more than half the price of a double. For more detail on the cost of accommodation, transport and eating, see the relevant sections.

VAT

Most goods in Britain, with the chief exceptions of books and groceries, are subject to a 20 percent **Value Added Tax** (**VAT**), which is almost always included in the quoted price. Visitors from non-EU countries can get a VAT refund when leaving the country on goods bought through the **Retail Export Scheme**: participating shops have a sign in their window. See Ⓦcustoms.hmrc.gov.uk for details.

Student and youth cards

The various official and quasi-official **youth/student ID cards** are of relatively minor use in

TOP 5 INDUSTRIAL HERITAGE SITES

Ironworks and the Big Pit Blaenafon. See p.108

Colliery Museum Cefn Coed. See p.121

Clywedog Valley Wrexham. See p.310

National Slate Museum Llanberis. See p.354

Llechwedd Slate Caverns Blaenau Ffestiniog. See p.369

Wales, saving only a few pence for entry to some sites. If you already have one, then bring it, but if you don't, it's barely worth making a special effort to get one.

Full-time students are eligible for the International Student Identity Card (ISIC, Ⓦisiccard.com), while anyone under 26 can apply for an International Youth Travel Card, which carries the same benefits. Both cost £9.

Several other travel organizations and accommodation groups also sell their own cards, good for various discounts. A university photo ID might open some doors, but is not as easily recognizable as the ISIC cards.

Tipping and service charges

In restaurants a service charge is sometimes included in the bill; if it isn't, leave a tip of 10–15 percent unless the service is unforgivably bad. Taxi drivers expect a tip in the region of ten percent. You do not generally tip bar staff – if you want to show your appreciation, offer to buy them a drink.

Tourist attractions

Many of Wales' most treasured sites – from castles, abbeys and great houses to tracts of protected landscape – come under the control of the privately run UK-wide National Trust or the state-run CADW, whose properties are denoted in the Guide by "NT" and "CADW".

Both organizations charge an entry fee for most places, and these can be quite high, especially for the more grandiose NT estates. We've quoted the standard adult entry price, but UK taxpayers are encouraged to pay the gift aid price, which adds around ten percent to the normal adult price, but through tax offsets gives the NT considerable benefit.

If you think you'll be visiting more than half a dozen NT places or a similar number of major CADW sites, it's worth buying an annual pass. Membership of the National Trust (Ⓣ0844 800 1895, Ⓦnationaltrust.org.uk; £50.50, under-26s £23.50, family £88.50) allows free entry and parking at its properties throughout Britain. Sites operated by CADW (Ⓣ01443 336000, Ⓦcadw.wales.gov.uk; £35, seniors £22, ages 16–20 £20, under-16s £16) are restricted to Wales, but membership also grants you half-price entry to sites owned by English Heritage and Historic Scotland.

CADW offers the Explorer Pass, which allows free entry into all CADW sites on three days in seven (adult £13.20, family £28), or seven days In fourteen (£19.85/£38.75). Entry to CADW sites is free for

TOP 5 CASTLES

Carreg Cennen Castle Llandeilo.
See p.152

Castell-y-Bere Castle Dysynni Valley.
See p.291

Gwydir Castle Betws-y-Coed. See p.346

Caernarfon Castle Caernarfon. See p.360

Conwy Castle Conwy. See p.409

Welsh residents over 60: check their website to obtain a pass.

Many other old buildings, albeit rarely the most momentous, are owned by the local authorities, and admission is often cheaper. Municipal **art galleries** and **museums** are usually free, as are sites run by the National Museums and Galleries of Wales (Ⓦmuseumwales.ac.uk), including the National Museum and St Fagans National History Museum, both in Cardiff. Although a donation is usually requested, **cathedrals** tend to be free, except for perhaps the tower, crypt or other such highlight, for which a small charge is made. Increasingly, **churches** are kept locked except during services; when they are open, entry is free. (You'll normally be able to find a notice in the porch or on a board telling you where to get a key if the church is locked.) Wales also has a number of superb showcases of its **industrial heritage**, mostly concerned with mining and mineral extraction (see box opposite).

Keen birders might consider joining the **RSPB**, where membership (Ⓦrspb.org.uk; £36 a year) gives you free entry to its reserves throughout Britain.

Entry charges given in the Guide are the full adult rates, but the majority of the fee-charging attractions located in Wales have 10–25 percent **reductions** for senior citizens and full-time students, and 20–50 percent reductions for under-16s – under-5s are admitted free almost everywhere. Proof of eligibility is required in most cases. Family tickets are also common, usually priced just under the rate for two adults and a child and valid for up to three kids.

Finally, foreign visitors planning on seeing more than a dozen stately homes, monuments, castles or gardens might find it worthwhile to buy a **Great British Heritage Pass** (£39 for 3 days, £69 for 7 days, £89 for 15 days, £119 for 30 days; Ⓦbritishher-itagepass.com), which gives free admission to over four hundred sites throughout the UK, over forty of them in Wales.

Climate

The climate is fairly consistent across Wales, though it is considerably wetter, and a little cooler along the mountainous spine, particularly in Snowdonia.

Electricity

In Britain, the current is 240V AC at 50Hz. North American appliances will need a transformer, though most laptops, phone and MP3 player chargers are designed to automatically detect and adapt to the electricity supply and don't need any modification. Almost all foreign appliances will require an adapter for the chunky British three-pin electrical sockets.

For details of how to plug your **laptop** in when abroad, phone country codes around the world, and information about electrical systems in different countries look at Ⓦkropla.com.

Emergencies and police

As in any other country, Wales' major towns have their dangerous spots, but these tend to be inner-city housing estates where you're unlikely to find yourself. The chief risk on the streets – though still minimal – is pickpocketing, so carry only as much money as you need, and keep all bags and pockets fastened. Should you have anything stolen or be involved in an incident that requires reporting, go to the local police station. The ☎999 (traditional British) or ☎112 (pan-European) numbers for police, fire and ambulance services should only be used in emergencies. There is also a non-emergency number for the police ☎101 (10p per call).

AVERAGE MONTHLY TEMPERATURES AND RAINFALL

Cardiff

	Jan	Feb	Mar	Apr	May	Jun	Jul	Aug	Sep	Oct	Nov	Dec
Max/min (ºC)	8/2	8/2	11/4	13/5	17/8	19/11	21/3	21/13	18/10	15/7	11/4	9/3
Max/min (ºF)	46/36	47/36	51/39	56/41	62/46	67/51	71/55	71/55	65/50	58/46	51/40	48/38
Rainfall (mm)	119	91	89	65	65	66	61	90	104	117	117	128

> **TOP 5 GARDENS**
> **Dyffryn Gardens** Barry. See p.101
> **National Botanic Garden** Tywi Valley.
> See p.149
> **Aberglasney** Tywi Valley. See p.150
> **Powis Castle** Welshpool. See p.248
> **Bodnant** Conwy. See p.414

Entry requirements

Citizens of all European countries – other than Albania, Bosnia Herzegovina and most republics of the former Soviet Union – can enter Britain with just a passport, generally for up to three months. US, Canadian, Australian and New Zealand citizens can travel in Britain for up to six months with just a passport. All other nationalities require a visa, available from the British consular office in the country of application.

For stays longer than six months, check details on the UK Border Agency website (ⓦ ind.homeoffice .gov.uk), where you can download the appropriate form. Do this before the expiry date given on the endorsement in your passport.

Embassy contact details are listed on the website of the Foreign and Commonwealth Office (ⓦ fco.gov.uk): look for links to "Find Embassies" and "Find a Foreign Embassy in the UK".

OVERSEAS REPRESENTATION IN BRITAIN

Foreign embassies are all found in London.

Australia ☏ 020 7379 4334, ⓦ uk.embassy.gov.au.
Canada ☏ 020 7258 6600, ⓦ canada.org.uk.
Ireland ☏ 020 7235 2171, ⓦ embassyofireland.co.uk.
Netherlands ☏ 020 7590 3200, ⓦ netherlands-embassy.org.uk.
New Zealand ☏ 020 7930 8422, ⓦ nzembassy.com.
South Africa ☏ 020 7451 7299, ⓦ southafricahouseuk.com.
USA ☏ 020 7499 9000, ⓦ usembassy.org.uk.

Customs and biosecurity

Travellers entering Britain directly from another EU country do not have to make a declaration to **customs** at their place of entry, and can effectively bring almost as much wine or beer as they like. It is supposed to be for personal use, so if you have more than 90 litres of wine and 110 litres of beer you may be questioned. If you're travelling from a non-EU country duty-free allowances are as follows:

Tobacco: 200 cigarettes; or 100 cigarillos; or 50 cigars; or 250g of loose tobacco.

Alcohol: Four litres of still wine, **plus** one litre of drink over 22 percent alcohol, or two litres of alcoholic drink not over 22 percent, or another two litres of still wine.

You're also allowed other goods (including perfume) to the value of £390.

For details, contact HM Revenue & Customs (ⓦ www.hmrc.gov.uk).

Biosecurity is also an issue. It is illegal to import meat, milk and other animal products from outside the EU: see ⓦ defra.gov.uk for more details. The website also has details of the fairly strict PETS scheme which allows pet **cats** and **dogs** to enter Britain without quarantine.

Gay and lesbian Wales

Homosexual acts between consenting males were legalized in Britain in 1967, but it wasn't until 2000 that the age of consent for gay men was made equal to that of straight men at sixteen. Lesbianism has never specifically been outlawed, apocryphally owing to the fact that Queen Victoria refused to believe it existed. In December 2005, civil partnerships between same-sex couples were legalized – marriage in all but name.

With such a rural culture, it's perhaps not surprising that Wales is less used to the lesbian and gay lifestyle than its more cosmopolitan English neighbour. That said, there's little real hostility, with the traditional Welsh "live and let live" attitude applying as much in this area as any other. Several Welsh musicians, academics, TV stars and politicians have come out in recent years, and no one's really batted an eyelid.

The organized gay scene in Wales is fairly muted. The main cities – Cardiff, Newport and Swansea – have a number of pubs and clubs, with Cardiff especially beginning to see a worthy and confident gay scene – a Mardi Gras festival in early September included – more in keeping with the capital's size and status. Details are given in the text of the Guide. Out of the southern cities, however, gay life becomes distinctly discreet, although university towns such as Lampeter, Bangor and Wrexham manage support groups and the odd weekly night in a local bar, while Aberystwyth is a significantly homo-friendly milieu. The ⓦ gaywales.co.uk website is the best resource for gay and lesbian events, venues and accommodation, and has links to other relevant sites. Alternatively, there are some informal but well-established networks, especially among the sometimes reclusive alternative lifestylers found in mid- and west Wales. **Border Women** (who should surely have called themselves Offa's Dykes;

(W)borderwomen.org) is a well-organized lesbian network for mid-Wales and the Marches.

Health

No vaccinations are required for entry into Britain. Citizens of all EU countries are entitled to free medical **treatment** at National Health Service hospitals; citizens of other countries are charged for all medical services except those administered by accident and emergency units at National Health Service hospitals. Thus a US citizen who has been hit by a car would not be charged if the injuries simply required stitching and setting in the emergency unit, but would be if admission to a hospital ward were necessary. Health insurance is therefore strongly advised for all non-EU nationals.

Pharmacies (known generally as chemists in Britain) can dispense only a limited range of drugs without a doctor's prescription. Most pharmacies are open during standard shop hours, though in large towns some may stay open as late as 10pm. Doctors' surgeries tend to be open from about 9am until early evening; outside surgery hours, you can turn up at the casualty department of the local hospital for problems that require immediate attention – unless it's a real **emergency**, in which case ring for an ambulance on ☎999 or ☎112.

Insurance

Wherever you're travelling from, it's a good idea to have some kind of travel insurance to cover you for loss of possessions and money, as well as the cost of any medical and dental treatment. Before paying for a new policy, however, it's worth checking whether you are already covered: some all-risks home insurance policies may cover your posses- sions when overseas, and many private medical schemes include cover when abroad. Students will often find that their student health coverage

extends during the vacations and for one term beyond the date of last enrolment.

After exhausting the possibilities above, you might want to contact a specialist travel insurance company, or consider the travel insurance deal we offer (see box below). A typical travel insurance policy usually provides cover for the loss of baggage, tickets and – up to a certain limit – cash or cheques, as well as cancellation or curtailment of your journey. Most of them exclude so-called dangerous sports unless an extra premium is paid: in Wales this can mean whitewater rafting, windsurfing and coasteering, though probably not ordinary hiking. If you take medical coverage, ascertain whether benefits will be paid as treatment proceeds or only after return home, and whether there is a 24-hour medical emergency number. When securing baggage cover, make sure that the per-article limit – typically under £500 – will cover your most valuable possession. If you need to make a claim, you should keep receipts for medicines and medical treatment, and in the event you have anything stolen, you must obtain an official statement from the police.

Internet

Throughout Wales, almost all public libraries now have free **internet access** with several computers and wi-fi. Typically you just front up, and sign in for the next available half-hour or hour-long slot. Cybercafés (where you can expect to pay £2–4 an hour) are a dying breed, supplanted by the plethora of free **wi-fi** hotspots at cafés and bars – the Wetherspoon pub chain, many Brains pubs and even McDonald's. Free wi-fi is also common (but not universal) at B&Bs and hotels.

Mail

Virtually all **post offices** (*swyddfa'r post*) are open Monday to Friday 9am to 5.30pm, Saturday 9am to 12.30pm. In small communities, you'll find sub-post

---

ROUGH GUIDES TRAVEL INSURANCE

Rough Guides has teamed up with Columbus Direct to offer you tailor-made **travel insurance**. Products include a low-cost **backpacker** option for long stays; a **short break** option for city getaways; a typical **holiday package** option; and others. There are also annual **multi-trip** policies for those who travel regularly. Different sports and activities (trekking, skiing, etc) can usually be included.

See our website ((W)roughguides.com/website/shop) for eligibility and purchasing options. Alternatively, UK residents can call ☎0870 033 9988, Australians ☎1300 669 999 and New Zealanders ☎0800 559 911. All other nationalities should call ☎+44 870 890 2843.

offices operating out of a shop, but these work to the same hours even if the shop itself is open for longer. Stamps can be bought at post office counters and from a large number of newsagents and other shops, although often these sell only books of four or ten stamps. A first-class letter to anywhere in Britain (up to 100g) costs 46p and should arrive the next day; second-class letters cost 36p, taking two to four days to arrive. Postcards cost 68p to EU countries, and 76p to everywhere else. For parcel rates visit Ⓦ royalmail.com.

Maps

Most bookshops will have a good selection of **maps of Wales** and Britain, though the best can be found in specialist travel bookshops. Virtually every petrol station in Britain stocks large-format **road atlases** produced by the AA, RAC, Collins, Ordnance Survey (OS) and others, which cover all of Britain at a scale of around three miles to one inch and include larger-scale plans of major towns. The best of these is the Ordnance Survey road atlas, which handily uses the same grid reference system as their accurate and detailed folding maps.

For hiking, go for the widely available maps by **Ordnance Survey** (Ⓦ ordnancesurvey.co.uk), renowned for their accuracy and clarity. The 204 maps in its 1:50,000 (a little over one inch: one mile) Landranger series (£6.99 each) cover the whole of Britain, while the more detailed 1:25,000 Explorer series (£7.99 each) also covers the whole country, has field boundaries to aid navigation, and is at an ideal scale for walkers.

Measurements

Like the rest of Britain, Wales is in very slow transition from imperial to metric measurements. Groceries are sold in packets quoted in grams and litres but usually in portions equivalent to a pound or a pint. Maps show mountain heights in metres but road distances are in miles and speeds in miles per hour. Petrol is sold by the litre. In pubs, beer is still sold in pints.

Money

The British **pound sterling** (£; *punt* in Welsh, and informally referred to as a "quid") is divided into 100 pence (p; in Welsh, c for *ceiniogau*). Coins come in denominations of 1p, 2p, 5p, 10p, 20p, 50p, £1 and £2. Notes come in denominations of £5, £10, £20 and £50. Shopkeepers will carefully scrutinize any £20 and £50 notes tendered, as forgeries are not uncommon.

Cards, cheques and ATMs

Most hotels, shops and restaurants in Wales accept the major **credit**, **charge and debit cards**, particularly Access/MasterCard and Visa/Barclaycard. American Express and Diners' Club are less widely accepted. Cards are even accepted at lots of B&Bs, though you should always be prepared to pay cash. Many businesses that do accept cards require a £10 minimum purchase. With a suitable PIN (ask at your bank before leaving home) your card will also enable you to get cash advances from most ATMs, though there may be a standard fee which makes it more cost-effective to withdraw larger sums. In addition, you may be able to make withdrawals from your home bank account using your ATM cash card – check before leaving home.

The safest way to carry your money is in **travellers' cheques**, available for a small commission (normally one percent) from any major bank. These can be exchanged at banks and bureaux de change and replaced if lost of stolen. Recognized brands – American Express, Thomas Cook, MasterCard and Visa – are accepted in all major currencies, but travellers' cheques (even in sterling) aren't accepted as cash.

Banks

Almost every Welsh town has a branch of at least one of the major banks: NatWest, Halifax, HSBC, Barclays and Lloyds TSB. As a general rule, opening hours are Monday to Friday 9 or 9.30am to 4.30 or 5pm, and branches in larger towns are often open on Saturday from 9am to 1pm. In the larger towns you may be able to find a bureau de change (often the post office), which will be open longer hours but may charge high commission.

Opening hours and public holidays

General **shop hours** are Monday to Saturday 9am to 5.30/6pm, although there's an increasing amount of Sunday and late-night shopping in the larger towns, with Thursday or Friday being the favoured evenings. The big supermarkets also tend to stay open until 8 or 9pm from Monday to Saturday, and open on Sunday from 10am to 4pm, as do many of the stores in the shopping complexes springing up on the outskirts of major towns. Note that not all **service stations** are open 24 hours, although you can usually get fuel around the clock in the larger towns

PUBLIC HOLIDAYS

New Year's Day January 1.
Good Friday late March to mid-April.
Easter Monday late March to mid-April.
Early May Bank Holiday first Monday in May.
Spring Bank Holiday (sometimes referred to as Whitsun) last Monday in May.

Late summer Bank Holiday Last Monday in August.
Christmas Day December 25.
Boxing Day December 26.
Note that if January 1, December 25 or December 26 falls on a Saturday or Sunday, the next weekday becomes a public holiday.

and cities. Also, most fee-charging sites are open on bank holidays, when Sunday hours usually apply.

In addition to the public holidays (see box, above) your travels around Wales may be disrupted by **school holidays**, when accommodation in popular areas (especially near beaches) is stretched by holidaying families. The main school holidays are two weeks around Christmas and New Year, two weeks around Easter, and six weeks from mid-July to early September. There is also a one-week break in the middle of each term, one usually falling in late May.

Phones

Given the near-ubiquity of mobile phones, most people don't have much need for public **payphones** (*teleffon*), which are operated by BT (🆆 bt.co.uk), and are still found all over the place. Some also allow SMS text messaging (20p) and have internet access (£1 for 15min). Calls to anywhere in the UK (except to mobiles and premium numbers) **cost** 60p for the first 30 minutes then 10p for every 15 minutes thereafter. Most payphones in out-of-the-way places no longer take coins, forcing you to use credit and debit cards (UK calls 20p/min, plus a £1 connection charge), or account-based phonecards available from post offices and some shops. When buying such cards, read the small print, as there are often all manner of extra charges and penalties.

Call costs vary greatly depending on whether you are calling from a private land line, public pay-phone or the mobile network you are on. We've given call cost guidelines below.

To **call Wales** from outside the UK, dial the international access code (🆃 011 from the US and Canada, 🆃 0011 from Australia and 🆃 00 from New Zealand), followed in all cases by 44, then the area code minus its initial zero, and finally the number.

PHONE NUMBER STYLES

🆃 **07xx** Mobile phone numbers. Calling one costs more than dialling a land line.

🆃 **0800** & 🆃 **0808** Free from a land-line and up to 40p a minute from a mobile.
🆃 **0845** & 🆃 **0870** reduced-rate national calls. Cheaper than calling long distance and free from some private lines.
🆃 **09xx** Premium-rated numbers cost 60p–£1.50 per minute.

USEFUL PHONE NUMBERS

National operator (freecall) 🆃 100.
International operator (freecall) 🆃 155.
National Directory Enquiry Several services including 🆃 118 118 (42p/min plus £1.29 connection charge).
International Directory Enquiry Several services including 🆃 118 661 (£1.86/min plus £2 connection fee).

Mobile phones

If you're bringing your own phone, you'll need to check with your phone provider whether it will work in Britain, and what the call charges are. The GSM system used in Britain is compatible with other European and Australasian systems, though most North American single-band phones don't work here. A better bet might be to bring your phone and buy a new pre-pay SIM card for it (under £5). With no contract you simply top up your account as you need to. Of course you'll have to tell your friends and colleagues your new number but you'll save on call costs. If your phone doesn't work on UK frequency bands you may need one that does. These are available from the numerous high-street outlets from as little as £15.

There's frenetic competition between the main operators – Vodafone (🆆 vodafone.co.uk), O2 (🆆 o2 .co.uk), Orange (🆆 orange.co.uk) and T-mobile (🆆 t-mobile.co.uk) – so shop around for a package that suits you.

Shopping

The quintessential Welsh memento is a **lovespoon** – an intricately carved wooden spoon that in centuries gone by was offered by suitors when courting. The meanings of the various designs range from a Celtic cross (symbolizing faith/

marriage) to vines (growing love) and a double spoon (commitment), with dozens of others available. Prices range from a few pounds for a small version, to several hundred pounds for a large, elaborate spoon by a well-known carver. You'll find them in craft shops all over the country, including some dedicated solely to these ornaments.

Other unique items include some superb paintings, jewellery, leatherwork and screen-printing from **arts and crafts** galleries throughout Wales; some are run by the artists themselves, and you can watch them at work. Given that Wales has an estimated three to four times as many sheep as humans, it's not surprising that there are some wonderful **woollen products** available.

A good online resource is the Wales Crafts Council (𝕎 walescraftcouncil.co.uk).

Smoking

Since 2007 smoking has been banned in restaurants, bars and clubs and on public transport. You'll now see clusters of die-hard smokers outside pubs and occupying café pavement tables in all weathers. Cigarettes are seldom on display (you'll have to ask for them) and may soon come in plain packaging.

Studying in Wales

There are numerous places around Wales where you might attend full-day or multi-day courses (residential or otherwise) to pursue all manner of interests. Some of the most interesting are:

Nant Gwrtheyrn 10 miles north of Pwllheli ☎ 01758 750334, 𝕎 nantgwrtheyrn.org. If you're keen on acquiring some Welsh beyond the basics, this is about the best bet there is. Residential courses are run for everyone from complete beginners to near-fluent speakers: either weekend (full board £225), three-day (£280) or five-day (£485). See p.388.

Plas Menai: The National Watersports Centre near Caernarfon ☎ 01248 670964, 𝕎 plasmenai.co.uk. All manner of predominantly two- and five-day courses covering sailing, windsurfing, kayaking and jet skiing in a beautiful location on the Menai Strait. For two-day courses expect to pay £185 (£125 non-resident), for five-day budget on £400 (£300).

Plas Tan y Bwlch near Porthmadog ☎ 01766 772 600, 𝕎 plastanybwlch.com. Snowdonia National Park Study Centre which runs residential courses focusing mainly on the environment and appreciation of the countryside. They extend to landscape photography (3 days, £160), botanical painting (5 days, £430), mushrooms and toadstools (2 days, £160), drovers and drovers' roads (4 days, £290), heritage railways (6 days, £465) and much more. Many are taught in Welsh or bilingually, and are suitable for Welsh-language beginners.

Plas y Brenin: The National Mountain Centre Capel Curig ☎ 01690 720214, 𝕎 pyb.co.uk. This internationally recognized outdoor training centre runs a huge range of residential courses and two-hour samplers at all levels up to expert, plus expedition training. Examples of beginner courses include: the two-day Navigation Skills course for hill-walkers (£230), the five-day Advanced Scrambling week (£560), the weekend introduction to rock climbing (£295), a five-day intro to sea kayaking (£475), a multi-activity weekend (£175), and many more. Also offers qualification courses for all levels of instructors. See p.348.

Time

Greenwich Mean Time (GMT) is in force from late October to late March, when the clocks go forward an hour for British Summer Time (BST). GMT is five hours ahead of New York, ten hours behind Sydney, and twelve hours behind New Zealand.

Tourist information

Wales promotes itself enthusiastically, broadly through **Visit Britain** and more specifically through **Visit Wales**, both with extensive websites offering a wealth of free literature, some of it just rose-tinted advertising copy, but much of it extremely useful – especially the maps, city guides and event calendars.

Visit Wales and tourist offices

Visit Wales (aka Croeso Cymru: ☎ 0870 830 0306, 𝕎 visitwales.com) operates a central information service that's excellent for pre-trip planning, with a detailed website and plenty of free brochures which can either be downloaded or sent by mail. There is also representation at Visit Britain, 1 Regent St, London SW1Y 4XT (☎ 020 8846 9000, 𝕎 visitbritain.com).

Tourist offices (usually called Tourist Information Centres or TICs) exist in many Welsh towns – you'll find their contact details and opening hours throughout the Guide. The average opening hours are much the same as standard shop hours, though in summer they'll often be open on a Sunday and for a couple of hours after the shops have closed on weekdays; opening hours are generally shorter in winter, and in more remote areas the office may well be closed altogether. All centres offer information on accommodation (which they can often book), local public transport, attractions and restaurants, as well as town and regional maps.

Areas designated as national parks (the Brecon Beacons, Pembrokeshire Coast and Snowdonia) also have a fair sprinkling of **National Park**

Information Centres, which are generally more expert in giving guidance on local walks and outdoor pursuits.

Travellers with disabilities

Visitors with disabilities will find travelling in Wales easier than in much of the world, though many older buildings (and especially cheaper places to stay) are difficult or impossible to adapt and it always pays to call ahead to check the situation. Disabled parking spaces are common, new buildings (including accommodation) are required to make appropriate provision, and a fair number of existing hotels, B&Bs and restaurants are retrofitting accessible bathrooms and ramps. Some YHAs (see p.35) also have disabled facilities.

Public transport companies are beginning to make more of an effort to accommodate passengers with mobility problems. Some rail services now cater for wheelchair users in relative comfort, and some assistance is available at stations if you call at least 24 hours in advance; call National Rail Enquiries (see p.29) to get the number of the appropriate rail company. You may be eligible for the Disabled Persons Railcard (£20 per year), which gives a third off most tickets for you and a companion. The link for "Passengers with disabilities" at Ⓦ nationalrail.co.uk has reams of information for journey planning, including maps identifying stations that have access to platforms without steps. There are no bus discounts for disabled passengers who are not Welsh citizens. Rental cars with hand controls are rare and expensive; Hertz offers models at the same rate as conventional vehicles, though in the more expensive categories. Call their dedicated line Ⓣ 0870 840 0084.

Access to monuments and museums is improving all the time. The National Trust (see p.48) produces a downloadable sheet detailing accessibility to NT properties in Wales; disabled visitors must pay entry fees, but they can bring a friend or carer in to assist them free of charge. CADW allows wheelchair users and the visually handicapped, along with their assisting companion, free entry to all monuments. You can download a booklet with detailed site access details. Access to theatres, cinemas and other public places is slowly improving.

Some public toilets are kept locked, but some local authorities have joined the National Key System (NKS) in which disabled people can gain access to facilities via a standard key (£3.50; contact RADAR, see below). Some tourist offices also hold a key which you can borrow.

There's no shortage of contact points for information, the best being RADAR and Disability Wales.

Contacts for travellers with disabilities

UK AND IRELAND

Disability Wales Ⓣ 029 2088 7325, Ⓦ disabilitywales.org. Welsh equivalent of RADAR (see below).

Irish Wheelchair Association Ⓣ 01 818 6400, Ⓦ iwa.ie. Useful information provided about travelling abroad.

RADAR: the disability network Ⓣ 020 7250 3222, TTY 7250 4119, Ⓦ radar.org.uk. Campaigning organization that's a good source of advice on holidays and travel in the UK. Produces the annual Open Britain guide to accessible travel and accommodation for £10.

Tourism For All UK Ⓣ 0845 124 9971, Ⓦ tourismforall.org.uk. Offers various guides and advice for access throughout Britain.

Wales Council for the Blind Ⓣ 029 2047 3954, Ⓦ wcb-ccd .org.uk. Though not specifically set up with visitors in mind, it does provide a good contact point.

Wales Council for the Deaf Ⓣ 01443 485687, minicom 01443 485686, Ⓦ wcdeaf.org.uk. Also not specifically set up with visitors in mind, but provides a good contact point.

NORTH AMERICA

Access-Able Ⓦ access-able.com. Online resource for travellers with disabilities.

Mobility International USA & TTY 541 343 1284, Ⓦ miusa .org. Information and referral services, access guides, tours and exchange programmes.

Society for Accessible Travel and Hospitality (SATH) Ⓣ 212 447 7284, Ⓦ sath.org. Long-standing non-profit educational organization with useful travel tips and access information on its website.

AUSTRALIA AND NEW ZEALAND

Disabled Persons Assembly Ⓣ & TTY 04 801 9100, Ⓦ dpa.org.nz. Resource centre with lists of travel agencies and tour operators for people with disabilities.

National Disability Services Ⓣ & TTY 02 6283 3200, Ⓦ nds.org.au. Formerly "ACROD"; provides lists of travel agencies and tour operators for people with disabilities.

Southeast Wales

KAYAKERS ON RHOSSILI BEACH

1

Southeast Wales

Home to some sixty percent of the country's population, the southeastern corner of Wales is one of Britain's most industrialized regions. Both people and industry are most heavily concentrated around the sea ports and former mining valleys, though quiet hills and beaches are only ever a few miles away. Wales unfolds from the English border in a beguilingly rural manner. The River Wye flows forth from its mouth at the fortress town of Chepstow, where you'll find one of the most impressive castles in a land where few towns are without one. In the Wye's beautiful valley lie the spectacularly placed ruins of Tintern Abbey, downstream from the old county town of Monmouth. Industrialization intensifies as you travel west to the River Usk which spills out into the Bristol Channel at Newport, Wales' third-largest conurbation, and home to the remains of an extensive Roman settlement in adjacent Caerleon.

To the west and north are the world-famous **Valleys**, once the coal- and iron-rich powerhouse of the British Empire. This is the Wales of popular imagination: hemmed-in valley floors packed with seemingly never-ending lines of slate-roofed terraced houses, slanted towards the pithead. Although all the deep mines have closed, the area is still one of tight-knit towns, with a rich working-class heritage displayed in some illuminating museums and colliery tours, such as the **Big Pit** at Blaenafon and the **Rhondda Heritage Park** in Trehafod. The valleys follow rivers coursing down towards the coast, where great ports shipped their products all over the world. The greatest of them all was **Cardiff**, once the world's busiest coal port, now Wales' upbeat capital. Stellar museums, a storybook castle, exciting rejuvenation projects and Wales' best cultural pursuits make the city an essential stop.

Immediately west of the capital, and a world away from the industrial hangover of the city and Valleys, is the lush **Vale of Glamorgan** and **Glamorgan Heritage Coast**, which stretches 28 miles westwards to include the neighbouring county of Bridgend. The entire area is dotted with stoic little market towns and chirpy seaside resorts – most notably **Barry** in the east and **Porthcawl** in the west.

West again is Wales' second city, **Swansea**. Bright, breezy and brash, Swansea is renowned for its nightlife and is undergoing rapid development, particularly along its historic waterfront. Like Cardiff, Swansea grew principally on the strength of its now revitalized docks, from where the coast arcs round from the **Port Talbot** steelworks in the east to the elegant holiday town of **Mumbles** on the jaw of the magnificent **Gower**

WELSH DRAGON ON FRONT OF MOTORPOINT ARENA, CARDIFF

Highlights

❶ Tintern Abbey Get your poetic juices flowing at Tintern's towering ruins, romantically situated in the Wye Valley. **See p.64**

❷ Caerleon Contemplate whether Wales' best-preserved Roman remains were the site of King Arthur's fabled court, Camelot. **See p.76**

❸ Cardiff Dazzling architecture, fine museums and some cracking nightlife mark the Welsh capital out as a must-visit destination. **See p.78**

❹ National History Museum, St Fagans Take a free and fascinating amble around this wonderful ensemble of Welsh buildings from the past. **See p.98**

❺ Blaenafon Strap on a hardhat and head-lamp and follow ex-coal miners into the Big Pit – one of the country's most poignant and powerful museums. **See p.108**

❻ Rhossili beach Surf some of Britain's best waves where the Gower peninsula ends in a flourish. **See p.135**

HIGHLIGHTS ARE MARKED ON THE MAP ON P.61

1

peninsula in the west. The Gower was Britain's first-ever designated Area of Outstanding Natural Beauty, and remains a microcosm of rural Wales, with its grand beaches, rocky headlands, ruined castles and bracken heaths roamed by wild horses.

GETTING AROUND   SOUTHEAST WALES

By car Southeast Wales is by far the easiest part of the country to travel around. Swift dual carriageways connect with the M4, bringing all corners of the region into close proximity.

By bus and train Public transport is similarly thorough: this is the only part of Wales with a half-decent train service, and most suburban and rural services interconnect with Cardiff, Newport or Swansea. Bus services fill in virtually all of the gaps, though often rather slowly. Check Getting around in Basics for discount fares and passes.

The Wye Valley

Only in the local government reorganization of 1974 was the **Wye Valley** finally recognized as part of Wales in; before this, the area was officially included as part of neither England nor Wales, so that maps were frequently headlined "Wales and Monmouthshire" (the county name). In this easterly corner, the two main towns are decidedly English in flavour: **Chepstow**, at the mouth of the Wye, with its massive castle radiating an awesome strength; and **Monmouth**, sixteen miles upstream, a spruce, old-fashioned town with the lingering air of an ancient seat of authority.

Six miles north of Chepstow, on the banks of the Wye, stand the inspirational ruins of the Cistercian **Tintern Abbey**, while across the river the southern segments of the **Offa's Dyke** earthworks are shadowed by a long-distance footpath (see box, p.43).

Chepstow

Of all the places that call themselves "the gateway to Wales", **CHEPSTOW** (Cas-Gwent) – the first Welsh town on the main road into the country – has probably the strongest claim. Situated on the western bank of the River Wye, just over a mile from where its tidal waters recede into the Severn estuary, Chepstow is an easy-going and engaging place, and worth a stop to visit its ancient castle.

Chepstow's position as a former river port is evident in the thirteenth-century **Port Wall**, encasing the castle precincts and the town centre in their loop of the river. The fifteenth-century **West Gate** marks the southern end of the **High Street**, a handsome thoroughfare sided by Georgian and Victorian buildings and sloping down from the gate towards the river. Here, the elegant five-arch cast-iron **Old Wye Bridge**, built in 1816, is still in use for cross-border traffic into England. This section of the Wye is tremendously tidal, with a mighty 49ft difference in the water level between high and low tides – one of the world's highest tidal drops. A short street with a riverside esplanade, The Back, runs southeast from the bridge; a plaque on the wall of the *La Bodega Susan'na* restaurant commemorates the quay as the site from which the three leaders of Newport's Chartist March of 1839 were dispatched to Van Diemen's Land (now Tasmania), in Australia.

A five-minute walk up the hill from The Back, **St Mary's Priory church** was founded at the same time as the castle, in around 1072, as a Benedictine priory. Much of what survived has been modernized over the centuries, but today you can still see its Norman origins, including an intricate arched eleventh-century doorway.

Chepstow Castle

Bridge St • March–Oct daily 9.30am–5pm, July & Aug till 6pm; Nov–Feb Mon–Sat 10am–4pm, Sun 11am–4pm • £4 • ☎ 01291 624065 • CADW

The strategic location of **Chepstow Castle** could scarcely be bettered. Built tight into a loop of the River Wye, it guards one of the most important routes into Wales.

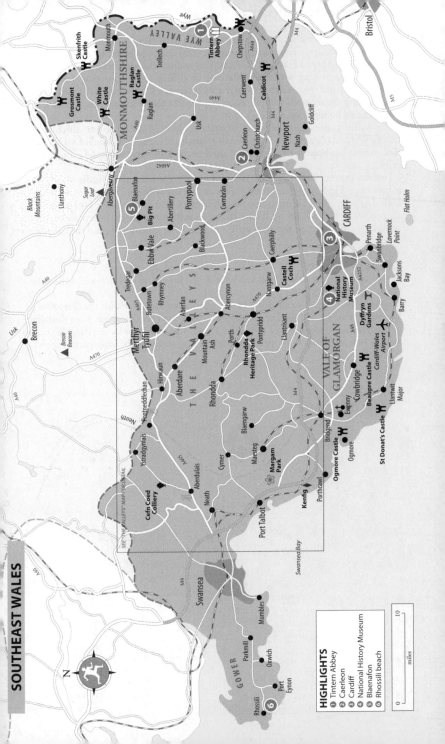

SOUTHEAST WALES

HIGHLIGHTS

1. Tintern Abbey
2. Caerleon
3. Cardiff
4. National History Museum
5. Blaenafon
6. Rhossili beach

0   10
miles

N

WYE VALLEY

MONMOUTHSHIRE

Skenfrith Castle
Monmouth
Grosmont Castle
White Castle
Raglan Castle
Trellech
Raglan
Usk
Tintern Abbey
Chepstow
Caldicot
Caerwent
Goldcliff
Nash
Newport
Christchurch
Caerleon
Cwmbrân
Pontypool
Abertillery
Blackwood
Caerphilly
Blaenafon
Big Pit
Ebbw Vale
Tredegar
Butetown
Rhymney
Aberfan
Abercynon
Nantgarw
Castell Coch
CARDIFF
Penarth
Lavernock Point
Swanbridge
Jacksons Bay
Barry
CARDIFF
National History Museum
Dyffryn Gardens
Cardiff-Wales Airport
VALE OF GLAMORGAN
Llantwit Major
St Donat's Castle
Beaupre Castle
Cowbridge
Ewenny
Bridgend
Ogmore Castle
Ogmore
Porthcawl
Kenfig
Port Talbot
Margam Park
Maesteg
Cymer
Blaengarw
Rhondda
Aberdare
Hirwaun
Rhondda Heritage Park
Porth
Mountain Ash
Pontypridd
Llantrisant
Merthyr Tydfil
THE VALLEYS
Pontneddfechan
Ystradgynlais
Aberdulais
Neath
Cefn Coed Colliery
SEE "THE VALLEYS" MAP FOR DETAIL
SWANSEA
Mumbles
GOWER
Parkmill
Oxwich
Port Eynon
Rhossili
Swansea Bay
Brecon
Brecon Beacons
Black Mountains
Llanthony
Sugar Loaf
Abergavenny
Bristol
Flat Holm
Wye

1

Chepstow was the first stone castle to be built in Britain, with its first Norman incarnation, the Great Tower keep, rising in 1067, just one year after William the Conqueror's victory at Hastings. William had realized the importance of subduing the restless Welsh, creating borderland Marcher Lordships and encouraging the title holders to expand into Welsh territory: a succession of Chepstow's lords attempted this, necessitating the renewed and increasingly powerful fortification of their castles over the next two hundred years.

The walled castle comprises three separate enclosures, the largest of which is the Lower Ward, dating mainly from the thirteenth century. Here, you'll find the **Great Hall**, which has been colourfully re-created as the Earl's chamber, and a fine vaulted cellar.

Twelfth-century defences separate the Lower Ward from the Middle Ward, which is dominated by the still-imposing ruins of the **Great Tower**, whose lower floors include the original Norman keep. Beyond the Great Tower is the far narrower Upper Ward which leads up to the Barbican **watchtower**, from where there are superlative views back over the castle and down the cliff to the mud flats of the river estuary.

Chepstow Museum

Bridge St • July–Sept Mon–Sat 10.30am–5.30pm, Sun 2–5.30pm; Nov–Feb Mon–Sat 11am–4pm, Sun 2–4pm; Oct & March–June Mon–Sat 11am–5pm, Sun 2–5pm • Free

Opposite the castle, a cream-painted Georgian townhouse contains the **Chepstow Museum**. Staid but comprehensive displays cover aspects of local life, with nostalgic photographs and paintings of the trades supported in the past by the River Wye, and records of Chepstow's brief spell as a shipbuilding centre in the early part of the twentieth century.

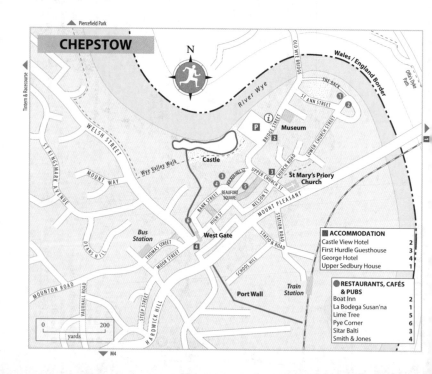

■ ACCOMMODATION	
Castle View Hotel	2
First Hurdle Guesthouse	3
George Hotel	4
Upper Sedbury House	1

● RESTAURANTS, CAFÉS & PUBS	
Boat Inn	2
La Bodega Susan'na	1
Lime Tree	5
Pye Corner	6
Sitar Balti	3
Smith & Jones	4

The Wye Valley Walk

From Chepstow, you can follow the first section of the fairly challenging, two-and-a-half-hour **Wye Valley Walk** to Tintern Abbey, which starts from the castle car park. A map – or the official route guide (£7.95), available from the tourist office – is advisable, as the path tucks and meanders around and above the twisting Wye. The walk brushes past the picturesque old estate of **Piercefield Park**, a mile north of town, part of which has metamorphosed into **Chepstow Racecourse** (☎01291 622260, ⌨www.chepstow-racecourse.co.uk), one of the country's premier racing venues, with regular, year-round meets, culminating in the Welsh National in December. The entrance is off the A466 north of town. You could return along the other side of the river on the Offa's Dyke Path, which passes the dramatic viewpoint of Devil's Pulpit (just off the B4228) and reaches its southern end at Sedbury Cliffs, a mile or so east of town on the English side of the border.

ARRIVAL AND DEPARTURE   CHEPSTOW

By train Trains between Cardiff and Birmingham stop at Chepstow's train station, 5min walk south of the High St. Destinations Cardiff (every 30–60min; 40min); Gloucester (every 30–60min; 30min); Newport (every 30–60min; 25min)

By bus The bus station is on Thomas St on the other side of the West Gate.

Destinations Bristol (hourly; 50min); Caerwent (hourly; 15min); Cardiff (hourly; 1hr 20min); Monmouth (hourly; 50min); Newport (every 30min; 50min); Penhow (hourly; 40min); Tintern (9 daily; 20min); Usk (5 daily; 35min).

INFORMATION

Tourist information The TIC is located in the castle car park, off Bridge St (daily: Easter–Oct 9.30am–5pm;

Nov–Easter 9.30am–3.30pm, closed 1–2pm; ☎01291 623772, ⌨chepstowtowncrier.org.uk).

ACCOMMODATION

Castle View Hotel 16 Bridge St ☎01291 620349, ⌨castleviewhotel.com. Bags of charm in this seventeenth-century building, with thirteen cosy rooms featuring crooked floors, thick oak beams and exposed stone walls; some have castle views. Good value. **£77**

First Hurdle Guesthouse 9 Upper Church St ☎01291 622189, ⌨thefirsthurdle.com. Rooms in this large, central and restful B&B have firm beds, attractive decor and shiny bathrooms. **£60**

George Hotel Moor St, next to the West Gate ☎01291 625363, ⌨thegeorgechepstow.com. A hostelry of sorts

for several centuries, the George's large, simply furnished rooms sit above a ground-floor bar and restaurant, though they are reasonably well insulated. **£50**

Upper Sedbury House Sedbury Lane ☎01291 627173, ⌨smoothhound.co.uk/hotels/uppersed. Friendly B&B a mile east over the Wye with comfortable en-suite rooms, residents' lounge and summertime outdoor pool. There's also a paddock for campers, who can use the facilities and take breakfast in the house. **£45**

EATING AND DRINKING

Boat Inn The Back ☎01291 628192. The most convivial of the waterside pubs, with black timber beams, bare brick walls, maritime paraphernalia, and a warm, welcoming atmosphere; decent selection of ales and a good, vegetarian-friendly menu. Daily 9.30am–11pm.

La Bodega Susan'na 18 The Back ☎01291 626868. Good-quality food in this handsome riverside restaurant, whose main focus is tapas and modern Mediterranean cuisine; the two-course lunch menu is good value. Mains £15–18. Tues–Sat 10am–11pm, Sun 10am–6pm.

Lime Tree 24 St Mary's St ☎01291 620959. Two-floored café/bar, with burgundy walls covered in local photographs, leather sofas and softly lit corners. It's a good spot for

breakfast (pancakes, smoothies) or lunch (burgers, filled breads, tapas), and there's regular nightly fun (jazz, acoustic and quizzes). Daily 8.30am–11pm.

Pye Corner Bank St ☎01291 630886. Homely three-in-one coffee shop, bar and restaurant, though the best reason to come here is to munch into one of the scrumptious home-made pies, such as minty lamb and Thai chook. Ciders and ales on tap too. Daily 11am–11pm, Fri & Sat till 1am.

Sitar Balti The Cellar, Beaufort Square ☎01291 627351. Well-regarded Indian restaurant in the basement of a townhouse, specializing in balti lamb and chicken dishes; the fish dishes are pretty special too. Mains £8–12. Daily 6pm–midnight.

Smith & Jones 9 Beaufort Square ☎01291 629683. Modern sandwich shop with soups, baguettes and panini, as well as a colourful salad bar; just the ticket for a castle or riverside picnic. Mon–Sat 8am–3pm.

Tintern Abbey and around

Six miles north of Chepstow, the roofless ruins of **Tintern Abbey** are spectacularly sited on one of the most scenic stretches of the River Wye. The abbey and its valley have inspired writers and painters ever since the Reverend William Gilpin published a book in 1782 extolling their picturesque qualities, and the "tall rock/The mountain, and the deep and gloomy wood" written about by Wordsworth are still evident today. Such is the abbey's enormous popularity, however, that it can get murderously busy, so it's best to go out of season or at the beginning or end of the day when the crowds have thinned out.

The best way to appreciate the scale and splendour of the abbey ruins is by walking along the opposite bank of the Wye. Just upstream from the abbey, a bridge crosses the river, from where a path climbs a wooded hillside. Views along the way and from the top are magnificent.

The ruins

March–Oct daily 9.30am–5pm, July & Aug till 6pm; Nov–Feb Mon–Sat 10am–4pm, Sun 11am–4pm • £3.80 • ☎01291 689251 • CADW

The abbey lasted as a monastic settlement from its foundation by the Cistercian order in 1131 until its dissolution in 1536, and the original order of monks was brought wholesale from Normandy, its members establishing themselves as major local landholders and agriculturalists. This increased the power and wealth of the abbey, attracting more monks and necessitating a massive rebuilding and expansion plan in the fourteenth century, when Tintern was at its mightiest. Most of the remaining buildings date from this time, after which the influence of the abbey and its order began to wane. Upon dissolution, many of the buildings were plundered and stripped, leaving the abbey to crumble. The fact that the ruins have survived at all is largely thanks to their remoteness, as there were no nearby villages to use the stone for rebuilding.

The church

The centrepiece of the complex was the magnificent Gothic **church**, built at the turn of the fourteenth century to encase its more modest predecessor. It retains an extraordinary sense of grandeur, and much of the building remains intact, including the remarkable tracery in the west window and intricate stonework of the capitals and columns.

The monks' quarters

Around the church are the less substantial ruins of the **monks' domestic quarters**, mostly reduced to one-storey rubble. Rooms are easily distinguishable, however, including an intact serving hatch in the kitchen and the square of the monks' **cloister**. The course of the abbey's waste disposal system can be seen in the **Great Drain**, an irregular channel that links kitchens, toilets and the infirmary with the nearby Wye. The **Novices' Hall** lies close to the Warming House, which, together with the kitchen and infirmary, would have been the only heated parts of the abbey, suggesting that novices might have gained a falsely favourable impression of monastic life before taking their final vows. In the dining hall, you can still see the **pulpit door** that would once have led to the wall-mounted pulpit, from which a monk would read the scriptures throughout each meal.

Tintern village

Now cluttered with teashops and overpriced hotels, the tiny village of **TINTERN** (Tyndyrn), immediately north of the abbey, is strung along a mile or so of the A466

The
Colliers

1

around a loop of the river. Some 200yd along the road, by the small stone arch bridge, the **Abbey Mill** centre (daily 10am–5.30pm) houses a restored nineteenth-century water wheel – which springs into action at half past each hour – as well as craft shops and a coffeehouse. Further along Monmouth Road, bibliophiles will want to browse through the rare and out-of-print titles – including some particularly rare children's titles – at Tintern's wonderful **bookshop**, Stella Books (daily 10am–5.30pm).

ARRIVAL AND DEPARTURE
TINTERN

By bus Buses stop at the abbey and at several points along the main village road and serve Chepstow (9 daily; 20min) and Monmouth (8 daily; 30min).

INFORMATION

Tourist information The excellent Old Station visitor centre (April–Oct daily 10.30am–5.30pm; ☎01291 689566) is located another few hundred yards towards Monmouth in the former Tintern station; two refurbished carriages house an exhibition on the Wye Valley, while you can pick up a good selection of leaflets on local walks, including the surrounding wild flower meadows and cliff rambles above the meandering river. For kids, there's a play area and a miniature railway which operates on the last Sunday of each month. Bus #69 stops outside.

ACCOMMODATION

Parva Farmhouse North of the abbey off the main road ☎01291 689411, ⓦparvafarmhouse.co.uk. Restful B&B accommodation in this pretty seventeenth-century farmhouse, with en-suite, mostly river-view rooms; downstairs there's an "honesty" bar and a cosy restaurant warmed by a beamed fireplace and serving British cuisine as well as wine cultivated from the owner's own vineyard. **£78**

Royal George Monmouth Rd ☎01291 689205, ⓦbw-royalgeorgehotel.co.uk. Located opposite the Abbey Mill, this neat hotel has modern, ground-level and first-floor rooms in a chalet-style building facing a large, willow-fringed garden. **£80**

CAMPING
Old Station ☎01291 689566. Tents can be pitched in the paddock behind the Old Station ; the only facilities are toilets and washbasins. April–Oct. Per person **£3.25**

EATING AND DRINKING

Kingstone Brewery Opposite the Old Station ☎01291 680111. Small microbrewery and café, offering brewery tours, ale-tasting and light lunches, such as a ploughman's salad. Mon–Wed, Fri & Sat 9am–4pm.

Old Station ☎01291 689566. The former waiting room of the old Tintern station is now a quaint Victorian-era tearoom, with a selection of sandwiches and cakes, and hot and cold drinks. April–Oct daily 10.30am–5.30pm.

Monmouth

Bordered on three sides by the rivers Wye and Monnow, elegant **MONMOUTH** (Trefynwy) retains the quiet charm of its days as an important border post and one-time county town. The centre of the town is **Agincourt Square**, a large and handsome open space at the top of the wide, shop-lined Monnow Street, gently descending to a distinctive thirteenth-century bridge over the River Monnow.

Shire Hall

Agincourt Square • Mon–Fri 10am–5pm, Sat & Sun till 4pm • Self-guided tours £2, plus guided tours on Wed at 2pm (£2.50) • ☎01600 775257

The cobbled square is dominated by old coaching inns, flanking the arched Georgian **Shire Hall**. Built in 1724 as a Court of Assize, it was here, in 1839, that the Chartists' trial was held, which resulted in the death penalty for its three ringleaders – Frost, Williams and Jones – though this was later commuted to transportation. The hall continued to function as a court until 1992, and you can still see the original courtrooms, as well as the holding cells below.

The hall's facade includes an eighteenth-century statue of the Monmouth-born King Henry V, victor at the 1415 Battle of Agincourt, which brought Normandy (and soon afterwards France) under the rule of the English Crown. In front is a florid statue of another local, the Honourable Charles Stewart Rolls, who in 1910 became the first man to pilot a double-flight over the English Channel, and also co-founded the Rolls-Royce empire.

The Castle and Regimental Museum

Regimental Museum Castle Hill • April–Oct daily 2–5pm; Nov–March Sat & Sun 2–4pm • Free • ☎ 01600 772175,
ⓦ monmouthcastlemuseum.org.uk

The **castle**, founded in 1068, was rebuilt in stone in the twelfth century and almost annihilated in the Civil War. The only notable part that remains is the Great Tower, in which Henry V is thought to have been born in 1387. Adjacent, the gracious seventeenth-century **Great Castle House**, built from castle bricks, now serves as the headquarters of the Royal Monmouthshire regiment. Their history is celebrated in the **Regimental Museum** along with intriguing finds from archeological digs such as oddly shaped twelfth-century bone dice.

Nelson Museum and Local History Centre

Priory St • Mon–Sat 11am–1pm & 2–5pm, Sun 2–5pm, Nov–Feb until 4pm • Free • ☎ 01600 710630

The market hall complex contains the **Nelson Museum and Local History Centre**, an attempt to portray the life of the great admiral through his personal artefacts – sword, medals, intimate letters and china – together with pictures, prints and naval equipment of the day. Charles Rolls' mother, Lady Llangattock, was an ardent admirer of Nelson and a voracious collector of related memorabilia, and it is her collection now on display in the museum.

Monnow Bridge

At the bottom of Monnow Street, a couple of hundred yards from Agincourt Square, the road narrows to squeeze into the confines of the fortified **Monnow Bridge** and its hulking stone gate, dating from 1262. This served both as a means of defence for the town and a toll collection point and is now the sole remaining medieval fortified river bridge in Britain where the gate tower actually stands on the bridge.

The Kymin and Round House

Kymin daily dawn–dusk • Free • ☎ 01600 719241 • **Round House** Easter–Oct Sat–Mon 11am–4pm • £2.30 • NT

Just over a mile east of Monmouth, a steep road climbs up to **The Kymin**, a fine viewpoint over the town and the Wye Valley. It's crowned by the crenellated Georgian **Round House**, built as a banqueting hall, and a Neoclassical **Naval Temple**, constructed in 1801 to cheer Britain's victories at sea.

ARRIVAL AND DEPARTURE   **MONMOUTH**

By bus Buses operate from the bus station at the bottom of Monnow St.

Destinations Monmouth to: Abergavenny (6 daily; 50min); Chepstow (hourly; 50min); Newport (hourly; 1hr); Raglan (hourly; 20min); Ross-on-Wye (6 daily; 35min); Tintern (9 daily; 35min); Usk (9 daily; 30min).

INFORMATION

Tourist information The TIC is in the foyer of the Shire Hall (Mon–Fri 10am–5pm, Sat & Sun 10am–4pm; ☎ 01600 775257, ✉ monmouth.tic@monmouthshire .gov.uk).

Canoeing The Monmouth Canoe & Activity Centre (☎ 01600 713461, ⓦ monmouthcanoe.co.uk), right by the Wye in Castle Yard, offers canoe rental, plus instruction if needed, and guided river trips. Advance booking required.

1

ACCOMMODATION

Bistro Prego 7 Church St ☎01600 712600, ⓦpregomonmouth.co.uk. Eight tightly packed en-suite rooms in a cosy B&B located above the town's finest restaurant. There's also a comfortable resident's lounge with wide-screen TV, sofas and skylight. **£65**

The Coach House St John's St ☎01600 775517, ⓦthecoachhousemonmouth.co.uk. Three crisp, white-coloured en-suite rooms in this sweet little family-run guesthouse just a short walk down from the Shire Hall. **£65**

Punch House 4 Agincourt Square ☎01600 713855, ⓔpunchhouse@sabrain.com. The rooms above this popular tavern are simple but agreeable, with timber beams and uneven floors and doors. Good value. Breakfast costs extra. **£40**

CAMPING

Monnow Bridge Campsite Drybridge St, over Monnow Bridge then right, behind the Three Horseshoes pub ☎01600 714004. Pitches **£10.50**

EATING AND DRINKING

Monmouth has a couple of classy restaurants, and boasts a large number of pubs, some of which date back several centuries.

★ **Bistro Prego** 7 Church St ☎01600 712600. The best place to eat in town is this sprightly bistro, offering separate lunch and dinner menus, with imaginative Italian-influenced dishes like tagliatelle with rabbit ragu, and salmon with Sicilian couscous salad. Mains £12–16. Booking advised at weekends. Daily 11am–10pm.

Gate House Old Monnow Bridge ☎01600 713890. Occupying an enviable spot by the medieval bridge, and with a veranda perched over the water, the *Gate House* is one of the most agreeable spots in town for a pint on a warm summer's day. Daily 11am–11pm.

Punch House 4 Agincourt Square ☎01600 713855. Standing adjacent to the Shire Hall, the Tudor-looking *Punch House* is the town's most popular hostelry, a rambling, reputedly haunted, inn serving mainly Brain's beers. Daily 11am–11pm.

Robin Hood 126 Monnow St ☎01600 713240. Diagonally across from the *Gate House*, this centuries-old boozer is where Shakespeare is believed to have once drunk; decent beers and a fun, relaxed atmosphere. Daily 11am–11pm.

★ **Stonemill** Just beyond the village of Rockfield 2 miles west of town on B4233 ☎01600 716273. Fine dining with seasonal menus created using locally sourced ingredients, most gathered from the surrounding woodland; treats include rack of new-season lamb with buttered leek, and roasted breast of wood pigeon. The restaurant itself, in a sixteenth-century barn with thick brick walls and chunky oak beams, looks gorgeous. Mains £17–23. Tues–Sat noon–3pm & 6–11pm, Sun noon–3pm.

The Three Castles

The fertile, low-lying land north of Monmouth, between the Monnow and the River Usk, was important as an easy access route into the agricultural lands of south Wales, and in the eleventh century the Norman invaders built a trio of strongholds here – **Skenfrith**, **Grosmont** and **White castles** – within an eight-mile radius of each other.

The castles' size and splendour demonstrate their significance in protecting the borderlands from the restless English, as well as the disgruntled Welsh, who first attacked nearby Abergavenny Castle in 1182, prompting King Ralph of Grosmont to rebuild the three castles in stone. In July 1201, all three were presented by King John to Hubert de Burgh, who fought extensively on the Continent and brought back sophisticated new ideas on castle design to replace earlier models with square keeps. He rebuilt Skenfrith and Grosmont, and his successor as overlord, Walerund Teutonicus ("the German"), worked on White Castle. In 1260, the advancing army of Llywelyn ap Gruffydd threatened the king's supremacy in south Wales, and the three castles were refortified in readiness.

Gradually, as the Welsh began to adapt to English rule, the castles were used more as living quarters and royal administrative centres than as military bases. The only return to military usage came in 1404–05, when Owain Glyndŵr 's army pressed down to Grosmont, only to be defeated by the future King Henry V. The castles fell into disrepair, and were finally sold by the Duchy of Lancaster to the Duke of Beaufort in 1825. The Beauforts sold the castles off separately in 1902, the first time since 1138 that the three had fallen out of single ownership.

White Castle

April–Oct daily 10am–5pm · £2.80 (generally free access rest of year) · ☎ 01600 780380 · CADW

Named for its white rendering (a few patches remain on the exterior walls), **White Castle** (Castell Gwyn) lies about eight miles west of Monmouth, and a mile south of the village of Llanvetherine. The most dramatic of the three castles, it's situated in open, rolling countryside with some superb views over to The Skirrid mountain (see p.223). From the grassy Outer Ward, a bridge leads over the moat into the dual-towered Inner Gatehouse, where the western tower, on the right, can be climbed for its vantage point. Here, you can appreciate the scale of the tall twelfth-century curtain walls in the Inner Ward. Of the domestic buildings within the walls, only the foundations and a few inches of wall remain. At the back of the ward, there are massive foundations of the Norman keep, demolished in about 1260 and unearthed in the early part of the twentieth century. The southern wall that took the place of the keep was once the main entrance to the castle, as can be seen in the postern gate in the centre, on the other side of which a bridge leads over to the Hornwork, one of the castle's three original enclosures, although now no more than a grass-covered mound.

Skenfrith Castle

Open access · Free · NT

Seven miles northeast of White Castle, alongside the River Monnow in the pretty border village of **SKENFRITH** (Ynysgynwraidd), is the thirteenth-century **Skenfrith Castle**, dominated by the circular keep that replaced an earlier Norman incarnation.

The castle's walls are built of sturdy red sandstone in an irregular rectangle. In the centre of the ward is the 21ft-high, roofless round keep, raised slightly on an earth mound to give archers a greater firing range, while below here are the vestiges of the great hall and private quarters. The Hall Range of domestic buildings includes an intact thirteenth-century window, complete with its original iron bars.

Grosmont Castle

Open access · Free · CADW

Five miles upstream of Skenfrith, right on the English border, the most dilapidated of the Three Castles, **Grosmont Castle** (Castell y Grysmwnt), sits on a small hill above the village of **GROSMONT**. Entering over the wooden bridge above the dry moat, you first pass through the ruins of the two-stage gatehouse. This leads into the small central courtyard, dominated on the right-hand side by the ruins of a large Great Hall, dating from the first decade of the thirteenth century. The village **church** is also worth a look, with some impressive Norman features, most notably the nave arches and the font. A memorial in the nave is popularly believed to be of John Kent, a fifteenth-century bard and magician believed by some to have been Owain Glyndŵr in hiding.

INFORMATION   THE THREE CASTLES

You can drive around all three castles in a couple of hours, though it's much more enjoyable to cycle or hike the nineteen-mile circuit of paths, which are detailed in a **booklet** (£3.95 from local tourist offices).

ACCOMMODATION

★ **The Bell** Skenfrith ☎ 01600 750235, ⓦ skenfrith .co.uk. Opposite the castle, this sumptuous sixteenth-century riverbank inn accommodates eleven thoughtfully styled rooms; most look out either over the hills or the river. **£110**

Great Tre-Rhew Farm Half a mile north of White Castle, off B4521 ☎ 01873 821268, ⓔ trerhew @btopenworld.com. In a 165-acre farm, this fifteenth-century farmhouse near the village of Llanvetherine (Llanwytherin) has three rooms with shared shower facilities. Tents **£1**; doubles **£60**

1

Hunter's Moon Inn Llangattock Lingoed ☎01873 821499, ⊛hunters-moon-inn.co.uk. Four floral (but not too floral) en-suite rooms are complemented by the intimate thirteenth-century pub (stone-flag flooring, bare brick walls and low ceilings) serving good food and superb guest ales. **£60**

EATING

★ **The Bell** Skenfrith ☎01600 750235. *The Bell's* restaurant is as top-drawer as its hotel. Many ingredients are sourced from the organic kitchen garden, resulting in sublime dishes like fillet of seabass with garden herb and pea risotto. In warmer weather pick a table out on the terrace. Mains £15–19. Daily 10am–11pm, Nov–March closed Tues evening.

Mid-Monmouthshire

The disputed past of mid-Monmouthshire, between Chepstow and Newport, is obvious from the yet more castles that dot the landscape, such as that at **Caldicot**, just off the M4 near the southern Severn Bridge. Nearby **Caerwent** is now a quiet village which was once a great Roman town.

To the north is an undulating land of forests and tiny villages, crisscrossed by winding lanes that offer unexpectedly delightful views – and quaint pubs – around each corner. The contours shelve down in the west to the valley of the **River Usk**, the former border of Wales as decreed in the sixteenth century by Henry VIII. Today, the A449 road roars through the valley, bypassing lanes, villages and the peaceful small town of **Usk** before joining the A40 near the spectacular ruins of **Raglan** castle.

Caldicot

Wedged between this road and the railway, **CALDICOT** (Cil-y-coed) is the first sight of Wales for train travellers using the main line from London and drivers using the second Severn bridge crossing from Bristol. This is a sprawling, overgrown village of modern housing, though its heavily restored castle – contained within a densely wooded country park – makes it worth a brief stop.

The castle

April–Oct daily 11am–5pm • £3.75 • ☎01291 420241, ⊛caldicotcastle.co.uk

Sited on the eastern side of the village, the **castle** dates from the twelfth century – one of the Norman Marcher castles built to keep a wary eye on the Welsh. The castle crumbled in the years leading up to the 1800s, before being rebuilt by a wealthy Victorian barrister, Joseph Cobb. The only original parts are a large fourteenth-century round tower and elaborate gatehouse, situated either side of a grassy courtyard, whose centrepiece is one of Nelson's battle cannons from his *Foudroyant* flagship. The tower contains a smattering of furniture and an intriguing collection of Cobb family photos.

Caerwent

Two miles northwest of Caldicot lies the historic village of **CAERWENT**. Almost two thousand years ago, the village was known by the Romans as Venta Silurum, the "market town of the Silures", a local tribe forcibly relocated here from a nearby hillfort by the conquering Romans in around 75 AD, after 25 years of battle.

The most notable remnants of the Roman town are the crumbling **walls** which form a large rectangle around the modern village. Access is easiest from the steps in front of the *Coach and Horses* pub, leading you up onto stone ramparts that command melancholic views around the quiet valley – a leisurely stroll around the walls should take no more than forty minutes. The South Wall is the most complete, still maintaining its fourth-century bastions. Follow the South Wall as it continues around to the old West Gate. Halfway along, a lane cuts up towards the village **church**: maps and diagrams in the porch explain the site of the village, and you can also see two inscribed stones, one a dedication from the Siluri tribe to their Roman overlord, Paulinus, and another, dedicated to Ocelus Mars, demonstrating the odd merging of Roman and Celtic gods for worship. Opposite the church, on the village's main street, the shin-high, rectangular outline of a Roman temple has been excavated.

Usk

Bypassed by the main A449, the quaint town of **USK** (Brynbuga) straddles the river of the same name. The town's hub is **Twyn Square**, where pastel-painted houses, flower boxes, shops and pubs make for an exceptionally pretty picture. At the top of the square – beyond the handsome clock tower – is a thirteenth-century **gatehouse**, once part of a Benedictine nunnery, and now guarding the passage to the impressive twelfth- and thirteenth-century church. Surviving features from its days as a nunnery in the 1200s include the nave and tower.

Usk Castle

Daily dawn to dusk • Free; donation requested • ☎ 01291 672563, ⓦ uskcastle.com

Looming up on a hilltop five minutes' walk from the centre of town stand the ivy-clad ruins of **Usk Castle**. Central to this eccentric little castle, which formed the backdrop to the Battle of Usk in 1405, are three impressive towers; the French-influenced Garrison Tower, the Great Tower with intact Norman windows, and the more complete Dovecot Tower. Meanwhile, geese and chickens roam freely among the vegetable, herb and flower gardens.

Usk Rural Life Museum

New Market St • April–Oct Mon–Fri 10am–5pm, Sat & Sun 2–5pm • £3 • ☎ 01291 673777, ⓦ uskmuseum.org.uk

At the bottom of Bridge Street, just before the bridge, the illuminating **Usk Rural Life Museum** is housed in a converted eighteenth-century malt barn. Aspects of farming are explained in a pleasantly haphazard way, and everything from animal-castrating implements to re-creations of domestic and farming interiors (including a dairy, stables and a cobbler's workshop) are packed into every available corner, while adjoining covered barns continue the exhibition with a vintage collection of tractors, ploughs and stagecoaches.

ACCOMMODATION   USK

Glen-yr-Afon House Pontypool Rd ☎ 01291 672302, ⓦ glen-yr-afon.co.uk. An elegant and gracious country house, a 5min walk west of town across the river, with rooms of differing architectural design, though all are furnished to a high standard. **£136**

King's Head 18 Old Market St ☎ 01291 672963, ⓦ kingsheadusk.com. This centuries-old inn, a couple of minutes' walk down from the museum, offers surprisingly

modern en-suite rooms, with hearty breakfasts to boot. **£60**

Three Salmons Hotel Bridge St ☎ 01291 672133, ⓦ threesalmons.co.uk. A hotel of sorts for some four hundred years, this striking listed building conceals the most contemporary rooms in town, each with fabulous beds, smart flat-screen TVs and DVD players, and sparkling bathrooms. **£85**

EATING AND DRINKING

La Cantina 61 Bridge St ☎ 01291 673433. A smart little bistro where Mediterranean food, and in particular fish, is the order of the day – there's seating in the warm interior or the neat terrace garden. Mains £12–14. Mon 9am–4pm, Tues–Sat 9am–11.30pm, Sun 10am–5pm.

Nag's Head Twyn Square ☎ 01291 672820. The most enjoyable of the town's pubs, an engagingly cluttered space with local memorabilia and brass plates scattered

around the bar; rabbit pie, guinea fowl and pheasant are among the dishes available, in addition to some terrific real ales. Daily 9.30am–2.30pm & 5–11pm.

Three Salmons ☎ 01291 672133. Cool, handsome restaurant in the hotel of the same name, which serves a lot of the wet stuff, though locally sourced game is never far from the menu. Mains £15–18. Daily noon–2pm & 6–11pm.

1

Raglan Castle

March–Oct daily 9.30am–5pm, July & Aug till 6pm; Nov–Feb Mon–Sat 10am–4pm, Sun 11am–4pm • £3.50 • ☎ 01291 690228 • CADW• Numerous buses daily from Monmouth, as well as hourly buses from Usk

Seven miles north of Usk is the village of **RAGLAN** (Rhaglan), lorded over by its glorious **castle**. The castle's ornate style and comparative intactness set it apart from other more crumbling Welsh fortresses. The late medieval castle was constructed on the site of a Norman motte in 1435 by Sir William ap Thomas. Various descendants added to the castle after his death, and building carried on into the late sixteenth century.

The **gatehouse** is still used as the main entrance, and the finest examples of the castle's showy decoration appear in its heraldic shields, intricate stonework edging and gargoyles. Inside, stonemasons' marks, used to identify how much work each man had done, can be seen on the walls. Ap Thomas' grandson, William Herbert II, was responsible for the two inner courts, built in the mid-fifteenth century around his grandfather's original gatehouse, hall and keep. The first is the cobbled **Pitched Stone Court**, designed to house the kitchen and servants' quarters. To the left is **Fountain Court**, once surrounded by opulent residences that included grand apartments and state rooms. Separating the two are the original 1435 **hall**, the **buttery**, the remains of the **chapel** and the **cellars** below.

Off Fountain Court, through the South Gate, is the pristine **bowling green**, standing on 12ft-high walls above the Moat Walk, and reached by a flight of stone steps from the green. The moated yellow ashlar **Great Tower**, off Fountain Court, manifests Continental influences in its construction, and has a surprisingly contemporary appearance. Two sides of the hexagonal tower were blown up by Cromwell's henchman, Fairfax, after an eleven-week onslaught against the Royalist castle in 1646. Climbing the tower gives you some marvellous views of the complex and surrounding countryside.

Newport and around

Wales' third-largest urban area, lively, gritty **NEWPORT** (Casnewydd-ar-Wysg) grew up around the docks at the mouth of the Usk and was finally granted city status in 2002. Evidence of Newport's rich history was largely erased by unfortunate twentieth-century development, but the city has recently undergone a massive regeneration project. Meanwhile, the city's profile received an even bigger boost in 2010 from the staging of the Ryder Cup at nearby Celtic Manor.

Vestiges of the city's history remain, however, particularly along the river by the monumental **Transporter Bridge**, while there are also the scant ruins of a riverside **castle** and, high on a hill above town, the **Newport Cathedral** of St Woolos, King & Confessor. The superb **museum** explores the town's vibrant past, including a memorable section on the nineteenth-century **Chartist movement**, formed to fight for universal franchise.

Predating Newport by at least a thousand years is **Caerleon** – the "old port" on the River Usk – which is now essentially a northern suburb of the city. Its well-preserved remains constitute one of the most important Roman military stations in Britain, but it's best known for its reputed association with King Arthur.

The heart of the city is **Westgate Square**, overlooked by the now defunct Westgate Hotel, an ornate Victorian successor to the hotel where soldiers sprayed a crowd of Chartist protesters with gunfire in 1839, killing nearly two dozen – the hotel's original pillars still show bullet marks. At the bottom of Commercial Street, **John Frost Square** (named after a former mayor and one of the 1839 Chartist leaders) is home to the Kingsway centre, which, among other things, incorporates the city museum.

The riverfront

Scything the city in two is the River Usk, whose tidal waters flow to the Severn estuary, three miles away. Between the rail and main road bridges are the risible remains of the town's **castle**, first built in 1191, rebuilt in the fourteenth century, sacked by Owain Glyndŵr in 1402 and refortified later in the same century.

On the other side of the Newport Bridge, a walkway leads along the riverbank past Peter Fink's giant red sculpture, **Steel Wave**, a nod to one of Newport's great industries. Nearby, building work in 2002 on the Riverfront arts centre revealed the remains of a medieval ship.

Transporter Bridge

Bridge times vary greatly, check ⓦ newport.gov.uk • Car toll £1, free for cyclists and pedestrians **Visitor centre** April–Sept Wed–Sat 10am–5pm, Sun 1–5pm; Oct–March Sat 10am–5pm, Sun 1–5pm

Dominating the Newport skyline is the 1906 **Transporter Bridge**, built to enable cars and people to cross the river without disturbing shipping, by hoisting them high above the Usk on a dangling blue gondola. Its comical, spidery legs flare out to the ground, connecting Brunel Street on the west bank and Stephenson Street opposite. The ride is smooth and the two-minute crossing has successfully cut commuting times since the

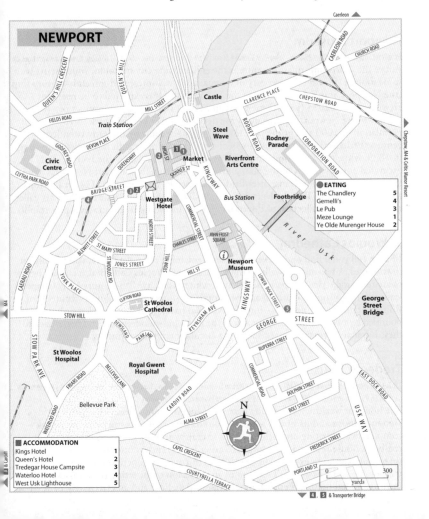

NEWPORT

EATING
The Chandlery	5
Gemelli's	4
Le Pub	3
Meze Lounge	1
Ye Olde Murenger House	2

ACCOMMODATION
Kings Hotel	1
Queen's Hotel	2
Tredegar House Campsite	3
Waterloo Hotel	4
West Usk Lighthouse	5

1

THE CHARTISTS

In an era when wealthy landowners bought votes from the enfranchised few, the struggles of the **Chartists** were a historical inevitability. Thousands gathered around the 1838 People's Charter that called for universal male franchise, a secret (and annual) ballot for Parliament and the abolition of property qualifications for the vote. Demonstrations in support of these principles were held all over the country, with some of the most vociferous and bloodiest taking place in the radical heartlands of industrial south Wales. On November 4, 1839, Chartists from all over Monmouthshire marched on Newport and descended Stow Hill, whereupon they were fired at by soldiers hiding in the Westgate Hotel, killing around 22 protesters. The leaders of the rebellion were sentenced to death, which was commuted to transportation, by the wealthy leaders of the town. Queen Victoria even knighted the mayor who ordered the arbitrary shooting.

bridge was reopened in the mid-1990s. A small **visitor centre** on the river's west bank elaborates on the bridge's history.

Newport Museum

John Frost Square • Mon–Thurs 9.30am–5pm, Fri 9.30am–4.30pm, Sat 9.30am–4pm • Free • ☎ 01633 656656, ⓦ www.newport.gov.uk

Above the tourist information centre is the enlightening city **museum**, which starts with some footage showing the recovery of a remarkably well-preserved fifteenth-century ship (the Newport Ship) on the banks of the Usk in 2002. It is expected to be ready for viewing around 2014 (see ⓦthenewportship.com). The museum continues by documenting Newport's spectacular growth from a small Uskside dock in 1801 with a population of 1000 to a grimy port town of 70,000 people by the early twentieth century. Perhaps the most interesting section, however, deals with the Chartist uprising in 1839, while there are some fine remains of a Roman mosaic ("The Four Seasons") excavated at Caerwent. On the floor above are some superb photos of Newport's iconic landmarks, such as the Transporter Bridge, Rodney Parade (Newport Gwent Dragon's rugby ground), and TJ's, the legendary former live music venue. The top-floor art gallery contains the **Wait Collection** of Edwardian kitsch, including three-hundred-plus teapots.

St Woolos Cathedral

In **Stow Hill** you'll find one of Newport's few remaining rows of Victorian and Georgian townhouses. A ten-minute walk up the hill leads to **St Woolos Cathedral**, a curious jigsaw of architectural styles and periods. The tiny, whitewashed twelfth-century Lady Chapel leads through a superb Norman arched doorway – supported by columns reputedly of Roman origin from Caerleon – into the Norman nave, notable for its clerestory windows, bounded by two fifteenth-century aisles. The cathedral's modern east end harks back to these original Norman features, sporting a circular marble east window.

Tredegar House

2 miles southwest of Newport, just off M4 junction 28 • **House** Easter–Sept Wed–Sun 11am–4pm **Park** daily 9am–dusk • House tour & gardens £6.95, park and gardens free • ☎ 01633 815880 • Buses #15 and #30 from Newport

The home of wealthy local landowners, the Morgan family, from 1402 until 1951, **Tredegar House** and its ninety acres of grounds have been transformed into a park complete with boating and fishing lake and craft workshops. The seventeenth-century red-brick house replaced the Morgans' earlier home, and its interior is far more lavish than its unassuming exterior suggests. Of its thirty rooms open to the public, most memorable is the first-floor Gilt Room: an explosion of glittering fruit bosses, an intricate gilded marble fireplace, mock-walnut panelling and an elaborately painted gold stucco ceiling. The formal walled gardens behind the housekeeper's shop have been relaid in patterns culled from eighteenth-century designs.

1

ARRIVAL AND DEPARTURE NEWPORT

By train The train station is on Queensway at the top of the High St.

Destinations Abergavenny (every 30–60min; 25min); Bristol (every 30min; 40min); Caldicot (hourly; 15min); Cardiff (every 15–30min; 15min); Chepstow (hourly; 20min); Hereford (hourly; 50min); London (hourly; 1hr 50min); Swansea (every 30–60min; 1hr 20min).

By bus The bus station is on Kingsway, just down from

John Frost Square.

Destinations Abergavenny (hourly; 1hr); Abertillery (every 30min; 1hr); Blaenafon (every 15min; 50min); Brecon (every 2hr; 2hr 20min); Caerwent (hourly; 40min); Cardiff (every 30min; 30min); Chepstow (every 30min; 50min); Monmouth (hourly; 1hr); Pontypool (every 15min; 30min); Raglan (hourly; 40min); Usk (hourly; 30min).

INFORMATION

Tourist information The TIC is in the museum complex on John Frost Square (Mon–Fri 9am–6pm, Sat 9am–4pm;

☏ 01633 842962, ⓦ newport.gov.uk).

ACCOMMODATION

Kings Hotel 7–8 High St ☏ 01633 842020, ⓦ kingshotelnewport.co.uk. Decently positioned at the top of the main High St, this large, long-established hotel offers fresh-looking, good-sized rooms. Breakfast is extra. **£90**

Queen's Hotel 19 Bridge St ☏ 01633 844900, ⓦ jdweatherspoon.co.uk. Despite its location above a busy, youthful pub, this is a very good-value central hotel, with modern, appealing rooms furnished in dark blue and burgundy colours. Breakfast is extra. **£50**

Waterloo Hotel 113 Alexandra Rd ☏ 01633 264266, ⓦ thewaterloohotel.co.uk. Opposite the Transporter Bridge, this stylishly refurbished hotel occupies a landmark turreted red-brick building. Rooms in the tower have four-poster beds, and many have dramatic views of the floodlit

bridge by night. Mod cons include underfloor heating in the bathrooms. **£95**

West Usk Lighthouse ☏ 01633 810126, ⓦ westusklighthouse.co.uk. Beyond the suburb of Duffryn, this place is set inside an 1821 lighthouse (decommissioned in 1922) at the mouth of the Usk on its western bank, with exquisite nautical-style rooms, holistic therapies including a flotation tank, and a life-size Dalek at the entrance signed by the third Doctor Who, John Pertwee. **£130**

CAMPING

Tredegar House 2 miles southwest of Newport ☏ 01633 815600. Picturesque, well-equipped campsite within the grounds of Tredegar House. Open all year. Pitches **£16**

EATING AND DRINKING

Newport can rate a couple of exceptional restaurants, but beyond this there's very little to shout about. Many of the town's pubs have fallen by the wayside, though Newport remains one of the centres of the buoyant Welsh **rock and dance music** scene – Goldie Lookin' Chain notwithstanding.

★ **The Chandlery** 77–78 Lower Dock St ☏ 01633 256622. Occupying a converted nineteenth-century ship's chandlery, this handsome place excels in fish- and steak-based dishes, such as spiced monkfish, and fillet of Usk Valley beef and confit of shin; the wine list includes many imported from South Africa. Stripped-wood floors, well-spaced and smartly laid tables, and charming service round things off admirably. Mains £16–22. Tues–Sun 11am–2.30pm & 6–11pm.

Gemelli's 42 Bridge St ☏ 01633 251831. Founded by chirpy Italian brothers Pasquale and Sergio, the food in this informal, artfully decorated restaurant is both inviting and authentic. Specialities include home-made tagliatelle with Welsh lamb sauce, and mushroom- and herb-stuffed ravioli. A gluten-free menu is also available. Mains £12–16.

Mon–Sat 9.30am–3pm & 6.30–10pm.

Le Pub 1 Caxton Place ☏ 01633 221477, ⓦ lepub .co.uk. A rip-roaringly fun music bar, with live bands and DJs most Fridays and Saturdays. Wed–Sun 8pm–1am, Fri & Sat till 3am.

Meze Lounge 6 Market St ☏ 01633 211432, ⓦ mezelounge.com. Following the sad demise of the legendary *TJ's* club, the city's best live music is now the preserve of this hip venue, with a prolific roster of indie-rock bands and some premier DJs.

Ye Olde Murenger House 53 High St ☏ 01633 263977. Dating from 1530 and featuring a beautiful Tudor frontage and inviting lamplit interior, this great old stager offers Sam Smith's beers as well as some good guest ales. Mon–Sat 11am–11pm, Sun noon–2.30pm & 7–10.30pm.

1

Caerleon

The compact town centre of **CAERLEON** (Caerllion) is northwest of the town bridge over the River Usk (Wysg), which gave Caerleon its old Roman name of Isca. This was a major administrative and legionary centre built by the Romans to provide ancillary and military services for smaller, outlying camps in the rest of south Wales. An enormous garrison housed up to five thousand members of the Second Augustan Legion in a neat, rectangular walled town. Its only near equivalents in Roman Britain were Chester, servicing north Wales and northwest England, and York, dealing with the Roman outposts up towards Hadrian's Wall and beyond.

Although the settlement gradually decayed after the Romans left, there were still some massive remains standing when itinerant churchman Giraldus Cambrensis visited in 1188, chronicling the "immense palaces, which, with the gilded gables of their roofs, once rivalled the magnificence of ancient Rome". Today, the remnants of the Roman town lie scattered throughout the present-day centre, including the excavated bathhouse and preserved amphitheatre, both of which retain a powerful sense of ancient history.

The fortress baths

High St • April–Oct daily 9.30am–5pm; Nov–March Mon–Sat 9.30am–5pm, Sun 11am–4pm • Free • ☎ 01633 422518 • CADW

The Roman **fortress baths** are atmospheric and cleverly presented. Excavations uncovered a section of the cold hall baths (the warm and hot hall baths are believed to be still buried under the town) and a splendidly intact communal pool, where people would go after the cold hall. Also clearly visible is the drain, in which a hoard of gemstones (see below), as well as teeth, buttons and food remnants, were found.

National Roman Legion Museum

High St • Mon–Sat 10am–5pm, Sun 2–5pm • Free • ☎ 01633 423134, ⓦ museumwales.ac.uk

A Victorian Neoclassical portico is the sole survivor of the original **National Roman Legion Museum**, now housed in the modern building behind. There are hundreds of artefacts dug from the remains of Isca and a smaller fortress at nearby Burrium (Usk): coinage, tools, pottery and glassware, military fittings and, best of all, nearly a hundred beautifully carved gemstones retrieved from the fortress bath drain. No less impressive is a collection of chunky funerary and dedication stones.

KING ARTHUR

The name **King Arthur** is ubiquitous in Wales – in history, folklore books and dozens of place names on the map (only the Devil has more places named after him across Britain). He has become one of the greatest Celtic allegories, a figure to be invoked for all manner of causes and one claimed by almost every part of the British Isles, but the earliest and strongest evidence for the reality of Arthur comes indisputably from Wales.

The first mention of King Arthur was around 800 AD in the *Historia Britonum* (History of the British), by the Welsh monk Nennius. Three centuries later, his compatriot Geoffrey of Monmouth used this work, among others, as the source material for his magisterial twelve-volume *Historia Regum Britanniae* (History of the Kings of Britain), in which he writes that Arthur was a sixth-century Celtic British king who defeated the invading Saxon army in the turbulent decades after the departure of the Romans. From sparse, semi-factual beginnings, epic stories developed. Arthur became an idealized medieval European knight, a totem of Celtic resistance and supernatural powers.

Caerleon is widely believed to be the location of Arthur's court, **Camelot**, although other claims place Camelot near Llangollen, in England at Glastonbury and in Cornwall, and in Brittany in France. Wales, however, remains perhaps the strongest contender; dozens of areas throughout Wales have Arthurian associations, and there is a plethora of books on the subject, such as Laurence Main's *In the Footsteps of King Arthur*, which has some great walks to get you to remote spots of Arthurian significance.

The amphitheatre
Broadway Lane • Daily 9.30am–5.30pm • Free

Opposite the museum, Broadway Lane leads down to the Roman **amphitheatre**, one of the best preserved in Britain, which was hidden under a grassy mound called King Arthur's Round Table until excavation work brought it to light in the 1920s. The amphitheatre was built around 80 AD, the same time as the Colosseum in Rome; legions of up to six thousand would sit tightly packed on the grassy stepped walls to watch the gory combat of gladiators, animal baiting or military exercises. It is still occasionally used for events and re-enactments, though of a somewhat less bloodthirsty kind. Over the road, alongside the school playing fields, are the extensive foundations of the legion's **barracks**, the only Roman barrack blocks still visible in Europe.

Ffwrwm Centre
High St • Most shops daily 9.30am–5.30pm

Within the **Ffwrwm Centre** are crafts workshops, an art gallery and a fine bistro. Scattered around this eccentric cobbled courtyard – where, it is alleged, Lord Tennyson came to investigate rumours that Caerleon was the seat of King Arthur's court (see p.76) – are dozens of sculptures inspired by ancient Celtic and Arthurian lore, while you can also clasp the gold horns of a Welsh fertility bull, an act that is supposed to lend you untold powers of procreation. It is also home to the largest-ever Welsh lovespoon (see p.53), carved from a 44ft cedar trunk.

ARRIVAL AND DEPARTURE　　　　　　　　　　　　　　　　　　CAERLEON

By bus From Newport, take bus #28 or #270 and get off by the post office on the High St. Returning to Newport, catch the bus from the same spot or from the Hanbury Arms.

INFORMATION

Tourist information The TIC is beside the Legionary Museum on the High St (daily: April–Oct 10am–5pm, Nov–March 10am–4pm; ☎01633 422656, ✉caerleon .tic@newport.gov.uk).

ACCOMMODATION

Pendragon House 18 Cross St ☎01633 430871, ⓦpendragonhouse.co.uk. Listed house near the baths, with three fresh white-on-white en-suite rooms, with super beds, cool linens, and flat-screen TV/DVD players. A warm welcome guaranteed, too. **£65**

Priory Hall High St ☎01633 421241, ⓦthepriorycaerleon.co.uk. A long, low stone-built twelfth-century building opposite the baths, this quiet, rambling place has reasonably decent, restful rooms. **£80**

Radford House Broadway ☎01633 430101, ⓦradfordhouse.co.uk. Opposite the museum, this grand Georgian guesthouse has three brilliantly conceived rooms, each one furnished in a different architectural theme; Georgian, Roman (with canopied bed) and Art Deco. There's also a handsome communal drawing room with plenty of books and a log fire. Terrific value. **£85**

Sarum House 13a Mill St ☎01633 431225, ⓦsarumhouse.co.uk. Warm, family-run guesthouse two blocks northeast of the museum, with a pair of charming rooms, one of which has its own lounge and balcony with Usk Valley views. **£60**

EATING AND DRINKING

Hanbury Arms Uskside ☎01633 420361. Located at the bottom of the High St, by the River Usk, the whitewashed *Hanbury* dates from the sixteenth century and is where Lord Tennyson spent several weeks in 1856 writing *Idylls of the King* – seek out the plaque. Beers include Brains and a selection of guest ales. Daily 11.30am–11pm, Fri & Sat till midnight.

The Lodge 28 High St ☎01633 423833. Modern, laid-back café and delicatessen offering a wide range of drinks and snacks; fresh subs and panini, home-made cakes and a terrific cheese and olive counter. Mon–Sat 7am–5.30pm, Sun 10am–4pm.

The Snug Ffwrwm courtyard ☎01633 430238. Warm, friendly daytime café which, on Friday and Saturday evenings, serves full meals, typically of an Italian bent, while the Sunday lunch is always a hit; there's outdoor seating in summer and a roaring log fire in winter. Mains £10–14. Daily 8.30am–4pm, plus Fri & Sat 7pm–midnight.

1

Cardiff

Official capital of Wales only since 1955, the buoyant city of **CARDIFF** (Caerdydd) has over the last fifteen years witnessed a remarkable evolution from a large town to a truly international city, with massive developments in recent years in the centre as well as on the rejuvenated Cardiff Bay waterfront.

Cardiff first gained significance in the nineteenth century with the international rise in importance of coal and iron – it was ideally located as a port for shipping these worldwide; the civic charter incorporating the city dates from 1905. As well as its cultural and political profile, particularly since devolution in 1999, Cardiff has a mighty reputation as a party town, and you need only wander around the centre on a weekend night to see the proof. With some seriously good nightlife, huge shopping malls, and a rapidly improving selection of accommodation, it's no surprise that Cardiff continues to be one of the fastest-growing city-break destinations in Britain.

Cardiff's sights are clustered around fairly small, distinct districts. Easily navigable on foot, the **commercial centre** is bounded by the River Taff – source of the nickname of generations of expatriate Welsh – on the western side. The Taff flows past the high stone walls of Cardiff's **castle** and the **Millennium Stadium**. Near the southeastern tip of the castle walls is Cardiff's main crossroads, where the great Edwardian shopping boulevards Queen Street and High Street conceal a world of arcades, great stores and run-of-the-mill malls. North of the castle, a series of white Edwardian buildings is home to the **National Museum and Gallery**, **City Hall** and **Cardiff University**.

A mile south of the commercial centre is **Cardiff Bay**, revitalized since the construction of a barrage to form a vast freshwater lake, home to the **National Assembly** and **Wales Millennium Centre**, as well as trendsetting bars and eateries.

Two miles northwest of the city centre above the banks of the Taff, the village-like suburb of **Llandaff** is built around the city's patchwork **cathedral**.

Brief history

Cardiff's origins date back to Roman times, when tribes from Isca settled here, building a small village alongside the Roman military fort. The fort was largely uninhabited from the Romans' departure until the Norman invasion, when William the Conqueror offered Welsh land to his knights if they could subdue the local tribes. In 1093, Robert FitzHamon built a simple fort on a moated hillock that still stands today in the grounds of the castle. A town grew up in the lee of the fortress, developing into a small fishing and farming community that remained a quiet backwater until the end of the eighteenth century.

Industrial expansion

The **Bute family**, lords of the manor of Cardiff, instigated new developments on their land, starting with the construction of a canal from Merthyr Tydfil (then Wales' largest town) to Cardiff in 1794. The second Marquis of Bute built the first dock in 1839, opening others in swift succession. The Butes, who owned massive swathes of the rapidly industrializing south Wales valleys, insisted that all coal and iron exports used the family docks in Cardiff, and it subsequently became one of the busiest ports in the world. By the beginning of the twentieth century, Cardiff's population had soared to 170,000 from its 1801 figure of around 1000, and the ambitious new Civic Centre in Cathays Park was well under way.

Changing fortunes

The twentieth century saw the city's fortunes rise, plummet and rise again. The dock trade slumped in the 1930s, and the city suffered heavy bombing in World War II, but since being created capital of Wales in 1955, the city's optimism and confidence have blossomed. Many government and media institutions have moved here from London, especially since the inauguration of the National Assembly in 1999, and the city's entertainment and leisure sectors are unrivalled in Wales.

The city centre

The city's main north–south thoroughfare is **The Hayes**, the focal point of which is **The Old Library**, home to the enlightening **Cardiff Story**. The neighbouring fifteenth-century grey limestone parish **church of St John** is worth a peek for its floridly pompous altar by prolific Victorian sculptor, Goscombe John. Running the entire length of one side of The Hayes is the **St David's Centre**, a gargantuan complex incorporating over 180 shops, as well as the **St David's Hall** concert venue.

On the north side of the St David's Centre, **Queen Street** is Cardiff's most impressive shopping street, pedestrianized and with many of its fine nineteenth-century buildings spruced up, albeit many now effaced by typical chain-store frontages. At the western end of the street, a statue of **Aneurin Bevan**, postwar Labour politician and classic Welsh firebrand, stands aloof from the bustle. Parallel to the Hayes, **St Mary Street** is flush with ornate Victorian and Edwardian shop frontages, although some have seen better days. This then becomes the High Street, beyond which lies **Cardiff Castle**, the city's premier tourist hangout, and, close by, the magnificent **Millennium Stadium**, which is well worth visiting for a guided tour.

Cardiff Market and the arcades

Off the High Street is the elegant Victorian **indoor market**, great for fresh food and specialist bric-a-brac stalls. Along both streets, renovated Edwardian arcades, with some of the city centre's most interesting shops inside, lead off between the buildings. Of these, **High Street** and **Castle arcades**, at the top of High Street, are the most rewarding, packed with great clothes shops, quirky gift shops, fab little coffee houses and a range of esoteric emporia where you can pick up fliers for clubs and events. Another arcade worth seeking out is the glorious **Morgan Arcade**, with original 1896 detailing and Venetian windows. It's also where you'll find **Spillers Records**, which was founded in 1894, making it the world's oldest record shop; you can easily spend a few hours browsing among its hard-to-find tracks of all genres including loads of local releases.

The Old Library and Cardiff Story

The Hayes • Mon–Sat 10am–5pm, Sun 11am–4pm • Free

The Hayes leads north to the beautifully colonnaded frontage of the **Old Library**, home to the city's tourist office and the **Cardiff Story**. Utilizing artefacts, hands-on gizmos and audiovisual displays, it's an enlightening romp through the city's colourful history, with particular emphasis on how the city has been shaped by the docks and the local coal industry. While here, don't miss the stunning **tiled corridor**; something of a hidden gem, this was the original library entrance, its ornate floor-to-ceiling tiles produced by Maw & Co in 1882.

Cardiff Castle

Daily: March–Oct 9am–6pm; Nov–Feb 9am–5pm • £11, premium ticket £14; admission includes an audio guide • ☎ 029 2087 8100, ⓦ www.cardiffcastle.com

The geographical and historical heart of the city is **Cardiff Castle**, an intriguing hotchpotch of remnants of the city's past. Having been the seat of several powerful families over the centuries, its most intense phase of development came under the ownership of the Bute family, in whose hands the castle remained for the best part of 150 years, from the late eighteenth century until the death of the fourth Marquess in 1947. The fortress hides inside a vast walled yard, each side measuring well over 200yd long and corresponding roughly to the outline of the original fort built by the Romans. Before entering, take a look at the exterior wall running along Castle Street to the river

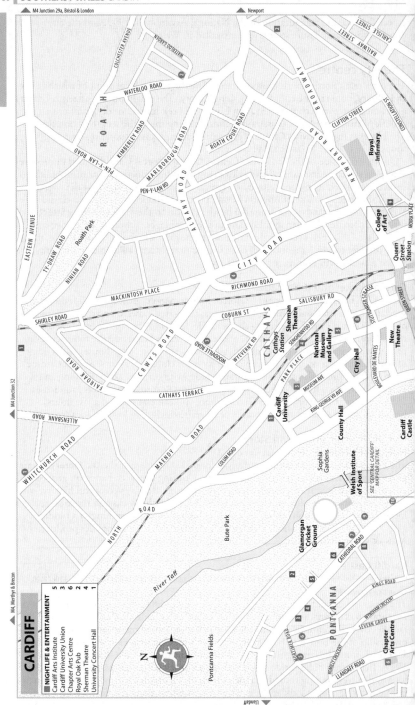

CARDIFF

■ NIGHTLIFE & ENTERTAINMENT

Cardiff Arts Institute	5
Cardiff University Union	3
Chapter Arts Centre	6
Royal Oak Pub	2
Sherman Theatre	4
University Concert Hall	1

M4 Junction 29a, Bristol & London

Newport

M4 Junction 32

M4, Merthyr & Brecon

Llandaf

Llandaf

COLCHESTER AVENUE

WATERLOO GARDEN

WATERLOO ROAD

R O A T H

KIMBERLEY ROAD

MARLBOROUGH ROAD

PEN-Y-LAN ROAD

PEN-Y-LAN RD

ALBANY ROAD

ROATH COURT ROAD

EASTERN AVENUE

TY-DRAW ROAD

Roath Park

NINIAN ROAD

C I T Y   R O A D

MACKINTOSH PLACE

RICHMOND ROAD

SHIRLEY ROAD

COBURN ST

SALISBURY RD

C A T H A Y S

Sherman Theatre

Cathays Station

CRWYS ROAD

WOODVILLE ROAD

WYEVERNE RD

SENGHENNYDD RD

National Museum and Gallery

FAIROAK ROAD

CATHAYS TERRACE

Cardiff University

PARK PLACE

MUSEUM AVE

City Hall

STUTTGARTER STRASSE

College of Art

MORIA PLACE

Queen Street Station

QUEEN STREET

New Theatre

BOULEVARD DE NANTES

Cardiff Castle

County Hall

KING GEORGE VII AVE

MAENDY ROAD

COLUM ROAD

WHITCHURCH ROAD

ALLENSBANK ROAD

N O R T H   R O A D

Welsh Institute of Sport

Sophia Gardens

SEE 'CENTRAL CARDIFF' MAP FOR DETAIL

Bute Park

River Taff

Pontcanna Fields

Glamorgan Cricket Ground

P O N T C A N N A

CATHEDRAL ROAD

KINGS ROAD

WYNDHAM CRESCENT

SÉVERN GROVE

MORTIMER ROAD

ROMILLY CRESCENT

LLANDAFF ROAD

Chapter Arts Centre

CLIFTON STREET

B R O A D W A Y

N E W P O R T   R O A D

CASTLETON ST

CARLISLE STREET

RAILWAY STREET

Royal Infirmary

N

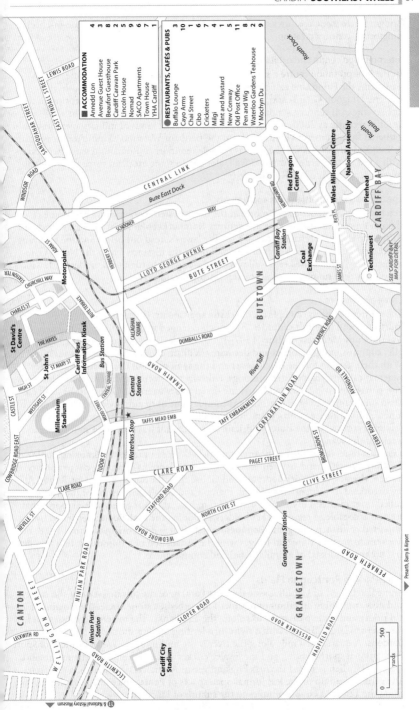

■ ACCOMMODATION
Annedd Lon 4
Avenue Guest House 3
Beaufort Guesthouse 8
Cardiff Caravan Park 2
Lincoln House 5
Nomad 9
SACO Apartments 6
Town House 7
YHA Cardiff 1

● RESTAURANTS, CAFÉS & PUBS
Buffalo Lounge 3
Cayo Arms 10
Chai Street 1
Cibo 6
Cricketers 7
Milgi 4
Mint and Mustard 1
New Conway 5
Old Post Office 11
Pen and Wig 8
Waterloo Gardens Teahouse 2
Y Mochyn Du 9

1

bridge, where stone creatures are frozen in impudent poses, a rather tongue-in-cheek nineteenth-century creation.

Interpretation centre and exhibition

In the **interpretation centre** a short film offers a concise history of the castle. In the basement, the **Firing Line exhibition** relays the distinguished heritage of both The Queen's Dragoon Guards and The Royal Welsh Regiment since their inception in the late seventeenth century – although the former gained their present title in 1959, the latter as recently as 2006. Cabinets are stacked with all kinds of military memorabilia garnered from numerous conflicts, from the Battle of Waterloo to more recent ventures in Iraq and Afghanistan. Here, too, is the sole reminder of Roman presence hereabouts, with a few dozen yards of exposed **wall**, along with some excellent three-dimensional murals depicting life in a Roman fort.

The Norman keep, battlements and tunnels

Perched atop a smooth grassy motte in the northwestern corner is the handsome, though much remodelled, eleventh-century **Norman keep**, built of Blue Lias limestone. At the top there are terrific views of the silky lawns spread out below and the gleaming white steel girders of the Millennium Stadium in the distance. From the North Gate immediately behind the keep, walkways lead along the **battlements**, underneath which are the **wartime tunnels**, used as shelters during World War II.

Castle apartments

The centrepiece of the complex is the **castle apartments**, dating in part from the fourteenth and fifteenth centuries, but much extended in Tudor times. Ultimately, it was the third Marquess of Bute (1847–1900) who lavished a fortune on upgrading his pile, commissioning architect and decorator William Burges (1827–81) to aid him. With their passion for the religious art and the symbolism of the Middle Ages, they systematically overhauled the buildings, radically transforming the crumbling interiors into palaces of vivid colour and intricate design, a style termed Gothic Revival. In all the rooms, fantastically rich trimmings complement the gaudy style so beloved of two nineteenth-century eccentrics, and it's worth remembering that, as one of over sixty residences owned by the Butes in Britain alone, Cardiff was only lived in for several weeks of the year.

Guided tours (available on the premium ticket) take in the **Winter Smoking Room**, the **Nursery**, with hand-painted tiles and silhouette lanterns depicting contemporary nursery rhymes, **Bachelor's Bedroom** and, above that, the **Summer Smoking Room**. All are decorated in rich patterns of gold, maroon and cobalt, with many of the images culled from medieval myths and beliefs. From here, the tour enters several rooms that are also accessible to regular ticket holders, including the **Arab Room**, decorated by imported craftsmen, the grand **Banqueting Hall**, which dates originally from 1428, but was transformed by Bute and Burges with the installation of a riotously kitsch fireplace, and **library**, possessed of a similarly fanciful chimneypiece.

Bute Park to Pontcanna Fields

Immediately west of Cardiff Castle lies **Bute Park**, once the private estate of the castle, and now containing an **arboretum**, superb flowerbeds, a stone circle, the remains of an old priory and some pleasant walks along the Taff banks. The main road crosses over the river at Cardiff Bridge, with a right turn leading up into the coolly formal **Sophia Gardens**. A quarter of a mile along the river is the multipurpose **Welsh Institute of Sport** (the national sports centre), and the Swalec cricket stadium, home to Glamorgan and, since 2009 when it staged the first England versus Australia Ashes match, a test arena. The gardens lead up to the less formal open spaces of **Pontcanna Fields**, which lead along the Taff for a couple of miles to the suburb of Llandaff.

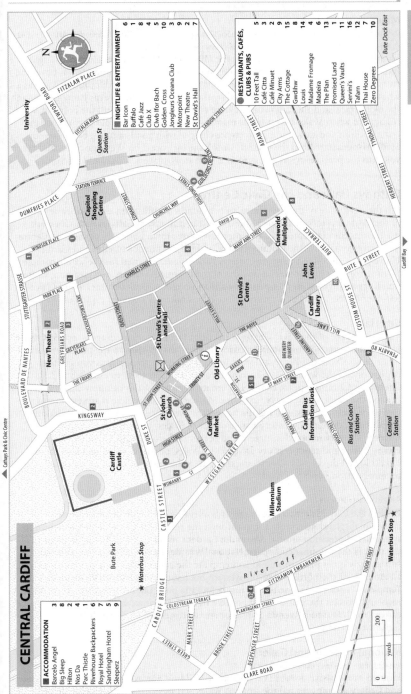

CENTRAL CARDIFF

■ ACCOMMODATION
Barcelo Angel	3
Big Sleep	8
Hilton	2
Nos Da	4
Parc Thistle	1
Riverhouse Backpackers	6
Royal Hotel	7
Sandringham Hotel	5
Sleeperz	9

■ NIGHTLIFE & ENTERTAINMENT
Bar Icon	6
Buffalo	1
Café Jazz	8
Club X	4
Clwb Ifor Bach	5
Golden Cross	10
Jongleurs Oceana Club	3
Motorpoint	9
New Theatre	2
St David's Hall	7

● RESTAURANTS, CAFÉS, CLUBS & PUBS
10 Feet Tall	5
Café Citta	3
Café Minuet	2
City Arms	9
The Cottage	15
Gwdihw	8
Louis	14
Madame Fromage	4
Madeira	6
The Plan	13
Promised Land	1
Queen's Vaults	11
Servini's	16
Tafarn	12
Thai House	7
Zero Degrees	10

1

Millennium Stadium

Daily tours, subject to events, hourly Mon–Sat 10am–5pm, Sun 10am–4pm • £6.65 • ☎ 029 2082 2228, ticket office: ☎ 08705 582582, ⓦ millenniumstadium.com; tickets for sporting events available from Ticketline, 47 Westgate St

Dominating the city from all angles is the **Millennium Stadium**. Shoehorned so tightly into its Taff-side site that the surrounding walkways had to be cantilevered out over the river, this 74,500-seat giant has become a symbol not only of Cardiff, but of Wales as a whole. The location was once occupied by the legendary Cardiff Arms Park, and though the old terraces and the famous name have now gone, the turf is still the home of Welsh rugby, and when Wales have a home match – particularly against old enemy England – the stadium and surrounding streets are charged with good-natured, beery fervour. **Stadium tours** start from the Cardiff Arms Store by Gate 3 on Westgate Street and take you into the press centre, dressing rooms, VIP areas, players' tunnel and pitchside.

Cathays Park and the Civic Centre

On the north side of the city centre, only a hundred yards from the northeastern wall of the castle precinct, is the area known most commonly as **Cathays Park**. The park itself forms the centrepiece for the impressive Edwardian buildings of the **Civic Centre** – the area containing the County Hall, City Hall, National Museum and Cardiff University – although the name Cathays Park is generally used for the whole complex. Dating from the first couple of decades of the twentieth century, the gleaming white buildings arranged with pompous Edwardian precision speak volumes about Cardiff's self-confidence, a full half-century before it was officially declared capital of Wales.

City Hall

The centrepiece of the Civic Centre is the magnificent, domed, dragon-topped **City Hall** (1905), an exercise in ostentatious civic self-glory that is open to the public in normal office hours. Note the Peace sculpture in the main entrance lobby as you go in: it depicts one of the women who marched from Cardiff in 1981 to establish the Greenham Common peace camp. The ornate interior is a riot of finery that reaches a peak in the particularly showy first-floor Marble Hall: all Sienese marble columns and statues of Welsh heroes. Among the figures are twelfth-century chronicler Giraldus Cambrensis, thirteenth-century native prince of Wales, Llywelyn ap Gruffydd, fifteenth-century national insurgent and perpetual hero, Owain Glyndŵr, Welsh king Henry Tudor and tenth-century architect of Wales' progressive codified laws, Hywel Dda (Howell the Good). Overseeing them all is the figure of Dewi Sant himself – the national patron saint, St David.

Alexandra Gardens and around

Behind the City Hall, two ruler-straight boulevards, evidently designed with ceremonial splendour in mind, run through the rest of the Civic Centre, arranged in symmetrical precision around **Alexandra Gardens** in the middle. At the very centre of the park is the colonnaded circular **National War Memorial** (1928), a popular and surprisingly quiet place to sit and contemplate the rush of civic and governmental duty all around. At the north end of the western boulevard, **King Edward VII Avenue**, is the **Temple of Peace** (1938), dedicated just before the outbreak of World War II to Welsh men and women the world over who were fighting for peace and relief of poverty. The eastern road, **Museum Avenue**, runs past an assortment of buildings belonging to Cardiff University.

National Museum and Gallery

Tues–Sun 10am–5pm • Free • ⓦ museumwales.ac.uk

Housed in a massive domed Portland-stone building, the exceptional **National Museum and Gallery** attempts to tell the story of Wales and reflect the nation's place in the

1

wider, international sphere. Occupying the ground floor is the "Evolution of Wales" exhibition, on either side of which are the natural history galleries, and the "Origins" archeological exhibition. Meanwhile, the upper floors are devoted to the museum's exceptional art galleries.

Evolution of Wales gallery

The museum's most obvious crowd-pleaser is the epic **Evolution of Wales** gallery, a natural history exhibition packed with high-tech gizmos and a staggering amount of information. It starts with a stirring large-screen video presentation, *Dyma Gymru* (This is Wales), full of stunning aerial footage taken over mountains, waterfalls and other natural Welsh wonders. It then goes on to explain, through fossils, rocks and footage of volcanoes, earthquakes and the galaxies, the slow beginnings of life on earth. Dinosaurs and the early mammals get a good look-in, and include a terrific Tyrannosaurus rex skull.

Natural History galleries

The environmental education continues in the adjacent **Natural History** galleries, with a magnificent collection of sparkling crystals, re-creations of assorted environments – mountain, wetland, seashore, dunes – and some great interactive technology and interpretive boards. It then heads upstairs with a display entitled "Man and the Environment", featuring numerous animals and their habitats, and culminates in the world's largest leatherback turtle, caught off Harlech in 1988.

Origins archeology gallery

Trumping both the above is the **Origins archeology gallery**, a dazzling assortment of mostly Bronze Age and Iron Age treasures. Pride of place, however, goes to the **Red Lady of Paviland Cave**; discovered in 1823 on the Gower (see p.130), the red-stained skeleton was later revealed to be that of a young man dating from around 26,000 years ago, which makes it the earliest-known burial in Britain. Among the most impressive artefacts is the superb **Caergwrle Bowl**, a boat-shaped gold votive container, more than 3000 years old and made of tin, shale and gold. No less exciting is the **Capel Garmon Firedog**, discovered near Conwy in 1852; originally one of a pair, this beautifully crafted Iron Age hearth stand with horned animals' heads most probably inhabited a chieftain's roundhouse. Heading towards the back, there's some exquisite Celtic jewellery, as well as an inspirational collection of stones and casts, spanning the earliest carved fragments (around the fifth century), through Celtic and early Christian standing stones to the more elaborate examples of the early medieval age.

Art Galleries One to Ten: Historic Art

Galleries One to Ten examine Wales' artistic heritage, with a particularly strong collection from the **eighteenth century**, an era that was perhaps the heyday of Welsh art, with its three main protagonists – Richard Wilson, William E. Parry and Thomas Jones – well represented.

Unsurprisingly, the Welsh landscape is to the fore, with the enlightening **Welsh Landscapes** in Gallery Seven well worth consideration. Here, Wilson's skill in capturing Wales' unique light can be seen to lustrous effect in his studies of castles at Caernarfon, Dolbadarn and Pembroke, as well as more emotionally intense pieces such as the beautiful *Pistyll Cain*. One of Wilson's protégés, William Hodges, also makes an appearance, most notably in his gentle evocation of *Llanthony Priory*. While the equally prolific Jones also dealt in landscapes – look out for *A View in Radnorshire* and his evocative images of Naples – his most notable offering is *The Bard*, a dramatic historical piece based upon Thomas Gray's tale of Edward I's massacre of the Welsh bards. The **Faces of Wales** in Gallery Five features an intriguing collection of portraits and photos of various esteemed natives, such as the travel writer Jan Morris. There's also a superb, and growing, collection of **ceramics**, one of Wales' most prolific areas of applied art.

1

Welsh Sculpture

In the rotunda beyond Gallery Fifteen is a fabulous **sculpture** collection, dominated by the celebrated one-man Welsh Victorian statue industry, Goscombe John. Far better here than on the dreary municipal plinths they usually adorn, his male studies verge on the homoerotic and his female forms are exquisite. Look out for the moving *Parting*, while, inevitably, there's a nod to Celtic mythology, in the shape of the playful, Rodin-esque *Merlin and Arthur*.

Art Galleries Eleven to Sixteen: Impressionists and Modern Art

Galleries Eleven through to Sixteen is where the real action is, however, with many works given at the bequest of two local wealthy sisters, Margaret and Gwendoline Davies. Gallery Eleven is dominated by nineteenth-century French Art, featuring the likes of Millet (the haunting, unfinished *Peasant Family* and lovely, pastoral *Goose Girl at Gruchy*), the watery landscapes of Boudin, and numerous works by Manet, including the intricately observed *Effect of Snow at Petit Montrouge*. Neighbouring Gallery Twelve concentrates on **modern art from the 1930s onwards**. Highlights include some stunning and wild pieces by Welsh supremo Ceri Richards, surrealists such as Magritte (*The Empty Mask*) and Trevelyan. Some sculpted pieces reside here too, including some fine works by Henry Moore, among them *Upright Motif*, and Barbara Hepworth's haunting *Oval Sculpture*. Gallery Fourteen, entitled **Art After Cézanne**, features a couple of pieces by Picasso, as well as sculptures by Matisse and Epstein, while, in Gallery Fifteen, the emphasis is very much on British art around 1900, with the likes of Walter Sickert, Sylvia Gosse, Gwen John, and Harold Gilman's colourful London scenes (*Café Royal* and *Mornington Crescent*).

Gallery Sixteen: Impressionists and Post-impressionists

Gallery Sixteen is unquestionably the museum's star room, owing to its fabulous collection of **Impressionists and Post-impressionists** works. Dominating the room are several pieces by Monet, including an uncharacteristically grey *Thames at London*, whose work sits alongside artists such as Cézanne, Sisley (including his views of Penarth and Langland Bay), Carnière, Degas, Pissarro and Renoir; his coquettish *La Parisienne* is a real standout. The centrepiece here, though, is Van Gogh's stunning *Rain at Auvers* – angry slashes of rain run right across the otherwise harmonious canvas – which was painted just weeks before his suicide. Mesmerizing pieces by Rodin also pepper the gallery, where there's a version of *The Kiss* and his original *Eve*.

Cardiff Bay

A must-see part of any Cardiff tour, **Cardiff Bay** has become one of the world's biggest regeneration projects, the downbeat dereliction of the old docks having been almost completely transformed into a designer heaven. Meanwhile, the imminent arrival of the BBC's Drama Village will only serve to further enhance the Bay's appeal – indeed, both *Doctor Who* and its spin-off, *Torchwood*, have been filmed in the area for a few years. In times gone by, when the docks were some of the busiest in the world, the area was better known by its evocative name of **Tiger Bay**, one that was immortalized by locally born chanteuse Shirley Bassey.

The Bay area now comprises three distinct parts, situated either side of **Roald Dahls Plass**, the main square named after the Cardiff-born children's author (1916–90) best known for his 1964 classic, *Charlie and the Chocolate Factory*: the swanky civic precincts around the glorious **Wales Millennium Centre**, on the eastern side, the shiny **millennium waterfront** to the west, including the retail and leisure complex known as **Mermaid Quay**, and, set back from the water's edge, the increasingly gentrified Taff-side suburb of **Butetown**.

1

Although the bay is an easy half-hour stroll from the city centre, the most relaxing way to reach it is by waterbus (hourly 11am–5pm from Bute Park and Taff's Mead Embankment), train (every 15min from Queen Street station) or the #6 Baycar bus from outside Central station (every 10–15min; £2 return).

The Wales Millennium Centre

Guided tours: daily 11am & 2pm • £5.50 • ☎ 029 2063 6464, ⓦ wmc.org.uk

Dominating the whole area is the mesmerizing **Wales Millennium Centre**, a vibrant performance space for theatre and music, and the resident home to many of Wales' premier arts organizations. Likened by critics to a copper-plated armadillo or aardvark, the WMC soars over the Bay rooftops, its exterior swathed in numerous Welsh building materials, including different slates, wood and stone, topped with a stainless-steel shell tinted with a bronze oxide to resist salty air.

Writ large across the frontage in 7ft-high letter windows, the inspirational bilingual inscription was crafted by poet Gwyneth Lewis; the phrases read downwards – in English "In these stones, horizons sing" and in Welsh "Creu gwir fel gwydr, o ffwrnais awen" ("Creating truth like glass, from the furnace of inspiration") – but, ingeniously, they also read across each line, in two languages, and still make crystal-clear poetry.

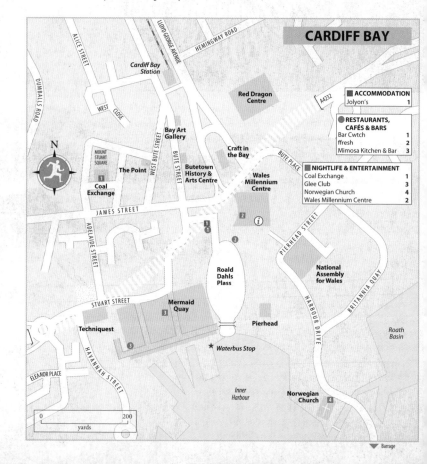

1

The grace and style continue throughout the interior, fashioned from materials that hark back to Wales' mineral-extracting past, from the native oak, ash, beech, sycamore, alder, birch, chestnut and cherry woods to the riveted steel and coal-like pillars. **Guided tours** of the building allow complete backstage access, as well as intimate views of the main auditorium, the acoustically sensational Donald Gordon Theatre.

The ground floor houses the main box office, music shop, souvenir shop, and the excellent *ffresh* bar and brasserie. Also located here is the Bay's **visitor centre** (daily 10am–6pm). Daily **free performances** of anything from poetry to hip-hop take place in the WMC foyer, usually at lunchtime and 6pm.

The Pierhead

Daily 10.30am–4.30pm • Free • ☎ 0845 0105500, ⓦ pierhead.org

Down by the water's edge is the magnificent red-brick **Pierhead Building**, which has beckoned ships into Cardiff port since its construction in 1897. A typically ornate neo-Gothic terracotta pile, it was built for the Cardiff Railway Company – formerly the Bute Dock Company which burnt down in 1892 – and perfectly embodies the wealth and optimism of the Bute family and their docks. It now houses a surprisingly enjoyable **exhibition** documenting the rise and fall of the coal-exporting industry hereabouts; the building became the administrative centre for the Port of Cardiff in 1947, and the last shipment of coal left here in 1964. There's also an exhibition on the genesis of the nearby **National Assembly for Wales**, a striking building designed by Richard Rogers.

Norwegian Church

Sun–Thurs 9am–6pm, Fri & Sat 9am–8pm; opening hours can vary depending on special events • ☎ 029 2087 7959, ⓦ norwegianchurchcardiff.com

A short walk around the Bay, on Harbour Drive, is the gleaming white **Norwegian Church**, an old seamen's chapel built in 1868 on land donated by the Marquis of Bute. Once one of the most important Scandinavian missions in Britain – it regularly served up to 70,000 sailors per year – the building is more well-known for being the place where Roald Dahl – whose parents were Norwegian – was christened. Its role today is as a prominent arts and performance centre, while there is also a charming little café here.

The Mermaid Quay district

Across from the Pierhead, **Mermaid Quay** is an airy jumble of shops, bars and restaurants that on a warm day is a fine place to hang out and watch the world amble by. The city's **waterbuses** leave from here, and information boards carry details of a variety of boat-rental opportunities to get you out onto the water.

Techniquest

Stuart St • Mon–Fri 9.30am–4.30pm, Sat & Sun 10am–5pm • £7; planetarium show £1.30 extra • ☎ 029 2047 5475, ⓦ techniquest.org

A few paces along from the quay you'll come to the metal-and-glass-crowned **Techniquest**, an impressive hands-on science museum packed full of exhibits and experiments. It also includes a planetarium and science theatre.

Cardiff Bay Barrage

Daily 7am–10pm • Free

Central to the whole Bay project is the half-mile-long **Cardiff Bay Barrage**, built right across the Ely and Taff estuaries, which transformed a vast mud flat into a freshwater lake and created eight miles of useful waterfront. Despite its controversies, the barrage is a phenomenal bit of engineering, and it's well worth having a wander along the embankment to see the lock gates, sluices, fish path and stunning views. If you don't fancy walking, yellow waterbuses (daily 10.30am–4.30pm; £4 return) shuttle between the waterfront and the southern end of the barrage at Penarth.

The Wetlands Centre

Jutting out over the water like an ocean-going liner, the **St David's Hotel**, east of Mermaid Quay, acts as a stylish full stop to the sweep of the bay. From its car park, a path leads a couple of hundred yards to a 20-acre **wetland reserve**, created partly to help offset the loss of wading-bird habitats when the barrage was built and the Bay flooded. It's a surreally peaceful spot in which to have a picnic or just stop and let the world go by for a while.

Cardiff International White Water

Watkiss Way • Mon, Tues, Thurs & Sat 9am–5pm, Wed & Fri 9am–8pm, Sun 9am–4pm • ☎ 029 2082 9970, ⓦ ciww.com • Bus #7 from Cardiff Bay

Rounding off the waterfront's many varied attractions is Cardiff International White Water, located within the International Sports Village down by the mouth of the River Ely. Rafting aside, the rapids course accommodates a number of adrenaline-fuelled watersports, including canoeing, kayaking and hydro-speeding. The variable river flows make it suitable for everyone, including beginners.

Butetown

The area immediately inland from the Bay is the salty old district of **Butetown**, whose inner-city dereliction still peeps through the rampant gentrification that has taken place here over the past couple of decades. James Street, a block north of Techniquest, is the main commercial focus, while to its north are the cleaned-up old buildings around **Mount Stuart Square**.

Coal Exchange Building

Mount Stuart Square • ☎ 029 2049 4917, ⓦ coalexchange.co.uk

While many of the buildings around Mount Stuart Square are now offices and bars, the most impressive is the mammoth **Coal Exchange Building**. Built in the 1880s as Britain's central Coal Exchange, the building was used as a base from where trade negotiations for the south Wales coal mining industries could take place; it also saw the world's first £1 million cheque signed in 1908. The old trading hall retains its splendid Corinthian columns and wood-panelled walls, a fitting setting for its present-day function as an arts and entertainment centre.

Butetown History & Arts Centre

4 Dock Chambers, Bute St • Tues–Fri 10am–5pm, Sat & Sun 11am–4.30pm • Free • ☎ 029 2025 6757, ⓦ bhac.org

The community-based **Butetown History & Arts Centre** aims to record and celebrate the remarkable multicultural pedigree of a district that is home, for example, to one of the oldest black communities in Britain; to that end, the centre mounts exhibitions, offers guided tours and maintains a growing archive.

Craft in the Bay

Lloyd George Ave • Daily 10.30am–5.30pm • Free

Set out rather stylishly in the middle of Lloyd George Avenue, one block further east of Bute Street, is **Craft in the Bay**. Occupying an old maritime warehouse, this fabulous, sheer-glazed building exhibits a range of contemporary applied art and craft from practitioners the length and breadth of Wales, as well as some from overseas. There's a cute café here too.

Llandaff Cathedral

Cathedral Rd, Llandaff • Daily 8am–7pm • Free • ☎ 029 2056 4554, ⓦ llandaffcathedral.org.uk • Bus #33 or #33A

A small, quiet ecclesiastical village, **Llandaff** lies two miles northwest of the city centre. The church that has now grown up into the city's **cathedral** is believed to have been founded in the sixth century by St Teilo, but was rebuilt in Norman style from 1120 well into the thirteenth century. From the late fourteenth century, the cathedral fell into disrepair, hurried along by the adverse attention of Cromwell's soldiers during the Civil War. In the early eighteenth century, one of the twin towers and the nave roof collapsed. Restoration only began in earnest in the early 1840s, and Pre-Raphaelite artists such as Edward Burne-Jones, Dante Gabriel Rossetti and the stained-glass firm of William Morris were commissioned to provide colourful new windows and decorative panels. In January 1941, a German landmine destroyed whole sections of it, but faithful and painstaking restoration was finally completed in 1960.

The fusion of different styles and ages is evident from outside, especially in the mismatched western towers. The northwest tower is by Jasper Tudor, a largely fifteenth-century work with modern embellishments, while the adjoining tower and spire were rebuilt from nineteenth-century designs.

The interior

Inside, Jacob Epstein's overwhelming *Christ in Majesty* sculpture, a concrete parabola topped with a circular organ case on which sits a soaring Christ figure, was the only entirely new feature added in the postwar reconstruction, and dominates the nave today.

At the west end of the north aisle, the **St Illtyd Chapel** features Rossetti's cloying triptych *The Seed of David*, whose figures – David the shepherd boy, David the King and the Virgin Mary – are modelled on Rossetti's Pre-Raphaelite friends. Along a little further, in the south presbytery, is the tenth-century Celtic cross that is the cathedral's only pre-Norman survivor. At the far end of the cathedral is the elegantly vaulted and beautifully painted **Lady Chapel**, notable for its gaudy fifteenth-century reredos on the back wall that contains, surrounded by golden twigs and blackthorn in each niche, bronze panels with named flowers (in Welsh) in honour of Our Lady. Over two dozen flowers take their Welsh names from the Virgin Mary.

The walled garden

Open access • Free

While you're here, it's worth having a quick look at the medieval **walled garden** of the Llandaff Bishops' Palace on the Cathedral Green. With herbaceous plants planted according to medieval patterns, it makes a pleasant – and fragrant – place to sit for a few minutes.

ARRIVAL AND DEPARTURE **CARDIFF**

BY PLANE

Cardiff international airport (☎01446 711111, ⓦcwlfly.com) is ten miles southwest of the city on the other side of Barry. The most direct way to reach the city centre is by Xpress bus #X91, which runs every two hours daily (£3.40) and takes you from the main terminal into the city. Alternatively, you can take a shuttle bus from the main terminal to Rhoose Cardiff International Airport train station and then a connecting train (Mon–Sat hourly, Sun every 2hr; £3.70 combined ticket). A taxi from the airport to Cardiff Central will cost around £26.

BY TRAIN

Cardiff Central train station handles all inter-city services, as well as many suburban and Valley Line services. Queen Street Station, at the eastern edge of the centre, is for local services only, including those to Cardiff Bay.

Destinations Abergavenny (hourly; 40min); Barry Island (every 20–30min; 30min); Bristol (every 30min; 50min); Caerphilly (every 15min; 20min); Carmarthen (hourly; 1hr 45min); Chepstow (hourly; 40min); Crewe (mostly hourly; 2hr 40min); Haverfordwest (10 daily; 2hr 30min); Holyhead (9 daily; 5hr); Llanelli (17 daily; 1hr 10min); Llantwit Major (hourly; 45min); Llwynypia (every 30min; 50min); London (every 30min; 2hr); Maesteg (hourly; 55min); Manchester (mostly hourly; 3hr 10min); Merthyr Tydfil (every 30min; 1hr); Neath (every 30min; 40min); Newport (every 15–30min; 15min); Penarth (every 15min; 15min); Pontypridd (every 15min; 30min); Swansea (every 30min; 1hr); Tenby (3 daily; 2hr 40min); Trehafod (every 30min; 35min); Ystrad Rhondda (every 30min; 50min).

BY BUS

The main bus station is next to Cardiff Central train station.

Destinations Abergavenny (hourly; 2hr 20min);

1

TRIPS AND TOURS

You can get a good introduction to Cardiff aboard an open-top double-decker **sightseeing bus tour** (daily: April–Oct every 30min 10am–6pm, Nov–March every 60min 10am–4pm; day-ticket £9), starting from outside the castle and carving a circuit around the city and Cardiff Bay, and which allows you to hop on and off at will. A scenic waterbus service (hourly; £3 single; ☎07500 556556, ⓦaquabus.co.uk) operates daily between Mermaid Quay and the city centre at Taff's Mead Embankment, diagonally across from the Millennium Stadium. Depending on the river flow, it also runs to Bute Park, by Cardiff Castle. For something a little more adrenaline-fuelled, Bay Island Voyages (☎01446 420692; ⓦbayisland.co.uk) offer various boat trips out to Flat Holm island (see p.101), plus high-octane trips in a rigid-hulled inflatable boat around the Bay. They have a kiosk near the Pierhead Building.

Aberystwyth (2 daily; 4hr); Barry Island (every 30min; 1hr); Blaenafon (hourly, 1 change; 1hr 30min); Brecon (5 daily; 1hr 25min); Bristol (10 daily; 1hr 10min); Caerphilly (every 20min; 40min); Cardiff–Wales Airport (every 30min; 30min); Chepstow (every 30–60min, 1 change; 1hr 20min); Cowbridge (every 30min; 40min); Lampeter (3 daily; 3hr); Llantwit Major (9 daily; 1hr); Merthyr Tydfil (every 30min; 55min); Nelson (hourly; 35min); Newport (every 30min; 30min); Penarth (every 20min; 20min); Pontypridd (every 15min; 30min); Senghenydd (hourly; 50min); Swansea (hourly; 1hr).

INFORMATION

Tourist information Cardiff's large tourist office is at the Old Library on The Hayes (Mon–Sat 9.30am–5pm, Sun 10am–4pm; ☎029 2087 3573, ⓦvisitcardiff.com). There's plenty of literature available, including free maps of the city, details of walking and bus tours, and copies of *Buzz*, a free monthly guide to arts and events in the city. For more esoteric information, including fliers for gigs and club nights, try some of the shops in the Castle and High St arcades. Staff can also book accommodation.

GETTING AROUND

Cardiff is an easy, flat and compact city to walk around; even the bay area is within a 30min stroll of Central station.

Public transport Out of the centre, there's an extensive and reliable bus network operated by the Cardiff Bus (Bws Caerdydd) company. Its sales and information kiosk is on Wood St (Mon–Fri 8.30am–5.30pm, Sat 9am–4.30pm; ☎029 2066 6444; ⓦcardiffbus.com).

Tickets A one-way fare anywhere in the city costs £1.50 (payable on the bus, exact money only). The last buses generally leave the city centre at around 11.30pm.

Travel passes Various travel passes offer good savings: a "Day to Go" ticket (£3) gives unlimited bus travel around Cardiff and Penarth for a day, a range which can be extended to Barry, the Vale of Glamorgan, the Caerphilly district and Newport with the Network Dayrider ticket (£7).

A "Weekly to Go" ticket (£14) is good for seven days' unlimited travel around Cardiff and Penarth, while the "Weekly to Go Plus" ticket (£18) covers the entire Cardiff area network. All are available from the Cardiff Bus sales office or on board buses themselves.

Taxis There are taxi ranks at Central station, Queen Street station, Duke St by the castle and St Mary's St; try Capital Cabs (☎029 2077 7777) or Dragon Taxis (☎029 2033 3333).

Bike rental Pedal Power offers an excellent bike rental scheme, with outlets at the Pontcanna Caravan Park and at a kiosk just beyond the Norwegian Church in Cardiff Bay (☎029 2039 0713; ⓦcardiffpedalpower.org; £6/hr, £18/day).

ACCOMMODATION

Cardiff has a decent, though by no means extensive, stock of accommodation. That said, a number of the big chain hotels have infiltrated the city in recent years. Most hotels are concentrated in the city centre, with a well-established belt of Victorian guesthouses lining the leafy Cathedral Rd, in the suburb of Pontcanna, a pleasant 15min walk northwest from the city centre. There is now a good spread of hostels, most of which are very centrally located.

HOTELS AND GUESTHOUSES

Barcelo Angel Castle St ☎029 2064 9200, ⓦbarcelo -hotels.co.uk; map p.83. Much-restored Victorian bauble occupying a prime city-centre location between the castle and the Millennium Stadium; although the building looks slightly jaded from the outside, the air-conditioned rooms are large and modern enough. __£75__

Big Sleep Bute Terrace ☎029 2063 6363, ⓦthebigsleephotel.com; map p.83. Snazzy budget option occupying a former 1960s office block turned retro-designer hotel with two categories of rooms; budget rooms with simple pine furnishings, and standard rooms in vivid shades of blue. Budget **£58**; standard **£69**

Hilton Kingsway ☎029 2064 6300, ⓦhilton.co.uk/cardiff; map p.83. Cardiff's most agreeable five-star hotel, offering warmly decorated, generously sized rooms, and sparkling bathrooms with large walk-in showers. First-rate facilities include heated lap pool, spa and gym. **£110**

★ **Jolyon's** 5 Bute Crescent ☎029 2048 8775, ⓦjolyons.co.uk; map p.88. Down in the Bay, this exquisite boutique hotel in a former seaman's house has six beautifully conceived rooms, each unique, perhaps with a wrought-iron or antique carved wooden bed, Indian teak fittings or slate-tiled bathroom walls. There's a delightful cellar bar here too. **£65**

Parc Thistle Park Place ☎0871 376 9011, ⓦthistle.com; map p.83. Smack-bang in the commercial heart of the city, this smart, contemporary hotel offers smoothly carpeted, air-conditioned rooms painted in gentle beige, brown and cream tones. **£95**

Royal Hotel 88 St Mary St ☎029 2055 0750, ⓦroyalhotelcardiff.com; map p.83. Despite its air of faded grandeur, this Victorian building conceals a modern interior; the bold red and black furnished rooms and limestone-finished bathrooms are well-appointed, if somewhat devoid of charm. Given that it's on one of the city's busiest streets, it's surprisingly quiet. **£90**

Sandringham Hotel 21 St Mary St ☎029 2023 2161, ⓦsandringham-hotel.com; map p.83. Pleasantly old-fashioned, family-run hotel offering plain but clean decor, good service and a friendly atmosphere. One of the better value for money places in the city. **£40**

★ **Sleeperz** Station Approach ☎029 2047 8747, ⓦsleeperz.com; map p.83. Cleverly utilizing the architectural space in between the rail line and two roads, this funkily designed hotel has light-filled rooms in breezy white/orange and black/grey colour schemes; the corner cabin bunk rooms are particularly neat. Terrific value. **£55**

HOTELS AND GUESTHOUSES ON CATHEDRAL ROAD

Annedd Lon 157 Cathedral Rd ☎029 2022 3349, ⓦanneddlon.co.uk; map p.80. Meaning "happy dwelling in Welsh, this Victorian guesthouse is indeed thoroughly welcoming; it has six simple but pleasantly furnished en-suite rooms, and there's off-street parking. **£55**

Avenue Guest House 163 Cathedral Rd ☎029 2023 2855, ⓦtheavenueguesthouse.com; map p.80. A few paces along from Annedd Lon, and in a similar vein, this is a very reasonable family-run Victorian-style place with fresh, sunny rooms, some en suite. **£60**

Beaufort Guesthouse 65 Cathedral Rd ☎029 2023 7003, ⓦbeauforthousecardiff.co.uk; map p.80. One of the most gracious Victorian guesthouses along this strip, with classic period furnishings in all the rooms, a great-looking dining room and secure parking. **£82**

Lincoln House 118 Cathedral Rd ☎029 2039 5558, ⓦlincolnhotel.co.uk; map p.80. The most upmarket accommodation hereabouts, this small Victorian hotel has rooms furnished with button-leather couches and heavy brocade. There's also a comfortable lounge bar for residents. **£90**

Town House 70 Cathedral Rd ☎029 2023 9399, ⓦthetownhousecardiff.co.uk; map p.80. One of the more modern guesthouses along Cathedral Rd, this restored Victorian house has stained-glass windows and a mosaic-tiled hall, and offers eight en-suite rooms, a residents' lounge and better-than-average facilities. **£65**

HOSTELS, SELF-CATERING AND CAMPING

Cardiff Caravan Park Pontcanna Fields ☎029 2039 8362, ⓦcardiff.gov.uk; map p.80. Very good council-run caravan park, an easy 25min walk from the city centre, with limited tent pitches, two service blocks, laundry and dishwashing facilities. The entrance is from Pontcanna Fields or at the end of Dogo St, off Cathedral Rd. Open all year. Per car **£3** plus per person **£5**

Cardiff University Cathays ☎029 2087 4616, ⓦcardiff.ac.uk/conferences. Thousands of en-suite student rooms near the city centre are available from the end of June to mid-Sept on a B&B or self-catering basis. A good, cheap option. Singles **£28**; doubles **£47**

Nomad 11 Howard Gardens ☎029 2025 6826, ⓦnomadcardiff.co.uk; map p.80. In a Victorian terrace building a 5min walk from the centre, this youth-orientated hostel accommodates a mix of small and large dorms; facilities include lounge with Sky TV, bar and games room with pool table. Dorms **£17**

★ **Nos da** 53–59 Despenser St ☎029 2037 8866, ⓦnosda.co.uk; map p.83. Hip hostel/budget hotel on the riverbank opposite the Millennium Stadium. Accommodation is in singles, doubles (some en suite) and four- to ten-bed dorms, with avant-garde decor like outsized artwork that flips down and transforms into beds. Also home to the popular *Tafarn* bar. Dorms **£19.50**; doubles **£44**

★ **Riverhouse Backpackers** 59 Fitzhamon Embankment ☎029 2039 9810, ⓦriverhousebackpackers.com; map p.83. Cosy, contemporary backpackers' hostel in a 120-year-old Victorian villa with mixed and female-only dorms and twin rooms, as well as a self-catering kitchen, welcoming dining/lounge area and a sunny wraparound BBQ deck. Dorms **£18**; doubles **£44**

1

SACO Apartments 76 Cathedral Rd ☎011 7970 6999, ⓦsacoapartments.co.uk; map p.80. Elegant one- and two-bedroom apartments in a large town house with full kitchens, washer/dryers, internet and private parking. **£85**

YHA Cardiff 2 Wedal Rd, Roath Park ☎0870 371 9311, ⓦyha.org.uk; map p.80. Large, purpose-built building just underneath the A48 Eastern Ave flyover at the top of Roath Park, almost 2 miles from the city centre and reachable via bus #28, #29 or #29B from the station (get off at the bus stop for Wedal Rd/Lake Rd West). No curfew. Dorms **£14.40**

EATING

The city's long-standing internationalism, particularly its Italian influence, has paid handsome dividends in its range of **restaurants** and **cafés**. That said, there's a paucity of top-drawer restaurants in the centre itself, and you'll have to head a little further out to sample the best of Cardiff's food, such as Pontcanna to the northwest. Mermaid Quay in Cardiff Bay is now home to a staggering number of restaurants, though many of these are style over substance.

CITY CENTRE
CAFÉS

★ **Madame Fromage** 21–25 Castle Arcade ☎029 2064 4888; map p.83. A small slice of Paris at this delightful corner café-cum-deli where cheese is king – the menu offers a lot more besides, however, from tartlets and quiche to lamb cawl and charcuterie platters. Afterwards, make a beeline for the shop's tempting stock of jams, pickles and chutneys. Mon–Fri 10am–5.30pm, Sat 9.30am–5.30pm, Sun noon–5pm.

The Plan 28–29 Morgan Arcade ☎029 2039 8764; map p.83. Great-looking two-floored café with floor-to-ceiling windows, offering a super range of coffees and light meals (breakfasts, baked potatoes, toasties and salads) derived from locally sourced organic produce. Mon–Sat 8.45am–5pm, Sun 10.30am–4pm.

Servini's 6–10 Wyndham Arcade ☎029 2039 4054; map p.83. Secreted away down another arcade, this cheery family-run local serves a wide variety of filling sandwiches and baguettes, among them some great veggie choices; there's also a colourful salad bar. Eat in or take away. Mon–Sat 8am–4pm.

RESTAURANTS

Café Citta 4 Church St ☎029 2022 4040; map p.83. A friendly, laidback pizzeria straight out of Italy, with a fine little log-burning oven knocking up freshly cooked pizzas using dough and sauces made on the premises, and locally sourced ingredients. Ideal spot for either a quick lunch or a quiet evening meal. Mains £7–8. Tues–Sat 11am–11pm, Sun noon–6pm.

★ **Café Minuet** 42 Castle Arcade ☎029 2034 1794; map p.83. Cheap, cosy and delightfully odd restaurant, whose hearty, authentic Italian regional cooking has been attracting a loyal band of locals for years. Park yourself at one of the check-clothed tables or out in the arcade itself, where there's a tiny hatch for takeaway snacks. Mains £6–8. Mon–Sat 10am–4.30pm.

Louis 32 St Mary St ☎029 2022 5722; map p.83. This place won't win any prizes for glamour, but it's a wondrously cheap and old-fashioned restaurant serving great heapings of well-cooked, traditional British comfort food such as cottage pie and roast chicken. Mains £5–6. Mon–Sat 8.30am–8pm, Sun 9.30am–4.30pm.

Madeira 2 Guildford Crescent ☎029 2066 7705; map p.83. Enjoyable, rustically decorated Portuguese restaurant known for its great skewers of meat (*espetadas*), steaks and other carnivorous delights. There are some beautifully cooked fish dishes too, including *Caldeirada*, a traditional Portuguese fish broth. The two-course lunch menu (£9) is great value. Mains £13–20. Mon–Sat noon–2.30pm and 6–11pm.

Thai House 3–5 Guildford Crescent ☎029 2038 7404; map p.83. The enduring popularity of this well-established venue is down to its seasoned yet varied menu, incorporating both imported Thai and local Welsh ingredients. Vegetarians are well catered for, as are those who prefer their dishes slightly hotter. With its restrained oriental decor and staff attired in traditional costume, the *Thai House* retains a genuinely authentic feel. Mains £10–15. Mon–Sat noon–2.30pm and 6–11pm.

CARDIFF BAY
RESTAURANTS

ffresh Wales Millennium Centre ☎029 2063 6465; map p.88. Deservedly a big hit with pre-show diners, this is as fresh as its name suggests. Nicely crafted lunch and dinner menus, featuring the likes of seafood terrine with tomato salsa, and Swansea Bay mussels with chips. Meanwhile, the crisp, minimalist lounge bar serves scrumptious burgers with onion marmalade and potato chips. Mains £12–16. Tues–Sat noon–2.30pm & 5–9.30pm, Sun noon–3.30pm.

★ **Mimosa Kitchen & Bar** Mermaid Quay ☎029 2049 1900; map p.88. The Bay's most rewarding restaurant, sporting a simple but striking design with a brushed steel bar, deep brown leather seating and slate flooring. The Welsh-oriented menu ranges from the simple (Gower lamb cutlets in mint oil) to the ambitious (roasted wild cod with chorizo), while the gut-busting gourmet burgers are a real standout. Mains £12–17. Mon–Thurs 10am–11pm, Fri & Sat till midnight, Sun till 10.30pm.

CARDIFF FARMERS' MARKETS

If you're looking to pack a picnic, you could do a lot worse than head to one of Cardiff's terrific **Farmers' Markets** (ⓦ riversidemarket.org.uk), where you can pick up some great local produce and sometimes other knick-knacks. The biggest and best is the Sunday **Riverside Market**, opposite the Millennium Stadium on Fitzhammon Embankment (10am–2pm). On Saturdays (9.30am–1pm) the **Roath Market**, at the Mackintosh Sports Club on Keppoch Street also has an arts and craft bazaar.

OUT FROM THE CENTRE

CAFÉS

Chai Street 132 Whitchurch Rd ☎ 029 2062 4519; map p.80. Daytime spin-off café to neighbouring *Mint and Mustard*, serving cheap but tasty and filling Indian street food (breakfasts and lunches) in super-colourful Bollywood-style surrounds. Unusual, but very good. Tues–Sun 8am–4pm.

Milgi 213 City Rd ☎ 029 2047 3150; map p.80. Quirky, boho chic café where (veggie) food, art and music all have equal sway. Weekly and monthly events here include the supper club, the art and curry club, and the Northcote Lane vintage market on the first Sunday of the month. The Sunday veggie roast is a real treat and the yurt out back is a perfect spot for a cool drink. Daily 10am–12.30am.

★ **Waterloo Gardens Teahouse** 5 Waterloo Gardens ☎ 029 2045 6073; map p.80. Upmarket teahouse, a 20min walk north of the centre in Roath; its reputation for artisan teas and home-made cakes is unrivalled anywhere in the city. Sample one of fifty or so loose-leaf teas alongside a slice of ginger and pear cake. Well worth the short trek. Mon–Sat 8am–6pm, Sun 9am–6pm.

RESTAURANTS

Cibo 83 Pontcanna St, off Cathedral Rd ☎ 029 2023 2226; map p.80. Small, moderately priced and tremendously busy but always welcoming trattoria serving ciabatta sandwiches, fragrant pastas, proper pizza and a blackboard of daily specials and desserts. Mains £8–10. Mon–Fri noon–11pm, Sat & Sun 9.30am–11pm.

★ **Mint and Mustard** 134 Whitchurch Rd ☎ 029 2060 0333; map p.80. Arguably Wales' finest Indian restaurant, with a menu as brilliant as it is bold; try the Tiffin sea bass wrapped in banana leaves, the stir-fried lamb with coconut chips and curry leaves, or one of the many exceptional vegetarian dishes – the melt-in-the-mouth Bombay chat is sensational. Mains £12–16. Mon–Sat 6–11pm.

New Conway 58 Conway Rd ☎ 029 2022 4373; map p.80. Fine gastropub with a daily blackboard menu offering a mix of upmarket pub classics (such as beer-battered fish and chips) and Nordic-inspired seasonal specials (chilli squid or pan-fried sea bass on ratatouille), courtesy of the Swedish chef. The living-room-style dining area, surrounding a central fireplace and shelves of books, is delightful. Mains £10–13. Daily noon–11pm.

★ **The Old Post Office** Greenwood Lane, St Fagans ☎ 029 2056 5400; map p.80. Located opposite the museum, this accomplished restaurant serves modern European dishes with a firm Welsh twist. The meats are fabulous, particularly the locally produced pork, and there are some imaginative variations on traditional dishes, such as duck shepherd's pie. Mains £17–20. Tues–Sat 6–11pm, Sun noon–3pm.

DRINKING

Cardiff's **pub life** has expanded exponentially in recent years, with chic cosmopolitan bars jostling for space alongside the more traditional Edwardian palaces of etched smoky glass and deep-red wood. You'll find plenty of both in the very centre, particularly along Mill Lane, Greyfriars Rd and Westgate St – weekend nights are legendarily raucous in Cardiff, during which time the city centre is not for the faint-hearted. The most agreeable pubs, however, are located out on the margins, notably along Cathedral Rd in the direction of Pontcanna, with more out towards the student quarter around Cathays. Brains still brews in Cardiff, making a great range of smooth and cask beers, as well as a fantastic "continental-style" golden ale, named "45", any or all of which should not be missed.

CITY CENTRE

10 Feet Tall 11a Church St ☎ 029 2022 8883, ⓦ thisis10feettall.co.uk; map p.83. Ultra-hip pastiche of north African and Mediterranean dining in its street-level café-cum-wine bar, in addition to a top floor for live music and the basement *Undertone* club for one-off events. Daily noon–late.

City Arms 10 Quay St ☎ 029 2064 1913; map p.83. Opposite the Millennium Stadium, this no-nonsense boozer is always popular, especially on international match days and before gigs at *Clwb Ifor Bach* just around the corner. Brains beers as well as some choice guest ales. Mon–Thurs 11am–11pm, Fri & Sat till 2.30am, Sun noon–10.30pm.

The Cottage 25 St Mary St ☎ 029 2033 7195; map p.83. Traditional Edwardian pub with cheerful staff serving up some of the best Brains in the city centre, alongside good cask options and a range of decent

1

home-made pies. Daily 11am–11pm, Fri & Sat till midnight.

★ **Gwdihw** 6 Guildford Crescent ☎029 2039 7933, ⓦgwdihw.co.uk; map p.83. Pronounced "goody-hoo", this is a wonderful little corner café/bar, its exterior painted bright orange and the interior decked out with stripped wood flooring, odd bits of furniture and retro-style accoutrements. Daily happenings include alternative film, poetry recitals, micro-festivals and regular bouts of live music on the dinky little stage. Mon–Thurs noon–midnight, Fri & Sat till 2am, Sun 4pm–midnight.

Pen and Wig 1 Park Grove ☎029 2064 9090; map p.80. Large boozer in a quiet residential street, popular with both local professionals and students for the fine selection of very reasonably priced guest ales. Unspoilt flagstone floored interior and decent beer garden. Mon–Fri 10am–midnight, Sat 10am–1am, Sun noon–11.30pm.

Promised Land 4 Windsor Place ☎029 2039 8998; map p.83. One of the most welcoming bars in the centre, this modestly sized two-floor venue has strong musical associations, as the many wall-mounted signed photographs and posters testify. Otherwise, it's a cracking spot for a daytime chill-out and bite to eat. Sun–Wed 10am–11pm, Thurs till midnight, Fri & Sat till 2am.

Queen's Vaults 29 Westgate St ☎029 2022 7966; map p.83. Cavernous rugby-memorabilia pub across from the Millennium Stadium, with antique fittings, large TV screens and pool tables, hence its enormous popularity with local sports fans. Mon–Thurs & Sun 10am–11pm, Fri & Sat till midnight.

Tafarn 53–59 Despenser St, Riverside ☎029 2037 8866; map p.83. Part of the *Nos da* hostel, with a heated outdoor deck overlooking the Taff, a cantina serving locally sourced meals and bar snacks, and an impressive range of Welsh beers, ciders and spirits. Daily noon–11.30pm.

Zero Degrees 27 Westgate St ☎029 2022 9494; map p.83. Shiny microbrewery in a lino-clad converted garage with friezes made from heat-compressed Wellington boots and discarded mobile phones. The £2 beer sampler lets you taste all five of its house brews, including mango and a couple of wheat beers. Great gourmet pizzas too. Mon–Sat noon–midnight, Sun till 1pm.

CARDIFF BAY

Bar Cwtch Jolyon's Hotel, 5 Bute Crescent ☎029 2048 8775 map p.88. Cosy by name, cosy by nature, this snug little bar in the basement of *Jolyon's* is a big hit with the locals; kick back on one of the squishy sofas with a glass of wine and a slice of pizza rustled up in the wood-burning stove. Mon–Thurs 5–11pm, Fri till 1am, Sat 3pm–1am, Sun 3–11pm.

OUT FROM THE CENTRE

Buffalo Lounge 34 Woodville Rd ☎029 2034 4822 ⓦbuffaloloungecardiff.com; map p.80. Relaxing daytime coffee house/evening bar over in the student quarter, with big windows, deep leather sofas and low hanging lampshades – and check out the bar made up from old VHS tapes. There's always lots going on here, such as the acoustic open mic night on Sundays. Mon–Fri 10am–midnight, Sat & Sun 11am–12.30am.

Cayo Arms 36 Cathedral Rd ☎029 2023 5211; map p.80. Within a six of the cricket ground, two conjoined Victorian townhouses have formed this large, busy and proudly Welsh pub, with Tomos Watkin beers, decent food and a lively crowd. Mon–Sat noon–11pm, Sun noon–10.30pm.

★ **Cricketers** 66 Cathedral Rd ☎029 2034 5102; map p.80. Set in a gorgeous Victorian townhouse, this combines a sunny interior – big sofas from which to admire the cricketing memorabilia – with lively beer gardens both front and back. The Welsh cask-conditioned beers are some of the best in Cardiff, and the food is very creditable too. Daily noon–11pm.

SPECTATOR SPORT IN CARDIFF

Cardiff's sporting pedigree is surprisingly strong and it now boasts several world-class sporting arenas. Inevitably, **rugby** takes centre stage, and there are few more atmospheric places to be than Cardiff on international match-day at the magnificent Millennium Stadium. The city's club side, **Cardiff Blues** (☎0845 345 1400; ⓦcardiffblues.com), play in the Magners League at Cardiff City Football Club's new stadium on Leckwith Road.

Despite playing second fiddle to rugby, **football** remains popular in the city, thanks to the success of **Cardiff City** (☎0845 365 1115; ⓦcardiffcityfc.co.uk), who have been regulars in the championship play-offs in recent years, though as yet have not been able to make the step up to the Premiership. Cardiff's **cricketing** profile has increased massively in recent years, thanks to the staging of test matches at the expanded Swalec Stadium in Sophia Gardens; the first England versus Australia test match of the 2009 series was played here to sell-out crowds. It's also where **Glamorgan**, Wales' sole first-class cricket team, play (☎029 2040 9380; ⓦglamorgancricket.com).

★ **Y Mochyn Du** Sophia Close, off Cathedral Rd ☎ 029 2037 1599; map p.80. Right in the shadow of the cricket ground, this old gatekeeper's lodge is a fine place to sup a pint of Welsh brewed beer, either in the conservatory or outside among the greenery. Popular with Welsh-speakers. Mon–Fri noon–11pm, Sat till midnight, Sun till 10.30pm.

NIGHTLIFE AND ENTERTAINMENT

There's plenty of choice when it comes to **nightlife** in Cardiff, whether your tastes run to banging clubs, sweaty rock gigs (in English or Welsh), or a night of soothing jazz or classical music. Despite the healthy state of Welsh music, there is a dearth of small- to medium-sized gig venues in the city, a situation not helped by the closure of a number of well-established places in recent times. In addition to those places listed here, both Cardiff Castle and the Millennium Stadium stage major events, particularly the latter, which is usually on major acts' world tours.

Theatre in Cardiff encompasses everything from the radical and alternative at the Sherman Theatre or Chapter Arts Centre, to big, blowzy productions at the New Theatre, or West End spectaculars at the Wales Millennium Centre, home of Welsh National Opera (ⓦ wno.org.uk). The WMC and St David's Hall are the main venues for classical music.

CLUBS

Buffalo 11 Windsor Place ☎ 029 2031 0312, ⓦ buffalocardiff.com; map p.83. Sister venue to the Buffalo Lounge, this upbeat retro restaurant/bar/club features fabulously quirky decor and a cool vibe from lunchtime until the wee hours. Electronica is Buffalo's real forte, though there's plenty else happening, including experimental art and fashion parties. Daily till 4am.

★ **Cardiff Arts Institute** 29 Park Place ☎ 029 2023 1252, ⓦ cardiffinstitute.org; map p.80. Anonymous red-brick building opposite the National Museum, concealing a sociable bar and arts venue, whose dynamic programme encompasses everything from live bands and DJ sets to all manner of art and multi-media events. You can even munch on a burger while playing with the wall-bound Lego board. Daily noon–late.

Cardiff University Union Park Place ☎ 029 2078 1400, ⓦ cardiffstudents.com; map p.80. With four venues under one roof, there's much going on here, from assorted dance nights to big-name live bands. Open to non-students.

★ **Clwb Ifor Bach** 11 Womanby St ☎ 029 2023 2199, ⓦ clwb.net; map p.83. Sweaty and massively fun live music and dance club on three floors with nightly gigs, sessions or DJs, including 70s and funk nights. Widely known as the "Welsh club", due to the prevalence of Welsh-language acts and punters, particularly on Sat. Tues–Sat 10pm–3am.

LIVE MUSIC VENUES

Café Jazz 21 St Mary St ☎ 029 2038 7026, ⓦ cafejazzcardiff.com; map p.83. Unassuming but popular venue, below the Sandringham Hotel, hosting a diverse range of jazz concerts Tuesdays through to Fridays; electric blues, funk, gypsy jazz and the like. Entrance typically £2–6.

Coal Exchange Mount Stuart Square, Cardiff Bay ☎ 029 2049 4917, ⓦ coalexchange.co.uk; map p.88. A fine Victorian building well converted for all manner of musical events, notably some top-drawer rock and indie bands.

Motorpoint Arena Mary Ann St ☎ 029 2022 4488, ⓦ livenation.co.uk/cardiff; map p.83. Large concrete venue rising high over the city centre's southern streets and playing host to major rock and pop gigs, classical concerts, opera and comedy.

Norwegian Church Harbour Drive, Cardiff Bay ☎ 029 2045 4899, ⓦ norwegianchurchcardiff.com; map p.88. Venue for all kinds of musical and performance evenings, though typically of a classical or operatic bent.

Royal Oak 200 Broadway, Newport Rd, Roath ☎ 029 2047 3984, ⓦ theroyaloakcardiff.co.uk; map p.80. Renowned music pub with acoustic and electric jam sessions on Wed and bands on Fri, all starting from 9pm, and all free.

St David's Hall The Hayes ☎ 029 2087 8444, ⓦ stdavidshallcardiff.co.uk; map p.83. Part of the massive St David's shopping centre, this large venue is home to visiting orchestras and musicians from jazz to opera, and is frequently used by the excellent BBC National Orchestra of Wales.

University Concert Hall Corbett Rd, Cathays Park ☎ 029 2087 4816, ⓦ cardiff.ac.uk/music; map p.80. Hosts public concerts by university and local orchestras, jazz groups and easy-listening ensembles.

Wales Millennium Centre Roald Dahls Plass, Cardiff Bay ☎ 029 2063 6464, ⓦ wmc.org.uk; map p.88. Stunning performance space that's home to Welsh National Opera, along with various other music and dance companies. Also used for touring West End and other mega-productions.

THE LESBIAN AND GAY SCENE

Cardiff's gay scene is far from massive, but robust all the same. The best source for current information and advice is the Mardi Gras website (ⓦ cardiffmardigras.co.uk). It doesn't take too much effort to discover what's going on, as the principal venues are on Charles St, just off Queen St in the city centre. All venues are for men and women unless otherwise noted.

Bar Icon 60 Charles St ☎029 2066 6505; map p.83. Trendy bar, with muted, comfy decor and a tendency to get funky towards the weekend. Mon–Thurs noon–midnight, Fri till 1am, Sat till 2am, Sun 5–11pm.

Club X 39 Charles St; map p.83. The city's premier gay club, which manages to span both cheesy and cutting edge. Also has a wonderful roof garden and a great atmosphere. Fri–Sun 8pm–6am.

Golden Cross 283 Hayes Bridge Rd; map p.83. Laidback restored Victorian pub, rich in atmosphere and with some beautiful tiled pictures of yesteryear Cardiff. Camp entertainment a speciality, as is the cheap food.

THEATRE AND COMEDY

Chapter Arts Centre Market Rd, Canton ☎029 2030 4400, ⓦchapter.org; map p.80. Although best known for its art-house movies, this superb multifunctional arts complex also hosts some fine British and touring theatre and dance companies.

Glee Club Mermaid Quay, Cardiff Bay ☎029 2023 0130, ⓦglee.co.uk; map p.88. Cardiff's best comedy club, with appearances by some of the biggest names on the British stand-up circuit; occasional live music too, featuring some well-established artists.

Jongleurs Oceana Club, Greyfriars Rd ☎0870 0111 960, ⓦjongleurs.com; map p.83. More corporate than the *Glee*, but dependable for decent comedy; shows on Fridays and Saturdays only.

New Theatre Park Place ☎029 2087 8889, ⓦnewtheatrecardiff.co.uk; map p.83. Splendid Edwardian city-centre theatre playing host to big shows, musicals and pantos.

Sherman Theatre Senghennydd Rd, Cathays ☎029 2064 6900, ⓦshermancymru.co.uk; map p.80. An excellent two-auditorium repertory theatre known for its strong line-up of plays in both Welsh and English. New and translated classic Welsh-language pieces, stand-up comedy, children's entertainment, drama, music and dance.

DIRECTORY

Hospital In the first instance, phone NHS Wales Direct on ☎0845 4647. The city's main hospital is the University Hospital of Wales, Heath Park (☎029 2074 7747).

Internet Cardiff Central Library (Mon–Wed & Fri 9am–6pm, Thurs 9am–7pm, Sat 9am–5.30pm; free for

30min); TIC (Mon–Sat 9.30am–5pm, Sun 10am–4pm; £1 for 30min).

Police Cardiff Central Police Station, King Edward VII Ave, Cathays Park ☎029 2022 2111; Cardiff Bay Police Station, James St (same tel number).

Post office Inside the Queen's Arcade, St David's Centre.

Around Cardiff

The fairy-tale thirteenth-century fortress of **Castell Coch** stands on a hillside in woodlands at the edge of the city's northern suburbs, while to the west, the **National History Museum** at St Fagans relates the country's history through buildings moved here from all corners of Wales.

Castell Coch

April–Oct daily 9am–5pm, July & Aug till 6pm; Nov–March Mon–Sat 9.30am–4pm, Sun 11am–4pm • £3.80 • ☎029 2081 0101 • CADW • Bus #26A from Cardiff bus station

Above the village of **TONGWYNLAIS**, four miles north of Llandaff, the coned turrets of **Castell Coch** rise mysteriously out of a steep wooded hillside. A ruined thirteenth-century fortress, Castell Coch was rebuilt into a fantasy castle in the late 1870s by William Burges for the third Marquess of Bute, complete with a working portcullis and drawbridge. Numerous similarities with Cardiff Castle include the lavish decor, culled from religious and moral fables, that dazzles in each room. Lady Bute's bedroom, at the top of one of the three towers, incorporates a fabulously painted double dome, around which 28 panels depict frolicking monkeys, some of which were considered lascivious for their day. However, the castle was hardly ever lived in and sees more life today, especially in the tearoom situated in the valet's room.

St Fagans National History Museum

Daily 10am–5pm • Free • ☎029 2057 3500, ⓦmuseumwales.ac.uk • Buses #320 and #322 from Cardiff bus station

Separated from Cardiff by a sliver of greenery, the village of **ST FAGANS** (Sain Ffagan), four miles west of the city centre, has a rural ambience only partly marred by the busloads of tourists that regularly roll in to visit the unmissable **St Fagans National History Museum**.

The castle and grounds

The museum is constructed on grounds near **St Fagans Castle**, a country house built in 1580 on the site of a ruined Norman castle and furnished in early nineteenth-century style, complete with heavy oak furniture and solemn portraits. Surrounding the castle are the formal gardens, from where grassy terraces slope down to a chain of eighteenth-century fishponds, which have also been restored to something akin to their original design. It's a lovely spot for a picnic.

Open-air museum

Beyond this parkland area is the **open-air museum**, an outstanding collection of period buildings – houses, shops, dwellings, churches – garnered from all corners of Wales and faithfully rebuilt on this site. There's much to see, and many of the structures can be entered, so give yourself a good couple of hours to take it all in.

Many of the domestic structures are farmhouses of different ages and styles – compare, for example, the grandeur of the seventeenth-century red-painted **Kennixton Farmhouse** from Gower or the homely Edwardian comforts of **Llwyn-yr-Eos Farm** with the threadbare simplicity of the Gwynedd farmworkers' **Llainfadyn Cottage**. An interesting variety of workplaces on the site include a **tannery**, a **pottery**, three **mills** and a **smithy**, most of which house people demonstrating the original methods. Indeed, the early twentieth-century **bakehouse** is still in good working order and you can purchase various goodies here.

The best demonstration of how life changed over the years for a section of the Welsh population comes in the superlative **Rhyd-y-car** ironworkers' cottages from Merthyr Tydfil. Built originally around 1800, each of the six houses, with their accompanying strip of garden, has been furnished in the style of a different era – stretching from 1805 to 1985. Even the frontages and roofs are true to their age, offering a wade through working-class Welsh life over the past two centuries. Next door are the Victorian **Gwalia Stores** from the mining community of Ogmore Vale; the smell of polished mahogany is as evocative as the starchy-aproned assistants and the jars of boiled sweets that they sell. In between the cottages and the store, take a quick look at the wonderfully grand Victorian **urinal**.

Other buildings to look out for include the diminutive whitewashed 1777 **Pen-Rhiw Chapel** from Dyfed, which is still used by a small Unitarian community, the pristine and evocative Victorian **St Mary's Board School** from Lampeter, and the ordered mini-fortress of a 1772 **Tollhouse** that once guarded the southern approach to Aberystwyth.

The Vale of Glamorgan

South of the capital, the **Vale of Glamorgan**'s rich pastoral landscapes and cliff-fringed coastline, broken by long, sandy beaches, are often overlooked by visitors, though they are worth at least a couple of days' exploration. Lively seaside resorts at **Porthcawl** in the west and **Barry** in the east contrast with the more refined atmosphere of **Penarth**, clinging to the coat-tails of Cardiff. In between lie yawning wide bays and tumbledown castles, linked by bracing coastal walks along spectacularly stratified cliffs. Inland, the lower parts of the Vale's urban features – such as Wales' international **airport** at Rhoose and occasional looming factories – are set against rolling green pastureland sprinkled with charming, low-key market towns like **Cowbridge**, **Llantrisant** and **Llantwit Major**.

The Vale's proximity to Cardiff makes it easy to explore using **public transport**. The main-line train route through the Vale has a stop at Bridgend, a handy interchange for

1

bus services to the coast and some of the larger inland settlements, while the Vale of Glamorgan line, an alternative route from Cardiff to Bridgend, has stops at Rhoose and Llantwit Major. Barry and Penarth, almost suburbs of Cardiff, are easily reached by bus and train.

Penarth and around

An easy and enjoyable day out from Cardiff, the increasingly upmarket Victorian seaside town of **PENARTH** lies just across the Barrage from Cardiff Bay, accessible by road and linked by half-hourly shuttle trains to Cardiff. From the train station, a path on the right leads up to Stanwell Road, which continues into the clean-cut Edwardian shopping streets of the town centre.

Turner House Ffotogallery and around
Plymouth Rd • Tues–Sat 11am–5pm • Free • ☎ 029 2070 8870, ⓦ ffotogallery.org

The fine red-brick **Turner House**, on the opposite side of the tracks, is home to the small but engaging **Ffotogallery**, which stages contemporary photographic and other lens-based media exhibitions. Running down the left-hand side of Turner House, the Dingle path leads into showy **Alexandra Park**, emblemizing the spirit of Penarth with its flowerbeds and bandstand. Continuing down the hill brings you onto the charmingly fusty **Esplanade**, a surprisingly short, but tidy, promenade with a rusting spearmint-green hall on the pier.

Lavernock Point and Flat Holm
Jutting out into the Bristol Channel two miles due south of Penarth, **Lavernock Point** provides a forlorn setting for assorted campsites and pubs, but is notable as the place in which conversation was first heard by means of radio waves. This – as a plaque on the wall of the Victorian church notes – took place on May 11, 1897, when Guglielmo Marconi sent the immortal words "Are you ready?" over to his assistant George Kemp on the island of **Flat Holm** (Ynys Echni), three miles out in the channel, officially Wales' most southerly point.

Over the years, Flat Holm has been used as a Viking anchorage, a cholera hospital and a lookout point. Today it's an interesting and beautifully remote **nature reserve**, the nesting place of thousands of gulls and shelducks.

INFORMATION   **PENARTH**

Tourist information The TIC is at the head of the pier on the Esplanade (Easter–Sept Fri–Sun 11am–5pm; ☎ 029 2070 8849, ⓔ penarthtic@valeofglamorgan.gov.uk).

ACCOMMODATION

Hickman Lodge 17 Hickman Rd ☎ 029 2070 1044, ⓦ hickmanlodge.co.uk. Peaceful guesthouse in a quiet tree-lined street sandwiched between the rail line and the busy Windsor Rd, with three soothingly decorated en-suite rooms; a single, twin and double. **£65**

Pier & Pebble Esplanade ☎ 029 2070 0333, ⓦ thepierandpebble.co.uk. Although somewhat plain-looking from the outside, this comely little hotel smack-bang on the seafront has six polished rooms, three of which possess expansive sea views, hence cost a little extra. **£55**

CRUISES

You can spend the day **cruising** the local coastline aboard the *Waverley*, a seagoing paddle steamer which makes regular visits to Penarth Pier between June and early September (though it's sometimes replaced by the more conventionally propelled but no less gracious *Balmoral*). Day-trips range from cruises around Flat Holm to longer journeys up the Severn estuary or across the Bristol Channel to Ilfracombe on the north Devon coast (£19–41; ☎ 0845 130 4647, ⓦ waverleyexcursions.co.uk).

BOAT TRIPS TO FLAT HOLM

Boats operated by the **Flat Holm Project** (T 029 2087 7912, W flatholmisland.com; £20), Cardiff Bay, sail roughly between six and twelve days a month between mid-March and late October; book well in advance. Most are day-trips giving three hours on the island (including a history, flora and fauna tour), though it's occasionally possible to stay overnight in a farmhouse **hostel** (£16.50 per person excluding boat transport) on the island if it's not booked out by groups.

EATING AND DRINKING

Fig Tree Esplanade T 029 2070 2512. The balcony terrace fronting this ornate Victorian building is a neat spot to rest up and try some Pembrokeshire mussels or beer-battered fish and chips. Mains £10–16. Tues–Sat noon–3pm & 6–11pm, Sun noon–4pm.

Foxy's 7 Victoria Buildings T 029 2025 1666. Opposite the train station, this sunny deli makes for an ideal lunch stop; stuffed panini, warm salads, mouth-watering cakes and a shop stacked with great local produce. Mon–Fri 8am–5.30pm, Sat 8.30am–5pm.

Olive Tree 21 Glebe St T 029 2070 7077. A gem of a restaurant sporting an inspiring choice of meat (herb-encrusted lamb, pork with capers, pheasant with cider sauce) and seafood dishes (oysters, scallops in pancetta). The three-course bistro menu (Tues–Fri 5.30–9pm; £22.50) is excellent value. Tues–Fri 5.30–11pm, Sat 7–11pm, Sun noon–3pm, plus 12.30–2.30pm Thurs–Sat.

Barry and around

Six miles southwest of Penarth, **Barry** (Barri) is the quintessential Welsh resort of old. Until the 1880s, when it was developed as a rival port to the Bute family's Cardiff, the main centre for activity, **Barry Island** (Ynys y Barri), was indeed an island due to its position on the tidal estuary, but the docks' construction saw the river diverted. Today, the "island" fronts Whitmore Bay, an expansive Blue Flag **beach**, behind which runs a cheerful promenade.

In recent years, the town has returned to its traditional roots as a family resort, with a **Pleasure Park** full of fairground attractions, crazy golf course on the prom (£3) and, inevitably, a handful of tacky arcades. If you're seeking a bit more solitude, head east around the headland to Jacksons Bay.

Barry is best known as one of the main settings for the TV sitcom *Gavin & Stacey*, which is mostly filmed here – the tourist office has details of shooting locations.

Dyffryn Gardens and around

Dyffryn, 7 miles north • Daily: March–Oct 10am–6pm; Nov–Feb 10am–4pm • £6.50 • T 029 2059 3328, W dyffryngardens.com

In the hamlet of **DYFFRYN**, are the magnificent **Dyffryn Gardens**, set around the Victorian home of a local merchant. Seldom busy, the gardens offer everything from formal lilyponds and billiard-table-smooth lawns to joyous bursts of floral colour and the russets, golds and greens of an arboretum. By the lane junction just south of the gardens is the **St Lythan Long Cairn**, over four thousand years old. It's nowhere near as impressive, however, as its near neighbour, the **Tinkinswood Long Cairn**, a huge, capstoned burial chamber, around 4500 years old. Legend has it that anyone who sleeps beneath the fifty-ton monolith for a night will either die, go raving mad or become a poet – a threat commonly ascribed to other megalithic sites in Wales. You'll find it on the other side of the Dyffryn Gardens entrance, just beside the wooded lane between Dyffryn and **St Nicholas**, a village on the A48 just two miles from Cardiff's Culverhouse Cross roundabout.

Llanerch Vineyard

4 miles northwest of St Nicholas and 1 mile south of M4 junction 34 • Daily 10am–5pm • Self-guided tours £7 • T 01443 222716, W llanerch-vineyard.co.uk

Among rolling hills, **Llanerch Vineyard** is Wales' most successful winery, producing around 20,000 bottles of white and rosé Cariad wine each year, most of it sold within

1

Wales. On a self-guided tour, you can nose around the vines and a patch of ancient woodland before sitting down to a taste of the finished product. Also on site is a wine shop, a conservatory café serving light bites, smart accommodation and a cookery school.

ARRIVAL AND DEPARTURE   BARRY

Frequent **trains** from Cardiff rattle through Barry Docks and Barry stations before terminating at Barry Island. There are also frequent **buses** from Cardiff.

INFORMATION

Tourist information The TIC is on Barry Island's promenade (Easter–Sept Tues–Sun 11am–5pm; ☎01446 747171, ✉barrytic@valeofglamorgan.gov.uk).

ACCOMMODATION

Acorns Guesthouse 17 Romilly Rd ☎01446 743238. While the rooms in this pleasant little B&B are decidedly average (and there are no en suites), they do have a TV, fridge and microwave, and it is the cheapest place in the area. **£45**

Llanerch Vineyard Hensol ☎01443 222716, ⓦllanerch-vineyard.co.uk. Smart, contemporary accommodation just outside Barry, with B&B-style rooms overlooking the vineyard, in addition to a couple of self-contained cottages sleeping four to six people. Rooms **£75**; cottages (minimum 2-night stay) **£300**

New Farm Port Rd West between Barry and Cardiff Airport ☎01446 735536, ⓦnewfarmbarry.co.uk. A welcoming early seventeenth-century farmhouse B&B that's still a working farm. The rooms are cosy enough with some nice touches, though not all are en suite. **£50**

The Vale coast

West of Barry, the **Vale of Glamorgan** coast alternates between craggy cliffs and wide, white-sand beaches. Considering its location between Wales' two great cities, it's surprisingly quiet, as most of the old-fashioned little towns and seashore villages seem to have escaped the effects of the surrounding industrialization.

Llantwit Major

At first glance, **LLANTWIT MAJOR** (Llanilltud Fawr) appears to be all modern housing estates and rows of shops, but at its heart is a tiny kernel of winding streets. This is where, in around 500 AD, the scholarly St Illtud educated a succession of young men at his monastery, giving the town the chance to claim the title of Britain's earliest centre of learning. Amongst Illtud's pupils were St David as well as St Patrick, who was abducted from the monastery by Irish pirates to become the patron saint of Ireland.

A miniature fifteenth-century **town hall** sits just before the quaint town square and serves as an informal **visitor centre**. From here, Burial Lane winds its way past the village square and down to the front of the magnificent **parish church**, sheltering in a hollow next to the trickle of the Col Huw River.

St Illtud's church

The first thing that strikes you about this superb church is its size: it is, in fact, two churches joined at the tower. The older west church, nearer the stream, dates from around 1100; aisles were added in the twelfth and thirteenth centuries to transform it into the nave of a new church. The main feature here is the collection of decorative Celtic crosses and stones arranged haphazardly inside. Prize among these is the exquisitely carved eighth-century boulder at the back of the church, on which the letters ILT and half of a U (remains of ILLTUD) can still be made out. Tagged on to the rear of the west church are the ruins of the roofless Galilee Chapel, which is currently being renovated and will eventually hold the aforementioned stones. The east church is notable chiefly for some fresco remains, the most impressive being the one of St Christopher on the north wall, dating from around 1400.

1

The beach

At the junction at the top of Burial Lane, Colhugh Street descends for a little over a mile along the scrubby valley of the Col Huw River to the rocky **beach**, popular for surfing and a great starting point for some wonderful walks along the caves and inlets of the stratified cliffs and back into the rolling countryside. There's a tidy little beach café here too.

St Donat's Arts Centre

☎ 01446 799100, ⓦ stdonats.com

From the beach the clifftop path runs for two miles westwards to reach **St Donat's Bay**, dominated by a mock-Gothic castle, dating back to the fourteenth century, that was bought and restored by US tycoon William Randolph Hearst in the 1930s, and is now the international Atlantic College and multipurpose **arts centre**, at the forefront of Welsh efforts to internationalize local culture. As well as theatre, film, dance, exhibitions and community outreach, the centre hosts the excellent **Beyond the Border Storytelling Festival** during the first weekend of July.

ARRIVAL AND DEPARTURE LLANTWIT MAJOR

By bus Buses drop passengers behind the modern shopping precinct, from where it's a short walk down East St into the town centre.
Destinations Barry (hourly; 50min); Cardiff (9 daily; 1hr);

Cowbridge (hourly; 40min).
By train The train station on the Vale line is yards away.
Destinations Barry (hourly; 20min); Bridgend (hourly; 20min); Cardiff (hourly; 45min).

INFORMATION

Tourist information The TIC is in the town hall on Church St (Easter–Sept Sat 10am–1pm & 2–6pm, Sun noon– 5pm; ☎ 01446 796086).

ACCOMMODATION

Acorn Camping Ham Lane South ☎ 01446 794024, ⓦ acorncamping.co.uk. Large, well-shaded site a mile or so south of town with excellent modern amenities, including a shop and children's play area. Per pitch with one adult **£10.15**
Bramble Cottage Flanders Rd, off the road down to the beach ☎ 01446 795838, ⓦ bramble-cottage.co.uk. Wonderful guesthouse in a converted seventeenth-century

barn with two sweet rooms and a pleasingly summery breakfast room overlooking a patio terrace and extensive lawns. **£60**
Curriers Wine St ☎ 01446 793506, ⓦ thecurriers .co.uk. Friendly little guesthouse a few paces up from the main square, offering six homely rooms with shared shower facilities, and a pretty, beamed-ceiling breakfast room. **£60**

EATING AND DRINKING

Illtud's 216 Church St ☎ 01446 793800. Satisfying restaurant with a menu drawing together some exceptional meat- and seafood-based dishes. Once beyond the front bar, you enter a seductive, hall-like interior graced by candle-topped tables, high ceiling drapes and splashes of artwork. Mains £12–15. Tues–Sat noon–2.30pm & 6–11pm, Sun noon–5pm.

The Old Swan Inn Church St ☎ 01446 792230. Dating back to the twelfth century, Llantwit's oldest public house is the most agreeable place for a pint. The sociable bar/dining room offers a better-than-average blackboard menu and a choice selection of beers sourced largely from local brewers. Mon–Sat noon–11pm, Sun till 10.30pm.

Southerndown

West of Llantwit Major, the coast ducks and dives past remote cliffs and sandy beaches. **SOUTHERNDOWN** is a diffuse holiday village of touristy pubs and one excellent restaurant. However, the real reason to come here is **Dunraven Bay**, a beautiful, wide beach backed by jagged cliffs of perfectly defined layers of limestone and shale.

1

Heritage Coast Centre

Opening times erratic but usually Mon, Thurs & Fri 9am–3pm • ☎ 01656 880157

In the busy car park by Dunraven Beach is the **Heritage Coast Centre**, a small information point about walks and drives along this splendid section of the south Wales coastline. Dunraven is at the western end of a magnificent fifteen-mile **coastal walk**, dipping down into tiny, wooded valleys and up across wide stretches of cliff and sand.

EATING AND DRINKING   **SOUTHERNDOWN**

Frolics 52 Beach Rd ☎ 01656 880127. It looks rather anonymous, but this is one of the finest restaurants along the coast, fusing Welsh ingredients and French flavours to produce some delicious cuisine, such as Provence-style fish stew and pan fried fillet of Gower hake. The restaurant itself is beautifully presented. Mains £15–20. Wed–Sun noon–2.30pm & 6.30–10pm.

Porthcawl

One of Wales' most enduring family resorts, **PORTHCAWL** possesses a quaint village centre, several sandy beaches and some fantastic **surf**, making it a great sojourn along the coast. The town also attracts large numbers of golfers, here to test themselves on the magnificent Royal Porthcawl course, consistently ranked one of Britain's finest.

John Street, the main pedestrianised street, extends down to the **Esplanade**, Porthcawl's extensive seafront promenade which stretches the full length of the town and changes its name throughout.

The section known as the **Esplanade** comprises a typical array of Victorian and Edwardian hotels along the rocky beach, where you'll find the domed **Grand Pavilion** (☎ 01656 815995, ⓦ grandpavilion.co.uk), home to assorted seaside entertainment shows and pantomimes. Eastwards, the Esplanade runs to a lifeboat station at the harbour before veering north alongside the coast under the name of Eastern Promenade, the home of Porthcawl's solid seaside attractions: the **Coney Beach amusement park**, behind whelk stalls and candy-floss shops looking out over the popular **Sandy Bay** and neighbouring **Trecco Bay**.

The Simon Tucker Surfing Academy

☎ 07815 289761, ⓦ asurfingexperience.com

On the northwest side of town, a twenty-minute walk from the centre, is the far quieter and more beautiful **Rest Bay**, locally famed as a swimming and **surfing beach**. The Simon Tucker Surfing Academy, run by the former champion surfer, operates from the beach and offers tuition (£30/hr), board (£10) and wetsuit rental (£5), plus loads of information on the local scene.

ARRIVAL AND DEPARTURE   **PORTHCAWL**

Half-hourly **buses** connecting Bridgend with Porthcawl stop at the top of the pedestrianized John St in the town centre.

INFORMATION

Tourist information The TIC is a 5min walk down from where buses stop, in the Old Police Station (Easter–Oct Mon–Fri 9am–5pm, Sat 9am–4pm, plus July & Aug Sun 9am–4pm; Nov–Easter Tues & Fri 9am–5pm, Sat 9am–4pm, closed noon–1pm; ☎ 01656 786639, ⓦ visitbridgend.com). They have good information on surf tide times.

> ## ALL SHOOK UP
>
> Each year, on the last weekend of September, Porthcawl becomes the unlikely destination for one of Europe's largest **Elvis Presley** celebrations. This rip-roaring festival sees the town overrun with thousands of Elvis impersonators keen to outdo each other in a host of tribute shows taking place at the Grand Pavilion and other venues throughout town. Check out ⓦ elvies.co.uk. The somewhat more refined **International Jazz Festival** takes place at the end of April (ⓦ porthcawl-jazz-festival.com).

ACCOMMODATION

Accommodation in Porthcawl is plentiful, good value and concentrated around Esplanade Avenue, Mary St and along the promenade in its various guises.

Fairways Hotel West Drive ☎01656 782085, ⓦthefairwayshotel.co.uk. Popular with visiting golfers to nearby Royal Porthcawl, this medium-sized shoreline hotel is one of the town's fancier options, accommodating smart, decently sized rooms, some with sea views. **£95**

Foam Edge 9 West Drive ☎01656 782866, ⓦfoam-edge.co.uk. Cheerful, family-run guesthouse with two warm and beautifully decorated rooms, one with an enclosed balcony, but both with sensational sea views; and there's a brimming cooked Welsh breakfast to round things off. **£80**

Olivia House 44 Esplanade Ave ☎01656 789022, ⓦoliviahouse.com. On the road running up from the pavilion, this townhouse has been converted into a showy boutique hotel sporting five lavish, individually styled rooms, with some thoughtful touches given to each. **£75**

CAMPING

Brodawel Moor Lane, Nottage ☎01656 783231. About a 15min walk north of town, this is a simple field site with basic facilities, but it's perfectly acceptable. April–Oct. Pitches **£12**

EATING AND DRINKING

Rava 29 Mary St ☎01656 773888. Atmospheric, family-run restaurant dishing up good value Italian fare, and there's invariably a cracking catch of the day. Mains £14–18. Tues–Sat 6–11pm.

A Touch of Class The Esplanade ☎01656 771383.

Upmarket coffee house near the pavilion that also does pancakes and waffles for breakfast, sandwiches and wraps for lunch, and evening tapas. Sun & Mon 8am–5.30pm, Tues–Sat 8am–11pm.

The inland Vale

The Vale of Glamorgan's hinterland is speckled with some intriguing towns, villages and ruined castles, connected by narrow, winding, high-hedged lanes.

Llantrisant

Ten miles west of Cardiff **LLANTRISANT** perches dramatically between two peaks which rise sharply from the rivers Ely and Clun. It was once encircled by fortifications to exploit its natural position as a watching post over the Vale of Glamorgan, and it retains a charmingly quaint atmosphere reminiscent of a French hilltop town.

The town centre is focused on the **Bull Ring**, where there's a suitably wild-eyed statue of **Dr William Price** (1800–93), dressed in his favoured druid's outfit of moons, stars and a fox fur on his head. Dr Price subscribed to radical beliefs for his time – vegetarianism, nudity, republicanism, the unhealthiness of socks, anti-smoking and free love – as well as pointing out the potential environmental disasters of mass industrialization. He is best remembered for burning the body of his dead infant son, Iesu Grist (Welsh for "Jesus Christ"), in an oil drum on Llantrisant Common in January 1884. He was arrested and, in a sensational trial at Cardiff, acquitted, after which cremation was made legal in the UK.

Clustered around this comely little square are a handful of quirky, artisan shops and craft outlets. A short walk from the square is the old guildhall, dating from 1733, the last remaining tower from the thirteenth-century castle and, 100yd along the lane, the parish church, offering glorious views across the Vale.

Cowbridge

High-class boutiques and restaurants line the long and handsome main street of **COWBRIDGE** (Y Bont Faen), Wales' wealthiest town. On the south side of the High Street, Church Street leads under the narrow gatehouse that is the sole survivor of the four that once punctuated the town's fourteenth-century walls.

1

Old Beaupre Castle

Open access • Free

A little more than a mile south of town, down St Athan Road, a quiet lane fringed with high hedges, there's a tiny lay-by opposite the Regency finery of Howe Mill. A path opposite leads along the bank of the River Thaw for a quarter of a mile to the gauntly impressive ruins of **Old Beaupre Castle**, largely an Elizabethan manor house. Built by the local noble family, the Bassetts, Beaupre is a huge shell of ruined Italianate doorways and vast mullioned windows in the middle of a quiet Glamorgan field.

ARRIVAL AND DEPARTURE   COWBRIDGE

Half-hourly **buses** connecting Cardiff with Cowbridge stop on Westgate, a short walk west of the High St.

ACCOMMODATION

Bear Hotel High St 📞01446 774814, 🌐bearhotel .com. An upgraded, long-established coaching inn now harbouring supremely comfortable, individually designed rooms, though all are typically furnished in classical style and some have four-poster beds. **£100**

EATING AND DRINKING

Huddart's 69 High St 📞01446 774645. At this upmarket restaurant warm pheasant salad, lobster bisque soup, and loin of fresh tuna are just some of the tempters on offer. Mains £16–18. Tues–Sat noon–2pm & 6.30–11pm, Sun noon–2pm.

Market Place 66 High St 📞01446 774800. Beautiful restaurant divided into different sections, with the graceful bare-brick interior of the listed seventeenth-century dining room contrasting with the modern garden terrace and

mezzanine bar. Exceptional menu featuring the likes of roast cod with rarebit crust, and asparagus and butternut squash risotto. Mains £14–18. Tues–Sat noon–11pm, Sun noon–4pm.

★ **The Quarter Penny Café** 54 High St 📞01446 774999. Park yourself in one of the little brick alcoves of this superb café and enjoy a steaming bowl of carbonara alongside a glass of wine. The summery terrace out the back is delightful. Mon–Sat 8.30am–5pm, Sun 9am–4pm.

The Valleys

No other part of Wales is as instantly recognizable as **the Valleys**, a generic name for the string of settlements packed into the narrow cracks in the mountainous terrain to the north of Newport, Cardiff and Swansea. Coming through Monmouthshire, the change from rolling countryside to sharp contours and a post-industrial landscape is almost instantaneous, though the greenery evident today is a far cry from the slag heaps and soot-encrusted buildings of a mere three or so decades ago.

Each of the valleys depended almost solely on coal mining (see p.110). This nearly defunct industry has left its mark on the staunchly working-class towns, where row upon row of brightly painted terraced houses, tipped along the slopes at incredible angles, are broken only by austere chapels, the occasional remaining pithead or the miners' old institutes and drinking clubs.

Although not traditional tourist country, this is without doubt one of the most fascinating corners of Wales. Some of the former mines have reopened as gutsy and hard-hitting museums, notably the absorbing **Big Pit** at Blaenafon and the **Rhondda Heritage Park** at Trehafod. You'll also gain a deeper impression of valley life from less conventional attractions such as the Utopian workers' village at **Butetown** and the iron gravestones of **Blaenafon**, as well as the dignified memorials, found in almost every community, to those who died underground – or, in the heart-rending case of **Aberfan**, while simply going about their daily lives. South Wales, perhaps more than any other part of Britain, demonstrates the true human cost of the world's first industrialized nation. In addition to the Valleys' industrial landmarks, there are some older historic sights here, notably the vast **Caerphilly Castle** and the sixteenth-century manor house of **Llancaiach Fawr.**

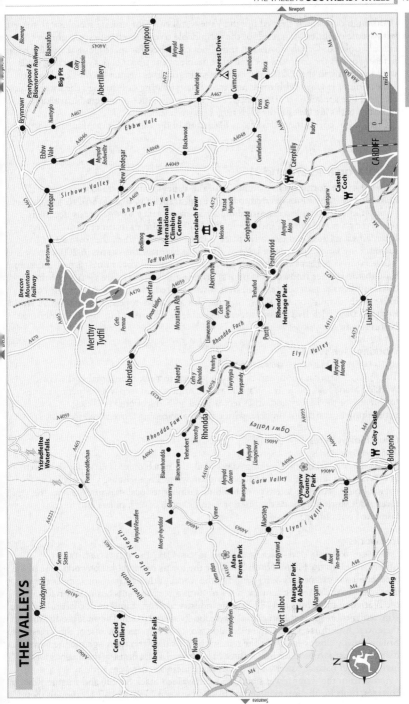

THE VALLEYS

1

Newport

Blorenge
Blaenafon
Pontypool & Blaenavon Railway
Big Pit
Coity Mountain
Abertillery
Pontypool
Brynmawr
Nantyglo
A4043
A472
Mynydd Maen
Forest Drive
Twmbarlwm
Cwmcarn
Risca
Newbridge
A467
Cross Keys
Ebbw Vale
Ebbw Vale
A4046
Blackwood
A4048
Cwmfelinfach
A468
Rudry
Caerphilly
Mynydd Bedwellte
New Tredegar
A4048
A4049
CARDIFF
A48 (M)
M4
Tredegar
Sirhowy Valley
A469
Rhymney Valley
Ystrad Mynach
Castell Coch
Nantgarw
Butetown
Welsh International Climbing Centre
Llancaiach Fawr
A472
Mynydd Meio
A470
Bedlinog
Nelson
Senghenydd
Pontypridd
Brecon Mountain Railway
Taff Valley
A4054
A470
Abercynon
A472
Llantrisant
Cefn Pennar
Aberfan
Cynon Valley
Mountain Ash
A4059
Cefn Gwyngul
Trehafod
Rhondda Heritage Park
A4119
Merthyr Tydfil
Llanwonno
Rhondda Fach
Porth
Ely Valley
Aberdare
Maerdy
Penrhys
Cefn y Rhondda
Mynydd Maendy
A4233
A4058
Llwynypia
Tonypandy
A4059
Rhondda Fawr
Treorchy
Rhondda
Ogwr Valley
Coity Castle
Ystradfelltre Waterfalls
A465
Treherbert
Blaenrhondda
A4061
Bridgend
A4107
Mynydd Llangeinwyr
M4
Pontneddfechan
Blaencwm
Mynydd Garth
A4060
Garw Valley
Tondu
Glyncorrwg
Bryngarw Country Park
A4221
Mynydd Rhiwfen
A4064
Cymer
Blaengarw
A4063
Maesteg
Llynfi Valley
Moel-yr-hyrddod
A4068
Seven Sisters
Vale of Neath
Ystradgynlais
A4109
Langynwyd
Afan Forest Park
Gwyn Afan
A4107
Moel Ton-mawr
A48
Kenfig
Cefn Coed Colliery
Aberdulais Falls
A4067
River Neath
Pontrhydyfen
Margam Park & Abbey
Margam
M4
Port Talbot
Neath
N

Swansea

0 ____ 5 miles

1

Although now much cleaned up, the Valleys still combine unique sociological interest with scenic qualities. As a result of the formidable terrain, each valley was almost entirely isolated. Canals, roads and train lines competed for space along the valley floor, petering out as the contours became untameable at the upper end. Connecting roads were built only in the 1920s, and even today transport is frequently restricted to the Valleys' outer reaches, with roads and train lines radiating out through the south Wales coalfield like spokes on a giant wheel. The Valleys also offer unforgettable **walking** holidays; paths are best on the high ridges between valleys.

This section covers the valleys from Blaenafon in the east to Cwm Afan and Port Talbot in the west.

Blaenafon and around

Situated in the northeastern extremities of the Valleys is the iron and coal town of **BLAENAFON** (sometimes referred to by its English spelling, Blaenavon). Its lofty hillside position makes it feel less claustrophobic than many valley towns, but its decline is testified by a population of little more than 5000, a third of its nineteenth-century size. It remains a spirited and evocative place, a fact recognized when the town and surrounding landscape gained UNESCO World Heritage Site status in 2000.

Blaenafon is perhaps best known for its **Big Pit**, an old coal mine-turned-museum, though the former ironworks is no less gripping, while there are vestiges of the town's industrial past scattered all over town. Indeed, the town's attractions could quite easily detain you for a day. In June, this all comes together in the town's **World Heritage Day**, with live music, street entertainers, Victorian fun fair and a heritage costume parade.

Working Men's Hall

High St • Films Mon–Thurs at 7pm, £3 • ☎ 01495 792661

The town's Victorian boom can be seen in its architecture, most notably the florid **Working Men's Hall**, built in 1895, and where miners used to pay a halfpenny a week for the use of the library and other recreational and educational facilities; entertainment is still put on here, with a **cinema** screening current-release films.

Church of St Peter

Church Rd • ☎ 01495 790292

Across the road from the Working Men's Hall, the much older (1805) parish **church of St Peter** is a good example of what became known as Enginehouse Churches – an engine house being the sole type of building familiar to local masons. Contact the reverend if you'd like to see the interior with its tomb covers, pillars and font, all fashioned out of iron.

Ironworks

North St • Easter–Oct: Mon–Fri 9.30am–4.30pm, Sat 10am–5pm, Sun 10am–4.30pm • Free • ☎ 01495 792615 • CADW

About 700yd up the hill on North Street are the town's remarkable **ironworks**, one of the most complete extant sites of its period in the world. Although iron smelting in the area dates back to the sixteenth century, it wasn't until three Midlands businessmen formed the Blaenafon ironworks in 1789 that the industry took off. Limestone, coal and iron ore – ingredients for successful smelting – were locally abundant, and at peak production there were five furnaces here. The Blaenafon works grew to become one of the largest in Britain, finally closing in 1900. The remains of the site offer a thorough picture both of the process used to produce iron – three furnaces and a cast house remain, alongside the hulking water balance tower – and the workers' lifestyles that went with it.

Across from the water tower stand the whitewashed Stack Square and Engine Row cottages, built for the foremen and craftsmen between 1789 and 1792, though they were inhabited until as recently as 1971. Two of these neat, four-room abodes remain *in situ*, with another housing an exhibition on the history of iron- and steel-making, and a model of how the site would have once looked. It was here, too, that the hit BBC docu-drama *Coal House* was filmed, with families trading twenty-first-century life for the conditions of the 1920s.

Blaenafon Community Heritage & Cordell Museum

Lion St • April–Sept Mon–Fri 10am–3.30pm, Sat 10am–1pm; Oct–March Mon, Tues & Thurs 10am–3.30pm, Sat 10am–1pm • £1 • ☎ 01495 790991

Adjoining the town library, the tiny **Blaenafon Community Heritage & Cordell Museum** proudly documents the roles played by various groups throughout the community. More absorbing are the exhibits on the life and works of author Alexander Cordell (1914–97), including his books, typewriter and Tippex-splattered desk. Born in Ceylon (now Sri Lanka), Cordell developed a deep affinity for Wales and its industrial past during the many years he spent living in the area, a theme which manifested itself in his renowned 1959 novel, *Rape of the Fair Country*; it was eventually translated into seventeen languages. Also available here are details of four local driving tours around "Cordell Country".

Pontypool and Blaenavon Railway

Easter –Sept: Sat & Sun 11am–4pm, plus specials days • £5 return • ☎ 01495 792263, ⓦ pontypool-and-blaenavon.co.uk

Between Easter and September, steam train buffs can ride on the **Pontypool and Blaenavon Railway**, which shunts between the Furnace Sidings (signposted just off the B4248 between Blaenafon and Brynmawr), Blaenavon High Level station and the *Whistle Inn*; a round-trip takes about fifty minutes. The Railway Shop in Blaenafon, at 13a Broad St (Mon–Fri 11am–5.30pm, Sat till 4pm) has some wonderful exhibits, as well as trains and other accessories to buy.

Big Pit

Signposted on west side of town, off B4246 • Feb–Nov; frequent one-hour tours daily 10am–3.30pm; Dec & Jan call for tour times and availability • Free • ☎ 01495 790311, ⓦ museumwales.ac.uk • Shuttle bus from Blaenafon every 30min

Three-quarters of a mile west of the town lies the marvellous **Big Pit National Coal Museum**, occupying a former colliery which opened in 1880 and closed exactly a century later.

The Pit

Of all the mining museums in south Wales, Big Pit brings you closest to the experience of a miner's work and life, as you descend 300ft, kitted out with lamp, helmet and heavy battery pack into a labyrinth of shafts and coal faces. The guides are ex-miners, who give you a personal insight into mining life as they lead you through examples of the different types of coal mining, from the old stack-and-pillar operation, where miners would manually hack into the coalface before propping up the ceiling with a wooden beam, to more modern mechanically worked seams. Constant streams of rust-coloured water flow by, adding to the dank and chilly atmosphere that terrified the small children who were once paid twopence for a six-day week (of which one penny was subtracted for the cost of their candles) pulling the coal wagons along the tracks. Just as integral to the working of the mines were the pit ponies, hardy creatures who worked at Blaenafon until 1972; as part of the tour you get to see the now forlorn-looking stables.

The Pithead Baths

Back on the surface are the superbly preserved pithead baths, dating from 1939 and just about the last ones surviving anywhere in the country. Beyond the rows of lockers, some of which contain miners' belongings, several rooms offer a compelling and moving insight into the lives and times of the miners and their families. The plight of

1

THE WELSH COAL INDUSTRY

The land beneath the inhospitable hills of the south Wales valleys had some of the world's most abundant and accessible natural seams of **coal**, as well as iron ore. During the boom years of the nineteenth and early twentieth centuries, wealthy English capitalists came to Wales and ruthlessly stripped the land of its natural assets, while paying paltry amounts to those who risked life and limb in the mines. The mine owners were in a formidably strong position – thousands of Welsh working class, bolstered by their Irish, Scottish and Italian peers, flocked to the Valleys in search of work and some sort of sustainable life. The Valleys – virtually unpopulated at the start of the nineteenth century – became blackened with soot and packed with people, pits and chapels by the beginning of the twentieth.

By 1920, there were 256,000 men working in the 620 mines of the south Wales coalfield, providing one-third of the world's coal resources. Vast **miners' institutes**, paid for by a wages' levy, jostled for position with the Nonconformist chapels, whose muscular brand of Christianity was matched by the zeal of the region's politics, trade-union-led and avowedly left-wing. Great socialist orators rose to national prominence, and even Britain's pioneering **National Health Service**, founded by a radical Labour government in the years following World War II, was based on a Valleys community scheme run by born Aneurin Bevan.

Over half of the original pits closed in the harsh economic climate of the 1930s. World War II saw a brief respite in the closure programme, which continued even more swiftly in the years immediately after. As coal seams became less economical (due to the additional distance to reach the coalface from the pitheads), and the political climate shifted, the number of people employed in the industry dipped down into four figures in the aftermath of the 1984–85 miners' strike. No coalfields were as solidly behind the strike as south Wales, whose workers and families responded wholeheartedly to the call to defend the industry, which their trade union, the **National Union of Mineworkers** (NUM), claimed was on the brink of being decimated. The year-long war of attrition between the Thatcher government and Arthur Scargill's NUM was bitter, finally seeing the government victorious as the number of miners returning to work outnumbered those staying out on strike. Over a quarter of a century on, all but a few privately run south Wales pits have now closed.

women is given due prominence, with emphasis on their role during the miners' strikes, when they organized food parcels and soup kitchens, and in many cases joined their men on the picket lines. The exhibition concludes with coverage of the explosive 1984–85 strikes; look out for the series of feisty testimonies from the miners made redundant here.

INFORMATION

Tourist information The Blaenavon Heritage Centre is on Church Rd (Tues–Sun: April–Sept 9am–5pm, Oct–March 9am–4pm; ☎01495 742333, ⓦ visitblaenavon

BLAENAVON

.co.uk). Also here is an enlightening exhibition on the history of the town's coal-mining and ironworking industries, as well as a café.

ACCOMMODATION

Rifleman's Arms Rifle St ☎01495 792297. A 10min walk north of town on the Abergavenny road, the friendly

Rifleman's offers five decent en-suite rooms above its pub, though it's by no means noisy. **£60**

Abertillery

It's worth taking a short detour down the Ebbw Vale Valley to Abertillery (ten miles southwest of Blaenafon), where the **Guardian monument** pays tribute to fallen miners of the Six Bells colliery disaster. In 1960, 45 miners were killed here by an underground explosion, an event commemorated some fifty years later with the unveiling of this, the largest memorial in the Valleys. The 40ft-high statue of a miner was constructed from some 20,000 individual slices of steel, while the names of the victims are cut into the handsome sandstone plinth on which the miner stands.

Cwmcarn Forest

1

8 miles south of Abertillery • **Forest drive** Easter–Aug daily 11am–7pm; July & Aug weekends until 9pm;
Sept daily 11am–6pm; March & Oct daily 11am–5pm; Nov–Feb Sat & Sun 11am–4pm • £5 per car **Visitor Centre**
☎ 01495 272001, ⓦ cwmcarnforest.co.uk

Offering plentiful opportunities for cycling and walking, the **Cwmcarn Forest** is best seen along the **Cwmcarn Forest Drive**. Setting out from the visitor centre, the seven-mile figure-of-eight drive takes in superb scenery, as well as kids' play areas, an Iron Age hillfort and numerous mountain bike trails. Information about some of these challenging downhill trails can be obtained from the visitor centre, which also has walking maps and guides, and a pleasant café on site.

There's also a very small, but neat and grassy **campsite** (£3 per pitch and £6 per adult) next to the visitor centre, with three basic wooden pods each sleeping two- to four-people (£35–40 per night).

Caerphilly

Now almost a suburb of Cardiff, just seven miles north of the capital at the foot of the **Rhymney Valley**, the town of **CAERPHILLY** (Caerffili) is wrapped around its staggering moated **castle**, a thirty-acre site that has become one of Wales' most visited tourist attractions. Caerphilly was also the birthplace of legendary comedian Tommy Cooper, a large bronze statue of whom stands opposite the castle.

The castle

April–June, Sept & Oct daily 9.30am–5pm; July & Aug daily 9.30am–6pm; Nov–March Mon–Sat 10am–4pm, Sun 11am–4pm • £4 •
☎ 029 2088 3143 • CADW

Built on the site of a Roman fort and an earlier Norman fortification, the present **castle** was begun in 1268 under Gilbert de Clare, who wanted to protect the vulnerable coastal plains around Cardiff from Llywelyn ein Llyw Olaf (Llywelyn the Last).

For the next few hundred years, Caerphilly was given at whim by various kings to their favourites – most notably by Edward II to his minion, and some say lover, Hugh le Despenser, in 1317. The Civil War necessitated the building of an armoury, which prompted Cromwell to seize it, drain the moat and blow up the towers. By the early twentieth century, the castle was in a sorry state, sitting amid a growing industrial town that saw fit to build in the moat and the castle precincts. It was during the late 1920s, under the supervision of the fourth Marquess of Bute, that the castle underwent an extensive period of restoration, followed, in 1958, by the demolition of houses and shops so that the moat could be reflooded.

The castle grounds

You enter the castle through the much-restored great **gatehouse** that punctuates the barbican wall by a lake. From here, a bridge crosses the moat, part of the wider lake, to the outer wall of the castle itself, behind which sits the hulking inner ward. Located here is the massive **eastern gatehouse**, which includes an impressive upper hall and oratory and, to its left, the wholly restored and reroofed **Great Hall**, largely built around 1317 by Hugh le Despenser. Running round from the eastern gatehouse, behind the Great Hall and down to the southwestern tower, is an elevated walkway. Walking along here, you'll pass the iconic southeastern **leaning tower**, with a dramatic cleft in its walls

---

CYCLE HIRE IN CWMCARN FOREST

Bikes can be rented one mile north of Cwmcarn in Abercan village, from PS Cycles, Bridge St
(☎ 01495 246555, ⓦ pscycles.co.uk).

1

THE BIG CHEESE

In addition to its castle, Caerphilly is also synonymous with its crumbly white **cheese**, which has inspired the vibrant **Big Cheese festival**, held over three days in late July in the shadow of the castle. There are all manner of events taking place, from street theatre to concerts, a funfair, falconry, historical re-enactments and craft market, a cheese race, and, of course, a food market selling cheese along with all manner of local produce. Throughout the rest of the year, the only place in town to buy actual Welsh Farmhouse Caerphilly cheese (rather than those made elsewhere but still carrying the Caerphilly label) is the visitor centre. For more see ⓦ caerphilly.gov.uk/bigcheese

where Cromwell's men are said to have attempted to blow it sky-high (though the tilt is more likely due to simple subsidence). With the exception of the ruined northeastern tower, the other corner turrets have been blandly restored since the Civil War, though the northwestern tower houses a reasonably interesting exhibition on the castle's restoration. A platform behind the barbican wall exhibits medieval war and siege engines, pointing ominously across the lake.

ARRIVAL AND DEPARTURE   CAERPHILLY

Both the castle and the visitor centre are a 5min stroll down Cardiff Rd from the **bus** and **train stations**. Regular trains and buses shuttle between here and Cardiff.

INFORMATION

Tourist information The town's red-brick visitor centre is just along from the castle entrance on Twyn Square (daily 10am–5pm; ☏ 029 2088 0011, ⓦ visitcaerphilly.com).

EATING AND DRINKING

Glanmors Tearooms Castle Court Precinct ☏ 029 2088 8355. For a spot of refreshment after visiting the castle, pop into this wonderfully genteel tearoom, with table service and tea served in china pots and teacups. Light lunches also available. Mon–Sat 8.30am–5.30pm.

The Rhymney and Sirhowy valleys

Following the traditional border between the former counties of Glamorganshire and Monmouthshire north of Caerphilly, the Rhymney Valley is light on worthwhile sights, and becomes increasingly industrialized as it steers past a seamless succession of small towns. That said, there are one or two points of interest if heading this way, as there are in the similarly low-key Sirhowy Valley across to the east.

Winding House

Cross St, off White Rose Way • Tues–Sun 10am–5pm • Free • ☏ 01443 822 666

Ten miles up the valley from Caerphilly is **NEW TREDEGAR**, where the **Winding House**, with its gleaming Victorian-era steam engine that once powered the colliery's high-speed lifts, is worth a visit. The engine usually runs only on Bank Holidays, though other dates are sometimes scheduled in. Otherwise, there's an enlightening exhibition on the history of Caerphilly and its surrounds. It's a ten-minute walk south of Tir-phil train station.

Butetown

At the head of the valley, a mile beyond Rhymney town and just short of the A465 Heads of the Valleys road, tiny **BUTETOWN** (Drenewydd) was constructed as a model workers' estate in 1802–03 by the idealistic Marquess of Bute, a member of Wales' richest land- and minerals-owning family, although only the central grid of houses was ever built.

1

Tredegar

A mile east of Butetown, at the head of the Sirhowy Valley, the little town of
TREDEGAR boasts **Bedwellty House and park**, a Georgian mansion built for the
Homfray family, co-founders of the Tredegar ironworks. Currently undergoing major
restoration work, the house is likely to feature a permanent exhibition when complete.
In the grounds (unrestricted access; free) you'll find an arboretum, ice house, and the
world's largest lump of coal, a fifteen-ton block exhibited as part of the 1951 Festival of
Britain. If you've time, head up into the centre to view the very fine cast-iron **town
clock**, erected in The Circle in 1858.

The Taff and Cynon valleys

Like the River Rhymney, the River Taff also empties into the Bristol Channel at Cardiff,
after passing through a condensed 25 or so miles of industry and population that obscure
the former **china works** at Nantgarw. The first town in the Taff Vale is **Pontypridd**, one of
the most cheerful in the Valleys, where the Rhondda River hives off west. Continuing
north, the river splits again at **Abercynon**, where the Cynon River flows in from
Aberdare. Just outside Abercynon is the enjoyable seventeenth-century **Llancaiach Fawr**
manor house, while to the north, the Taff is packed into one of the tightest of all the
Valleys, passing **Aberfan** five miles short of the valley head town of **Merthyr Tydfil**.

China Works Museum

Wed–Sun 10am–4.30pm • Free • ☎ 01443 841703

Barrelling north along the A470, you'd never suspect that the **China Works Museum** is
tucked behind a thicket of trees just by the junction for **NANTGARW**. For less than five years
in the 1810s, the pottery here produced some of the finest porcelain in the world, the few
florid examples on display only serving to whet your appetite for the extensive collection in
the National Museum and Gallery in Cardiff. Master porcelain painter William Billingsley
set up the works with high ambition using Valleys coal and Cornish clay, but the extremely
difficult "soft paste porcelain" process resulted in just a ten-percent firing success rate and
the enterprise soon folded. One of the firing kilns has now been rebuilt and the main
building contains small displays on the process and the history of the site.

Pontypridd

Home town of crooner Tom Jones, **PONTYPRIDD** is today rapidly gentrifying as Cardiff
commuters move in, but retains its own unique spirit. Arriving in Pontypridd, you're
greeted by the town's distinctive arched **bridge** of 1775, once the largest single-span
stone bridge in Europe. Featuring three holes either side to lessen the bridge's overall
weight and allow gusty winds through, it was built by local amateur stonemason
William Edwards, whose previous attempts crumbled into the river below. Wednesdays
and Saturdays are good days to be here, with the old-fashioned **market** spilling out
onto Market Street and the surrounding squares.

Ynysangharad Park

On the far side of the river from the town centre is **Ynysangharad Park**, established after
World War I as a memorial park, but now the town's popular green space. Here you'll
find Sir W. Goscombe John's cloying allegorical statue and tomb in honour of Pontypridd
weaver Evan James, who in 1856 composed the stirring *Hen Wlad Fy Nhadau* (*Land of
My Fathers*), which that subsequently became the Welsh national anthem.

Pontypridd Museum

Taff St • Mon–Sat 10am–5pm • Free • ☎ 01443 490748

Right next to the bridge, the **Pontypridd Museum** is housed in what was one of the
town's great chapels. Built in 1861, it has been lovingly restored, and boasts unusually

1

ornate ceiling bosses, pillars, pulpit, stained-glass window and organ that all contribute to the reverential atmosphere. The centre's contents are a real treasure trove of photographs, video, models and exhibits which succeed in painting a warm picture of the town and its outlying valleys. Tom Jones and local opera star and actor Sir Geraint Evans are also celebrated among the exhibitions here.

John Hughes' Grogg Shop

159 Broadway • Mon–Fri 9am–5pm, Sat 10am–5pm

Near the elegant and impressive train station, the wonderfully quirky **John Hughes' Grogg Shop** has been producing figurine caricatures of Welsh rugby stars, as well as other sporting and world celebrities, in oddball sculpture for some 45 years – also on display are photos and memorabilia donated by some of those who've been made into a "Grogg", and an autograph wall signed by various stars. It's well worth a visit even if you don't plan on buying anything.

ARRIVAL AND DEPARTURE   PONTYPRIDD

By train The train station is a 10min walk south of the old bridge on The Graig.

Destinations Abercynon (every 15min; 10min): Aberdare (every 30min; 35min); Cardiff (every 15min; 30min); Merthyr Tydfil (every 30min; 35min); Treherbert (every 30min; 40min).

By bus The bus station is directly above the old bridge on the western bank.

Destinations Abercynon (every 15min; 10min); Aberdare (every 45min; 15min); Caerphilly (every 30min; 30min); Cardiff (every 15min; 40min); Merthyr Tydfil (every 15min; 25min).

INFORMATION

Tourist information The TIC is inside the Pontypridd Museum (Mon–Sat 10am–5pm; ☎ 01443 490748).

ACCOMMODATION

Blueberry Hotel Market St ☎ 01443 485331, ⓦ blueberryhotel.com. Appropriately appealing name for this sparkling little hotel, whose nine rooms are fashioned in one of two styles; cool, crisp white-on-white, or classic French furnished. **£80**

EATING AND DRINKING

★ **Bunch of Grapes** Ynysangharad Rd ☎ 01443 402934. A terrific combination of restaurant/pub, whose imaginative menu (braised rabbit with chard and spinach, Breconshire ox cheek with tarragon mash) is the best for miles around. There are typically more than half a dozen real ales on at any one time, while the festival bar testifies to the many regular beer events held here. Located in a residential street beyond the park and A470 flyover. Daily 11am–11pm.

Llanover Arms Bridge St ☎ 01443 403215. Retaining a certain worn charm, the stone-fronted *Llanover*, situated right by the bridge, is one of the town's better watering holes. The beer is good too, with a couple of decent guest ales. Daily noon–11pm.

ENTERTAINMENT

Pontypridd boasts one of the country's finest **male voice choirs**. Visitors are welcome to watch rehearsals, which take place inside the museum building on Saturday evenings. Concerts are at the Tabor Hall on Vaughan St (In the Pwllgwaun neighbourhood); the tourist office has schedules.

Clwb-y-Bont Off Taff St ☎ 01443 491424. Down a narrow lane just behind Boots, this thick-set building is the town's principal club and live music venue, with open mic evenings and the occasional jazz concert. Mon–Thurs 5pm–midnight, Fri & Sat 11am–1am.

Llancaiach Fawr Manor

Tues–Sun 10am–5pm (last admission one hour before closing) • £6.50 • ☎ 01443 412248, ⓦ llancaiachfawr.co.uk • Mon–Sat hourly bus #X38 from Pontypridd

The river divides at **Abercynon**, four miles up the Taff Valley, with the Cynon River flowing in from Aberdare in the northwest. Two miles east of Abercynon, just north of the village of **NELSON**, is **Llancaiach Fawr Manor**, a Tudor house built around 1530 which has been transformed into a living-history museum set in 1645, the time of the Civil War, with guides dressed as house servants and speaking seventeenth-century English. Although the whole experience could easily be nightmarishly tacky, it's actually very deftly done, with well-researched period authenticity and numerous fascinating anecdotes from the staff. The three-floored residence – reputedly one of Britain's most haunted – was originally built for the Prichard family, erstwhile Sheriff of Glamorgan and Justice of Peace, the latter a position he held throughout the Civil War. During the tour you get to view the kitchen and dining room, the Great Hall (which was used as a courtroom), the bed chambers and counting house (an arms store).

Special tours are also available, including seventeenth-century evenings, and, between October and March, ghost and candlelit tours. The International Cider Festival is also held in the grounds in mid-August, with cider and perry bars, live music and on-site camping.

The Summit Centre

Mon–Fri 10am–10pm, Sat & Sun noon–6pm • ☎ 0844 8000 222, ⊕ www.rockuk.org

A couple of miles north of Llancaiach Fawr, just beyond the village of **Trelewis**, the old Taff Merthyr colliery has been transformed into the **Summit Centre**. As well as vast climbing walls (£15 for a 1hr taster session, £7 entry for experienced climbers), it offers a wide range of adventure options, including caving instruction in a purpose-built artificial cave system (£40 for a minimum group size of eight). It's popular with groups, so it's worth booking your visit ahead.

Aberfan

North of Abercynon, the Taff Valley village of **ABERFAN** contains one sight that's impossible to forget: the two lines of arches that mark the **graves** of the 144 people killed in October 1966 when an unsecured slag heap slid down a hill and onto the Pantglas Primary School in the village. The death toll – including 116 children – is beyond comprehension. Official enquiries revealed the sorry inevitability of the disaster, given the cavalier approach to safety so often displayed by the coal bosses. Over four decades later, the tragedy lives on in the memory of the thousands of people from all over southeast Wales and beyond who came to help recover the bodies.

Aberdare

Eight miles northwest of Abercynon, towards the top of the Cynon Valley, is the sprawling town of **ABERDARE** (Aberdâr). The town was built on the local iron, brick and brewing industries, in addition to playing a prominent role in the development of early Welsh-language publishing. Aside from the rows of terraced houses, the centre offers a handful of good shops, **cafés** and **pubs**, such as the lively *Yr Ieuan ap Iago* on the High Street.

Cynon Valley Museum & Gallery

Depot Rd • Mon–Sat 9am–4.30pm • Free

A short walk from the train station brings you to one of the Valleys' best museums, the **Cynon Valley Museum & Gallery**, housed in an old tram depot next to the Tesco superstore. Exhibits convey the social history of the valley, from the appalling conditions of the mid-nineteenth century, when nearly half of all children born here died by the age of five, to stirring memories of the 1926 General Strike and the 1984–85 miners' strike. Alongside are some videos and displays on Victorian lantern slides, teenage life through the ages, the miners' jazz bands and the local publishing industry. To round things off, there's also a bright art gallery and decent café on site.

1

Dare Valley Country Park

Visitor centre April–Sept Mon–Fri 9am–5.30pm, Sat & Sun till 7pm; Oct–March daily 9am–4pm • ☎ 01685 874672,
ⓦ darevalleycountrypark.co.uk

On the western flank of town is the **Dare Valley Country Park**, where you can participate in one of three waymarked trails, ranging between two and four miles. There's good birdwatching here, too, with a platform to view nesting peregrines, while the chain of small lakes harbours moorhen, little grebe and coots. The **visitor centre** has an exhibition on the park's formation, in addition to the inevitable café; it's also the starting point of the 32-mile **Glamorgan Forest Way** to Afan Argoed and Margam Country Park (see p.121). Bike rental is available between April and September.

Merthyr Tydfil

On the cusp of the grand, windy heights of the Brecon Beacons to the north and the industrial valleys to the south, the fortunes of **MERTHYR TYDFIL** (Merthyr Tudful) have risen and fallen more than once. Merthyr's strategic location was first exploited by the Romans as an outpost of their base at Caerleon. In 480 AD, Tydfil, Welsh princess and daughter of Brychan, Prince of Brycheiniog, was captured as she rode through the area, and murdered for her Christian beliefs. She became St Tydfil the Martyr, and her name was bestowed on the area. Throughout the rest of the twentieth century and into the twenty-first, the town has suffered from unemployment that continues to be among the highest in the UK, but its relatively cheap house prices have made it an attractive proposition for commuters from Cardiff.

Cyfarthfa Castle

April–Sept daily 10am–5.30pm; Oct–March Tues–Fri 10am–4pm, Sat & Sun noon–4pm • Free

Merthyr's key site is **Cyfarthfa Castle**, located north of the centre just beyond the A470 Brecon road. Built in 1825 as an ostentatious mock-Gothic castle for William Crawshay II, boss of the town's original ironworks, it's set within an attractive, 160-acre **park** that slopes down to the river and once afforded Crawshay a permanent view over his iron empire.

Cyfarthfa's current incarnation, however, is as a museum, and a great one at that. You start in a well-re-created Valleys traditional Welsh café on the ground floor, then go downstairs into the old wine cellars for a gutsy history of the town. Starting with tales of the martyr Tydfil, the Penydarren Roman fort and ruined Morlais Castle, the

---

THE MERTHYR RADICALS

In the seventeenth century, Merthyr became a focal point for Dissenters and Radicals, movements which, through poverty and oppression, gained momentum in the eighteenth century as the town's four massive ironworks were founded to exploit locally abundant seams of iron ore and limestone. Merthyr became the largest iron-producing town in the world, and by far the most populous settlement in Wales: in 1831, the town had a population of 60,000, more than Cardiff, Swansea and Newport combined. Workers flocked from all over Britain and beyond, finding themselves crammed into squalid housing, while the ironmasters built themselves great houses and palaces nearby. Merthyr's **radicalism** bubbled furiously: it was here that the red flag was first raised, when rioters in 1831 gathered around a standard dipped in the blood of a killed calf; another martyr, union organizer Dic Penderyn, was hanged unjustly for his role in the riots. Later, the town saw the election of Britain's first-ever socialist MP, Keir Hardie, in 1900.

Merthyr's precipitous development saw it peak and trough earlier than anywhere else: of its four mighty ironworks, only one was still open at the end of World War I, and that closed in the 1930s. In 1939, a Royal Commission suggested that the town be abandoned and the inhabitants shifted to the coast. The plan was forgotten when war broke out.

narrative soon leads into Merthyr's industrial and political heritage. Merthyr's place in working-class history is well examined, with an interesting set of panels and pamphlets on the 1831 riot. Other exhibits examine Aberfan, the 1984–85 miners' strike, pubs and the temperance movement, as well as the beleaguered 1980s Sinclair C5 car, constructed here at the Hoover plant – "built by Hoover, driven by suckers" as the local phrase memorably had it.

Upstairs, the castle's opulent main rooms, all chandeliers and acres of curtains, house a superb collection of Welsh and international **art**. Welsh highlights include an uncharacteristically gentle study of *The Elf* by monumental sculptor Goscombe John, and works by local painters Penry Williams, Augustus John, Cedric Morris, Kyffin Williams and Alfred Jones, whose double portrait of Salome is quite mesmerizing. More surprisingly, there is a portrait of Crawshay by Rolf Harris, whose grandfather George Frederic was born in the town; he, too, contributes several paintings.

The surrounding **park** contains landscaped walks, a plant nursery, café, bowling green, tennis courts, and a stage set next to the main lake.

Joseph Parry's Cottage

Chapel Row • April–Sept Thurs–Sun 2–5pm • Free

Tucked among modern houses just off the A4102 (Bethesda Street), alongside the River Taff, is **Chapel Row**, a line of cottages built in the 1820s for skilled ironworkers. One of these is **Joseph Parry's Cottage**, where the composer was born, though this mini-museum is most interesting as a social record of slightly better-than-average workers' domestic conditions of the nineteenth century. Parry's music, including the national favourite *Myfanwy*, is piped between rooms, and the upstairs section of the house is given over to a display of his life and music.

ARRIVAL AND DEPARTURE
MERTHYR TYDFIL

By train Merthyr's train station lies east of the town centre, a minute's walk from the High St, and serves Cardiff (every 30min; 1hr); Pontypridd (every 30min; 30min).
By bus The bus station is right in the centre on Wheatsheaf Lane and serves Abergavenny (hourly; 1hr 30min); Brecon (every 1–2hr; 40min); Cardiff (every 20min; 50min); Swansea (6 daily; 1hr 15min).

INFORMATION

Tourist information The TIC is behind the bus station at 14a Glebeland St (Mon–Sat 9.30am–4pm; ☏ 01685 379884, ✉ tic@merthyr.gov.uk).

ACCOMMODATION

The town's accommodation possibilities are limited, though it's unlikely you'll need, or want, to hang around after visiting the castle anyway.

Chaplins 30–31 High St ☏ 01685 387272, ⓦ chaplinshotel.co.uk. Central, family-run place with fourteen comfortable en-suite rooms, all of which vary slightly. Filling breakfast in the downstairs bistro. **£59** cheapest place in town. Rooms also available in an annexe. **£50**

CAMPING

Tregenna Hotel Park Terrace, next to Penydarren Park ☏ 01685 723627, ⓦ tregennahotel.co.uk. It's far from inspiring, with rather austere and dated rooms, but the low-key *Tregenna* is in a quiet location and is just about the

Grawen Farm Cwm Taf ☏ 01685 723740. Located four miles north of town on A470, this family-run farm has modern, well-equipped facilities. Open April–Oct. Per tent **£10**; plus per person **£2**

EATING AND DRINKING

Chaplins 30–31 High St. In the hotel of the same name, down in the somewhat optimistically titled café quarter, this perky little place is best known for its Jumbuck's pies, a selection of Aussie-inspired creations, such as The Outback (chunky steak) and Aussie Rules (steak, bacon and cheese). Not a bad place for a pint either. Daily 10am–11pm.

1

The Rhondda

The twin valleys of the **Rhondda** – Rhondda Fach (Little Rhondda) to the east and Rhondda Fawr (Great Rhondda) to the west – are each sixteen miles long yet less than a mile wide. Between them they once formed the heart of the massive south Wales coal industry. Hollywood romanticized the area in the 1947 Oscar-winning weepie *How Green Was My Valley*, although the story was based on author Richard Llewellyn's early life in nearby Gilfach Goch, outside the valley.

Early records show that in 1841 the Rhondda had a population of under a thousand, but that exploded with the discovery of coal and, by 1924, 167,000 people had squeezed into the available land in ranks of houses packed around sixty or so pitheads. Poverty and hardship were rife, but so were pride, self-reliance, radical religion and firebrand politics. The Communist Party ran the town of Maerdy (nicknamed "Little Moscow" by Fleet Street in the 1930s) for decades. The 1984–85 miners' strike saw solidarity in the Welsh pits on a greater scale than any other part of Britain until the Rhondda's last pit closed in 1990. Aside from the excellent **Rhondda Heritage Park**, there's some rewarding hillwalking, with astounding views over the densely packed houses below.

Rhondda Heritage Park

Daily 9am–6pm, last admission 4.30pm; closed Mon Oct–March • £5.60 • ☎ 01443 682036, ⓦ rhonddaheritagepark.com

The Rhondda starts just outside **Pontypridd**, winding through the mountains alongside railway, road and river to **Trehafod** and the colliery museum of the **Rhondda Heritage Park**. Although the first pits were sunk here in 1850, it wasn't until William Lewis (later Lord Merthyr) reopened the site in 1880 that the pit began to prosper, and by 1900 some 5000 men were producing in excess of a million tons of coal a year. Production at the Lewis Merthyr colliery ceased in 1983, seven years before the last pit closed in the Rhondda. Wandering around the yard, you can see the 140ft-high chimney stack, which fronts two iconic latticed shafts, named Bertie and Trefor, after Lewis's sons.

Guided tours (10am, noon & 2pm) take you through the engine winding houses, lamp room, fan house and a simulated "trip underground", with stunning visuals and sound effects, re-creating life (and death) in the late nineteenth century and 1950s through the eyes of colliers. The Trehafod **train station** is just a five-minute walk from the Heritage Park.

Rhondda Fach

The Rhondda's two valleys divide at the bustling town of **PORTH** ("Gateway"), a mile beyond the museum, from where the Rhondda Fach (Little Rhondda) River twists its way northwards through the smaller and frequently forgotten valley of the same name, passing endless archetypal Valleys towns like Ynyshir, Pontygwaith, Tylorstown, Ferndale and Maerdy – row after row of tiny houses clinging to sheer valley walls.

Rhondda Fawr

The **Rhondda Fawr** (Great Rhondda) stretches from the outskirts of Pontypridd to Blaenrhondda and is blessed with a train line, a decent road and most of the sights. The first notable settlement is **TONYPANDY**, followed a mile later by **LLWYNYPIA**, wedged in between walkable, forested hillsides. From here, a steep two-mile climb leads up to **Mynydd y Gelli**, where the remains of an Iron Age hut settlement and a Bronze Age burial chamber and stone circle can be seen.

Treorchy

The road, river and train line wind tortuously past an endless stream of towns to **TREORCHY** (Treorci), best known internationally for its famed **Treorchy Male Choir**, Wales' oldest. Visitors are welcome to rehearsals, which usually take place at 7pm each

1

MALE VOICE CHOIRS

Although Wales' **male voice choirs** can be found all over the country, it is in the southern, industrial heartland that they are loudest and strongest. The roots of the choirs lie in the Nonconformist religious traditions of the seventeenth and eighteenth centuries, when Methodism in particular swept the country, and singing was a free and potent way of cherishing the frequently persecuted faith. Throughout the breakneck nineteenth-century industrialization in the Valleys, choirs of coal miners came together to praise God in the fervent way that was typical of the packed, poor communities. Classic hymns like *Cwm Rhondda* and the Welsh national anthem, *Hen Wlad Fy Nhadau* (*Land of My Fathers*), are synonymous with the choirs, whose full-blooded interpretations render all other efforts insipid.

Despite the collapse of coal mining in the twentieth century, most choirs continue to perform in Wales and abroad. Each small Valleys town has its own choir, most of whom happily allow visitors to sit in on rehearsals. Ask at the local tourist office or library, and take the chance to hear one of the world's most distinctive choral traditions in full, roof-raising splendour.

Tuesday and Thursday at Treorchy primary school on Glyncoli Road; phone ahead for confirmation (☎01443 422935). Most concerts by the choir take place at the splendid **Parc and Dare Theatre** on Station Road (☎08000 147111), a multipurpose arts venue that's always busy.

Treherbert

North of Treorchy, at the top of the Rhondda Fawr, is **TREHERBERT**, its straggle of houses continuing up the valley at **BLAENCWM** and **BLAENRHONDDA**, two communities effectively bypassed since a new road was built in the 1930s by unemployed miners, connecting Treherbert to the forests and lakes of Hirwaun Common en route to Brecon.

ARRIVAL AND DEPARTURE   **THE RHONDDA**

By train A train line, punctuated with stops every mile or so, runs the entire length of the Rhondda Fawr from Pontypridd to its terminus at Treherbert.

By bus Buses also cover the route; change in Merthyr Tydfil for connections to the Brecon Beacons.

The Ogwr, Garw and Llynfi valleys

To the southwest of the Rhondda, the Ogwr, Garw and Llynfi valleys are different to their bigger, better-known neighbour: the contours are slightly softer, the open spaces wider and the towns less bustling.

The Ogwr Valley

South from Treorchy, the **Ogwr Valley** plunges through the Rhondda Fawr to the ancient settlement and now county town of **BRIDGEND** (Pen-y-bont ar Ogwr), itself a useful transport interchange. Just over a mile northeast of the town are the substantial remains of **Coity Castle** (free access; CADW), built around the end of the twelfth century by one of the earliest Norman knights in the area. Bridgend is also handy for Porthcawl, detailed in the Vale of Glamorgan section.

The Garw Valley

The dead-end **Garw Valley** consists of a road, river and the disused railway crammed in on the valley floor, before they all peter out into wooded hillsides. Most of the scars of the valley's mining past have now been levelled and landscaped, leaving it surprisingly pretty, and, as it's well off any tourist track, very rewarding for walks and congenial company in local pubs and shops. At the southern end of the valley, the **Bryngarw Country Park** (daily dawn–dusk; free, but charges for special events) is a pleasant

1

diversion, with landscaped gardens, exceptional flower collections and mature woodlands gathered around the restored Bryngarw House, which now houses a bistro and conference centre.

The Llynfi Valley

Stretching up from Bridgend and Tondu along the A4063 is the broad-bottomed and leafy **Llynfi Valley**, the main settlement being **MAESTEG**, from where the main road links up with the A4107 at Cymer, for Cwm Afan. On top of the mountain to the south of Maesteg is the beautiful village of **LLANGYNWYD**. Birth- and burial-place of bard Wil Hopcyn, it has an ancient atmosphere in stark contrast to the ex-mining towns below. The splendid *Yr Hen Dŷ* pub is said to be the oldest inn in south Wales, where revellers traditionally congregate on New Year's Day for the hallowed Welsh custom of the **Mari Llwyd** (Grey Mare), during which a horse's skull is paraded through the village to ward off evil spirits during the forthcoming year.

Cwm Afan

Winding its way between the top of the Llynfi Valley and the coast at Port Talbot, the main attraction in bucolic **CWM AFAN** is the **Afan Forest Park**, whose 9000 acres of hilly forest has become one of the country's premier mountain bike destinations.

Afan Forest Park Visitor Centre

April–Sept Mon–Fri 9.30am–5pm, Sat & Sun 9.30am–6pm; Oct–March Mon–Fri 9.30am–4pm, Sat & Sun 10.30am–5pm • Free; parking £3.25; museum £2 • ☎ 01639 850564, ⓦ afanforestpark.co.uk

Situated three miles west of little **CYMER**, the excellent visitor centre houses the small **South Wales Miners' Museum**, where a mock-up miners' tunnel leads through to all manner of mining-related memorabilia, such as equipment, documents and photographs. The five waymarked **mountain bike** trails here are fairly demanding, so not best suited to families or those seeking a gentler time of it. Bikes can be rented from Skyline Cycles, just below the visitor centre (☎ 01639 851100; from £30 per day). Some five miles further up the valley, the **Glyncorrwg Mountain Bike Centre** (daily: May–Oct 8am–5pm, till 8pm Wed–Fri; Nov–April 9am–4pm; ☎ 01639 851900; ⓦ glyncorrwgpondsvisitorcentre.co.uk) is a dedicated biking centre, and the starting point for several difficult trails; its great facilities include a bike shop, bike park, showers, camping (£5 per person; open all year), jet wash and café.

ACCOMMODATION   CWM AFAN

Afan Lodge Duffryn Rhondda ☎ 01639 852500, ⓦ afanlodge.com. On the main road between the forest park visitor centre and Cymer, this former miners' institute building has been converted into a great-looking alpine-style chalet; popular with mountain bikers, many of the bright, cool a/c rooms have fantastic views down towards the lush forest. Bike wash and lock-up available. **£90**

Pontrhydyfen

The valley descends for a couple of miles towards the village of **PONTRHYDYFEN**, picturesquely sited at the confluence of the Afon and Afon Pelenna rivers. Slicing through the village are two monuments that further testify to the region's proud industrial heritage; a magnificent four-arch aqueduct dating from 1827, and, a little further downstream, an equally impressive nine-arch viaduct, built in 1898. The village is best known, however, as the birthplace of actor Richard Burton, who was born in a (unmarked) house at the foot of the aqueduct. From here, roads either side of the river continue south to the industrial sprawl of **PORT TALBOT**, still dominated by its massive steelworks.

Margam

1

A couple of miles southeast of Port Talbot, on the other side of junction 38 of the M4, **MARGAM** was originally a Cistercian settlement and later the home of various industrial magnates. The first left turn after the motorway junction leads to the arcaded twelfth-century **abbey church**, the sole remaining Cistercian house of worship in Wales.

Margam Stones Museum

April–Sept Wed–Sun 10.30am–4pm; Oct–March Wed & Fri only by appointment • £2.10 • ☎ 01443 336000 • CADW

Within a nineteenth-century school house is the little-known **Margam Stones Museum**. Often bypassed in the rush to get to the neighbouring country park, this outstanding collection of memorial stones, sculptured crosses, grave slabs and tomb covers dates mostly from Celtic and medieval times. The most prized exhibit is the tenth-century Cynfelin (or Conbelin) stone, an intricately carved wheel-headed cross. Take a close look, too, at the figures and gargoyles from destroyed Welsh churches and monasteries.

Margam Country Park

Castle and grounds April–Sept daily 10am–5pm; Oct–March park only Mon–Tues 1–4.30pm, Wed–Sun 10am–4.30pm • Free; parking £3.70 • Bus #1 (from Bridgend or Port Talbot) stops outside the park entrance

The 850-acre **Margam Country Park** has enough to see and do to keep you occupied for the best part of half a day, longer if the weather is kind. The park is centred around the nineteenth-century Gothic pile of **Margam Castle**, much of which was gutted by fire in 1977. It's essentially off-limits, but you can still wander into the lobby and peer up the octagonal lantern tower and see a few models and photos. One of these is of Eisenhower, taken when he visited American troops stationed here during World War II.

Down from the castle, and tucked in by the abbey church walls, are the impressive remains of the original Cistercian abbey, most notable for the vaulting of its twelve-sided chapterhouse, which survived the dissolution of the monasteries only to have its roof collapse under the weight of weeds in 1799. Alongside is Margam's showpiece **orangery**, a splendid Georgian outhouse, built in 1790 and, at 327ft long, reputedly the longest in Britain. There's plenty for kids to do here, including a miniature railway (which runs from the entrance up to the castle; £1.60), a "fairyland" play area, adventure playground, farm trail and, for older kids, a Go Ape centre.

Vale of Neath

Although the town of **NEATH** (Castell-Nedd) is not particularly worthy of a visit, the **Vale of Neath**, spearing northeast, boasts several fascinating remnants from both the Industrial Revolution and the coal-mining industry.

The Aberdulais Tinworks and Waterfalls

2 miles northeast of Neath • Jan & Feb Sat & Sun 11am–4pm; March & Nov–Christmas Fri–Sun 11am–4pm; April–Oct daily 10am–5pm • £4.50 • ☎ 01639 636674 • NT • Bus #154 from Neath

Aberdulais was once one of the world's largest tinplate manufacturing centres, thanks largely to its position at the confluence of the Dulais and Neath rivers. Its **waterfalls** have been harnessing hydroelectric power here since the sixteenth century – initially for the manufacture of copper – though the present-day water wheel was installed in 1982. Among the impressive extant remains is the tinning house and chimney stack; the old smithy building now accommodates an illuminating exhibition on the industry. The falls themselves provide a picturesque backdrop to the site. There's also a tempting tearoom.

Cefn Coed Colliery Museum

A4109, 3 miles north of Aberdulais • April–Oct daily 10.30am–5pm • Free • ☎ 01639 750556 • Bus #158 from Neath

Once the world's deepest anthracite mine is now the **Cefn Coed Colliery Museum**. Dubiously nicknamed "The Slaughterhouse" – owing to the extreme dangers faced

1

by miners working at depths in excess of 2250ft – the colliery closed in 1968, with workers transferred to the nearby Blaenant drift mine, which subsequently closed in 1990. This is more low-key than many of the Valleys' other heritage sites, but a walk around the mining gallery and boiler house through to the magnificent steam winding engine gives yet another stark reminder of a region's once proud but now lost way of life. Crowning the site are the colliery's iconic latticed steel pithead frames.

Swansea

Over half a century ago, Dylan Thomas dubbed his native **SWANSEA** (Abertawe) an "ugly, lovely town" – a scathing but affectionate epithet which was once well deserved, although the famous poet probably wouldn't recognize the place these days. The city was devastated by bombing in World War II and hastily rebuilt, but since the turn of the millennium has been undergoing something of a renaissance, with bright, bold new developments springing up across the city.

Swansea's wide seafront overlooks the huge sweep of **Swansea Bay**, the focal point of much of the redevelopment, particularly around the old docks, and the city now boasts some of the best-funded **museums** in Wales. The seafront arcs around to the Gower peninsula, with the elegant but relaxed seaside resort of **Mumbles**, as well as some of Britain's best **surfing**, on its doorstep.

Swansea's train station faces out onto the **High Street**, which heads south into **Castle Street** and the main square, from where streets disperse in all directions. Running south is **Wind Street** (so named because it's winding – or at least gently curving), nocturnal Swansea's main drag, chock-full of bars, pubs and restaurants; evenings are quite something along here. The remaining streets hereabouts are largely the preserve of shops, with just the occasional place of interest for the visitor.

Brief history

The city's Welsh name, Abertawe, refers to the settlement at the mouth of the River Tawe, now being coaxed back to life as part of Swansea's redeveloped waterfront after centuries of use as a repository for Swansea's metal trades. The English name derives from Viking sources, suggesting that a pre-Norman settlement existed in the area. The first reliable records of Swansea date back to 1099, when a Norman castle was built here as an outpost of William the Conqueror's empire. A small settlement subsequently grew near the coalfields and the sea, developing into a mining and shipbuilding centre that, by 1700, was the largest coal port in Wales.

Metal-smelting days

Copper-smelting became the area's dominant industry in the eighteenth century, soon attracting other activities to pack out the lower Tawe Valley. Drawn by the town's flourishing activities, a swiftly growing port and the arrival of the Swansea Canal, thousands of emigrants moved to the city from all over Ireland and Britain; by the nineteenth century, the town was one of the world's most prolific metal-bashing centres.

Decline and revival

Smelting was already on the wane by the beginning of the twentieth century, although Swansea's port continued to thrive. Britain's first oil refinery was opened on the edge of the city in 1918, with dock developments growing up in its wake. Civic zeal, best exemplified by the graceful 1930s Guildhall, was reawakened after the establishment of an important branch of the University of Wales here in 1920. Swansea was devastated during World War II, however, when thirty thousand bombs rained down on the city in just three nights in 1941. Initial rebuilding left the city disjointed, although now,

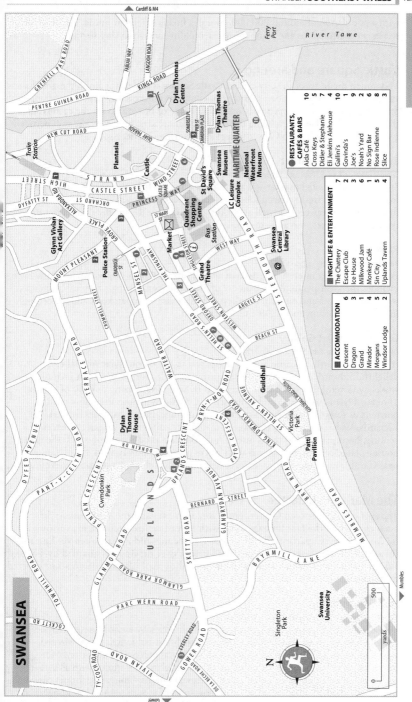

SWANSEA

River Tawe

Cardiff & M4

Ferry Port

MARITIME QUARTER

Train Station

Glynn Vivian Art Gallery

Plantasia

Castle

Dylan Thomas Centre

Dylan Thomas Theatre

Swansea Museum

National Waterfront Museum

St David's Square

LC Leisure Complex

Quadrant Shopping Centre

Market

Bus Station

Grand Theatre

Police Station

Swansea Central Library

Guildhall

Dylan Thomas' House

Cwmdonkin Park

Victoria Park

Patti Pavilion

Singleton Park

Swansea University

N

Mumbles

Gower

0   500   yards

with a population of around 200,000, Swansea boasts resurgent music, club and surf scenes, new attractions and some spirited rebuilding and redevelopment.

Castle Square and around

Very much the heart of the city centre, **Castle Square** is a pleasant amphitheatre of steps surrounding a fountain, albeit slightly ruined by an unnecessarily large TV screen. Standing somewhat incongruously on the west side of the square are the **castle ruins**, the most obvious landmark being the semicircular arcades, built into the wall between 1330 and 1332 by Bishop Gower to replace a Norman predecessor.

Swansea Indoor Market

Oxford St • Mon–Fri 8am–5.30pm, Sat 7.30am–5.30pm

Swansea's glass-roofed **market** – Wales' largest – is a lively bustle of colourful stalls, fresh flowers and freshly baked food, including local delicacies like laver bread (made from laver, aka seaweed), as well as cockles trawled from the nearby Loughor estuary, typical Welsh cakes, fish and cheeses.

Plantasia

Parc Tawe • Daily 10am–5pm • £3.95 • ☎ 01792 474555

Possibly of greater interest to kids than adults, the retail park on the Strand, Park Tawe, includes the great pyramidal glasshouse of **Plantasia**, comprising a tropical hothouse with exotic plants and tamarin monkeys, a bird house with parakeets and numerous insects, an aquarium and a 20ft Burmese python.

Glynn Vivian Art Gallery

Alexandra Rd • Tues–Sun 10am–5pm • Free • ☎ 01792 516900

A short walk north of Castle Square brings you to the **Glynn Vivian Art Gallery**, a delightful Edwardian venue housing an inspiring collection of Welsh art including works by Gwen John, her brother Augustus (whose mesmerizing portrait of Caitlin Thomas, Dylan's wife, is a real highlight), and Kyffin Williams; the grimy mining portraits of Josef Herman; and a whole room of huge, frantic canvases by Ceri Richards, Wales' most respected twentieth-century painter. In the early nineteenth century, Swansea was a noted centre of fine porcelain production, of which the gallery houses a large collection, together with pieces of contemporary work from Nantgarw, near Cardiff. Look out too for the excellent frequently changing temporary exhibitions.

The Maritime Quarter

The spit of land between Oystermouth Road, the sea and the Tawe estuary has been christened the **Maritime Quarter**, with its vast centrepiece marina surrounded by contemporary apartments, cafés, shops, museums and a leisure centre. Entering the quarter from the east, the main road bridge over the Tawe is guarded by a World War II ack-ack gun which stands as a memorial to the Luftwaffe decimation suffered by Swansea.

Swansea Museum

Victoria Rd • Tues–Sun 10am–5pm • Free • ☎ 01792 653763

Founded in 1835 as the Royal Institution of South Wales, **Swansea Museum** is Wales' oldest public museum. Much of it is still appealingly old-fashioned, with a wizened Egyptian mummy, lots of archeological finds, and local porcelain and pottery. More interesting is the Cabinet of Curiosities room, full of glass cases stuffed with all sorts of oddments such as offbeat household items, memento moris – miniature shrines containing photos and models of the deceased – and some intriguing local photos, including several

of Winston Churchill taken during his visit to the city in World War II. There's also a
marble bust of Gower son, Edgar Evans, who perished with Scott in Antarctica in 1912.

Dylan Thomas Centre
Somerset Place • Daily 10am–4.30pm • Free • ☎ 01792 463980

In the former nineteenth-century guildhall is the **Dylan Thomas Centre**, where a superb
exhibition offers a compelling insight into the life and times of the eponymous poet.
Entitled Man and Myth, there is some unique archive material on display; original
worksheets, bar tabs, the writer's only known painting, and the last photos of Thomas
before his death, taken, appropriately enough, in a New York bar. Also on display are
the doors of the shed in which Thomas wrote at Laugharne. In the meantime, a
fascinating video on his life and work plays continuously. Also located here is a superb
little bookshop-cum-café hosting some terrific literary events throughout the year.

National Waterfront Museum
Oystermouth Rd • Daily 10am–5pm • Free • ☎ 01792 638950, Ⓦ museumwales.ac.uk

Down by the marina is the fine **National Waterfront Museum**. Carved out of the shell of
the old Industrial and Maritime Museum, the original building has been stunningly
extended to accommodate wide-ranging exhibitions on Wales' history of innovation
and industry. The museum is divided into fifteen zones, each with an interactive take
on topics such as energy, landscape, coal, networks and money. Much else besides is
celebrated here, such as Wales' success in the field of sport and its contribution to the
music industry, with coverage of the much loved colliery brass bands, awards won by
the likes of the Super Furry Animals and a pair of bejewelled wellies worn by Dame
Shirley Bassey at Glastonbury in 2007. Look out too for the many superb heritage
pieces, such as the 1907 Robin Goch (Redbreast) monoplane, one of the very few
pre-World War I planes still in existence.

West Swansea

Aside from being one of the greenest parts of the city, thanks to a generous spread of
parks and gardens, the area west of the centre counts a brace of worthwhile attractions
in the shape of some architectural gems, a couple of fine little museums, and Dylan
Thomas' birthplace.

The Guildhall and Brangwyn Hall

St Helen's Road dips down to the seafront near the tall white tower of the **Guildhall** – a
soaring piece of 1930s civic architecture. Within the Guildhall, **Brangwyn Hall** takes its
name from Sir Frank Brangwyn, who painted the eighteen enormous British Empire panels
lining the hall. Its function today is as one of the city's premier classical concert venues.

Patti Pavilion

Immediately behind the Guildhall, down by the coast road, the most prominent feature
of **Victoria Park** is the **Patti Pavilion**, a graceful green-roofed, glass-paned hall that was a
gift from opera singer Adelina Patti, brought here from her home at Craig-y-nos in the
Brecon Beacons. Today the pavilion is home to a function hall and Indian restaurant.

Ceri Richards Gallery and Egypt Centre
Swansea University, Mumbles Rd • **Ceri Richards Gallery** Mon–Fri 10am–6pm, Sat 10am–4pm • Free • ☎ 01792 295526 **Egypt Centre**
Tues–Sat 10am–4pm • Free • ☎ 01792 295960

Along the coast road, the **Swansea University** campus affords a commanding view over
the bay stretching to Mumbles Head. On site is an imaginative performance space, the
Taliesin Arts Centre, which also incorporates the **Ceri Richards Gallery**, specializing in
touring exhibitions by contemporary Welsh and Celtic artists.

1

Also housed here, the **Egypt Centre** is Wales' pre-eminent Egyptology display. The collection is split in two: The House of Death, with its funerary paraphernalia, and The House of Life, covering day-to-day existence, although most of the artefacts come from tombs.

Clyne Gardens

Blackpill • Open access • Free

Midway between Swansea city and Mumbles are the **Clyne Gardens**, the grounds of the Vivian family's old estate, which has lovely walks through rhododendron glades, bog gardens, woods, meadows and past a few follies.

Cwmdonkin Park and Dylan Thomas' birthplace

5 Cwmdonkin Drive • Daily 10.30am–6pm • £4.95 • ☎ 01792 405331, ⓦ 5cwmdonkindrive.com

In the Uplands area, a thirty-minute walk from the city centre, shaded avenues rise up the slopes past the sharp terraces of **Cwmdonkin Park**, where there is a memorial to Dylan Thomas inscribed with lines from *Fern Hill*, one of his best-loved poems.

On the eastern side of the park, a blue plaque at 5 Cwmdonkin Drive denotes this solid Victorian semi as **Dylan Thomas' birthplace**. Thomas actually lived here until he was twenty, and while nothing remains from his time, the house has been sympathetically restored to re-create the atmosphere of early twentieth-century life in Swansea. **Guided tours** of the surprisingly spacious interior take in the house's many rooms, including the grand lounge, his father's study, the kitchen (where you'll be invited to have a cup of tea) and Thomas' boxy bedroom. It's even possible to sleep here, but to do so you must contact the house well in advance.

ARRIVAL AND DEPARTURE   SWANSEA

Swansea is the main interchange station for services out to the west of Wales and for the slow but scenic line across the middle of the country to Shrewsbury in Shropshire. The **train station** is at the top end of the High St, a 10min walk from the **bus station**, sandwiched between the Quadrant shopping centre and the Grand Theatre.

BY TRAIN
Destinations Cardiff (every 30min; 50min); Carmarthen (hourly; 50min); Ferryside (11 daily; 40min); Haverfordwest (9 daily; 1hr 30min); Kidwelly (11 daily; 30min); Knighton (4 daily; 3hr); Llandeilo (4 daily; 1hr); Llandovery (4 daily; 1hr 20min); Llandrindod Wells (4 daily; 2hr 20min); Llanelli (hourly; 20min); Llanwrtyd Wells (4 daily; 1hr 45min); London (hourly; 3hr); Milford Haven (9 daily; 2hr); Narberth (8 daily; 1hr 35min); Newport (every 30min; 1hr 20min); Pembroke (8 daily; 2hr 10min); Tenby (8 daily; 1hr 40min); Whitland (hourly; 1hr 10min).

BY BUS
Destinations Aberdulais (every 45–60min; 45min);

Aberystwyth (4 daily; 3hr); Brecon (5 daily; 1hr 35min); Cardiff (every 30min; 1hr); Carmarthen (every 30min; 1hr 20min); Dan-yr-ogof (5 daily; 1hr); Llangennith (3 daily; 1hr 20min); Merthyr Tydfil (6 daily; 1hr 15min); Mumbles (every 10min; 15min); Neath (hourly; 20min); Oxwich (9 daily; 1hr); Pennard (hourly; 30min); Port Eynon (9 daily; 50min); Porthcawl (hourly; 1hr 20min); Rhossili (Mon–Sat 10 daily, Sun 3; 1hr).

BY FERRY
Ferries to Cork depart from the Kings Dock on the eastern side of the River Tawe (☎ 0844 5768831, ⓦ fastnetline.com).

GETTING AROUND

As most of the sights are within walking distance of each other, getting around Swansea is easy.

Buses The thorough bus network is useful for further-flung areas, including the suburbs near the University such as Uplands and Sketty (a bracing half-hour walk from the centre) and Mumbles and Gower. A day ticket covering the city centre area is £4, and a ticket covering the bay area

(including southern Gower to Rhossili) is £4.40. Weekly tickets are £16.50 and £18 respectively.
Bike rental There's good bike rental available at Action Bikes, 5 St David's Square (☎ 01792 464640, ⓦ actionbikes swansea.co.uk; £10 for half a day, £15 for a full day).

FROM TOP TINTERN ABBEY (P.64); FACADE OF WALES MILLENNIUM CENTRE, CARDIFF (P.88); TRANSPORTER BRIDGE, NEWPORT (P.73) >

1

INFORMATION

Tourist information The TIC is on Plymouth St, behind the Grand Theatre next to the bus station (all year Mon–Sat 9.30am–5.30pm; June–Sept also Sun 10am–4pm; ☎01792 468321, ⓦvisitswanseabay.com); there's stacks of material here on both the city and the Gower, and you also can pick up the comprehensive bimonthly magazine *What's On*. The staff here can also book accommodation.

ACCOMMODATION

For a reasonably large city, Swansea is not exactly endowed with a surfeit of great **accommodation**. That said, there are some inexpensive hotels and B&Bs lining the seafront Oystermouth Rd, with slightly pricier options in the leafy Uplands district. Moreover, it's just a stone's throw to the Gower, where there are further, albeit slightly pricier, options. There are no hostels in Swansea, while the nearest campsite is west of the city towards Mumbles.

Crescent 132 Eaton Crescent, Uplands ☎01792 465782, ⓦcrescentguesthouse.co.uk. Large, sky-blue Edwardian guesthouse with pretty, pastel-shaded en-suite rooms, half of which have superb views over the city and the bay. **£65**

Dragon Kingsway Circle ☎01792 657100, ⓦdragon-hotel.co.uk. Despite its officious-looking facade, this landmark central hotel is an elegant and modern establishment with plush, a/c rooms coloured vivid red; the luxury amenities including a gym, indoor pool and beauty salon, plus a lounge and piano bar, and restaurant. **£89**

Grand Hotel Ivey Place, High St ☎01792 645898, ⓦthegrandhotelswansea.co.uk. Accomplished yet pleasingly informal hotel opposite the train station with softly coloured, a/c rooms with flat-screen TV/DVD player, and sparkling bathrooms with fantastic showers. There's also a basement spa with steam room and hot tub. **£75**

★ **Mirador** 14 Mirador Crescent ☎01792 466976, ⓦthemirador.co.uk. Swansea's most inspirational accommodation, a family-run townhouse in the Uplands area with seven rooms, each themed on a particular country and furnished accordingly (African, Oriental, Egyptian, and so on). **£69**

★ **Morgans** Somerset Place ☎01792 484848, ⓦmorganshotel.co.uk. Swansea's showpiece boutique hotel, split between the sumptuously converted old Port Authority HQ and the beautiful Regency terrace townhouse opposite. Superbly appointed rooms boasting hardwood flooring, polished wood fittings and Egyptian cotton bed linen and goosedown duvets. **£65**

Windsor Lodge Mount Pleasant ☎01792 642158, ⓦwindsor-lodge.co.uk. Like a country hotel in the city, this 200-year-old house has nicely decorated, if slightly dated, rooms, and the bathrooms are a little poky, but it's in a good location. **£70**

EATING, DRINKING AND NIGHTLIFE

Swansea boasts a small but select core of superb **restaurants**, which are fairly evenly spread across the city. There's no shortage of nightlife here, with a proliferation of **bars** and **clubs** to the fore; most of the action is overwhelmingly centred on Wind St – not a place for the faint-hearted on a Friday or Saturday evening – though the Uplands area now has its fair share of good-time party places. The city's theatrical and high **cultural** life is also robust and varied.

RESTAURANTS AND CAFÉS

Aida Café 3 Fishmarket Quay ☎01792 456285. Away from the hurly burly of the city centre, kick back with a fresh cup of coffee and take in the view across the marina. Mon 10.30am–5.30pm, Tues–Thurs till 10.30pm, Fri & Sat till 12.30am.

Didier and Stephanie 56 St Helen's Rd, Uplands ☎01792 655603. Small French restaurant in a beautiful Victorian house, with pastel-painted walls and stripped-wood flooring. The menu specializes in some fairly obscure regional Gallic surprises. Mains £16–19. Tues–Sat noon–2.30pm & 7pm–midnight.

Gallini's 3 Fishmarket Quay ☎01792 456285. Directly above Aida, this somewhat ordinary-looking but cheery Italian restaurant is the place in town to come for fresh pasta and seasonally caught fish such as tiger prawns in ginger, garlic and white-wine sauce. Mains £10–15. Mon–

Sat noon–2.30pm & 6pm–midnight.

Govinda's 8 Craddock St ☎01792 468469. Simple and clean vegetarian restaurant in the Hare Krishna tradition, selling ultra-cheap, wholesome meals, for around £4–5, and freshly pressed juices. Mon–Sat 11am–5pm.

Joe's 85 St Helen's Rd ☎01792 653880. This perennially popular outlet has been doling out some of the country's finest ice cream since 1922. All the classic flavours are here, as well as many specialist creations, such as raspberry crumble, hazelnut fudge and lemon meringue. Daily 11am–9pm, Sat & Sun noon–8pm.

★ **Rose Indienne** 73–74 St Helen's Rd, Uplands ☎01792 467000. The pick of Swansea's many Indian restaurants, the beautifully appointed *Rose Indienne* offers some genuinely exciting and unusual dishes, for example Goan duck curry, and salmon marinated in masala with mint chutney, in addition to a dozen or so lentil- and vegetable-

FESTIVALS

Swansea Bay Summer Festival features music, theatre and outdoor concerts, and takes place from May to September. **Swansea Live** is a celebration of local music on the last weekend of May, with stages in front of Derricks record shop and around town. The highbrow **Swansea Festival of Music and the Arts** lasts throughout October, while the **Dylan Thomas Festival** is in November.

based dishes. Charmingly staffed too. Mains £10–12. Mon–Sat noon–2.30pm & 5.30–11pm, Sun noon–4pm.

⭐ **Slice** 73–75 Everley Rd ☎ 01792 290929. Located out in the Sketty area, the diminutive *Slice* – so named because of the quirkily shaped building – offers a level of cuisine unmatched anywhere in the city, with confident contemporary dishes such as venison pie with parsnip purée and roast duck breast with Sichuan pepper. There are only a handful of tables, so booking is essential. Mains £15–20. Thurs–Sun noon–2pm & 6.30–11pm.

BARS, PUBS AND CLUBS

The Chattery 59 Uplands Crescent ☎ 01792 473276. Although nominally a restaurant, this long-standing venue is also well regarded for the quality of its musical guests (both local and touring UK/US acts), with gigs typically taking place on two or three Saturdays a month. Daily 10am–5pm, plus gig nights 7.30pm–midnight.

Cross Keys Inn 12 St Mary St ☎ 01792 630921. Dating from the 1700s, Swansea's oldest hostelry is a deceptively large affair, offering good ales, a sunny beer garden (BBQs in summer), and a loyal band of rugby followers. Mon–Sat 11am–11pm, Sun noon–10.30pm.

Eli Jenkins Ale House 24 Oxford St ☎ 01792 641067. Named after a Dylan Thomas character, this pleasant, popular locals' pub sits surprisingly well amid the surrounding shopping precincts, and the beer is pretty good too. Mon–Thurs 8am–11pm, Fri & Sat till midnight, Sun 11am–11pm.

Ice House Kings Rd ☎ 01792 649060. Just across the bridge in the ever-expanding SA1 district, this laidback venue is housed inside one of only two remaining ice houses in Wales. The regular mix of rock and blues music (Fridays and Sundays) and comedy (last Saturday of the month) provides for some of the city's best live entertainment. Sun–Tues 8.30am–8pm, Wed–Sat till 11pm.

Milkwood Jam 50 Plymouth St ⓦ milkwoodjam.co.uk (no phone). Cracking city-centre club which packs them in for its regular programme of live music, typically rock and blues, though the open mic night every Wednesday is well attended. Daily 8pm–late.

⭐ **Monkey Café** 13 Castle St ☎ 01792 480822, ⓦ monkeycafe.co.uk. Groovy, inexpensive, mosaic-floored café with a relaxed atmosphere that draws a pretty diverse crowd. Happenings almost daily, including live music, DJs, burlesque, tango and salsa classes, and even

cookery classes. Art exhibitions are regularly held here too. On a good night, it's the best place in town. Daily 11am–2am, Fri & Sat till 4.30am.

Noah's Yard 38 Uplands Crescent. Classy wine bar with big bay windows, bare brick walls and Art Deco lighting, Chesterfield sofas and trunks for tables, as well as lots of post-modern artwork including a piece by Banksy, the infamous street artist. Live music on Mondays by the very accomplished house jazz band. Mon–Thurs 4pm–midnight, Fri & Sat till 12.30am, Sun till 11pm.

No Sign Bar 56 Wind St ☎ 01792 465300. A narrow frontage leads into a long, warm pub interior, one of the oldest in town and easily the best on Wind St. The meaning of the name is explained in depth in the window. Daily 11am–1am.

Sin City 14–16 Dillwyn St ☎ 01792 468892, ⓦ sincityclub.co.uk. Along with *Milkwood Jam*, this is the city's premier live music venue, though the emphasis here is firmly on indie and heavy rock. Riotous club nights too, especially the Friday-night indie/rock face-off. Thurs–Sat 10pm–late.

Uplands Tavern 42 Uplands Crescent ☎ 01792 458242. Next to Noah's Yard, this former haunt of Dylan Thomas – the walls of the Dylan snug corner are plastered with some fabulous photos – is today a bastion of local live music, especially rock and blues, usually Thursdays through to Saturdays. Daily 11am–11pm, Fri & Sat till midnight.

THEATRE, CINEMA AND CLASSICAL MUSIC

Brangwyn Hall The Guildhall, Guildhall Rd South ☎ 01792 635432. Vastly impressive music hall in the Art Deco civic centre which hosts regular concerts by the BBC National Orchestra of Wales and others.

Dylan Thomas Theatre Dylan Thomas Square, Maritime Quarter ☎ 01792 473238, ⓦ dylanthomastheatre.org.uk. Thriving community operation staging reruns of Thomas's classics, intertwined with other modern works in the Little Theatre.

Grand Theatre Singleton St ☎ 01792 475715, ⓦ swanseagrand.co.uk. One of Britain's best provincial theatres, with a wide-ranging diet of visiting high culture, comedy, farce and music.

Taliesin Arts Centre Swansea University ☎ 01792 602060, ⓦ taliesinartscentre.co.uk. Welsh, English and international visiting theatre, film, dance and music (jazz, world), including offbeat and alternative fare.

1

DIRECTORY

Hospital Singleton Hospital, Sketty Park Lane, Singleton, West Swansea (☎01792 205666).

Internet Swansea Central Library, Civic Centre, Oystermouth Rd (Tues–Fri 8.30am–8pm, Sat & Sun 10am–4pm; ☎01792 636464).

Police The main station is on Grove Place (☎01792 456999).

Surfing Information and equipment (including secondhand boards) from Big Drop Surf Shop, 1 St David's Square, St David's Centre. (☎01792 480481, ⊛big-drop .com).

Swimming Swansea has two excellent swim facilities; the Wales National Pool (☎01792 513513, ⊛walesnational poolswansea.co.uk) on Sketty Lane near the university, and the waterpark at the LC leisure complex on Oystermouth Rd (☎01792 484672, ⊛thelcswansea .co.uk).

Gower

Thrusting into the Bristol Channel west of Swansea, the nineteen-mile **GOWER** (Gŵyr) peninsula is fringed by sweeping yellow bays and precipitous cliffs, caves and blowholes to the south, and wide, flat marshes and cockle beds to the north. Brackened heaths with prehistoric remains and tiny villages lie between, interspersed with castle ruins, curious churches and the scent of wild garlic.

Gower starts in Swansea's western suburbs, along the coast of Swansea Bay which curves round to a point in the charmingly old-fashioned and increasingly swish resort of **Mumbles** and Mumbles Head, marking the boundary between the sandy sweep of Swansea Bay and the rocky inlets along the southern Gower's serrated coastline. This southern coast is punctuated by sites exploited for their defensive capacities, best seen in the eerie isolation of the sandbound **Pennard Castle**, high above **Three Cliffs Bay**. West, the wide sands of **Oxwich Bay** sit next to inland reedy marshes, beyond which is the picturesque village of **Port Eynon**. West again, the coast becomes a wild, frilly series of inlets and cliffs, capped by a five-mile path that stretches all the way to the peninsula's glorious westernmost point, **Worms Head**.

Rhossili Bay, a breathtaking four-mile span of sand backed by the village of Rhossili, occupies the entire western end of Gower from Worms Head to the islet of **Burry Holms**, and, when conditions are right, provides some of the best **surfing** in Wales. The northern coast merges into the tidal flats of the estuary, running past the salted marsh of **Llanrhidian**, overlooked by the gaunt ruins of **Weobley Castle**, and on to the famous cockle beds at **Penclawdd**. Mumbles aside, there's not an abundance of **accommodation** on the Gower, so you'd do well to make reservations in advance, including for campsites.

GETTING AROUND   GOWER

By bus There are no train services on Gower, but with its proximity to urban Swansea, bus transport is reasonably comprehensive. Gower Explorer buses (services 115 to 118) run regularly from Swansea's bus station to Rhossili, Port Eynon, Parkmill and Oxwich in South Gower; and through North Gower to Llanrhidian Llangennith and Llanmadoc. A Gower Explorer day pass costs £4.40.

Driving, cycling and walking Traffic at the height of the summer can be heavy, so take care when driving, especially when rounding blind corners on the narrow – often single-lane – twisting lanes. Cycling and walking are ideal ways to tour the area, as the peninsula's attractions are all within a short distance of each other and, in many cases, well off-road.

Mumbles

At the westernmost end of Swansea Bay on the cusp of Gower, **MUMBLES** (Mwmbwls) is a lively, enjoyable and increasingly glamorous seaside town. Its name comes from French sailors who dubbed the twin islets off the end of Mumbles Head *mamelles* (French for "breasts"). Today, the name "Mumbles" also refers interchangeably to the entire loose sprawl of **Oystermouth** (Ystumllwynarth), the area between Swansea and Mumbles.

1

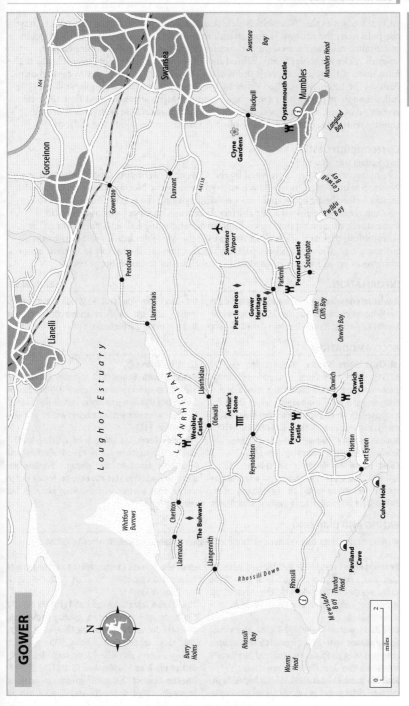

GOWER

Swansea Bay

Mumbles Head

Swansea

Blackpill

Oystermouth Castle

Mumbles

Langland Bay

Clyne Gardens

Gorseinon

M4

Gowerton

Dunvant

A4118

Caswell Bay

Pwlldu Bay

Pendawdd

Swansea Airport

Parc le Breos

Gower Heritage Centre

Parkmill

Pennard Castle

Southgate

Llanmorlais

Three Cliffs Bay

Llanelli

Loughor Estuary

L L A N R H I D I A N

Llanrhidian

Oxwich Bay

Oxwich

Oxwich Castle

Weobley Castle

Oldwalls

Arthur's Stone

Penrice Castle

Horton

Reynoldston

Port Eynon

Whitford Burrows

Cheriton

The Bulwark

Llanmadoc

Llangennith

Culver Hole

Rhossili Down

Pavilland Cave

Thurba Head

Rhossili

Mewslade Bay

N

Rhossili Bay

Burry Holms

Worms Head

0 _____ 2

miles

1

Once known as the "Mumbles Mile", thanks to the stags and hens that used to trawl the pubs here, the seafront is now an uninterrupted curve of stylish hotels and B&Bs, restaurants, cafés and ice-cream parlours leading down to the old-fashioned **pier**, towards rocky Mumbles Head. Behind the promenade, a warren of streets climbs the hills, lined with boutiques, craft shops and galleries and further places to eat and drink. Around the headland, reached either by the longer coast road or a short walk over the hill, is **Langland Bay**, with a sandy beach popular with **surfers**. A good time to be here is the end of April for the good-natured **Mumbles Musical Mile Festival**, a four-day shindig with gigs and events taking place at various venues along the seafront.

Oystermouth Castle
April–Sept daily 11am–5pm • £1.20

The hilltop above town is crowned by the ruins of **Oystermouth Castle**. Founded as a Norman watchtower, the castle was strengthened by the Normans to withstand Welsh attacks before being converted into a residence during the fourteenth century. Today you can see the remains of a late thirteenth-century keep next to a more ornate three-storey ruin incorporating an impressive banqueting hall and state rooms. The surrounding parkland affords lush views over the Mumbles headland, Swansea and its sweeping bay. The castle is only partially open at present, owing to a long-term major restoration project which is scheduled to continue for several more years.

INFORMATION   MUMBLES

Tourist information The small but very helpful TIC is in the Methodist church on Mumbles Rd, just beyond the Newton Rd junction (Easter–Sept Mon–Sat 10am–5pm, Oct–Easter 10am–4pm; ☎01792 361302, ⓦmumblesinfo .org.uk). Staff can advise on accommodation both in Mumbles and around the Gower.

ACCOMMODATION

★ **Clyne Farm Centre** Westport Ave ☎01792 403333, ⓦclynefarm.com. Superb self-catering accommodation at this eco-minded farm, where a range of cottages sleep between four and eight people. There's also a campsite (£5 per person, minimum two-night booking during summer weekends). It's located just off the A4118 in Blackpill, roughly midway between Mumbles and Swansea. For a weekend in summer, from **£465**

Coast House 708 Mumbles Rd ☎01792 368702, ⓦthecoasthouse.co.uk. Welcoming and very affordable seafront guesthouse with six fresh-looking rooms decorated predominantly in Laura Ashley-style floral tones.

Closed Dec & Jan. **£65**

Patrick's with Rooms 638 Mumbles Rd ☎01792 360199, ⓦpatrickswithrooms.com. This has sixteen fantastically stylish en-suite rooms, individually furnished in bold, contemporary colour schemes and all with sea-facing views. **£115**

★ **Tides Reach** 388 Mumbles Rd ☎01792 404877, ⓦtidesreachguesthouse.co.uk. Seven spacious and immaculate rooms in this elegant, cheerfully run guesthouse, where you can also enjoy the homely lounge and delightful courtyard garden bursting with roses and honeysuckle. **£60**

EATING AND DRINKING

Mumbles is one of Wales' culinary havens, with some really superb **restaurants**, in addition to some inviting cafés.

Beaufort Arms 1 Castle Rd ☎01792 425404. Up behind *Tides Reach*, a popular, down-to-earth locals' pub with two lounge areas, one for heads-down drinking and socializing, and another, slightly formal one, for simple dining. Daily noon–midnight.

Café 93 93 Newton Rd ☎01792 368793. Cheery, two-floored pink and white café at the top of the road, with tea, coffee and cakes, alongside crisp pizzas and juicy burgers. Mon & Tues 9am–5pm, Wed–Sat 9am–11pm.

Joe's 524 Mumbles Rd ☎01792 368212. Next to the TIC, this sister outlet to Joe's in Swansea has been making ice

cream here for nearly a century, offering a dizzying array of flavours and concoctions. Mon–Sat 9.30am–5.30pm, Sun 11am–6.30pm.

The Kitchen Table 626 Mumbles Rd ☎01792 367616. Comforting café-cum-restaurant, sporting kitchen-style tables and chairs and serving organic, home-made burgers and tasty veggie dishes. Mains £10. Tues–Sat 9.30am–5.30pm, plus 6.30–9.30pm Thurs–Sat.

Out of the Blue 698 Mumbles Rd ☎01792 361616. First-class seafood restaurant offering an array of beautifully crafted dishes like crab linguine, loin of monkfish wrapped in Parma ham, and red mullet on tomato and pea risotto. Mains £18-22. Tues–Sat noon–2pm & 6–9.30pm.

★ **P.A.'s Wine Bar** 95 Newton Rd ☎01792 367723. Mumbles' most rewarding restaurant, whose myriad seafood possibilities complement perfectly its outstanding repertoire of wines. There's a gut-busting Sunday lunch too. The vine-covered terrace is a fine spot to eat in warmer weather. Mains £15–25. Mon–Sat noon–2.30pm & 6–11pm, Sun noon–2.30pm.

Verdi's Knab Rock ☎01792 369135. Overlooking the sea near the pier, this Welsh–Italian institution is hugely well regarded for its superb pizzas and ice creams, sorbets and sundaes. Mon–Thurs 10am–6pm, Fri–Sun 10am–9pm.

The south and west Gower coasts

From Mumbles Head, the limestone crags of the **southern Gower coast** twist and delve the fifteen miles or so to Worms Head, at the bottom of Rhossili Bay. Many of the sandy bays between the cliffs are easily accessible by car, so they tend to be extremely crowded in peak season.

From Mumbles Head to Three Cliffs Bay

The first few miles of the southern Gower coast are highly developed, including the popular **surf beach** of **Langland Bay**, between two headlands. The narrow, golden-sanded **Caswell Bay** comes next, from where you can follow the cliff path to the tiny and remote former smugglers' haunt of **Brandy Cove**, or pebbly **Pwlldu Bay**. Brandy Cove and Pwlldu Bay are inaccessible by car; park in Bishopston village and walk the last mile or so.

Three miles along, huge **Three Cliffs Bay** is one of Gower's finest beaches, at the end of a silent valley fringed by dunes and the eerie ruins of **Pennard Castle**. The best approach is from the car park at **Southgate**, from where you hike a mile or so west along clifftops to Three Cliffs Bay, where you turn inland and follow the boundary of the golf course to the castle.

Gower Heritage Centre

Daily 10am–5pm • £5.90 • ☎01792 371206, ⓦ gowerheritagecentre.co.uk

You can also reach Three Cliffs Bay from the **Gower Heritage Centre** on the main A4118 in the village of **PARKMILL**. A large crafts and rural life museum, it comprises working water and corn mills, woollen mill and smithy house, as well as various attractions for kids, such as a farm, adventure play area and a puppet theatre. Take a peek, too, inside *La Charrette*, a disused railway carriage that was converted into Wales' smallest cinema, seating just 23 people – today, it just shows a film on the Gower. At reception you can pick up several useful leaflets outlining local walks, such as the one to Three Cliffs Bay.

Parc le Breos

A mile north of Parkmill (reachable via the lane that heads past the Heritage Centre) is the Neolithic burial chamber (3000–1900 BC) known, in honour of the thirteenth-century lords of Oystermouth Castle, as **Parc le Breos**. Although over-restored, the roofless chamber is impressive for its age and sheer size – 70ft long and divided into four separate chambers. In 1869, the skeletons of two dozen people were found inside. Just beyond the chamber and to the right, a deep fissure in a limestone outcrop marks the position of the dank and musty **Cathole Rock Cave**, in which flint tools, dating back over 12,000 years, have been found.

ACCOMMODATION	MUMBLES HEAD TO THREE CLIFFS BAY
Maes-Yr-haf ☎01792 371000, ⓦ maes-yr-haf.com. On the main load across from the heritage centre, the "Fields of Summer" has half a dozen impeccably	furnished rooms in deep purple and black colour schemes, and all fitted with combined TV/DVD, ipod dock and playstation. **£100**

1

Parc-le-Breos House ☎01792 371636, ⓦparc-le-breos.co.uk. A mile up a lane beside the Heritage Centre, this old shooting lodge was one of the original Gower manor houses, but is now a grand B&B offering tidy, Victorian-era furnished rooms, as well as horseback sightseeing trips from £28 per half day. **£74**

CAMPING

Three Cliffs Caravan Park North Hills Farm ☎01792 371218, ⓦthreecliffsbay.com. Spectacularly positioned over Three Cliffs Bay between Parkmill and Penmaen, this is a small but well-equipped site with kitchen and laundry facilities, and a farm shop. Open April–Sept. Pitches **£13**

Oxwich

One of the most curious landscapes in Gower is the reedy **nature reserve** around **Oxwich Burrows**, a flatland of salt and freshwater marshes reached via the lane that forks left off the A4118 at the ruined gatehouse of the privately owned Penrice Castle. Close by on the coast, the scattered village of **OXWICH** is grouped next to the gaping sands of Oxwich Bay. The sands and sea around here regularly receive awards, including the coveted blue flag.

Oxwich Castle

April–Sept daily 10am–5pm • £2.80 • ☎01792 390359 • CADW

Crowning a headland above the beach, **Oxwich Castle** is a fine example of early sixteenth-century house gentrification by Sir Rice Mansel, member of a powerful Welsh dynasty. His son Edward added the many-windowed eastern range, a pile of rooms with a highly fashionable long gallery that fell into ruin shortly afterwards. Standing just outside the walls is the substantial ruin of the dovecote, whose nesting holes would have been used for the storage of eggs, meat and other provisions.

ACCOMMODATION   **OXWICH**

Oxwich Bay Hotel ☎01792 390329, ⓦoxwichbayhotel .co.uk. Set in splendid isolation just above the sands, this strangely plain-looking hotel has well-turned-out rooms, in addition to rooms in cottages a short walk away. The grassy terrace is an alluring spot for a beer on a warm day. **£75**

Oxwich Camping Park Penrice road over a mile back from the beach ☎01792 390777. Extensive grounds with modern wash facilities, a laundry and on-site swimming pool. Open April–Sept. Pitches **£8**

Horton and Port Eynon

The rocky cliffs from Oxwich Point fade into wide stony bays towards the quiet village of **HORTON**, with a decent beach, and the more touristy **PORT EYNON** and its deep, sweeping bay.

The villages' sands and dunes are sheltered by a prominent headland, easily reached by a series of paths that wind their way along the shore from the car park above the bleak ruins of the old shoreline salt house and oyster pools. Owned by the National Trust, the lichen-spattered limestone headland is a wild and windy spot, where tufted grass gives way to sharp limestone crags. A natural cave at the tip can be seen from above, a great dome-shaped chasm that plunges into the hillside. Around the headland to the west is the quite remarkable, but fairly hard to find, **Culver Hole**, built into the cliffs. A man-made cave, it may originally have been a stronghold for the long-gone Port Eynon castle, and has served its time subsequently as a smugglers' retreat, dovecote and armoury.

The **coastal path** west from here is the most spectacular walk on Gower, veering along crags above thundering waves for five miles. The only real beach along this stretch is the secluded **Mewslade Bay**, just short of Rhossili and accessible by the path from Pitton. Along the coast walk, about midway between the two villages, is **Paviland Cave**, the site of an astonishing find in 1823, when the skeleton of a Stone Age hunter, at least 26,000 years old, was unearthed. At **Thurba Head**, on the eastern side of Mewslade Bay, there are a few scant remains of an Iron Age hillfort sited magnificently a few hundred feet above the waves.

Carreglwyd Camping and Caravan Park Above the YHA hostel ☎ 01792 390795, ⦿ porteynon.com. Backing onto the beach and surrounded by cliffs, this large and picturesque site comprises five hedged-off fields and good facilities (modern showers, laundry, shop). Pitches **£18**

Culver House ☎ 01792 720300, ⦿ culverhousehotel .co.uk. Nineteenth-century dwelling nicely tucked away behind the sand dunes offering eight apartment-style suites, each one comprising one or two bedrooms and an open-plan kitchen/lounge area. All have sea-facing balconies. **£70**

YHA Port Eynon ☎ 0870 770 5998, ⦿ yha.org.uk. Occupying a tremendous beachside location, this Victorian-era lifeboat station has been converted into a super hostel, with four- to eight-bedded dorms as well as double rooms. Shared shower facilities, self-catering kitchen and lounge. Between November and March it is available to groups only. Dorms **£18**

Rhossili, Worms Head and Llangennith

Heading west, Gower saves the best for last. The sublimely sited village of **RHOSSILI** (Rhosili) has wraparound views up into the hills and out to sea. It's a great place for coastal walking, particularly out to **Worms Head**, an isolated string of rocks with the spectacular appearance of a basking Welsh dragon, accessible for only five hours around low tide. Take care in this area: the **tidal currents** are extremely dangerous and people have lost their lives here. If you do get cut off, don't attempt to wade back – wait on the promontory until the tide recedes.

Below the village, a great curve of white sand stretches away into the distance, a dazzling coastline vast enough to absorb the crowds, especially if you are prepared to head a little way north towards **Burry Holms**, an islet three miles distant that is cut off at high tide. These coastal waters were notorious for **shipwrecks** in the nineteenth century, and towards the Rhossili end of the beach you can see (at low tide) the black ribs of the hull of the *Helvetia*, which foundered here in 1887. The northern end of the beach can also be reached along the small lane from Reynoldston, in the middle of the peninsula, to **Llangennith**, on the other side of the towering sandstone **Rhossili Down**, rising up to 633ft.

Church of St Mary

Standing in the heart of the village, the thirteenth-century **church of St Mary** is a typical Gower church, a thick-set stone construction with a distinctive saddleback tower. The church manifests some delightful detail, notably the late Norman carved door archway, to the left of which is a scratch sundial. Inside, take a look at the wall-mounted tablet dedicated to Rhossili son, Edgar Evans, who was the first member of Scott's Antarctic team to die.

Tourist information The National Trust Centre, at the head of the road beyond the village, stocks plenty of literature and some excellent local walking maps (Jan–March & Nov–Dec Wed–Sun 11am–4pm; Easter–Oct daily 10.30am–5pm; ☎ 01792 390707).

ACCOMMODATION

King's Head Llangennith ☎ 01792 386212, ⦿ kingsheadgower.co.uk. The most prominent accommodation in the village offers rooms of a high standard (some with sea views), both in the newer stone building up from the pub, and in an annexe attached to the pub itself. **£65**

Rhossili Bunkhouse ☎ 01792 391509, ⦿ rhossili bunkhouse.com. A mile or so back out of Rhossili, near the village of Middleton, this bunkhouse, attached to the village hall, offers clean and simple two-, four- and seven-bedded rooms. Note, though, that a minimum two-person, two-night stay is required. **£72**

Western House Llangennith, on the lane towards the beach ☎ 01792 386620, ⦿ westernhousebandb .co.uk. Three cool and wildly colourful rooms in this red limewashed B&B, whose remarkably chilled-out proprietors will ensure nothing less than a totally relaxing stay. **£60**

Worm's Head ☎ 01792 390512, ⦿ thewormshead .co.uk. Spectacularly sited on the cliff top, this small, welcoming hotel has fairly ordinary rooms, but the views are nothing short of sensational. Even if you're not staying here, take a coffee on the terrace. **£86**

1

CAMPING

Hillend ☎01792 386204, ⓦhillendcamping.com. Large, fabulously sited campsite behind the dunes and with direct access to the glorious beach. Two of the four fields are set aside for families and couples. Open April– Oct. Pitches **£18**

Pitton Cross Caravan and Camping Rhossili ☎01792 390593, ⓦpittoncross.co.uk. The only campsite in the vicinity of Rhossili is an excellent, compact site with segregated paddocks and magnificent sea views; in fact you can walk directly down to the beach. There's a great kite shop here too. Pitches **£11**

EATING AND DRINKING

Bay Bistro ☎01792 390519. Easy-going café serving light meals (salads, sandwiches, burgers), homemade cakes, coffee and tea; park yourself inside on one of the sunken armchairs or out on the windy terrace, although the coastal views are not as good as those from the *Worm's Head* next door. Daily 10am–5.30pm.

Mid- and north Gower

The great sweep of land that rises to the north of the main Gower road does not attract anything like the number of visitors that the south and west do, due to the lack of comparable coastline. Gower's northern fringe comprises a flattened series of marshes and mud flats merging indistinguishably with the sands of the Loughor estuary. Wading birds, gulls and bedded cockles, as well as herds of cattle and wild horses, are all found among the flats, dunes and inlets burrowing into the land from the estuary.

The central plateau is a pleasant patchwork of pastoral farmland. Its backbone, the 500ft-high sandstone ridge Cefn Bryn, stretches across the centre of the peninsula, with wiry peat and grass dotted with hardy sheep, ancient stone cairns and holy wells. The best views over the peninsula are from the road brushing over its roof.

Reynoldston and Arthur's Stone

The **Cefn Bryn** ridge makes a sublime walk, most easily explored from the quiet village of **REYNOLDSTON**, grouped around a sheep-filled village green and the *King Arthur Hotel*. From Reynoldston, a dramatic road rises up the slope of Cefn Bryn before skating across its summit in a perfect, straight line. Several tracks lead off from the road giving clear views to both Gower coasts, but you might be best off stopping at the small car park about a mile east of Reynoldston; from here, a path leads about half a mile across the boggy moor to **Arthur's Stone** (see box opposite).

ACCOMMODATION   MID- AND NORTH GOWER

Fairyhill ☎01792 390139, ⓦfairyhill.net. A grand, ivy-clad country-house hotel with eight rooms of supreme luxury; the dinner, bed and breakfast package is compulsory on Friday and Saturday nights; dinner is optional the rest of the week. **£180**; Fri & Sat night (with dinner) **£250**

SURFING AND OTHER ACTIVITIES ON THE GOWER

Gower has some of the finest surf in Britain, and its profile is certainly on the increase. The best surf is to be had around the bays and beaches of Langland, Caswell, Oxwich and Rhossili, though the most consistent is at Llangennith, which is also suitable for beginners. ⓦgowerlive .com has live webcams and tide times.

Surfing For equipment rental, the best place is PJ's Surfshop in Llangennith (☎01792 386669, ⓦpjsurfshop.co.uk), which has a wide range of rental surfboards (£11/day), boogie boards (£6/day) and wetsuits (£11/day). A mile away at the *Hillend* campsite, the Welsh Surfing Federation's Surf School (☎01792 386426, ⓦwsfsurfschool.co.uk) runs half-day surfing courses costing £25 for the first lesson and £20 for subsequent lessons. In Rhossili, Sam's Surf Shack (☎01792 390519, ⓦsamssurfshack) has both equipment hire and a surf school (£25/hr).

Other activities Euphoria Sailing (☎01792 234502, ⓦeuphoriasailing.com) offer tuition and rental for sailing, waterskiing and wakeboarding. Also in Rhossili, the Fly West Wales Summer School (ⓦflyspain.co.uk/fly-west-wales) offers paragliding trips and tuition, including day-taster courses and tandem flights (both £100), which can be extended to a four-day pilot course (£390).

ARTHUR'S STONE

Gower is littered with more dolmens, standing stones and other prehistoric remains than any other landscape in Wales. The most celebrated of all is **Arthur's Stone** (near Reynoldston and sometimes referred to as King Arthur's Stone), a massive and isolated burial chamber topped by a quartz capstone weighing over 25 tons. The dolmen is thought to be anything up to 6000 years old, while the thrusting, ruptured capstone (which, before it split sometime around 1693, rested on six supporting stones) is mentioned, often as *Maen Ceti*, in documents dating back a thousand years.

Some believe that it's part of an astronomical alignment along with Lady's Well, a spring deemed holy and now enclosed in a hut, across the road; and Penmaen's ruined chapel and Neolithic burial chamber, some three miles southeast. This alignment is allegedly charged with a special energy that has, in fact, shown up in some curious photographs with streaks and dots in otherwise clear skies. Whatever the case, the views from up here are extraordinary.

★ **King Arthur Hotel** ☏01792 390775, ⓦ kingarthurhotel.co.uk. The village's convivial pub has half a dozen comfortable en-suite rooms upstairs, though the annexe offers larger, more attractive rooms, with French windows and cast-iron beds and tables. **£70**

Llanrhidian

The small village of **LLANRHIDIAN** sits above the largely inaccessible marsh of the same name, which is virtually indistinguishable from the sands of the Loughor estuary.

Weobley Castle

Daily: April–Oct 9.30am–6pm; Nov–March 9.30am–5pm • £3.80 • ☏01792 390012 • CADW

Standing gaunt against the backdrop of the marsh and the estuary a mile and a half further west, **Weobley Castle** was built as a fortified manor in the latter part of the thirteenth century. Its first residents were the de la Bere family, who remained here until the fifteenth century, after which time it was variously lived in by a succession of wealthy landowners, such as Rhys Thomas and the Mansels, the latter owners of Oxwich Castle. The most intact parts of the complex are the north and west portions, formerly the hall, kitchen and accommodation block. The views across the marshes and mud-flats are quite wonderful.

EATING AND DRINKING | LLANRHIDIAN

Dolphin Inn ☏01792 391069. Warmly run eighteenth-century pub with a cosy interior and some fine real ales. The garden is a great place to kick back, and has a children's play area with a few farm animals. Mon 6–11pm, Tues–Sun 1–11pm.

Welcome to Town ☏01792 390015. Opposite the *Dolphin*, a superb but expensive country bistro whose menu has been created using produce cultivated almost exclusively from the Gower, such as roast lamb with wild garlic polenta, and new-season Gower asparagus with Carmarthenshire ham. Mains £20–25. Tues–Sat noon–2pm & 7–11pm, Sun noon–2pm.

Llanmadoc

West of the village of **Cheriton**, with its charming thirteenth-century church, is **LLANMADOC**, where you can park and venture onto the land spit of **Whitford Burrows**, a soft patch of dunes now open as a nature reserve, with the only sea-washed cast-iron lighthouse in the UK. Steep paths lead from Llanmadoc village up **Llanmadoc Hill** to the south. **The Bulwark**, a lonely and windy hillfort, can be seen at the eastern end of Llanmadoc Hill's summit ridge.

ACCOMMODATION | LLANMADOC

Tallizmand Guesthouse ☏01792 386373, ⓦ tallizmand.co.uk. The main accommodation option along Llanmadoc's main road is the *Tallizmand Guesthouse*, with three en-suite rooms and a cosy communal lounge warmed by an open fire. **£65**

Southwest Wales

ATLANTIC PUFFIN, SKOMER

Southwest Wales

The most westerly outpost of Wales, the counties of Carmarthenshire and, in particular, Pembrokeshire harbour fabulous scenery: bucolic and magical inland, where Carmarthenshire follows the Tywi Valley into the heart of the country; rocky, indented and spectacular around the Pembrokeshire Coast National Park and its 186-mile path. Industrial south Wales peters out at Llanelli, before the undistinguished county town of Carmarthen. A glorious road winds along the Tywi Valley, past ruined hilltop forts and the National Botanic Garden of Wales on the way to Llandeilo and Wales' most impressively positioned castle, Carreg Cennen, high up on a dizzy plug of Black Mountain rock. Further inland, the sparsely populated countryside of remote hills and tiny valleys is broken only by endearing small market towns such as Llandovery, the gloomy ruins of Talley Abbey and the Roman gold mines at Dolaucothi.

The wide sands of southern Carmarthenshire, just beyond Dylan Thomas' adopted home town of **Laugharne**, merge into the popular south Pembrokeshire seaside resorts of **Tenby** and **Saundersfoot**. Tenby sits at the entrance to the south Pembrokeshire peninsula, divided from the rest of the county by the Milford Haven and Daugleddau estuary, bringing tidal waters deep into the county's pastoral heart. The peninsula's turbulent, rocky coast is ruptured by some remote historical sites, including the Norman baronial castle at **Manorbier** and the tiny **St Govan's chapel**, wedged into a rocky cliff near Bosherston. At the neck of the peninsula is the old county town of **Pembroke**, dominated by its fearsome castle; to the north beyond the Milford Haven estuary is the market town and transport interchange of **Haverfordwest**, dull but hard to avoid. St Bride's Bay's rutted coastline is one of the most glorious parts of the coastal walk, leading north towards the village-sized city of **St Davids**, where the exquisite cathedral shelters in a protective hollow. Close by are opportunities locally for spectacular coast and hill walks, hair-raising boat crossings to local islands, surf galore and numerous other outdoor activities.

The coast turns towards the north at St Davids, becoming the southern stretch of Cardigan Bay. The northernmost section of the Coast Path, from the pretty ferry port

ST GOVAN'S CHAPEL, PEMBROKESHIRE

Highlights

❶ The Tywi Valley Castles, follies and the National Botanic Garden set among one of Wales' lushest and most atmospheric valleys. **See p.149**

❷ Carreg Cennen Castle The region's most dramatically sited fortress, perched on a vertiginous plug of rock and framed by green hills and glowering mountains. **See p.152**

❸ Laugharne A must for all Dylan Thomas devotees, but much more than that, this quirky place is the quintessential small Welsh coastal town. **See p.156**

❹ St Govan's chapel A tiny grey chapel wedged into a fissure in the cliffs, just above the

churning sea: a phenomenal statement of faith and an awesome sight. **See p.174**

❺ Skomer, Skokholm and Grassholm Rough and rugged islands, where squawking colonies of birds rule the roost. **See p.180**

❻ St Davids The jewel of Pembrokeshire, Britain's smallest city is surrounded by fabulous scenery and fosters a burgeoning surf scene with superb après-surf. **See p.183**

❼ Carn Ingli One of Wales' holiest mountains, with great views over the mysterious Mynydd Preseli and the charming little seaside town of Newport. **See p.194**

HIGHLIGHTS ARE MARKED ON THE MAP ON P.142

of **Fishguard** to the outskirts of Cardigan and past the delightful little town of **Newport**, is the most dramatic and remote. Inland are the eerie **Mynydd Preseli**, relic-spattered mountains overlooking windswept plateaux of heathland and isolated villages – none more remote than the leafy valley of **Cwm Gwaun**.

GETTING AROUND   SOUTHWEST WALES

Despite the remoteness of much of southwestern Wales, public transport is surprisingly efficient and comprehensive, though you'll have to plan carefully, even in summer. Bus and train **timetables** are widely available locally, and online at ⓦ pembrokeshiregreenways.co.uk and ⓦ carmarthenshire.gov.uk. Check Getting around in Basics for **discount fares** and **passes**.

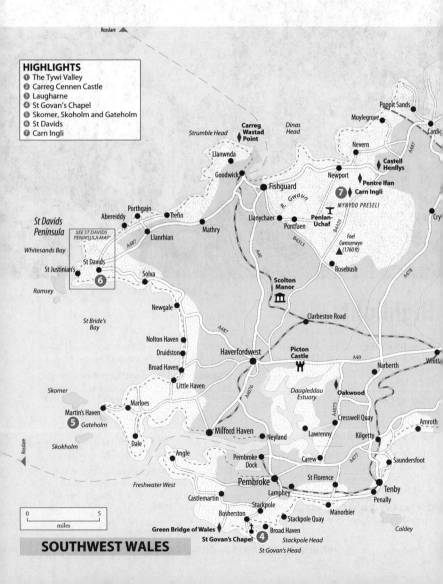

HIGHLIGHTS
1. The Tywi Valley
2. Carreg Cennen Castle
3. Laugharne
4. St Govan's Chapel
5. Skomer, Skoholm and Gateholm
6. St Davids
7. Carn Ingli

SOUTHWEST WALES

BY TRAIN

Direct train services connect Cardiff and Swansea with Llanelli, Carmarthen, Tenby, Pembroke, Haverfordwest, Milford Haven and Fishguard, while the Heart of Wales line shuffles out of Swansea and Llanelli to Llandeilo and Llandovery before delving into Powys. A West Wales Day Ranger ticket (£8.80) is valid after 8.45am Mon–Fri, any time weekends and bank holidays, and gives free travel on all trains west of Carmarthen.

BY BUS

Bus services out to the smaller towns and villages are regular and dependable, especially in high summer, when most coastal villages have a fairly regular service. Carmarthen and Haverfordwest are the main hubs, with some services from Tenby, Pembroke and Fishguard. The Pembrokeshire coast is well catered for, with various winsomely titled services – the Coastal Cruiser, the Puffin Shuttle, the Poppit Rocket – operating year-round under the banner of Pembrokeshire Coastal Bus Services.

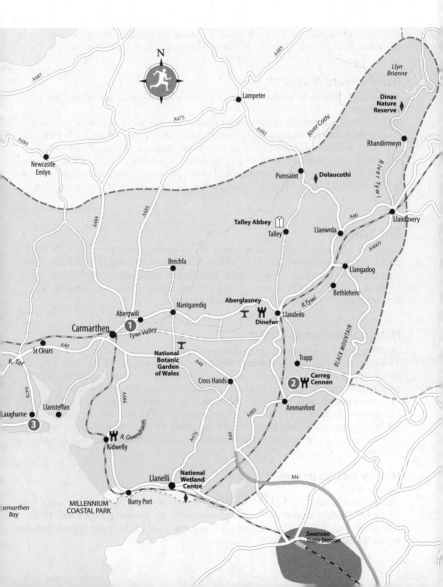

BY BIKE

Only in the deserted lanes of northern and eastern Pembrokeshire does bus travel become difficult, although it's excellent walking and cycling country, and there are ample places to rent bikes throughout the area.

BY BOAT

Most of the offshore islands are connected by regular (seasonal) boat services, although few of these allow for overnight stops.

Llanelli and around

LLANELLI marks the border between anglicized southeast Wales and the *bro*, Welsh Wales, where the native language is part of everyday life. Once a major industrial hub, the town's steelworks have almost all now been cleared and replaced with massive retail developments, sucking out what life was left in the town centre; but rugby very much remains a local passion while the National Wetlands Centre is a rewarding visit.

Parc Howard Museum

April–Sept Mon–Fri 11am–1pm & 2–6pm, Sat & Sun 2–6pm; March–Oct Mon–Fri 11am–1pm & 2–4pm, Sat & Sun 2–4pm • Free • ☎ 01554 772029

To learn something of the metalworking days when the town was known as Tinopolis, visit the **Parc Howard Museum**, half a mile north of the centre, off the A476 Felinfoel road. The Italianate mansion, set in a lovely park, has good coverage of the town's industrial boom, from 1800, when its population was 3000, to 1891, when it reached 33,464, as well as samples of the famous Llanelli pottery. By the parish church in the centre of town, historic **Llanelly House**, built in 1714, is also to open as a museum in 2012.

The Scarlets

Llanelli is famed for its rugby club, one of Wales' leading teams since 1875. In 2003 they became the **Scarlets** (☎ 01554 783900, ⓦ scarlets.co.uk), one of Wales' four new regional teams, although a Llanelli RFC team continues to play in the Premier Division. In 2008 they both moved from historic Stradey Park to the modern Parc y Scarlets stadium, on the A484 just east at Pemberton.

National Wetlands Centre

Daily 9.30am–5pm; grounds open till 6pm in summer • £8.20 • ⓦ wwt.org.uk

Two miles east of town, the **National Wetlands Centre** overlooks an extensive area of salt marsh dotted with bird hides and landscaped walkways. Uneconomic farmland has been returned to nature, with "natural" ponds created around existing hedgerows. Important populations of lapwing, redshank, and over-wintering pintail, wigeon and teal draw birdwatchers, but the centre caters just as well to kids and the curious. The wilder western section is best explored on **free bikes** available here in school summer holidays only, when free canoe safaris are also offered (both daily mid-July to early Sept noon–4pm).

Millennium Coastal Park

Open access • Free

The wetlands centre is linked to Llanelli by the fourteen-mile **Millennium Coastal Park**, formerly industrial land along the Loughor estuary incorporating a cycle path that's part of the 300-mile Celtic Trail (see p.44) and National Cycle Route 4, from London to St Davids.

ARRIVAL AND DEPARTURE

LLANELLI

By train Half a mile south of the town centre. Destinations Cardiff (20 daily; 1hr 20min); Carmarthen (25 daily; 30min); Llandeilo (4 daily; 40min); Llandovery (4 daily; 1hr); Llandrindod Wells (4 daily; 2hr); Llanwrtyd Wells (4 daily; 1hr 25min); Pembrey & Burry Port (23 daily; 5min); Shrewsbury (4 daily; 3hr 30min); Swansea (29 daily; 20min).

By bus On Island Place, immediately east of the centre. Destinations Carmarthen (2 hourly; 1hr); Kidwelly (2 hourly; 30min); Swansea (4 hourly; 1hr).

INFORMATION

Tourist information and bike hire The TIC (daily: mid-May to Sept 10am–8pm; Oct to mid-May 10am–5pm; ☎ 01554 777744) is in the Discovery Centre at North Dock, 0.5 miles southwest of the town centre beside the Coast Path. There's a good café (same hours) as well as Merlin Cycle Tours (☎ 01554 756603, 07875 060815, ⊛ merlincycletours.co.uk), which rents bikes for £7/hr or £25/day.

ACCOMMODATION

Coastal Park 86 Queen Victoria Rd ☎ 01554 755357, ⊛ coastalpark.co.uk. Not actually on the coast but not far west from the train station, this fairly ordinary B&B also has a grill-bar (Thurs–Sat noon–3pm, Tues–Sat 5–10pm). **£60**

Llwyn Hall Llwynhendy ☎ 01554 777754, ⊛ llwynhall.co.uk. The best of the town's guesthouses, almost two miles east off B4297, this has a good restaurant. **£65**

EATING AND DRINKING

Langostinos 1 Murray St ☎ 01554 773711, ⊛ langostinosllanelli.co.uk. Serves up classy tapas, pasta (£12), steaks and fish dishes (£15–20) and a three-course dinner for £20. Daily 9am–3pm, Tues–Sat 6–11pm.

Sheesh Mahal 53 Stepney St ☎ 01554 773773. Offers some of south Wales' finest curries; starters £2.50–4.95, mains £6–10, baltis £7.50–8. Sun–Thurs 5.30–11pm, Fri & Sat 5.30pm–midnight.

Kidwelly

KIDWELLY (Cydweli) is a sleepy little town dominated by an imposing **castle**, strategically sited overlooking the River Gwendraeth and a vast tract of coast.

The castle

March–June, Sept & Oct daily 9.30am–5pm; July & Aug daily 9.30am–6pm; Nov–Feb Mon–Sat 10am–4pm, Sun 11am–4pm • £3.50 • ☎ 01554 890104 • CADW

The castle was established around 1106 as a satellite of Sherborne Abbey in Dorset, transformed in the 1270s and extended in the fourteenth century. Entering through the massive gatehouse (completed in 1422), you can still see portcullis slots and murder holes, through which noxious substances could be tipped onto intruders. The **gatehouse** forms the centrepiece of the impressively intact semicircular outer ward walls, which date from around 1275. Views from the musty solar and hall, packed into the easternmost wall of the inner ward, show the castle's defensive position at its best, with the river directly below. Although the whole castle is long since roofless, the remains are some of the most intact of any medieval Welsh castle that has not been extensively restored. A fourteenth-century town **gate** shields the castle approach from Castle Street, which is the main road through Kidwelly.

Kidwelly Industrial Museum

June–Sept Mon–Fri 10am–5pm, Sat & Sun noon–5pm • Free • ☎ 01554 891078, ⊛ kidwellyindustrialmuseum.co.uk

A 167ft brick chimney just over a mile north of town (up Priory Street) marks the modest but informative **Kidwelly Industrial Museum**, housed in a former tinplate works. Many of the works' old features have been preserved, including the rolling mills, where blocks of tin were rolled and spun into wafer-thin slices.

Carmarthen and around

The ancient capital of its region and county town of Carmarthenshire, **CARMARTHEN** (Caerfyrddin) is a lively market town with 15,000 inhabitants, but does not entirely live up to the promise of its status. Unlike Llanelli, new shopping developments have been built right in the centre, but there's still little reason to stay – fortunately, with so many beautiful and interesting places nearby, there's little need to. It's the first major town in west Wales where the native language is widely heard, and was once – in the early eighteenth century – the largest town in all of Wales, thanks to its position at the tidal limit of the River Tywi.

Two miles east of central Carmarthen, **Abergwili** is of interest for the Carmarthen County Museum, and its role as Merlin's resting place.

Carmarthen

Founded as a Roman fort, **CARMARTHEN**'s most popular moment of mythological history dates from the Dark Ages and the supposed birth of the wizard **Merlin** just outside the town (see box opposite) – its Roman name, Moridunum, may have given him his Welsh name, Myrddin. The Normans built a castle in 1095, and in 1313 Carmarthen was granted its first charter by Edward I, helping the town flourish as a centre of the wool trade. It was later taken by Owain Glyndŵr in the early fifteenth century. The town grew in importance, attracting trade and new commerce, industrial works and a key port.

Across the river from the train station, the stern facade of the 1930s **Shire Hall** stands within the uninspiring remains of the **castle**, Edward I's reworking of a Norman fortress destroyed by Glyndŵr in 1405. It can be entered (until around 5.30pm; free) from **Nott Square**, beneath which spreads the most picturesque eighteenth- and nineteenth-century part of town, around King Street. From Nott Square, the broad, sloping Darkgate leads down to Lammas Street, a wide Georgian thoroughfare flanked by coaching inns. To the north, the St Catherine's Walk shopping precinct leads to the striking new **market** (Mon 9.30am–4.30pm, Tues–Sat 9.30am–5pm), a great centre for

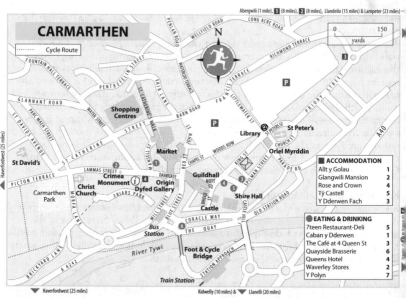

MERLIN

Merlin (Myrddin) is a difficult character to pin down. A mythic figure throughout Europe's Celtic fringe, he is variously described as a wizard and prophet, though over the centuries he has also been called a half-demon and Antichrist, as well as being credited with building Stonehenge. His most common association, of course, is with King Arthur (see box, p.76) to whom he was tutor, wizard and advisor. It was Merlin who arranged Arthur's rise to the throne through the sword-in-the-stone contest, Merlin who founded the Round Table, and Merlin who accompanied Arthur to the Isle of Avalon at the end of his life.

This interpretation dates back to the twelfth-century writings of Geoffrey of Monmouth who, in his *Historia Regum Britanniae* of 1134, drew on all sorts of tales and folklore (plus a fair bit of fabrication) to create the Merlin we know today. He is even credited with inventing the Latinized "Merlin" form to avoid his character being associated with "merde", the French for excrement.

According to Geoffrey and, half a century later, Giraldus Cambrensis (see box, p.380) , Merlin was born in Carmarthen. Geoffrey built on stories of very different Merlins under different names – Myrddin Wyllt (Merlin the wild), Merlin Caledonensis (Scottish Merlin), and the most Welsh, Myrddin Emrys (Merlin Ambrosius) – perhaps separate people whose stories have blended, or the same person whose stories diverged over centuries of telling.

Local legend has it that Merlin sleeps under Merlin's Hill, where he will remain until the country is in great danger and King Arthur and his men rise up. Another story tells of Merlin predicting that "when Merlin's tree shall tumble down, then shall fall Carmarthen town". The oak, which once stood in the town centre, died a few years back, but Carmarthen remains. A piece of the tree can be seen in the Carmarthen County Museum.

Today Carmarthen celebrates its legendary connection with the **Gŵyl Myrddyn** (Merlin Festival; ⓦ carmarthenshire.gov.uk), in mid-August, with a funfair, coracle racing, medieval village, fortune tellers and, of course, wizards.

2

local produce, secondhand books, antiques and endearingly useless tat. On the main market days – Wednesday and Saturday – stalls spill outside.

Origin Dyfed Gallery

26 Blue St • Mon–Sat 10am–5pm • Free • ☎ 01267 220377

The excellent **Origin Dyfed Gallery** is the public face of a local art and craft cooperative. Here you can browse a range of cards, jewellery, glass, ceramics, photography, sculpture and metalwork, textiles and woodcarving, including love spoons.

Oriel Myrddin

Church Lane • Mon–Sat 10am–5pm • Free • ☎ 01267 222775, ⓦ orielmyrddingallery.co.uk

Opposite **St Peter's church** is a Victorian art school that has metamorphosed into the excellent **Oriel Myrddin**, a craft centre and art gallery displaying the work of local artists.

Abergwili

The severe grey Bishop's Palace at **ABERGWILI**, two miles east of Carmarthen, was the seat of the Bishop of St Davids between 1542 and 1974, and now houses the **Carmarthen County Museum**, a spirited amble through the history of the area.

Carmarthen County Museum

Tues–Sat 10am–4.30pm • Free • ☎ 01267 228696, ⓦ carmarthenmuseum.org.uk

Local pottery, archeological finds, wooden dressers and a lively history of local castles are well presented, along with material on crime and policing, geology, education, coracles and Carmarthen's role in the development of the eisteddfod tradition. There's a surprisingly interesting display on the first Welsh translation of the New Testament,

2

produced here in 1567. Upstairs there's an art display plus the bishop's chapel and a re-created schoolroom and farmhouse interior.

Merlin's Hill Centre

Daily: April–Oct 10am–7pm; Nov–March 10am–5pm • £3 • ☎ 01267 237808, ⓦ www.merlinshill.com

A mile north of Abergwili rise the sharp slopes of **Merlin's Hill** (Bryn Myrddin), reputedly the sleeping place of the great wizard. Alltyfyrddin Farm, on whose land this lies, has cashed in with the cheesy **Merlin's Hill Centre**, full of sub-Harry Potter exhibits aimed mainly at kids, but which at least gives access to the Iron Age hillfort.

ARRIVAL AND DEPARTURE   CARMARTHEN

Unless otherwise stated, frequencies for trains and buses are for Monday to Saturday services; on Sundays there are very few buses, and 4–6 trains on most lines, though the main line east from Carmarthen is served more frequently.

BY TRAIN

Trains between Swansea and Pembrokeshire stop at the train station, on the south side of the River Tywi.

Destinations Carmarthen to: Cardiff (20 daily; 1hr 45min–2hr 10min); Fishguard Harbour (4 daily; 1hr); Haverfordwest (11 daily; 40min); Kidwelly (15 daily; 15min); Llanelli (28 daily; 25min); Milford Haven (11 daily; 1hr); Narberth (9 daily; 25min); Pembroke (9 daily; 1hr 10min); Swansea (26 daily; 50min); Tenby (9 daily; 50min).

BY BUS

All buses terminate at the bus station on Blue Street, north of the river.

Destinations Carmarthen to: Aberaeron (hourly; 1hr 45min); Aberystwyth (hourly; 2hr 20min); Brechfa (2 daily; 35min); Cardigan (hourly; 1hr 25min); Cenarth (hourly; 1hr 10min); Drefach Felindre (hourly; 50min); Haverfordwest (3 daily; 1hr); Kidwelly (every 30min; 25min); Lampeter (hourly; 1hr); Laugharne (6 daily; 30min); Llandeilo (10 daily; 40min); Llandovery (8 daily; 1hr 20min); Llanelli (every 30min; 1hr); Llansteffan (7 daily; 20min); Narberth (3 daily; 50min); National Botanic Garden of Wales (3 daily; 20min); Swansea (every 30min; 1hr 20min); Tenby (1 daily; 1hr 10min).

INFORMATION

Tourist information The TIC is at 113 Lammas St, near the Crimea Monument (July & Aug daily 10am–5pm; April–June, Sept & Oct Mon–Sat 10am–5pm; Nov–March Mon–Sat 10am–4pm; ☎ 01267 231557, ⓦ carmarthenshire .gov.uk). For free internet access visit the library (Mon–Sat 9.30am–5pm) on King St opposite St Peter's church.

ACCOMMODATION

The range of **accommodation** in Carmarthen is limited, and few places are truly notable, so we also list a selection of places in the nearby Tywi Valley.

Allt y Golau Felingwm Uchaf, 8 miles northeast of Carmarthen ☎ 01267 290455, ⓦ alltygolau.com. Superb sustainability-minded B&B in a renovated 1812 farmhouse with three tastefully decorated rooms and sumptuous breakfasts. Close to the Botanic Garden. **£68**

Glangwili Mansion Llandllawdog, 7 miles northeast ☎ 01267 253735 ⓦ glangwilimansion.co.uk. A beautiful designer guesthouse, with lots of bright abstract art, hens, alpacas and an eagle owl; it's near Brechfa Forest, for hiking or biking. **£105**

Rose and Crown Lammas St ☎ 01267 232050,

ⓦ roseandcrowncarmarthen.co.uk. Ancient coaching inn well refurbished with chic rooms, free wi-fi, DVD players, and full Welsh breakfasts in the bar downstairs. **£60**

Tŷ Castell B&B Station Rd, Nantgaredig, 6 miles east of Carmarthen along A40 ☎ 01267 290034, ⓦ ty-castell .co.uk. Wonderful outdoors-oriented farmhouse B&B by the Towy, with a licensed restaurant on site. **£56**

Y Dderwen Fach 98 Priory St ☎ 01267 234193. The best of the central budget B&Bs, in a simple seventeenth-century house. Some rooms have bathtubs. **£50**

EATING AND DRINKING

7teen Restaurant-Deli 17 Queen St ☎ 01267 229599, ⓦ restaurant7teen.co.uk. In a beautifully restored building, 7teen serves simple meals of the best local ingredients, such as cockles, laver bread and coracle-caught sea trout and sea bass. Lunch costs £12/15 for 2/3 courses; in the evenings starters/desserts cost around £5, mains £14–15.50, with steaks up to £20, and good vegetarian options. Mon & Sun noon–3pm, Tues–Sat 6–9pm.

Caban y Dderwen 11 Mansel St. The best spot in town for snacks and light lunches, including pan-fried laver bread with cockles (£6). Named after the famous oak tree that once stood outside. Mon–Sat 9am–5pm, Thurs closes 3.30pm.

The Café at 4 Queen St 4 Queen St ☎ 0870 042 4176. A stylish café, serving good coffee, teas and cakes, and light lunches including club sandwiches and soups with home-made bread. Mon–Sat 9am–5pm.

Quayside Brasserie Coracle Way ☎ 01267 223000. Cosy restaurant with some outside seating. It's great for fresh local meat, fish and seafood (mains £11–17), and especially popular at lunchtime. Mon–Thurs noon–3pm, 6–11pm, Fri–Sun noon–11pm.

Queens Hotel 10 Queen St ☎ 0871 951 1000. The best beer in town, in a wood-panelled coaching inn that also offers a long menu of home-cooked dishes, notably cawl (Welsh broth; 3.50/4.50). Mon–Sat 10am–midnight, Sun 11am–10.30pm; food Sun–Thurs noon–3pm, Fri/Sat 10am–6pm.

Waverley Stores 23 Lammas St ☎ 01267 236521. A large health-food shop with a vegetarian café and tea garden, also serving tasty lunch dishes for around £5. Mon–Sat 10am–3pm.

★ **Y Polyn** Capel Dewi, Nantgaredig, B4310 2 miles north of National Botanic Garden ☎ 01267 290000, ⓦ ypolynrestaurant.co.uk. A country pub offering some of the best food in the area. The Modern British cuisine makes superb use of local ingredients and everything is served with relaxed panache. Set dinners cost £24 for two courses, £30 for three. Open for lunch Tues–Fri & Sun, dinner Tues–Sat.

The Tywi Valley

The **River Tywi** curves and darts its way east from Carmarthen through some of the most spellbinding scenery in south Wales. It's not hard to see why the Merlin legend has taken such a hold in these parts – the landscape does seem infused with a kind of eerie magic. The thirty-mile trip from Carmarthen to **Llandovery** is punctuated by gentle, impossibly green hills topped with ruined castles, notably the wonderful **Carreg Cennen** near the appealing town of Llandeilo. Two fine gardens have sprung up here in recent years: one completely new in the form of the **National Botanic Garden of Wales**; the other a faithful restoration of the original walled gardens around the long-abandoned house of **Aberglasney**.

Brechfa Forest

Ten miles northeast of Carmarthen in the lovely Cothi valley, Brechfa is becoming increasingly renowned for its mountain-biking trails, but it's a beautiful area for walking too. Quiet narrow lanes cut through the 16,000 acres of mixed ancient forest and recent plantations, emerging near Talley and Dolaucothi.

ACCOMMODATION, EATING AND DRINKING   **BRECHFA FOREST**

Black Lion Abergorlech, 5 miles northeast of Brechfa ☎ 01558 685271, ⓦ blion.co.uk. A fine old inn close to the start of the main MTB trails; with a flagstoned bar, a restaurant extension and bike washing facilities; closed Mon in winter. Mains are around £8–14. Mon–Fri bar noon–3pm, 7–10pm, food noon–2pm, 7–9pm; Sat & Sun bar noon–11pm, food Sat noon–3pm, 6–9pm, Sun noon–2.30pm, 7–9pm.

Gilfach-Wen Barn Brechfa ☎ 07970 629726, ⓦ brechfa-bunkhouse.com. Useful, well appointed and pleasantly located self-catering bunkhouse accommodation. Per person £16

Ty Mawr Country Hotel Brechfa ☎ 01267 202332, ⓦ wales-country-hotel.co.uk. Upmarket accommodation as well as a microbrewery and bar. £108

The National Botanic Garden of Wales

Daily: April–Sept 10am–6pm; Oct–March 10am–4.30pm • £8.50, Nov–Feb £5; £7 for those arriving by bike; £4.25 for those arriving by public transport • ☎ 01558 668768, ⓦ gardenofwales.org.uk • Bus #166 runs three times daily from Carmarthen

Though only opened in 2000, the great glass "eye" of the **National Botanic Garden of Wales** has quickly become the centrepiece of the Tywi Valley. Just a mile north of the

A48 and seven miles east of Carmarthen, it occupies what's left of the vast estate of the nineteenth-century banker William Paxton. His house, Middleton Hall, burnt down in 1931, though the servants' quarters remain as a conference centre. The garden has gradually come to warrant its considerable hype, and enough of the elements are in place to see its huge potential.

A central walkway leads past lakes (drained in 1939 and restored in the 1990s), sculpture and geological outcrops from all over Wales, with walks down towards planted areas and different wood and wetland habitats. Paxton's double-walled garden has been teased back to life (providing vegetables for the rather unexciting café/restaurant), and enhanced by the addition of a small but exquisite Japanese garden, a tropical house, and a bee garden that's home to a million bees.

The glasshouse and Millennium Square

At the top of the hill is the garden's most audacious feature: the vast oval **glasshouse**, a stunning piece of architecture by Norman Foster. It houses endangered plants from regions with a Mediterranean climate in South Africa, Australia, Chile and California, as well as the Mediterranean itself. Outside, paths lead through the Waun Las National Nature Reserve all the way to the three-cornered Paxton's Tower (built to honour Nelson in 1809; always open, NT) on a hilltop two miles to the northeast.

The stableyard houses a restaurant and an excellent exhibition on medicinal plants and the dynasty of Welsh herbalists known as the Physicians of Myddfai (Meddygon Myddfai, supposedly descended from the Lady of the Lake), abutting **Millennium Square**, a venue for open-air concerts and performances. The entire garden is sustainably managed: rainwater is used for irrigation; the glasshouses are heated by burning wood coppiced on the grounds; and wastewater is purified through a series of reed beds. A large tract of surrounding land is being turned over to organic farming using Welsh breeds of cattle and sheep, as well as re-creations of moorland, woodland and other native Welsh habitats.

Aberglasney

Daily: April–Sept 10am–6pm; Oct–March 10.30am–4pm • £7 • ☎ 01558 668998, ⓦ aberglasney.org

A natural twin to the Botanic Garden lies five miles northeast at **Aberglasney**, half a mile south of the A40 near Broad Oak. Locals had long known about the decaying and abandoned manor house – which supposedly had protected status – but it was only in 1994, when the grand double portico (added in 1830) came up for auction, that the authorities took notice. The portico was withdrawn from sale and reattached to the house as part of a major restoration undertaken by the Aberglasney Trust from 1998, although the house's stabilized shell is destined to play second fiddle to its remarkable **gardens**. Much smaller and more intimate than the National Botanic Garden, they are being steadily re-created as living historical documents.

The walled gardens

Once massively overgrown, these mostly sixteenth- to eighteenth-century walled gardens have regained much of their original formal splendour, while archeological work has uncovered their history. Especially noteworthy are the replanted kitchen garden and what is thought to be the only secular cloister garden in Britain, dating from the late sixteenth century. A walkway around the top of the cloister gives access to a set of birdless Victorian aviaries, and great views over the Jacobean Pool Garden to mature woodlands beyond. On the lawn near the gatehouse (long thought to be a Victorian folly but now dated to c.1600) is a line of five yews planted three centuries ago, and trained over to root on the far side, a feature unique in Britain.

The courtyard garden

In 2005, the central courtyard of the manor house was glassed in to form an atrium populated with subtropical plants – tree ferns, cycads, orchids and more. Dubbed a Ninfarium (after gardens at Ninfa, near Rome), it makes a beautiful counterpoint to the outdoor gardens. You'll also find a video history of the estate and arts and crafts displays in the unplastered entrance hall. Leave time for tea and cakes outside the tempting **café** built into the wall of the Pool Garden.

2

Llandeilo and around

Beautifully set below the magnificent Black Mountain, **LLANDEILO** is in transition. It remains a quiet market town, but is becoming known as an upmarket rural retreat for the aspirational of Swansea, Cardiff and beyond, with a couple of boutique hotels, some fancy shops and galleries, and a handful of delis, cafés and restaurants. It also hosts an up-and-coming music festival in mid-July (ⓦllandeilomusicfestival.org.uk). Llandeilo makes an excellent base for exploring the area, particularly Dinefwr and Carreg Cennen.

Church of St Teilo

Llandeilo Fawr Gospels display: Easter–Oct Tues–Sat 11am–4pm

Spend a few minutes in the parish **church of St Teilo** (rebuilt from 1848 by George Gilbert Scott) on Rhosmaen Street, home to a pair of eighth-century Celtic crosses. The base of the tower houses an interactive display on the **Llandeilo Fawr Gospels**, an eighth-century parchment manuscript which contains the earliest-known example of written Welsh. The book itself is in Lichfield Cathedral in England, but you can browse its digitized text and learn something of both these gospels and the closely related (and more famous) Lindisfarne Gospels.

Dinefwr Castle

Open access • Free

The strategic importance of the Tywi Valley is underlined by the tumbledown ruins of **Dinefwr Castle**, set in the extensive Dinefwr Park a mile west of Llandeilo. High on a wooded bluff over the river, the castle was built in 877 by Rhodri Mawr, King of Wales, and became the seat of the rulers of Deheubarth. It was rebuilt in stone from 1165 by the Lord Rhys (Rhys ap Gruffudd), who united the warring Welsh princes against the Normans, and then strengthened by Edward I after 1282. It was never lost by the English until the seventeenth century, after which it was allowed to fall into "Romantic" ruin.

There's free access by public footpaths through the park, and you can climb to the highest point of the largely thirteenth-century ruins for stunning views across the valley and, in the other direction, Newton House. With a car, it's easiest to park at Newton House and follow the well-marked walk from there.

Newton House

Mid-Feb to Oct daily 11am–5pm (July/Aug to 6pm); Nov to mid-Feb Fri–Sun 11.30am–4pm • £6.30 • ☎ 01558 668998 • NT

By Tudor times Dinefwr Castle had become ill-suited to the needs of the Lord Rhys' descendants, who built a new residence half a mile away. Now named **Newton House**, it was much transformed over the centuries, being rebuilt in the 1660s and given corner towers in the 1750s and a new "Venetian Gothic" facade in the 1860s; it then fell into disrepair before being saved in the 1990s. It isn't the most distinguished of stately homes, but the basement and ground floor have been imaginatively set up as though it were a Sunday in 1912. Below stairs you can try your hand at brushing a top hat or correctly folding a shirt before progressing upstairs, where a formal lunch is laid out and a gramophone plays in the drawing room. Up the splendid staircase there are interesting displays on the Rhys family genealogy, the estate's heritage and the impact of World War II. The lovely **park**, mostly landscaped in the 1770s following suggestions by Capability Brown, now contains rare White Park cattle and fallow deer.

Carreg Cennen Castle

4 miles southeast of Llandeilo • Daily: April–Oct 9.30am–6.30pm; Nov–March 9.30am–4pm • £4 • ☎ 01558 822291, ⓦ carregcennencastle.com • CADW

Isolated in the rural hinterland southeast of Llandeilo is the most magnificently sited castle in Wales. **Carreg Cennen Castle** was constructed on its fearsome outcrop in 1248 (though Sir Urien, one of King Arthur's knights, is said to have built a fortress here earlier), but fell to Edward I in 1277. It remained in use until 1462, when it was partly destroyed by the Earl of Pembroke for being a rebel base.

The castle's most striking aspect is its vertiginous location, three hundred feet above a sheer drop into the green valley of the Cennen River. From the car park and **farm**, with rare breeds of cows and sheep, a path climbs sharply upwards, with astounding **views** towards the severe purple lines of the Black Mountain, in utter contrast to the velvet greenery of the Tywi and Cennen valleys. The castle seems impenetrable, its crumbling walls merging with the limestone on which it defiantly sits. The highlights of a visit are the views down into the valley and the long, damp descent into a pitch-black cave that served as a shelter in prehistoric times. Torches (which can be rented for £1.50 from the excellent tearoom near the car park) are essential; continue as far as possible and then turn them off to experience absolute darkness.

ARRIVAL AND DEPARTURE

LLANDEILO

By train The train station is on the eastern edge of the town centre and is on the scenic Heart of Wales railway, whichh runs from Swansea and Llanelli to Llandovery and Shrewsbury.

Destinations Llandovery (4 daily; 20min); Llandrindod Wells (4 daily; 1hr 20min); Llanelli (4 daily; 40min); Shrewsbury (4 daily; 2hr 50min); Swansea (4 daily; 1hr 10min).

By bus Buses stop on New Road. Buses along the A40 between Carmarthen and Llandeilo give access to Aberglasney and Dinefwr.

Destinations Carmarthen (10 daily; 40min); Llandovery (9 daily; 40min).

ACCOMMODATION

Abermarlais Caravan Park A40, 6 miles east of Llandeilo ☎ 01550 777868, ⓦ abermarlais caravanpark.co.uk. Spacious riverside campsite that's perfect for families. Closed Nov–Feb. Per pitch with one adult **£9**

The Cawdor 70 Rhosmaen St ☎ 01558 823500, ⓦ thecawdor.com. Llandeilo's focal point, this former coaching inn has been given a postmodern makeover with

delightful, simply decorated rooms (all different) and stunning attic suites. **£65**

★ **Fronlas** 7 Thomas St ☎ 01558 824733, ⓦ fronlas .com. This large terraced house has been creatively transformed into a modern three-room B&B, all bare boards, funky lighting, wild wallpapers and minimalist design. Breakfasts are largely organic and of local ingredients. The lounge has an honesty bar and good DVDs. **£80**

EATING AND DRINKING

★ **Angel Hotel** 62 Rhosmaen St ☎ 01558 822765, ⓦ angelbistro.co.uk. Convivial pub serving superb bar meals featuring daily specials, with a slightly more formal restaurant at the rear (mains £11–15). From Monday to Wednesday you'll pay £10 for two courses or £12 for three, or £12/14 on Friday and Saturday; Thursday is an internationally themed buffet. Food Mon–Sat 11.30am–3pm, 6–11pm (bar open Mon–Sat 11.30am–11pm, Sun 11am–11pm).

Barita 139 Rhosmaen St ☎ 01558 823444. A great deli (for fine Welsh cheeses) and health-food shop, with seating

upstairs to savour the coffee. Mon–Fri 9.30am–5.30pm, Sat 9.45am–5pm.

Carolita's Tex-Mex at The Sal 33 New Rd ☎ 01558 823325, ⓦ carolitas.co.uk. Behind the Salutation Inn (a fine locals' pub) is a walled courtyard and a real Tex-Mex grill, dishing up large portions of authentic food – save space for the Mexican wedding cookies. Thurs–Sat from 6pm (last orders 9pm), Sun 5–8pm.

The Cawdor 70 Rhosmaen St ☎ 01558 823500, ⓦ thecawdor.com. Excellent semi-formal restaurant serving sumptuous two- or three-course lunches

(£12/15) and dinners (£17/19.50), which might include grilled duck breast with sautéed celeriac and a red wine sauce. Good wine, guest ales and deep leather sofas also attract a broad clientele for bar snacks, cream teas or just a drink. Daily noon–2pm, 7–9pm, bar snacks 11am–6pm.

Heavenly 60 Rhosmaen St ☎01558 822800, ⓦ heavenlychoc.co.uk. Great organic ice cream and hand-made chocolates that are, well, heavenly.

Mon–Thurs 9.30am–5pm, Fri/Sat 9.30am–5.30pm, Sun 11.30am–3pm.

Plough Inn Rhosmaen ☎01558 823431, ⓦ ploughrhosmaen.com. Just a mile north of town, this famed pub-restaurant uses the best local ingredients to offer a set lunch (Mon–Sat; £8–16 for 1 to 3 courses) and dinner (Sun–Thurs; £14.50–18.25 for 2/3 courses), as well as an à la carte menu that's less exciting, apart from the curry of the day. Daily 11.30am–2.30pm, 5.30–9.30pm.

Llandovery and around

Twelve miles northeast of Llandeilo, the former cattle drovers' town of **LLANDOVERY** (Llanymddyfri) makes a natural base for exploring the Tywi Valley and the breathtaking countryside around Llyn Brianne and Dolaucothi to the north and west. The town's architecture and layout have changed little for centuries, the main Broad Street lined with solid early nineteenth-century townhouses and older inns, much as it was when itinerant writer George Borrow visited in 1854, remembering it as the "pleasantest little town in which I have halted in the course of my wanderings". The market hall, built in 1840, was new then, and is now the Dinefwr Crafts Centre, housing a café and stalls selling crafts such as oak furniture, love spoons and raku pottery.

The castle ruins

Open access • Free

On a grassy mound on the south side of Broad Street, the scant ruins of a thirteenth-century **castle** give fine views over Llandovery's huddled grey buildings and the Bran River, but the real draw is a ridiculously shiny stainless-steel sculpture of local lord Llywelyn ap Gruffydd Fychan, the "Welsh Braveheart", raised on the six-hundredth anniversary of his execution in the Market Square in front of the English king Henry IV, for supporting the rebel prince Owain Glyndŵr in 1401.

Llandovery Heritage Centre

Kings Rd • Easter–Sept daily 9.30am–5pm; Oct–Easter Mon–Sat 10am–4pm, Sun 11am–1pm • Donation appreciated

Above the tourist office, the community-run **Llandovery Heritage Centre** contains interesting displays on the legend of the Lady of the Lake from Llyn y Fan Fach; sixteenth-century outlaw Twm Sion Cati, the "Welsh Robin Hood"; seventeenth-century vicar Rhys Prichard, author of *Canwyll y Cymry* ("The Welshmen's Candle"); the Physicians of Myddfai (see p.150); and on the cattle drovers and their Black Ox bank, now part of LloydsTSB.

The Dolaucothi Gold Mine

Off A482, 10 miles northwest of Llandovery • Mid-March to June, Sept & Oct daily 11am–5pm; July & Aug 10am–6pm • Site £3.60, Roman & Victorian underground tours £3.80 each, £5.70 combined, level-access Long Adit tour £2.50 • ☎01558 650177 • NT

West of Llandovery the countryside is blissfully quiet, with a web of lanes that see little traffic. The principal route is the A482, which heads six miles from the A40 between Llandeilo and Llandovery to the **Dolaucothi Gold Mine**.

This is the only place in Britain where we can be sure the Romans mined gold, using remarkably advanced systems to extract the precious metal from the rock; an opencast mine and a few water channels can still be seen. The mine lay abandoned from around 350 AD until 1872, when new shafts were sunk and sporadically exploited until 1938. The site appears much as it was in the 1930s, and there are good displays, but you'll get a much better appreciation by joining one of the hard-hat underground tours.

Near the entrance to the mine is a stone used by the Romans for crushing gold ore; it's marked with indentations supposedly left by five saints who slept here one night, an event which gives its name to the straggling village of **PUMSAINT** (Five Saints). A former coach house in the centre of the village houses displays on village history and wildlife.

Talley Abbey

B4302, 9 miles west of Llandovery • Daily 9.30am–6.30pm • Free • CADW

The crumbling twelfth-century tower of Wales' only Premonstratensian **abbey** dominates the village of **TALLEY**, also home to the serene lakeside **church of St Michael**, rebuilt in 1773 (largely from the stones of the abbey) and still including its original box pews. Talley's more recent claim to fame is as the home of Wales' famous **Tipi Valley**, a hippy encampment set up in the 1970s just south near Cwmdu. Controversy has dogged the place ever since, but there now seems to be a stoic truce between the locals and the tipi dwellers. The *Cwmdu Arms* is a characterful community-run pub (the National Trust owns this and the Dolaucothi Arms in Pumsaint, which they also hope to reopen).

Dinas Nature Reserve

Four miles beyond Rhandirmwyn at the Ystradffin chapel, there's a car park (£1) for the RSPB's **Dinas Nature Reserve**, deep within which is the reputed hideout cave of Twm Sion Cati (see p.153). You're discouraged from seeking out the bandit's lair lest you disturb the woodpeckers, nuthatches, dippers, redstarts and pipits, but a spectacular trail loops through the gorge and ancient woodland.

Llyn Brianne

The **Llyn Brianne** reservoir, built in the 1970s (to supply Swansea) fits well into the hilly contours and offers peaceful shoreline walks. The land to the north is remote and spectacular, with walks following the Tywi valley into the Elenydd hills and to the Dolgoch hostel.

ARRIVAL AND DEPARTURE   LLANDOVERY

By bus Buses leave from the station and the car park by the Heritage Centre.
Destinations Brecon (5 daily; 40min); Carmarthen (8 daily; 1hr 20min); Dolaucothi (4 weekly; 25min); Lampeter (8 weekly; 45min); Llandeilo (9 daily; 40min).

By train The train station is on the main A40 just west of the town centre.
Destinations Llandeilo (4 daily; 20min); Llandrindod Wells (4 daily; 1hr); Llanelli (4 daily; 1hr 10min); Shrewsbury (4 daily; 2hr 30min); Swansea (4 daily; 1hr 30min).

INFORMATION

Tourist information On Kings Rd, by the central car park, the joint TIC and Brecon Beacons National Park visitor centre (Easter–Sept daily 9.30am–5pm; Oct–Easter Mon–Sat 10am–4pm; ☎ 01550 720693) is well stocked with leaflets on local walks and natural history, and has an interpretive centre on the Black Mountain. There's also a community tourism office in the train station in 2011, along with a café and the Pedal Power bike rental shop (☎ 01550 721420).

ACCOMMODATION

Cwmgwyn Farm Llangadog Rd, A4069 2 miles southwest ☎ 01550 720410, ⊕ cwmgwyn-holidays .co.uk. Charming farmhouse B&B with spacious rooms, tasty breakfasts and a wood-beamed lounge complete with inglenook fireplace. **£64**

Cynyll Farm A4069 5 miles southwest ☎ 01550 777316, ⊕ cynyllfarm.co.uk. Great-value, long-standing farmhouse B&B just northeast of Llangadog, where there are some great pubs. **£54**

The Drovers 9 Market Square ☎ 01550 721115, ⊕ droversllandovery.co.uk. Six elegant rooms, and a huge lounge with books and board games, in an eighteenth-century townhouse; superb breakfasts. **£65**

Henllys Estate 2 miles northwest ☎ 01550 721332, ⊕ henllysestate.co.uk. The best-value of the rural B&Bs hereabouts, with lovely oak-floored en-suite bedrooms, digital TV and good breakfasts. **£65**

New White Lion 43 Stone St ☎ 01550 720685, ⊕ newwhitelion.co.uk. An understated exterior hides

Llandovery's finest accommodation, combining modern style and selected antiques. **£110**

Royal Oak Inn Rhandirmwyn, 7 miles north of Llandovery ☎01550 760201, ⓦtheroyaloakinn.co.uk. Tucked away on quiet lanes, this popular pub offers pleasant B&B accommodation. **£75**

CAMPING

Erwlon 1 mile east of Llandovery off A40 ☎01550 720332, ⓦerwlon.co.uk. The nearest campsite to town, with caravan sites and camping. Pitches **£13**

Gellifechan 7 miles north, just beyond Rhandirmwyn ☎01550 760397. This basic tap-in-a-field campsite occupies an idyllic riverside site. Pitches **£6**

EATING AND DRINKING

Castle Hotel Kings Rd ☎01550 720343, ⓦcastle-hotel-llandovery.co.uk. The town's leading hotel has been given a cool makeover and is now also its classiest place to eat. There are plenty of leather sofas where you can enjoy coffee and cakes, plus bar areas and a more formal restaurant. Highlights of the menu include good cheese and seafood platters (£8.50–12.75), Welsh faggots (£9), Welsh lamb (£12.50) and steaks (from £17.50). Breakfast Mon–Fri 7–11am, Sat 8–11.30am; light refreshments 8am–6pm; lunch daily noon–3pm; dinner Mon–Thurs 6–9.30pm, Fri–Sat 6–10pm, Sun 6–8.30pm; bar Mon–Thurs 11am–11pm, Fri–Sat 11am–midnight, Sun 11am–10.30pm.

Karahi 34 High St ☎01550 720022. Great curry restaurant with a standard selection of north Indian curries plus unusual specialities such as fresh salmon kufta (£10) and a creamy lamb pasanda (£9). Daily noon–2.30pm, 5.30–11pm.

King's Head Inn 1 Market Square ☎01550 720393, ⓦkingsheadcoachinginn.co.uk. Come to this former drover's coaching inn for bar meals (£5–12), flaky drovers' beef pie (£9) or lamb shank (£13). Food daily noon–2.30pm, 6–9.30pm (8.30pm Sun); bar 10am–11pm.

Red Lion 2 Market Square. An eccentric old-fashioned pub (with beer served in jugs from the barrel) in an unsigned red, colonnaded house nestled in an easy-to-miss corner. Fri & Sat only; often closed by 10pm.

Royal Oak Inn Rhandirmwyn, 7 miles north of Llandovery ☎01550 760201, ⓦtheroyaloakinn.co.uk. Country pub that's well worth the trip for its imaginative menu of nicely cooked classics, and for its beer – it's been CAMRA's Carmarthenshire pub of the year four times already in the 21st century. Food daily noon–2pm, 6.30–9.30pm.

Southern Carmarthenshire

Frequently overlooked in the stampede towards the Pembrokeshire resorts, southern Carmarthenshire is a quiet part of the world, its coastline broken by the triple estuary of the Tywi, Taf and Gwendreath rivers. **Llansteffan** huddles below its ruined castle alongside the Tywi, while the Taf estuary is home to **Laugharne**, the region's sole big tourist attraction and a place of pilgrimage for Dylan Thomas lovers.

Llansteffan

The pretty village of **LLANSTEFFAN**, on the Tywi estuary ten miles southeast of Carmarthen, is overshadowed by a dramatic ruined **castle** (unrestricted access). This prime example of Norman fortifications was built between the eleventh and thirteenth centuries. The entrance used today is not the original gatehouse, which was converted into living quarters in the fourteenth century. In both gatehouses, however, the portcullis and murder holes can still be seen. Atop the towers, it's easy to appreciate the site's defensive position, with far-reaching views in all directions; long before the present castle, an Iron Age fort was occupied by 600 BC. Returning from the castle to where the path doubles back to the right near a house, continue straight ahead past the house for half a mile then left down the lane towards the beach. The door in the wall on the right conceals **St Anthony's Well** (Bwthyn Sant Antwn), which can supposedly heal lovesickness. At anything but high tide you can return via the beach.

2

Regular buses run from Carmarthen to Llansteffan (7 Mon–Sat; 3 Sun).

ACCOMMODATION

Bay Tree High St ☎ 01267 241237, ⓦ baytreellansteffan
.com. Opposite the Village Store, this friendly simple B&B
also sells fresh coracle-caught sea trout. **£60**

Pantyrathro Country Inn 2 miles towards

Carmarthen ☎ 01267 241014, ⓦ backpackers
hostelwales.co.uk. Slightly poky hostel-style
accommodation plus one double room, with a bar serving
Mexican food. Dorms **£14**; double **£30**

EATING AND DRINKING

The Village Store High St ☎ 01267 241888. The post
office shop houses an off-beat little café serving breakfasts,
light lunches (and a full Sunday lunch), sandwiches, coffee
and home-baked cakes; also themed evenings such as tapas
or Chinese food. Mon–Fri 9am–5pm, Sat & Sun 9am–1pm.

Yr Hen Dafarn High St ☎ 01267 241656. A superb
restaurant that's a real labour of love (booking essential).
The menu is seasonal and portions are large. Fri & Sat
nights only.

Laugharne

When quiet, the village of **LAUGHARNE** (Talacharn) is a delightful spot, with a ragged
castle looming over the reeds and tidal flats and narrow lanes snuggling in behind. But
Laugharne has increasingly been taken over by the legend of Dylan Thomas, the nearest
Wales has to a national poet.

Dylan Thomas Boathouse
Daily: May–Oct & Easter 10am–5.30pm; Nov–April 10.30am–3.30pm • £4 • ☎ 01994 427420, ⓦ www.dylanthomasboathouse.com

Down an exceedingly narrow lane (unsuitable for cars) beside the estuary, you'll reach

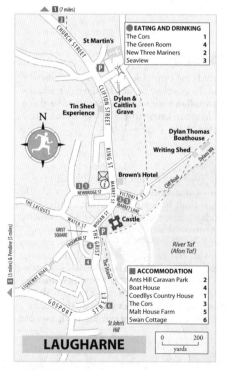

the **Dylan Thomas Boathouse**, the
simple home of Thomas, his wife
Caitlin and their three children from
1949 until 1953 when he died on a
lecture tour in New York. His death
was attributed to "a massive insult to
the brain" (spurred by numerous
whiskies), but it's possible he was a
victim of pneumonia or diabetes and
incompetent doctors. It's an
enchanting museum with a feeling of
inspirational peace above the
ever-changing water. In the bedrooms
upstairs are a video on Thomas' life
and a selection of local artists' views
of the estuary and the village.
Downstairs, the family parlour has
been preserved intact, with the rich
tones of the man himself reading his
work via a period wireless set. A small
tearoom (free entry) and outdoor
terrace look over the water.

Back along the lane, you can peer
into the green garage where Thomas
wrote: a wood-burning stove, curling
photographs of literary heroes, pen
collection and numerous
scrunched-up balls of paper under the
cheap desk suggest that he could

DYLAN THOMAS

Dylan Thomas (1914–53) was the quintessential Celt – fiery, verbose, richly talented and habitually drunk. Born into a snugly middle-class family in Swansea, Dylan's first glimmers of literary greatness came when he was posted, as a young reporter, on the *South Wales Evening Post* in Swansea; some of the most popular tales in his *Portrait of the Artist as a Young Dog* were inspired by his time working on the newspaper.

Rejecting the provincialism of Swansea and Welsh life, Thomas arrived in London as a broke twenty-year-old in 1934, weeks before the appearance of his first volume of poetry. Another volume soon followed, cementing the engaging young Welshman's reputation. Married in 1937, he and Caitlin returned to Wales, settling in the backwater of Laugharne, before moving to New Quay in Cardiganshire for part of World War II. Short stories – crackling with rich and melancholy humour – tumbled out as swiftly as poems, widening his base of admirers, although they remained few until well after his death. Despite his evident hedonism and his long days boozing in *Brown's Hotel*, Thomas was a self-disciplined writer, honing some of the most instantly recognizable poetry of the twentieth century. Perhaps better than anyone, he wrote in an identifiably Celtic, rhythmic wallow. Although Thomas knew little Welsh – he grew up when the native language was stridently discouraged – his English usage is definitively Welsh in its cadence and bold use of words.

Thomas, especially in public, liked to adopt the persona of an archetypal stage Welshman: sonorously loquacious, romantic and fond of a stiff tipple. This role was particularly popular in the United States, where he made lucrative lecture tours, and died in 1953. Just one month earlier, he had put the finishing touches to what many regard as his masterpiece: *Under Milk Wood*, the "play for voices". Describing the dreams, thoughts and lives of a Welsh seaside community over 24 hours, the play has never dipped out of fashion and has lured Wales' greatest stars, including Richard Burton and Anthony Hopkins, to the narrator's role. The small town of Llareggub (spelt Llaregyb by the BBC, which wouldn't allow the use of the expression "bugger all" backwards) is loosely based on Laugharne, New Quay, and a vast dose of Thomas' own imagination.

return at any minute. Thomas is buried with Caitlin, who died in 1994, in the graveyard of the parish church at the northern end of the village, marked by simple white crosses. Inside the church door is a painting by Benjamin West (the Anglo-American second president of the Royal Academy), plus a tenth-century Celtic cross in the south transept.

Brown's Hotel

Dylan's old boozing hole, **Brown's Hotel** on the main King Street, reopened as a hotel in 2012 – the nicotine-crusted front bar, probably fitted in the 1960s but inextricably associated with Thomas, has been reinstated.

Tin Shed Experience

Clifton St • Daily 10am–5.30pm • £3 • ⓦ tinshedexperience.co.uk

Just north of the village centre, the **Tin Shed Experience** is literally a tin garage housing mementoes of World War II; it's a key venue for The Laugharne Weekend (ⓦ thelaugharneweekend.com), a popular and relaxed arts festival in mid-April that's beginning to attract big names.

Laugharne Castle

April–Sept daily 10am–5pm • £3.20 • ☎ 01994 427906 • CADW

The main street courses down to the imposing ruins of **Laugharne Castle**. Built in the twelfth and thirteenth centuries, most of the original buildings were obliterated in Tudor times when Sir John Perrot transformed it into a splendid mansion. The "castle brown as owls" (Dylan Thomas) was largely destroyed in the Civil War. The mix of medieval might and Tudor finery is intriguing, especially in the Inner Ward, dominated by two towers, the domed roof of one giving sublime views over the huddled town. This is now surrounded by an attractive formal garden with fine mature trees; a gazebo contains an explanatory panel on another Welsh writer, Richard Hughes, best known for his novel *A High Wind in Jamaica*, who rented the adjoining Castle House from 1934 to 1942 and first brought Thomas to Laugharne.

Town hall

The tiny toytown **town hall** is the seat of Laugharne's unique Corporation, which has run the town since c.1290, with citizens electing a portreeve (mayor) and jury (council). The building is topped by a whitewashed Italianate bell tower, which once served as a single-cell prison.

INFORMATION	LAUGHARNE

Tourist information At Corran Books, opposite *Brown's Hotel* on King St (Mon–Sat 10am–5pm).

ACCOMMODATION

Ants Hill Caravan Park 1 mile north of Laugharne, on A4066 ☎07977 110095, ⓦantshill.co.uk. The closest camping and caravan park to town. March–Oct. Pitches **£20**

Boat House 1 Gosport St ☎01994 427263, ⓦtheboathousebnb.co.uk. Stylish, comfortable four-room B&B right in the centre. Great breakfasts might include vanilla waffles or smoked salmon. **£70**

★ **Coedllys Country House** Llangynin, 7 miles north of Laugharne ☎01994 231455, ⓦcoedllys countryhouse.co.uk. Wonderful, thoughtfully run farmhouse accommodation comprising three rooms, each with antique furniture, classy bedding and a comfy sofa. Visit the farm animal sanctuary or the fitness centre, which

has an exercise pool, spa and sauna. **£90**

The Cors Newbridge Rd ☎01994 427219 ⓦthecors .co.uk. A small, gracious country house amid lovely gardens. There are just two "shabby-chic" but comfortable rooms and a classy restaurant. **£80**

Malt House Farm ☎01994 427251, ⓦmalthouse farmbedandbreakfast.co.uk. Very friendly B&B on a real working organic beef farm 3 miles southwest, with two rooms with small bathrooms and two rooms sharing a big bathroom. Open all year. **£50**

Swan Cottage 20 Gosport St ☎01994 427409. Appealing one-room B&B with a nice garden and good rates for singles and extended stays. **£56**

EATING AND DRINKING

★ **The Cors** Newbridge Rd ☎01994 427219, ⓦthecors.co.uk. Excellent modern Welsh cuisine served casually by candlelight might include smoked haddock crème brûlée or grilled sewin (sea trout), with mains for around £20. Booking essential. The gardens are delightful, and there are two rooms (£80). Thurs–Sat evenings from 7pm.

New Three Mariners High St ☎01994 427426. Cheery

pub that offers the best drinking in town. No food. Bar open Mon–Fri 4–11pm, Sat & Sun noon–midnight.

Seaview Market Lane ☎01994 427030 ⓦseaview -laugharne.co.uk. An exquisite little restaurant with rooms (£80) in Dylan Thomas' home from 1938 to 1941; you can have 2/3 courses for £22/26, but the speciality is the nine-course tasting menu (£55, or £90 with selected wines). Tues–Sat 7–9pm, Sun noon–2.30pm.

Narberth and the Landsker Borderlands

Edging west into Pembrokeshire, the first town of any significance is **Narberth**, a cheerful little place with a burgeoning reputation for its upmarket shopping. It's also the "capital" of the **Landsker Borderlands**, a quiet, charming region dotted with some beautiful but little-visited villages. *Landsker* is a Norse word meaning "frontier", referring to the division between Cymric north Pembrokeshire and the anglicized south. The division goes back to the Norman colonization of the south of the county, though the name has only been used since the 1930s. The area is also home to Europe's largest wooden roller coasters at the **Oakwood** theme park, as well as the wonderful Celtic cross, castle and tidal mill at **Carew**.

Narberth

According to *The Mabinogion*, a collection of ancient Celtic folk tales and legends, NARBERTH (Arberth) was the court of Pwyll, and its ruined **castle** was probably the old home of the Welsh princes. Today, though, it has a growing reputation as Pembrokeshire's prime boutique **shopping** destination, with a dozen or so delis, galleries and clothing and homeware shops along High Street. You'll certainly notice the curious, spiky **town hall**, midway down High Street, built in the 1830s with a clock tower added in 1881, and now housing a gift shop. Outside, a plaque marks the cell where the leaders of the Rebecca Riots (see p.234) were imprisoned.

Further down the hill at 11 Market St, the Narberth Museum Bookshop (Mon–Fri 10.30am–4.30pm) is the public face of the town's **museum** project – opening in the former Bonded Stores on Church Street in the spring of 2012, it will display items from old shops and businesses, especially brewing and bottling, as well as nineteenth- and twentieth-century fans, costumes and military uniforms, and a geared penny-farthing bicycle, one of only six in the world.

The Queen's Hall

44 High St · ☎ 01834 861212, ⓦ thequeenshall.org.uk

At the top of High Street, **The Queen's Hall** is one of Pembrokeshire's best emerging venues, hosting concerts, comedy, theatre, art exhibitions in the Oriel Q gallery (Wed–Sat 10am–5pm) and on Thursday afternoons a farmers' market. You'll also find tourist information here.

ARRIVAL AND DEPARTURE

NARBERTH

By bus Buses stop at the top of High St and serve Carmarthen (3 daily; 40min); Haverfordwest (hourly; 20min); Tenby (hourly; 45min).

By train The train station is on the edge of the town a mile east from High St and serves Carmarthen (every 2hrs; 30min); Pembroke (every 2hr; 45min); Swansea (every 2hr; 1hr 25min); Tenby (every 2hr; 30min).

ACCOMMODATION

The Grove Molleston ☎ 01834 860 915, ⓦ thegrove-narberth.co.uk. Derelict in 2007, this Georgian mansion, under two miles southwest of Narberth, has been restored as one of Wales's finest country-house hotels, with delightful rooms and a superb restaurant. **£140**

Highland Grange Farm Robeston Wathen, 2 miles west on A40 ☎ 01834 860952, ⓦ highlandgrange.co.uk. Reliable guesthouse on a working farm with Shetland ponies. **£60**

Jabajak Banc y Llain, Llanboidy Rd, 3 miles north of

LITTLE ENGLAND BEYOND WALES

Ever since the Normans stormed their way through Wales, securing their rule with castles, Pembrokeshire has been effectively divided. But its colonization began even earlier, when seaborne Viking raiders seized the best land – the sandy southern coast and the fertile pasture of the Daugleddau estuary – and the Normans only continued an established practice by intermingling with the Vikings (to produce a very English racial mix) and restricting the Celtic Britons (the Welsh) to the northern part of the country.

Today, the racial divide of the past is still evident, delineated by what has become known as the **Landsker Line**, a vestigial boundary through the heart of Pembrokeshire. Along the line are some sixteen castles or castle mounds (such as Roche, Haverfordwest, Llawhaden and Narberth), while on either side of it, the village names are either demonstrably Welsh or anglicized. This historical partition explains why the area south of the line, dubbed "**Little England Beyond Wales**", has appealed to English migrants and tourists, while the north tends to attract Celts and other Europeans. Whereas the Tenby and Pembroke area has inclined towards the most Unionist of UK parties, the Conservatives (who hold very little sway in the rest of Wales), the north dallies between the old Liberal tradition and modern Welsh nationalism in the shape of Plaid Cymru.

Whitland ☎ 01994 448786, ⓦ jabajak.co.uk. Relaxed small hotel beside a budding vineyard. The emphasis is mainly on the food, but the rooms, some with four-poster beds, are comfy. **£90**

Plas Hyfryd Country Hotel Moorfield Rd, at the north end of town ☎ 01834 869006, ⓦ plashyfrydhotel.com. Comfortable fourteen-room hotel in a former rectory with restaurant and bar. **£76**

EATING AND DRINKING

The Angel High St, close to The Queen's Hall ☎ 01834 860579. The best spot in town for pub food such as steak and kidney pudding or veggie lasagne (both £7), and there's also a beer garden. Food daily 10am–9pm.

Jabajak Banc y Llain, Llanboidy Rd, 3 miles north of Whitland ☎ 01994 448786, ⓦ jabajak.co.uk. Bareboards and rock-walled restaurant where you might order half a dozen pan-fried local scallops (£9) followed by Welsh lamb with a citrus and cranberry sauce (£22.50). The wine list is very good, with their own white wine available from 2012. Mon–Sat evenings; bookings only.

Kirkland Arms St James St ☎ 01834 860423. Memorabilia-filled pub that's great for a beer or a game of pool. Daily 11am–11pm.

Sospan Fach 44 High St. Modern restaurant and café in The Queen's Hall serving tasty daytime snacks, soups, salads, mussels (£7), pasta (£8) or a Mexican platter (£9). Mon & Wed 9.30am–5pm, Tues & Thurs 11.30am–5pm, Fri & Sat 9.30am–8pm.

★ **Ultracomida** 7 High St ☎ 01834 861491, ⓦ ultracomida.co.uk. Perfect for lunch, this little slice of Spain tucked in behind a fabulous deli has hams hanging from the ceiling, large shared tables and a menu featuring delicious authentic Spanish tapas (around £4) or larger *raciones* (£9), washed down with Iberian wines. Deli, drinks and takeaways Mon–Sat 10am–6pm; restaurant Mon–Thurs noon–5pm, Fri & Sat to 9pm.

Oakwood

April–Oct daily 10am–5pm, mid-July to Aug to 6pm • £20 • ☎ 01834 891373, ⓦ oakwoodthemepark.co.uk

The A4075 heads south from the main A40 past **Oakwood**, Wales' largest theme park, and an exciting day out. Its forte is roller coasters, including Megafobia, the largest wooden roller coaster in Europe, and the stomach-churning Vertigo. There's also tobogganing, boating, go-karting and numerous smaller rides.

Blue Lagoon

School holidays daily 10am–9pm; school terms Mon–Thurs 10am–7pm (no swimming after 5pm), Fri 10am–9pm, Sat & Sun 10am–7pm • £6–10 for 3hr • ☎ 01834 862410, ⓦ bluelagoonwales.com

Near Oakwood is the new **Blue Lagoon** water park, with a wave pool, flumes and Lazy River; from 6pm every evening during school holidays there's a "beach party" with music, light effects and water fun getting steadily wilder. There's also the indoor Adventure Centre (£9–16 combined with the water park), with soft play, climbing wall, mini-golf, Wii gaming, Lego Room and the Techniquest interactive science centre, plus a ropes course (£20 extra).

The Eastern Cleddau

West of Narberth, quiet lanes wind down towards the muddy banks of the Cleddau estuary amid a charming landscape with inconsequential little settlements and some great, if sometimes slightly overgrown, walking following the waymarked **Knight's Way** and **Landsker Borderlands Trail**.

Lawrenny

Pretty **LAWRENNY** village, eight miles southwest of Narberth, is dominated by the magnificent twelfth-century **St Caradoc's church**. Half a mile away, the Cresswell and Carew rivers meet at **Lawrenny Quay** – there's good eating here at the *Quayside* café (see p.162), where you can borrow a laminated sheet for a lovely **loop walk** (3 miles; 1–2hr; 200ft ascent), weaving through the ancient oaks of Lawrenny Wood and giving fine views of the privately owned **Benton Castle** across the estuary.

2

ACCOMMODATION LAWRENNY

Knowles Farm 1 mile north of Lawrenny village ☎01834 891221, ⓦlawrenny.org.uk. A great organic farmhouse B&B, handy for some wonderful walks. **£70**
Millennium Youth Hostel ☎01646 651270,

ⓦlawrennyvillage.co.uk/hostel. An independent hostel in a Victorian schoolhouse 300yd beyond the church, with dorms and family rooms. Dorm beds **£15**

EATING AND DRINKING

Quayside Lawrenny Quay ☎01646 651574, ⓦquaysidelawrenny.co.uk. The staff really care about their food. Super-fresh panini compete with Welsh rarebit

or crab sandwiches (£8), served either in the airy pine interior or outside, where you can look out to yachts moored midstream. Easter–Sept daily 11am–5pm.

Carew

The pretty village of **CAREW** (Caeriw), four miles east of Pembroke, is famed for its 13ft **Celtic cross**, by the road just south of the river crossing. Erected as a memorial to Maredydd, ruler of Deheubarth, who died in 1035, the gracefully tapering shaft is covered in fine tracery of ancient Welsh designs.

Carew Castle and Tidal Mill

Daily: April–Oct 10am–5pm; Nov–March 11am–3pm • April–Oct £4.50; Nov–March £3 (castle only) • ⓦcarewcastle.com

An Elizabethan walled garden houses the ticket office for **Carew Castle and Tidal Mill**. Here you can pick up an explanatory leaflet and audioguide (free) for the castle, a hybrid of defensive necessity (c.1100) and Elizabethan whimsy. It offers an excellent example of the organic nature by which castles grew, from the Norman tower (probably the original gatehouse) and thirteenth-century battlements to the Tudor gatehouse and Elizabethan mansion grafted onto them.

Carew Tidal Mill

A few hundred yards west of the castle is the **Carew Tidal Mill**, probably established in the sixteenth century, rebuilt around 1800 and last used in 1937. The impressive exterior of the only restored tidal mill in Wales belies the pedestrian exhibitions and moderately interesting audiovisual displays of the milling process inside.

EATING AND DRINKING CAREW

Carew Inn ☎01646 651267, ⓦcarewinn.co.uk. A fine traditional inn for real ale and pub grub; an outdoor pool table is a feature of the pleasant garden. Lunch & dinner daily.
Cresselly Arms Cresswell Quay, 2 miles north ☎01646

651210. Ancient waterfront pub where beer comes in frothing jugs but food is conspicuously absent. On a fine evening when the tide is in, there can be few finer spots for a beer in west Wales. Mon–Fri noon–3pm, 5–11pm; all day Sat & Sun.

South Pembrokeshire coast

The southern zigzag of coast on either side of Tenby is a strange mix of caravan parks and Ministry of Defence shooting ranges above some spectacularly beautiful bays and gull-covered cliffs. For walkers, the coast is constantly beguiling, as it nips and tucks past some excellent, comparatively quiet beaches, many also accessible by car.

Northeast of Tenby, **SAUNDERSFOOT** and **AMROTH** have popular beaches, separated by cliffs topped by caravan parks. West of Tenby, worthwhile destinations include **MANORBIER**, with its dramatic castle above a small bay, and quintessentially pretty **ST FLORENCE**. You can stroll along the beautiful sandy **Barafundle Bay** and past the **BOSHERSTON** lily ponds at the National Trust's Stackpole Estate, then cross MOD land to the ancient **St Govan's chapel**, squeezed into a rock cleft above the crashing waves. The limestone sea arch known as the **Green Bridge of Wales** is the highlight of the dramatic scenery hereabouts, which gradually softens towards the village of **ANGLE**, facing the petrochemical installations across the actual harbour of Milford Haven.

Amroth

Six miles northeast of Tenby, the tiny beach village of **AMROTH** marks the eastern end of the 186-mile Pembrokeshire Coast Path, winding around every cove and cliff in the county, all the way to St Dogmael's, just outside Cardigan. The Carmarthen Bay Coast Walk starts half a mile to the east, with a surprisingly rugged five-mile hike to the tatty seaside resort of Pendine via Marros Beach.

Colby Woodland Gardens

Mid-Feb to Oct daily 10am–5pm • £4.60 • ☎ 01834 811885 • NT

The attractive Colby Woodland Gardens are wedged into a wooded valley a mile inland from Amroth, an area which was extensively mined for anthracite and iron ore until the nineteenth century. Highlights include the sloping walled garden and gazebo and, in May and June, the explosion of colour in the numerous rhododendron bushes. There are art and craft galleries (11am–5pm) and a useful tearoom (April–Oct 10am–5pm).

Saundersfoot

The cliffs between Amroth and Tenby are lined with caravan parks, although the Coast Path and cycle route pass below them from Wiseman's Bridge to Saundersfoot through former tramway tunnels. The only break is the picturesque harbour of **SAUNDERSFOOT**, built in the 1830s for the export of coal and anthracite. The industry has long since folded and the predictable clutch of cafés, tacky shops and boisterous pubs make the town a popular, good-natured place to hang out beside the wide yawn of sand.

ARRIVAL AND INFORMATION SAUNDERSFOOT

By bus and train Saundersfoot's train station is over a mile northwest up The Ridgeway from the harbour. Buses run roughly hourly to Tenby from the centre of the village.

Tourist information The TIC (Easter–Oct daily 10am–4pm; winter Thurs–Mon 10am–1pm; ☎01834 813672, ⓦvisit-saundersfoot.com) is on the harbourfront.

ACCOMMODATION

Cliff House Wogan Terrace ☎01834 813931, ⓦcliffhousebbsaundersfoot.co.uk. A lovely former ship-owner's home, this has great sea views. **£65**

St Brides Hotel St Brides Hill ☎01834 812304, ⓦstbridesspahotel.com. High on the hill overlooking the beach, this is one of Pembrokeshire's finer hotels, with contemporary style, an elegant restaurant and a spa with an infinity hydrotherapy pool. **£150**

EATING AND DRINKING

Royal Oak Inn Corner of the High St and Wogan Terrace. A homely freehouse for good food and beer in the centre of the village. Daily from 11am with food served noon–10pm (in season).

Swallow Tree Gardens caravan park Just south of town off B4316 ☎01834 812398, ⓦswallowtree.com. The restaurant here is a glorious surprise, offering quality British-pub-style cuisine with stylish twists, such as Thai chicken curry or goat's cheese ravioli (£8–10), or specials such as John Dory fillet with asparagus (£12–15), and a good Sunday lunch (£14/17 for 2/3 courses). Daily noon–4pm, Mon–Sat 5–10pm.

Wiseman's Bridge Inn 1.5 miles north ☎01834 813236, ⓦwisemansbridgeinn.co.uk. This thoroughly enjoyable beachside pub is good for a drink or a meal. Bar 11am–11pm, food noon–1.30pm, 6–9pm.

2

THE PEMBROKESHIRE NATIONAL PARK AND COAST PATH

Of the fifteen national parks in Britain, the **Pembrokeshire Coast National Park** is the only one that is predominantly sea-based, hugging the rippled coast around the entire southwestern section of Wales. Established in 1952, the park is not one contiguous mass, but rather a set of occasionally unconnected patches of coast and inland scenery. Starting at its southeastern corner, the first segment clings to the coast from Amroth through to the Milford Haven waterway, an area of sweeping limestone cliffs and some fabulous beaches. The second (and much the quietest) part lies around the pastoral landscape of the Daugleddau estuary, plunging deep into the rural heart of Pembrokeshire southeast of Haverfordwest. Superb for scenic cliff walking, the third section is around the beaches and resorts of St Bride's Bay, a great chunk scooped by the sea out of Wales' westernmost land. Finally, beyond Fishguard to the north, the park boundary runs far inland to encompass the Mynydd Preseli, a barren but invigoratingly beautiful range of hills dotted with ancient relics.

Following almost every wriggle of the coast, the **Pembrokeshire Coast Path** winds 186 miles from Amroth in the south, to its northernmost point at St Dogmael's near Cardigan. Mostly the path clings to the clifftops, overlooking rocks frequented by sunbathing seals, craggy offshore islands, unexpected gashes of sand and shrieking clouds of sea birds. Only on the southwestern end of the Castlemartin peninsula, given over to army training camps and firing ranges, does the path veer inland for any major length; it also ducks briefly inland along the Milford Haven estuary, where the huge expanse of hill-backed water lined by oil refineries provides one of the route's many surprises.

The Coast Path's most ruggedly inspiring segments are around St Davids Head and the Marloes peninsula, either side of St Bride's Bay; the stretch from the castle at Manorbier to the tiny cliff chapel at Bosherston along the southern coast; and the undulating contours, massive cliffs, bays and old ports along the northern coast, either side of Fishguard. These offer miles of windswept walking among great flashes of gorse, heather and seasonal plants, as well as close-quarter views of thousands of sea birds. Basking seals frequent some of the more inaccessible beaches, particularly around the time when pups are born in the autumn.

Spring is perhaps the finest season for walking: the crowds have yet to arrive and the clifftop flora is at its most vivid. The national park's excellent free newspaper, *Coast to Coast*, detailing special walks, boat trips and other events, is published every spring and can be picked up from visitor centres across the area. The best websites are the park's general site Ⓦ pembrokeshire coast.org.uk, and Ⓦ nt.pcnpa.org.uk, which concentrates on trail-specific info with plenty of trip-planning advice.

Readers with walking difficulties should pick up the *Easy Access Routes* booklet (£3), detailing flatter sections, many of which have been remodelled with gates rather than stiles.

Tenby and around

Beguilingly old-fashioned **TENBY** (Dinbych-y-Pysgod) is everything a seaside resort should be, wedged on a promontory between two sweeping beaches fronting an island-studded seascape. Narrow streets wind downhill from the medieval centre to the harbour, past miniature gardens fashioned to catch the afternoon sun. Steps down the steeper slopes give magical views of the dockside arches, while rows of brightly painted houses and hotels are strung along the clifftops. Simply walking around the streets and along the beaches at low tide is a delight, but Tenby is best visited during quiet times such as May or late September – in busy months, you'll be fighting for space with hordes of fellow holiday-makers.

Tenby is also one of the major stopping-off points along the **Pembrokeshire Coast Path**, providing walkers with a welcome interlude of glitter and excitement amid mile upon mile of undulating cliff scenery. A few miles offshore from Tenby, the monastic **Caldey Island** makes for a pleasant day-trip.

Tenby's old centre is triangular, with two sides meeting at the castle and the third following the remaining **town walls**, built in the late thirteenth century and massively strengthened in 1457 by Jasper Tudor, Earl of Pembroke and uncle of the future king,

Henry VII. Tenby was further fortified in the 1580s, when it was seen as a likely target for the Spanish Armada. The only town gate still standing is **Five Arches** (roughly halfway along the wall), a semicircular barbican with hidden lookouts and acute angles to surprise invaders, now busy with oblivious pedestrians. The wall continues south to the Esplanade, with a line of snooty hotels facing out over South Beach.

St Mary's church

The town centre's focal point is the 152ft spire of the largely fifteenth-century **St Mary's church**, between Tudor Square and St George's Street. Its light interior shows the elaborate ceiling bosses in the chancel to good effect, while fifteenth-century tombs attest to Tenby's mercantile tradition. On the church's western side runs Upper Frog Street, replete with craft shops and an arcaded indoor **market**, containing craft stalls and gift shops.

Tudor Merchant's House

Quay Hill • Mid-March to Oct Sun–Fri; Feb half-term & mid-July to end Aug daily 11am–5pm • £3 • ☎ 01834 842279 • NT

Quay Hill runs down towards the harbour past some of Tenby's oldest dwellings, including a **Tudor Merchant's House**, built in the late fifteenth century, when Tenby was second only to Bristol as a west-coast port. The compact house with its Flemish-style chimneypieces is on three floors, and has been filled with reproduction Tudor furniture that you are welcome to sit on. The rear herb garden gives a good view of the huge Flemish chimney.

The harbour

When it's not too crowded, the **harbour** can look idyllic. Sheltered by the curving headland and fringed by pastel-hued Georgian and Victorian houses, it's ideal for an evening stroll. By day, it's the departure point for numerous excursion boats, especially the short trip to Caldey Island.

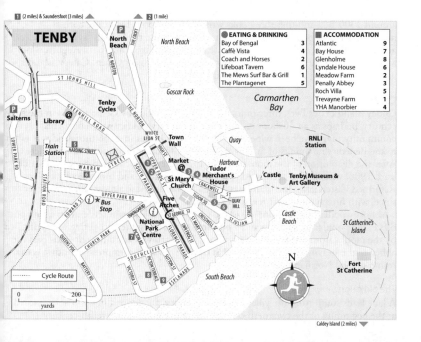

Caldey Island (2 miles) ▼

2

Castle Hill

Above the harbour is the headland of **Castle Hill**, its grassy slopes rife with Victoriana in the form of huge flowerbeds (including an indigenous small daffodil in springtime), benches, a bandstand and a pompous memorial to Prince Albert – upstaging the ruins of the Norman **castle**, notable for the all-round view from its windswept tower. On the north side of the headland, the modern RNLI **lifeboat station** (daily 8.30am–5.30pm; free) has photos of wrecked ships, videos, a viewing gallery and a schedule of launch exercises, plus a souvenir shop.

Castle Hill offers great views over the quieter **South Beach**, where the sea recedes so far at low tide that the tiny St Catherine's Island (no access) becomes fully beached. The island is topped by the remains of the 1869 St Catherine's Fort, one of Palmerston's Follies (see box, p.172).

Tenby Museum & Art Gallery

Castle Hill • Easter–Oct daily 10am–5pm; Nov–Easter Mon–Fri 10am–5pm • £4 • ⓦ tenbymuseum.org.uk ☎ 01834 842809

The **Tenby Museum & Art Gallery** presents a broad history of the town and harbour since the tenth century with a scale model showing the town in 1586, before it burst the town walls. The geology section includes ancient axes and a skull dated from around 1300 BC, and there are books written in the 1550s by locally born mathematician Robert Recorde, who was the first to use the "equals" symbol. The real attraction, though, is the art collection, featuring work by Tenby-born Augustus John and Nina Hamnet, as well as John Piper and Augustus' sister Gwen. Caldey Island also gets a look-in, with a replica of its Ogham Stone.

Caldey Island

Caldey Island (Ynys Pyr), three miles off Tenby, was settled by Celtic monks in the sixth century, perhaps as an offshoot of St Illtud's monastery at Llantwit Major. This community may have been wiped out in Viking raids, but in 1136 the island was given to the Benedictine monks of St Dogmael's at Cardigan, who founded a priory here. After the dissolution of the monasteries in 1536, the island changed hands willy-nilly until 1906, when it was again sold to a Benedictine order, and subsequently to Reformed Cistercians. The island has been a monastic home almost constantly ever since, with fifteen monks currently in residence.

A short woodland walk from the island's jetty leads to its main settlement: a tiny post office, the popular tea gardens and a **perfume shop** selling the herbal fragrances distilled by the monks from Caldey's abundant flora. The narrow road to the left leads past the abbey to the heavily restored **chapel of St David**, whose most impressive feature is the round-arched Norman door.

The old priory

A lane leads south from the village to the old **priory**, abandoned in 1536 and restored at the beginning of the twentieth century. Its centrepiece is the twelfth-century

GETTING TO CALDEY ISLAND

Boats leave Tenby Harbour (or Castle Beach when the tide is out) every 20–30 minutes for the twenty-minute journey to the island (Easter–Sept Mon–Sat, Oct Mon–Fri 10am–3pm, returning until 5pm; £10 return; ☎01834 844453, ⊛caldey-island.co.uk). Tickets (not for any specific sailing) are sold at the kiosk at the harbour.

St Illtud's church, distinguished by its curiously blunt (and leaning) steeple, and by the presence of one of the most significant pre-Norman finds in Wales. The sandstone **Ogham Stone**, with an inscription from the sixth century (added to, in Latin, during the ninth), was discovered under the stained-glass window on the south side of the nave. The church's rough sixth-century flooring consists largely of pebbles from the island's beaches. The lane continues south, climbing up to the gleaming white island **lighthouse**, built in 1828. Views from here are memorable.

ARRIVAL AND DEPARTURE   TENBY

By train The train station is just west of the town centre, at the bottom of Warren St.

Destinations Carmarthen (9 daily; 50min); Lamphey (9 daily; 20min); Narberth (9 daily; 20min); Pembroke (9 daily; 20min); Pembroke Dock (9 daily; 30min); Saundersfoot (9 daily; 10min); Swansea (8 daily; 1hr 45min); Whitland (9 daily; 30min).

By bus Local buses stop on South Parade at the top of Trafalgar Rd and on Upper Park Rd; National Express coaches call on Upper Park Rd.

Destinations Amroth (8 daily; 40min); Carew/Cresswell (4 daily; 40min); Carmarthen (1 daily; 1hr); Haverfordwest (hourly; 1hr); Manorbier (hourly; 20min); Narberth (hourly; 45min); Pembroke (hourly; 45min); Saundersfoot (2 hourly; 15min).

By car A word of warning: cars are banned in central Tenby from mid-July to the first weekend of September (daily 11am–5pm). Free shuttle buses (daily 10am–6pm) run from the Salterns and North Beach car parks (both pay-and-display), at the west and north side of the town centre, respectively.

INFORMATION

Tourist information The TIC (Easter–Oct Mon–Fri 9.30am–5pm, Sat & Sun 10am–4pm; Nov–Easter Mon–Sat 10am–4pm; ☎01834 842402, ⊜tenby.tic @pembrokeshire.gov.uk) is just along from the bus shelter on Upper Park Rd. You can also enquire at the Town Council at the top of Upper Frog St (Mon–Thurs 9am–5pm, Fri

9am–4.30pm).
The National Park Centre on South Parade (April–Sept daily 9.30am–5pm, Oct–March Mon–Sat 10.30am–3.30pm; ☎01834 845040, ⊜tenbycentre@pembrokeshirecoast .org.uk) has interesting child-friendly displays on the Pembrokeshire coast and around.

ACCOMMODATION

As a major resort, Tenby has dozens of hotels and guesthouses, all pressed from much the same mould. Prices are a little higher than elsewhere in west Wales, and in high summer (mid-July to early Sept) the place is close to bursting; at other times it's not hard to find reasonable **accommodation**. Otherwise, you might consider staying in Saundersfoot, Manorbier or St Florence. There are caravan sites all around Tenby: most take **tents**, especially those around the village of New Hedges, a mile or so north on the A478. In the peak summer season you'll also find tap-in-a-field sites which spring up for a couple of months.

HOTELS AND GUESTHOUSES

Atlantic The Esplanade ☎01834 842881,

⊛atlantic-hotel.uk.com. The best hotel along the South Beach, with fine rooms (some with sea views), a good

GHOST WALKS AND MORE

A nice way to explore Tenby is to join Marion Davies for her **Ghost Walk of Tenby** (mid-June to mid-Sept Mon–Sat at 8pm; £4.50; reservations recommended on ☎01834 845841 or 07970 420734, ⊛guidedtourswales.co.uk), which leaves from the Lifeboat Tavern in Tudor Square at 8pm and spends an hour and a half exploring the town's past and its inhabitants. She also leads other themed walks and offers out-of-season specials – see the notices at the tourist office or contact her directly.

2

restaurant and a pool and spa. Rates include breakfast. **£128**

★ **Bay House** 5 Picton Rd ☎01834 849015, ⓦbayhousetenby.co.uk. Considerable thought has gone into every aspect of this excellent three-room B&B, from the comfortable, restrained decor to the delicious breakfasts – especially the Glamorgan sausages. **£85**

Glenholme Picton Terrace ☎01834 843909, ⓦglenholmetenby.co.uk. Agreeable eight-room B&B near the town centre, with en-suite rooms and cycle storage. **£52**

Lyndale House Warren St ☎01834 842836, ⓦlyndalehouse.co.uk. Small, well-maintained B&B near the train station. Good single rates. **£68**

Penally Abbey 1 mile west of Tenby, close to Penally station ☎01834 843033, ⓦpenally-abbey.com. Luxurious country-house hotel on the site of a sixth-century abbey, with great sea views. Standards are very high, but the atmosphere is relaxed and the food unpretentious. **£145**

Roch Villa 1 Harding Villas ☎01834 843096, ⓦrochvillabandb.com. Budget B&B with three shared

bathrooms; rooms all have video or DVD player. Bed only **£20**

HOSTEL AND CAMPING

Meadow Farm Northcliffe ☎01834 844829. Under a mile north of town on the Coast Path, this campsite in a grassy field has only limited facilities but long views over the town towards Caldey Island – a great alternative to the family fun-park-style places. April–Oct. Per person **£7**

Trevayne Farm Monkstone, 2 miles north off A478 ☎01834 813402, ⓦcamping-pembrokeshire.co.uk. Family-oriented caravan and campsite with superb views over Saundersfoot and the sandy arc sweeping round to Amroth and Pendine. Closed Nov–March. Per tent with two adults **£10**

YHA Manorbier Skrinkle Haven ☎0845 371 9031, ⓔmanorbier@yha.org.uk. Modern hostel in an old MOD building overlooking the cliffs five miles west of Tenby, near the Manorbier bus route. Meals and camping facilities available. Closed Nov–Feb. Dorms **£14**

EATING AND DRINKING

There are dozens of **cafés** and **restaurants** around the town, and in high season the beachfronts (especially North Beach) are packed with cheap places that shut up shop in the winter.

Bay of Bengal 1 Crackwell St ☎01834 843331. Reliable BYOB curry restaurant. Ask for a seat downstairs, for great bay views. Daily all year from 5/5.30pm.

Caffè Vista 3 Crackwell St ☎01834 849636. Great little Greek-Australian-run café with excellent panini, espresso and cakes, plus a small selection of dishes such as beef or butterbean stew. Great harbour views from the small terrace, free wi-fi and it's licensed. Daily 9am–5pm, Thurs–Sat to 10.30pm in summer.

Coach and Horses Upper Frog St ☎01834 842704. Animated, wooden-beamed pub (said to be the oldest in Tenby) with good beer, well-prepared bar meals and some tasty Thai dishes. Bar noon–midnight; food noon–3pm, 6–9pm.

Lifeboat Tavern St Julian's St ☎01834 844948. Popular and enjoyable pub, with a youthful clientele; live music Tues & Sun. Daily noon–midnight.

★ **The Plantagenet** Quay Hill ☎01834 842350. This cosy and thoroughly enjoyable restaurant makes optimum use of local produce. It's in one of the oldest houses in Tenby – ask for a table inside the massive tenth-century Flemish chimney. Dinner mains go for £18–23 (£15 for vegetarian), but lunch is cheaper (£8 dishes), or just have a drink in the intimate bar. April–late Oct & Christmas/New Year daily, restaurant noon–2.30pm, 5–10pm; closed most of Jan & Feb; late Oct–March Fri dinner, Sat lunch/dinner, Sun lunch.

DIRECTORY

Banks The main banks are on Tudor Square and have ATMs and currency-changing facilities.

Bike rental Tenby Cycles, 16a The Norton (☎01834 845573, ⓦtenbycycles.co.uk), rents hybrids (£12 a day) as well as tag-a-longs and trailers.

Internet Free access at the library on Greenhill Rd (Mon–Fri 9.30am–5pm, Sat 9.30am–12.30pm); paid-for at

Café No.25, 25 High St. There's also free wi-fi at *Caffè Vista* (see above).

Leisure centre Marsh Rd ☎01834 843574. Facilities include swimming pool and gym.

Police Warren St ☎0845 330 2000.

Post office Warren St.

Taxis Tenby Taxis ☎01834 842371.

FESTIVALS

The week-long **Tenby Arts Festival** (ⓦtenbyartsfest.co.uk) in mid-Sept is fairly highbrow but has a rowdy and lively Fringe. The three-day **Tenby Blues Festival** (ⓦtenbyblues.co.uk) in mid-Nov is gaining in profile.

Manorbier and St Florence

Three miles southwest of Tenby around **Manorbier** and **St Florence** the Coast Path reaches the glorious, privately owned beach of **Lydstep Haven**; it's a beautiful spot, with limestone caverns to explore in the craggy Lydstep Point, and worth the small fee. Although some of the caverns are only accessible at low tide, the **Smugglers' Cave** is safe at all times.

Manorbier

As it proceeds west, the Coast Path veers inland to avoid the artillery range on Old Castle Head, then leads into the quaint village of **MANORBIER** (Maenorbŷr), pronounced "manner-beer", birthplace of Giraldus Cambrensis, Gerald of Wales (see p.380), who described the castle here, in which he was born in 1146, as "excellently well defended by turrets and bulwarks, and ... situated on the summit of a hill extending on the western side towards the sea".

Manorbier Castle

April–Sept & Oct half-term daily 10am–6pm • £4 • ☎ 01834 871394, Ⓦ manorbiercastle.co.uk

Founded in the early twelfth century as a baronial residence, the **castle** sits above the village and its beach on a hill of wild gorse. The Norman walls are very well preserved, surrounding walled gardens and a grass courtyard in which the extensive remains of the castle's chapel and staterooms jostle for position with the nineteenth-century domestic residence. Views from the ramparts are wonderful, taking in the corrugated coastline, bushy dunes, deep-green fields and smoking chimneys of the tinted village houses. In the walls and buildings is a warren of dark passageways to explore, occasionally opening out into little cells populated by lacklustre wax figures, including Gerald himself.

St James' church

Daily 9.30am–5.30pm

The lane below the castle leads past the curious, elongated tower of **St James' church**, a Norman structure whose rough stonework has recently been rendered with a "buttermilk limewash" to mimic how the whole church would apparently once have looked. It's a striking sight but not universally popular.

The beaches

Below the church, a sandy break in the red sandstone cliffs reveals Manorbier's shell-shaped **cove**. For more secluded bathing, follow the path on the left of the beach (as you face the sea) over the headland called the Priest's Nose, past a Neolithic cromlech (burial chamber) known as the **King's Quoit**, and round for just over half a mile to the steep steps down to often-deserted **Presipe Beach**. High tides can cover the whole beach, so check times. Alternatively, follow the Coast Path two-and-a-half miles right/west to Swanlake Bay, known for its stunning rock pools and formations.

St Florence

Three miles north of Manorbier is the delightful little village of **ST FLORENCE**, whose whitewashed stone cottages, many with their original medieval Flemish chimneystacks, huddle around tiny lanes. St Florence was once an important port, though its inlet has long since silted up, leaving a lovely walk down to Penally (on the edge of Tenby, three miles southeast) beside the usually dry bed of Ritec stream.

Mid-Pembrokeshire

Central Pembrokeshire is generally ignored by visitors intent on reaching the more obvious coastal pleasures to the south and west. None of the towns is especially interesting, but they're the county's largest settlements.

Historically, the most significant is **Pembroke**, the old county town on the Pembroke River, a continuation of the massive **Milford Haven** waterway, described by Nelson as the greatest natural harbour in the world. Yet despite its location and its formidable **castle** (and the nearby ruins of the Bishop's Palace at **Lamphey**), Pembroke is rather dull.

The river links Pembroke to **Pembroke Dock**, on the southern banks of the magnificent Daugleddau River estuary, from where ferries leave for Ireland. Across the water, American Quakers founded the town of **Milford Haven**, which has a dramatic setting and a good museum but probably won't detain you long.

Seven miles to the north, the region's chief town, **Haverfordwest**, is an important market and transport centre. Despite some handsome architecture, it remains rather soulless, though it's made more palatable by its proximity to **Scolton Manor**, housing the county museum, and **Picton Castle**.

A branch line leaves the main Swansea–Fishguard railway at Whitland, calling at Narberth and Tenby en route to Pembroke and Pembroke Dock. A second spur peels off the main line at Clarbeston Road for Haverfordwest and Milford Haven. There's a reasonable **bus** service throughout the area, with most routes starting at either Pembroke or Haverfordwest.

Pembroke and beyond

The old county town of **PEMBROKE** (Penfro) grew up solely to serve its castle, the mightiest link in the chain of Norman strongholds across southern Wales and the base for the invasion of Ireland in 1171. Drawn out along a ridge, the walled town flourished as a port shipping local goods to all parts of Britain, as well as Ireland, France and Spain. Though it chose the winning side during the Wars of the Roses, Pembroke was less fortunate in the Civil War, being besieged and captured by Cromwell.

Though it subsequently became a centre of leather-making, weaving, dyeing and tailoring, Pembroke never regained its former importance, and was in grave decline by the twentieth century, its port long since overtaken by nearby rivals. Happily this means that central Pembroke was spared postwar redevelopment, although the fringes around the main street are largely modern and bland.

History buffs shouldn't pass up a trip out to the ruined Bishop's Palace in **Lamphey**, though unless you're off to Ireland you might skip **Pembroke Dock**.

The town's sole thoroughfare, **Main Street** stretches from the **train station** (as Station Rd) in the east to the mighty walls of the castle. Partway along, Blackhorse Walk runs north beside **St Michael's church**, down to the lovely **Mill Pond** and the most impressive remnants of the thirteenth-century town **walls**, between the demolished East Gate and **Barnard's Tower**, a medieval towered house attached to the walls. The mill pond is now a nature reserve (unrestricted access) and home to swans and otters.

The castle

Daily: April–Sept 9.30am–6pm; March & Oct 10am–5pm; Nov–Feb 10am–4pm • £5.25 • ☎ 01646 684585, ⓦ pembrokecastle.co.uk

In the early years following the Norman invasion, the people of Deheubarth (west Wales) avoided conquest thanks to a tacit agreement between Rhys ap Tewdwr and the Normans, but after Rhys' death fighting the Normans in 1093, Lord Roger de Montgomery immediately invaded and raised a castle, rebuilt in stone after 1189. Protected by a hill on its southern side and water on the other three, **Pembroke Castle** proved impregnable for the next four centuries, enforcing the rule of "Little England Beyond Wales" (see p.159). In 1452, Henry VI granted the castle to Jasper Tudor, whose nephew Harri was born here, later becoming the Lancastrian heir to the throne, and, in 1485, King Henry VII. During the Civil War, Pembroke was a Parliamentarian stronghold until its military governor suddenly switched to the

Royalist side in 1648. Cromwell's 48-day siege of the town only succeeded after he cut off its water supply. There's a new café, gift shop and a brass-rubbing centre here, very handy on a rainy day.

The gatehouse

Despite Cromwell's battering and centuries of subsequent neglect, the castle's sheer, bloody-minded bulk still inspires awe, even if it's largely due to extensive restoration over the last century. You enter through the soaring **gatehouse**, home to some excellent displays on the history of the castle, the Tudor empire and the Civil War. The intact walls and towers contain many walkways and dark passages that give ample chance to chase around spiral stairways into great oak-beamed halls. Eventually you'll descend into the large, grassy courtyard, enclosed by battlements and punctuated by hulking towers where the town walls formerly joined the fortress.

The keep and Wogan Cavern

In the inner ward, the 75ft-high Norman **keep** has walls 18ft thick and a high domed interior. Alongside, you can peer down into the gloomy cell below the Dungeon Tower, housing a model of its last prisoner.

Steps beside this lead far down into **Wogan Cavern**, a huge natural cavern, dank and slimy, where light beams in through a barred hole in the wall facing out over the waterside path. Inhabited at least 12,000 years ago, the cavern was fortified by the Normans, who built the spiral staircase by which you enter.

ARRIVAL AND DEPARTURE   **PEMBROKE**

By train The train station is off Upper Lamphey Rd, east of the town centre.

Destinations Lamphey (9 daily; 3min); Manorbier (9 daily; 12min); Pembroke Dock (9 daily; 10min); Swansea (8 daily; 2hr 10min); Tenby (9 daily; 20min); Whitland (9 daily; 50min).

By bus Buses stop near the castle on Main St.

Destinations Angle (6 daily, Oct–April Mon, Thurs & Sat 4 daily; 30min/1hr 25min); Bosherston (6 daily, Oct–April Mon, Thurs & Sat 4 daily; 35min/1hr); Carew/Cresswell (4 daily; 20min); Castlemartin (6 daily, Oct–April Mon, Thurs & Sat 4 daily; 40min/1hr 10min); Haverfordwest (hourly; 55min); Manorbier (hourly; 20min); Milford Haven (hourly; 50min); Pembroke Dock (3 hourly; 10min); Stackpole (6 daily, Oct–April Mon, Thurs & Sat 4 daily; 30min/1hr 15min); Tenby (hourly; 40min).

INFORMATION

Tourist information and **internet** The TIC (Easter–Oct Mon–Fri 10am–4pm, Sat 10am–1pm; winter Tues–Sat 10am–1pm; ☎01646 776499, ✉pembroke.tic @pembrokeshire.gov.uk), on Commons Rd parallel to Main Street, can provide a useful free town guide and information on the Pembrokeshire National Park and Coast Path. The library, in the same building, offers free internet access.

ACCOMMODATION

Beech House B&B 76–78 Main St ☎01646 683740, ⓦbeechhousepembroke.com. Rooms here only have shared bathrooms, but for comfort, style and hospitality it easily outdoes places charging twice as much. Per person **£20**

Poyerston Farm Off A477 3 miles northeast of Pembroke ☎01646 651347, ⓦpoyerstonfarm.co.uk. Open all year, this is a top-quality farmhouse B&B. **£70**

Tregenna 7 Upper Lamphey Rd ☎01646 621525, ⓦtregennapembroke.co.uk. If *Beech House* is full, try one of the four en-suite rooms here, about 800m beyond the train station. **£55**

EATING AND DRINKING

The Courtyard Trewent Court, rear of 25 Main St ☎01646 622144. A good new place for coffee, cakes and light lunches. Mon–Sat 9am–5pm.

Old King's Arms 13 Main St ☎01646 683611. This pub serves good bar meals and more substantial restaurant dishes. Food served noon–2.15pm, 6.30–10pm.

Quayside Café The Cornstore, North Quay ☎01646 684290. Down by the river, this serves good espresso and light meals. Mon–Sat 10am–5pm.

2

PALMERSTON'S FOLLIES

The coast of southern Britain, and particularly that of south Pembrokeshire, is littered with what are known as **Palmerston's Follies**, nineteenth-century naval defences that never saw action. As Prime Minister in 1860, Lord Palmerston felt that Britain was ill-prepared to withstand an attack by Napoleon III, who was newly equipped with iron-clad battleships. Britain's navy had barely been upgraded since Nelson's victory at Trafalgar half a century earlier, so a Royal Commission recommended building a series of forts to protect naval dockyards while the navy modernized.

Palmerston wholeheartedly backed the recommendation and had forts built right along the south coast of England and around Milford Haven and Pembroke. By the time they were completed in the 1880s, Anglo-French relations had improved, and the forts were never attacked. Arguably, the forts had been an effective deterrent, but in the public eye they became known as Palmerston's Follies. Most remain inaccessible to the public, though you can visit the Gun Tower at Pembroke Dock.

The best examples around Pembrokeshire are at Tenby, West Angle Bay, West Blockhouse Point and Milford Haven.

Pembroke Dock

Workaday **PEMBROKE DOCK** (Doc Penfro), three miles north of Pembroke, is principally of interest for its ferries to Rosslare in Ireland and its naval dockyard, active from 1814 to 1926 and now slowly awakening from suspended animation. The Garrison Chapel, the only Neoclassical Georgian church in Wales, has been restored, along with the adjoining Town Market, and is to become a heritage centre. The **Flying Boat Centre** at the western end of the docks (Gate 4; Tues–Sat 10am–4pm; free; ⓦsunderlandtrust.org.uk) recalls the time during World War II when this was the world's largest flying boat base, with informative panels, models and relics from sunken planes.

The Gun Tower

Front St · Easter–Oct Sun–Fri 10am–4pm · £2.50 · ☎ 01646 622246, ⓦ guntowermuseum.org.uk

The harbourside **Gun Tower**, one of Palmerston's Follies (see box above), was built in 1851 and now houses a few moderately diverting exhibits on the history of the town and dockyard. There's a smaller Martello tower (not open) at the western end of Fort Road, just beyond the Flying Boat Centre.

ARRIVAL AND DEPARTURE   PEMBROKE DOCK

By train Pembroke Dock's train station is in the centre of town, 0.5 miles east of the ferry terminal.
Destinations Carmarthen (every 2hr; 1hr 20min); Pembroke (every 2hr; 8min); Swansea (every 2hr; 2hr 15min); Tenby (every 2hr; 30min).
By bus Buses stop on Laws St, just west of the train station.

Destinations Carew (4 daily; 15min); Haverfordwest (hourly; 40min); Milford Haven (hourly; 30min); Pembroke (3 hourly; 10min); Tenby (hourly; 1hr).
By ferry Irish Ferries (☎ 08705 329543, ⓦ irishferries .com) sail to Rosslare; ships currently depart at 2.45am and 2.45pm, and the journey takes four hours.

CLEDDAU BRIDGE

One of the most impressive sights in this part of Wales is the view from the 1970s **Cleddau Bridge** (car toll 75p) between Pembroke Dock and Neyland on the north bank; it's open to pedestrians and cyclists, with National Cycle Network route 4 continuing to Haverfordwest on the traffic-free Brunel Trail. The views are magical, especially at sunset, with the masts of boats far below and the full skies reflected in the clear water. Even the refineries look attractive from this far up.

ACCOMMODATION

Borders 25 Park St ☏01646 689089 ⓦbandbwith theborders.co.uk. A warm and friendly B&B near the station; pick-ups from the ferry can be arranged, as can evening meals. There's a sunny patio with barbecue, wi-fi, and bike storage. **£50**

Lamphey

The pleasant village of **LAMPHEY** (Llandyfai), two miles east of Pembroke, is best known for the ruined **Bishop's Palace**, off a quiet lane to the north of the settlement.

Bishop's Palace

Daily April–Oct 10am–5pm • £3.20 • ☏01646 672224 • CADW

Dating from at least the thirteenth century and abandoned at the Reformation in the mid-sixteenth century, the palace was built as a country retreat for the bishops of St Davids. Stout walls surround the scattered ruins, and many of the palace buildings have long been lost under the grassy banks. Most impressive are the remains of the Great Hall at the eastern end of the complex, topped by the fourteenth-century Bishop Gower's hallmark arcaded parapets, similar to those he added to the Bishop's Palace of St Davids. Lit only by narrow slits, the gloomy undercroft below the Great Hall has the feeling of a crypt.

ACCOMMODATION   LAMPHEY

Lamphey Court Hotel & Spa ☏01646 672273, ⓦlampheycourt.co.uk. Grand if slightly over-the-top accommodation, with spa, opposite the palace ruins. **£134**
Lower Lamphey Park ☏01646 672906, ⓦlowerlampheypark.co.uk. A characterful three-room Georgian farmhouse, with some outbuildings converted into self-catering cottages. **£60**

Portclew House Freshwater East, 2 miles south of Lamphey ☏01646 672800, ⓦportclewhouse.co.uk. Half a mile from the superb beach of Freshwater East, this Grade II-listed Georgian house offers seven spacious rooms, plus self-catering units. **£56**

Stackpole Quay to Angle

One of the best starting points for breathtaking clifftop walks is the National Trust's **Stackpole Estate**, encompassing a few miles of coast and some beautiful inland waterways and woods.

Stackpole Quay

Road access is at two main points, the westernmost being the gorgeous harbour of **Stackpole Quay** (parking £2.50). It's one of the smallest harbours you'll find anywhere, with barely room for four boats between its slabs of stratified limestone. A half-mile walk brings you to **Barafundle Bay**, inaccessible by car and one of the finest beaches in Wales, with clear water and a soft, sandy beach fringed by wooded cliffs.

South of the beach, a spectacular stretch of the Coast Path leads to **Stackpole Head**, a tufted plateau on craggy arches jutting into the sea. The Stackpole estate is home to around twenty pairs of choughs, about five percent of the British population.

ACCOMMODATION, EATING AND DRINKING   STACKPOLE

Boathouse Tearoom Stackpole Quay ☏01646 672687. Tasty lunches are served in a sheltered, sunny courtyard by the quay. Easter–Oct daily; winter Fri–Sun 11am–4pm.
Stackpole Inn Jason's corner, Stackpole village ☏01646 672324, ⓦstackpoleinn.co.uk. Serves real ales and does superb pub meals with straightforward lunches

(mains £5–8) and more elaborate dinners (not Sun; mains £13.50–20) such as pan-fried sea bass or Moroccan lamb cutlets. They also have spacious and pleasant nautically themed rooms. Food served Mon–Fri noon–2pm, 6.30–9pm, Sat noon–11pm, Sun noon–2.30pm, 6.30–9pm. **£90**

Bosherston Lily Ponds

Open access • Free

The Coast Path continues through the dunes of **Stackpole Warren** to **BROAD HAVEN** – the next spot on the coast accessible by car – where a nice small beach overlooks several rocky islets owned by the National Trust. Just inland are the **Bosherston Lily Ponds**, three reed-fringed fingers of water created in the late eighteenth century for coarse fishing, and now beautifully landscaped, though the lilies no longer carpet its surface as they once did. The westernmost lake remains the prettiest, especially in June and July, when the flowers are in full bloom. You can still fish here, with a permit (£6 a day; closed mid-March to mid-June) from *Ye Olde Worlde Café*, a hundred yards away in the village of **BOSHERSTON**.

St Govan's chapel

From Bosherston it's a mile to the coast across the army training grounds, by a road that is usually open at weekends but frequently closed Monday to Friday. Firing orders are posted outside *Ye Olde Worlde Café* or call ☎01646 662367 after 4.30pm for the next day's programme. Follow the lane through the MOD checkpoint to a spot overlooking the cliffs where **St Govan's chapel** is wedged. This tiny grey structure is at least eight (and possibly as much as fourteen) centuries old. Legend has it that when St Govan was attacked here by pirates in the sixth century, the cliffs opened up and folded gently around him, saving him from certain death; he later chose to be buried here. Steps descend into the sandy-floored chapel, with its simple stone altar, and thence to a small cell hewn from the rock, containing the fissure that reputedly sheltered Govan. The steps continue all the way down to the spume-flecked sea for a magnificent close-up view of the precarious crags, caves and arches.

The Castlemartin Ranges

The area west of Broad Haven is the MOD's **Castlemartin Ranges** and is entirely out of bounds except for a four-mile clifftop strip on which the Coast Path and bridleway lead past the striking cleft of **Huntsman's Leap** and two isolated beaches at **Bullslaughter** and **Flimston Bay**, to **Stack Rocks**. This area, known as Range East, is open to the public when firing is not taking place, ie at weekends, bank holidays, August, Christmas and New Year, and most evenings after about 4.30pm – call ☎01646 662367 for recorded information. National Park rangers lead occasional walks here and in the otherwise closed Range West (☎01834 845040; £4/evening (4hr), £8/day); despite the military activity, the ranges are rich in wildflowers, butterflies and choughs. An inland alternative is the new offroad trail from Bosherston to the army camp of **MERRION**, on the B4319. The only vehicle access to the coast is a lane (open only as above) from Merrion to Stack Rocks past the mournful little chapel at **FLIMSTON**, a hamlet forcibly abandoned to the army.

Stack Rocks jut out of the sea here like a series of tall, lichen-spattered stepping stones. A hundred yards further west (as far as you're allowed to go), a graceful limestone arch rises from a wave-flattened rock platform, known as the **Green Bridge of Wales**. On a quiet day, the only company you will have are the shrieking gulls, guillemots and kittiwakes swooping to their perches on the limestone ledges.

Freshwater West

The Coast Path (or the Coastal Cruiser bus) follows the B4319 a couple of miles to **Freshwater West**, a beach that's great for **surfing**, though the currents can be too strong for swimming. Behind the beach, desolate wind-battered dunes, recently used as locations for Robin Hood and Harry Potter films, make for interesting walking; there's also good birdwatching here.

Angle

The B4319 meets the B4320 from Pembroke near the **Devil's Quoit**, a Neolithic burial chamber topped by an impressive capstone. It continues down the final finger of the peninsula, to the remote village of **ANGLE** at the western end of a wide curve of mud known as **Angle Bay**, much frequented by migrating waders such as redshank, curlew, whimbrel, dunlin and turnstone. Angle consists of one long street, bounded by old, coloured cottages. **West Angle Bay**, a secluded spot a mile to the west of the village, is better for swimming, and overlooks one of Lord Palmerston's forts (see p.172) on **Thorn Island**.

2

EATING AND DRINKING   ANGLE

Hibernia Inn ☎ 01646 641517 ⓦ thehibernia.co.uk. A convivial pub in the heart of the village, serving home-cooked food that's great value for money. Daily noon–2pm, 7–9pm.
Old Point House ☎ 01646 641205. A delightful rustic inn (reached by walking behind the church and 10min east along the shore), whose fire is said to have burned

continuously for over three hundred years until the mid-1990s, since when it has only been lit in winter. Quality meals come in large portions: the specials board usually includes several examples of the day's catch. Mon–Sat 12.30–2.30pm, 6.30–8.30pm; Sun lunch only 12.30–2.30pm; closed Tues Nov–March.

Milford Haven

Taking its name from the waterway, the town of **MILFORD HAVEN** (Aberdaugleddau), four miles west of Neyland, was founded in 1790 by Quakers from Nantucket, brought here to work as whalers. Their grid pattern – principally three streets rising sharply parallel to the waterway – survives today, although the town stagnated until developing as a major fishing port from the 1880s. Despite a magnificent site and interesting heritage, Milford Haven hasn't got much going for it. The town centre has seen hard times of late, receiving little of the funding pumped into the sterile marina development in the old docks.

The only reasons to stray from the docks into the town proper are to enjoy the view of the haven from Hamilton Terrace, and to visit the Torch **theatre** (ⓦ www.torchtheatre .co.uk), on St Peter's Road, home to west Wales' only professional theatre company as well as a cinema and a good café.

The waterside

The waterside is undeniably impressive, with ferries and tankers ploughing the glittering waters of the Haven that stretch out below the pleasant public gardens. Hamilton Terrace runs past the gardens and down to the revamped docks, where you'll find the interesting **Milford Haven Museum** and, on the other side, the **Waterfront Gallery** in The Old Sail Loft (Mon–Sat & summer Suns 10.30am–5pm; ⓦ thewaterfrontgallery.co.uk; free).

Milford Haven Museum

Easter–Oct Mon–Sat 11am–5pm, Sun during school holidays & bank holiday weekends noon–5pm • £1.50 • ☎ 01646 694496

In the former Customs House (1797), the museum's exhibits include photographs and mementos from the fishing trade, details of the town's Quaker origins, some fascinating material on Milford Haven in wartime, when massive convoys formed here, and coverage of the modern oil industry.

ARRIVAL AND DEPARTURE   MILFORD HAVEN

By train Milford Haven train station is located under the Hakin road bridge, next to the docks.
Destinations Carmarthen (11 daily; 1hr); Haverfordwest (11 daily; 15min); Swansea (8 daily; 2hr 20min).
By bus Buses stop at Tesco near the train station and on

Charles St (westbound)/Hamilton Terrace (north/eastbound).
Destinations Dale (3 daily; 30min); Haverfordwest (every 30min; 25min); Marloes (3 daily; 40min); Pembroke (hourly; 50min).

2

THE PEMBROKESHIRE ENERGY INDUSTRIES

On both sides of the magnificent Milford Haven waterway, the most prominent landscape features belong to the **refineries** fringing the haven since 1960. Storage tanks, observation towers and security fences litter the Coast Path here, the most blighted stretch being the five miles between the west side of the Pembroke River estuary and Angle Bay, facing the town of Milford Haven.

The presence of so much polluting and potentially hazardous industry seems totally out of place in this rural setting. The situation has improved over the years, with one refinery closing down and the two remaining plants cleaning up their acts considerably. But controversy continues as Milford Haven gears up to become the UK's major importer of liquefied natural gas (LNG). As the nation's North Sea reserves run out, Britain is looking to the Middle East to supply its needs. Around £4 billion worth of the stuff is supposed to arrive in massive supertankers over the next fifteen years, mainly from Qatar. A couple of huge new storage and gasification installations have recently been commissioned, and a new gas-fired power station will open in 2012. To connect these to the gas supply network, a new, buried pipeline threads across south Wales, intruding into the Brecon Beacons National Park.

Though the project is enthusiastically backed by the Welsh Assembly and Pembrokeshire County Council, many locals are less keen. Fears over the safety of tankers and general discontent over the disruption during construction have seen numerous protests, but the project rolls inexorably on.

INFORMATION

Tourist information The TIC is in the library at 19 Cedar Court, in the retail park just west of the train station ☎ 01437 771818, ✉ milford.tic@pembrokeshire.gov.uk (April–Oct Mon–Fri 10am–4pm, Sat 10am–1pm; Nov–March Mon, Wed, Fri & Sat 10am–1pm).

ACCOMMODATION

Belhaven House 29 Hamilton Terrace ☎ 01646 695983, ⓦ westwaleshotel.com. One of the nicer places in town, overlooking the gardens and haven; all rooms en suite. **£65**

Sandy Haven Near Herbrandston ☎ 01646 698844, ⓦ sandyhavencampingpark.co.uk. A quiet little site right by the water two miles west of town. Closed mid-Sept till just before Easter. Two-person tents **£12**

EATING AND DRINKING

The Harbourmaster Nelson Quay ☎ 01646 695493, ⓦ theharbourmaster.co.uk. A bar-restaurant at the marina, offering an all-day bar menu (c.£7) and an Italian-influenced evening menu using fresh local produce (£13–16). Daily noon–11pm, Fri & Sat till midnight.

Martha's Vineyard On the Marina ☎ 01646 697083, ⓦ marthas-vineyard.co.uk. A good eating option, offering soups and sandwiches (c.£4), salads and Mediterranean-style mains as well as cod fillet (£10.50). Daily noon–2pm, 6–9.15pm.

Haverfordwest and around

Ancient but dull **HAVERFORDWEST** (Hwlffordd), seven miles north of Milford Haven, grew up around the castle that dominates the skyline to this day. Built in earth and timber by the Flemish Tancard around 1110, it was rebuilt in stone by the mid-thirteenth century and demolished after the Civil War. This was one of the largest towns in Wales in Tudor times, prospering as a port and trading centre, but the Civil War and an outbreak of plague in 1651–52 put an end to that. Haverfordwest is once again the county town of Pembrokeshire, but despite a slew of rich architecture from its glory days, it's hardly a place in which to linger. The diminutive Castle Square forms the heart of the town. Beside the Castle Hotel, a small alleyway ascends to the **castle**, which fails to live up to the expectations created by views of it from below, since there's nothing to see except the bare shell of the thirteenth-century inner ward.

Haverfordwest Town Museum

Castle St • Easter–Oct Mon–Sat 10am–4pm • £1 • ☎ 01437 763087, ⓦ haverfordwest-town-museum.org.uk

In the imposing governor's house (1779) next to the castle is the **town museum**, a motley collection of fairly interesting local history exhibits, such as the first ballot paper used here, Nelson's freedom of the borough charter, and lots of good historical photos.

The lower town

Below the castle, the Riverside Shopping Centre follows the River Cleddau from Castle Square to the Old Bridge, by the bus terminus and tourist office. The more architecturally appealing parts of Haverfordwest lie up the handsome High Street, rising from Castle Square towards the thirteenth-century St Mary's church.

Picton Castle

April–Sept daily 10.30am–5pm; also Feb & Oct half-terms & pre-Christmas events (castle tours start 12.15–2.15pm) • £9 (grounds only £6, all year) • ☎ 01437 751326, ⓦ pictoncastle.co.uk

Three miles east of Haverfordwest on the main A40, signs lead two miles south to **Picton Castle**, a chunky mansion built in the thirteenth century and remodelled between 1790 and 1800. Set in glorious **grounds** with walled garden, maze and play area, the castle still has its original contents, notably wonderful marble fireplaces by Sir Henry Cheere, a circular library and long thin chapel, as well as family portraits (some by Graham Sutherland) plus a Renoir and the earliest-known fake Van Gogh (from the 1920s).

Scolton Manor

4 miles northeast of Haverfordwest via B4329 **House/museum** April–Oct daily 10.30am–5.30pm • £2 **Park** Daily: April–Oct 9am–6pm; Nov–March 9am–4.30pm; parking £1 • ☎ 01437 731328, ⓦ www.pembrokeshirevirtualmuseum.co.uk

A modest stately home completed in 1842, **Scolton Manor** is home to the Pembrokeshire County Museum. Buy tickets in the shop next to the agreeable café (10am–5pm daily), then head to the barn-like shed beyond the stables and a preserved steam locomotive, housing agricultural machines, corn dollies, a preserved shop and cottage interior, as well as a room of railway history and a display on the local impact of World War II. In the house itself you can appreciate the lifestyle of a rich Victorian family: the gilt, brocade and fine furnishings upstairs contrasting with the servants' quarters below. Next, check out the surrounding **country park**, whose visitor centre emphasizes environmental awareness.

ARRIVAL AND DEPARTURE   HAVERFORDWEST

By train Trains stop a 10min walk to the east.
Destinations Cardiff (7 daily; 2hr 25min); Carmarthen (11 daily; 40min); Milford Haven (11 daily; 25min); Swansea (7 daily; 1hr 30min).
By bus The bus station is across the Old Bridge from the town centre, near the TIC.
Destinations Broad Haven (6 daily; 20min); Cardigan (hourly; 1hr 20min); Carmarthen (3 daily; 1hr); Dale (3 daily; 55min); Fishguard (hourly; 40min); Manorbier (hourly; 1hr 10min); Milford Haven (every 30min; 25min); Narberth (hourly; 20min); Newgale (hourly; 25min); Newport, Pembrokeshire (hourly; 1hr); Pembroke (hourly; 55min); Rosebush (1 on Tues only; 45min); St Davids (hourly; 45min); Solva (hourly; 40min); Tenby (hourly; 1hr).

INFORMATION

Tourist information The TIC (April–Oct Mon–Fri 9.30am–5pm, Sat 10am–4pm; Nov–March Mon–Sat 10am–4pm; ☎ 01437 763110, ⓔ haverfordwest.tic @pembrokeshire.gov.uk) is at 19 Old Bridge.
Bike rental Mike's Bikes, 17 Prendergast (☎ 01437 760068, ⓦ mikes-bikes.co.uk; Mon–Sat 9am–5.30pm), 400yd northeast of the bus station, rents mountain bikes and hybrid tourers (both £12 a day) with panniers, lock and helmet, and tag-a-longs for kids.

ACCOMMODATION

College Guest House 93 Hill St ☎ 01437 763710, ⓦ collegeguesthouse.com. One of several decent B&Bs near the Leisure Centre (free parking) at the top of Hill. **£70**
Lower Haythog Farm Spittal ☎ 01437 731279,

2

ⓦ lowerhaythogfarm.co.uk. Comfortable farmhouse B&B near Scolton Manor, with welcoming hosts and superb evening meals for £23. **£70**

EATING AND DRINKING

★ **Black Sheep** High St ☎ 01437 767017 ⓦ black sheeprestaurant.co.uk. This ambitious restaurant, recently relocated to the Old Shire Hall (1835), concentrates on local produce and indeed meat from its own farm. Exotic flavours from Jamaica or Morocco, for example, are mixed with hearty, nostalgic British food such as steak and baby onion pie or pork liver and onions with mash. Main courses cost £6–8 at lunchtime and around £12 in the evening, or £16–20 for duck or steak. All year Mon–Sat noon–3pm, Tues–Sat from 6pm.

Casa Maria 2 Castle Square ☎ 01437 779194, ⓦ casamariadeli.co.uk. At the start of the walk up to the castle, this classy deli sells Spanish, French and Welsh

CAMPING

Rising Sun Inn A487 at Pelcomb Bridge ☎ 01437 765171. Sited two miles northwest. Pitches **£8**

cheeses, meats and olives, with a café upstairs serving tapas with wine. Mon–Sat 10am–4pm; shop 9.30am–5.30pm.

The George's 24 Market St ☎ 01437 766683, ⓦ thegeorges.uk.com. A great option for lunch or evening meals, taking a wholefood approach to delicious peasant dishes. You can eat in a lovely walled garden if the weather allows, or the cellar bistro if not. Tues–Sat 10am–5.30pm, Fri & Sat 6–11pm.

Mambo Italiano High St ☎ 01437 760009 ⓦ mamborestaurant.co.uk. In the former Shire Hall, this cheerful family-friendly place serves pizza and pasta from just £4.50. Tues–Sat 11am–3pm, 5pm–late (all day in high season).

St Bride's Bay

At the westernmost end of Wales, **St Bride's Bay** is one of the country's most enchanting areas, with rocky outcrops, islands and broad, sweeping beaches curving around between two headlands that sit like giant crab pincers facing out into the warm Gulf Stream. The southernmost of these, St Ann's Head, offers calm, east-facing sands at **Dale**, sunny expanses of south-facing beach at **Marloes** and wilder west-facing sands at **Musselwick**. From **Martin's Haven**, boats depart for the islands of **Skomer**, **Skokholm** and **Grassholm**.

The golden sands of the main scoop of St Bride's Bay are backed by popular holiday villages such as **Little Haven**, **Broad Haven** and **Newgale**. From here, the lacerated coast veers west as **St Davids peninsula**, the stunning cliffs interrupted only by occasional gashes of sand. Just north of **St Non's Bay**, the tiny cathedral city of **St Davids**, founded in the sixth century by Wales' patron saint, is a justified highlight. Rooks and crows circle above the impressive ruins of the huge **Bishop's Palace**, beside the more delicate bulk of the **cathedral**, the most impressive in Wales. The peninsula, more windswept and elemental than any other part of Pembrokeshire, tapers out just west of the city at the popular **Whitesands Bay** and the hamlet of **St Justinian's**, staring out over the crags of **Ramsey Island**.

GETTING AROUND   ST BRIDE'S BAY

Transport around the region is excellent, courtesy of the **Pembrokeshire Coastal Bus Service**, assorted routes centred on Milford Haven and St Davids running daily in summer and three days a week (Mon, Thurs, Sat) in winter. Timetables are published online (ⓦ pembrokeshire.gov.uk/bustimetables) and in the national park's free newspaper *Coast to Coast*. Note that at busy times **parking** can be hard to come by and is almost always pay-and-display.

Dale

The tiny village of **DALE**, fourteen miles west of Haverfordwest, huddles at the head of a huge bite out of the coast. Blighted by views of oil refineries, Dale is not especially attractive, but it's surprisingly sunny and its sheltered, east-facing beach makes it a popular yachting and **watersports** centre.

Allenbrook ☎01646 636254, ⓦwww.allenbrook -dale.co.uk. A luxurious, charming, richly furnished country house close to the beach. **£70**

Richmond House ☎07974 925009, ⓦrichmond-house.com. A comfortable B&B next to the pub (which does decent bar meals) on the Dale waterfront; open all year. **£90**

Along the coast from Dale

The calm waters of Dale are deceptive, and as you head south towards **St Ann's Head** the wind gets wilder, with waves and tides to match. This was the site of the 1996 *Sea Empress* tanker wreck, though thankfully all visible reminders of the oil slick have now vanished.

Around the Dale peninsula

The coastline here offers invigorating walking. The Coast Path sticks tight to the undulating coastline, passing tiny bays en route to St Ann's lighthouse. Tucked in the eastern lee of St Ann's Head is **Mill Bay**, where Henry VII landed in 1485, marching the breadth of his native Wales and gathering an army to face Richard III at Bosworth Field.

The coast turns and heads north from St Ann's Head, reaching the sandstone-backed **West Dale Bay**, less than a mile from Dale on the opposite side of the peninsula; the seven-mile walk around the peninsula is highly worthwhile, but swimming here is hazardous, due to currents and hidden rocks.

Marloes and around

A mile north of Dale, the village of **MARLOES** backs the great sandy curve of **Marloes Sands**, known for its stunning cliffs of grey, gold and purple folds of rock, alternate layers of grey shale and old red sandstone. At **Three Chimneys**, two-thirds of the way along the beach, three vertical lines of hard Silurian sandstone and mudstone were formed horizontally and forced up by ancient earth movements.

Gateholm Island

The beach at Marloes is crowned at its western end by **Gateholm Island**, accessible at mid-tide and below (most easily reached from the YHA hostel – see below – a hundred yards before which is a large National Trust car park). Over 130 Iron Age hut circles, pottery and pieces of jewellery have been found here, on what is thought to have been an ancient monastic community. Today, Gateholm is powerfully atmospheric, though getting topside involves a tricky scramble: head around the left side as you look at the island.

The Deer Park

Inexplicably bypassed by the Coast Path is the sublime headland of the **Deer Park**, the very western tip of this peninsula, reached by a small gateway in the wall just beyond the car park. It was never actually stocked with deer; the National Trust now grazes the park with Welsh mountain ponies. Paths radiate out all over the headland, all with stunning views over the offshore islands and St Bride's Bay, and the prospect of a glorious sunset. Next to the small Skomer Marine Nature Reserve information point, with videos of underwater life, is a battered Celtic ring cross; just below, the basic jetty of **Martin's Haven** is the main departure point for **boats** to the islands of Skomer,

---

WATER ACTIVITIES

Activities around are focused on the beachside shack of West Wales Wind, Surf and Sailing (☎01646 636642, ⓦsurfdale.co.uk), which offers lessons (April–Oct; £35–65 per half day) in windsurfing, sailing and kayaking. With adequate proficiency you can rent equipment: a basic windsurfer costs £35 a half day; a superior ensemble £45; and a kayak £20.

Skokholm and Grassholm. Covering the coast of the headland as well as the island, the reserve harbours soft coral, forty species of sea anemone and over seventy species of sponge, as well as octopus, crabs and lobster.

Musselwick Sands and St Bride's Haven

Musselwick Sands, just north of Marloes, is a beautiful and unspoilt beach, though it can be dangerous at high tide. Further north along the peninsula is the narrow **St Bride's Haven**, a tiny, sheltered inlet with a small beach at the end of the lane that peters out by the tiny chapel of St Bride. There are some good rock pools around the beach.

ACCOMMODATION, EATING AND DRINKING   MARLOES

The Clock House ☎01646 636527, **◍**clockhouse marloes.co.uk. There's not much to the village of Marloes, but you can stay centrally at *The Clock House*, which has six white and airy rooms with wi-fi. Breakfast is served in their quality *Clock House Café*, also open for evening meals of local lobster, fish and meat; £19/24 for 2/3 courses. Easter–Oct Tues–Sun, 6.30–8.30pm. **£86**

YHA Marloes Sands ☎0870 770 5958. Converted farm buildings overlooking the northern end of Marloes Sands. Open May to mid-Sept. Dorms **£14**

CAMPING
West Hook Farm ☎01646 636424. Usefully placed basic site a couple of miles east of Martin's Haven and right beside the Coast Path; closed Oct–Easter. Per person **£4**

Skomer and the offshore islands

One of the highlights of this stretch of coast is a boat trip out around the offshore islands, though the only one day-trippers can land on is **Skomer**, a 722-acre flat-topped island that dominates the near horizon. It has the largest **sea bird** colonies in southern Britain, the remains of hundreds of ancient hut circles, a stone circle, collapsed defensive ramparts and settlement systems and a Bronze Age standing stone known as Harold's Stone, near the narrow neck where boats land. The stars of Skomer are the 200,000-plus Manx shearwaters, which only leave their burrows at night, though there's a live video of one in a burrow for day visitors to see. There are also puffins (best May to July), gulls, guillemots, razorbills, storm petrels, cormorants, shags and kittiwakes. Land birds include buzzards, skylarks, jackdaws, chough, owls and peregrines. On Skomer's north side, facing out over the Garland Stone, there's a good chance of seeing grey seals, especially from late August to October. In spring and early summer, wild flowers carpet the island.

Skokholm

Two miles south of Skomer is the 240-acre island of **Skokholm**, whose warm red

---

BOAT TRIPS TO AND AROUND THE ISLANDS

Boats operate from April to October; the only company authorized to land on **Skomer** is Dale Sailing (**☎**01646 603123, **◍**pembrokeshire-islands.co.uk), operating from Dale and Martin's Haven (Tues–Sun & bank holidays 10am, 11am & noon; £18), giving you several hours to explore the island. They also have one-hour, round-the-island cruises (daily 1pm; £10), a two-hour evening trip that's great for sea birds (May–July Tues, Wed & Fri at 7pm; £13), and Sea Safari trips in fast, rigid-inflatables around Skomer and Skokholm (daily 3.30pm & 6.30pm; 2hr 30min; £30).

Dale also operate landing trips from Martin's Haven to **Skokholm** on just four Mondays a summer, booked through the Wildlife Trust of South and West Wales (**☎**01239 621 600/621 212, **◍**welshwildlife.org; £25).

Dale's trips around **Grassholm** are either on the *Dale Princess* from Martin's Haven (early April to mid-Aug Mon at 2pm; 3hr; £30), or from Martin's Haven or Dale on its Grassholm Gannetry Experience sea safari (daily 12.30pm; 2hr 30min; £30). Thousand Islands Expeditions (**☎**01437 721721, **◍**thousandislands.co.uk) also offer a **whale- and dolphin-watching** trip from St Justinian's, near St Davids) to Grassholm and beyond (daily 9am, 3.15pm; £60).

sandstone cliffs are a sharp contrast to Skomer's grey severity. Britain's first bird observatory was founded here in the 1930s, and the island is still rich in birdlife.

Grassholm

Six miles west of Skomer, the tiny islet of **Grassholm** resembles a small iced cake: the "icing" is, in fact, a swarming mass of 80,000 gannets, one of the northern hemisphere's largest colonies, covering well over half the island.

ACCOMMODATION	SKOKHOLM

Wildlife Trust of South and West Wales accommodation ☎ 01239 621600, ⓦ welshwildlife .org. Self-catering accommodation (April–Oct) in the old farm in the centre of the island; perfect for birders and those in search of solitude. The boat costs £25 and goes on Monday and Friday. Per person for 3/4 nights **£125**; 7 nights **£250**

Little Haven to Solva

The long, straight west-facing back of St Bride's Bay, with its sublime Atlantic surf, is flanked by dramatic stretches of cliffs from Little Haven to Druidston, and on either side of the miniature fiord of Solva.

Little Haven

Steep streets descend to the sheltered stony beach of **LITTLE HAVEN**, five miles north of Marloes, a picturesque old fishing village and former coal port that's extremely popular with divers and swimmers in summer. At low tide, walks along the shore towards Broad Haven are superb: you can explore caves and rock pools or just enjoy the full westerly skies. There's some striking geology between Little Haven and Broad Haven, with alternating bands of hard and soft rocks producing caves and blowholes.

Broad Haven

The Coast Path cuts inland from Little Haven for a mile to reach brash, popular **BROAD HAVEN**, a dramatic contrast to its unassuming neighbour, especially in summer, with cars cruising its waterfront and holiday-makers spilling out of its pubs. Still, it has a wide beach fringed by fissured and shattered cliffs.

Druidston Haven

A couple of miles north of Broad Haven, the quiet sandy beach at **DRUIDSTON HAVEN** is hemmed in by steep cliffs and reached along small paths at the bottom of the sharply sloping lane from Broad Haven. The best access is from the unique *Druidstone Hotel*.

Newgale

The next bay north of **Nolton Haven** (little more than a pub and a few houses and caravans around a sheltered shingle cove) is the vast, west-facing **Newgale Sands**,

---

BEACH ACTIVITIES AROUND ST BRIDE'S BAY

Haven Sports Marine Rd, Broad Haven, just behind the Galleon Inn ☎ 01437 781354, ⓦ havensports.co.uk. Rental of sit-on-top kayaks and bodyboards. Mon–Fri 10am–5pm, Sat & Sun 9am–5.30pm.

Big Blue Newgale ☎ 07816 169359, ⓦ thebigblueexperience.com. Kiteboarding, starting with land-based kiting (£40 for 2hr).

Newsurf Newgale ☎ 01437 721398, ⓦ newsurf .co.uk. Rental of surfing gear and offers surfing lessons for £35 a half day.

Nolton Stables Just inland from Nolton Haven ☎ 01437 710360, ⓦ noltonstables.com. Fantastic beach riding, particularly the 90-minute trip to Druidston (£42).

virtually untouched at its southern end, but popular with families and surfers around the uninspiring **NEWGALE**.

Immediately north, Brandy Brook disgorges onto the beach, marking the boundary of "Little England Beyond Wales" (see box, p.159) and the limit of Norman colonization of Pembrokeshire.

Solva

Beyond Newgale the coast turns west, rising abruptly to craggy cliffs that make this a wilder, more Celtic landscape than that of southern Pembrokeshire. The Coast Path from Newgale to **SOLVA**, three miles west, is marvellous, with easy clifftop walking, magnificent coastal views and, in the lee of the Dinas Fach headland, a secluded sandy beach at **Porthmynawyd**. Solva itself is a touristy, picture-postcard village at the top of an inlet running down to **Gwadn beach**. Above this, the **Gribin Headland** between the valleys of the Solva and Gribin rivers gives memorable views and has an imposing Iron Age earthwork on its summit.

ACCOMMODATION LITTLE HAVEN TO SOLVA

BROAD HAVEN

Belmont Barn ☎01437 781372, ⍾belmontbarn .co.uk. B&B a mile inland, with sea views and use of a kitchenette. **£70**

Bower Farm ☎01437 781554, ⍾bowerfarm.co.uk. A welcoming farmhouse B&B, reached by a narrow twisty road from Broad Haven. **£76**

YHA Broad Haven ☎01437 781688 or 0870 770 5728, ⊜broadhaven@yha.org.uk. Almost on the seafront at the northern end of the village, the modern, spacious hostel comes with bunks and a good-value café-bar. Closed Nov–Feb. Dorms **£17**; en-suite rooms **£60**

DRUIDSTON HAVEN

★ **Druidstone Hotel** ☎01437 781221, ⍾druidstone .co.uk. A rambling and easy-going place on the cliff with a quirky array of B&B rooms, some with superb sea views, self-catering cottages, including an old circular croquet pavilion, and a cellar bar that spills out onto the clifftops.

Under the stairs is the smallest bookshop in Wales. Rooms are frequently booked months in advance, especially at weekends. **£80**

Shortlands ☎01437 781234, ⍾bumpylane.co.uk. Just inland in the tiny hamlet of Druidston, this small and friendly campsite (July and Aug) is on a rare-breeds organic farm with showers and great views of St Bride's Bay. It also has a static caravan and a low-allergen self-catering cottage, both open all year and let by the week or for short breaks. Caravan per week **£290**; cottage **£460**

NEWGALE

Newgale Camping Site ☎01437 710253, ⍾newgalecampingsite.co.uk. Just across the road from the beach. Closed Nov–Feb. Per person **£5**

SOLVA

Gamlyn 17 Y Gribin ☎01437 721542. B&B in the pretty Lower Village beside the river. **£50**

EATING AND DRINKING

LITTLE HAVEN

Ceri's Café at Captain Morgan's ☎01437 781233. In the former post office, near the beach, this cheery place is open for breakfast, sandwiches/rolls, cakes and hot food including pizza. Daily 9am–4pm (winter), 9am–9.30pm (summer).

The Swan ☎01437 781880, ⍾theswanlittlehaven .co.uk. This beachside gastropub offers quality bar meals at lunch (around £9) and more refined evening dining with dishes like rib-eye in béarnaise sauce, and asparagus and pea risotto (£15–18), followed by rosewater crème brûlée (£6). Food daily 10am–9pm, bar daily 10am–11pm.

DRUIDSTON HAVEN

Druidstone Hotel ☎01437 781221, ⍾druidstone .co.uk. The dinner menu changes nightly, but expect

anything from lamb kofte (£7) to sea bass with tapenade (£19). Tuesdays are feast nights, with a buffet of, say, Cajun or Jamaican food for £12.50 (vegetarian £9.50). There's a lighter lunch menu and vegetarians are well catered for. Daily 12.30–2.30pm & 7–9.30pm (10pm Fri).

NEWGALE

Sands Café ☎01437 729222. A great place for baguettes, panini, espresso, ice creams and the likes of green pea and pesto soup (£4.50) and smoked mackerel pâté (£6). Daily 9.30am–5pm.

SOLVA

Lavender Café The Old Chapel, Main St ☎01437 721907. Run by a Cuban artist/musician, this is a great place for a sandwich or a ploughman's; there's often live

music too. Closed Jan & Feb.
The Old Pharmacy 5 Main St ☎01437 720005, ⓦtheoldpharmacy.co.uk. An excellent restaurant: expect the likes of Solva crab with samphire and red onion (£7) followed by local lamb or pork (£16–18). Open evenings from 5.30pm, & lunch Easter–Oct.

St Davids

Perched at the very western point of Wales on a windswept, treeless peninsula, **ST DAVIDS** (Tyddewi) is a miniature city – really just a large village. It clusters around its cathedral, Wales' spiritual and ecclesiastical centre and totally independent of Canterbury.

St Davids High Street courses down to the triangular Cross Square, with its centrepiece **medieval cross**, and continues under the thirteenth-century **Tower Gate**, the entrance to the serene **Cathedral Close**. The cathedral lies down to the right, hidden in a hollow by the River Alun. This apparent modesty is explained by reasons of defence: a towering cathedral, visible from the sea on all sides, would have been far too vulnerable. On the other side of the babbling Alun lie the ruins of the Bishop's Palace.

There are numerous small commercial **art galleries** and craft outlets throughout St Davids: some are tacky, but most reflect the quality of the many artists attracted to this spirited corner of Wales by the unique quality of the area's light.

The cathedral

Cathedral Daily 9am–5.30pm · £4 donation requested · ☎ 01437 720202, ⓦ stdavidscathedral.org.uk **Tower Gate** Daily 10am–5pm · £1

The gold-and-purple 125ft sandstone tower of the **cathedral** is approached down the Thirty-Nine Steps (traditionally known as the Thirty-Nine Articles, after Thomas Cranmer's key tenets of Anglicanism). They descend from beyond the doughty **Tower Gate**, the last of four medieval originals, which now houses an exhibition about the history of St Davids (daily 10am–5pm; £1) above a tiny display of carved stones (free).

The nave

The cathedral tower has clocks on only three sides (the people of the northern part of the parish couldn't raise enough money for one facing them), and is topped by pert golden stone pinnacles that seem to glow a different colour from the rest of the building. The most striking feature of the low twelfth-century nave is its intricate latticed oak **roof**, built to hide sixteenth-century emergency repairs. The nave floor still has a pronounced slope and the support buttresses inserted in the northern aisle of the nave look incongruously new and temporary.

The organ and choir stalls

At the crossing, an elaborate **rood screen** was constructed under the orders of fourteenth-century Bishop Henry Gower to incorporate his own tomb. Behind the rood screen and the organ, the choir sits directly under the tower's magnificently bold and bright lantern, another addition by Gower. The round arch over the organ was built in Norman times, contrasting with the other three underpinning the tower, which are pointed and date from

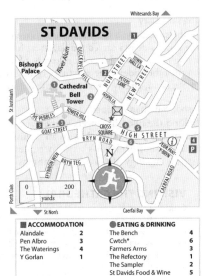

■ ACCOMMODATION		● EATING & DRINKING	
Alandale	2	The Bench	4
Pen Albro	3	Cwtch*	6
The Waterings	4	Farmers Arms	3
Y Gorlan	1	The Refectory	1
		The Sampler	2
		St Davids Food & Wine	5

2

A PILGRIMAGE CITY

Founded by the Welsh patron saint himself in 550, the shrine of St David has drawn pilgrims for a millennium and a half – William the Conqueror included – and by 1120, Pope Calixtus II decreed that two journeys to St Davids amounted to the spiritual equivalent of one pilgrimage to Rome. The cathedral was built from 1181, the settlement growing around it, and St Davids today still relies on the imported wealth of newcomers to the area, attracted by its savage beauty. St Davids was officially declared a city in 1995, despite having just 1600 inhabitants.

---

rebuilding work in the 1220s. At the back of the right-hand choir stalls is a unique **monarch's stall**, complete with royal crest, for, unlike any other British cathedral, the queen is an automatic member of the St Davids cathedral Chapter. The misericords under the choir seats display earthy medieval humour; there's one of a chaotic wild boar hunt and another of someone being seasick. Behind the left-hand choir stalls, the **north transept** contains the tomb of St Caradoc, with two pierced quatrefoils in which it is believed people would insert diseased limbs in the hope of a cure.

Cathedral Library and Treasury

Cathedral Library Mon 2–4pm; summer holidays Mon–Fri 11am–1pm & 2–4pm • £1

Off the north transept, steps from St Thomas' chapel lead up to the **Cathedral Library**, which includes the Royal Charter of 1995 that granted St Davids city status. On the far side of the transept, the Treasury (free) recounts the cathedral's history through a small, well-presented display of its treasures.

The presbytery

Separating the choir and the presbytery is an unusual **parclose screen** of finely traced woodwork; beyond this is the tomb of Edmund Tudor, father of King Henry VII. The back wall of the **presbytery** was once the eastern extremity of the cathedral, as can be seen from the two lines of windows. The upper row is intact, while the lower three were filled with delicate gold mosaics in the nineteenth century, surrounded by over-fussy stonework. The colourful fifteenth-century roof, with its deceptively simple medieval pattern, was restored by Sir George Gilbert Scott in the 1860s.

The sanctuary

In the **sanctuary**, a few fragmented fifteenth-century tiles remain around the altar. On the south side is a carved sedilla, a seat for the priest and deacon celebrating Mass. To its right are thirteenth-century tombs of bishops Iorwerth and Anselm de la Grace, and on the other side of the sanctuary is the disappointingly plain thirteenth-century tomb of St David, largely destroyed in the Reformation.

Bishop Vaughan's chapel

Behind the filled-in lancets at the back of the presbytery altar is the Perpendicular **Bishop Vaughan's chapel**, with an exquisite fan tracery roof built between 1508 and 1522. Bishop Vaughan's statue occupies the niche to the left of the altar. To the right is an effigy of Giraldus Cambrensis, Gerald of Wales, his mitre placed not on

---

VISITING THE CATHEDRAL

Guided tours of the cathedral (Aug Mon at 11am & Fri at 2.30pm, other times ☎01437 720199, ✉toursofstdavidscathedral@yahoo.co.uk; £3) are arranged at the bookshop in the nave. Also worth noting are the choral **evensong** (every Sun 6pm) and the superb annual **music festival**, held in late May/early June (🌐stdavidscathedral.org.uk). Leave time for a visit to *The Refectory* **café** (see below), beyond the modern **cloister**, built on the ruins of the fourteenth-century original.

his head, but at his feet – a reminder that he never attained the status of bishop to which he evidently aspired. Opposite, a peephole looks west into the presbytery. Around the opening, the four crosses may well predate the Norman church. The bottom cross is largely obscured by a casket, reputedly containing some of the intermingled bones of St David and his friend, St Justinian. Behind Bishop Vaughan's Chapel is the ambulatory and the simple **Lady Chapel** with its sentimental Edwardian stained glass.

The Bishop's Palace

March–Oct daily 9am–5pm (July–Aug to 6pm); Nov–March Mon–Sat 10am–4pm, Sun 11am–4pm • £3.20 • CADW

From the cathedral, a path leads over the River Alun to the splendid **Bishop's Palace**, built by bishops Beck and Gower in the early fourteenth century. Its huge central quadrangle is enclosed by an array of ruined buildings in extraordinarily rich colours: the green, red, purple and grey tints of volcanic rock, sandstone and many other types of stone. The **arched parapets** along the top of the walls were a favourite motif of Gower, who did more than any of his predecessors or successors to transform the palace into an architectural and political powerhouse. Off the quadrangle, the ruinous yet still impressive **Bishop's Hall** and the enormous **Great Hall**, with its glorious rose window, overlay a myriad of rooms adorned by eerily eroded corbels. Beneath the Great Hall, dank vaults contain an interesting exhibition on the palace and the indulgent lifestyles of its occupants. The destruction of the palace is largely due to Bishop Barlow (1536–48), who supposedly stripped the buildings of their lead roofs to provide dowries for his five daughters' marriages to bishops.

ARRIVAL AND DEPARTURE   ST DAVIDS

By bus From mid-April to September, the Celtic Coaster bus (#403) connects the Grove car park (by the tourist office) and the centre of St Davids with Whitesands Bay, St Justinian's and Porth Clais. Buses to/from Fishguard and Whitesands Bay stop on New St (arriving) and Nun St (leaving).

Destinations Broad Haven (3 daily; 45min); Fishguard (7 daily; 50min); Haverfordwest (hourly; 45min); Marloes (3 daily; 1hr 20min); Porthgain (3 daily; 30min); Solva (hourly; 10min); Whitesands Bay (mid-April–Sept hourly, May–Aug every 30min; 30min).

INFORMATION

Tourist information Entering St Davids, the main road from Haverfordwest (here called the High Street) passes the National Park tourist office (Easter–Oct daily 9.30am–5.30pm; Nov–Easter Mon–Sat 10am–4.30pm; ☎01437 720392, ✉info@orielyparc.co.uk, ⊛stdavids .co.uk). This houses Oriel y Parc, the National Park's

---

ACTIVITIES

Several local companies run **boat trips** to the outlying islands (see p.189). There are a number of other outdoor activities available, most run through TYF, 1 High St (☎01437 721611, ⊛tyf.com), which pioneered **coasteering**, an exhilarating multi-sport combination which involves scrambling over rocks, jumping off cliffs and swimming across the narrow bays of St Davids peninsula. This is possible for just about anyone (there are even itineraries for non-swimmers) and operates throughout the year, as do **surfing**, **kayaking** and **rock climbing** (all £58 half day, £99 full day; £62/105 in July/Aug); TYF can also organize multi-day sessions and longer courses. Preseli Venture, halfway to Fishguard near Mathry (☎01348 837709, ⊛preseliventure.co.uk), also offer coasteering, sea kayaking, surfing, walking and biking; a half day costs £55 (£59 weekends May–Sept), and a full day £105 (£115), and they also have superb hostel-style accommodation in their Eco Lodge (£39 B&B, £59 full board).

   Ma Simes Surf Hut at 28 High St (☎01437 720433, ⊛masimes.co.uk) is the place to rent **surfboards** (£12/day) or book a lesson (£35/half day).

2

THE REALLY WILD FESTIVAL

Held in a field on Whitesands Road, on the outskirts of St Davids, on the last weekend in July, **Really Wild** (ⓦ reallywildfestival.co.uk) brings together local food producers, wild food gatherers and artisans such as instrument makers, spinners, weavers and feltmakers, to celebrate the delights of West Wales' food and crafts; there's more raucous fun in pig racing, welly-wanging and other events, and on the Verge (festival fringe).

landscape gallery (same hours; free), which features works by Graham Sutherland and rotating loans from the National Museum of Wales.

Bike rental There's no bike rental in town itself, but re-Cycles Bike Hire (ⓣ 01437 711123,

ⓦ pembrokeshireonline.co.uk/re-cycle) rent out bikes (£10/day) and will deliver to any location.

Internet access For internet access and wi-fi, visit Oriel y Parc or *The Bench* (see p.187).

ACCOMMODATION

There are numerous places to **stay** on and around St Davids peninsula, with prices fairly high in season at the larger hotels, but falling dramatically for the rest of the year. Campsites abound in and around the city.

HOTELS AND GUESTHOUSES

Alandale 43 Nun St ⓣ 01437 720404; map p.183. Small, friendly, central guesthouse with five en-suite rooms, some with long views; healthy breakfasts. £80

★ **Crug Glas** Abereiddi, 4 miles northeast of St Davids ⓣ 01348 831302, ⓦ crug-glas.co.uk; map p.188. Luxurious country house on a working farm. The five large rooms are elaborately decorated with gold fittings, tasselled cushions and either half-tester or four-poster beds, plus there's a spacious attic suite. Breakfasts are excellent (great bacon) and delicious four-course dinners cost around £25. Rooms £90, suite £130

Pen Albro 18 Goat St ⓣ 01437 721865; map p.183. More a Bed & Snack than a B&B; but it's the cheapest in town, with no en-suite rooms; right beside the *Farmers Arms*. Per person £20

Ramsey House Lower Moor ⓣ 01437 720321, ⓦ ramseyhouse.co.uk; map p.188. Quality B&B on the road to Porth Clais, with six boutique-style rooms and excellent breakfasts which may include home-made apple and sage sausages. They also do three-course dinners for £35 and have a bar. Closed Nov–Feb. £100

The Waterings Anchor Drive ⓣ 01437 720876, ⓦ waterings.co.uk; map p.183. Very comfortable en-suite rooms and suites in a former marine research establishment, which retains a maritime theme. There are lovely grounds and you can play croquet on the lawn. £85

Y Gorlan 77 Nun St ⓣ 01437 720837; map p.183. Central guesthouse with en-suite rooms, in a Victorian

house that's in the centre of town yet has great views across towards Whitesands Bay. Open all year. £80

HOSTEL AND CAMPSITES

All the following are marked on the map on p.188.

Caerfai Farm Caerfai Bay, 1 mile south of St Davids ⓣ 01437 720548, ⓦ cawscaerfai.co.uk. The best campsite around, on an organic dairy farm and with great coastal views. No caravans. Closed Oct–April. £2.50 discount if arriving on foot or by bike; per person £7

Glan-y-môr Caerfai Rd, 0.5 mile south of town ⓣ 01437 721788, ⓦ glan-y-mor.co.uk. The nearest campsite to town, with a pub and restaurant on site. No bookings – just turn up on spec. Closed Oct–Feb. Tent with 2 adults £12

Lleithyr Farm Just off B4583, 1 mile northwest, 0.5 mile short of Whitesands Bay ⓣ 01437 720245, ⓦ lleithyrfarm.co.uk. High-standard campsite and caravan park with heated shower rooms in winter. Closed Jan & Feb. Per person £5

Rhoson St Justinian's ⓣ 01437 721911, ⓔ info @stdavidscamping.co.uk. Basic field campsite with no showers but handy for the boats to Ramsey Island. Closed Nov–Easter. Per person £3

YHA St Davids Llaethdy, 2 miles northwest near Whitesands Bay ⓣ 0870 770 6042, ⓔ stdavids@yha .org.uk. Large, renovated hostel in a former farmhouse and outbuildings. Daytime lockout and 11pm curfew. Closed Nov–March. Dorms £18.40; rooms £60

EATING, DRINKING AND ENTERTAINMENT

On the surface a bit of a backwater, St Davids is in fact a real magnet for surfers, outdoor types and musicians. In the summer, and over Christmas/New Year, parties are likely to break out just about anywhere. It's also a good place to eat, with something for all tastes and budgets.

The Bench 11 High St ☎01437 721778, ⓦbench-bar .co.uk. Versatile Italian bar-restaurant with a sunny conservatory and garden, which does decent pizza and fresh pasta dishes (£7–9), plus good panini and espresso, and great Italian ice cream to go (including alcoholic ices for over-18s). There's also internet access. 9am–9pm.

★ **Cwtch*** 22 High St ☎01437 720491. Some of the finest dining in Pembrokeshire can be found at *Cwtch** (pronounced "cutsh"), an intimate and easy-going restaurant that's all slate and wood and blackboard menus. Top-quality local ingredients are sourced for unfussy dishes such as roasted red pepper and tomato soup, and hake with lime and anchovy butter. Open for dinner (£26/30 for two/three courses) Mon–Sat and Sun lunch; booking recommended. Closed Mon & Tues in winter.

Farmers Arms Goat St ⓦfarmersstdavids.co.uk. Lively and very friendly pub, with a terrace overlooking the cathedral – especially enjoyable on a summer's evening.

Good food also available, such as panini, salads, jacket potatoes, and mains for £6–10. Daily 11am–midnight.

The Refectory St Davids Cathedral. The beautiful St Mary's Hall is a great spot for tea and cakes, and also serves delicious meals at moderate prices. Free wi-fi. Daily Nov–Easter 11am–4pm, Easter–July & Oct 10am–5pm, Aug–Sept 10am–8pm.

The Sampler 17 Nun St. Daytime coffee shop serving delicious clotted-cream teas. The walls are covered with an impressive collection of needlework samplers. Generally March–Nov and about 2 weeks over Christmas, Mon–Thurs 10.30am–5pm (last orders), plus Sat in summer and Sun in Aug.

St Davids Food & Wine High St ⓦstdavids foodandwine.co.uk. A splendid deli, selling organic local cheeses and over 30 Welsh beers; the best place to pick up filled rolls or picnic makings. Mon–Sat 8.30am–5.30pm.

St Davids peninsula

Surrounded on three sides by inlets, coves and rocky stacks, St Davids is an easy base for excellent walking around the headland of the same name. A mile south, the popular **Caerfai Bay** is a sandy gash in the purple-sandstone cliffs, from which masonry for the cathedral was quarried. Half a mile to the west is the craggy indentation of **St Non's Bay**, where, according to legend, St Non gave birth to St David during a tumultuous storm around 500 AD. A spring opened up between Non's feet, and despite the crashing thunder all around, an eerily calm light filtered down onto the scene.

St Non's Bay

This point on the coast south of St Davids received pilgrims for centuries, resulting in the foundation of a tiny Celtic chapel, whose successor's thirteenth-century ruins now lie in a field to the right of the car park, beyond the simple well and shrine where Wales' patron saint is said to have been born. The 1934 **chapel**, in front of the austere 1929 **Retreat House**, was built in simple Pembrokeshire style from the rocks of ruined houses, which, in turn, had been built from the stone of ancient, abandoned churches. Just to the west, **Porth Clais** was the city's main harbour from Roman times, the spruced-up remains of which can still be seen at the bottom of the turquoise river creek.

WALKS AROUND ST DAVIDS

OS 1:25,000 Explorer map OL35 (North Pembrokeshire) is advised.

There's some fabulous **coastal walking** around St Davids, largely on the Pembrokeshire Coast Path, while the Celtic Coaster bus service means that you won't need to retrace your steps. The visitor centre stocks a number of leaflets (50p), each detailing a short coastal walk. One good and relatively leisurely **day walk** is from Caerfai Bay, past Porth Clais and round Treginnis Head to St Justinian's. At half tide the waters between here and Ramsey Island churn up into an impressive maelstrom. Another good day walk makes a loop from Whitesands Beach around St Davids Head, one of the most mysterious and magical places in Wales. Evidence of ancient civilization is everywhere, and numerous mystics and seers have pinpointed the area as a focus of the earth's natural energies. Highlights include the rocky summit of **Carn Llidi** (595ft), approached on the south side past two cromlechs (capped burial stones), and **Carreg Coetan Arthur** (Arthur's Quoit), a 6000-year-old burial chamber.

St Justinian's

Running due west out of St Davids, Goat Street ducks past the ruins of the Bishop's Palace and over the plateau for two miles to the harbour at **ST JUSTINIAN'S**, little more than a ruined chapel (no access), lifeboat station (open daily in summer 10am–4pm) and ticket hut for the frequent **boats** over to **Ramsey Island** (see p.189).

Whitesands Bay

Two miles to the north and reached via the B4583 off the Fishguard road, **Whitesands Bay** (Porth Mawr) faces west and offers good **surfing**, especially for intermediates. The spectacularly beautiful **Porthmelgan**, a narrow slip of cove reached by a fifteen-minute walk northwest along the Coast Path from Whitesands car park, is far less crowded, largely on account of the dangerous swimming. The thin spit of rock and cliff that juts

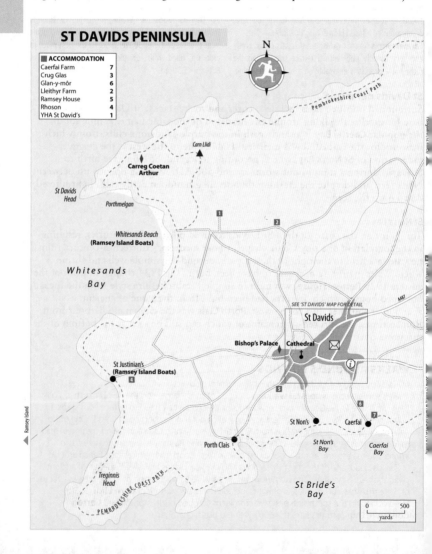

ST DAVIDS PENINSULA

N

ACCOMMODATION

Caerfai Farm	7
Crug Glas	3
Glan-y-môr	6
Lleithyr Farm	2
Ramsey House	5
Rhoson	4
YHA St David's	1

Pembrokeshire Coast Path

Carn Llidi

Carreg Coetan Arthur

St Davids Head

Porthmelgan

Whitesands Beach (Ramsey Island Boats)

1

2

Whitesands Bay

A487

SEE 'ST DAVIDS' MAP FOR DETAIL

St Davids

Bishop's Palace **Cathedral**

✉

ⓘ

St Justinian's (Ramsey Island Boats)

4

5

6

7

St Non's   Caerfai

Porth Clais

St Non's Bay

Caerfai Bay

Treginnis Head

PEMBROKESHIRE COAST PATH

St Bride's Bay

Ramsey Island

0	500
yards	

CRUISES TO RAMSEY ISLAND

Several operators run trips to Ramsey either from St Justinian's or Whitesands Beach.

Thousand Islands Expeditions Cross Square in St Davids (April–Oct daily; ☎01437 721721, ⓦthousandislands.co.uk; £15). The only operator allowed to land you on the island. Boats depart from St Justinian's at 10am and noon, returning at noon and 4pm; you can come back on either boat, allowing you up to six hours' exploration. Perhaps the best deal is their combined Landing & Around trip (Easter–Oct 10am, 10.30am & noon; £35), which gives you a good look at the wildlife all around. There's also the evening Puffin & Shearwater trip (6pm; £30) and the Whale & Dolphin experience (9am, 3.15pm; £60).

Voyages of Discovery 1 High St (☎01437 720285, 0800 854367, ⓦramseyisland .co.uk); **Ramsey Island Cruises** New St (☎01437 721423, 0800 028 6212, ⓦramseyislandcruises .co.uk); and **Aquaphobia** High St opposite the tourist information centre (☎01437 720471, ⓦaquaphobia -ramseyisland.co.uk). All have similar offerings (bar landing on the island) and charge from roughly £25 for one hour to £60 for a two-and-a-half-hour trip to Grassholm. **Venture Jet** From Whitesands Bay (☎01348 837764, 0800 0854786, ⓦventurejet.co.uk). Operates jet boats to Ramsey and Grassholm, from £24 for an hour to £55 for three-and-a-half hours.

2

out into the ocean less than a mile to the west is **St Davids Head**, site of an Iron Age coastal fortress, its outline most visible in spring. Rising behind Whitesands and Porthmelgan, the gnarled crag of **Carn Llidi** tops a pastoral patchwork of fields.

Ramsey Island

The dual-humped plateau of **Ramsey Island** (Ynys Dewi), three miles west of St Davids and half a mile offshore, has been under the able care of the RSPB since 1992 and is quite enchanting. Birds of prey circle the skies above it, but the island is better known for the tens of thousands of sea birds that noisily crowd the sheer cliffs on the western side. On the beaches, seals laze sloppily below the paths worn by a herd of red deer. There's something to see all year round, but spring is great for nesting birds (especially puffins and shearwaters), and autumn for seals with their pups.

North Pembrokeshire coast

The stretch of coast just north of St Davids forms the very southern sweep of Cardigan Bay and is noticeably less commercialized than the touristy littoral of south and mid-Pembrokeshire. From the crags and cairns above St Davids Head, the Coast Path perches precariously on the cliffs, where only the thousands of sea birds have access.

Although the area's major source of income is now tourism, the remains of old mines, quarries and ports at **Abereiddi** and **Porthgain** bear witness to the slate and granite industries that once employed hundreds of people. Industry dies down towards **Trefin** and up to the more remote beaches and inlets that punctuate the coast as it climbs up to the splendid knuckle of **Strumble Head**. To the east is **Carregwastad Point**, the site of the last invasion of Britain in 1797. The event is also remembered in the port town of **Fishguard**, where the invading French surrendered at the *Royal Oak Inn*.

Abereiddi to Abercastle

The fantastic stretch of coast northeast of St Davids combines rugged cliffs and birdlife with remnants of long-closed industry and even more ancient cultures.

Abereiddi

Five miles north of St Davids, a small lane tumbles down into the bleak hamlet of **ABEREIDDI**, where you can find tiny fossilized animals in the shale of the black-sand beach. At the back of the beach are remains of workers' huts and a tramway that once climbed over the hill to Porthgain, all part of the slate quarry that closed in 1904. The quarry itself was dynamited for safety reasons, producing a "blue lagoon" due to the minerals suspended in the seawater.

Porthgain

The lane parallel to the coast passes the hamlet of Cwmwdig Water and leads to tiny **LLANRHIAN**, where a left turn takes you a mile down to the rambling village green of **PORTHGAIN**. This fascinating little port grew up from 1850 below its slate works, the stumpy remains of which huddle around the tiny quay, together with an old brickworks, lime kiln and eerie ruins of workers' cottages. It also has a couple of small art galleries and the eighteenth-century *Sloop Inn* (see below). There's a superb circular walk (4 miles, 2 hrs) back to Abereiddi, which is largely level after the steep climb out of Porthgain, returning inland or by the Strumble Shuttle bus.

Abercastle

The coastal lane continues east to **ABERCASTLE**, past the 4500-year-old **Carreg Samson** cromlech (burial chamber) at Longhouse, precariously topped by a 16ft capstone. If you're walking, continue past the cromlech and down to the Coast Path to the attractive and popular harbour of Abercastle, once used for the export of limestone and coal. From there, one of the most scenic parts of the Coast Path zigzags east along the wild, vertiginous cliffs to the point at **Trwyn Llwynog**, about two miles away.

ACCOMMODATION	**ABEREIDDI TO ABERCASTLE**

PORTHGAIN

★ **Caerhafod Lodge** Porthgain, 0.5 mile north of Llanrhian ☎ 01348 837859, ⓦ caerhafod.co.uk. Within walking distance of Porthgain, this is a brilliant independent hostel with a tranquil atmosphere, good views and helpful hosts. They offer self-catering facilities and mostly four-bedded rooms (sheets supplied). Per person **£16**

TREFIN

The Old School Hostel Ffordd-yr-afon, Trefin ☎ 01348 831800, ⓦ theoldschoolhostel.co.uk. There are also bunks a mile or so east of Porthgain at *The Old School Hostel*, a former YHA hostel that has been revamped and rejuvenated. They have ultra-cheap private rooms, do light breakfasts and packed lunches, and operate eco-incentives such as a £1 discount for those arriving without a car; they also plant a tree for every booking and run on green electricity. Per person **£17**

EATING AND DRINKING

PORTHGAIN

The Shed Porthgain ☎ 01348 831518, ⓦ theshed porthgain.co.uk. As well as a tearoom and a fresh fish and cheese deli, this is a classy fish & chips bistro (from £9), with most of the produce caught locally. Shop & tearoom 10.30am–5pm; bistro noon–9pm; closed Sun

evenings except in school holidays.

Sloop Inn Porthgain ⓦ sloop.co.uk. This charming pub has numerous photographs of the port in its sepia heyday and a perfect terrace to while away the evening, as well as good bar food. Food served 9.30am–9.30pm.

Strumble Head

The headland – known as **Pen Caer** – that rises to the north of Abercastle, peaking at **STRUMBLE HEAD**, is delightful: tiny hedge-backed lanes bump around between rocky cairns, with fields of wild flowers and sudden glimpses of the shimmering sea. From this remote and spectacular section of the Coast Path there's access to the sandy stretch of **Aber Mawr**, smaller **Aber Bach**, and the west-facing gash of **Pwllcochran**.

Nearly two miles further north, there's the simple but fabulously sited *Pwll Deri* YHA **hostel**. Looming large on the inland side of the hostel are the three crags of **Garn Fawr** (699ft): by following a path from the car park at their eastern edge, on the lane up to Strumble Head, you can explore the vestiges of Iron Age ditches, ramparts and hut circles.

Strumble Head, just over a mile north of Garn Fawr, is reached either by the rugged Coast Path – with astounding views over the two-mile-long "wall" of cliffs to the south – or along a floral country lane. At the headland, the 1908 **lighthouse** is perched atop **Ynys Meicel**, connected to the mainland by a metal footbridge that's closed to the public. It's a peaceful yet invigorating spot that's perhaps the best in Wales for sea bird spotting, with gannets, fulmars, kittiwakes, Manx shearwaters, guillemots and fulmars, and four other types of shearwaters, as well as porpoises. On land you may see stonechats, linnets, choughs, peregrines, buzzards and ravens.

Almost three miles on, the hamlet of **LLANWNDA** merits a historical footnote as the site of the **last invasion of Britain** (see box below). The **church of St Gwyndaf** is also well worth a visit for its charming setting, an ancient history which winds back beyond the eighth century, and the collection of pre-Norman carved stones embedded in its walls.

Carregwastad Point

The 1.5-mile **walk** from Llanwnda to **Carregwastad Point** is fabulous, coasting gently down fields and across the top of a craggy cwm. Start by going over the stile and along the path across the track from the church entrance. At the coast turn left to reach Carregwastad Point and the plaque commemorating the invasion (see box), or right to **Aber Felin**, a bay often littered with grey seals.

Fishguard and Goodwick

Fishguard (Abergwaun) occupies a lofty headland between the pretty Lower Town and the port of **GOODWICK** (Wdig). Though often seen only as somewhere from which to catch a ferry to Ireland, it's an enjoyable place in its own right, with fine views from the easy coastal walks around town.

In the centre of town, the **Royal Oak Inn** was the scene of the surrender of the "last invasion of Britain" in 1797. The episode's heroine, Jemima Nicholas, is buried beside the Victorian **parish church** behind the pub.

Last Invasion Gallery

Mon–Sat 9.30am–5pm, Thurs until 6.30pm; Oct–March closes 1pm on Sat • Free

Inside the Town Hall, the **Last Invasion Gallery** contains the 100ft-long **Fishguard**

THE LAST INVASION OF BRITAIN

In 1797, while Napoleon was absent fighting in Italy, a newly formed Franco-Irish revolutionary command was trying to make its mark in Paris. Believing that the oppressed countryfolk of Britain would sympathize with their revolutionary views and join their cause, a motley band of "liberators" – some just out of prison and still shackled – hatched a madcap plan to invade Britain. Winds blew their ships from their planned landing at Bristol and they ended up at **Carregwastad Point**, just south of Fishguard, now marked with a memorial stone. The disorganized army of 1400 made its base at Trehowel Farm, midway between Strumble Head and Llanwnda, which was stocked with food and drink for an imminent family wedding. Indeed most local farms were full of contraband liquor plundered from a recent Portuguese shipwreck. The would-be conquerors set to with gusto, swiftly becoming too drunk to do anything except loot the silver plate in Llanwnda's church.

After two days the invasion had collapsed and the invaders surrendered on 24 February to a local militia at the **Royal Oak** in Fishguard, claiming they had seen "troops of the line to the number of several thousand". No such army was in the vicinity and some say the bleary-eyed French mistook several hundred local women clad in stovepipe hats and red flannel shawls for British Redcoats. While that may not be true, it's a fact that fourteen soldiers were rounded up with a pitchfork by a 47-year-old cobbler's wife, Jemima Nicholas – dubbed ever since the "Welsh Heroine".

FISHGUARD'S FESTIVALS

Over the bank holiday weekend at the end of May, Fishguard hosts the increasingly popular **Fishguard Folk Festival** (ⓦpembrokeshire-folk-music.co.uk), while in late July there's the **Fishguard International Music Festival** (ⓞ01348 875s538, ⓦfishguardmusicfestival.co.uk) combining classical, choral, jazz and blues. **Theatr Gwaun** on West St (ⓞ01348 873421, ⓦtheatrgwaun.co.uk) mainly shows films but also has the occasional music or drama event.

2

Tapestry, inspired by the famous Bayeux model and made to mark the event's bicentenary in 1997. The tapestry offers a wonderful depiction of the invasion, including debauched French soldiers, with one unfortunate thief shown on the lower border with his throat cut. A video tells the story of the local artists and embroiderers who made it all happen, and the bicentenary re-enactment.

Lower Town

Main Street winds northeast, then plummets down around the coast to **Lower Town** (Cwm), a cluster of old-fashioned cottages around a muddy, thriving, herring-fishing and pleasure-boat port. Views from above Lower Fishguard over the town headland and out to the Goodwick breakwater are superb. Lower Fishguard's moment of glory came in 1971, when Richard Burton and Elizabeth Taylor filmed Dylan Thomas' *Under Milk Wood* here.

ARRIVAL AND DEPARTURE   FISHGUARD AND GOODWICK

By train Fishguard Harbour train station is on Quay Road in Goodwick.
Destinations Cardiff (3 daily; 2hr 45min); Carmarthen (7 daily; 50min); Swansea (4 daily; 1hr 45min).
By bus Buses stop by the town hall in the central Market Square, right outside Fishguard's tourist office, and on The Parrog in Goodwick.
Destinations Cardigan (hourly; 40min); Haverfordwest

(hourly; 40min); Newport, Pembrokeshire (hourly; 15min); Rosebush (1 on Tues only; 25min); St Davids (6–8 daily; 45min); Trefin (6–8 daily; 30min).
By ferry Fishguard harbour, for ferries and catamarans to Rosslare, Ireland (3 daily; 2hr–3hr 30min), is on Quay Road in Goodwick Most buses stop 0.5 mile away at Station Hill. A taxi (ⓞ01348 873075, 875129) into Fishguard costs about £4.

INFORMATION

Tourist information The TIC (Easter–Oct Mon–Fri 9.30am–5pm, Sat 9.30am–4pm; Aug also Sun 10am–4pm; Nov–Easter Mon–Sat 10am–4pm; ⓞ01347 776636, ⓔfishguard.tic@pembrokeshire.gov.uk) is in the town hall on the central Market Square, which also hosts markets on Tues, Thurs and Sat mornings. They also have free internet access (15min maximum, or for longer sessions visit the library upstairs; Mon–Sat 9.30am–5pm, Thurs until 6.30pm). Just steps away, Seaways bookshop

on West St is the best source of books on Wales plus information on Ireland in town.
There's also a tourist office (daily: Easter–Oct 9.30am–5pm (summer holidays to 6pm), Nov–Easter 10am–4pm; ⓞ01348 874737, ⓔfishguardharbour.tic@pembrokeshire. gov.uk) on The Parrog on the Goodwick foreshore; it's in the Ocean Lab, an education centre with an exhibition on marine life and detailed information on the Coast Path, as well as a coffee shop with wi-fi.

ACCOMMODATION

★ **Cefn-y-Dre** 1 mile south along Hamilton St ⓞ01348 875663, ⓦcefnydre.co.uk. There's a relaxed and understated elegance to this lovely country house with parts dating from the early sixteenth century. Just three rooms, attractive grounds, tasty breakfasts, and superb home-cooked meals (£25; reserve in advance) prepared by wonderful hosts. **£75**
Gwaun Vale Caravan Park 1.5 miles southeast on B4313 ⓞ01348 874698, ⓦgwaunvale.co.uk. Well-appointed site on the fringes of Cwm Gwaun that is relatively wind-free even when the Coast Path is getting battered. Pitches **£15**

Hamilton Lodge 21–23 Hamilton St ⓞ01348 874797, ⓦhamiltonbackpackers.co.uk. Cosy, very central and well set-up hostel with dorms, doubles and twins, and a free light breakfast. Bedding is provided. Dorm beds **£16**; rooms **£32**
Plain Dealings Tower Hill ⓞ01348 873655. Peaceful and attractive top-quality B&B 0.5 mile from the centre, with views of the Lower Town. March–Oct. **£70**
YHA Pwll Deri 4 miles west of Fishguard ⓞ0870 770 6004, ⓔpwllderi@yha.org.uk. Recently revamped, this is a superbly sited clifftop hostel, with dorms and a couple of private double rooms. Dorms **£15**; doubles **£60**

EATING AND DRINKING

Bar Five 5 Main St ☎01348 875050, ⓦbarfive.net. Chic, modern restaurant and bar with great harbour views, sunny terrace and good meals (three courses for £15), majoring on local produce and especially lobster. Wed–Sat 6–9.30pm, Sun 11am–3pm.

Café Celf 16 West St ⓦwestwalesartscentre.com. Arty café that's great for a restful cake and espresso or a lunch platter with smoked salmon, salami or roast vegetables (£5–9). High season: Mon–Sat 10am–4pm; low season: Tues–Sat 10am–3pm; dinner: Fri & Sat 7pm.

Royal Oak Market Square ☎01348 872514. Historic pub with real ales and a separate dining area for good pub meals (baguettes £4–5, mains £9). There are also good-value Sunday lunches, and folk nights on Tues – participants very welcome. Daily 10.30am–11pm; food noon–2pm, 6–9pm.

Ship Inn Lower Town ☎01348 874033. Eccentric, unmissable pub with lots of interesting clutter all over the walls and ceiling, including black-and-white photos of the filming of *Under Milk Wood* and *Moby Dick*. Daily noon–11pm.

Mynydd Preseli

In a county famed for its magnificent coastal scenery, Pembrokeshire's interior is frequently overlooked. The **Mynydd Preseli** (Preseli Mountains) occupy a triangle of land in the north of the county, flecked with prehistoric remains and roughly bounded by the coast in the north, the B4313 to the west and the A478 to the east.

The main A487 coast road is the area's only major **bus** route, cruising from Fishguard to Cardigan through delightful **Newport**, handy for the historic peak of **Carn Ingli**, the bucolic church at **Nevern** with its "bleeding" yew, and the reconstructed Iron Age settlement at **Castell Henllys**. This is also the final (or initial) stretch of the Pembrokeshire Coast Path and the cognoscenti's favourite, with awesome solitude, abundant natural life and stunning cliff formations.

Inland from Fishguard, the **Gwaun River** wriggles southeast through its green cwm, with tiny villages and remote churches seemingly untouched by modernity. Formed around 200,000 years ago, this is Europe's oldest glacial meltwater valley and the subject of many a geology field trip. The brooding mountains hereabouts shelter innumerable standing stones, stone circles, hillforts, cairns and earthworks, several linked by a hike along the **Golden Road**.

Newport

The A487 winds through **NEWPORT** (Trefdraeth), an ancient, proud and wealthy little town that is without doubt the best base in north Pembrokeshire. Set on a gentle slope coursing down to the estuary of the Afon Nyfer, it is a quietly enjoyable place, with superb accommodation, food and drink, welcoming inhabitants and a selection of fine coastal and hill walks on its doorstep. Newport still appoints a mayor annually, a legacy of its days as the seat of the Norman Marcher Lordship of Cemaes. One visible manifestation of this heritage is the annual custom, on the third Friday of August, of "Beating of the Bounds", when the mayor marks out the town's boundaries. The town's festival, Ffair Gurig, is held the week of June 27, with a carnival on its last Saturday.

South of the main thoroughfare, **Bridge Street**, a number of pretty lanes rise up to the intriguing **castle** (private), a nineteenth-century residence fashioned out of the thirteenth-century gatehouse. The other obvious landmark is **St Mary's church**, with its original Norman font and a massive fifteenth-century tower.

The Nyfer estuary and beaches

Long Street and Lower St Mary Street head down to the **Nyfer estuary**, over which squawking sea birds circle and skim the water's edge. A path hugs its southern shore – turn east (or take Parrog Road if you're driving) for a gentle stroll to the **Parrog**, Newport's nearest beach, mostly shingle but with sandy stretches at low tide. A better beach is the vast dune-backed **Traethmawr**, on the north side of the estuary, reached over the town bridge down Feidr Pen-y-Bont – note the pilgrims' stepping stones on the upstream side of the bridge. The footpath that follows the river either side of the bridge is marked as the Pilgrims' Way, and makes a delightful riverbank stroll to Nevern (see p.195), a couple of miles east. Just short of the bridge, on the town side, **Carreg Coetan Arthur**, a well-preserved capped burial chamber, can be seen behind holiday bungalows.

Carn Ingli

Follow Church Street past St Mary's for the relatively easy two-hour ascent of **Carn Ingli** (Hill of Angels), once the core of an active volcano and one of Wales' holiest mountains. It gets its name from St Brynach who lived here in quiet contemplation, supposedly with angels as his companions. More certainly, stone embankments of the Iron Age hillfort and the nearby Bronze Age hut circles prove that the hill once had a sizeable community.

ARRIVAL AND INFORMATION   NEWPORT

By bus Buses stop on Bridge St in the centre of town.
Destinations Cardigan (hourly; 20min); Fishguard (hourly; 15min); Haverfordwest (hourly; 1hr).
Tourist information The cheerful National Park tourist office (☎01239 820912, ✉newportTIC @pembrokeshirecoast.org.uk; Easter–Oct Mon–Sat 10am–5.30pm, plus mid-July to Aug Sun

10am–1.15pm; Nov–Easter Mon & Fri 10am–3pm, Tues, Wed, Thurs & Sat 10.30am–1pm) is on Long St and offers paid internet access.
Bike hire Wholefoods of Newport, on East St, is an outlet for Newport Bike Hire (☎01239 820773, ⌖newportbikehire.com), with bikes for £15/day and tag-a-longs for kids for £10.

ACCOMMODATION

Cnapan East St ☎01239 820575, ⌖cnapan.co.uk. Five comfortable rooms and an old-fashioned friendly welcome are the hallmarks of this long-standing favourite above a great restaurant. Closed Jan & Feb. **£82**
The Globe Upper St Mary St ☎01239 820296. About the cheapest place around, with shared bathroom and continental breakfast included. **£60**
★ **Llys Meddyg** East St ☎01239 820008, ⌖llysmeddyg.com. Stylish restaurant-with-rooms fashioned from a Georgian residence. All rooms (and the more spacious suites) have great bedding, classy toiletries and individual decor. Free wi-fi. Rooms **£100**; suites **£180**
Morawelon The Parrog ☎01239 820565 ✉carreg@morawelon.fsnet.co.uk. Seaside campsite 300yd from

town, nicely set in pleasant gardens and with its own café overlooking the beach, and coin-op showers. March–Oct. Per person **£6**
Y Bryn Fishguard Rd, 200yd west of town ☎01239 820288, ⌖brynbedandbreakfast.co.uk. Great-value B&B with four unfussy rooms, all with private bathroom (three also have sea views); the spacious attic room is particularly appealing. A full breakfast is served and there's off-street parking. **£70**
YHA Newport Lower St Mary St ☎01239 820080 or 0870 770 6072, ✉reservations@yha.org.uk. Tucked in behind the Eco Centre Wales, this classy conversion of an old school has dorms and a couple of private rooms. Dorms **£14.40**; rooms **£72**

EATING AND DRINKING

The Canteen Market St ☎01239 820131, ⌖thecanteen. org.uk. Casual café-restaurant with slate floors and modern wooden tables: a great setting for a good espresso or a meal from the short but well-chosen menu such as venison sausages and mash (£9.50), with interesting wines by the bottle or the glass. Mon–Thurs 10am–4pm, Fri & Sat 10am–8.30pm; takeaway fish & chips from 5–7pm.
★ **Cnapan** East St ☎01239 820575, ⌖cnapan.co.uk. Fresh local produce informs the menu at this classic dinner-only restaurant, where spicy mussel chowder might be followed by guinea fowl with gooseberry and elderflower sauce. £26/32 for two/three courses. Booking essential. Open from 6.30pm, last orders 8.30–8.45pm; closed Tues, and Jan & Feb.
Golden Lion East St ☎01239 820 321,

⌖goldenlionpembrokeshire.co.uk. Bare stone and timber-beamed pub with real ales and a superb menu of carefully prepared pub meals (£10) and fancier restaurant-style dishes (£13–20), both served either in the bar or more formally out the back. Food daily noon–2pm, 6–9pm.
Llys Meddyg East St ☎01239 820008, ⌖llysmeddyg .com. A Georgian dining room, the cellar bar or the partly walled kitchen garden provide the settings for exquisite dinners (£27.50/33 for 2/3 courses) which might include local baby crab cakes with papaya mustard then wild bass with a sweet-and-sour mushroom broth. Lunches (£16/18.50 for 2/3 courses) are no less appealing. Closed Sun evening (except bank holidays) & Mon in winter; summer hours Tues–Sat & bank holiday Sundays noon–3pm, 6–9pm, other Sundays noon–3pm only.

Morawelon The Parrog. Waterfront café specializing in seafood, with crab and prawn sandwiches (£5–6.65) and baked crab (£16), as well as vegetable lasagne (£9.25), waffles (£5) and cream teas. 9am–5pm daily April–Sept, Wed–Sun Oct & Dec–March; also some evenings.

Around Newport

Either side of Newport, the Coast Path runs through some sublime scenery. To the **west**, the trail edges around the protuberant Dinas Head, en route to Fishguard. Two miles west of Newport's Parrog beach, a very narrow road leads to the popular strand at **Cwm-yr-Eglwys**, where the scant seafront ruins of the twelfth-century **St Brynach's church** are all that survived a huge storm on the night of October 25, 1859, when the rest of the church and some 114 ships at sea were wrecked.

Along the coast

The three-mile walk around Dinas Head offers splendid views over the huge cliffs, where thousands of sea birds nest between May and mid-July. On the western side of the headland, accessible by car off the A487, is the grey-sand beach of **Pwllgwaelod**.

The stretch of Coast Path running **east from Newport** to the fringes of Cardigan at St Dogmael's is perhaps the wildest and toughest of the whole path: it plummets and climbs, passing rocky outcrops, blowholes, caves, natural arches, ancient defensive sites and thousands of sea birds. The only part accessible by car is at the spectacularly folded cliffs of **Ceibwr Bay**, eight miles from Newport near the pretty pastel village of **MOYLEGROVE** (Trewyddel).

Nevern

Just over a mile east of Newport by road, but about double that by the pleasant riverside walk, the straggling village of **NEVERN** (Nanhyfer) is darkly atmospheric, with a couple of intriguing sights. High on a bluff above the village, the ruins of the Norman **castle**, abandoned in 1195, are being excavated and restored a bit; it's open all year, with visitors welcome at the dig in June or July.

The church of St Brynach

The brooding bulk of the **church of St Brynach**, founded in the sixth century and with an intact Norman tower, has many features of interest. The churchyard's ancient yews give it a dank, dark presence. Note the second tree on the right, the famous "**bleeding yew**", so called for the brown-red sap that oozes mysteriously from its bark. Legend has it that it will continue to bleed until a Welsh lord of the manor is reinstated in the village castle – unlikely in the foreseeable future, given its tumbledown state. Also outside the church, just by the main doorway, is the stunning **Great Cross**, an inscribed tenth-century Celtic masterpiece standing some 13ft high. St Brynach's interior is no less interesting. Standing at the back, you can easily see how the chancel has been built slightly out of alignment with the nave, supposedly to represent Christ's inclined head on the Cross. Built into the windowsills of the south transept are two ancient inscribed stones: the **Maglocunus Stone**, with Latin and Ogham inscriptions from about the fifth century AD, and the **Cross Stone**, marked with a very early Celtic cross.

Pentre Ifan

2 miles south of Nevern • Open access • Free

The well-signposted cromlech at **Pentre Ifan** is a vast burial stone – the largest in Wales – with its 16ft arrowhead top-stone precariously balanced on large stone legs, and dating back over four thousand years. The views from here are superb, situated as it is on the cusp of the stark, eerie Mynydd Preseli with the pastoral rolls of the countryside to the east.

Castell Henllys

2 miles east of Nevern • Daily 10am–5pm • Winter 11am–3pm • April–Oct £4.75, Nov–March £3 • ☎ 01239 891319, ⓦ castellhenllys.com

Signposted off the A487, excavations of the Iron Age hillfort of **Castell Henllys** are turning up more and more of its past. Four roundhouses and a granary, complete with thatch, have been reconstructed on their 2000-year-old foundations, and throughout the summer the National Park lays on opportunities to watch ancient skills and learn what Iron Age life was like here. Children's activities (during the school holidays; £2.50 for 90min; book ahead) give kids a chance to try wool dyeing and basket making or train as a warrior. A sculpture trail through the woods and river valley brings to life the tales of *The Mabinogion*, and further trails lead into the ancient oak woodlands of the adjacent Pengelli Forest. Free one-hour guided tours (April–Oct 11.30am & 2.30pm) come with a strong environmental message, looking at land usage, wood management and conservation.

Cwm Gwaun and the inland hills

Cwm Gwaun, the valley of the burbling River Gwaun, is one of the great surprises of Pembrokeshire – a bucolic vale of impossibly narrow lanes, surrounded by the bleak shoulders of bare mountains. It is a timeless place whose residents retain an attachment to the pre-1752 Julian calendar, celebrating New Year on January 13.

Llanychaer

The B4313 heads two miles southeast from Fishguard to tiny **LLANYCHAER** where, opposite the *Bridge End Inn*, a lane runs almost half a mile steeply uphill to the **church** and "**cursing**" **well** of the lost settlement of **Llanllawer**. The well had a pre-Christian reputation for cementing curses and ill omens if you left a bent pin, although most pilgrims sought miraculous cures, particularly for eye conditions. The lane running east opposite the well and church leads to seven large standing stones – the longest megalithic alignment in Wales – in **Parc y Merw** (the Field of the Dead), just short of Trellwyn Farm.

Back on the B4313, nearly a mile beyond Llanychaer, a lane branches left and drops down into Cwm Gwaun, soon crossing the river near a picnic site from where there are some good walks up into the old oak forests that line the valley.

Pontfaen

Three miles off the B4313 you reach the scattered settlement of **PONTFAEN**, complete with its time-warped pub, the rustic and remote *Dyffryn Arms* (see p.197). By turning sharp right before the pub and following the lane across the river and up a sharp hill for a quarter of a mile, you'll reach Pontfaen's exquisitely restored **church** (open daily), dedicated, like so many round here, to St Brynach. The circular graveyard indicates pre-Christian origins before the church was founded, according to tradition, by the wandering Breton saint in 540 AD. In the graveyard are two impressive but very worn stone crosses, dating from between the sixth and ninth centuries.

Gerddi Penlan-Uchaf

2 miles northeast of Pontfaen • March–Nov daily 9am–dusk • £3 • ⓦ penlan-uchaf.co.uk

Well tucked away, the delightful **Gerddi Penlan-Uchaf** is a set of hillside gardens cut through by a stream with wonderful views over the valley. They contain thousands of miniature flowering and alpine plants, and acres of herbs and wild flowers together with some impressive dwarf conifers.

ACCOMMODATION	CWM GWAUN AND THE INLAND HILLS
Erw-Lon Farm B4313 between Pontfaen and Rosebush ☎ 01348 881297 ⓦ erwlonfarm.co.uk. In an area where accommodation is limited, welcoming B&B. **£60** **Gwaun Valley Brewery** Kilkiffieth Farm, Pontfaen, on	B4313 five miles from Fishguard ☎ 01348 881304, ⓦ gwaunvalleybrewery.co.uk. Friendly microbrewery with a simple all year campsite. Daily 10am–6pm & evenings on request; acoustic music sessions Sat 7–10pm. Pitches **£5**

EATING AND DRINKING

★ **Dyffryn Arms** Known as *Bessie's* after its aged proprietor, you can enjoy good company here in an old-fashioned living room. There's a small beer garden, or you can take your drinks into the riverside field across the road. Open all day.

Rosebush

As you head east, the brooding nature of the Mynydd Preseli makes itself most apparent. This is bleak, invigorating countryside, the wild, open hills scattered with the relics of ancient civilizations. The characteristic **Preseli bluestone**, which was used between 2000 and 1500 BC to construct Stonehenge, some 140 miles away, came from these slopes.

Slate is also found hereabouts, and was quarried until 1905 near the weird little village of **ROSEBUSH**, just off the B4313 around ten miles southeast of Fishguard. The Klondike atmosphere of the place is partially explained by the fact that it was built quickly as a would-be resort following the arrival of the railway in 1876.

Foel Cwmcerwyn

A good hike leads from Rosebush along the eastern edge of the coniferous Pantmaenog Forest to the 1760ft summit of **Foel Cwmcerwyn** (4 miles return; 2hr; 800ft ascent), the highest point in Pembrokeshire. Topped by a Bronze Age cairn, the rounded hill sits above **Craig y Cwm**, the most recently glaciated valley (c.8000 BC) in the area.

ACCOMMODATION	ROSEBUSH

Rosebush Caravan & Camping Park ☎ 01437 532206, ⓦ ukparks.co.uk/rosebush. Campers are well served at this well-maintained, lakeside site; open mid-March to Oct. Pitches £10

EATING AND DRINKING

Old Post Office ☎ 01437 532205. Though noted for its vegetarian and vegan specialities, this also serves steaks and fish. Tues–Sun noon–11pm, lunch & dinner Tues–Sat, lunch Sun.

Tafarn Sinc ("Zinc Tavern") ☎ 01437 532214, ⓦ tafarnsinc.co.uk. The largest of several corrugated-iron shacks contains the sawdust-floored bar, a good spot for a pint and a meal (£8–11) in the garden on a fine day. Tues–Sun noon–11pm.

The Golden Road

The main range of the Preselis lies just northeast of the village, crossed by an ancient track, in use for at least 3500 years, known as the **Golden Road**. A hike (8 miles one-way; 4–5hr; 1000ft ascent) taking in the best section runs due north out of Rosebush past the old slate quarries through Pantmaenog Forest and up onto the Golden Road.

Turn right to reach many of the Preselis' cairns and ancient sites, such as **Beddarthur**, an eerie stone circle that is supposed to be the great king's burial place, **Carn Menyn**, probably the quarry from which most of the Stonehenge bluestones were cut, and **Foeldrygarn** ("the Hill of Three Cairns"), with its hugely impressive Iron Age ramparts and hut circles. Public transport is of little use, so plan for a full day out and hike both ways: the perspective is quite different on the way back.

WALKERS' BUSES

The Preseli Rural Transport Association runs its Green Dragon walkers' buses (July–Sept; 3 daily Tues & Thurs): the Gwaun Valley Bus runs from Fishguard to Pontfaen and Newport, and the Preseli Hills Bus runs from Crymych (connecting with Narberth–Cardigan buses) to Rosebush. They meet at the Bwlch Gwynt car park, near Rosebush, from where it's a one-hour hike to the top of Foel Cwmcerwyn (see above).

The Brecon Beacons and Powys

SUGAR LOAF, NEAR ABERGAVENNY

The Brecon Beacons and Powys

The vast inland county of Powys takes up a full quarter of Wales. Often traversed quickly en route to the coast, it's well worth exploring in its own right. The most popular area is the Brecon Beacons National Park at the county's southern end, an area of moody heights, wild, rambling moors and thundering waterfalls. The main centres within the Beacons are Wales' culinary capital, Abergavenny, in the far southeast, and Brecon. The bleaker part of the Beacons lies to the west, around the raw peaks of the Black Mountain (Mynydd Ddu) and Fforest Fawr geopark, and includes the immense Dan-yr-ogof caves and the mighty waterfalls around Ystradfellte. Architecturally charming towns such as Crickhowell and Talgarth, set in quiet river valleys, also make good bases for walkers. At the northern corner of the national park, the border town of Hay-on-Wye is famous for its dozens of secondhand bookshops and attracts thousands to its annual literary festival.

Northwest of Hay lie the old spa towns of Radnorshire and Brecknockshire, namely **Llanwrtyd Wells**, **Llandrindod Wells** and the largest, **Builth Wells**. Crossed by spectacular mountain roads such as the **Abergwesyn Pass** from Llanwrtyd, the countryside to the north is supremely beautiful, dotted with ancient churches and remote hill-farming hamlets, from the lively border communities of **Presteigne** and **Knighton** to inland centres like **Rhayader**, the nearest centre of population for the grandiose reservoirs of the **Elan Valley**.

The northern portion of Powys, **Montgomeryshire**, is as sparsely populated and remote as its two southern siblings. In common with most of mid-Wales, country towns here such as **Llanidloes** have a sizeable stock of New Age health-food shops, healing groups and arts activity. To the west, the inhospitable mountain of **Plynlimon** is flecked with boggy heathland and gloomy reservoirs, beyond which the hearty town of Machynlleth (covered in Chapter 4) sits out on a limb of Powys. The eastern side of Montgomeryshire is home to the anglicized old county town, **Montgomery**, between the robust towns of **Welshpool** and **Newtown**. The northern segment of the county is even quieter, with the only crowds being found along the banks of **Lake Vyrnwy**, a flooded-valley reservoir.

Highlights

❶ Ystradfellte waterfalls Explore the trio of great waterfalls in the limestone country around Ystradfellte. **See p.207**

❷ Glasbury Canoe downstream along the tranquil River Wye. **See p.216**

❸ Abergavenny Dine on locally sourced Welsh cuisine from some of the country's finest chefs at Abergavenny's restaurants, or hit town for its prestigious food festival. **See p.218**

❹ Hay-on-Wye Browse millions of secondhand books at over thirty bookshops in this bibliophile's paradise. **See p.225**

❺ Llanwrtyd Wells Get your festival fix at the home of Welsh wacky events, such as the Man versus Horse Marathon or the Real Ale Wobble. **See p.228**

❻ Presteigne Step back in time at the 1868 Judge's Lodging, now an evocative museum. **See p.236**

❼ Offa's Dyke Walk along this massive earthwork through the ever-changing borderlands. **See p.240**

HIGHLIGHTS ARE MARKED ON THE MAP ON P.203

By train Services are restricted to the Heart of Wales line from Shropshire to Swansea via Knighton, Llandrindod Wells, Llanwrtyd Wells and smaller stops in between, and the Shrewsbury–Machynlleth route through Welshpool and Newtown.

By bus Many larger centres such as Brecon, Llanidloes, Rhayader, Builth Wells and Hay-on-Wye rely on sporadic bus services, although most places can be reached via a handful of daily services.

Check Getting around in Basics for discount fares and passes.

Brecon Beacons National Park

With the lowest profile of Wales' three national parks, the **Brecon Beacons** are refreshingly uncrowded, primarily attracting local urban walkers. Spongy hills of grass and rock tumble and climb around river valleys that lie between sandstone and limestone uplands peppered with glass-like lakes and villages that seem to have been hewn from one rock. Known for their vivid quality of light, the hills of the Beacons disappear and re-emerge from hazy blankets of cloud, with shafts of sun sharpening the lush green patchwork of fields.

Covering 520 square miles, the national park straddles southern Powys and northern Monmouthshire from west to east. The most remote parts are around the Black Mountain peaks to the west, with miles of tufted moorland and bleak, often dangerous, summits, plummeting to the porous limestone country in the southwestern section, a rocky terrain of rivers, deep caves and spluttering waterfalls. To the northeast, the lonely Black Mountains (not to be confused with the entirely separate Black Mountain to the west) are separated from the Beacons themselves by the Monmouthshire and Brecon Canal, which forges a passage along the Usk Valley. Built around the beginning of the nineteenth century to support coal mining, iron ore and limestone quarrying, the canal is an impressive feat of engineering, successfully steering a 25-mile lock-free stretch (Britain's longest) through some of the most mountainous terrain in Wales.

Getting around the largely rural territory of the Brecon Beacons National Park can be difficult without your own wheels.

Trains Abergavenny is the only town with a train station, though Merthyr Tydfil, on the southern flank of the park, is well connected by rail to Cardiff.

Buses With relatively frequent services (often 4–6 daily) along the major routes, buses are a much better bet than trains; a smattering of services only run on certain days. The main routes are from Abergavenny to Brecon and on to Libanus, Merthyr and Cardiff (#X43); Brecon to Talgarth, Hay-on-Wye and Hereford (#39); Brecon to Swansea via

Sennybridge, Craig-y-nos and the Dan-yr-ogof Showcaves (#X63); Brecon to Llandrindod (#X704). Detailed listings of services in the area are contained in the free *Discover the Brecon Beacons* leaflet, available from tourist offices and bus companies. From the second May bank holiday weekend until the end of September, the Beacons Bus (all day £8) loops around various routes within the park on Sundays and bank holidays – timetables can be downloaded from ⓦ www.travelbreconbeacons.info. The Cardiff service tows a bike trailer, enabling you to bus it here (£5) and cycle back down the Taff Trail (p.210).

Cycling The relatively compact nature of the region, the

ACCOMMODATION IN THE BRECON BEACONS

The Brecon Beacons offers plenty of diffuse **accommodation**, including plenty of low-budget options. *Camping on Farms* (downloadable at ⓦ www.breconbeacons.org/content/visit-us/where-to-stay/camping-on-farms/view) lists around forty low-cost and free sites scattered throughout the park, while *Bunkhouse Accommodation in the Brecon Beacons* covers two dozen bunkhouses – most charge £10–15 a night. There's also a list at ⓦ bunkhousesinwales.co.uk. If you're interested in self-catering accommodation, the best locally are *Brecon Beacons Holiday Cottages* (ⓣ 01874 676446, ⓦ breconcottages.com) and the *Abergavenny Farm Holidays Group* (ⓦ afhg.co.uk).

THE BRECON BEACONS & POWYS

HIGHLIGHTS
1. Ystradfellte Waterfalls
2. Glasbury
3. Abergavenny
4. Hay-on-Wye
5. Llanwrtyd Wells
6. Presteigne
7. Offa's Dyke (Knighton)

Trawsfynydd

Bala

Llangollen

Oswestry

Pennant Melangell
Llangynog
Pistyll Rhaedr
Llanrhaeadr-ym-Mochnant

Lake Vyrnwy
Llanwddyn
Llanfyllin

Mallwyd
Llanmynech

River Severn

Llanfair-Caereinion
Welshpool
Welshpool & Llanfair Light Railway
Powis Castle

Machynlleth

Berriew

Dylife
Staylittle
Gregynog Hall
Dolforwyn
Montgomery

ENGLAND

Plynlimon (2469ft)
Llyn Clywedog
HAFREN FOREST
Caersws
Newtown

Llanidloes

Llangurig

A483

Abbeycwmhir
Llananno

Knighton
7

Elan Valley
Rhayader
Cross Gates

Llanfihangel Rhydithon

RADNOR FOREST
6
Presteigne

Claerwen Reservoir
Elan

Disserth
Llandrindod Wells
New Radnor
Old Radnor

Abergwesyn Pass

Abergwesyn
Beulah
Cilmeri

Garth
Builth Wells
Llanwrtyd Wells
5
Llangammarch Wells

River Wye

N

Mynydd Eppynt

Glasbury
2
Hay-on-Wye
4

Sennybridge
Talgarth
Capel-y-ffin

Llangorse Lake

Brecon
Llanthony
BLACK MOUNTAINS

Black Mountain
Dan-yr-ogof

Tretower Court
Partrishow

BRECON BEACONS NATIONAL PARK
Brecon Beacons (2907ft)
Bwlch
Crickhowell

Craig-y-nos
FFOREST FAWR

River Usk
A40

Ystradfellte
1

3
Abergavenny

Coelbern

0   2
miles

profusion of narrow lanes and the many opportunities to get off-road make this a great place to travel by bike: rental locations include Brecon, Abergavenny and Hay-on-Wye.

Horseriding is also extremely popular and well organized; see the listings throughout this chapter, or visit ⓦ horseridingbreconbeacons.com.

The western Beacons

The western half of the Brecon Beacons National Park comprises the bleak uplands of Black Mountain and Fforest Fawr, and the sparsely populated valleys in between. It is evident everywhere that this is limestone country: caves, sinkholes and waterfalls dot the map. From the valleys, invigorating walks or bike rides thread up to the lonely moors for sweeping views across the Beacons.

Black Mountain

The most westerly expanse of upland in the national park is known as the **Black Mountain** (Mynydd Ddu). Despite being named in the singular (as distinct from the Black Mountains further east), the "mountain" actually covers an unpopulated range of barren, smooth-humped peaks that break suddenly at rocky escarpments towering over quiet streams and glacial lakes.

The area provides the most challenging and exhilarating walking in south Wales. Paths cross the wet, wild landscape from Dan-yr-ogof in the east, and from the soaring ruins of Carreg Cennen Castle, just short of Llandeilo in the west. Other good starting points for forays into the open Black Mountain uplands are Tyhwnt, near Ystradgynlais, in the south and, in the north, the hamlet of **LLANDDEUSANT**, seven miles south of Llandovery.

ACCOMMODATION	BLACK MOUNTAIN
YHA Llanddeusant ☏ 0845 371 9750, ⓦ yha.org.uk. A cosy hostel in the former village pub, with four-, six- and	eight-bed dorms as well as family rooms. You can camp here too. Closed Nov–Jan. Dorms **£14.40**

The Fforest Fawr geopark

Covering a vast expanse of hilly landscape between the Black Mountain and the central Beacons southwest of Brecon, **Fforest Fawr** (Great Forest) seems something of a misnomer for an area of largely unforested sandstone hills dropping down to a porous limestone belt in the south. The "forest" tag refers more to the old definition of a forest as land used as a hunting ground. In 2005, Fforest Fawr was recognized – and is now subsequently administered – by UNESCO as a geopark, becoming part of the Europe-wide network of other geoparks.

The hills rise up to the south of the A40 west of Brecon, with the dramatic A4067 Sennybridge–Ystradgynlais road scoring the western side of the range and the A470 Brecon–Merthyr road defining the Fforest's eastern limit.

A WALK AROUND LLANDDEUSANT

The OS Explorer 1:25,000 map #OL12 (Brecon Beacons – Western & Central Area) is recommended. Passing both Llyn y Fan Fach and Llyn y Fan Fawr, this bleak and lonely ascent weaves through classic post-glacial scenery: valleys slashed with tumbling streams cut between purple hills, while occasional mounds and moraines of rock debris indicate the force of the ice that pushed through the valleys. Such heaps sometimes grew to a size large enough to form a natural dam, building up lakes, such as Llyn y Fan Fach, in their wake.

The walk (12 miles; 4–5hr; 1400ft ascent) starts in Llanddeusant and climbs steeply to Llyn y Fan Fach, from where a precarious path leads around the top of the escarpment, following the ridge to **Fan Brycheiniog** (2630ft), above the glassy black waters of Llyn y Fan Fawr. Return the same way.

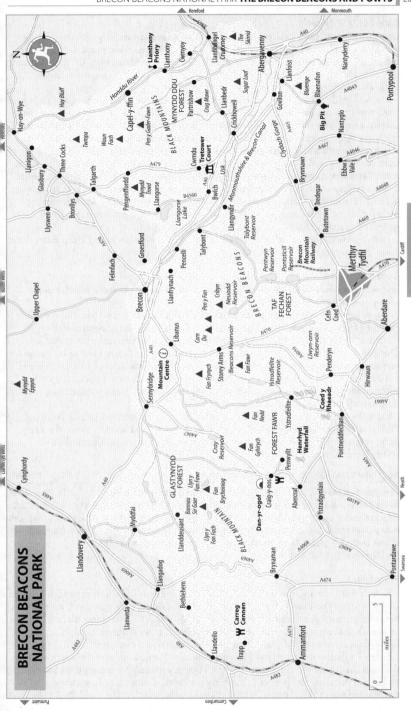

BRECON BEACONS NATIONAL PARK

3

Dan-yr-ogof Showcaves

Just west of A4067 • April–Oct daily 10am–3pm • £13.50 • ☎ 01639 730284, ⓦ showcaves.co.uk

The upper reaches of the valley of the Afon Tawe, Swansea's river, mark the limestone belt, as seen in the hamlet of **Glyntawe** at the **Dan-yr-ogof Showcaves**. Only discovered in 1912, and opened to the public in 1939, it's claimed the caves form the largest system of subterranean caverns in northern Europe.

In a self-guided tour, with commentary resonating from loudspeakers, the path first leads you into the **Dan-yr-ogof** cave, the longest showcave in Britain, and a warren of caverns framed by stalactites and frothy limestone deposits. Although the whole cave is known to be around ten miles long, you'll be steered around a circular route of about a mile and a half. Back outside, you pass a re-created Iron Age "village" and walk past some of the many life-size fibreglass dinosaurs sprinkled around the site to reach **Cathedral Cave**, a succession of spookily lit caverns leading into the "cathedral" itself, a hugely impressive 150ft-long, 70ft-high cave. Reachable via a precarious path behind the dinosaur park is **Bone Cave**, the third and final cavern, known to have been inhabited by Bronze Age tribes, with some 42 human (and many animal) skeletons found here.

There's plenty more to see and do here, especially for kids, including a museum, shire horse centre, playground and farm.

Craig-y-nos Castle

400yd south of Dan-yr-ogof Showcaves • ☎ 01639 730205, ⓦ craigynoscastle.com • Free self-guided tour of ground floor; historian led-tours £10 (on request)

The nineteenth-century **Craig-y-nos Castle** is a grand folly built in 1842 and fancifully extended from 1878, when it was bought by Adelina Patti, the celebrated Italian-American opera singer. In her forty years of residence, she turned the place into a diva-esque castle, even adding a scaled-down version of the Drury Lane opera house for performances. After Ms Patti's reign, Craig-y-nos suffered decades of chronic neglect, until it was bought in the mid-1990s, renovated and turned into an oddball **hotel** and entertainment venue. The Grade I listed opera house, which was once used as a hospital, still stages the occasional concert.

Some 44 acres of the castle's grounds form part of the Brecon Beacons National Park and operate as **Craig-y-nos Country Park** (unrestricted access). From the car park, there are signposted walks around a landscaped site along the banks of the young River Tawe.

ACCOMMODATION, EATING AND DRINKING FFOREST FAWR

Changing Seasons ☎ 07535 488009. Above the car park next to the castle, this lovely tea room and restaurant keeps local walkers satisfied with its selection of home-made pies and pasties, cakes and ice cream. There's lots of seasonal and organic produce to buy, too. Mon–Thurs & Sun 10am–6pm, Fri & Sat 10am–10.30pm.

Craig-y-nos Castle ☎ 01639 730284, ⓦ craigynos castle.com. Various blocks and rooms within the castle have been converted into a whole range of high-class rooms and apartments sleeping two to four people, with quite a few family rooms. **£140**

Ystradfellte

A wonderful, twisting mountain road between Pontneddfechan to the south and the A4067 crosses the Fforest Fawr and drops down into the valley of the Afon Llia and the limestone crags around the hamlet of **YSTRADFELLTE**. Little more than a handful of houses, a church and a pub, this is, nonetheless, a phenomenally popular centre for walking, as a result of the dazzling countryside on its doorstep. Lush, deep ravines – a total contrast to the barren mountains immediately to the north – carve through the limestone ridge south of the village, with great pavements of bone-white rock littering fields next to cradling potholes, disappearing rivers and thundering waterfalls.

The River Mellte waterfalls

A mile south of Ystradfellte, the River Mellte tumbles into the dark and icy mouth of the **Porth-yr-ogof** cave, emerging into daylight a few hundred yards further south. A signposted path heads south from the Porth-yr-ogof car park and into the green gorge of the River Mellte. Continue for little more than a mile to the first of its three great waterfalls, **Sgwd Clun-Gwyn** (White Meadow Fall), where the river crashes 50ft over two huge, angular steps of rock before hurtling down course for a few hundred yards to the other two falls, the graceful **Sgwd Isaf Clun-Gwyn** (Lower White Meadow Fall) and, a little further on, the mighty **Sgwd y Pannwr** (Fall of the Fuller).

The path continues through the foliage to the confluence of the rivers Mellte and Hepste, half a mile further on. A quarter of a mile along the Hepste is arguably the most impressive of the area's falls, the **Sgwd yr Eira** (Fall of Snow), where the rock below the main tumble has eroded back 6ft, allowing people to walk directly behind a dramatic 20ft curtain of water – particularly dazzling in afternoon or evening light.

Pontneddfechan waterfalls

Just off the A465 along the forested valley of the River Nedd (or Neath), near the village of **PONTNEDDFECHAN**, are some spectacular waterfalls. The most famous of these is the **Sgwd Gwladus** (The Lady Falls), an easyish mile's walk along the river from Pontneddfechan, which, like Sgwd yr Eira, overhangs enough to allow you to walk behind. A few hundred yards further, though accessible only via stepping stones and a bit of a scramble that can be tricky after heavy rain, is perhaps the best of all, the sublime **Sgwd Einion Gam** (The Fall of Crooked Einion).

INFORMATION　　　　　　　　　　　　　　　　　　　**PONTNEDDFECHAN**

The Waterfalls Centre in the centre of the village (Easter–Sept daily 9.30am–5pm (closed 1–1.30pm), Oct–Easter Sat & Sun 9.30am–3pm; ☎01639 721795) can provide lots of good information on walks to the many falls. There's also an exhibition on the Fforest Fawr geopark.

Penderyn Welsh Whisky Distillery

Daily 9.30am–5pm • Tours £6 • ☎01685 813300, ⓦ welsh-whisky.co.uk

Four miles east of Pontneddfechan in the village of **PENDERYN** is the **Welsh Whisky Distillery**. When it opened in 2000, Penderyn became Wales' first working distillery for more than one hundred years, and today it produces three single malt whiskies, matured in bourbon barrels and finished in Madeira wine casks. Hour-long **guided tours** of the centre take in an exhibition on the working of the distillery and an explanation of the distillation and bottling processes; uniquely, the process here at Penderyn involves the use of a single copper pot still – as opposed to the conventional two or three – before the whisky is matured for between four and seven years; you'll also get a little taster at the end of the tour.

The central Beacons

The **central Brecon Beacons** – after which the whole national park is named – are well set up for walking and pony trekking. The area, to the immediate south of Brecon town, centres on the two highest peaks in south Wales, **Pen y Fan** (2907ft) and **Corn Du** (2863ft), half a mile to the west. Although neither reaches 3000ft, the terrain is unmistakably and dramatically mountainous: classic old red sandstone country with sweeping peaks rising out of glacially carved land.

The combined ascent of **Pen y Fan** and **Corn Du** is the most popular walk in the park. The most direct route up is the well-trampled red-mud path that starts from Pont ar Daf, half a mile south of Storey Arms on the A470 midway between Brecon and Merthyr Tydfil. The ascent is a comparatively easy five-mile round trip, gradually climbing up the southern flank of the two peaks. A longer and generally quieter route

A CIRCULAR WALK AROUND CORN DU AND PEN Y FAN

The OS Explorer 1:25,000 map #OL12 (Brecon Beacons West & Central) is recommended.
Few walkers visiting the Brecon Beacons for the first time can resist making an ascent of the two highest peaks: Corn Du and Pen y Fan. Most take one of the shorter routes from the A470 south of Brecon, but connoisseurs prefer this longer and infinitely more rewarding **circular "Gap" route** (8 miles; 4–5hr; 1400ft ascent) that makes an anticlockwise circuit around a ridge-top horseshoe of the Beacons.

The hike starts at the car park by the late Victorian Neuadd reservoirs and crosses the dam of the lower, smaller reservoir, then climbs westwards up the hill in front. Head right (north) along a well-defined path along the ridge top including Graig Fan Ddu. Follow the obvious path that strikes up the sandstone ridge to the first summit, then down to a shallow saddle and up again to the peak of Pen y Fan, the highest point in south Wales. Either carry on to the next summit, Cribyn, and then descend to the Gap, or turn right by the stream in the valley between Pen y Fan and Cribyn, around the base of Cribyn and then back to the Neuadd reservoirs.

3

leads up to the two peaks from the "Gap" route – the pre-nineteenth-century (and possibly Roman) main road winding north from the Neuadd reservoirs through the only natural break in the central Beacons' sandstone ridge to the bottom of the lane. The route eventually joins the main street in the Brecon suburb of Llanfaes as Bailihelig Road. Although the old road is no longer accessible for cars, car parks at either end open out onto the track for an eight-mile round-trip ascent up Pen y Fan and Corn Du from the east.

Brecon and around

The handsome Georgian buildings of **BRECON** (Aberhonddu) stand at the northern edge of the Beacons, bearing testimony to the town's past importance. A Roman fort was built near here, but the town only started to grow with the building of a Norman castle and Benedictine monastery, founded in 1093 on the banks of the Honddu River, which gives the town its Welsh name. To the dual strands of military and ecclesiastical importance was added the status of regional market centre and cloth-weaving town. In the seventeenth-century Civil War, the townsfolk demonstrated their neutrality between the forces of Parliament and the Crown by demolishing most of the castle and large sections of the town walls, dissipating the appeal for either side of seizing their town. Today, it's a lively base for walkers and less active visitors alike, with good accommodation, and plenty of places to eat and drink.

Brecon's imposing central square, at the western end of **The Bulwark**, is flanked by the solid-red sixteenth-century tower of **St Mary's church**, an assortment of old-fashioned shop frontages, and the elegant Georgian portico of the **Wellington Hotel**. The grid of streets north and west of The Bulwark is packed with some delightful Georgian and Victorian buildings. Northwest, at the crossroads of High Street Inferior, Ship Street descends down to the **River Usk**, the bridge crossing the Usk next to the point where the smaller Honddu River flows in from the north.

Brecknock Museum

Captain's Walk • Mon–Fri 10am–5pm, Sat 10am–1pm & 2–5pm • £1 • ☎ 01874 624121
At the junction of The Bulwark and Glamorgan Street is the neo-Grecian frontage of the **Brecknock Museum**, where there's an interesting walk-through history of Wales and a nineteenth-century assize court, last used in 1971 and preserved in all its ponderous splendour, overseen by the high judge's throne. Elsewhere, there are galleries on town and rural life, though more impressive is the archeology gallery, featuring inscribed stones dating back to the fifth century and a selection of painstakingly carved Welsh love spoons – some over four hundred years old – that were betrothal gifts for courting

Welsh lovers. The prize exhibit, however, is a remarkably well-preserved, 15ft-long *crannog* (log boat or dug-out canoe), dredged up from Llangorse Lake in 1925 and reckoned to date from around 760 AD.

Regimental Museum

The Watton. Easter–Sept Mon–Fri 10am–5pm, Sat 10am–4pm, plus certain Sun; Oct–March Mon–Fri 10am–5pm • £4 • ☎ 01874 613310, ⓦ rrw.org.uk

Beyond the foreboding frontage of the South Wales Borderers' **barracks** is its **Regimental Museum**, packed with mementos from the regiment's three-hundred-year existence. As well as an extraordinary stache of guns and medals, there's coverage of campaigns in Burma, the Napoleonic and Boer Wars, both World Wars and the ongoing mission in Afghanistan. Most absorbing, though, are the tales of the 1879 Zulu War when 140 Welsh soldiers faced an attack by 4000 Zulu warriors. There's even a piece of the Berlin Wall here.

The Monmouthshire and Brecon Canal

A series of colourful terraced streets runs down to the town's theatre and the northern terminus of the **Monmouthshire and Brecon Canal**, where afternoon cruises aboard the *Dragonfly* (March–Oct; ☎07831 685222, ⓦdragonfly-cruises.co.uk; £7) ease their way out of town for enjoyably relaxed two-and-a-half hour trips. Inside the old tollhouse at the same spot, Beacon Park Day Boats (☎0800 612 2890, ⓦbeaconparkdayboats. co.uk) have boats and canoes for hire.

Brecon Cathedral

Cathedral Close, Priory Hill • ☎ 01874 623857, ⓦ breconcathedral.org.uk

Over the rushing waters of the Honddu, Priory Hill climbs up to the stark grey

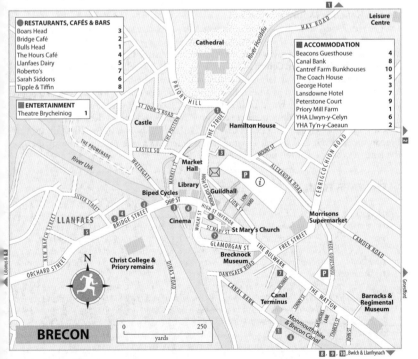

3

buildings of the monastery settlement, centred on the **cathedral**, or Priory Church of St John the Baptist. Its surprisingly lofty interior, framed by a magnificent timber roof, is graced with a few Norman features intact from the eleventh-century priory that was built here on the site of a probable earlier Celtic church. The hulking Norman font sits at the western end of the nave, near the entrance, as does the unusual **Cresset Stone**, a large boulder indented with thirty scoops in which to place oil or wax candles; it's thought to be the last remaining one in the country. From here the south aisle runs down to the most interesting of the many family memorials, the **Games monument** (1555), made up from three oak beds and depicting an unknown woman whose hands remain intact in prayer, but whose arms and nose have been unceremoniously hacked off.

Heritage Centre

Cathedral Close, opposite the cathedral • April–Oct daily 10.30am–4.30pm, Nov–March Mon–Sat noon–4pm • Free • ☎ 01874 625222

A converted seventeenth-century tithe barn houses the cathedral's **heritage centre**, holding a small and intermittently interesting collection of gilded vestments, Bibles, crucifixes and the like. The star piece, though, is an oversized chair believed to have been used by King Charles I when he stayed at Priory House in 1645. The attached *Pilgrims* tearoom is extremely popular.

The castle and riverbank

Between the cathedral and the River Usk, the few remains of the town's **castle** are moulded into the walls of the *Castle Hotel*. The end result is a powerful, if bizarre, amalgam that looks its best from along **The Promenade** by the River Usk, reached from the town-centre side of the river bridge. In high summer, motor and rowing boats can sometimes be rented along the riverbank.

Brecon Beacons Mountain Centre

6 miles southwest of Brecon, off A470 (turn off at Libanus) • Daily: March–June & Sept–Oct 9.30am–5pm; July & Aug 9.30am–5.30pm; Nov–Feb 9.30am–4.30pm • Free • ☎ 01874 623366, ⊛ breconbeacons.org

Scenically placed outside town is the National Park Visitor Centre, also known as the **Brecon Beacons Mountain Centre**. It's chiefly useful for its well-stocked shop of maps, books and guides. There are also interesting displays on the flora, fauna, geology and history of the area, as well as an excellent café serving hot meals. You can walk straight out from the door onto Mynydd Illtud Common, laced with gentle paths looking across to some major peaks. Staff here can give experienced hikers details of walks tackling the more challenging peaks of Corn Du and Pen y Fan (see p.207). Buses leave Brecon for Merthyr and stop at Libanus, from where it's a one-mile uphill walk along the lane next to the church up to the centre.

THE TAFF TRAIL

Running from Brecon to Cardiff Bay, the 55-mile **Taff Trail** (⊛ tafftrail.org) passes through a spectacular cross section of south Wales scenery: the Usk Valley, the Brecon Beacons uplands, the former coal-mining Taff Valley and urban parkland. Most of the route – which is open to hikers and bikers – is on forest trails, designated pathways and country lanes and is seldom steep. Pubs and restaurants along the way are marked on the free *Taff Trail* map, available from tourist offices and park information centres, which also shows the location of train stations and the occasional trail-side campsite.

Perhaps the best way to tackle the whole trail is to start in Brecon (where there's bike rental), ride to Cardiff – downhill much of the way – then catch a train back to Merthyr Tydfil and ride the fifteen miles back over the hills to Brecon. Keen riders could do this in a day, though you might prefer to break the journey in Pontypridd or Cardiff. Also see p.202 for details of the Beacons Bus Cardiff bike service.

ARRIVAL AND DEPARTURE

By bus Buses stop above the car park on Heol Gouesnou. Destinations Aberdulais (4 daily; 1hr 10min); Abergavenny (hourly Mon–Sat; 1hr 40min); Builth Wells (7 daily Mon–Sat; 40min); Cardiff (5 daily; 1hr 30min); Craig-y-nos/Dan-yr-ogof (6 daily; 40min); Crickhowell (hourly Mon–Sat; 25–45min); Hay-on-Wye (6 daily; 45min); Hereford (5 daily; 1hr 45min); Libanus (every 30–60min; 15min); Llandrindod Wells (7 daily Mon–Sat; 1hr); Merthyr Tydfil (hourly; 40min); Sennybridge (9 daily; 15min); Swansea (2–3 daily; 1hr 30min); Talgarth (6 daily; 25min); Talybont (6 daily Mon–Sat; 20min).

INFORMATION

Tourist information The TIC is in the large car park off Lion St, (April–Oct Mon–Sat 9.30am–5.15pm, Sun 10am–4pm; Nov–March daily 10am–4pm; ☎01874 622485, ⓦbreconbeacons.org); its vast stock of material includes a comprehensive range of walking maps for the Brecons.

Internet access At the TIC (£1 for 15min) and free at the town library on Ship St (Mon & Wed–Fri 9.30am–5pm, Tues 9.30am–7pm, Sat 9.30am–1pm).
Bike rental Biped Cycles, 10 Ship St (Mon–Sat 9am–5.30pm; ☎01874 622296, ⓦbipedcycles.co.uk), has a good stock of bikes for all ages and levels for around £25 a day.

ACCOMMODATION

Ample **accommodation** to suit all pockets exists in Brecon's compact town centre, while the suburb of Llanfaes, across the river from the main town, has a handful of smaller hotels and B&Bs on its main street. There's also a decent stock of hostel-style accommodation around the fringes of town. Places get booked up months in advance for the jazz festival in August.

HOTELS AND GUESTHOUSES

Beacons Guesthouse 16 Bridge St, Llanfaes ☎01874 623339, ⓦthebreconbeacons.co.uk. Converted townhouse concealing a large number of differently coloured rooms (some with shared showers and one with a four-poster), all leading off a central spiral staircase. Pleasant guest lounge and a dinky cellar bar with just two tables. **£58**

★ **Canal Bank** Ty Gardd ☎01874 623464, ⓦaccommodation-breconbeacons.co.uk. Picturesquely pitched right on the canal just a 5min walk from town, this wonderful three-room guesthouse comes with super home comforts, genuine hospitality and a superb breakfast. **£90**

Cantre Selyf 5 Lion St ☎01874 622904, ⓦcantreselyf.co.uk. Large and imposing seventeenth-century townhouse, all creaking floors and moulded plaster ceilings, but sensitively modernized with smart bathrooms and firm cast-iron beds in its three generously sized rooms. Delicious breakfasts. **£75**

The Coach House 12/13 Orchard St ☎01874 620043, ⓦcoachhousebrecon.com. High-class and very hospitable guesthouse with up-to-the-mark rooms painted in smooth creams and browns and furnished with designer lamps, mirrors and suchlike. Delicious Welsh breakfasts including vegetarian options. They also offer a range of holistic treatments and can organize transport for walkers. **£70**

George Hotel George St ☎01874 623421, ⓦgeorge-hotel.co.uk. The building itself is the most appealing thing about this centrally located seventeenth-century hotel, though the rooms are perfectly acceptable, if somewhat dowdily furnished. **£80**

Lansdowne Hotel 39 The Watton ☎01874 623321, ⓦlansdownehotel.co.uk. Pleasantly old-fashioned hotel in a handsome Georgian corner house, offering nine smallish en-suite rooms, including some for families, but they are pretty good value. £65, family rooms **£85**

Peterstone Court Llanhamlach, 3.3 miles east of Brecon ☎01874 665387, ⓦpeterstone-court.com. Historic country manor set in lush countryside blending antique and contemporary furnishings. There are also spa facilities, a swimming pool and a good restaurant. **£115**

HOSTELS, BUNKHOUSES AND CAMPSITES

Cantref Farm Bunkhouses Cantref Pony Trekking Centre, four miles southeast of Brecon off A40 ☎01874 665223, ⓦcantref.com. Dormitory-style accommodation with rooms in two large stone farm buildings, both with kitchen, lounge and showers.; minimum two-night stay on weekends. Campers can pitch tents in the grounds. Pitches **£3.50**, dorms **£14.50**

Priory Mill Farm Hay Rd ☎01874 611609, ⓦpriorymillfarm.co.uk. Lovely, low-key riverside campsite, with wooden cabins for showers and trays for log fires. It's on the northern edge of town, reached by a 10min walk along the riverbank. Open March–Oct. Pitches **£7**

YHA Brecon Groesffordd, just over 2 miles east of Brecon ☎0845 371 9506, ⓦyha.org.uk. Large Victorian farmhouse close to Brecon, reached via the path (Slwch Lane) from Cerrigcochion Rd in town or a mile from bus stops at either Cefn Brynich lock (Brecon–Abergavenny buses) or Troedyrharn Farm

BRECON JAZZ FESTIVAL

Held over the second or third weekend of August, the **Brecon Jazz Festival** is one of Britain's most prestigious music gatherings. The line-up is invariably outstanding, with artists of the calibre of Femi Kuti, Zoe Rahman and the Matthew Herbert Big Band playing venues as diverse as Brecon Cathedral, Christ's College and the Market Hall. Tickets typically cost £8–15. For more information visit ⓦhayfestival.com/breconjazz. The Brecon Fringe Festival (ⓦbreconfringe.co.uk) encompasses alternative, predominantly local, bands playing cafés, pubs and galleries.

(Brecon–Hereford buses). Open all year. Dorms **£16.40**, doubles **£48**

YHA Llwyn-y-Celyn 7 miles southwest of Brecon, near Libanus ☎0845 371 9029, ⓦyha.org.uk. Traditional farmhouse hostel, just off the A470 and main bus route to Merthyr. March–Oct, Nov–Feb weekends only. Dorms **£16.40**, doubles **£48**

EATING AND DRINKING

Brecon has a select number of decent places **to eat**, though the **drinking** options are fairly low-key and not quite so inviting. While here, be sure to try real ales from the local **Breconshire Brewery**, which you'll find on tap in many local pubs.

RESTAURANTS AND CAFÉS

Bridge Café 7 Bridge St ☎01874 622024. Good-looking café/bistro by the bridge featuring a homespun interior with oak flooring, kitchen-style tables and chairs and fireside sofas. The menu changes monthly but expect a range of interesting dishes like Welsh beef goulash and Catalan fish stew. Mains £11. The only letdown is its very limited opening hours. March–Oct, Thurs–Sat 6.30am–11pm, Sun 9–11am.

★ **The Felin Fach Griffin** Felinfach, A470 3 miles northwest ☎01874 620111. High-end gastropub that's well worth a visit for its superb modern Welsh cuisine; the meat is sourced locally (Bwlch venison with artichoke) and the fish is delivered from Cornwall (monkfish tail with chicory). Mains £15–20. Daily 11.30am–11pm.

The Hours Café 15 Ship St ☎01874 622800. Cheerful daytime café-cum-bookshop, with sloping floors and black timber beams, where you can enjoy warm salads and toasted sandwiches, hearty soups, cakes and a good range of free-trade coffees. Tues–Sat 10am–5pm.

Llanfaes Dairy 19 Bridge St ☎01874 625892. Colourful ice-cream parlour just across the river, serving scrumptious and exotic home-made flavours like maple walnut and mascapone orange. Daily 10.30am–5.30pm.

Roberto's St Mary's St ☎01874 611880. Diminutive place occupying the town's former post office, offering a little slice of Italy, with vines adorning the beams, wine bottles lining the walls and Italian/Welsh classics like home-made ravioli with leeks and cheese. Mains £10–15. Mon–Sat 5.30–10pm.

★ **Tipple & Tiffin** Theatr Brycheiniog, Canal Wharf ☎01874 611866. A fetching waterside setting and easy-going atmosphere mark this place out as Brecon's most inviting restaurant; tapas-style dishes designed for sharing, along with a few more substantial options chalked up daily on a blackboard. Largely frequented by the pre-theatre crowd, but a terrific place to come any time. Mains £8–10. Tues–Sat 10am–10pm, Sun noon–4pm.

PUBS

Boars Head Ship St ☎01874 622856. Two very different bars: the front is basic and frequented mainly by locals, whereas the back bar is younger and louder; there's also a not all together convincing stone terrace overlooking the water. Daily noon–midnight, Fri & Sat till 2am.

Bull's Head 86 The Struet ☎01874 622044. Small and cheery locals' pub, with views over the Honddu River and towards the cathedral. Some decent local ales on offer and occasional live music. Daily noon–midnight, Fri & Sat till 2am.

Sarah Siddons 47 High St Inferior ☎01874 610666. Named after the famous actress, born here in 1755 when the pub was then known as the *Shoulder of Mutton*. It's a small, fairly ordinary-looking boozer, but it's extremely popular, especially with off-duty soldiers. Daily 11am–midnight, Fri & Sat till 1.30am.

ENTERTAINMENT

The **Theatr Brycheiniog** at the canal basin (☎01874 611622, ⓦbrycheiniog.co.uk) offers a rich programme of music, comedy, theatre and dance; while the old-fashioned Coliseum **cinema** is on Wheat Street near the central crossroads (☎01874 622501, ⓦcoliseumbrecon.co.uk).

A CIRCULAR WALK AROUND THE EASTERN BEACONS

The OS Explorer 1:25,000 map #OL11 (Brecon Beacons Central Area) is recommended.

A very rewarding eastern objective (but requiring careful map-reading) is Craig y Fan Ddu and the path skirting the top of the moorland rim beyond it, around the Caerfanell valley. By starting at the Blaen-y-glyn car park (grid reference SO 064169), on the lane between Talybont and Pontsticill/Merthyr, you begin the ascent through forest. The walk starts across the road, follows the River Caerfanell, crosses a concrete bridge, and forks left uphill, first along the edge of the forest, then through the forest itself, then left at the Torpantau car park entrance, and up the steep bank. You later face a hard climb up to the ridge of Craig y Fan Ddu, then carry on north a mile to Bwlch y Ddwyallt, where five paths converge. Bear southeast, past a monument, lying between two heaps of twisted metal, marking the spot of a wartime RAF plane crash. Climb to the top of the ridge, and then walk southeast along the rim. After half a mile, at a spur of land, head straight on, down the steep grassy slope, later following a fence, down into the valley, then alongside the river on a path past some little waterfalls towards the starting point.

3

The Usk Valley

Home to the majority of the national park's residents, and hence the greatest concentration of facilities for visitors, the wide, fertile Usk Valley leads southeast from Brecon, running parallel to the Monmouthshire and Brecon Canal and effectively dividing the Brecon Beacons proper from the Black Mountains to the northeast. The A40 connects Brecon and Bwlch with Tretower, Crickhowell and Abergavenny, providing a backbone for dozens of minor lanes which twist south over the Brecon Beacons or north into the bucolic headwaters of some of the Usk's tributaries.

Talybont and around

Six miles southeast of Brecon, **TALYBONT-ON-USK** is idyllically situated for walks, bike rides or canal trips. The lane heading south of the village over the canal heads towards a number of **reservoirs**, starting with the 323-acre **Talybont Reservoir**. It then wiggles up onto the rocky hillsides, past the waterfalls on the Nant Bwrefwr and beyond to the isolated and hauntingly beautiful Neuadd (or Beacons) reservoirs to the north, a good starting point for walks to the summits of Pen y Fan and Corn Du along the old "Gap" route; or, to the south, the more popular (and hence busier) **Pentwyn** and **Pontsticill** (aka Taf Fechan) **reservoirs**. Two eastbound paths at either end of the Pontsticill Reservoir enable escape from fellow walkers in favour of a fairly steep climb up the rocky slopes for wonderful views over the lakes.

Brecon Mountain Railway

Jan–March 3 trains Sat & Sun, April–Oct 5 trains daily • £10.50 return trip • ☎ 01685 722988, ⏹ breconmountainrailway.co.uk

Below Pontsticill, the tiny **Brecon Mountain Railway** shuttles passengers along a two-mile section of track on the eastern bank of the reservoir down to Pant station, which is the main station and from where trains depart. There are good visitor facilities at Pant, including a restaurant. The round trip takes just over an hour.

ARRIVAL AND DEPARTURE   TALYBONT-ON-USK

By bus Regular Brecon–Crickhowell buses stop at Talybont.

ACCOMMODATION

Usk Inn Station Rd ☎ 01874 676251, ⏹ uskinn.co .uk. Upmarket village pub transformed into a country restaurant with ten polished and fragrant-smelling rooms named after birds you'll spot along the River Usk. **£80**

White Hart Inn ☎ 01874 676227, ⏹ breconbunkhouse.co.uk. Pressed up hard against the canal, this big pub has an upstairs bunkhouse with four- and six-bed rooms and shared shower facilities.

Popular with walkers and cyclists. Cooked breakfast £6. Dorms £18

YHA Danywenallt ☎ 0845 371 9548, ⓦ yha.org.uk. Around a mile south of Talybont, at the northern end of the reservoir, this converted farmhouse offers small, bright dorms, a warming woodstove and meals by request (though no self-catering facilities). Dorms £20.40, doubles £51

EATING AND DRINKING

Star Inn ☎ 01874 676635. The most convivial of the village pubs, which stands out for its lengthy list of real ales, regular beer festivals and lively music nights. Daily 11.30am–11pm.

Travellers Rest ☎ 01874 676233. A homely spot with a roaring fire and good-looking restaurant, and a lovely menu featuring the likes of lamb shank on braised leeks, and pan fried shallots with cider. Mains £15. Wed–Sun 7–10pm, plus Sun 12.30–2.30pm.

Bwlch

A few miles northeast of Talybont, the little village of **BWLCH** is strung out along the A40 with spectacular valley views. The village makes a good, central base for **walks** in the surrounding mountains and for day-trips further afield, and also has a couple of outstanding budget **accommodation** options.

ARRIVAL AND DEPARTURE BWLCH

By bus Bwlch is served by Regular Brecon–Crickhowell buses.

ACCOMMODATION

Beacons Backpackers ☎ 01874 730215, ⓦ beaconsbackpackers.co.uk. Part of the *New Inn*, accommodating very tidy four- and six-bed en-suite dorms overlooking the valley. Dorms £20

Gliffaes Country House Hotel ☎ 01874 730371, ⓦ gliffaeshotel.com. Impressive Italianate manor set back from the A40 midway between Bwlch and Crickhowell (2 miles from both), has grand rooms, which have either a river or garden view, and serves sumptuous high teas. £104

The Star Bunkhouse ☎ 01874 730080, ⓦ starbunkhouse.com. Directly opposite Beacon Backpackers, and of a similar style, with three- and four-bed dorms and a self-catering kitchen. Dorms £17

EATING AND DRINKING

New Inn ☎ 01874 730215. Bwlch's only pub, the *New Inn* is an ancient former coaching house and quintessential Welsh village pub with decent food (including award-winning chilli), real ales and local events such as quiz nights. Daily 6–11pm.

Llangorse

North of Talybont and Bwlch, the B4560 threads its way four miles through rolling countryside to **LLANGORSE** (Llangors), sheltered in the western lee of the Black Mountains. The village is a mile northeast of the reed-shored **Llangorse Lake** (Llyn Syfaddan), which was notorious in medieval times for its supernatural properties (blood-red water, eerie sounds and mythical lost city). Its *crannog* (artificial lake island), the only one of its kind in Wales, is thought to have been a ninth-century seat of the royal house of Brycheiniog. Today, a reconstructed *crannog* at the water's edge has information panels interpreting the lake's history and legends.

Llangorse Riding & Ropes Centre

Gilfach Farm, 1 mile southeast of Llangorse • Mon–Sat 9am–10pm, Sun 9am–5pm • ☎ 01874 658272, ⓦ activityuk.com

Experienced climbers can rent gear cheaply here, and for beginners there are Learn to Climb sessions (£15 for 1hr; £26 for 2hr). Multi-activity indoor sessions (climbing, abseiling, scrambling) cost £25 for half a day and £45 for a full day, while there are many more outdoor pursuits available. The centre also offers off-road horseriding for beginners and intermediates (£14.50 for 1hr, £30 for half a day) and hacking for the experienced (£38 for half a day).

Lakeside Caravan and Camping ☏ 01874 658226, ⊛ llangorselake.co.uk. Well-equipped site with modern shower blocks, laundry, play area, shop, bar and restaurant. Also has boats and bikes for rental. Closed Nov to mid-March. Per adult £7.25, electricity £4

Llangorse Riding & Ropes Centre Gilfach Farm ☏ 0333 600 2020, ⊛ activityuk.com. There are a couple of bunkhouses on site, and although preference is generally given to groups using the centre, it's worth asking; there's also a small but neat campsite overlooking the lake. Bunkhouse £15.50, camping £5

Pen-y-Bryn House ☏ 01874 658606. A mile up the road in Llangorse itself, there's top-quality B&B at this delightful farmhouse. There's also a self-catering unit in the gardens which sleeps four. B&B £60, self-catering £140

Talgarth

Five miles north of Llangorse, **TALGARTH** is a spirited and friendly village built around its unusual town hall and the hulking **St Gwendoline's church** tower, constructed in the fourteenth century but harking back to Talgarth's position as a defence centre against the Norman invasion.

Talgarth Mill

The Square • April–Oct daily 10am–4pm • £3.50 • ☏ 01874 711352, ⊛ talgarthmill.org.uk

Originating from the mid-eighteenth century, **Talgarth Mill** fell into disuse in the 1940s, but a lengthy restoration programme has returned it to something like its former glory. And as before, it now harnesses the local waters to grind the corn to produce flour for the on-site bakery, which in turn supplies the café with a delicious array of breads and cakes. Once done with your refreshments, there's a tempting riverside walk along the banks of the River Ennig.

Tourist information The village's independently run and very well stocked TIC is inside the Tower Shop on the main square (April–Oct Mon–Sat 10am–4pm, Sun 10am–1pm; Nov–March Mon–Sat 10am–3.30pm, Sun 10am–1pm; ☏ 01874 712226, talgarthcentre.org.uk).

Gliding Black Mountains Gliding Club offers 30min trial flights costing £75 (☏ 01874 711463, ⊛ blackmountainsgliding.co.uk).

ACCOMMODATION, EATING AND DRINKING

Castle Hotel Bronllys Rd ☏ 07789 682335, ⊛ talgarthhotel.co.uk. Heading out of town in the direction of Bronllys, this roadside hotel/pub has three smart-looking rooms with snazzily designed bathrooms. They also own the cracking little fish and chip shop next door. £65

Strand Café Regent St ☏ 01874 711195. Part café, part secondhand bookshop, this quaint little establishment offers a gamut of snacky-style meals, from pies and salads to pizzas and puddings. Mon & Thurs–Sat 10am–9pm, Sun 10am–4pm.

Tower Hotel The Square ☏ 01874 711253, ⊛ towerhoteltalgarth.co.uk. The *Tower* has five standard rooms, as well as a bunkhouse with small dorms and shared bathroom facilities. The downstairs pub is nothing special, save for its decent range of local ales, some of which it brews on site. Hotel room £60, bunkhouse £20

Bronllys and around

Between Talgarth and the neighbouring village of **BRONLLYS** is **Bronllys Castle**, of which only a large twelfth-century cylindrical tower remains – climb to the top for stunning views up the Llynfi River valley and beyond to the light-washed peaks of the Black Mountains. There are some sparkling little places to **eat** and **sleep** around here.

Wye Valley Canoes

April–Oct • ☏ 01497 847213, ⊛ wyevalleycanoes.co.uk

Four miles northeast of Bronllys, just off the A438 on the B4350, the riverside village of **GLASBURY** is home to **Wye Valley Canoes**, where you can rent a kayak to paddle the gentle currents of the River Wye. Rental for a five-mile trip downstream to Hay-on-Wye (around two to three hours) costs £20 including minibus pick-up at the other end; longer trips, including multi-day rentals, are also possible.

ACCOMMODATION

Llangoed Hall ☎01874 754525, ⓦllangoedhall .co.uk. A couple of miles north of Llyswen on the A470, this luxurious pile is actually an ancient castle remodelled in the early twentieth century by Portmeirion's Clough Williams-Ellis. The large, decadent rooms are furnished in fabrics by Elanbach (the on-site textile printing company) and adorned with some lovely touches such as antique mirrors and old-fashioned wireless radios. **£210**

River Café at Wye Valley Canoes in Glasbury ☎01497

BRONLLYS

847007, ⓦwyevalleycanoes.co.uk. Four bright and refreshingly simple en-suite rooms above the restaurant, with splendid views across to the river. **£70**

Wye Knot Stop Llyswen ☎01874 754247, ⓦwyeknotstop.co.uk. This village café also possesses two spacious and uncluttered en-suite rooms, one of which sleeps up to four people, and the other is a downstairs, wheelchair-friendly room. Pleasantly restful place to stop over. **£65**

EATING AND DRINKING

Honey Café Just north of Bronllys on the main road, ☎01497 711904. A fixture since 1933, and still hugely popular for its home-made cakes and desserts, though the real pull is its spicy Tex-Mex evening menu. Summer daily 9am–9pm; winter Wed–Sat 9am–9pm, Sun–Tues 9am–6pm.

River Café At Wye Valley Canoes in Glasbury ☎01497 847007. Very fine Italian restaurant right by the river, whose fresh, Mediterranean-influenced fish and pasta

menu (crab pasta, pasta ricotta, grilled sea bass) is an absolute winner – alternatively, stop by for a heart-starting coffee and a home-baked treat out on the terrace. Mains £9–15. Wed–Sat 9am–11.30pm, Sun 9am–5.30pm.

Wye Knot Stop Llyswen ☎01874 754247, ⓦwyeknotstop.co.uk. Breezy daytime café serving the best coffee for miles around, alongside cream teas and a scrummy selection of cakes and pastries. Thurs–Tues 10am–4pm. Closed Jan.

Tretower Castle and Court

April–Oct daily 10am–5pm; Nov–March Fri & Sat 10am–4pm, Sun 11am–4pm • £3.50 • ☎01874 730279 • CADW

Rising from the valley floor twelve miles south of Talgarth, the solid round tower of the **castle and court** at **TRETOWER** (Tre-tŵr) was built to guard the valley pass, and still dominates the skyline from both the A40 and A479. Having replaced an earlier Norman fortification, the high, circular thirteenth-century tower is pretty much all that remains of the castle building, alongside a few sections of wall adjoining a farm. More impressive is the late fourteenth-century manor house, whose downstairs rooms contain a mock-up kitchen, pantry and buttery. The upstairs rooms, which can be viewed from an upper-level walkway, are now mostly stripped bare, but do still retain a certain faded grandeur.

Crickhowell

One of the gems of the Brecon Beacons, **CRICKHOWELL** (Crucywel; locally referred to as "Crick") lies on the northern shore of the wide and shallow Usk. Many a local myth has been spawned by its grand seventeenth-century **bridge** with thirteen arches visible from the eastern end but only twelve from the west. Bridge Street rises from the river and up to the uninspiring mound of the ruined **castle** and the wide **High Street**, which is lined with many coloured, rough-hewn tenements, handsome-looking shops and several old-fashioned butchers. New Road runs parallel to Bridge Street from the river, passing the steeple of the town's fourteenth-century **church of St Edmund**.

CRICKHOWELL'S FESTIVALS

Crickhowell stages two superb annual festivals. The big one is the **Green Man Festival** (ⓦgreenman.net), a three-day music jamboree in mid-August embracing folk, indie and Americana and featuring the likes of the Fleet Foxes and the Super Furry Animals. In addition, there are drum workshops, literary events, a cinema tent, kids' activities, performance art, comedy and a "healing field". At the beginning of March, Crickhowell hosts a popular eight-day **Walking Festival** (ⓦcrickhowellfestival.com) with guided walks ranging from tough all-day treks to easy strolls, costing £5–6.50 per walk, per person. A range of special-interest walks and talks is also part of the programme.

Table Mountain

Crickhowell's spectacular northern backdrop is **Table Mountain** (1481ft), whose brown cone presides over the rolling green fields below. The most scenic route up it is along the path that goes off by the electricity substation past The Wern off Llanbedr Road. At the summit are remains of the 2500-year-old hillfort (*crug*) of Hywel, from which Crickhowell takes its name. A steeper, and far shorter, route to Table Mountain starts from the village of **LLANBEDR**, some two miles north of Crickhowell, and heads up alongside the stream behind the *Perth-y-pia* bunkhouse. The views are among the best in the area. Many walkers follow the route to the north from Table Mountain, climbing two miles up to the plateau-topped limestone hump of **Pen Cerrig-calch** (2302ft).

INFORMATION AND ACTIVITIES   CRICKHOWELL

Tourist information The Crickhowell Resource and Information Centre on Beaufort Street (daily 10am–5pm; ☎01873 811970, ⓦcrickhowellinfo.org.uk) also incorporates a café, internet (£1.50 for 30min) and an upstairs gallery selling quality local art.

Activities Crickhowell Adventure Gear shop opposite the market cross at 1 High St (Mon–Sat 9am–5.30pm, Sun 10am–4pm, ☎01873 810020) sells caving and walking paraphernalia, while Mountain and Water (☎01873 831825, ⓦmountainandwater.co.uk) offers boating, caving, climbing, orienteering and other mountain activities (£85 for a full-day activity for 2 to 3 people).

ACCOMMODATION

Bear Hotel Beaufort St ☎01873 810408, ⓦbearhotel.co.uk. A grand old coaching inn whose architectural quirks have lent themselves to some highly idiosyncratic rooms; those in the hotel itself possess more character, while those in the old courtyard stables are a touch more polished. **£92**

Dragon High St ☎01873 810362, ⓦdragoncrickhowell .co.uk. Salmon-pink building at the quieter, far end of the High St, with fairly contemporary rooms, some adorned with Welsh artwork. Relaxing and friendly option. **£70**

★ **Tt Gwyn** Brecon Rd ☎01873 811625, ⓦtygwyn .com. Impressive eighteenth-century stone gatehouse a 5min walk north of town, offering three warm and sunny rooms, each one conceived on a Welsh literary theme and stocked accordingly (Dylan room, Cordell room, Vaughan room). Breakfast is taken in the delightful conservatory dining room and there are extensive gardens for rambling. Superb value. **£65**

CAMPING

Riverside Caravan Park New Rd ☎01873 810397, ⓦriversidecaravanscrickhowell.co.uk. A level, nicely manicured site with decent facilities located just before the bridge, though it's over 18s only. March–Oct. Pitches **£6**

EATING AND DRINKING

Bear Hotel Beaufort St ☎01873 810408. Romantic candlelit restaurant that is ideally suited to winter dining, while the outdoors garden is just the job for a summertime splurge of game or fish. Mains £12–20. The hotel's low-beamed pub is pretty much the town's social hub, sporting bags of charm and serving terrific beer. Daily noon–2pm & 6–11pm.

Bridge End Inn Bridge St ☎01873 810338. Comprising part of the town's former tollhouse, a truly old-fashioned pub with flagstone flooring, a stone fireplace and brass, copper pots hanging from the walls and ceilings, and a sweet riverside garden. Daily 11am–11.30pm.

★ **Nantyffin Cider Mill** Brecon Rd ☎01873 810775. Housed in a great stone barn a mile or so along the A40 towards Brecon, the old mill (with the cider press still intact) is now a tip-top restaurant serving innovative starters such as chicken liver and brandy parfait, followed by the likes of home-smoked fish pie with spinach. There's a serious wine list here too and a choice of ciders. Mains £15–18. Tues–Sat noon–3pm & 6–11pm, Sun noon–3pm.

Number 18 18 High St ☎01873 810337. Smart, glassed-in restaurant with downstairs and mezzanine-level seating, and a fresh and seasonal menu; the chargrilled venison, lamb and chicken dishes are particularly worth considering. Mains £12–15. The café, which fronts the restaurant, has some terrific coffees. Mon–Sat 9am–6pm, Sun 10am–5pm; restaurant Wed–Sat 6–11.30pm, Sun noon–4pm.

Abergavenny

Six miles southeast of Crickhowell, Wales' culinary mecca, **ABERGAVENNY** (Y Fenni), is a vibrant, confident town, though its history is somewhat more chequered. The first main settlement was around the Norman castle, which was built by the English king

Henry I's local appointee, Hameline de Ballon, with the express aim of securing enough power to evict local Welsh tribes from the area, an important through route into Wales. Hostility to the Welsh reached its peak at Christmas 1175, when William de Braose, then lord of the town, invited Gwent chieftains to the castle, only to murder them all. The town was shaken badly by the Black Death (1341–51) and a routing by Owain Glyndŵr in 1404, but continued to grow, thanks largely to the weaving and tanning trades that developed from the sixteenth century. The industries prospered alongside Abergavenny's flourishing **market**, still the focal point for a wide area every Tuesday. In World War II, Hitler's deputy, Rudolf Hess, was imprisoned in the town's mental asylum after his plane crash-landed in Scotland in 1941. Today, Abergavenny's combination of urban amenities and countrified setting makes it an ideal jumping-off point for forays into the central and eastern sections of the Brecon Beacons.

From the train station, Monmouth Road rises gently into the town centre, becoming Cross Street and, finally, High Street. Off to the right are Monk Street and, next to the turreted Victorian Gothic town hall, the wonderful covered **market** (Tues, Fri & Sat for produce, Wed flea market, regular weekend antiques fairs and Farmers' Market on fourth Thurs of every month).

The castle and museum

Any street heading south off Cross or High streets leads to Castle Street, where the dark, fragmented remains of Abergavenny's medieval **castle** (free access) languish

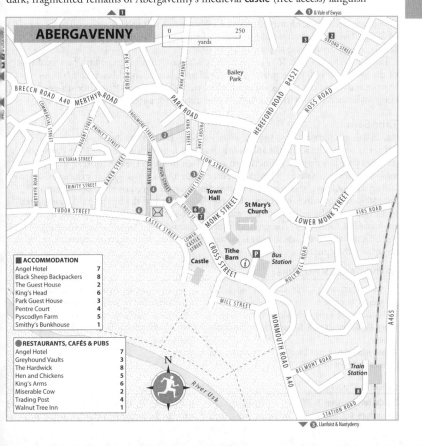

serenely above the River Usk. Entrance to the eleventh-century castle is through the sturdy, though now roofless, gatehouse, to the right of which stands an extensive portion of the curtain wall. The castle's keep, meanwhile, was remodelled in the nineteenth century, and sits in the middle of the forsaken ruins like an incongruous Lego model. Glorious views aside, the grounds are a lovely spot for a picnic.

Town museum

March–Oct Mon–Sat 11am–5pm, Sun 2–5pm, closed 1–2pm • Nov–Feb Mon–Sat 11am–1pm & 2–4pm • Free ☎ 01873 854282, ⓦ abergavennymuseum.co.uk

While in the castle grounds it's worth visiting the quirky **town museum**, where displays cover the town's history, using photographs and billboards, and re-created interiors including a saddlery, a sanitized Border farmhouse kitchen of 1890 and Basil Jones' grocery shop, once on Main Street. After the death of Jones' son in 1989, the contents of the shop were transported to the museum lock, stock and biscuit barrel. Some of it is recent, but much of it dates from the 1930s and 1940s.

Church of St Mary

Abergavenny's parish **church of St Mary**, on Monk Street, contains effigies and tombs spanning the entire medieval period. Originally built as the chapel of a small twelfth-century Benedictine priory, the existing building goes back only as far as the fourteenth century, although some of the monuments within predate the building itself. The interior manifests a wealth of outstanding detail, not least the **Jesse Tree**, one of the finest late medieval sculptures anywhere in Britain; a recumbent, twice-life-size statue of King David's father, it would once have formed part of an altarpiece tracing the family lineage from Jesse to Jesus.

There are effigies of Sir John de Hastings, who contributed greatly to the rebuilding of the priory, as well as members of the de Braose family, in addition to a host of marble and stone-cut tombs. Take a look, too, at the finely crafted fifteenth-century choir stalls, complete with (relatively) contemporary eighteenth-century graffiti.

Tithe Barn

Mon–Sat 10am–4pm, Food Hall Café 9am–5pm, plus Sun 11am–3pm • Free • ☎ 01873 858787, ⓦ stmarys-priory.org

Adjacent to the church is the splendidly restored fourteenth-century **Tithe Barn**, which in times past has variously functioned as a coach house, a theatre for travelling actors and even a disco. It's now a heritage centre, with a well-put-together exhibition on the history of the town, though this is somewhat overshadowed by the **Abergavenny Tapestry**, an expansive, brightly coloured visual record of the town's past. Completed just in time for the millennium, it was stitched by over fifty devoted volunteers and took around four years. The ground floor is occupied by a small information point and the bright *Food Hall Café*, which is an agreeable spot for some refreshments after absorbing the church.

ARRIVAL AND DEPARTURE   ABERGAVENNY

By train Abergavenny's train station is half a mile southeast of the centre.
Destinations Cardiff (every 30–60min; 45min); Hereford (every 45–60min; 25min); Newport (every 30–60min; 30min).
By bus Buses depart from Swan Meadows bus station, at the bottom of town on Cross St.

Destinations Brecon (hourly; 40min–1hr); Cardiff (hourly; 2hr); Clydach (hourly; 40min); Crickhowell (hourly Mon–Sat; 15min); Llanfihangel Crucorney (7 daily; 15min); Merthyr Tydfil (hourly; 1hr 30min); Monmouth (6 daily; 45min); Newport (hourly; 1hr 10min); Raglan (6 daily; 25min).

INFORMATION

Tourist information The TIC is adjacent to the bus station (daily: April–Oct 10am–5pm; Nov–March 10am–4pm;
☎ 01873 853254, ⓦ visitabergavenny.co.uk) and shares space with the Brecon Beacons National Park office.

Bike rental Hopyard Cycles in Govilon, a couple of miles west of town (☎01873 830219, ⓦ hopyardcycles.co.uk; from £15 for the day), can deliver bikes throughout the area.
Canal boats To explore the Monmouthshire and Brecon Canal, you can rent narrowboats (and day-rental motorboats as well as canoes) from Beacon Park Boats at Llanfoist (☎01873 858277, ⓦ beaconparkboats.com), a mile south of town.

ACCOMMODATION

Accommodation in the very centre of Abergavenny is fairly limited, though you don't have to go far to find some very reasonable guesthouses.

HOTELS AND GUESTHOUSES

Angel Hotel 15 Cross St ☎01873 857121, ⓦ angelhotelabergavenny.com. Occupying an old coaching inn, Abergavenny's premier central hotel is a warren of corridors with a range of very classy rooms, most of which possess big comfy beds and large bathrooms replete with posh toiletries. **£96**

★ **The Guest House** 2 Oxford St ☎01873 854823, ⓦ theguesthouseabergavenny.co.uk. Fun, popular guesthouse with six sunny rooms. Guest lounge with Sky Sports and a Wii console, a resident parrot in the dining room, and a backyard petting area with aviary. No credit cards. **£70**

King's Head 59 Cross St ☎01873 853575, ⓦ kingsheadhotel.co.uk. Smartly refurbished eighteenth-century town-centre pub next to the market hall; the fourteen en-suite rooms are not exactly bursting with character, but they are furnished to a high standard **£85**

Park Guest House 36 Hereford Rd ☎01873 853715, ⓦ parkguesthouse.co.uk. Exceptionally good-value B&B in a beautiful Georgian townhouse a short walk north of the centre. Six low-key rooms, three of which are en suite, offering a simple mix of styles and colours. **£55**

Pentre Court Brecon Rd ☎01873 853545, ⓦ pentrecourt.com. Small and friendly Georgian country house out on the road to Brecon, keeping four big and pleasantly old-fashioned en-suite rooms, a couple of which have views of the Usk Valley. There's a swimming pool for use during the summer and wooded gardens to amble around. Entrance is opposite the *Lamb & Flag* pub. **£70**

HOSTELS, BUNKHOUSES AND CAMPING

Black Sheep Backpackers 24 Station Rd ☎01873 859125, ⓦ blacksheepbackpackers.com. A few paces down from the station, this converted railway hotel has accommodation in twin, quad and dorm rooms, all with separate shower facilities. Continental breakfast included. Dorms **£16**; doubles **£39**

Pyscodlyn Farm Llanwenarth Citra, 2 miles west of town off A40 ☎01873 853271, ⓦ pyscodlyn caravanpark.com. Primarily a caravan site, but there is one sheltered field for campers. Good access as all Brecon or Crickhowell buses pass by. Also sells day fishing licences. Pitches **£8**

Smithy's Bunkhouse Lower House Farm, Pantygelli ☎01873 853432, ⓦ smithysbunkhouse.com. Self-catering dormitory accommodation under the slopes of the Sugar Loaf a couple of miles north of town. Good facilities including a well-equipped kitchen and common room with wood-burning stove. Dorms **£12.50**

EATING AND DRINKING

Abergavenny's reputation as Wales' culinary hotbed is more than justified, boasting as it does the finest concentration of restaurants anywhere in the country. The best of these, though, are outside town.

RESTAURANTS

★ **The Foxhunter** Nantyderry, 7 miles southeast of town ☎01873 881101, ⓦ thefoxhunter.com. Modern British cuisine by TV chef Matt Tebbutt, served in a lovingly restored former stationmaster's house. There's a fantastic wild food menu available (£35), or you can partake in a specially tailored foraging trip. Mains £16–20. Tues–Sat noon–3pm & 7–11pm.

Greyhound Vaults Market St ☎01873 858549. Don't be fooled by the dull, pub-like exterior and earthy interior, this place serves a wide range of tasty, moderately priced Welsh and English specialities, such as Welsh Black steak with leeks, and topside of beef with Yorkshire pudding. Mains £10–15. Tues–Sat 12–2pm, Sun 12–2.30pm, plus Fri & Sat 7–9pm.

★ **The Hardwick** Old Raglan Rd ☎01873 854220,

ABERGAVENNY FOOD FESTIVAL

Abergavenny's annual **Food Festival** (ⓦ abergavennyfoodfestival.co.uk) in mid-September is one of the most prestigious in Britain. It's tremendous fun, two bumper days of markets, master classes, tastings and talks, and pretty much any other take on food you can think of. The festival also has several spin-off events throughout the year, full details of which are on the main website.

ⓦthehardwick.co.uk. Headed up by TV chef Stephen Terry, this fabulous-looking pub, two miles east of town, offers a huge choice of brilliantly inventive dishes such as pan-fried salmon with grilled fennel, sea greens and cucumber butter sauce. Mains £17–25. Daily noon–3pm & 6.30–10pm; bar open all day.

Trading Post 14 Neville St ☎01873 855448. The former eighteenth-century *Cow Inn* – cast your eyes up to the row of cows' heads on the front of the building – is now a classy coffee house and bistro, and an ideal spot for reading the paper over a cappuccino or tucking into a steaming jacket potato. Mon–Sat 9am–5pm.

★ **Walnut Tree Inn** B4521 at Llanddewi Skirrid, 2 miles north of town ☎01873 852797, ⓦthewalnuttreeinn.com. Legendary foodies' paradise now under the helm of Shaun Hill, drawing diners from afar for its Mediterranean-accented British cuisine like turbot with spiced mussel and clam broth, and iced tiramisu parfait. Mains £18–25. Tues–Sat noon–3pm & 7–11pm.

CAFÉS AND PUBS

Angel Hotel 15 Cross St ☎01873 857121. High tea within the hotel's gracious dining room is a good enough reason alone to come to Abergavenny; the lavish spread typically includes a selection of sandwiches, pastries and scones, and costs £14.80 per person. Daily 3–5.30pm.

Hen and Chickens Flannel St, off High St ☎01873 853613. Timeless, traditional pub popular with locals and visitors alike, serving some of the best beer in town and staging regular live music, including jazz most Sunday evenings. Daily 10.30am–11pm.

Kings Arms 29 Neville St ☎01873 855074. Handsome pub combining old (stone fireplace and wonderful curving beams on the low ceiling) and new (neat modern furnishings) to smart effect. Good beer and very creditable food in the restaurant section. Daily 11am–11pm, Fri & Sat till 1am.

Miserable Cow Cibi Walk Precinct ☎07910 460548. Not in the most exciting of locations, but this friendly and colourful open-air café, with formica-covered tables and separate smoking/no smoking sections, serves fine coffee. Mon–Sat 8am–5.30pm, Sun 9am–3.30pm.

Court Cupboard Gallery

New Court Farm, Llantilio Pertholey, off A465 2 miles northeast of Abergavenny • Daily 10.30am–5pm, Jan & Feb open until 4pm • ☎01873 852011, ⓦcourtcupboard.com

Within a 500-year-old farm, the **Court Cupboard Gallery** is an artists' enclave of workshops, selling leather crafts (including beautiful handmade bags), jewellery, sculptures, handmade soaps and more. You can often chat with the artists as they work, and the gallery also mounts regular exhibitions as well as art and craft courses.

The Black Mountains

Appearing only partly tamed by human habitation, the northeastern-most section of the Brecon Beacons National Park, known as the **Black Mountains** (plural, as distinct from the Black Mountain forty miles west) is made up of a series of high, finger-like ridges enclosing, remote, secretive valleys dotted with tiny villages. The wide valley of the River Usk divides the Beacons heartland from the Black Mountains, whose sandstone range rises to more clearly defined individual peaks than those in the western end of the park.

The **Vale of Ewyas** stretches along the extreme eastern boundary of the Brecon Beacons National Park, making one of the most enchanting and reclusive regions in Wales, most memorably seen by car by the narrow road past Llanthony Priory, over the Gospel Pass and on to Hay-on-Wye.

The most rewarding areas to **walk** are around Llanthony and the hilltops above, Hay Bluff and along the southern band of peaks, notably Pen Cerrig-calch, Table Mountain and the Sugar Loaf. The mass of rippling hills in the centre and to the north is less easy to reach, although a couple of good paths follow the contours around them.

Llanfihangel Crucorney

Some six miles north of Abergavenny, on the main village street of **LLANFIHANGEL CRUCORNEY** (Llanfihangel Crucornau, the "Sacred Enclosure of Michael at the Corner of the Rock"), are the odd fifteenth-century **church** and the reputedly haunted *Skirrid Mountain Inn*.

BLACK MOUNTAINS SUMMITS

Blorenge (1834ft) The simplest way up is from the road that strikes off the B4246 a mile short of Blaenafon: the open road climbs the shale- and sheep-covered slopes to the car parks near the radio masts. An easy walk from here leads across boggy heathland to a long cairn at the summit, from which there are some glorious views. There is a steeper ascent of the Blorenge from **Llanfoist**, a mile southwest of Abergavenny, which cuts past the church and under the canal before zigzagging up the mountain.

Sugar Loaf (1955ft) The broad and smooth cone of Sugar Loaf commands the Black Mountains foothills to the northwest of Abergavenny. The easiest ascent is from the south, taking the right fork of Pentre Lane off the A40, half a mile west of Abergavenny, and following the road that climbs Mynydd Llanwenarth.

The Skirrid (1595ft) Shooting up from the Gavenny Valley, three miles northeast of Abergavenny, the Skirrid (Ysgyryd Fawr) is the most eye-catching mountain in the area. The Skirrid has long been held to be a holy mountain; the almighty chasm that splits the peak is said to have been caused by the force of God's will on the death of Christ, a theory that drew St Michael and legions of other pilgrims to this bleak but breathtaking spot. Another theory claims that Noah's Ark clipped it as it passed by. The best path, although it's still a steep ascent, leads from the lay-by on the B4521 just short of the *Walnut Tree Inn*. At the summit, a few leaning boulders are all that remains of a clandestine chapel built by persecuted Catholics.

Hay Bluff (2220ft) Giving terrific views from its often windy summit, this is easily climbed from the top of the road at the Gospel Pass south of Hay-on-Wye. A prominent track runs up to the summit cairn, from which you can continue southeast around the rim of the hill until turning left down the Offa's Dyke Path which drops steadily to the road to make a magnificent three-mile circuit.

3

EATING AND DRINKING **LLANFIHANGEL CRUCORNEY**

Skirrid Mountain Inn 01873 890258. First mentioned in 1110 and thus thought to be the oldest pub in Wales. During the seventeenth century, some 180 people are believed to have been hanged here – you can still see the beam inside the inn, which bears the scorch marks of the rope. It's an atmospheric spot for a drink and a bite to eat. Mon–Sat 11.30am–1pm, Sun noon–5pm.

Partrishow

From Llanfihangel Crucorney, the main road through the valley heads north into the Vale of Ewyas. After a mile, a lane heads west towards the enchanting valley of the **Grwyne Fawr**, lost deep in the middle of quiet hills. The road is well worth following to the hamlet of **PARTRISHOW**, where a bubbling tributary of the Grwyne Fawr trickles past the delightful **church** and **well** of St Issui (confirm opening times with the Abergavenny tourist office). First founded in the eleventh century, the tiny church features a lacy fifteenth-century rood screen, carved out of solid Irish oak and adorned with crude symbols of good and evil, most notably in the corner, where an evil dragon consumes a vine, a symbol of hope and well-being – the rest of the whitewashed church breathes simplicity by comparison. Of special note are the wall texts painted over the apocalyptic picture of a skeleton and scythe. Before the Reformation, such images were widely used with the intent of teaching an illiterate population about the scriptures; however, King James I ordered it to be whitewashed over and repainted with scripture texts. Here, the ghostly grim reaper is once again seeping through the whitewash. Encased in glass by the pulpit is a rare example of a 1620 Bible in Welsh.

Cwmyoy

If you're prepared for some adventurous driving, take the little lane that peels off the the Vale of Ewyas road, as it dips down over the river and into the village of **CWMYOY** and its wonky **parish church of St Martin**, which has subsided substantially due to geological twists in the underlying rock. Nothing squares up: the tower leans at a severe angle from the bulging body of the church and the view inside from the back of the nave towards the sloping altar, askew roof and straining windows is unforgettable; a wry smile is guaranteed. No less stunning are the views back down through the valley.

Downey Barn Gallery

Mon–Fri 10am–noon, Sat & Sun 10am–4.30pm • ☎ 01873 890993, ⓦ galleriesintheblackmountains.co.uk

A few yards below Cwmyoy church, the **Downey Barn Gallery** occupies a timber barn adjacent to the home of artist and children's author Caroline Downey. Her artwork largely takes the form of shadowy, moonlit landscapes, which complement the enchanting series of illustrated tales set in the Black Mountains, entitled *Proper Dragon Tales*; you may also get to meet her ginger cat, Merlin, who features in her books. Although there are opening times for visiting, it's best to make an appointment.

Llanthony

In the heart of the Vale of Ewyas is the secluded hamlet of **LLANTHONY**, where a handful of houses, an inn and a few farms cluster around the remains of **Llanthony Priory** (daily 10am–4pm; free; CADW), whose ruins retain a real sense of spirituality and peace, set against an inspiring backdrop of river and mountain. It's believed the priory was founded on the site of a ruined chapel around 1100 by Norman knight William de Lacy, who was allegedly so captivated by the site that he renounced worldly life and founded a hermitage, attracting like-minded recluses and forming Wales' first Augustine priory. The church and outbuildings still standing today were constructed in the latter half of the twelfth century. Roving episcopal envoy Giraldus Cambrensis visited the emerging priory church in 1188, noting that "here the monks, sitting in their cloisters, enjoying the fresh air, when they happen to look up at the horizon behold the tops of mountains, as it were touching the heavens". A track behind the ruins winds up to the Offa's Dyke Path, which runs along a lofty, windy ridge.

ACCOMMODATION
LLANTHONY

Court Farm ☎ 01873 890359, ⓦ llanthony.co.uk. Just behind the priory, *Court Farm* offers superb self-catering units in the farmhouse, together with a lovely bunkhouse in an old stone barn called The Wain House (usually taken by groups, so minimum charges may apply). There's also a field for camping, as well as pony trekking between April and October (half/full day from £28/52). Self-catering per week from £340, bunkhouse £12, camping £3

Llanthony Priory Hotel ☎ 01873 890487, ⓦ llanthonyprioryhotel.co.uk. Fashioned out of part of the tumbledown priory, the hotel was built in the eighteenth century as a hunting lodge. Even the most easily accessed of the four antique-laden rooms (with shared bathrooms) involves scaling a narrow spiral staircase, and the tower rooms are several steep flights up. Minimum two-night stay at weekends. £80

EATING AND DRINKING

Llanthony Priory Hotel ☎ 01873 890487, ⓦ llanthonyprioryhotel.co.uk. Characterful restaurant and hugely atmospheric cellar bar beneath medieval arches. May–Oct Tues–Fri 11am–3pm & 6–11pm, Sat 11am–11pm, Sun noon–10.30pm, July & Aug Mon–Sat 11am–11pm, Sun noon–10.30pm; Nov–April Fri 6–11pm, Sat 11am–11pm, Sun noon–4pm.

Capel-y-ffin

From Llanthony, the road climbs alongside the narrowing Honddu River before coasting by ruined farmhouses for four miles to the isolated hamlet of **CAPEL-Y-FFIN**. Locked in the middle of sheer hills, it has a devotional feel, due to the fact that the village is made up of little more than two tiny chapels (one accommodating a congregation of just twenty) and a curious ruined monastery. A lane forks off by the phone box, leading up to the ruins of the privately owned (and confusingly named) **Llanthony Monastery**, founded in 1870 by the Reverend Joseph Lyne. The religious order failed to survive his death in 1908, but the place later became a self-sufficient outpost of the art world when, in 1924, it was bought by English sculptor, typeface designer and eccentric Eric Gill, whose commune, a motley collection of artists and their families, drew much of their creative inspiration from the area.

The Gospel Pass

From Capel-y-ffin, the hedge-lined road narrows further still as it weaves a tortuous route up into the **Gospel Pass** and out onto the glorious roof of the Black Mountains. A howling, windy moor by **Hay Bluff**, five miles up from Capel-y-ffin, gives panoramic views and terrific walking over springy hills. The road drops just as suddenly as it climbed, descending five miles into Hay-on-Wye.

ACCOMMODATION	**CAPEL-Y-FFIN**
The Grange ☎ 01873 890215, ⓦ grangetrekking .co.uk. A comfortable B&B with extensive gardens in which you can pitch a tent (£5). You can also get well-priced	evening meals here, and staff can organize pony trekking (from £14/hr). Closed Nov–Easter.

3

Hay-on-Wye

The quaint border town of **HAY-ON-WYE** (Y Gelli), at the northern tip of the Brecon Beacons, is synonymous with secondhand books. Since the first bookshop opened here in the 1960s, just about every spare inch of space has been given over to the trade, including the old cinema, houses, shops and even the crumbling stone castle. There are now well over thirty bookshops in town, many of which are highly specialized, including ones dedicated solely to travel, poetry, children, and even "murder and

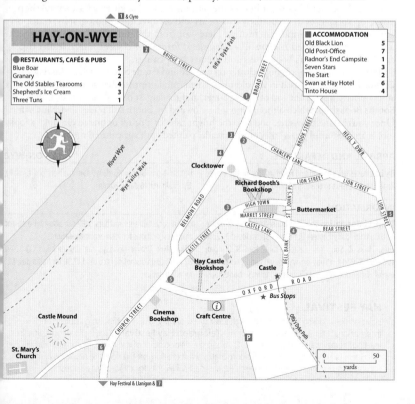

HAY-ON-WYE

⬤ **RESTAURANTS, CAFÉS & PUBS**
Blue Boar	5
Granary	2
The Old Stables Tearooms	4
Shepherd's Ice Cream	3
Three Tuns	1

◼ **ACCOMMODATION**
Old Black Lion	5
Old Post-Office	7
Radnor's End Campsite	1
Seven Stars	3
The Start	2
Swan at Hay Hotel	6
Tinto House	4

RICHARD BOOTH AND THE HAY BOOK BUSINESS

Richard Booth, whose family originates in the area, opened the first of his Hay-on-Wye **secondhand bookshops** in 1961. Since then, he has built an astonishing empire and attracted other booksellers to the town, turning it into the greatest market of used books in the world.

Whereas so many mid-Welsh and border towns have seen populations ebb away over the past half-century, Hay is booming on the strength of its bibliophilic connections. Booth views this transformation of a hitherto ordinary little market town as a prototype for reviving rural economies, based on local initiatives and unusual specialisms. This, coupled with Hay's geographical location slap-bang on the Wales–England border and Booth's own self-promotional skills, led him to declare Hay independent of the UK in 1977, with himself, naturally, as king. He appoints his own ministers and offers "official" government scrolls, passports and car stickers to visitors. Although such a proclamation carries no weight officially, most of the people of Hay seem to have rallied behind King Richard and are delighted with the publicity – and visitors – that the town's continuing high profile attracts.

Booth's avant-garde ideas and the events surrounding the 1977 declaration are laid out in his entertaining autobiography, *My Kingdom of Books*.

mayhem". Sprouting up alongside are an increasing number of antique shops, galleries and fine-food haunts.

The written word is the chief concern of this small market town, and the ideal place to start sampling the wares is up the track towards the castle, a fire-damaged Jacobean mansion built into the walls of a thirteenth-century fortress and owned by Hay's ruling "monarch", Richard Booth. It houses the pleasantly ramshackle **Hay Castle Bookshop**. The shop specializes in an unlikely mix of art and architecture, photography, transport, humour and Native American history. Here – or from the tourist office – you can pick up the annually revised *Hay-on-Wye Booksellers, Printsellers & Bookbinders* leaflet (free), detailing all the town's booksellers and literary happenings.

Most of the town's bookshops cluster on and around Castle Street, such as the **Hay Cinema Bookshop**, housed in the old town cinema and great for new remaindered editions at low prices. Just off the top of Castle Street, and the largest bookshop in Hay, is **Richard Booth's Bookshop**, which although no longer owned by Booth still trades under his name. Once you're done browsing, pop into the bright café for a drink or bite to eat. Take a look, too, at the beautiful glazed tiles on the facade, painted with agricultural motifs.

ARRIVAL AND DEPARTURE — HAY-ON-WYE

By bus Buses from Brecon and Hereford stop by the Oxford Road car park, next to the tourist office.

Destinations Brecon (6 daily; 45min); Hereford (5 daily; 1hr); Talgarth (6 daily; 20min).

INFORMATION

Tourist information The TIC is housed in the craft centre on Oxford Rd (daily: Easter–Oct 10am–5pm, closed 1–2pm Tues, Thurs & Sun; Nov–Easter 11am–1pm & 2–4pm; ⓣ 01497 820144, ⓦ hay-on-wye.co.uk), and publishes a useful free booklet detailing the town's bookshops, galleries, restaurants and bars. Staff can also advise on and make reservations for local accommodation.

Bike Hire Drover Holidays can deliver bikes (ⓣ 01497 821134, ⓦ droverholidays.co.uk; £17.50 for half a day, £25 for a full day).

HAY FESTIVAL

Hay positively bursts at the seams in the last week of May, when fashionable London and international literati decamp here for the **Telegraph Hay Festival** (ⓦ hayfestival.com), Britain's leading literary gathering, bar none. Dubbed the "Woodstock of the mind" by former festival attendee, Bill Clinton, the festival incorporates a raft of high-profile keynote readings alongside top-rank music and comedy, while there are loads of events for children of all ages.

ACCOMMODATION

As a major tourist venue, Hay is well served for accommodation, although prices are a little higher here than in other places nearby, and there are no hostels. Just about everywhere gets booked up months in advance during the Hay Festival.

HOTELS AND GUESTHOUSES

★ **Old Black Lion** Lion St ☎01497 820841, ⓦ oldblacklion.co.uk. Very well-regarded thirteenth-century inn which has charming en-suite rooms both above the pub and in the neighbouring annexe, though those in the annexe are slightly more appealing. **£90**

Old Post Office Llanigon, 2 miles south of Hay ☎01497 820008, ⓦ oldpost-office.co.uk. A wonderful seventeenth-century vegetarian B&B which is well placed for walks, including the Offa's Dyke Path. Two-night minimum stay at weekends. **£70**

Seven Stars 11 Broad St ☎01497 820886, ⓦ theseven-stars.co.uk. Former town pub near the clock tower, with eight modestly sized but cosy rooms, some with the original oak beams and window frames; there's also an indoor swimming pool and sauna. Closed Jan. **£84**

The Start Hay Bridge ☎01497 821391, ⓦ the-start.net. Neatly renovated Georgian house on the riverbank, with three rooms boasting antique furnishings and linen, and handmade quilts. The vegetable garden provides many of the ingredients for breakfast, including scrummy Glamorgan sausages and organic porridge. **£70**

Swan at Hay Church St ☎01497 821188, ⓦ swanathay .co.uk. The town's most formal hotel, with spotless and attractively furnished rooms, some of which sport period features and garden views. **£99**

★ **Tinto House** 13 Broad St ☎01497 821556, ⓦ tinto-house.co.uk. Charming old house possessing three large and sumptuous rooms, each a different style and colour, in addition to a self-contained unit in the old stable block which has splendid garden views. **£80**

CAMPING

Radnors End ☎01497 820780, ⓦ hay-on-wye.co.uk /radnorsend. A 10min walk from town across the Wye bridge on the road to Clyro; small, neat field in a beautiful setting overlooking Hay, with on-site showers and laundry facilities. March–Oct. Pitches **£5**

EATING AND DRINKING

Blue Boar Castle St ☎01497 820884. Tasteful, wood-panelled real ale pub centred around a gently curving bar and two stone fireplaces, with a separate dining area to one side. Daily 9am–11pm.

The Granary Broad St ☎01497 820790. White rough-hewn walls and simple wooden tables and chairs mark this thoroughly unpretentious café and bistro out as one of the most enjoyable venues in town; a wide range of excellent vegetarian and meat-based meals, many made from local produce. Save space for the wonderful desserts and good espresso. Mains £10. Daily 9am–5.30pm, school holidays till 9pm.

★ **The Old Stables Tearooms** Bear St ☎07796 484766. Barely half a dozen tables crammed into this delightful eatery, with boards chalked up all over the place offering superb Welsh produce, including a fantastic array of speciality teas and home-made tarts. On a warm day, the flower-filled yard is a lovely spot to come and eat. Tues–Sat 10.30am–4pm.

Shepherd's Ice Cream 9 High Town ☎01497 821898. Popular Georgian-style café/ice-cream parlour doling out local ice cream made from sheep's milk, often in offbeat flavours like raspberry cheesecake and banana toffee crunch. Mon–Fri 9.30am–5.30pm, Sat 9.30am–6pm, Sun 10.30am–5.30pm.

★ **Three Tuns** Broad St ☎01497 821855. Set in Hay's second-oldest building (after the castle), the ancient stonework, outdoor terrace and crackling open fires make for an atmospheric dining spot. Food includes creations such as honey-glazed Welsh lamb shank with spring onion mash, and Black Mountain smoked salmon with rocket. Mains £12–18. Daily 11am–11pm.

Radnorshire and Montgomeryshire

Even quieter than the quiet Brecon Beacons, the northern tranche of Powys – comprising the old counties of Radnorshire and Montgomeryshire – is a hugely rewarding area to explore. This is farming country, where urban life comes no bigger than a few small market towns. Between the towns, the contours of the impossibly green, sheep-flecked farmland are shaped by the glassy lakes and lively rivers that run down from the open moorland of the Cambrian Mountains, which form Wales' spine. Despite the area's remoteness, the quality and pace of life here has proved irresistible to "alternative" lifestylers over the years, resulting in wholefood cafés and quirky festivals.

In the south of **Radnorshire** and in bordering Brecknockshire, four distinctly different communities jointly form the **Wells towns** (spa towns), each of which grew up around a reputedly health-giving spring. There's more water in the **Elan Valley**, to the west, centred around four interlocking reservoirs and graced by an abundance of red kites. To the east, close to the English border, **Presteigne** is a charmingly villagey town with a great museum, while for walkers, **Knighton** is ideally situated at the start of **Glyndŵr's Way**, as well as midway along the eighth-century **Offa's Dyke**.

The northernmost section of Powys is mellow **Montgomeryshire**. Good bases include the cheerily offbeat little town of **Llanidloes**, the laidback northern outpost of **Llanfyllin**, the stately old county town of **Montgomery** and its much larger and more bustling replacement, **Welshpool**.

The Wells towns

Straddling the old border of Brecknockshire and Radnorshire, around fifteen miles north of Brecon, mid-Wales' four former spa towns are strung out along the Heart of Wales rail line and the main A483. All were obscure villages up until the eighteenth century, until royalty and nobility spearheaded the fashion for taking a cure. Once the railway arrived, the four Welsh spas became much more egalitarian, each developing its own distinct clientele and atmosphere.

The westernmost spa of **Llanwrtyd Wells**, hunkered down beneath the hills, is best known for its weird array of offbeat festivals and unusual events, while close by is tiny **Llangammarch Wells**. Both **Builth Wells** and **Llandrindod Wells** are worth a stop, the latter having retained some exceptional Victorian-era architecture, though both places are struggling these days.

Llanwrtyd Wells and around

Around twenty miles northwest of Brecon, **LLANWRTYD WELLS** was the spa to which the Welsh – farmers of Dyfed alongside the Nonconformist middle classes from Glamorgan – came to great eisteddfodau in the valley of the Irfon. One of the smallest towns in Britain, these days it's more well-known for being the Welsh capital of wacky events. Moreover, it boasts the finest coterie of restaurants in mid-Wales.

Main Street runs through the centre of town, crossing the Irfon River just below the main square, Y Sgwar, which is framed by an assortment of boldly coloured buildings and dominated by a striking sculpture of a red kite by Sandy O'Connor. Although the sulphurous aroma had been apparent in the area for centuries, it was "discovered" in 1732 by the local priest, Theophilus Evans, who drank from a vile-smelling spring after seeing a healthy frog pop out of it. The spring, named **Ffynnon Drewllyd** (Stinking Well), bubbles up among the dilapidated spa buildings on Dolecoed Road.

WACKY EVENTS

Belying its appearance as a sleepy kind of place, Llanwrtyd Wells has its distinctly zany moments. Although a host of events take place here throughout the year, three in particular take precedent. In mid-June, the **Man Versus Horse Marathon** is a punishing 22-mile endurance test between man and beast over various types of terrain. Then, at the end of August, it's the turn of the **World Bog-Snorkelling Championships**, in which competitors must complete two lengths of a water-filled trench cut through a peat bog – the current world record, posted here in 2010, is one minute thirty seconds. Then in November, there's the wonderfully named **Real Ale Wobble**, two days of combined mountain biking and beer drinking, an event for the somewhat less serious-minded cyclist. Visit ⓦ green-events.co.uk for full event listings.

Mynydd Eppynt

To the south of Llanwrtyd Wells, the remote **Crychan Forest** and the rippling mountains of the **Mynydd Eppynt** make up the northern outcrops of the Brecon Beacons, best seen from the roads that snake across the moors from the towns of Garth and Builth. The bulk of the Eppynt, however, has been appropriated by the British Army, as evidenced by the many red flags flying stiffly, warning you not to stop or touch anything.

Llangammarch Wells

A tiny ex-spa with its own rail station, **LLANGAMMARCH WELLS** is beautifully positioned on the Ithon, beneath the Eppynt, from where the B4519 descends dramatically. The main reason for coming here is the excellent spa at the posh *Lake Country House*, while there is also excellent fishing and walking at hand.

Abergwesyn

Five miles north of Llanwrtyd, the lane from Llanwrtyd meets up with another road from Beulah at the riverside hamlet of **ABERGWESYN**, home to the **Coed Trallwm Mountain Bike Centre** (☎01591 610546, ⓦcoedtrallwm.co.uk), from where three graded trails fan out, which are either four or five kilometres in distance. You'll need to bring your own bike, however, as there's no rental here. The centre's visitor centre occupies a log cabin with an organic café (Wed–Mon noon–4pm).

The Abergwesyn Pass

A magnificent winding road twists up from Beulah to the **Abergwesyn Pass**, threading its way up through dense conifer forests to wide, gorse- and heather-strewn valleys bereft of any sign of human habitation, framed by craggy peaks and waterfalls. At the little bridge over the tiny Tywi River, a track heads south past the wonderfully isolated, gaslit *Elenydd Wilderness Hostel* at **Dolgoch**.

On the other side of the river, a new road channels past the thick forest on to Llyn Brianne (see p.154), a couple of miles further on. This is as remote a walking holiday as can be had in Wales – paths lead from Dolgoch, through the forests and hillsides to the exquisitely isolated chapel at **Soar-y-Mynydd** and beyond, over the mountains to the next *Elenydd Wilderness Hostel*, Ty'n Cornel (also spelt Tyncornel), five strenuous miles from Dolgoch.

From Dolgoch, the road continues over expansive terrain before dropping down along the rounded valley of the Berwyn River and into Tregaron. Although the entire Llanwrtyd–Tregaron route is less than twenty miles in length, it takes a good hour for drivers to negotiate the twisting, narrow road safely. The old drovers, driving their cattle to Shrewsbury or Hereford, would have taken at least a day or two over the same stretch.

ARRIVAL AND DEPARTURE **LLANWRTYD WELLS**

By train The train station is a 5min walk east of town on Station Rd and serves: Builth Wells (4 daily; 20min); Knighton (4 daily; 1hr 10min); Llandrindod Wells (4 daily; 30min); Shrewsbury (4 daily; 2hr); Swansea (4 daily; 2hr).

By bus Buses serve Builth Wells (5 daily; 25min).

INFORMATION

Tourist information Llanwrtyd's hot-pink-painted, independently run tourist office is just off the main square (April–Dec daily except Wed & Sun; Jan–March daily except Tues, Wed & Sun 10am–5pm; ☎01591 610666, ⓦllanwrtyd.com). A welcoming place, it also has cheap internet access, sells local art and crafts and has a small café.

Bike rental and guided cycling tours Green Dragon Activities, Victoria Rd (☎01591 610508, ⓦgreendragonactivities.co.uk; £25 full day hire).

Pony trekking At the Ffos Farm Riding Centre, northeast of town on Ffos Rd, you can saddle up for pony trekking (☎01591 610459, ⓦffosfarm.co.uk; £20/hr, £65 full day).

ACCOMMODATION

★ **Ardwyn House** Station Rd ☎01591 610768, ⓦardwynhouse.co.uk. Stunning turn-of-the-twentieth-century period piece with three, richly detailed en-suite rooms, including roll-top baths, and downstairs a book-lined billiards room and honesty bar. **£70**

Carlton Riverside Irfon Crescent ☎01591 610248, ⓦcarltonriverside.com. Striking stone building nestled alongside the river, offering four differently sized, individually designed rooms, with glass and leather furnishings and wall prints. **£75**

The Drover's Rest The Square ☎01591 610264, ⓦfood-food-food.co.uk. On the opposite side of the bridge from the Carlton, another fine restaurant with rooms; the four cottage-like rooms are located above the restaurant, and they also have accommodation a few minutes' walk away in *High View House*. **£60**

Elenydd Wilderness Hostel Dolgoch and Ty'n Cornel: bookings ☎0870 7708868 or 01443 790720, ⓦelenydd-hostels.co.uk. Two converted farmhouses with nice, clean dorms, and there's also space for camping at both. Advance bookings for both hostels is essential in winter. Dorms **£12**, camping pitches **£6**

Lake Country House Llangammarch Wells ☎01591 620202, ⓦlakecountryhouse.co.uk. A mile before the village, this exquisite, half-timbered country house is the home of a now defunct barium well that attracted Lloyd George and foreign heads of state seeking cures. It now offers a range of luxury accommodation, in addition to a decadent pool with hot tub, nine-hole golf course, and fishing on the two lakes. **£195**

★ **Lasswade** Station Rd ☎01591 610515, ⓦlasswadehotel.co.uk. A few paces down from Ardwyn House, a lovely Edwardian residence overlooking lush fields with eight tranquil, florally decorated rooms. There's a five percent discount for those arriving by train. **£75**

Stonecroft Inn Dolecoed Rd ☎01591 610332, ⓦstonecroft.co.uk. Self-catering guesthouse adjoining the pub, with both en-suite and shared bathrooms, and access to a fully equipped kitchen. Beds **£16**

EATING AND DRINKING

For such a small place, Llanwrtyd Wells is blessed with an exceptional number of terrific places to eat.

★ **Carlton Riverside** Irfon Crescent ☎01591 610248. The food at this well-regarded place is modern British, prepared with flair and imagination, and with a wine list to match. The restaurant itself has well-spaced, crisply laid tables offering river views. Two-course Carlton menu £19.50; à la carte £34. There's also a cool little cellar bar serving home-baked pizza. Mon–Sat 7–11pm.

Drover's Rest Riverside Restaurant ☎01591 610264. Bric-a-brac and other accoutrements fill this warm, cottagey-like restaurant, where wholesome traditional Welsh dishes are the order of the day; Brecon venison in red wine, Celtic pork tenderloin, as well as some delicious cheese-based vegetarian dishes. Cookery and art classes are also run here. Mains £15–20. Tues & Thurs–Sun 10.30am–3.30pm & 7.30–10pm.

★ **Lasswade Hotel** Station Rd ☎01591 610515. Consummate restaurant that is highly regarded for its sustainable food policy. The menu, which changes daily, is wonderfully ambitious, featuring the likes of warm salad of woodland mushrooms with smoked bacon, and roasted cod with chilli jam. Three-course meal £28. Booking required. Daily 7.30–9pm.

Neuadd Arms The Square ☎01591 610236. Lively place and home to the Heart of Wales Brewery, which produces five fabulous ales that you can soak up with good bar food, including some great curries. Note the memorial top hat on the exterior wall, in honour of Screaming Lord Sutch, who performed here on several occasions. Daily 11am–midnight.

Stonecroft Inn Dolecoed Rd ☎01591 610332. The riverside beer garden at this superb pub is a particularly idyllic spot to down a pint of one of the locally brewed real ales, and there's regular live music to boot. Mon–Thurs 5pm– late, Fri–Sun noon–late.

Builth Wells

Once the spa of the Welsh working classes, **BUILTH WELLS** (Llanfair ym Muallt) still has a vibrant, welcoming feel, as well as good amenities and transport links. The town

ROYAL WELSH SHOWGROUND

On the other side of the river is Builth's major modern source of prosperity, the **Royal Welsh Showground** (☎01982 553683, ⓦrwas.co.uk), which hosts numerous agricultural events, together with monthly flea markets and occasional specialized collectors' fairs. The highlight on its calendar is the animated **Royal Welsh Show**, Europe's largest agricultural fair, which takes place over four days in mid- to late July, attracting over 100,000 visitors.

stretches along the Wye below its architecturally jumbled High Street, a narrow, winding thoroughfare lined with a hardy array of time-worn shops, an old-fashioned butcher's and the odd café and pub. This becomes Broad Street as it descends to the town bridge, where you'll find an eye-catching mural of Prince Llewelyn and the multipurpose **Wyeside Arts Centre** (☎01982 553683, ⓦwyeside.co.uk), converted out of the town's Victorian Assembly Rooms.

ARRIVAL AND DEPARTURE
BUILTH WELLS

By train Builth Road train station is nearly three miles north of the town and inaccessible by public transport – a taxi (☎01982 551159 or 553210) costs about £5.
Destinations Knighton (4 daily; 55min); Llandrindod Wells (4 daily; 15min); Llanwrtyd Wells (4 daily; 20min).

By bus Buses depart from the car park by the river bridge. Destinations Brecon (7 daily; 40min); Llandrindod Wells (hourly Mon–Sat; 20min); Llanwrtyd Wells (4 daily Mon–Sat; 30min).

INFORMATION

There's no TIC here, but the *Lion Hotel* can furnish you with basic information on the town and its surrounds.

ACCOMMODATION

Bron Wye 5 Church St ☎01982 553587, ⓦbronwye.co.uk. Backing onto parkland by the River Wye, this family-run, nineteenth-century residence offers the best-value accommodation in town: five pleasant rooms, a homely guest lounge and a filling breakfast in the park-facing dining room. **£60**

Greyhound Hotel Garth Rd ☎01982 553255, ⓦthegreyhoundhotel.co.uk. The grey-brick exterior of this establishment, located a few minutes west of the centre, is far from enticing, but the rooms are thoroughly modern and nicely sized. **£75**

Lion Hotel 2 Broad St ☎01982 553311, ⓦlionhotelbuilthwells.com. The impeccably restored *Lion Hotel*, near the bridge, has contemporary, autumnal-hued rooms with big beds and thick carpets. **£85**

White House Campsite Hay Rd ☎01982 552255, ⓦwhitehousecampsite.co.uk. Located right by the River Wye, just 5min walk south of the centre, this is a level field site with modern amenities, particularly popular with caravanners. Per person **£8**

EATING AND DRINKING

Fountain Inn 7 Broad St ☎01982 553888. Restored fourteenth-century inn that's still predominantly a pub, though there's also an adjoining café and a rooftop terrace restaurant, both with oversized TVs. Daily 10am–midnight; café 10am–5pm.

The Strand 2 Groe St ☎01982 552652. Genteel two-floored café specializing in home-made treats, especially cakes and puddings, as well as all-day breakfasts, toasted sandwiches and pies. Mon–Sat 9am–5pm.

Llandrindod Wells

Following the 1864 arrival of the railway, **LLANDRINDOD WELLS** (Llandrindod; locally referred to as "Llandod" or simply "Dod") was once Wales' most elegant spa resort. Its Victorian heyday is long since over, however, and although many of the fine buildings from the era still stand, today the town is struggling, both economically and socially. That said, it's well worth a stop to admire the faded glamour of its ornate architecture, and there are a couple of very worthwhile museums. You can wander past the once-lavish **spa pump room** in **Rock Park**, the site of the mineral-rich springs, from where a walking path leads to "**Lovers' Leap**", a Victorian fake cliff overlooking the river.

Local **walks** from Llandrindod include routes to the Iron Age hillfort on Cefnllys, taking in the witch's-hat spire of the thirteenth-century **St Michael's church** and **Bailey Einon Wood** nature reserve.

The signal box

June–Aug Fri & Sat 11am–3pm • Free

On the station platform is an old London North Western Railway **signal box**, dating from 1865, but actually moved here in 1986 from the level crossing a little further up the tracks. Still with its original fixtures and fittings, it now houses an interesting little display about the railway and its spirited survival in the face of repeated plans for closure over the last fifty years.

Radnorshire Museum

Temple St • April–Sept Tues–Fri 10am–4pm, Sat 10am–4pm; Oct–March same but Sat 10am–1pm • £1 • ☎ 01597 824513

The small but hugely entertaining **Radnorshire Museum** evokes the area's history with exhibits ranging from archeological finds to items from Victorian spa days. Among the pick of these is a Sheela-na-gig, a typically crude, though remarkably well-preserved, carved relief of a vulva, found in the local parish church, and a log-boat dredged up from the Ifor River in 1929 and thought to date from around 1200 AD. Elsewhere, look out for the original clock from the station signal box, and an elegant needle shower of the kind used at the old pump room.

National Cycle Collection

Temple St • Open 10am–4pm: May–Oct Mon–Fri; Nov–April Tues, Thurs & Sun • £3.50 • ☎ 01597 825531, ⓦ cyclemuseum.org.uk

Further down the street is the marvellous **National Cycle Collection**, a nostalgic collection of over 280 velocipedes, including ordinaries (aka penny-farthings), trikes, racers, and an 8ft-high "Eiffel Tower" advertising bike from 1899. The museum also holds some notable machinery, including the bike belonging to serial record-breaking time trialist Eileen Sheridan, and the reserve bike and racing skin belonging to 1992

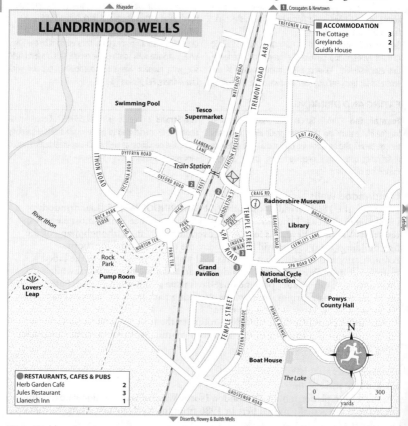

LLANDRINDOD WELLS

■ ACCOMMODATION	
The Cottage	3
Greylands	2
Guidfa House	1

● RESTAURANTS, CAFES & PUBS	
Herb Garden Café	2
Jules Restaurant	3
Llanerch Inn	1

Olympic gold medallist Chris Boardman. Look out, too, for the Bianchi bike ridden by the legendary Fausto Coppi, twice winner of the Tour de France.

ARRIVAL AND DEPARTURE LLANDRINDOD WELLS

By train The train station is in the heart of town between the High St and Station Crescent.
Destinations Builth Wells (4 daily; 15min); Knighton (4 daily; 40min); Llanwrtyd Wells (4 daily; 30min); Shrewsbury (4 daily; 1hr 40min); Swansea (4 daily; 2hr 30min).

By bus Buses leave from outside the train station.
Destinations Aberystwyth (2 daily; 2hr); Brecon (7 daily Mon–Sat; 1hr); Builth Wells (hourly; 20min); Newtown (6 daily; 55min); Rhayader (6 daily; 30min).

INFORMATION

Tourist information The TIC is in front of the Radnorshire Museum on Temple St (Easter–Oct Mon Fri 10am–4pm, Sat 10am–1pm; Nov–Easter Mon–Sat 10am–1pm; ☎ 01597 822600, ⓦ llandrindod.co.uk).

ACCOMMODATION

The Cottage Spa Rd ☎ 01597 825435, ⓦ thecottagebandb.co.uk. Handsome Edwardian property fronted by a pretty, tree-filled garden, with seven differently configured rooms, all laden with period-style furnishings. No TVs in the rooms but guests are welcome to use the lounge. **£62**

Greylands High St ☎ 01597 822253, ⓦ greylandsguesthouse.co.uk. Tall Victorian red-brick house in the town centre, near the station, with seven comfortable, good-value rooms. **£58**

Guidfa House Crossgates, 3 miles north on A44 ☎ 01597 851241, ⓦ guidfa-house.co.uk. This is a relaxing Georgian guesthouse with seven pretty rooms, an elegant sitting room with log fire, and great meals made from local produce. **£77**

EATING AND DRINKING

Herb Garden Café 5 Spa Centre ☎ 01597 823082. Fresh, organically produced salads and platters, juicy house burgers and a stack of sweet treats at this attractive, friendly diner, the big windows and squashy sofas make this a great venue to kick back. Mon–Sat 9.30am–5pm.

Jules Restaurant Temple St ☎ 01597 824642. Brashly coloured restaurant and wine bar offering a menu of great variety (pan-fried duck breast with Thai red curry, roasted sea bass) which includes some tempting vegetarian options (stuffed pepper melt, pan-fried polenta with ratatouille). The Light Bite menu (£10) is good value. Mains £10–15. Mon–Sat noon–2pm & 5.30–11pm, Sun noon–2pm.

Llanerch Inn Llanerch Lane ☎ 01597 822234. Directly opposite the train station, this sixteenth-century hostelry is central Llandrindod's only pub, and predates most of the surrounding town by quite some time; a pint in front of the stone fireplace or a well-cooked, classic pub meal are two good reasons to come here. Daily 11am–11pm.

North and east Radnorshire

Before the reorganization of British counties in 1974, Radnorshire was the most sparsely populated county in either Wales or England, and it's still a remote area, especially to the north and east. In the northwest, **Rhayader** is the only settlement of any real size. Most people base themselves here to explore the wild countryside to the west of the town, a hilly patchwork of waterfalls, bogland, bare peaks and the four interlocking reservoirs of the **Elan Valley**, built at the beginning of the twentieth century and displaying a grandiose Edwardian solidity.

The countryside to the northeast of Rhayader is slightly tamer, with lanes and bridlepaths delving in and around the woods and farms, occasionally brushing through minute settlements like the village of **Abbeycwmhir**, named for the scant ruins of the Cistercian abbey in the dank, eerie valley of the Clywedog Brook. From here, the hills roll eastwards towards the English border and some of the most intact parts of **Offa's Dyke**, the eighth-century King of Mercia's border with the Welsh princes. The handsome border town of **Knighton** is well geared-up for walkers and cyclists. Seven miles south and inches from England, the dignified town of **Presteigne** contains some intriguing reminders of its former role as the county capital. The River Lugg flows through Presteigne from the Radnorshire hills, passing the isolated church at **Pilleth**, where Owain Glyndŵr captured Sir Edmund Mortimer, agent of the English king, in 1402.

Rhayader

Ten miles west of Llandrindod Wells lies the small, bustling town of **RHAYADER** (Rhaeder Gwy, literally "waterfall on the Wye"). Although the waterfall invoked by the town's name virtually disappeared when the town bridge was built in 1780, the Wye still frames the town centre, running in a loop around the western and southern sides. Rhayader was a centre of the mid-nineteenth-century "**Rebecca Riots**", when local farmers disguised themselves in women's clothing in order to tear down tollgates that were prohibitively expensive for travellers and local workers. Rhayader's four main streets – named North, South, East and West – meet at a small clock tower in the centre of town.

Gilfach Farm Nature Reserve

Visitor & exhibition centre: April–Sept Mon & Fri–Sun 10am–5pm • Free • ☎ 01597 870301, ⓦ rwtwales.org

Three miles north of Rhayader, just off the A470, is the peaceful **Gilfach Farm Nature Reserve**, the showpiece of the Radnorshire Wildlife Trust. Within the 418 acres are meadows, oak forest, moorland, an old railway tunnel that's home to some bats, and river habitats supporting a huge variety of wildlife and flora. The restored longhouse barn has now been kitted out as a **visitor and exhibition centre**, showing live video footage from ten birds' nests around the reserve.

Gigrin Farm Red Kite Feeding Station

Daily: summer 1–5pm, winter 1–4pm • £4 • ☎ 01597 810243, ⓦ gigrin.co.uk

One of the best places anywhere in Europe to watch **red kites feeding** is at **Gigrin Farm**, off South Road (the A470 from Builth) on the outskirts of Rhayader. Each day at 3pm (2pm in winter), these magnificent birds are lured here, with as many as five hundred descending at any one time – it's a quite fantastic sight. A handful of hides are used for viewing, including some specialized photography/filming hides, though a fee is payable for the use of these and they must be pre-booked. There's also a scenic one-and-a-half-mile-long nature trail here as well as a small visitor centre.

ARRIVAL AND DEPARTURE   RHAYADER

By bus Buses stop in the main Dark Lane car park behind the leisure centre and serve: Builth Wells (hourly; 20min); Llandrindod Wells (6 daily; 25min).

GETTING AROUND

Bike rental Available from Clive Powell Mountain Bikes on West St (daily 9am–5.30pm, closed Thurs; ☎ 01597 811343, ⓦ clivepowell-mtb.co.uk; £5/hr, £20/day); also all-inclusive cycling packages.

ACCOMMODATION

Beili Neuadd 2 miles northeast of town off the B4518 ☎ 01597 810211, ⓦ midwalesfarmstay.co.uk. A laidback farmhouse B&B, this also has a sixteenth-century stone barn bunkhouse containing kitchen and lounge. B&B £60; bunkhouse bed £16

Elan Hotel West St ☎ 01597 810109, ⓦ elanhotel .co.uk. Ten rooms above a pub, each one furnished in simple pinewood, with wall-mounted TVs and decent enough bathrooms. £67

★ **Ty Morgans** East St ☎ 01597 811666, ⓦ tymorgans .co.uk. Superb building housing nine effortlessly cool rooms, most of which still feature their original red or grey bare brick walls and oak-beamed ceilings. Thick carpets, low-slung beds and numerous mod cons round things off in great style. £70

CAMPING

Gigrin Farm ☎ 01597 810243, ⓦ gigrin.co.uk. A quiet, fairly basic option at the red kite feeding station; open year-round. Tents £5

Wyeside Immediately north of town off A470 ☎ 01597 810183, ⓦ wyesidecamping.co.uk. On the banks of the Wye, a smart site with separate camping and caravan areas and clean, modern amenities. Feb–Nov. Pitches £3 plus per adult £6.50

EATING AND DRINKING

Crown Inn North St ☎ 01597 811099. Most agreeable of the town's several boozers, with lots of small, dark wooden tables gathered around a large stone fireplace, and Brains beer. Daily noon–11pm.

Old Swan Corner of West and South sts ☎ 01597 811060. Tuck into steaming jacket potatoes and fabulous cakes in this agreeably old-fashioned daytime tearoom with faded red Formica tablecloths and plenty of clutter.

Mon–Sat 9am–5pm, Sun 11am–5pm.

Ty Morgans East St ☎ 01597 811666. Great-looking bar/ bistro offering dishes ranging from the simple (fish and chips, sausage and mash) to the sophisticated (ham hock roulade, pan-seared red swordfish). Three-course bistro menu £20. The bistro opens out into the bustling Strand coffee house, complete with a sweet little deli selling artisan chocs. Daily 8am–11pm.

Elan Valley

Until the last decade of the nineteenth century, the untamed countryside west of Rhayader received few visitors, although the poet Shelley did holiday here: his honeymoon retreat at Nantgwyllt was among the couple of dozen buildings submerged by the waters of the **Elan Valley** reservoirs, a nine-mile-long string of four lakes created between 1892 and 1903 to supply water to the rapidly growing industrial city of Birmingham, 75 miles away; in the 1950s, a supplementary reservoir at Claerwen, to the immediate west, was opened. Although the lakes enhance an already beautiful and idyllic part of the world, the colonialist way in which Welsh valleys, villages and farmsteads were seized and flooded to provide water for England is something tourist promotions prefer to gloss over.

The "appeal" of the Elan Valley is, nonetheless, extremely strong, not only for the landscape but for the profusion of rare plants and birds in the area. **Red kites** are especially cherished – in the 1930s, when numbers were down to just a couple of breeding pairs, the Elan Valley looked set to enter the history books as their last outpost in Britain. Loss of habitat, along with nest robbing by collectors and poisoning at the hands of farmers, was largely to blame, but conservation work undertaken by a few dedicated individuals saved the day. Since then, these birds of prey have staged an impressive recovery, becoming so common they've started repopulating surrounding areas. There is also a healthy population of peregrines, merlins, buzzards and goshawks.

Claerwen Reservoir

From the Elan Valley visitor centre, a road tucks in along the bank of Caban Coch to the **Garreg Ddu** viaduct, from where you can follow the bank for four spectacular miles to the vast, rather chilling 1952 dam on **Claerwen Reservoir**. More remote and less popular than the Elan lakes, Claerwen is a good base for the more determined walker with paths for eight to ten miles across the harsh terrain to the abbey of Strata Florida or the lonely **Teifi Pools**.

Pen-y-garreg

From the Garreg Ddu viaduct, a more popular road continues north along the long, glassy finger of **Garreg Ddu** Reservoir, before doubling back on itself just below the awesome **Pen-y-garreg** dam and reservoir; if the dam is overflowing, the vast wall of foaming water is mesmerizing. At the top of Pen-y-garreg lake, it's possible to drive over the dam at **Craig Goch** for a close-up view of its gracious curve, elegant Edwardian arches and green cupola. The lake beyond it is fed by the Elan River, which the road crosses just short of a junction. A bleak, invigorating moorland pass heads west from here before dropping into the eerie moonscape of Cwmystwyth (see p.280), while the eastbound road funnels into a beautiful valley back to Rhayader. On the way back, fork off the Elan Valley Road in Rhayader onto the smaller Aberystwyth Road.

INFORMATION ELAN VALLEY

Elan Valley visitor centre Just below the dam of the first reservoir, Caban Coch (mid-March to Oct daily 10am–5.30pm; ☎ 01597 810898, ⓦ elanvalley.org.uk).

Incorporates a permanent exhibition about the history and ecology of the area and a tearoom. You can also pick up a series of useful leaflets on walks around the valley.

ACCOMMODATION

Elan Valley Hotel ☎ 01597 810448, ⊚ elanvalleyhotel .co.uk. Delightful, privately run country house on the Rhayader side of Elan village, which offers eleven subtly decorated, individually styled rooms, good food in its well regarded restaurant and a lively bar. **£75**

Abbeycwmhir

ABBEYCWMHIR (Abaty Cwm Hir), seven miles northeast of Rhayader, takes its name from the abbey whose meagre ruins (open access; free) lie beneath the village. Cistercian monks founded the abbey in 1146, planning one of the largest churches in Britain, whose 242ft nave has only ever been exceeded in length by the cathedrals of Durham, York and Winchester. Destruction by Henry III's troops in 1231 scuppered plans to continue the building, however. The sparse remains of what they did build – a rocky outline of the floorplan – lie in a conifer-carpeted valley alongside a gloomy green lake, lending weight, if only by atmosphere, to the site's melancholic associations. Llywelyn ap Gruffydd's body, after his head had been carted off to London, was rumoured to have been brought here from Cilmeri (near Builth Wells) in 1282, and a new granite slab, carved with a Celtic sword, lies on the altar to commemorate this last native prince of Wales. It should look incongruous, but somehow it only adds to the eerie presence of the ruins and the village.

The Hall at Abbey-Cwm-Hir

Tours daily – advance booking essential – at 10.30am, 2pm & 7pm • Daytime/evening tours £14/20, gardens only £5 • ☎ 01597 851727, ⊚ abbeycwmhir.com

Presiding over the ruins is the resplendent privately owned manor house **The Hall at Abbey-Cwm-Hir**, set in twelve acres of flower-filled gardens and woodlands. Built in 1834, this Gothic Victorian pile possesses 52 rooms – mostly restored in the late 1990s – each and every one of which can be viewed on a guided tour conducted by one of the family members. Among the highlights is the beautifully tiled entrance hall with its decorative plasterwork, and the magnificent snooker room complete with stained-glass ceiling. Afterwards, have a wander around the gardens and grounds.

Presteigne

Twenty miles east of Llandrindod Wells, the charming town of **PRESTEIGNE** (Llanandras) has attracted refugees from the rat race ever since the 1960s, which partly accounts for the craft, antique and bookshops and laidback cafés occupying the town's gracious and old-fashioned buildings. The town tucks in between the B4362 town bypass and the River Lugg, the border with England, which flows under the seventeenth-century bridge at the bottom of Broad Street. Just before the bridge, the solid parish **church of St Andrew** contains Saxon and Norman fragments, as well as a sixteenth-century Flemish tapestry.

The end of the High Street is the site of the town's most impressive building, the Jacobean **Radnorshire Arms**, built as a private home for Sir Christopher Hatton, Lord Chancellor of England and, allegedly, lover of Queen Elizabeth I, who owned neighbouring property.

Judge's Lodging

Broad St • March–Oct Tues–Sun 10am–5pm; Nov Wed–Sun 10am–4pm; Dec 1–22 Sat & Sun 10am–4pm • £6.50 • ☎ 01544 260650, ⊚ judgeslodging.org.uk

The town's standout attraction is the **Judge's Lodging**, a fabulously interpreted trawl through the rooms where circuit judges stayed while presiding over the local assizes. Many of its original furnishings had been stashed in the attic, rediscovered only during its recent restoration to its 1868 grandeur. You now follow an audio tour, being "introduced" to characters along the way. Nothing is roped off or hidden behind screens, and it feels more like visiting a private home than a museum, while the oil lamps that light the upper floors and the gas-flame lighting in the servants' quarters

---

PRESTEIGNE FESTIVAL

During the last week of August, Presteigne stages the prestigious **Presteigne Festival** (ⓦ presteignefestival.com), a classical music arts event, with concerts held in venues such as St Andrew's church, the Assembly Rooms and other churches in nearby villages.

---

provide a whiff of authenticity. Finally you emerge in the courtroom, where an alleged thief that you've "met" in the cells is being tried.

ARRIVAL AND INFORMATION   PRESTEIGNE

By bus Buses from Knighton, Kington and Leominster stop outside the *Radnorshire Arms* or at the coach park on the bypass.

Tourist information The TIC is housed within the Judge's Lodging (March–Oct Tues–Sun 10am–5pm; Nov Wed–Sun 10am–4pm; Dec 1–22 Sat & Sun 10am–4pm; ☎01544 260650, ⓦ www.presteigne.org.uk).

ACCOMMODATION

Gumma Farm Nearly 2 miles west on the road to Discoed ☎01547 560243. Homely charms abound at *Gumma Farm*, which has one double en suite, and a twin and single sharing a bathroom; you can also camp here. Rooms **£60**, camping per person **£3**

★ **Old Vicarage Norton** 2 miles north on the road to Knighton ☎01544 260038, ⓦ www.oldvicarage -nortonrads.co.uk. Sumptuous Victorian country house with three gorgeous, antique-furnished rooms, each with fine views across the Marches. **£108**

Radnorshire Arms High St ☎01544 267406, ⓦ www .radnorshirearmshotel.com. Classy Jacobean inn with both period (complete with oak wood panelling) and contemporary rooms in the main building, as well as rooms in the garden lodge to the rear. Main building **£90**, Garden Lodge **£65**

EATING AND DRINKING

Hat Shop Restaurant 7 High St ☎01544 260017. This perky little eatery, with its sunflower yellow interior, is a delightful spot to try out some adventurous dishes like rump steak with whiskey and tomato sauce, and Andalucian paprika-encrusted pork loin. Mains £12–14. Daily noon–2pm & 6.30–11pm.

No. 46 Wine Bar 46 High St ☎01544 267675. Cool, modern wine bar with stripped wood flooring and coloured plastic chairs, serving fine wines and Trappist beers. Occasional live music too. Daily 11am–2pm & 5pm–late.

Radnorshire Arms High St ☎01544 267406. Above-average pub fare in this historic boozer's warmly fashioned restaurant, featuring the likes of fillet of cod on linguine, and duck breast with mixed summer berries. The family-friendly tented beer garden is also a good spot to chow down. Mains £10–12. Daily noon–3pm & 6–10pm.

Old Radnor

Just off the A44 six miles southwest of Presteigne, **OLD RADNOR** was once the home of King Harold, killed at the Battle of Hastings by William the Conqueror's troops. The site of his vanished castle is down the lane running southeast from the large, very English-looking **church of St Stephen**, looking across to Radnor Forest. Inside, beyond the elaborately carved 15th-century rood screen and dating from the 16th century, is Britain's oldest organ case (though the organ is newer), and there's a chunky pre-Norman font on four stone feet.

ACCOMMODATION, EATING AND DRINKING   OLD RADNOR

★ **Harp Inn** ☎01544 350655, ⓦ harpinnradnor.co.uk. In a rambling, fifteenth-century former farm building, the *Harp Inn* serves delicious Welsh meals (mains £10–16) like bacon-wrapped wild rabbit in mustard and cream, plus a few Mediterranean excursions and hard-to-find real ales. They also have atmospheric rooms, some with four-poster or wrought-iron beds. Bar & restaurant: Tues–Fri 6–11pm, Sat & Sun noon–3pm and 6–11pm. **£75**

Radnor Forest

North of New Radnor, the deep ravines and wooded hillsides of **Radnor Forest** offer some memorable high-level walking and birdwatching. A good starting point is the village of **New Radnor** from where a lane called Mutton Dingle gives access to a couple of routes around the isolated summit of **The Whimble** and above spectacularly deep Harley Dingle towards the prominent mast on Black Mixen. Further west just off the A44, a track signposted from the car park leads into a thick forest and to the rushing cascade of the **Water-break-its-neck waterfall**, at its icicle-adorned best in winter.

Knighton

Lively, attractive **KNIGHTON** (Tref-y-clawdd, "the town on the dyke"), six miles north of Presteigne, straddles King Offa's eighth-century border and the modern Wales–England divide, and has come into its own as a base for those walking the **Offa's Dyke Path** and the **Glyndŵr's Way** footpath.

So close is Knighton to the border that the town's **train station** is actually in England. From here, Station Road crosses the River Teme into Wales and climbs a couple of hundred yards into the town, joining the pretty Broad Street at Brookside Square. Further up the hill is the town's Victorian clock tower, where Broad Street becomes West Street and the steep High Street soars off up to the left, past rickety Tudor buildings and up to the mound of the old **castle**.

Spaceguard Centre

Wed–Sun & bank holiday tours at 2pm & 4pm, plus May–Oct at 10.30am • ☎ 01547 520247, ⓦ www.spaceguarduk.com • £6

Looming high above Knighton, a mile off the A4113, the **Spaceguard Centre** is housed in the former Powys County Observatory and has a planetarium, camera obscura and solar telescope. Call ahead if you're visiting in winter, as it tends to shut for a few days.

ARRIVAL AND INFORMATION   KNIGHTON

By train The train station is at the bottom of Station Rd, a few minutes' walk from the centre.
Destinations Llandrindod Wells (4 daily; 40min); Llanwrtyd Wells (4 daily; 1hr 10min); Shrewsbury (4 daily; 1hr); Swansea (4 daily; 3hr 10min).
By bus Buses serve Ludlow (5 daily; 1hr 10min); Presteigne (5 daily; 20min).
Tourist information The excellent Offa's Dyke Centre on West St (Easter–Oct daily 10am–5pm; Nov–Easter Mon–

Sat 10am–4pm; ☎ 01547 528753, ⓦ www .offasdyke.demon.co.uk) also houses the tourist office, who can advise on and book local accommodation. There's also a worthwhile exhibition on Offa's Dyke here.
Cycle hire The local bike rental firm, Wheely Wonderful (☎ 01568 770755, ⓦ www.wheelywonderfulcycling .co.uk), is over the border in Shropshire at Petchfield Farm, Elton, near Ludlow, but will deliver to Knighton.

ACCOMMODATION

Fleece House Market St ☎ 01547 520168, ⓦ www .fleecehouse.co.uk. Quiet, three-roomed guesthouse decked out with slate-tiled walls and home-made wooden furnishings. **£60**
Knighton Hotel Broad St ☎ 01547 520530, ⓦ www .theknighton.com. This smart hotel offers sixteen beautifully appointed rooms positioned around a

gorgeous double staircase, though it is fairly expensive. **£130**

CAMPING
Panpwnton Farm ☎ 01547 528597. Cheap camping in a field over the river and half a mile up the lane that forks left at the station. Per person **£3.50**

GLYNDŴR'S WAY

One of the UK's newer National Trails, **Glyndŵr's Way** (ⓦ nationaltrail.co.uk/glyndwrsway) weaves for 135 miles through the solitary rural landscapes of Montgomeryshire and northern Radnorshire, from Knighton to Welshpool. Well signposted all the way, though depending rather a lot on lane and road walking, Glyndŵr's Way is far quieter than the Offa's Dyke Path, both in the number of settlements en route and the number of hikers on the trail. Varied scenery includes barren bog, exhilarating uplands, reservoirs, undulating farmland and sections of river-valley walking. You can pick up an official route guide for £12.99 from tourist offices in the region, or order it online at ⓦ powystrails.org.uk.

EATING AND DRINKING

Horse and Jockey Wylcwm Place ☎01547 520062. This thirteenth-century coaching inn features a tidy restaurant with a sunny courtyard. The vast menu includes lots of steak, chicken and fish, as well as pizzas and spicy Mexican-style dishes. Mains £8–14. Daily: pub noon–11pm, restaurant noon–2pm & 6–9pm.

Montgomeryshire

The northern part of Powys is made up of the old county of **Montgomeryshire**, an area of enormously varying landscapes and few inhabitants. The best base for the spartan and mountainous southwest of the county is the spirited little town of **Llanidloes** ten miles north of Rhayader on the River Severn (Afon Hafren), which arrives in the town after rising nearby in the dense **Hafren Forest** on the bleak slopes of **Plynlimon**.

From Llanidloes, one of Wales' most dramatic roads rises past the chilly shores of the **Llyn Clywedog** Reservoir, squeezed into sharp hillsides, and up through the remote hamlet of **Dylife**. This stark, uplifting scenery contrasts with the gentler, greener contours that characterize the east of the county, where the muted old county town of **Montgomery**, with its fine Georgian architecture, perches above the border and Offa's Dyke. The Severn runs a few miles to the west, near the village of **Berriew**, home of the offbeat **Andrew Logan Museum of Sculpture** and below the dank hilltop remains of **Dolforwyn Castle**. Further south, the Severn runs through **Newtown**, good as a transport interchange and for followers of **Robert Owen**.

In the north of the county, **Welshpool** is the only major settlement, packed in above the wide flood plain of the Severn and linked by an impossibly cute toy rail line to **Llanfair Caereinion**. On the southern side of Welshpool is Montgomeryshire's one unmissable sight, the sumptuous **Powis Castle** and its exquisite terraced gardens. The very north of the county is pastoral, deserted and beautiful, particularly around **Lake Vyrnwy**.

Llanidloes and around

Transforming itself from rural village to weaving town and, more recently, into a centre for artists and craftspeople, **LLANIDLOES** (pronounced Thlann-idd-loiss) has managed to avoid the decline of so many other small market towns. It's a charming little place which receives few visitors, but is well worth a detour.

The town centres on four main streets, which all meet at the market hall – the main thoroughfare is Great Oak Street, a wide, handsome street framed by well-proportioned, two- and three-storey buildings variously accommodating shops, restaurants and

---

OFFA'S DYKE

George Borrow, in his classic book *Wild Wales*, noted that it was once "customary for the English to cut off the ears of every Welshman who was found to the east of the dyke, and for the Welsh to hang every Englishman whom they found to the west of it". Certainly, **Offa's Dyke** has provided a potent symbol of Welsh–English antipathy ever since it was created in the eighth century as a demarcation line by King Offa of Mercia, ruler of the whole of central England. It appears that the dyke was an attempt to thwart Welsh expansionism.

Up to 20ft high and 60ft wide, the earthwork made use of natural boundaries such as rivers in its run north to south, and is best seen in the sections near Knighton in Radnorshire and Montgomery. Today's England–Wales border crosses the dyke many times, although the basic boundary has changed little since Offa's day. The glorious **long-distance footpath** (ⓦwww.nationaltrail.co.uk), opened in 1971, runs from Prestatyn on the north Clwyd coast for 177 miles to Sedbury Cliffs, just outside Chepstow, and is one of the most rewarding walks in Britain – neither too popular to be unpleasantly crowded, nor too monotonous in its landscapes. The path is maintained by the Offa's Dyke Association, whose headquarters are in the Offa's Dyke Centre in Knighton.

tenements. Worth popping into is the **Great Oak bookshop** at no. 35 (Mon–Fri 9.30am–5.30pm, Sat till 4.30pm), with loads of Celtic and Welsh-interest stuff and a barn full of good new and secondhand fiction. Running in the opposite direction, west of the market hall, is Short Bridge Street, a line of fine buildings running down to the River Severn, past two imposing nineteenth-century chapels – one Zionist, one Baptist – staring across the road at each other. North and south of the market hall are China Street and Long Bridge Street – the latter is good for interesting little shops.

The Market Hall and exhibition centre

Open usually late May–Sept Tues–Sun 11am–4pm • Free • ☎ 01686 412388

At the junction of the four mains streets is the superb black-and-white **market hall**, built on timber stilts in 1600, allowing the market – now long since moved – to take place on the cobbles underneath. Also known as the Booth Hall, it remained a popular trading place until the early twentieth century and is the only surviving timber-framed market hall in Wales. Today it houses an **exhibition centre** with displays on other similarly timbered buildings in the region.

St Idloes church

Church St (off Bridge St) • Usually daily 10.30am–3.30pm • Call ☎ 01686 412370 to confirm opening hours

The glory of the **church of St Idloes** is its impressive fifteenth-century hammerbeam

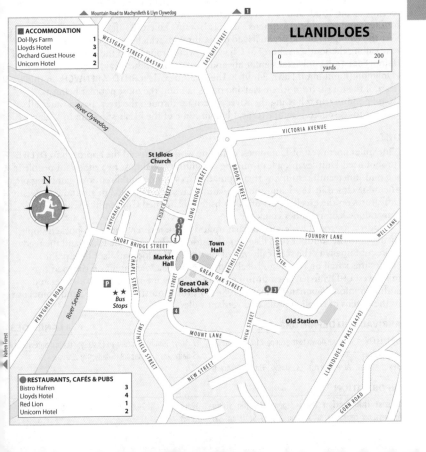

roof, said to have been poached from Abbey Cwmhir. The adjoining tower, meanwhile, is typical of those found in the county, a massive square block crowned by a wooden belfry and pyramidal roof.

The town hall

At the centre of Great Oak Street is the **town hall**, originally built as a temperance hotel to challenge the boozy **Trewythen Arms** opposite. A plaque on the closed hotel commemorates Llanidloes as an unlikely-seeming place of industrial and political unrest, when, in April 1839, Chartists stormed the hotel, dragging out and beating up special constables who had been dispatched to the town in a futile attempt to suppress the political fervour of the local flannel weavers.

Museum

Great Oak St • June–Aug Tues, Thurs & Fri 11am–1pm & 2–4pm, Sat 10am–1pm & 2–5pm; Sept–May Sat 11am–2pm • Donation requested • ☎ 01686 413777

Forming part of the town hall complex, the eclectic **museum** offers a diverting collection, ranging from old local prints and mementos, including pictures of boomtown Dylife, to a stuffed two-headed lamb, born locally in 1914.

Llyn Clywedog

Four miles northwest of Llanidloes, the beautiful **Llyn Clywedog Reservoir** was built as recently as the 1960s and has settled well into the folds of the Clywedog Valley. At its southern end, the modern concrete dam is Britain's tallest (237ft), towering menacingly over the remnants of the **Bryntail lead mine**, through which a signposted path runs. The roads along the southern shores of Clywedog wind around into the dense plantation of **Hafren Forest**, the only real sign of life and vegetation on the bleak, sodden slopes of **Plynlimon** (Pumlumon Fawr, 2469ft). There's a car park at **RHYD-Y-BENWCH**, in the heart of the forest, from where **walking paths** fan out, the most popular being a six-mile round trip following the River Severn up through the trees, past a waterfall and out to its source, a saturated peat bog in some of the harshest terrain in Wales.

Dylife

Nine miles northwest of Llanidloes, old mine workings herald the approach to **DYLIFE** (pronounced Duh-levah), a lead-mining community of almost two thousand people in the mid-nineteenth century, with a reputation as a lawless and licentious gambling pit. The mine closed in 1896, and the population has since dwindled to around just twenty (it features on the excellent historical website, Abandoned Communities, at ⓦabandonedcommunities.co.uk).

Good walks from Dylife include that up to Pen-y-crocbren, the mine-pocked slope that rises to the south of the village, and west to **Glaslyn**, or "blue lake", and the reedy shores of **Bugeilyn**. The scenically varied **Glyndŵr's Way** footpath (see box, p.238) crosses this patch on its way to Machynlleth. A popular viewpoint on the road two miles west of Dylife has been furnished with a cheery memorial to broadcaster and author **Wynford Vaughan-Thomas** (1908–87), whose outstretched slate hand points out to the dozens of rippling peaks and verdant valleys.

ARRIVAL AND DEPARTURE

LLANIDLOES

By bus China St curves down to the car park from where all bus services operate.

Destinations Aberystwyth (3 daily; 1hr); Newtown (7 daily; 30min); Ponterwyd (3 daily; 40min); Shrewsbury (5 daily; 2hr); Welshpool (6 daily; 1hr 20min).

INFORMATION

Tourist information The independently run visitor information centre is at 3 Long Bridge St (Mon–Sat 10am–1pm & 2–4pm; ☎ 01686 412287, ⓦ llanidloes .com).

ACCOMMODATION

★ **Lloyds Hotel** Cambrian Place ☎ 01686 412284, ⓦ lloydshotel.co.uk. Superbly run, highly idiosyncratic hotel possessing seven beautifully conceived rooms, each one awash with colour and character. Lots of lovely personal touches, right down to the wall-mounted sepia prints and watercolours. **£76**

Orchard Guest House 10 China St ☎ 01686 414847, ⓔ karenjohnson127@btinternet.com. Quiet guesthouse whose three rustic rooms (named after Scottish islands) have been invested with a host of brilliantly quirky features, though none is better than the bedstead constructed out of thick wooden logs. **£80**

Star Inn Dylife ☎ 01650 521345, ⓦ starinndylife .co.uk. This unpretentious village pub makes a good spot for a meal or bed for the night. Rooms with and without showers. Daily 6.30–11pm, plus Sat & Sun noon–3pm. **£55**

Unicorn Hotel 4 Long Bridge St ☎ 01686 411171, ⓦ unicornllanidloes.co.uk. A small hotel of considerable charm and quality, hosting six crisp, generously sized and impeccably clean rooms; there's a substantial breakfast to look forward to as well. **£70**

CAMPING

Dol-llys Farm Trefeglwys Rd ☎ 01686 412694, ⓦ dolllyscaravancampsite.co.uk. Large site around a 15min walk north of town, where you can choose from a pitch on the level field near the facilities, or a more secluded spot down by the river, where campfires are permitted. Easter–Oct. Per person **£6**

EATING AND DRINKING

Bistro Hafren 2 Great Oak St ☎ 01686 414936. Simple unfussy restaurant with little about it by way of decor, but which has a broad range of dishes including several good-value set menus; two-course lunch £6.95, dinner £10. Mon–Sat (except Tues) 9am–3pm & 6–11pm, Sun noon–2pm.

★ **Lloyds Hotel** Cambrian Place ☎ 01686 412284, ⓦ lloydshotel.co.uk. For a totally unique dining experience, Lloyds is the place to come; pre-dinner drinks are served at 7.30pm followed by a surprise five-course menu (£39.50), finishing around 11pm – contact the hosts in advance if there is anything you don't eat. Advance booking is essential. One sitting daily, starting 7.30pm.

Red Lion 8 Long Bridge St ☎ 01686 412270. The tatty, exposed brick frontage conceals the town's most agreeable pub; the main lounge bar has comfy leather seating huddled around an imposing stone fireplace, while the other room is principally for bar games. Daily 11am–midnight.

★ **Unicorn Hotel** 4 Long Bridge St ☎ 01686 411171, ⓦ unicornllanidloes.co.uk. Fabulous restaurant offering a seductive, game-heavy menu (wild boar steak on a potato and apple rosti, pan-roasted guinea fowl in red pepper sauce) alongside some wet treats (monkfish tail with scallop mousse). Mains £15–20. Tues–Sat 10.30am–2pm & 6.30–11pm, Sun noon–2pm.

Newtown and around

Despite its name, **NEWTOWN** (Y Drenewydd), thirteen miles northeast of Llanidloes, was founded in the thirteenth century, growing steadily until experiencing a massive population explosion in the nineteenth century as a centre for weaving and textiles – the town once boasted 50 pubs and six breweries. Today, its activity is much reduced and it's hardly awash with great amenities, but its compact town centre, straddling the River Severn, has a certain appeal.

W.H. Smith museum

24 High St • Mon–Sat 9am–5.30pm • Free

The **W.H. Smith** shop here on the High Street opened in 1927, and it was decided, amid the company's modernization programme in the 1970s, to restore this particular branch to its original state, hence the marvellous oak shelving and other 1920s fixtures and fittings. The upstairs floor, which used to be a W.H. Smith's lending library, now houses an intermittently interesting **museum** about the company and its growth since it was established in 1792. Take a look, too, at the original tiling on the frontage.

Oriel Davies Gallery

The Park • Mon–Sat 10am–5pm • Free • ☎ 01686 625041, ⓦ orieldavies.org

Adjacent to the car park and bus station, the **Oriel Davies Gallery** is a contemporary art gallery comprising three separate spaces hosting imaginative temporary exhibitions, ranging from multimedia to ceramics and experimental artworks. There's a decent café here too.

Robert Owen Memorial Museum

The Cross, Broad St • Tues–Fri 10am–3pm • Free • ☎ 01686 626345, ⓦ robert-owen-museum.org.uk

Opposite the nineteenth-century red terracotta **clock tower** is the house in which early socialist **Robert Owen** was born in 1771, now open as a **Memorial Museum** that explains this remarkable man's life (see box opposite). The museum's visitors' book indicates just how much of a shrine the place has become, with a roll call of socialist politicians and trade unionists scrawling their thanks for Owen's work in its pages. Among the many personal effects are some of his furnishings, his funeral procession card and a lock of hair. A two-minute walk down the road, on the outside wall of St Mary's church, is Owen's tomb, enclosed by a high black railing.

Textile Museum

5–7 Commercial St • June–Aug Mon, Tues & Thurs–Sat 2–5pm • Free • ☎ 01938 622024

Over the river from the town centre, the **Textile Museum** sits above six cramped old weavers' cottages. Exhibits show the dramatic ebb and flow of the town's staple trade, from the flannel and handloom factories of the 1790s, through the social unrest and industrial decline of the 1830s and 1840s (Wales' first Chartist demonstration took place here in 1838), the revival of trade thanks to local entrepreneur Pryce Jones' world-first mail-order service, and its subsequent dwindling to nothing by 1935.

Gregynog Hall

Five miles north of Newtown, the mock-Tudor **Gregynog Hall** was the home from 1920 of Gwendoline and Margaret Davies, aesthete sisters who inherited a vast fortune from their port-building father and spent much of it on a world-class art collection, most of which now resides in Cardiff's National Museum of Wales. Gregynog became the headquarters for their artistic revival, including the establishment of a world-famous small press, which is up and running once more. It's now a tertiary institution, offering public courses in Welsh language and culture and hosting an annual **music festival** in late June (ⓦ wales.ac.uk/gregynog); the hall is not generally open to the public but you can wander through the grounds at any time.

ARRIVAL AND DEPARTURE   NEWTOWN

By train Newtown's train station is on the southern edge of the town centre.
Destinations Aberystwyth (8 daily; 1hr 20min); Machynlleth (8 daily; 50min); Welshpool (8 daily; 15min).
By bus A path heads past the Victorian parish church of St

David and up Back Lane to the bus station.
Destinations Llandrindod Wells (6 daily; 50min); Llanidloes (7 daily; 30min); Machynlleth (6 daily; 55min); Montgomery (4 daily; 40min); Welshpool (8 daily; 40min).

INFORMATION

Tourist information There's no TIC here, but the Customer Service Centre (Mon–Fri 9am–5pm) by the bus station has a limited amount of info; otherwise, contact the Welshpool tourist office.

ACCOMMODATION

Yesterdays Severn Square ☎ 01686 622644, ⓦ yesterdayshotel.com. Located in the square behind the clock tower, this homely little B&B offers a mix of single, double and triple rooms and locally sourced Welsh breakfasts. **£70**

EATING AND DRINKING

Oriel Café Oriel Gallery ☎ 0 1686 625041. The location, next to the bus station, won't inspire, but the funky-coloured, atrium-like interior is a fun place to try one of the imaginative daily specials. Mon–Sat 10am–4pm.

ROBERT OWEN, PIONEER SOCIALIST

Born in Montgomeryshire in the late eighteenth century, **Robert Owen** (1771–1858) left Wales to enter the Manchester cotton trade at the age of 18 and swiftly rose to the position of mill manager. His business acumen was matched by a strong streak of philanthropy towards his subordinates. Fundamentally, he believed in social equality between the classes and was firmly against the concept of competition between individuals. Poverty, he believed, could be eradicated by cooperative methods. Owen recognized the potential of building a model workers' community around the New Lanark mills in Scotland and joined the operation in 1798, swiftly setting up the world's first infant school, an Institution for the Formation of Character and a model welfare state for its people.

Owen's ideas on cooperative living prompted him to build up the model community of New Harmony in Indiana, USA, which he had established between 1824 and 1828, before handing the still-struggling project over to his sons. Before long, and without the wisdom of its founder, the idealistic tenets of New Harmony collapsed under the weight of greed, ambition and too many vested interests. Undeterred, Owen, by now back in Britain, was encouraging the formation of the early trade unions and cooperative societies, as well as leading action against the 1834 deportation of the **Tolpuddle Martyrs**, a group of Dorset farm labourers who withdrew their labour in their call for a wage increase. Owen's later years were dogged by controversy, as he lost the support of the few sympathetic sections of the British establishment in his persistent criticism of organized religion. He gained many followers, however, whose generic name gradually changed from Owenites to "socialists" – the first usage of the term. Owen returned to Newtown in his later years, and died there in 1858.

3

Parker's Café 1 Short Bridge St ☏01686 626095. Smart, civilized daytime café next to the clock tower that is equally good for a sandwich or a slice of quiche, as it is a lunchtime glass of wine. Mon–Sat 9am–5pm.
The Sportsman 17 Severn St ☏01686 623978.

A rough-hewn red-brick frontage hides a clean, good-looking place serving a good range of ales from the local Monty's brewery. The town's one standout pub. Tues–Sun noon–11pm.

Montgomery and around

Eight miles northeast of Newtown, the tiny, anglicized town of **MONTGOMERY** (Trefaldwyn) lies at the base of a dilapidated **castle** on the Welsh side of Offa's Dyke and the present-day border. Construction of the castle began in 1233 under the English king, Henry III, and today's remains are not on their own worth the steep climb up the lane at the back of the town hall, although the view over the lofty church tower, handsome Georgian streets and the gargantuan green bowl of hills around the town is stunning. The symmetrical main thoroughfare, Broad Street, swoops up to the red-brick **town hall**, crowned by a trim clock tower.

Old Bell Museum

Arthur St • April–July & Sept Wed–Fri & Sun 1.30–5pm, Sat 10.30am–5pm; Aug Mon–Fri & Sun 1.30–5pm, Sat 10.30am–5pm • £1 • ☏ 01686 668313, ⓦ oldbellmuseum.org.uk

A few paces along from the town hall is the **Old Bell Museum**, formerly a temperance house and butcher's, but now an unusually enjoyable local history collection. Crammed into every nook and cranny of this marvellous little building are artefacts from excavations, scale models of local castles, mementos from Montgomery civic life and displays on the region's various trades, with due prominence given to the likes of clogmakers, clockmakers, carpenters and tanners.

Church of St Nicholas

At the other end of Broad Street, the rebuilt tower of Montgomery's parish **church of St Nicholas** dominates the diminutive buildings around it. Largely thirteenth-century, the highlights of its spacious interior include the 1600 canopied tomb of local landowner, Sir Richard Herbert, his wife, Magdalen, and their eight children (including Elizabethan poet

George Herbert). The two medieval effigies on the floor at the end of the tomb are of uncertain origin, although the farther one is thought to be of Sir Edmund Mortimer ("revolted Mortimer", as Shakespeare had him), son-in-law of Owain Glyndŵr, brother-in-law of Hotspur and once Constable of Montgomery Castle. Equally impressive are the elaborately carved fifteenth-century double screen and accompanying loft, believed to have been built from sections removed from a priory over the border in Cherbury.

Offa's Dyke

Montgomery is near one of the best-preserved sections of **Offa's Dyke**, which the long-distance footpath shadows either side of the B4386 a mile east of the town. Ditches almost 20ft high give one of the best indications of the dyke's original look, twelve hundred years after it was built.

Dolforwyn Castle

Open access • Free • CADW

Four miles southwest of Montgomery, a small left turn off the A483 leads up to the gaunt remains of **Dolforwyn Castle**. Described by Jan Morris as "the saddest of all the Welsh castles", this was the last fortress to be built by a native Welsh prince on his own soil – Llywelyn ap Gruffydd in 1273 – as a direct snub to the English king, Edward I, who had forbidden the project. Llywelyn built his fortress and started to construct a small adjoining town as a Welsh fiefdom to rival the heavily anglicized Welshpool, just up the valley. Dolforwyn only survived for four years in Welsh hands before being overwhelmed after a nine-day siege by the English, and the castle was left slowly to rot. In the past twenty years, the remains have been excavated, and significant portions of the fragile old castle have emerged on the wind-blown hilltop, with astounding views over the Severn Valley, 400ft below. Note that, if driving, you must park in the car park, from where it's a stiff fifteen-minute uphill climb to the castle.

ACCOMMODATION

MONTGOMERY

Brynwylfa 4 Bishops Castle St ☎01686 668555, ⓦbrynwylfa.co.uk. Just off the main square, there are just two rooms in this beautiful townhouse, one with exposed brick walls, the other with a gorgeous roll-top bath. **£60**

Dragon Hotel ☎01686 668359, ⓦdragonhotel.com. Next to the town hall, the rambling black-and-white *Dragon Hotel* is showing its age a little and is slightly overpriced, but the rooms are plentifully furnished (some have four-poster beds) and there is an indoor pool. **£96**

EATING AND DRINKING

Castle Kitchen 8 Broad St ☎01686 668795. Sociable café/restaurant with an open kitchen doling out soups, quiches and tarts, and on two evenings a week, more substantial fare like lamb and olive tagine with fruity couscous. The busy downstairs area extends to a vine-covered terrace, and upstairs is all wonky flooring and stripey walls. Mon–Sat 9.30am–4.30pm, Sun 11am–4pm, plus Fri & Sat 7–9.15pm.

Ivy House Church Bank ☎01686 668746. Sweet, two-floored florally decorated tearoom serving veggie snacks, teas and cakes, as well as foodstuffs to take away; head to the cosy upstairs dining room for lovely head-on views of the main square. Daily 9am–5pm.

Berriew

Three miles northwest of Montgomery, the black-and-white Tudor houses in the village of **BERRIEW** (Aberrhiw) are grouped prettily around a small church, the shallow waters of the Rhiw River, and the posh half-timbered *Lion Hotel*.

Andrew Logan Museum of Sculpture

June–Sept Sat & Sun noon–4pm • £3 • ☎01686 640689, ⓦandrewlogan.com

Just over the river bridge from the centre of Berriew, the flamboyant **Andrew Logan Museum of Sculpture** seems an improbably high-camp addition to the tidy Berriew landscape. In the 1970s, British sculptor Logan inaugurated the Alternative Miss

World Contest, a drag-and-grunge ball. Dazzling contestant outfits share space with Logan's oversized sculptures, a gaudy Shiva-figure *The Goddess of the Void* and a 12ft-high encrusted glass *Cosmic Egg*.

Glansevern Hall Gardens

May–Sept Thurs–Sat & bank holidays noon–5pm • £6 • ☎ 01686 640644, ⓦ www.glansevern.co.uk

A mile southeast of Newtown and across the main A483, you'll find **Glansevern Hall Gardens**, spreading around a stately Georgian mansion. Sited on the banks of the River Severn, there's much to enjoy among the 25 acres of land, including a lake, wildflower meadow, a walled garden with orangery, and a collection of unusual trees.

ACCOMMODATION, EATING AND DRINKING   BERRIEW

Lion Hotel ☎ 01686 640452, ⓦ thelionhotelberriew .com. A fine country inn with seven beautifully furnished rooms above the excellent pub/restaurant. The pub – all brass-topped tables and cushioned bench seating – is known for the quality of its cask ales, while the restaurant serves excellent home-cooked meals (expect the likes of fish pie topped with parsley mash and leeks). Daily noon–11pm. **£85**

Welshpool

Three miles from the English border and five miles north of Berriew, eastern Montgomeryshire's chief town, **WELSHPOOL** (Y Trallwng), was formerly known merely as Pool, acquiring its prefix in 1835 to distinguish it from the English seaside town of Poole in Dorset. The town's well-proportioned roads are lined with some Tudor and many good Georgian and Victorian buildings, but it's sumptuous **Powis Castle**, one of the greatest Welsh fortresses, that puts Welshpool on most people's agenda.

Powysland Museum

Canal Wharf • Mon, Tues, Thurs & Fri 11am–1pm & 2–5pm; June–Aug also Sat & Sun 10am–1pm & 2–5pm; Oct–April also Sat 11am–2pm • Free • ☎ 01938 554656,

This large wharfside warehouse has been carefully restored as the **Powysland Museum**, an impressively wide collection covering the history of the local area. The entrance is heralded by Andrew Logan's spangly blue outsized handbag, beyond which displays include archeological finds from a local Neolithic timber circle and Roman remains through to exhibits showing the changing patterns of domestic and civic life, as well as surprises like an intricate model of a guillotine carved from mutton bones, left behind by prisoners of the Napoleonic Wars, and a slice of wallpaper that was allegedly taken from Napoleon's residence on St Helena. There's also a nostalgic look at the Welshpool & Llanfair Railway, with a ceremonial spade, bugle and the like.

Broad Street and the Cockpit

Broad Street is the most architecturally interesting of the streets leading off from the town's central crossroads, with the ponderous Victorian town hall and its dominating clock tower overlooking Tudor and Jacobean town-houses. On New Street, behind the NatWest bank, you can wander around an early eighteenth-century circular **cockpit**, where cockfights were held until 1849, after which time the practice was made illegal. To visit, contact the town council (☎ 01938 553142; free).

Welshpool & Llanfair Railway

Generally 2–3 trains a day; June–Aug daily; April, May, Sept & Oct holidays & weekends only • £11.90 return • ☎ 01938 810441, ⓦ wllr.org.uk

Broad Street changes name five times as it rises up the hill towards the tiny Raven Square terminus station of the **Welshpool & Llanfair Railway**, half a mile beyond the town hall. The eight-mile narrow-gauge line originally operated for less than thirty years, closing in 1931 – these days, scaled-down engines once more chuff along the equally small-scale valleys of the Sylfaen Brook and Banwy River to the quiet village of **LLANFAIR CAEREINION**.

Powis Castle

1 mile southwest of town up Park Lane • April–Sept Mon & Wed–Sun castle 1–5pm, gardens 11am–5.30pm; March & Oct Mon & Wed–Sun castle 1–4pm, gardens 11am–4.30pm; Nov & Dec Fri–Sun castle noon–4pm, gardens 11am–4pm • Castle and gardens £12.40, gardens only £9.10 • ☎ 01938 551944 • NT

Located on the site of an earlier Norman fort, work on the outstanding Powis Castle was started in the reign of Edward I by the Gwenwynwyn family; to qualify for the site and the barony of De la Pole, they had to renounce all claims to Welsh princedom. In 1587, Sir Edward Herbert bought the castle and began to transform it into the Elizabethan palace you see today.

Inside, the **Clive Museum** – named after the son of Clive of India, who married into the family in 1784 – provides a lively account of the British in India, through diaries, notes, letters, paintings, tapestries, weapons and jewels, although it's the sumptuous period rooms that impress most, from the vast and kitsch frescoes by Lanscroon above the balustraded staircase to the mahogany bed, brass and enamel toilets and decorative wall hangings of the state bedroom. The elegant Long Gallery has a rich sixteenth-century plasterwork ceiling overlooking winsome busts and marble statuettes of the four elements, in between glowering family portraits.

Designed by Welsh architect William Winde, the **gardens** are spectacular in their own right. Dropping down from the castle in four huge stepped terraces, the design has barely changed since the seventeenth century, with a charmingly precise orangery

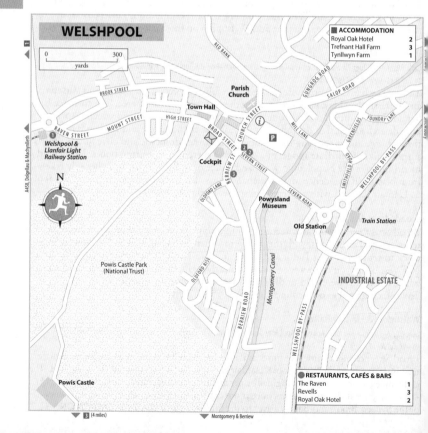

and topiary. Summertime outdoor concerts, frequently with firework finales, take place in the gardens.

ARRIVAL AND DEPARTURE WELSHPOOL

By train The train station is at the bottom of Severn St, with the neo-Gothic turrets of the old Victorian station (now with shops and a restaurant) just in front of it.
Destinations Aberystwyth (8 daily; 1hr 30min); Birmingham (8 daily; 1hr 30min); Machynlleth (8 daily; 1hr); Newtown (8 daily; 15min); Pwllheli (2 daily; 3hr 30min); Shrewsbury (8 daily; 25min).

By bus Buses depart from the Old Station on Severn Rd.
Destinations Berriew (8 daily Mon–Sat; 20min); Llanidloes (6 daily; 1hr 15min); Llanfyllin (5 daily Mon–Sat; 35min); Llanymynech (5 daily; 30min); Montgomery (3 daily Mon–Sat; 25min); Newtown (9 daily; 35min); Oswestry (4 daily; 45min); Shrewsbury (6 daily; 45min).

INFORMATION

Tourist information The TIC is just off Church St in the Vicarage Gardens car park (Mon–Sat 9.30am–5pm, Sun 10am–4pm; ☎01938 552043, ⍟welshpool.org). It's one

of the few tourist offices within the region, so you can get stacks of information here, while the staff can also advise on and book accommodation.

ACCOMMODATION

Royal Oak The Cross ☎01938 552217, ⍟royaloakhotel .info. Traditional Georgian coaching inn with a range of crisply presented rooms, which come in two categories; standard and the marginally more polished contemporary rooms. **£89**
Trefnant Hall Farm 4 miles southwest of Welshpool, beyond Powis Castle ☎01686 640262, ⍟trefnanthall .co.uk. You'll need wheels to get to this isolated Georgian farmhouse, whose three florally decorated rooms have

delightful head-on views towards green sloping fields. Guests are free to use the lounge with its gorgeous fireplace. **£60**
Tynllwyn Farm Groes-Pluen, 1 mile west of town on A490 ☎01938 553175, ⍟tynllwynfarm.co.uk. Warmly-run B&B offering good-sized, homely rooms, a fabulous breakfast and extremely generous hospitality. They've also got a couple of self-catering cottages. **£60**

EATING AND DRINKING

The Raven Inn Raven Square ☎01938 553070. The perky *Raven* has a great reputation for its menu featuring carnivorous treats such as steak pepper grilled kebabs, and fillet steak with blue stilton and spinach as well as home-made burgers. Mains £10–15. Tues–Sun noon–11pm.
Revells Berriew St ☎01938 559000. Housed within a striking muddy-green Art Deco cinema building, this welcoming restaurant combines a simple early evening menu (5.30–7pm) with a more sophisticated main evening

bistro menu. Mains £12–16. Thurs–Sat 5.30–11pm, Sun noon–3pm.
Royal Oak The Cross ☎01938 552217. Comfortable hotel restaurant with armchair-style seating, shelves of books and black-and-white photos on the walls. The food is a mix of classic (steak and ale pie, pork and leek sausages) and contemporary (pan-fried duck breast with black cherry sauce), while the tapas nights on Thursday and Friday are good fun. Mains £10–15. Daily 11am–11pm.

Llanfyllin

The hills and plains of northern Montgomeryshire conceal a maze of deserted lanes and farms as the land rises towards the foothills of Denbighshire's Berwyn Mountains. The only real settlement of any size is **LLANFYLLIN**, a handsome and friendly hillside town, ten miles northwest of Welshpool in the valley of the River Cain. The High Street is busy with bright pubs, cafés, shops and a weekly Thursday market, while the square-cut, red-brick parish church is a rare example of eighteenth-century church building in Wales.

ARRIVAL AND DEPARTURE LLANFYLLIN

By bus Bus destinations include: Llanrhaeadr-ym-Mochnant (3 daily Mon–Sat; 20min); Oswestry

(4 daily Mon–Sat; 35min); Welshpool (5 daily Mon–Sat; 35min).

ACCOMMODATION, EATING AND DRINKING

★ **Cyfie Farm** south of Llanfihangel-yng-Ngwynfa towards the village of Dolanog ☎01691 648451, ⍟cyfiefarm.co.uk. The tranquil, ivy-draped

seventeenth-century *Cyfie Farm* has three first-class self-catering cottages, each with glorious countryside views. It also serves four-course evening meals (£27.50), while

3

the terraced gardens are something of an attraction themselves. **£120**

★ **Seeds** 5 Penybryn Cottages, High St ☎01691 648604. Sixteenth-century seed merchant's house (it also hosted Napoleonic War prisoners) that now boasts a superb restaurant; take your place at one of the six small tables in front of the log burner and enjoy grilled Cornish sardines, pan-fried lamb's kidneys, and lemon sorbet and vodka; there's a serious wine list to boot. Three courses £27.50. Wed–Sat noon–2pm & 7–11pm.

The Tanat and Rhaeadr valleys

Parallel to the valley of the River Cain, north of Llanfyllin, are the lush valleys of the Afon Tanat and its tributary, the Rhaeadr – a beguiling and sparsely populated backwater, set against the looming Berwyn Mountains.

Llanrhaeadr

The small, low-roofed village of **LLANRHAEADR-YM-MOCHNANT**, six miles north of Llanfyllin, is best remembered as the parish of Bishop William Morgan, who translated the Bible into Welsh in 1588, a pivotal act which ensured the survival of the old tongue.

Llanrhaeadr lies at the foot of the wild walking country of the southern Berwyn Mountains. From the middle of the village, Waterfall Street becomes a lane that courses northwest for four miles to a dead end at the enchanting **Pistyll Rhaeadr**, Wales' highest waterfall at 240ft. The river tumbles down the crags in two stages, flowing under a natural stone arch known as the Fairy Bridge. It's well worth walking to the top of the falls for the dizzying views down the valley, as well as the chance to follow further paths leading up into the moody Berwyns. Pistyll Rhaeadr is rich in legend, which you can absorb at the riverside *Tan-y-Pistyll* licensed **café**.

ACCOMMODATION, EATING AND DRINKING LLANRHAEADR

Bron Heulog Waterfall St ☎01691 780521, ⓦ bronheulog.co.uk. Grand Victorian house with three beautifully decorated rooms, each themed on a different flower, namely bluebell, sunflower and orchid. **£70**

Plough Inn ☎01691 780654, ⓦ ploughcountryinn .com. Just two rooms (a twin and double, both en suite) in this delightful country pub, which itself is a great spot for a pint or bite to eat. Mon–Thurs 4–11pm, Fri–Sun noon–11pm. **£55**

Tan-y-Pistyll Café Pistyll Rhaeadr ☎01691 780392, ⓦ pistyllrhaeadr.co.uk. Easy-going café with two en-suite rooms (£85), a cottage sleeping five (£140) and a lovely campsite (£5.50 per person) in the back field, where fires are allowed, and they also operate various spiritual retreats. Café open summer 9.30am–6pm, winter 10am–4pm.

Sycarth

East from Llanrhaeadr, the B4396 runs along the Tanat Valley and through the village of **LLANGEDWYN**. A mile or so after the village, few visitors make it up one of the left turns leading to **SYCARTH**, only a mile from the English border, but one of the most Welsh of all shrines: a grass mound marks the site of Owain Glyndŵr's ancestral court, reputedly a palace of nine grand halls. Bard Iolo Goch immortalized this Welsh Shangri-la as a place of "no want, no hunger, no shame/No-one is ever thirsty at Sycarth".

Just east of Sycarth, the English–Welsh border tightly encircles the 740ft limestone crag of **Llanymynech Rocks** (now a nature reserve), before cutting down to run right through the middle of the village of **LLANYMYNECH**.

Llangynog

Heading northwest from Llanrhaeadr, the B4391 hugs the river as far as the sleepy former mining village of **LLANGYNOG**, where it heads north into the Berwyn Mountains and Denbighshire. A lane by the bridge leads to a stunning four-mile hike over the top of Y Clogydd and down to the elfin charms of Pistyll Rhaeadr.

Pennant Melangell

Less strenuously, you can walk (or, less strenuously still, drive) two miles further up the

Tanat Valley to the hamlet of **PENNANT MELANGELL**, sitting low in a quiet, sheer-sided valley of sparkling brooks, and the site of one of Wales' most enduring sites of pilgrimage. Legend has it that the eighth-century saint Melangell was praying in the valley when a hare being chased by a hunt pack led by Prince Brochwel took refuge in her skirts. The hounds drew to a sudden stop before her and fled howling. The prince drew his horn to his lips to call them, only to find himself unable to remove it. The prince was so moved by Melangell's gentle humanity that he granted her the valley, in which she built a religious community. The little **church** here dates from the eighth century; inside, a twelfth-century shrine and supposed effigy of St Melangell lie beneath an exquisite barrel roof. Melangell's grave is in the semicircular *cell y bedd* at the back of the church. Intact Norman features include a window in the main church, the south door porch and the font.

Lake Vyrnwy

A few miles south of Pennant Melangell, the magnificent **Lake Vyrnwy** (Llyn Efyrnwy) combines its functional role as a water supply for Liverpool with Victorian self-aggrandizement in the shape of the huge nineteenth-century dam and Disneyesque turreted straining tower. Constructed during the 1880s, Vyrnwy was the first of the massive reservoirs of mid-Wales. The village of **Llanwddyn** was flattened and rebuilt at the eastern end, its people receiving only meagre compensation for the loss of their homes.

The lake makes a terrific base for birdwatching, with a couple of hides for the more enthusiastic twitcher; the Coed-y-Capel hide, at the northern end, is dedicated to spotting peregrines, typically between April and July; there's usually an expert resident here too. In the small hide across the road from the RSPB Visitor Centre, you can sit and watch forest birds attacking the feeders outside the windows. The lake is well stocked with fish, and particularly brown trout; fishing on the lake is permitted – boats can be rented from the *Lake Vyrnwy Hotel*.

INFORMATION

LAKE VYRNWY

Information, bike rental and fishing On the western side of the dam, the excellent RSPB Visitor Centre (a shop really) can advise on the best places to birdwatch, and they also offer free guided walks of the lake area at 11.30am and 2pm on summer weekends (April–Oct daily 10.30am–5pm, Nov–March Sat & Sun 10.30am–4pm; ☎01691 870278, ⓦrspb.org.uk/lakevyrnwy). Just below the centre, the *Artisans Coffee Shop* (☎01691 870317, ⓦartisanslakevyrnwy.co.uk; £5/hr, minimum two hours) rents out bikes. Between mid-March and mid-October, fishing permits can be obtained from the Lake Vyrnwy Hotel (£40 per boat per day).

ACCOMMODATION, EATING AND DRINKING

Lake Vyrnwy Hotel ☎01691 870692, ⓦlakevyrnwy.com. The most prominent accommodation hereabouts is this lavish spa retreat overlooking the waters above the southeastern shore. Top-notch rooms with either hill or (more expensive) lake views. **£130**

The Oaks ☎01691 870250, ⓦvyrnwyaccommodation.co.uk. An old-fashioned but very pleasant B&B just beyond the visitor centre offering three pastel-coloured rooms, two of which share a bathroom. Small TV and tea-making facilities in each room. **£70**

CAMPING

Fronheulog ☎01691 870662, ⓦfronheulog-caravanpark.co.uk. There are a handful of pitches at this decent site, positioned at the top of the hairpin bends two miles from the lake on the road to Llanfyllin. April–Oct. Per person **£2.50**

EATING AND DRINKING

Artisans Coffee Shop The Old Sawmill ☎01691 870317. Large and well-stocked café serving teas, coffees, cakes and snacks. Daily 9.30am–4.30pm.

Lakeview Tearoom ☎01691 870286. Daytime snacks and full evening meals are available at this sweet, mildly quirky tearoom on the lakeside road some two miles beyond the *Lake Vyrnwy Hotel*. Fantastic views over the lake. Mon–Fri noon–3pm, Sat & Sun 11.30am–4.30pm, restaurant daily from 7.30pm.

The Cambrian coast

THE COAST NEAR ABERYSTWYTH

The Cambrian coast

Cardigan Bay (Bae Ceredigion) takes a huge bite out of Wales' west coast, bordered by the Pembrokeshire peninsula in the south and the Llŷn in the north. Between these two rugged projections lies the Cambrian coast, which starts where the rugged seashore of Pembrokeshire ends, continuing in much the same vein of great cliffs, isolated beaches and swirling sea birds, punctuated with sarnau, stony offshore reefs largely exposed at low tide. This coast is split by tumbling rivers, while with the bulwark of the Cambrian Mountains lies to the east. Before the nineteenth-century construction of the railway and improved roads, these served to isolate this stretch of coast from the rest of Wales, with only narrow passes and cattle-droving routes pushing through the rugged terrain to the markets in England. Today development is still low-key, with large sand-fringed sections sprinkled with enchanting coastal resorts.

4

North of the charismatic town of **Cardigan**, the coast breaks at some popular seaside resorts – the best being **Llangrannog** and **New Quay** – before the tiny Georgian harbour town of **Aberaeron**, with its concentration of good places to stay and eat.

A bucolic **inland** alternative to the coastal resorts follows the **River Teifi**, which meets the sea at Cardigan and meanders eastwards through lush meadows past a clutch of small towns: the stalwart market centre of **Newcastle Emlyn**, the pint-sized university town of **Lampeter** and the charmingly old-fashioned community of **Tregaron**.

The coastal and inland routes connect at the cosmopolitan "capital" of mid-Wales, **Aberystwyth**, built on the estuary of the **Rheidol**, a fast-falling river with dramatic ravines that make for great walking country. A narrow-gauge railway, an attraction in itself, climbs out of Aberystwyth to **Devil's Bridge**, where three bridges, one on top of the other, span a plunging chasm of cascading waterfalls.

Machynlleth, at the head of the Dyfi estuary, was once the seat of Owain Glyndŵr's putative fifteenth-century Welsh parliament and is still a thriving market centre. Just outside the town is the **Centre for Alternative Technology**, Britain's renowned showpiece for sustainable living and renewable energy.

The train line and narrow coastal road then skirt west around **Cadair Idris**, the monumental mountain that dominates the southern third of **Snowdonia National Park**. Each of the mountain's crag-fringed faces invites exploration, but it is best approached from the south, where the narrow-gauge **Talyllyn** rail line reaches the tiny settlement of **Abergynolwyn**, a great base for the unhurried delights of the **Dysynni Valley**. Cadair

WILDLIFE PHOTOGRAPHERS AT BWLCH NANT YR ARIAN

Highlights

❶ New Quay Follow Dylan Thomas' footsteps through the salty seaside town that inspired *Under Milk Wood* and provided much of the backdrop for film *The Edge of Love*. **See p.261**

❷ Aberaeron Hit town for Aberaeron's Seafood Festival, or simply stroll around its colourful Georgian harbour, lined by great places to sleep and eat. **See p.264**

❸ Aberystwyth Hang out in this lively, seaside university town rooted firmly in Welsh culture and language. **See p.271**

❹ Devil's Bridge Ride the scenic narrow-gauge, steam-powered Vale of Rheidol Railway from Aberystwyth to this towering triplet of bridges and series of cascades. **See p.279**

❺ Bwlch Nant yr Arian Visit mid-afternoon for the impressive sight of dozens of red kites squabbling over a heap of beef and lamb. Combine that with some of the best single-track mountain biking in Wales. **See p.278**

❻ Cadair Idris Hike up southern Snowdonia's highest peak for swooping views and the chance to become a poet … or go mad. **See p.282**

❼ Machynlleth Learn about ways to reduce your impact on the planet at the cutting-edge Centre for Alternative Technology. **See p.283**

HIGHLIGHTS ARE MARKED ON THE MAP ON P.256

Idris' northern flank slopes down to the market town of **Dolgellau**, base for the mountain bike mecca and woodland pursuits of **Coed-y-Brenin**.

Dolgellau is at the head of the scenic Mawddach estuary and linked by waterside path to the likeable resort of **Barmouth**. The coastal strip then broadens out with complex dune systems protecting the approaches to **Harlech** and its virtually intact castle, the southernmost link in Edward I's chain of thirteenth-century fortresses, perched high on its rocky promontory.

THE CAMBRIAN COAST

HIGHLIGHTS
1. New Quay
2. Aberaeron
3. Aberystwyth
4. Devil's Bridge
5. Bwlch Nant yr Arian
6. Cadair Idris
7. Machynlleth

GETTING AROUND   THE CAMBRIAN COAST

BY TRAIN
Cambrian Line The most relaxing way to get fairly swiftly to, and along, the Cambrian coast is on the Cambrian Line (Ⓦ thecambrianline.co.uk) from Shrewsbury in England through to Machynlleth. At Machynlleth, the line splits: one branch runs south to Aberystwyth, from where you can pick up the Vale of Rheidol line to Devil's Bridge; the other swings north, calling at 25 stations in under sixty miles before terminating at Pwllheli on the Llŷn. The Day Ranger ticket (see Basics) offers flexible travel at moderate prices.

Cambrian steam train To experience this fine line behind a steam locomotive, join this train (☏ 0845 128 4681, Ⓦ westcoastrailways.co.uk) which runs between Machynlleth and Porthmadog (late July to late August

Monday to Friday (£28 return) and, on Wednesday and Friday only, on to Pwllheli (£33 return); you can also join it in Tywyn and Barmouth.

BY BUS
Buses All towns and many villages in the region can be reached by bus. Check Getting around in Basics for discount fares and passes. Useful routes are:

X32 Aberystwyth–Machynlleth–Dolgellau–Porthmadog–Caernarfon.

X40 Swansea–Carmarthen–Lampeter–Aberaeron–Aberystwyth.

X50 Cardigan–Aberaeron–Aberystwyth.

From Cardigan to Aberaeron

The southern section of the Ceredigion coastline has Wales' highest sea-cliffs, safe, sheltered beaches, great coastal walking, and a resident pod of bottlenose dolphins. Many of the coast's settlements retain a timeless, salty charm: the one-time smuggler's port of **New Quay** uncoils down the hair-raisingly steep hillside to the craggy coastline, while smaller places like **Llangrannog**, **Penbryn**, **Mwnt** and **Tresaith** juxtapose rolling pastoral countryside and wide, sweeping beaches, and brightly painted cottages huddle around the boat-filled harbour at **Aberaeron**. Just inland, at the mouth of the Teifi, is the pretty and cheerful old county town of **Cardigan**.

The main A487 road runs parallel to the coast, meeting the sea at Aberaeron. The regular #550 bus service links the larger seaside villages and towns along this stretch. The Cardi Bach bus (summer daily except Wed; winter 3 days a week) connects all the villages and coves between Cardigan and New Quay. Tourist offices have timetables and route maps.

Cardigan and around

Until the River Teifi silted up in the nineteenth century, **CARDIGAN** (Aberteifi) was one of the greatest sea-ports in Britain, although these days there's little evidence of its former status. It is, however, a sprightly little town, with some great diversions and a relaxed ambience. The **castle** bulges at the town end of Cardigan's **medieval bridge** from where the picturesque High Street leads up to the spiky turrets of the **Guildhall** and the town's bustling **covered market** (daily except Wed & Sun), an eclectic mix of

---

CEREDIGION COAST PATH

Cardigan is the start and end of both the Pembrokeshire Coast Path and the **Ceredigion Coast Path** (Ⓦ ceredigioncoastpath.org.uk), which opened in 2008 and follows the coast for 63 wind-blown miles from Cardigan to Ynyslas. Both paths will be part of the encircling Wales Coast Path, due for completion in 2012.

You can walk the whole thing over several days making use of the Cab-a-bag service with local taxis delivering your luggage to your next stop for £1.50 a mile. Alternatively, just walk short sections using the Cardi Bach buses to loop back to your start point. Tourist offices sell leaflets detailing short sections of the route, or you can download descriptions from the website.

There is no shortage of wonderful walking, but some of the most dramatic sections are from Llangrannog north to New Quay.

locally produced food and plenty of browsable oddities. Leading off the High Street, narrow thoroughfares come crammed with Georgian and Victorian buildings. Gradually being rescued from dereliction, the town's **castle** was founded by the Norman lord Roger de Montgomery in 1093 and was the site of the first Welsh eisteddfod in 1176. It is unlikely to open to the public for a few years yet.

There's more pleasure in visiting the surrounding particularly the delightful **Teifi Marshes** and a rugged section of coast centred on the ancient church at **Mwnt**.

Teifi Marshes Nature Reserve

The extensive **Teifi Marshes Nature Reserve** hugs the banks of the Teifi right on the fringes of Cardigan. It encompasses several important habitats – reed beds, meadows, marshes and untouched oak woodland – for otters, badgers, butterflies and birds, including Wales' largest resident group of Cetti's warblers. A herd of **buffalo**, brought in to control invasive bulrushes, wanders incongruously among the native inhabitants and can be seen from the various trails which access viewing hides.

You can drive from Cardigan (a very roundabout route of about four miles), but the best approach is to simply walk (or cycle) from Cardigan's river bridge along the bed of an old railway. It is an inviting route past reed beds and a couple of bird hides, and in fifteen minutes you'll be at the Welsh Wildlife Centre.

Welsh Wildlife Centre

Teifi Marshes • Easter–Dec daily 10.30am–5pm, Nov to mid-Dec Wed–Sun 10.30am–4pm • Free; parking £3 • ☎ 01239 621600, ⓦ welshwildlife.org

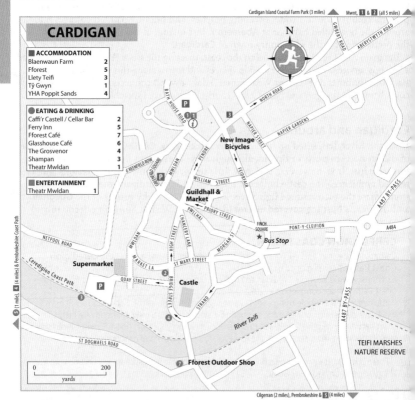

The elegant, modern timber-and-glass structure in the centre of the Teifi Marshes is the **Welsh Wildlife Centre**, home to informative displays and an airy café with expansive views over the reserve and an adventure playground to keep kids entertained. You can easily spend half a day here exploring the two main walks, one around the reed beds, the other along an enticing gorge section of the Teifi. This is the area explored on **kayak** or **canoe trips** run by Fforest Outdoor.

Cardigan Island Coastal Farm Park
Gwbert, 3 miles north of Cardigan • April–Oct daily 10am–6pm • £3.90 • 📞 01239 623637, 🌐 cardiganisland.com

The B4548 follows the Teifi Estuary north to the straggling seaside village of **GWBERT**, a peaceful spot with good sea views best enjoyed from the **Cardigan Island Coastal Farm Park**, a great place for kids, offering the chance to spot dolphins and fur seals on a coastal walk. The farm itself has llamas, emus and wallabies, as well as more traditional British stock – ponies, chickens, ducks and a donkey.

Mwnt
Five miles north of Cardigan, tiny lanes bump down to the isolated little hamlet of **MWNT**, where the exquisite sandy beach and cliffs are under the custodianship of the National Trust. Set in windswept solitude above the cliffs, the tiny, whitewashed church is the oldest in Ceredigion – its foundation dates back to the sixth century, although most of today's thickset building dates from the thirteenth century. Mwnt's finest hour came in 1155, when invading Flemings landed here, only to be routed by the Welsh. The occasion, which became known as *Sul Coch y Mwnt*, the Bloody Sunday of Mwnt, has been periodically remembered through the whole skeletons and other human bones that have been unearthed en masse in the vicinity.

ARRIVAL AND DEPARTURE CARDIGAN

By bus Buses stop on Finch Square.

Destinations Aberaeron (7 daily; 50min); Aberystwyth (12 daily; 1hr 30min–2hr); Carmarthen (13 daily; 1hr 30min); Cenarth (13 daily; 15min); Cilgerran (5 daily; 5min); Dre-fach Felindre (13 daily; 30min); Llangrannog (3 daily; 50min); Newcastle Emlyn (13 daily; 20min); New Quay (hourly; 1hr).

INFORMATION AND ACTIVITIES

Tourist information The TIC is inside Theatr Mwldan on Bath House Road (July–Aug daily 10am–5pm; Sept–June Mon–Sat 10am–5pm; 📞 01239 613230, ✉ cardigantic@ceredigion.gov.uk).
Bike rental New Image Bicycles, 29 Pendre (📞 01239 621275, 🌐 niboc.co.uk), charge from £18 a day for a standard MTB or hybrid.

Canoeing and kayaking Fforest Outdoor Shop, adjacent to the Heritage Centre (📞 01239 613961, 🌐 www.coldatnight.co.uk), runs gentle, guided canoeing trips along the Teifi (£35), and more adventurous kayaking trips (£35) bumping over a few rapids.

ACCOMMODATION

Blaenwaun Farm Mwnt 📞 01239 613456, 🌐 blaenwaunfarm.com. Well-equipped family-run caravan site a walk up through the wooded ravine from the Mwnt church. There's a modern amenities block, kids' play area and unlimited showers. Come supplied, as there are no shops nearby. Closed Nov–Feb. Pitches **£15**

Fforest Cwmplysgog, Cilgerran just off A478 at Pen y Bryn, 2 miles south of Cardigan 📞 01239 623633, 🌐 www.coldatnight.co.uk. Luxury goes outdoors at this wonderful farmland site beside the Teifi Marshes. They provide the tents (all sleeping at least four) – geodesic dome, tepee, bell etc – all with their own fully equipped cooking area. There's loads of privacy but also an on-site

"pub", sauna and occasional meals. Closed Nov–March. Summer prices from **£230**

Llety Teifi Pendre 📞 01239 615566, 🌐 llety.co.uk. A raspberry-pink boutique guesthouse with ten contemporary rooms in a Victorian townhouse with its own restaurant/bar. **£75**, deluxe **£85**

Tŷ Gwyn Mwnt, 5 miles north 📞 01239 614518. A fairly basic campsite with pitches in a field plus showers, some 200yd beyond the Mwnt church. Come supplied, as there are no shops nearby. Pitches **£11**

YHA Poppit Sands Poppit, 4 miles northwest of Cardigan 📞 0845 371 9037, ✉ poppit@yha.org.uk. Remote hostel at the northern end of the Pembrokeshire

Coast Path, with great views. Get there on the Poppit Rocket bus service (May to late Sept 3 daily, late Sept to April 3 per week); the year-round #407 stops within half a mile. Camping is allowed in the hostel grounds. Closed Nov–Feb. Dorms **£16**

EATING, DRINKING AND ENTERTAINMENT

Caffi'r Castell/Cellar Bar Corner of Quay and High sts ☎ 01239 621882. The home-made cawl at this café is wonderfully warming on a chilly day. Their Cellar Bar is the best spot for live music – open mic on Thursday, and all sorts on Friday and Saturday. Daily 9am–6pm.

Ferry Inn St Dogmael's, just over a mile west ☎ 01239 615172, ⓦ sabrain.com/ferry-inn. A great spot with loads of seating beside the Teifi, great beer and range of wonderfully tasty meals in hearty portions at moderate prices. Mon–Sat 10am–11.30pm, Sun noon–11.30pm.

Glasshouse Café Welsh Wildlife Centre ☎ 01239 621600. You're almost entirely surrounded by glass in this café in the centre of the Teifi Marshes where you can tuck into home-made soup, vegetable flan and salad, filled baguettes and perhaps polenta lemon cake. Daily 10.30am–5pm, closed Mon & Tues in winter.

Fforest Café Castle St ☎ 01239 615286. Great little café run by the folks who operate the Fforest outdoor shop and camp. Come for cream teas, smoothies and home-made cakes and free wi-fi. Mon–Sat 9am–5pm.

The Grosvenor Bridge St ☎ 01239 613792. Recent renovations make this the smartest pub in town, with well-kept ales, bar meals well above the norm and some outdoor seating overlooking the river. Mon–Thurs 11am–10pm, Fri & Sat 11am–11pm, Sun noon–10pm.

Shampan Quay St ☎ 01239 621444. Smart floating Indian restaurant moored on the riverbank and serving curries done to a very high standard. Mains £6–8. Daily 5–11pm.

Theatr Mwldan Bath House Rd ☎ 01239 621200, ⓦ mwldan.co.uk. Cardigan's centre for exhibitions, films and ballet, and offers a lot more than you might expect for a small town.

4

Tresaith, Llangrannog and around

Between Cardigan and New Quay the coast is a mass of impossibly narrow, hedgerow-hemmed lanes leading down to gorgeous little bays – especially **Tresaith**, **Penbryn** and **Llangrannog** – that aren't much more than clefts in the rugged cliffs.

Tresaith

At the scenic hamlet of **TRESAITH**, eight miles northeast of Cardigan, there's a great little beach, a kiosk renting wetsuits and aquatic playthings, and the *Ship Inn*. Fifty yards around the rocks to the east, a sandy cove has its own natural after-sea shower – a **waterfall** crashing down from the River Saith above. There's often good **surf** (heed the signs if you're swimming), as well as **dinghy races** on calmer summer Sundays.

Penbryn

The wide, sandy, National Trust beach at **PENBRYN**, a mile northeast of Tresaith, is accessed by yet more impossibly narrow lanes (and by the clifftop Ceredigion Coast Path). Almost a mile in length, its unspoilt shallow waters make it ideal for children. Parking is 400yd back from the beach beside the small café.

Llangrannog

Three miles northeast of Penbryn, **LLANGRANNOG** is the most attractive village on the Ceredigion coast, wedged in between hills covered with bracken and gorse. The very narrow streets wind their way to the tiny seafront, catering for visitors with a couple of cafés and pubs and assorted sporting activities. The beach can become congested in midsummer, though the madness is easily escaped on a clifftop walk.

ACCOMMODATION, EATING AND DRINKING   TRESAITH AND LLANGRANNOG

★ **Ffynnon Fendigaid** Rhydlewis, 3 miles south of Llangrannog ☎ 01239 851361, ⓦ ffynnonf.co.uk. This eclectically decorated rural B&B in an eighteenth-century farmhouse in extensive semi-wild grounds has two guest rooms (very good breakfasts) plus a self-catering cottage for four. Walkers and cyclists welcome (pick-ups and drop-offs possible) the owners also have a self-catering Swedish chalet (Caban Cwtch; ⓦ UnderTheThatch.co.uk). **£75**

Glandŵr At the top of Tresaith village on the road to Aberporth ☎01239 811442, ⓦglandwrtresaith.co.uk. Three contemporary rooms in a rich Georgian country house that's only a 5min walk from the beach but feels a world away in its seven acres of woodland and gardens. **£90**

The Penrallt Off B4333, Aberporth ☎01239 810227, ⓦthepenrallt.co.uk. Classy 26-room hotel in a sixteenth-century mansion peacefully set in 42 acres. Rooms are modern and beautiful, and both the casual *Terrace* (mains £11–16) and the Modern British *Bay Restaurant* (mains £15–25) are among the finest places to eat you'll find in these parts. Terrace: daily noon–9.30pm; Bay Restaurant: Wed–Sat 6.30–9.30pm, Sun noon–3pm. **£100**

The Ship Llangrannog ☎01239 654510. Gentrified pub with a patio for summer relaxing and a fire in winter. Good food, a decent range of wines and a changing roster of real ales. Daily 11am–11pm.

Ship Inn Tresaith ☎01239 811816, ⓦwww.shiptresaith.co.uk. Tresaith's only pub has had the blanding treatment that the Brains brewery is meting out to many a traditional pub around Wales, but it is still worth visiting for its low-cost food, good beer (supped on the terrace on a sunny day) and four comfy rooms all with fantastic sea views. Food served Mon–Fri noon–3pm & 6–9pm, Sat & Sun noon–9pm. **£60**

CAMPING

Llety Caravan Park Tresaith ☎01239 810354, ⓦlletycaravanpark.co.uk. Amid the static caravans there's a wonderful (if significantly sloping) clifftop field for tents and tourers with a pretty footpath which descends straight to the beach. Good toilets and showers. Pitches **£15**

New Quay

NEW QUAY (Cei Newydd) lays claim to being the original Llareggub in **Dylan Thomas'** *Under Milk Wood*. Certainly, it has the little tumbling streets, pastel-painted Victorian terraces, cobbled harbour and dreamy isolation that Thomas evoked so successfully in his "play for voices", as well, perhaps, as the darkly eccentric characters he describes.

New Quay's main road cuts through the upper, residential part of town, past **Uplands Square**, from where acutely inclined streets plunge down to a pretty harbour, formed

4

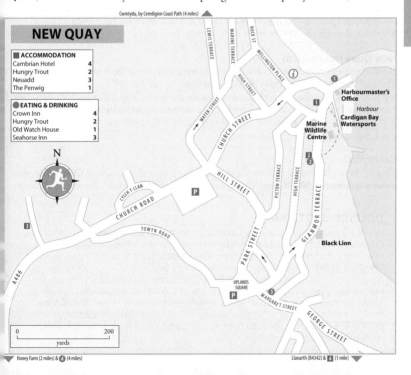

NEW QUAY

ACCOMMODATION

Cambrian Hotel	4
Hungry Trout	2
Neuadd	3
The Penwig	1

EATING & DRINKING

Crown Inn	4
Hungry Trout	2
Old Watch House	1
Seahorse Inn	3

N

Cwmtydu, by Ceredigion Coast Path (4 miles)

Harbourmaster's Office

Harbour

Cardigan Bay Watersports

Marine Wildlife Centre

Black Lion

UPLANDS SQUARE

0   200
yards

Honey Farm (2 miles) & (4 miles)

Llanarth (B4342) & (1 mile)

DYLAN THOMAS IN NEW QUAY

Dylan Thomas and his young family lived in New Quay during the last half of World War II, and his experiences here showed him the odder side of human nature. Thomas' metropolitan ways and poetic demeanour did not go down too well in such a close-knit little town, particularly so with an ex-commando officer, fresh home from the war, with whom he had a row in the *Black Lion* pub. The soldier, convinced that his wife was in a *ménage à trois* with Thomas and his wife Caitlin, followed the writer home and shot at his rented bungalow, the *Majoda*, with a machine gun, while the family was inside. The officer was charged with attempted murder in June 1945, and acquitted. Dylan Thomas and family left the area soon afterwards. The story forms the centrepiece of the 2008 film, *The Edge of Love*, much of which was filmed in the area.

Two free leaflets from the tourist office each highlight places where the poet spent time: *Dylan Thomas' Ceredigion*, which guides you through local villages, and *Dylan Thomas' New Quay* **walking trail**, concentrating on places he lived and his favourite pubs. One is the *Black Lion*, on Glanmore Terrace, which promises to reopen its collection of Thomas memorabilia: go and ask.

by its sturdy stone quay, and with a small, curving main beach. Back from the sand, the higgledy-piggledy lines of multicoloured shops and houses comprise the lower town, the more traditionally seaside part of New Quay, full of standard-issue cafés, pubs and beach shops.

Cardigan Bay Marine Wildlife Centre (CBMWC)

Glanmore Terrace • April–Oct daily 9am–5pm • Donation requested • ☎ 01545 560032, ⓦ cbmwc.org

Tucked away down the slipway above the main harbour beach, the **Marine Wildlife Centre** contains some interesting exhibits on the dolphins, sea birds and seals that inhabit Cardigan Bay. Staff will point you to the best spots on land from which to see dolphins, though you'll have more luck on their boat trips.

New Quay Honey Farm

Off A486 at Cross Inn, 2 miles inland • May–Oct Tues–Sat 10am–5.30pm • £3.75 • ☎ 01545 560822, ⓦ thehoneyfarm.co.uk

The well-signposted **New Quay Honey Farm** does a great job of illustrating the life and works of bees, together with chances to sample the honey and delicious mead produced here. Several glassed-in exhibits have bees busily creating hives in tree branches and logs, and don't miss the fascinating and very active leaf-cutter ant colony. There's a good tearoom.

Cwmtydu

One of the highlights of the coast is the glorious cave-walled beach at **CWMTYDU**, two miles southwest of New Quay (though almost five miles by road). Approached along

DOLPHIN-SPOTTING

One of only two pods in Britain, the Cambrian coast's **bottlenose dolphins** are one of New Quay's major attractions, and can often be seen frolicking by the harbour wall, particularly when the tide is full and the weather calm. A mile-wide strip of the coastal waters forms the Ceredigion Marine Heritage Coast, in summer plied by boat trips geared around sightings. The pleasure jaunts run by **New Quay Boat Trips**, based at the harbourmaster's office on the harbour wall (April–Oct daily; £8 for 1hr, or £15 for 2hr; ☎ 1545 560800, ⓦ newquayboattrips .co.uk), are the cheapest, but chances of a sighting are even better on the **CBMWC trips** (April–Oct daily; ☎ 01545 560032, ⓦ cbmwc.org; £12 for 1hr, or £18 for 2hr), which go further offshore and up along the heritage coast. Your fee goes towards marine mammal research, partly done by the on-board ranger.

WALKING THE COAST PATH: NEW QUAY TO LLANGRANNOG

It's easy to escape New Quay's bustle (such as it is) using one of the most spectacular sections of the Ceredigion Coast Path, easily broken into two very manageable sections. The terrain is fairly undulating the whole way; explanatory leaflets are available at local TICs. The Cardi Bach bus service usually provides access to Cwmtydu and Llangrannog.

New Quay to Cwmtydu (4 miles; 2–3hr). Start around the rocky promontory of **New Quay Head**, where an invigorating path steers along the top of the sheer drops to **Bird Rock**, aptly named for the profusion of razorbills and guillemots nesting here. There's a good chance of seeing dolphins too. Continue past Cwm Soden, an area of interesting folded geology, and on to Cwmtydu.

Cwmtydu to Llangrannog (6 miles; 3–4hr). A wonderful section of path, often cut into the coastal slopes high above the water with long views both ways. It also runs through the National Trust lands of **Ynys Lochtyn** and can be turned into a loop walk using an alternative route through a wooded valley.

---

tiny lanes winding steeply down from above, Cwmtydu was once a smugglers' cove, is often visited by dolphins and seals, and the mainly shingle beach makes a relatively safe spot for water sports.

ARRIVAL AND DEPARTURE
NEW QUAY

By bus Buses stop at the south end of town on Park St. Destinations Aberaeron (hourly; 20min); Aberystwyth (hourly; 1hr); Cardigan (hourly; 1hr).

INFORMATION AND ACTIVITIES

Tourist information The TIC is at the corner of Church St and Wellington Place (April–Sept Mon–Sat 10am–5pm; closed Nov–March), offer various watersports courses and can rent you yachts (£10–20/hr), windsurfers (£10–15/hr) and sit-on-top kayaks that are perfect for exploring the rocky coast to the south.
☎ 01545 560865, ✉ newquaytic@ceredigion.gov.uk).
Watersports Cardigan Bay Watersports, Main Beach (☎ 01545 561257, ✇ cardiganbaywatersports.org.uk;

ACCOMMODATION

Cambrian Hotel New Rd, 1 mile southeast along B4342, towards Gilfachreda ☎ 01545 560295, ✉ cambrianhotel@newquay.co.uk. Clean, well-presented and friendly landmark hotel with beautiful, understated rooms and original features like stained-glass leadlight windows. Good restaurant too. Single **£45**, rooms **£70**

Hungry Trout 2 South John St ☎ 01545 560680, ✇ thehungrytrout.co.uk. A couple of delightful rooms, both with sea views but only one with en suite, set above a seafood restaurant, where breakfast is served. **£85**, en suite **£95**

The Penwig South John St ☎ 01545 560910, ✇ penwig.co.uk. Seven smart, modernized rooms above a pub which has been revamped by the Brains brewery. Three have great sea views and there's a bar with low-cost meals downstairs. **£50**

CAMPING

Neuadd Behind the Penrhiwllan Inn at the top of the hill on A486 to Synod Inn ☎ 01545 560709, ✇ neuaddcaravanpark.com. The nearest campsite to town with tent pitches on a grassy site overlooking the rooftops and the sea. 50p tokens for showers. Pitches **£11**

EATING AND DRINKING

New Quay has some fine places to eat and drink, though pubs around the area greatly enhance the selection. Fuelled by a huddle of pubs and a transient young population, summer nights can be boisterously good-natured. New Year's Eve here is legendary, when virtually the whole town gets kitted out in fancy dress and spends most of the night locked in the pubs or dancing out in the streets.

★ **Crown Inn** Llwyndafydd, 4 miles south of New Quay ✇ the-crown-inn.moonfruit.com. Excellent pub famed for its straightforward food in hearty portions (burgers £6; most mains £9–12) and the Sunday carvery lunches (noon–2pm; £6). Real ales and a kids' menu and play area. Daily noon–10pm or later.

4

Hungry Trout 2 South John St ☎01545 560680, ⊛thehungrytrout.co.uk. New Quay's finest seafood restaurant with much of the produce caught in the waters seen out of the window. The menu typically includes monkfish wrapped in Carmarthen ham and salmon on a bed of bok choy with teriyaki sauce. Most mains are £11–15 and there's outside seating for those summer evenings. Daily 8am–10pm.

Old Watch House Church St. The best of the mainstream cafés, serving fish and chips, grills and sandwiches all day.

Or just drop in for a cream tea overlooking the ocean. Daily 9am–5pm.

Seahorse Inn Margaret St. This fine, traditional local, a world away from the holiday bustle down the street, is little more than one room with exposed stonework, fake beams, pool and a limited range of good ales. It was known to Dylan Thomas as the *Commercial* and was the model for the *Sailor's Arms* in *Under Milk Wood*. Daily 11am–10pm or later.

Aberaeron and around

In complete contrast to the precipitous, zigzagging streets of New Quay, **ABERAERON**, seven miles up the coast, faces away from the ocean, its brightly coloured Georgian houses and level streets clustered instead around the town's internal harbour. It is a beguiling sight which, combined with a handful of superb places to stay and eat, has helped make Aberaeron *the* weekend getaway of the Cambrian Coast. The well heeled of Cardiff, Swansea and even London descend for a few days of good eating and breezy walks along the coast path.

Aberaeron's harmonious maritime appearance results from its being built en masse after the 1807 Harbour Act paved the way for port development. Reverend Alban Gywnne spent his wife's inheritance dredging the Aeron estuary as a new port for mid-Wales and constructing a formally planned town around it – reputedly from a design by John Nash. Georgian planning is most evident around the central **Alban Square**, with graceful, small-scale terraces of quoin-edged buildings and the odd pedimented porch.

From the square, a grid of narrow streets stretches away to the sea at **Quay Parade**, a neatly ordered line of colourful houses on the seafront. The southern end of Aberaeron's stony **beach** is marginally better than its northern extent, but the most agreeable activity is simply ambling around the waterfront and grazing in the cafés and pubs.

ARRIVAL AND DEPARTURE   ABERAERON

By bus Stop on the A487/Bridge St.
Destinations Aberystwyth (every 30min; 40min); Cardigan (7 daily; 50min); Carmarthen (12 daily; 1hr 40min); Lampeter (10 daily; 40min); New Quay (hourly; 20min).

INFORMATION

Tourist information The TIC is at Pen Cei (July–Sept daily 10am–5pm; Oct–June Mon–Sat 10am–5pm; ☎01545 570602, ✉aberaerontic@ceredigion.gov.uk) and lends out free "town trail" audio guides for a two-hour stroll around the sights.

Bike rental Cyclemart, Cilcennin, 6 miles east ☎01570 470079, ⊛cyclemart.co.uk. A wide range of bikes from £12 a half day or £18 a day. Daily except Mon 10am–6pm.

ACCOMMODATION

★ **3 Pen Cei** 3 Pen Cei ☎01545 571147, ⊛pen-cei-guest-house.co.uk. There's a great sense of style,

meticulous attention to detail and some of the finest breakfasts around at this five-room B&B, with a couple of

---

FESTIVALS IN ABERAERON

The town is positively hopping during its fun-filled **festivals**, notably the annual **Seafood Festival**, held on a Sunday in early July, with live entertainment and loads of free food and drink. Other festivities include the **Cob Fair** (mid-Aug; ⊛aberaeronfestival.co.uk), with horses and local art and crafts taking over the streets; and the **Aberaeron Carnival** (last Mon in Aug), when the town swings to live jazz.

rooms overlooking the harbour. **£95**

★ **Harbourmaster Hotel** 1 Pen Cei ☏ 01545 570755, ⓦ harbour-master.com. Wonderful hotel that put the Aberaeron hospitality scene on the map a decade ago and still leads the charge. It is ultramodern with thirteen superbly appointed rooms over three buildings. Step up to one of the suites for more space, a terrace and great views. **£110**

Llys Aeron Lampeter Rd, 1 mile out ☏ 01545 570276, ⓦ llysaeron.co.uk. You'll get fresh flowers in your spacious room, a warm welcome and a top-rate breakfast at this upscale B&B on the outskirts of town. Coast Path walkers might fancy the hot tub in the back garden (£4 a head) and

there's self-catering for four (£130 a night; min 2 nights). **£85**

The Monachty Market St ☏ 01545 570389. These seven modernized rooms over a Brains pub are the cheapest in town and some have great views. There's free wi-fi but breakfast is not included. **£55**

CAMPING

Drefnewydd Farm A487, 400yd north ☏ 07971 402201, ⓦ campingonthefarm.co.uk. Laidback shoreline campsite without fixed caravans but with clean toilets and hot showers. Closed Nov to mid-April. Pitches **£16**

EATING AND DRINKING

Cadwgan 10 Market St ☏ 01545 570149. Great, unpretentious local that provides a wonderful antidote to Aberaeron's gentrification. It's like walking into someone's living room; someone who serves a rotating roster of real ales and a few bar snacks, that is. Daily 11am–10pm or later.

★ **Harbourmaster Hotel** 1 Pen Cei ☏ 01545 570755, ⓦ harbour-master.com. Two places in one. The wonderfully convivial bistro/bar is perfect for sinking into a sofa with one of their excellent Welsh ales or something from the two dozen wines by the glass. There's no attempt to be flash, but these people cook with aplomb. Expect the likes of cheeseburger, pepper steak, Moroccan lamb stew or classic pizza (all £10–14), plus delicious desserts. The restaurant is only open for dinner, which might be pork belly with creamed celeriac or pan-fried scallops (mains £16–18). Bistro open all day-food served daily

8–11.15am & noon–9pm; restaurant daily 6.30–9pm.

The Hive Cadwgan Place ☏ 01545 570599, ⓦ thehiveaberaeron.com. Smart waterside café and restaurant that's strong on seafood but spans the spectrum with their light bites, Catalan-style pizza, and more substantial dinners. They also have a long-standing reputation for wonderful honey-sweetened ice creams sold from the kiosk outside. Restaurant daily 9am–10pm; ice cream kiosk daily 10.30am–6pm.

Naturally Scrumptious Market St ☏ 01545 574733, ⓦ naturallyscrumptious.co.uk. Excellent deli groaning with Welsh cheese, pies, posh sausages and panini. The cakes are best eaten with a coffee or one of their fine teas in the cute little café behind. Daily 9am–4pm.

New Celtic Market St ☏ 01545 570369. The best fish and chips around, to take away or eat in their new restaurant terrace. Daily 8am–9pm.

Llanerchaeron

Ciliau Aeron, A482, 3 miles east of Aberaeron • April–Oct daily 11am–5pm plus June & July Wed 5–8pm; reduced hours in winter • £7.10
Parkland all year dawn–dusk • Free • ☏ 01545 570200 • NT

Llanerchaeron is the substantially restored remains of a late eighteenth-century Welsh country estate that was bequeathed to the National Trust in 1989. It is a remarkable example of a type of holding once common in these parts. Over the last decade or so, a century of decline has been arrested and partially reversed, leaving the Nash-designed main house in pristine shape. The original, mostly Edwardian set-piece rooms only hint at the fact that this was someone's home little more than two decades ago. This is much more apparent in the servants' quarters and the serviced courtyard which acted as laundry, dairy, salting room and home brewery. The estate is a working organic farm, with a considerable vegetable- and fruit-growing enterprise in the **walled garden**, a time capsule of horticultural history, featuring early greenhouses and hotbeds with underground heating styled on Roman hypocausts.

ARRIVAL AND DEPARTURE   LLANERCHAERON

By bus The #X40 bus from Aberaeron to Lampeter passes within half a mile of the site.

By bike You might find it just as easy to ride (or walk) the two and a half miles along the cycle path connecting

Aberaeron with Llanerchaeron. Apart from a small hill in town, the route is flat, as it follows the old railway line: access is off South Rd in Aberaeron.

The Teifi Valley

The meandering Teifi is one of Wales' most eulogized rivers for its spawning fish, otter population and the coracles that were a regular feature from pre-Roman times. The river flows through undulating, vivid-green countryside to the river's estuary at Cardigan, dotted with a string of pleasant little market towns with a strong Welsh ambience. To foodies it is the centre of Welsh cheesemaking (ⓦ teifivalleycheese producers.com), and you'll often find the good stuff on restaurant cheese platters.

The river is tidal almost as far up as the massive ramparts of **Cilgerran Castle**, though it narrows appreciably by the time it reaches the rapids at **Cenarth**. Further upstream, it swirls around three sides of another fortress at **Newcastle Emlyn**, and also takes in the tiny university town of **Lampeter**. Beyond here, the river passes through harsher landscapes to **Tregaron**, a good base for nearby **Llanddewi Brefi**, with some spectacular walks up into the Abergwesyn Pass and the reedy bogland of **Cors Caron**. The river's infancy can be seen in the solid village of **Pontrhydfendigaid**, famed for its annual eisteddfod, and the nearby ruins of **Strata Florida Abbey**, beyond which the river emerges from the dark and remote **Teifi Pools**.

Cilgerran Castle

Cilgerran • April–Oct daily 10am–5pm; Nov–March daily 10am–4pm • April–Oct £3.20; free Nov–March • ☎ 01239 621339 • NT

Just a couple of miles up the Teifi from Cardigan (four miles by road) is the commandingly situated village of **Cilgerran**. Park considerately on the wide main street to visit the massive ramparts of **Cilgerran Castle** that rise on a high wooded bluff above the river, which was still navigable for seagoing ships during the castle's construction in 1100. A few years later, in 1109, Nest (the "Welsh Helen of Troy") was abducted here by a lovestruck Prince Owain of Powys. Nest's husband, Gerald of Pembroke, escaped by slithering down a toilet waste chute through the castle walls.

The massive dual entry towers still dominate the castle, and the outer walls are some 4ft thicker than those facing the inner courtyard. Walkways high on the battlements – not for vertigo-sufferers – connect the other towers. The outer ward is a good example of the evolution of the keepless castle throughout the thirteenth century. Any potential attackers would be waylaid instead by the still-evident ditch and the outer walls and gatehouse, of which only fragmentary remains can be seen. Another ditch and drawbridge pit protect the inner ward underneath the two entry towers.

A **footpath** runs from the castle to the river's edge. If you want to see coracles in action, the best bet is Cilgerran's fun annual **coracle races**, which take place in mid-August.

Cenarth

A lure for tourists since the nineteenth century, tiny **CENARTH**, six miles upstream from Cilgerran, is still chock-full of tearooms and gift shops thanks to its pretty (though hardly impressive) **rapids**, caused by the Teifi tumbling and churning its way over the craggy limestone. The **cafés** and a couple of **pubs** provide sustenance.

National Coracle Centre

Easter–Oct daily 10.30am–5.30pm; other times by appointment • £3.50 • ☎ 01239 710980, ⓦ coraclemuseum.co.uk

By the river is the **National Coracle Centre**, a small museum with intriguing displays of original coracles from all over the world, half of them from Wales. You may still see people fishing for salmon from these traditional boats, which the fishermen strap to their backs to haul upstream.

Newcastle Emlyn and around

An ancient farming and droving centre, **NEWCASTLE EMLYN** (Castell Newydd Emlyn) still retains an earthy agricultural feel, particularly during the busy and bellowing Thursday market. The swooping meander of the Teifi River made the site a natural defensive position, first built on by the Normans. The "new" **castle** – of which only a few stone stacks and an archway survive – replaced this original fortress in the mid-thirteenth century. Although the ruins aren't impressive, the river setting, surrounded by grazing sheep and rugby fields, is quintessentially Welsh. The castle is tucked away at the bottom of dead-end Castle Terrace, which peels off the main street by a squat little stone **market hall**. That's about it for sights, but there are some great pubs and decent enough places to eat, along with a strong sense of community, an eclectic range of shops and an unhurried charm.

National Wool Museum

Dre-fach Felindre, 3 miles east • Daily April–Sept 10am–5pm; Oct–March Tues–Sat 10am–5pm • Free • ☎ 01559 370929, ⓦ museumwales.ac.uk

At the beginning of the twentieth century, the village of Dre-fach Felindre was at the heart of the Welsh wool trade, with 43 working mills in and around the village. One of these, the Cambrian Mills, has been turned into the **National Wool Museum**. The lower Teifi's prolific past as a weaving centre is told through excellent exhibits spanning the entire process – from the different wools produced by Wales' eleven million sheep, through demonstrations of working presses and looms to stunning examples of the finished flannels, shawls and blankets. Throughout, video footage and informative wall displays put the industry into its social and cultural contexts.

Llandysul

The region's pace slows down even further as the lanes reach **LLANDYSUL**, sitting pretty above the Teifi some eight miles east of Newcastle Emlyn. Two main streets run parallel through the village, the lower one brushing past the massive Early English-style **church of St Tysul**. Two centuries ago, the church porch served as a goalpost in the annual match of *cnapan*, an anarchic and extremely rough, day-long football-like game which ran the length of the village. Inside the church, there's an inscribed altar stone, thought to date from the sixth century, in the Lady Chapel.

Llanybydder Horse Market

Llanybydder, 10 miles east of Llandysul • Last Thursday of every month

The biggest reminder of the area's strong agricultural pedigree takes place in the otherwise sleepy village of **Llanybydder**. The monthly **horse market** brings buyers, sellers and neighing horses together from all over the country, and evokes a bygone era.

ARRIVAL AND DEPARTURE   NEWCASTLE EMLYN

By bus The #460, which stops on New Road, serves: Cardigan (13 daily; 20min) and Carmarthen (13 daily; 1hr).

ACCOMMODATION, EATING AND DRINKING

The Daffodil A475, 4.5 miles east at Penrhiwllan ☎ 01559 370343, ⓦ daffodilinn.co.uk. This stylish revamp of a village inn has become hugely popular with locals drawn from around the district to the light and airy atmosphere, cosy bar and a wide-ranging menu (mains £9–14). Book ahead for the Sunday roast (£10). Food served Mon–Sat noon–2pm & 6–9pm, Sun noon–2.30pm & 6–8.30pm.

Emlyn Arms Bridge St ☎ 01239 710317, ⓦ gwestyremlynhotel.co.uk. Nicely refurbished old coaching inn with stylish, modern rooms, gym and sauna. Quality light meals are served in the two bars and there's a separate smart restaurant (mains £10–15). Food served daily noon–2.30pm & 6–9pm. **£95**

La Calabria Ffostrasol, 6 miles northeast ☎ 01239 851101, ⓦ la-calabria.co.uk. Without detailed instructions you'll never find this unlikely place run by Welsh-Italian, Tony, in the converted cowshed of a farm. The food is rustic southern Italian – pizza, pasta, saltimbocca – kids are well catered for, and the soundtrack is opera. Be sure to try the ice cream made with milk from their own herd. Mains £10–15. Tues–Sat noon–2.30pm & 6–10.30pm, Sun noon–2.30pm.

Ludo's at The Cooper's Station Rd, B4571 ☎01239 710588. The finest Welsh ingredients get a Breton twist in this fine little gastropub on the northern outskirts of town. Start perhaps with pork fritters in a cider reduction (£6) followed by roast chicken with tarragon barley risotto (£14). Wed–Sun noon–2.30pm & 6–10pm.

Maes-y Derw 0.5 mile towards Cardigan on A484 ☎01239 710860, ⓦmaes-y-derw.co.uk. Classy B&B with spacious rooms in a beautifully restored house on the edge of town. Great breakfasts, evening meals by arrangement and there's a self-catering cottage. **£80**

Lampeter

The old-fashioned town of **LAMPETER** (Llanbedr Pont Steffan), twenty miles east of Newcastle Emlyn, is best known as a remote outpost of the British university system, known as Trinity St David. It was founded in 1822 by the Bishop of St Davids to aid Welsh theological students unable to travel to England for their education. Though the town has fewer than three thousand residents, it's a lively place, with frequent gigs and theatre performances and an eclectic population of current students, graduates who forgot to leave, hippies and farmers.

The town's three main streets – High, Bridge and College – meet at **Harford Square**, named after the local landowning family responsible for the construction of the early nineteenth-century **Falcondale Hall**, now an opulent hotel on the northern approach to Lampeter. Stick your head into **Conti's Café** with ageing accolades for its rich home-made ice cream.

St David's Building

Off College Street are the main buildings, which include C.B. Cockerell's **St David's Building**, the original stuccoed quadrangle dating from 1827 and modelled along the lines of an Oxbridge college. Tucked right underneath the main buildings, the motte of Lampeter's long-vanished **castle** forms an incongruous mound amid such order.

The High Street

The **High Street** is the most architecturally distinguished part of town, its eighteenth-century coaching inn, the *Black Lion*, dominating the streetscape; you can see its old stables and coach house through an archway.

ARRIVAL AND DEPARTURE — LAMPETER

By bus Most buses stop outside the NatWest Bank on the High St.
Destinations Aberaeron (12 daily; 40min); Aberystwyth (hourly; 1hr 15min); Carmarthen (12 daily; 1hr); Llanddewi Brefi (6 daily; 25min); Tregaron (9 daily; 25–35min).

INFORMATION

Information There's no tourist office, but ⓦlampeter.org has contact details for accommodation. Noticeboards in the *Mulberry Bush* (see below) carry information about local B&Bs and longer lets.

ACCOMMODATION, EATING AND DRINKING

Black Lion High St ☎01570 422490. Comfortable-enough en suite rooms above the bar in this ancient coaching inn are nothing flash but the price is right (not including breakfast). Reasonable bar meals are a good evening option. **£40**

Falcondale Mansion Hotel Falcondale Drive ☎01570 422910, ⓦfalcondalehotel.com. Italianate Victorian mansion in spacious parkland, 600yd west along High St then twice that along its stately drive. Rooms (which vary enormously) are beautifully opulent, the meals are wonderful (set dinner £40) and you're immediately made to feel welcome. Even if you're just passing through, consider afternoon tea (book for the full cream tea: £13) or the excellent Sunday lunch (£17). Food service daily noon–2.30pm, 3–5pm & 6–10pm. **£140**

Haulfan Guest House 6 Station Terrace, behind University College ☎01570 422718, ⓦhaulfan guesthouse.co.uk. Modest but modernized B&B, one room without en suite. There's also a single, and one child under 12 stays free. **£50**

King's Head 14 Bridge St ☎01550 720393. Friendly and fairly studenty pub with well-kept beer and a range of music, quiz and open mic nights. Daily 11.30am–11pm.

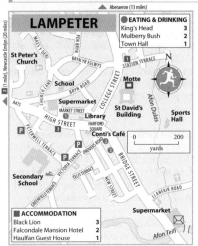

Mulberry Bush 2 Bridge St. Airy café above a long-standing wholefood shop, serving a limited range of soups, salads, vegan lasagne, juices and daily specials at modest prices. Occasional music nights. Mon–Sat 9am–6pm.

Town Hall High St ☎ 01570 421599. Smart, light-filled café and deli in the Town Hall with a short menu of cheeses, cold meats, olives and salads turned into some tasty sandwiches and platters. Good coffee and cakes, and heaps of foodie books to browse. Mon–Fri 8am–5pm, Sat 9am–4pm.

Tregaron and around

On the cusp of the verdant Teifi Valley and the desolate moors rising above it, the small town of **TREGARON**, ten miles northeast of Lampeter, was for long seemingly untouched by the modern world, but is now gradually being drawn into the twenty-first century.

All roads to Tregaron lead into the spruced-up market square, hemmed in by solid eighteenth- and nineteenth-century buildings. The **statue** in the centre of the square is of Tregaron-born Henry Richard (1812–88), the founder of the Peace Union, forerunner of the League of Nations and, subsequently, the United Nations.

Rhiannon Welsh Gold Centre

Cnr Dewi Rd & Market Square • July & Aug daily 10am–5.30pm; rest of year Mon–Sat 10am–5.30pm • ☎ 01974 298415, ⓦ rhiannon.co.uk

You might even see Rhiannon Evans at work in the classy Rhiannon Welsh Gold Centre, which stocks jewellery in Celtic designs fashioned from Welsh gold and other materials. It is backed up with galleries of painting, glassware, woollen throws and assorted knick-knacks, plus a good café.

Tregaron Red Kite Centre and Museum

100 yards south on Dewi Rd • Easter–Sept daily 10.30am–4.30pm; Oct–Easter Sat & Sun noon–4.30pm • Donation requested • ☎ 01974 298977

Community-run, the **Tregaron Red Kite Centre and Museum** is housed in an old Victorian school (with one intact schoolroom) and exhibits an eclectic mixture of material drawn from the area's farming and droving tradition along with tales of the resurgence of the red kite.

Llanddewi Brefi

Through the mid-2000s the single shop in the village of **LLANDDEWI BREFI**, three miles south of Tregaron, did a roaring trade in souvenir T-shirts commemorating the fictitious home of Dafydd, the "only gay in the village" from the BBC comedy *Little Britain*.

Llanddewi Brefi's previous claim to fame was the legend of 118 Welsh churchmen who met here in 519 AD and summoned Dewi Sant (St David). On appearing, Dewi began to speak to the men, but had trouble being heard, until the ground beneath him shuddered ominously and suddenly rose, giving him a natural platform to continue speaking – the massive **parish church** of St David sits on the mound to this day. Part of the church wall consists of two discernible stones inscribed with fragments of Latin script. These were originally part of a single memorial that dated from within a century of David's death – the first recorded mention of the Welsh patron saint – but they were broken up, reportedly, by an illiterate eighteenth- or nineteenth-century mason.

Cors Caron

B4343, 2 miles north of Tregaron • Open access • Free • ⓦ www.ccw.gov.uk

The Afon Teifi meanders through a wide, flat valley into the eerie wetland of **Cors Caron** (Tregaron Bog), a national nature reserve of peatland which was once cut for fuel. It is one of the most prodigious wildlife areas in Wales, home to rare marsh grasses, black adders, buzzards and red kites. A couple of walks lead off from a parking area beside the **Tregaron–Aberystwyth cycle trail** which follows an old railway line along the bog's flanks. Easiest is a wheelchair-accessible **boardwalk** (2-mile loop; 1hr; flat) which weaves out through cotton grass, bog mosses and birch to a hide with huge windows and explanations on how Cors Caron was created over the last 15,000 years. Part way round you can spur off on the **Riverside Walk** (4 miles; 2–3hr; uneven), which extends into a large loop along the infant Teifi and back along the disused railway.

Strata Florida

6 miles north of Tregaron and 1 mile east of Pontrhydfendigaid • April–Sept daily 10am–5pm; Oct–March daily 10am–4pm • £3.20 April–Sept; free Oct–March • ☎ 01974 831261 • CADW

In glorious rural solitude against wide-open skies and sheep-flecked hills stand the atmospheric ruins of **Strata Florida Abbey**, originally located in Ystrad Fflur, "the valley of the flowers", two miles away, but relocated in its early years to this equally fertile spot. This Cistercian abbey was founded in 1164, swiftly growing into a centre for milling, farming and weaving, and becoming an important political centre for Wales. In 1238, a dying Llewelyn the Great, fearful that his work of unifying Wales under one ruler would disintegrate, summoned the lesser Welsh princes here to command them to pay homage to his son, Dafydd.

Although very little survived Henry VIII's dissolution of the monasteries, the huge, Norman west doorway gives some idea of the church's vast dimensions. Fragments of side chapels include beautifully tiled medieval floors, and there's also a serene cemetery. A yew tree in the neighbouring graveyard shades the spot where Dafydd ap Gwilym, fourteenth-century bard and contemporary of Chaucer, is said to be buried.

ARRIVAL AND DEPARTURE   TREGARON

Buses, which arrive at the market square, serve: Aberystwyth (10 daily; 1hr); Lampeter (9 daily; 25–35min); Llanddewi Brefi (6 daily; 10min).

ACCOMMODATION, EATING AND DRINKING

Llew Du Pontrhydfendygaid ☎ 01974 831624, ⓦ blacklionhotel.co.uk. The *Llew Du* (Black Lion) is a great local pub. It is particularly welcoming to cyclists and walkers, and has a roaring fire when the temperature drops. Bar meals are unsophisticated but well made, and there are comfortable rooms. Daily 11am–11pm. **£70**

Talbot Hotel Market Square ☎ 01974 298208, ⓦ ytalbot.com. Classically symmetrical old drovers' inn now with a contemporary gloss while retaining beams in the old bar and a fabulous inglenook fireplace. Ales and bar meals are very good (and come with tempting kids' choices) plus there's a spacious Modern British restaurant (mains £18–24) which does a fine Sunday lunch (two courses for £16, three for £20). Rooms are stylishly spare and well appointed. Restaurant open daily 11am–11pm. **£80**

Aberystwyth

Midway along the Cambrian coast, spirited **ABERYSTWYTH** (or "Aber", as it's known locally) is a blast of fresh sea air. Two long bays skirted by pebbly beaches curve between twin rocky heads: Constitution Hill to the north, and Pen Dinas to the south above the town harbour's marina, where both the Rheidol and Ystwyth rivers empty into the sea. East of the town centre, the district of Penglais is home to the graceful Portland stone buildings of the National Library and the modernist blocks of Aberystwyth University, one of the UK's most prestigious educational institutions (the

ABERYSTWYTH

ACCOMMODATION	
Bodalwyn	1
Conrah Hotel	7
Glan-y-mor Leisure Park	6
Gwesty Cymru	4
Helmsman	2
Maes-y-Môr	3
Yr Hafod	5

EATING & DRINKING	
Gwesty Cymru	1
MG's Café	5
Rummers	9
Shilam Tandoori	8
Ship and Castle	4
Treehouse	3
Ultracomida	2
Y Cwps	7
Yr Hen Lew Du	6

ENTERTAINMENT	
Aberystwyth Arts Centre	4
Commodore Cinema	1
Côr Meibion Aberystwyth	2
Drwm	3

CARDIGAN BAY

North Beach

South Beach

River Rheidol

Constitution Hill
Cliff Railway

Pier
Pavilion
Old College
War Memorial
Castle
St Michael's
Castle Hotel

Ceredigion Museum
Library
Market
RAFA Club

Town Hall

Bronglais Hospital

School of Art

Aberystwyth University
Students Union

National Library of Wales

Sports Ground and Plascrug Leisure Centre
Plascrug Leisure Centre

Bus Stops
Train Station
Vale of Rheidol Railway

MARINE TERRACE
BATH STREET
NORTH ROAD
QUEEN'S ROAD
PORTLAND ST
PORTLAND ROAD
NORTH PARADE
TERRACE ROAD
MARKET STREET
EASTGATE
DARKGATE STREET
PIER ST
NEW ST
KING STREET
NEW PROMENADE
VULCAN ST
SEA VIEW PL
HIGH ST
BRIDGE ST
SOUTH ROAD
GRAYS INN RD
QUEENS ST
MILL STREET
ALEXANDRA ROAD
PARK AVENUE
NORTHGATE ST
POPLAR ROW
STANLEY ROAD
ELM TREE AVENUE
QUEEN'S ROAD
PENGLAIS ROAD
LLANBADARN ROAD
BOULEVARD ST. BRIEUC
A487
A44
TREFECHAN RD
PEN-YR-ANGOR
PENPARCAU ROAD
NEW PROMENADE
SOUTH MARINE TER.
Marina
CEFN LLAN

6 (3 miles), Borth (5 miles) & Machynlleth (20 miles)

Llanbadarn Fawr (0.5 miles)

A487 (3 miles) & Cardigan (40 miles)

Bow House (0.5 miles)

N

0   200   yards

Prince of Wales, Prince Charles, studied here). Wales' National Library here makes the city home – it's claimed – to more books per capita than anywhere else in the world. There are plenty of other cultural and other diversions in town too, as well as an array of Victorian and Edwardian seaside trappings including a cliff railway.

Aberystwyth's anti-establishment past and anarchic soul manifest in diverse ways. Pubs – and there are loads – stay open late, the political scene is green-tinged, and the town overall is emphatically Welsh – making it an easy-going and enjoyable place to gain an insight into the national psyche.

The precursor of Aberystwyth is the inland village of **Llanbadarn Fawr**, the seat of Wales' oldest bishopric between the sixth and eighth centuries, whose massive parish church still reeks of past power. Aberystwyth and Llanbadarn grew together around the church and the seafront thirteenth-century castle, minting its own coins and headquartering Owain Glyndŵr's revolutionaries in the Middle Ages. The *Cymdeithas yr Iaith* (Welsh Language Society) was founded in Aberystwyth in 1963 and is still located in the town, while the National Library was established here in 1907.

Constitution Hill and the cliff railway

Railway daily mid-March to early Nov 10am–5pm; early Nov to mid-March Wed–Sun 10.30am–4pm • £3.50 return • ☎ 01970 617642, Ⓦ aberystwythcliffrailway.co.uk

The 430ft-high **Constitution Hill** (Y Graig Glais) rises sharply from the rocky beach at the long Promenade's northern end. It's accessible on foot, though if you don't fancy the invigorating but stiff walk up, you can take the clanking 1896 **cliff railway**, which creeps up the crooked tracks at scarcely more than walking pace from the grand terminus building at the top of Queen's Road, behind the Promenade.

Camera obscura

Daily mid-March to early Nov 10am–5pm; early Nov to mid-March Wed–Sun 10.30am–4pm • £1 • ☎ 01970 617642, Ⓦ aberystwythcliffrailway.co.uk

At the top of Constitution Hill you'll find a café, picnic area, telescopes and an octagonal **camera obscura**, a device popular in the pre-TV era using a mirror and hefty lens to project close-up and long-shot views over the town, the surrounding mountains and bays, plus a vista of the hordes of caravans to the north, resembling legions of tanks poised for battle. The existing structure was built in 1985 on the ground plan of the Victorian original, but with its scale expanded to make it the largest of its type in the world.

The seafront

From the bottom of Constitution Hill, the **Promenade** – officially Marine Terrace – arcs away to the south, past ornate benches decorated with snakes, a continuous wall of hotels and guesthouses, a prim bandstand and a shingle beach.

Ceredigion Museum

Easter–Oct Mon–Sat 10am–5pm; Nov–Easter Mon–Sat noon–4.30pm • Free

The **Ceredigion Museum** is atmospherically housed over three floors in the ornate Edwardian Coliseum music hall. Mementos of the building as a theatre and cinema give a sense of place to an otherwise disparate collection, including cosy reconstructed cottages, dairies complete with separating and churning equipment, a nineteenth-century pharmacy, exhibits on the local geology and a surprisingly interesting look at the history of weights, measures and coinage.

Old College

West of Marine Terrace and the spindly **pier**, the seafront is dominated by the dazzling, John Nash-designed, turreted villa known as the **Old College**. Dating from 1790, the villa was massively extended in the 1860s, as a hotel designed to soak up the anticipated masses arriving on the new rail line. The venture failed, and in 1872 it was sold to the fledgling university, whose property it remains.

The castle and around
Open access • Free

At the southern end of the Promenade a rocky headland is occupied by the **castle** ruins which stare blankly out to sea. Built by Edward I as part of his conquest of Wales, the thirteenth-century fortress is more notable for its breezy position than for the buildings themselves, of which the two outer gates are the most impressive remains.

While in the area, wander past the Art Nouveau **Castle Hotel**, 37 South Rd, built in the style of an ornate Edwardian gin palace, and still with etched glass windows designating "Public Bar", "Lounge Bar" and "Luncheon Bar".

The harbour and Pen Dinas
South of the castle is the quiet, sandy beach along South Marine Terrace, which peters out by the wide **harbour**, the mouth of the Rheidol and Ystwyth rivers. The quietest beach is further south still, across the other side of the rivers' mouth, at **Tanybwlch**. High above the shingle strand is the Iron Age hillfort of **Pen Dinas** (413ft), crowned with what looks like a chimney – actually an 1853 memorial to the Duke of Wellington. Paths lead to the top from the car park at Tanybwlch.

4 The University and around

Aberystwyth's cultural heart beats strongest around the hillside suburb of Penglais, home to the **National Library of Wales** and the **Aberystwyth Arts Centre**. At the foot of the hill the **School of Art Gallery & Museum** deserves a short visit, perhaps on your way out to see the ancient **church of St Padarn** at Llanbadarn Fawr.

School of Art Gallery & Museum
Buarth Mawr • Mon–Fri 10am–5pm • Free

A hundred yards north of the station, Stanley Road leads to the splendid **School of Art**. Originally bequeathed to the university by the Davies sisters of Gregynog Hall (see p.244), this impressive Edwardian building, topped with a distinctive cupola, has been the home of the art department since 1995. The public galleries on the ground floor mount both touring exhibitions and rotating exhibitions from the university's extensive permanent collection, with an emphasis on Welsh art.

National Library of Wales
A487, 1 mile east • Mon–Fri 9.30am–6pm, Sat 9.30–5pm • Free; free 1hr guided tours Mon 11am & Wed 2.15pm • ☎ 01970 632800, Ⓦ www.llgc.org.uk

Housed in a massive white stone Edwardian building overlooking the town, the **National Library of Wales** possesses fine manuscripts including the oldest extant Welsh text, the twelfth-century *Black Book of Carmarthen*, and the earliest manuscript of *The Mabinogion*. Occasionally these form part of the typically excellent temporary exhibitions held in the corridors near the entrance, the upstairs Gregynog Gallery and the downstairs Peniarth Gallery. Displays from the library's permanent collection of books, manuscripts and papers include the **World of the Book**, which looks at the history of the written word and publishing in Wales. You can easily spend a few hours here, aided by a good café.

As one of the UK's copyright repositories, the library holds copies of every new book published in Britain. If you're tracing family history you'll want access to the **Reading Rooms**, for which you'll need two forms of ID, including one that shows your current address.

Aberystwyth Arts Centre

A487, 1 mile east • ☎ 01970 623232, ⓦ aberystwythartscentre.co.uk

The excellent **Aberystwyth Arts Centre**, a quarter of a mile uphill from the National Library, sits in the middle of the university's main campus. A curious mix of 1960s brutalism and postmodern elegance, the Arts Centre is a great place to while away an hour or two, taking in the various temporary art and ceramics exhibitions, browsing the designer crafts and bookshops, catching a film or enjoying a drink in the café, which affords sublime views over the town and bay.

Church of St Padarn

At Llanbadarn Fawr, just off A44, 1 mile southeast • Generally daily 10am–4pm

The suburb of Llanbadarn Fawr is the original settlement from which Aberystwyth grew but warrants little attention except for the stunning sight of the massive, thirteenth-century **church of St Padarn**. The site's religious association goes back to the Breton St Padarn who established a monastic settlement here in the second half of the sixth century, decades before even St Augustine's mission to the English of 597 AD.

Inside the church, opposite the main door, hangs an enlargement of a page from *Rhygyfarch's Psalter* of 1079, one example of the beautifully decorated texts for which the monks of Llanbadarn became renowned. In the south transept, there's a fascinating exhibition on St Padarn's monastic foundation and the area's history that includes two fine tenth-century crosses, moved inside from the churchyard in 1916. The taller one, about 8ft high, is woven with exquisite Celtic tracery. Perhaps the most entertaining part of the exhibition deals with poet **Dafydd ap Gwilym** (c.1320–70) and his upbringing in Llanbadarn parish. His poem *Merched Llanbadarn* ("Women of Llanbadarn") tells of his frustration at sitting in the church watching the beautiful parish girls:

Plygu rhag llid yr ydwyf,	*Passion doubles me over,*
Pla ar holl ferched y plwyf!	*Plague take all the parish girls!*
Am na chefais, drais drawsgoed,	*Because, frustrated trysting,*
Onaddun'yr un erioed,	*I've had not a single one.*
Na morwyn fwyn ofynaig,	*No lovely, longed-for virgin,*
Na merch fach, na gwrach, na gwraig.	*Not a wench nor witch nor wife.*

ARRIVAL AND DEPARTURE
ABERYSTWYTH

By train Main line and Vale of Rheidol trains use the same train station on Alexandra Rd, a 10min walk from the seafront.
Destinations Borth (9 daily; 12min); Machynlleth (9 daily; 30min).
By bus Local and long-distance buses stop outside the train station on Alexandra Rd.

Destinations Aberaeron (every 30min; 40min); Borth (hourly; 20min); Caernarfon (3 daily; 3hr); Cardigan (12 daily; 1hr 30min–2hr); Carmarthen (mostly hourly; 2hr 20min); Lampeter (hourly; 1hr 15min); Machynlleth (hourly; 45min); New Quay (hourly; 1hr); Pontrhydfendigaid (3 daily; 50min); Tregaron (10 daily; 1hr); Ynyslas (hourly; 30min).

INFORMATION

Tourist information The TIC is close to the seafront on Terrace Rd (July & Aug daily 10am–5pm; Sept–June Mon–Sat 10am–5pm; ☎ 01970 612125; ⓔ aberystwythtic@ ceredigion.gov.uk). Staff can help with accommodation

and sell tickets for local events.
Internet Free at the library on Corporation St (Mon–Fri 9.30am–6pm, Sat 9.30am–5pm).

ACCOMMODATION

Accommodation is generally quite reasonably priced and easy to find, though everywhere fills up to the gills during graduation week (usually the second or third week of July), when prices invariably jump. Guesthouses and B&Bs predominate; anywhere on the seafront is likely to charge a premium.

4

HOTELS AND GUESTHOUSES

Bodalwyn Queens Ave ☎ 01970 612578, ⓦ bodalwyn .co.uk. Quiet and roomy eight-room guesthouse blending contemporary furnishings with original features. All rooms have well-appointed en-suite bathrooms, and breakfast is served in a sunny conservatory. **£72**

Conrah Hotel A487, 4 miles south ☎ 01970 617941, ⓦ conrah.co.uk. This stately Georgian hotel has a bit of a businessy feel, but the rooms are very comfortable and the restaurant and lounges have great views over the spacious grounds. **£95**

★ **Gwesty Cymru** 19 Marine Terrace ☎ 01970 6122252, ⓦ gwestycymru.com. Classy seafront "restaurant with rooms", eight of them, all with crisp white cotton sheets, big bathrooms and a very modern Welsh feel. Four rooms have sea views and there's a wonderful attic room. Breakfast is served in the half-basement restaurant. **£100**

Helmsman 43 Marine Terrace ☎ 01970 624132, ⓦ helmsmanguesthouse.co.uk. Traditional seafront guesthouse with fairly drab public areas but tidy rooms. There's no premium for sea views. **£70**

★ **Yr Hafod** 1 South Marine Terrace ☎ 01970 617579, ⓦ yrhafod.co.uk. Good-value seafront accommodation, with spacious, well-maintained and tastefully decorated rooms (some en suite and several with sea views), appealingly situated south of the castle. **£62**

HOSTELS, CAMPING AND SELF-CATERING

Aberystwyth University Penglais ☎ 01970 621960, ⓦ aber.ac.uk/en/visitors. During the university's summer recess (mid-June to mid-Sept) the university offers some single-bed accommodation in self-contained flats including bed linen, full cooking facilities and access to the university facilities, including two sports halls and a heated pool. Per person **£23.50**

Glan-y-mor Leisure Park Clarach Bay, 3 miles north ☎ 01970 828900, ⓦ sunbourne.co.uk. Situated on the other side of Constitution Hill, with a variety of options including on-site caravans and tent pitches, plus a superb range of leisure facilities including (for an extra fee) a heated indoor pool and gym. Pitches **£19**

Maes-y-Môr 25 Bath St ☎ 01970 639270, ⓦ maesymor.co.uk. Brightly painted and very central hostel-style place with a good kitchen for guests, laundry and free wi-fi. Each room has TV, tea and coffee. Breakfast not included. **£55**

EATING AND DRINKING

Aberystwyth's cultural and gastronomic life is a cosmopolitan, year-round affair, thriving on students in term time and visitors in the summer. As well as a varied range of **pubs** and **restaurants**, the town is a good place to hear Welsh **music** and a lively centre for theatre and cinema. Daytime **café** culture is booming in the town centre, and the Arts Centre is home to two fabulous cafés and two bars.

RESTAURANTS AND CAFÉS

Gwesty Cymru 19 Marine Terrace ☎ 01970 6122252, ⓦ gwestycymru.com. Accomplished slate-floored restaurant that's one of the smartest places in town to eat. Expect the likes of crispy duck with mango and lychee salsa (£7), followed by mains such as hake florentine (£16) and daily specials. The £8 lunches (Mon–Fri only) are excellent value and the seaview terrace out front makes an ideal spot for a pre-dinner drink. Daily noon–2.30pm & 6–9pm.

MG's Café 26 Chalybeate St. Comfy sofas, newspapers and Aberystwyth's best espresso make this one of the most tempting places in town to hang out on a grotty day. There's a good range of savoury dishes and tasty cakes. Mon–Thurs 8am–6pm, Fri 8am–11pm, Sat 8.30am–5pm.

Shilam Tandoori Alexandra Rd ☎ 01970 615015, ⓦ shilam.co.uk. Superb modern Indian restaurant in the train station with unusual specialities and good vegetarian choices such as shabjee khufta with vegetable balls. The daytime buffet (daily noon–5pm) is great value at £5.50. Daily noon–11pm.

★ **Treehouse** 14 Baker St ☎ 01970 615791, ⓦ treehousewales.co.uk. Upbeat, mostly vegetarian café over two levels, located above a wholefood shop. It is good for pizza slices, salads, good coffee, plus daily specials made from local ingredients. They also bake their own breads and cakes. Mon–Fri 10am–5pm, Sat 9am–5pm.

★ **Ultracomida** 31 Pier St ☎ 01970 630686, ⓦ ultracomida.co.uk. Spain comes to Aber in this fabulous deli, its wall lined with Iberian wines, French and Welsh cheeses, olives and all manner of goodies. It's great for freshly made sandwiches to take away but also a fine café for tapas, Spanish breakfast (served 10–11.30am for £6). Also tapas-style dinners on Friday and Saturday nights (£20). Mon–Thurs 10am–5pm, Fri & Sat 10am–9pm, Sun 1–3.30pm.

PUBS

Rummers Bridge St. Studenty, late-closing pub with slate floors, outside seating by the river and live music most weekends. It calls itself a wine bar but you're better sticking to beer and spirits. Daily 11am–11pm.

Ship and Castle Corner of Vulcan and High sts ☎ 01970 612334, ⓦ shipandcastle.co.uk. Nicely refurbished, youthful pub with a pool table, a great jukebox and considerable pride in having the best selection of real ales in town. Daily 11am–11pm.

Y Cŵps (Coopers Arms) ☎ 01970 624 050 Llanbadarn Rd.

Fun and friendly Welsh local, with regular folk and jazz nights and jam sessions. Daily 11am–11pm.
Yr Hen Lew Du *(The Old Black Lion)* 14 Bridge St ☎ 01970

615378. Boisterous, very Welsh and hugely enjoyable pub. Easily the best place in Aberystwyth to catch an international match on the big screen. Daily 11am–11pm.

ENTERTAINMENT

Aberystwyth Arts Centre The University, Penglais ☎ 01970 623232, ⒲ aberystwythartscentre.co.uk. The town's main venue for art-house cinema, touring theatre, classes, events and wide-ranging temporary exhibitions. From late July through Aug there's always some kind of music on – anything from classical music to popular shows.
Commodore Cinema Bath St ☎ 01970 612421. Screens

mainstream current releases.
Côr Meibion Aberystwyth RAFA Club on Bridge St ☎ 01970 615320. Visitors are welcome to attend rehearsals of this Male Voice Choir (Thurs 7–8.30pm).
Drwm National Library, Penglais ☎ 01970 632800, ⒲ drwm.llgc.org.uk. Hip centre for film, lectures and concerts.

DIRECTORY

Horseriding Rheidol Riding Centre, off A44, 5 miles east of Aberystwyth ☎ 01970 880863, ⒲ rheidol-riding-centre. co.uk. Offers a variety of lessons and leisure rides for all standards in farmland in the Vale of Rheidol.

Swimming Plascrug Leisure Centre, off Llanbadarn Rd ☎ 01970 624579. Has two indoor pools, a sauna and solarium, squash and tennis courts, and a multi-gym.

Around Aberystwyth

Immediately inland of Aberystwyth lies the **Vale of Rheidol**, a region of forested glades and remote villages easily accessed by road. A more enjoyable approach is on the narrow-gauge steam train that terminates at the spectacular **Devil's Bridge**. Further exploration takes you into the **Vale of Ystwyth** and the bleak mining landscape around **Cwmystwyth**.

The coast north of Aberystwyth draws sunseekers to the beach at **Borth** and the dunes close to the mouth of the Dyfi estuary. Birdwatchers will prefer to head further northeast to the RSPB's **Ynys-Hir Nature Reserve**, with its complex series of habitats.

The Vale of Rheidol

The River Rheidol winds its way down to Aberystwyth through a secluded, wooded valley, where occasional old industrial workings have moulded themselves into the contours, past waterfalls and minute villages. Devil's Bridge is easily accessed by the Vale of Rheidol Railway (see below), the Rheidol Cycle Trail (see box below) and by car. For a **day out**, drives can head straight for Devil's Bridge (along the A4120), then the lead mines in time for the kite feeding at Bwlch Nant yr Arian. If you've stayed for the kite feeding you're probably too late for side trips to the Cwm Rheidol Reservoir and the butterfly house on the same day.

Vale of Rheidol Railway
April–Oct 2–4 trains most days • £14.50 return • ☎ 01970 625819, ⒲ rheidolrailway.co.uk
The glorious Vale of Rheidol is best seen from the 23.5in-gauge **Vale of Rheidol Railway**,

---

CYCLING THE VALE OF RHEIDOL AND THE YSTWYTH TRAIL

You can also explore the valley by bike using the **Rheidol Cycle Trail**, a combination of designated cycle paths and quiet country lanes which runs eighteen miles from Aberystwyth to Devil's Bridge: the tourist office in Aberystwyth has a free leaflet outlining the route. Unfortunately bikes can't be taken on the Vale of Rheidol Railway.

The twenty-mile **Ystwyth Trail** from Aberystwyth to Tregaron is another winner, partly following the trackbed of the Manchester & Milford Railway across Cors Caron.

a narrow-gauge steam train which huffs and puffs along twelve miles of steep hillsides, climbing over 600ft in the process. It was built in 1902, ostensibly for the valley's lead mines but with a canny eye on its tourist potential. For many years it operated as part of British Rail's network, running steam trains until 1989 (over twenty years after steam locos had ceased operating elsewhere). It was then sold to the private group which now operates it using authentic Rheidol rolling stock. The trip takes one hour each way, and is most enjoyable from the comfortable first-class observation carriage (£2.50 extra each way) or the open-sided "summer car". There's also an excellent GPS-triggered audio guide to the line and valley for a small extra charge.

Cwm Rheidol Reservoir

On a side road 4 miles east of Capel Bangor **Visitor centre** Easter & May–Sept 10.30am–4.15pm • Free **Power station tours** 11am–3.30pm • Free • ☎ 01970 880667

Midway along the valley, the Rheidol is dammed at the **Cwm Rheidol Reservoir**, the final element in a small, showpiece hydroelectric scheme that starts high in the headwaters at the Nant-y-moch Reservoir. It is all explained at the visitor centre, where you can join a free 45-minute tour of the **power station**, where impressive sluices and channels funnel the water according to need.

Magic of Life Butterfly House

On a side road 4 miles east of Capel Bangor • Easter–Sept daily 10am–5pm; Oct 10am–4pm • £6.50 • ☎ 01970 880928, ⓦ magicoflife.org

Behind the Cwm Rheidol Reservoir visitor centre, the **Magic of Life Butterfly House** houses dozens of beautiful butterflies and moths – including the lovely blue morpho – in a wild garden and tropically heated polytunnel. It is the work of committed environmentalist, Neil Gale; talking to him makes the whole place come alive.

Bwlch Nant yr Arian

A44, 9 miles east of Aberystwyth • Visitor centre daily: Easter–Sept 10am–5pm; Oct–Easter generally 10.30am to dusk • Free; parking £1.50 • ☎ 01970 890453, ⓦ www.forestry.gov.uk/bwlchnantyrarian

In recent years, **Bwlch Nant yr Arian** has become famous for its red kites, easy walks and varied mountain biking. From the visitor centre, which has a decent café with a pleasant deck, three well-marked walking trails (30min, 1hr & 2hr) head out into the evergreen forest and among the abandoned detritus of lead mining.

The easiest trail loops around a lake past the kite hide, a superb spot for watching the daily **red kite feeding** (3pm during daylight saving, 2pm in winter) when some 20lb of beef and lamb are placed on a grassy patch by the lake. In 1999, when this practice first started, fewer than a dozen birds would come; now it isn't uncommon to see 200 kites all squabbling over the pickings.

If you've brought a **bike** along, the woods also offer top-class mountain biking, notably on the 16km Summit Trail, which is classed as difficult and will take at least an hour and a half. A bike trail map (£2) covers the mostly moderate to hard red and black runs, but the nearest bike rentals are in Machynlleth, Cardigan and near Aberaeron.

Llywernog Mine Museum & Caverns

A44, 1 mile east of Bwlch Nant yr Arian • April–June, Sept & Oct daily 10.30am–5pm; July & Aug 10am–6pm • £7.50 • ☎ 01970 890620, ⓦ silverminetours.co.uk

Bwlch Nant yr Arian forest's lush foliage makes it difficult to imagine how stark the valley once looked. A truer picture unfolds in the impressively barren scenery around the **Llywernog Mine Museum & Caverns**, which opened in the 1740s and closed in the early twentieth century, then reopened in the early 1970s. The site has since expanded in an appropriately rustic manner. A low-key mock-up of a working mine, housing an interesting museum, leads on to a collection of rusted machinery and the dank, dark mine itself, visitable on a rewarding thirty-minute underground tour. Topside, you can pan for "fool's gold" or dowse for veins of galena, a silver-rich mineral once mined locally – the remains of waste tips scarring hillsides and shafts pockmarking former sites are now mostly hidden among the evergreens of the Rheidol Forest; in the latter half of the 1800s, the whole of northern Ceredigion lured galena speculators and opportunists by the trainful.

EATING AND DRINKING   **BWLCH NANT YR ARIAN**

Druid Inn Goginan, 2 miles west of Bwlch Nant yr Arian ☎ 01970 880650, ⓦ goginan.com/druid. A classic country pub that maintains high standards with well-kept real ales and great bar meals largely using local produce. Particularly noted for their Sunday lunches. Mon–Thurs & Sun noon–midnight, Fri & Sat noon–1am.

Devil's Bridge

Folk legend, incredible scenery and travellers' lore combine at **DEVIL'S BRIDGE** (Pontarfynach), a tiny settlement twelve miles east of Aberystwyth – reached by road (A4120) or the Vale of Rheidol Railway – built largely for the long-established visitor trade. To avoid the congestion, visit at the beginning or end of the day, or out of season.

The main attraction is the Devil's Bridge itself, where three roads (the A4120, the B4343 and the B4574) converge and cross the churning River Mynach yards above its confluence with the Rheidol to form three bridges, one on top of the other. The road bridge in front of the alpine *Hafod Arms* hotel is the most recently built of the three, dating from 1901. Immediately below it and wedged between the rock faces are the stone bridge from 1753, and, at the bottom, the original bridge, dating from the eleventh century and reputedly built by the monks of Strata Florida Abbey.

The Punch Bowl
£1 coin in the turnstile

The classic view of the **three stacked bridges** is from the Punch Bowl path. Standing by the modern road bridge with your back to the hotel, take the right-hand turnstile for a ten-minute loop.

Slippery steps lead down to the deep cleft in the rock, where the water pounds and hurtles through the gap crowned by the bridges. The Punch Bowl is the name given to a series of rock bowls scooped by the sheer power of the thundering river, which rushes through past bright-green mossy rocks and saturated lichen.

Mynach Falls
Pay at the ticket office Easter–Oct daily 9.45am–5pm • £3.50; at other times pay £2 in the turnstile

There are more extensive trails and many more steep steps across the road from the Punch Bowl. A path leads down into the valley and ultimately to the crashing **Mynach Falls**. The scenery here is magnificent: sharp, wooded slopes rising away from the frothing river, with distant mountain peaks surfacing on the horizon. A platform overlooks the series of falls, from where a steep flight of steps takes you further down to a footbridge dramatically spanning the river at the bottom.

ACCOMMODATION, EATING AND DRINKING   **DEVIL'S BRIDGE**

Hafod Hotel A4120, Devil's Bridge ☎ 01970 890232, ⓦ thehafodhotel.co.uk. Newly revitalized hotel that is once again the social hub of this scattered community. Mainly frequented for its restaurant, bars and tearooms, though it does have comfortable rooms. Food and drink daily 9am–10pm or later. **£85**

Woodlands Caravan Park A4120, Devil's Bridge ☎ 01970 890233, ⓦ woodlandsdevilsbridge.co.uk. Reasonably priced camping with a few static caravans, spacious and picturesque touring sites, showers, kids' playground, camp store and tearooms. Pitches **£12.50**

The Vale of Ystwyth

The Ystwyth River runs pretty much parallel to the Rheidol, a couple of miles to the south. Four miles south of Devil's Bridge is the quiet village of **PONTRHYDYGROES**, the former centre of local lead-mining activity. The B4574 climbs out of the village and past the country estate of **Hafod**, once the seat of a great house belonging to the wealthy Johnes family. Their last mansion was demolished in 1958 as an unsafe ruin, and all that remains is the beautiful estate Thomas Johnes landscaped and forested two hundred years ago. The church, off the B4574, is the best place to embark on the waymarked **trails** that lead through the estate, past its trickling streams, monumental relics and planted glades, down to the river. A bridge spans the river, where paths fan out along its banks and up through the tiny valley of the Nant Gau.

Cwmystwyth

From Devil's Bridge, a small road grinds seven miles eastwards and uphill into the bizarre moonscape surrounding **CWMYSTWYTH**, a small, semi-derelict village at the bottom of a valley of old lead mines, deserted in the late nineteenth century when the mines were exhausted. The river shimmers past abandoned shafts, tumbledown cottages, twisted tramways and grey heaps of spoil littering spartan hillsides. The isolated road continues to climb the uninhabited slopes, before dropping down into the Elan Valley and its reservoirs.

ACCOMMODATION CWMYSTWYTH

Tyllwyd Cwmystwyth, 6 miles southeast of Devil's Bridge ☎ 01974 282216. Head just east of Cwmystwyth to reach this farm campsite beside the River Ystwyth with green hills all about. It is a wonderfully peaceful spot, but bring all you need as there are no shops or pubs anywhere nearby. Toilets and showers are across the road at the farmhouse. Pitches **£12**

North from Aberystwyth

The A487 runs north from Aberystwyth towards Machynlleth, slicing between the mountains to the east and the flat lands bordering the vast Dyfi estuary. The seaward plain is essentially a raised bog, **Cors Fochno**, visible from the main road but better viewed from the rail line or the coastal B4353. This road sneaks through **Borth**, stretching for nearly two miles along the seafront, to the **nature reserve** at **Ynyslas**, the best place to explore the sand dunes, flanking a supremely scenic **beach** looking across the Dyfi estuary.

Inland, the eighteenth-century iron foundry at **Furnace** heralds **Ynys-hir**, an RSPB nature reserve with an impressive range of bird habitats, and **Cors Dyfi**, where ospreys can be viewed for most of the summer.

Borth

Hemmed in by the sea on one side and a vast peat bog on the other, **BORTH**, five miles north of Aberystwyth, is an old fishing village that gradually adapted to caravan park tourism. The village is strung out along ruler-straight High Street, which regularly gets battered by weather fronts from the Atlantic. Its three-mile-long shallow **beach** is excellent: swimming is fine as long as you don't go too far up towards the mouth of the Dyfi.

ARRIVAL AND DEPARTURE BORTH

By train Trains from Aberystwyth head direct to Borth (9 daily; 12min) and continue to Ynyslas (9 daily; 20min) and Machynlleth (9 daily; 30min).

ACCOMMODATION AND EATING

Tir a Mor High St ☎ 01970 871042. Relaxed café where you can sink into sofas in the loft and use the binoculars to gaze out across Cors Fochno. Mon–Fri 9am–5pm, Sat & Sun 9am–6pm.

YHA Borth High St ☎ 0845 371 9724, ✉ borth@yha .org.uk. Edwardian YHA hostel at the northern end of town, with dorm beds and some family rooms, as well as a licensed bar. Easter–Oct. Dorms **£17**

Ynyslas Nature Reserve

Reserve Open access **Visitor centre** Just off B4353, 3 miles north of Borth • Easter–Sept daily 9.30am–5pm • Free • ☏ 01970 872901, ⓦ www.ccw.gov.uk

Northwards from Borth, the flat landscape meets the formidable sand dunes that line the southern side of the Dyfi estuary. The road follows the coast a couple of miles to the dramatic estuary-side **Ynyslas nature reserve**. In winter, wading and sea birds feed among the dunes and mud flats, while in summer, butterflies flit among vibrant sand plants growing in the grass. The views here stretch inland to the mountains, along the estuary and coast, and over the river to the colourful huddle of Aberdyfi.

The reserve's **visitor centre** is the starting point for guided walks and tours most summer weekends. Walk half a mile along the beach to a **fossilized forest** where, at low tides, the sands near the water's edge are studded with the petrified stumps of a dozen or so 5000-year-old trees, a reminder that the coast was some twelve miles away when these trees were in their prime. A more romantic explanation is the Welsh legend that tells of a drowned land known as Cantre'r Gwaelod which was protected by sea walls and floodgates. Their keeper, Seithenyn, happened to get drunk the night of an almighty storm and the sea burst through, drowning a thousand people and fourteen settlements.

Dyfi Furnace

A487, 11 miles north of Aberystwyth • Open access • Free • CADW

During the latter half of the eighteenth-century the barn-like **Dyfi Furnace** was the centre of the silver and iron smelting activities. The power of the Einion River was harnessed using an immense water wheel driving the bellows, and with the recent installation of a generator the water wheel is once again producing power. Take two minutes to stroll around the back to a picturesque waterfall that feeds the water wheel.

Cwm Einion

A narrow lane from Dyfi Furnace follows the river through a forest and out into the idyllic **Cwm Einion**, known as "Artists' Valley" because of its popularity with nineteenth-century landscape painters. A parking area about a mile and a half along the lane gives access to footpaths which head up into the deserted foothills of Plynlimon, across the spongy moors and through dark conifer forests to the remote glacial lakes of **Llyn Conach** and **Llyn Dwfn**, three miles away. It is a landscape which may soon be massively changed by the installation of huge wind turbines.

Ynys-hir

A487, 0.5 mile north of Dyfi Furnace • **Reserve** daily 9am–9pm or dusk if earlier • £3 **Visitor centre** April–Oct daily 10am–5pm, Nov–March Wed–Sun 10am–4pm • ☏ 01654 700222, ⓦ rspb.org.uk/wales

The thousand-plus-acres of **Ynys-hir Nature Reserve** comprise five distinct habitats. Redstarts, pied flycatchers and warblers flit about the ancient hanging oak woodland so typical of mid-Wales, while cormorants flock to the estuarine salt marshes, and red-breasted mergansers and elusive otters inhabit the freshwater streams and pools. The remnant peat bogs are a riot of wild flowers in spring; winter brings water rails to the reed beds to join the herons. The attractions are obvious to the birders who return time and again to the network of hides, but there's enough along the one- or two-hour designated trails to interest anyone, and most weekends there are special-interest guided walks.

Cors Dyfi

A487, 5 miles north of Dyfi Furnace • **Cors Dyfi** daily 10am–6pm • Free **Osprey Project** April–Aug daily 10am–6pm • Free

At **Cors Dyfi**, a short wheelchair-accessible boardwalk leads out among the reeds, ponds and bog plants inhabited by water buffalo that have been brought in to manage the invasive birch and willow that would otherwise turn the place into a forest. It is a nice enough stroll, enhanced during spring and summer by the opportunity to see **ospreys** nesting on the top of a pole some 700yd away from a viewing platform. Better still,

CCTV cameras give you a real close-up of the nest: in May you might see the chicks hatch, while later you'll see them fledge.

Southern Cadair Idris and the Dyfi and Talyllyn valleys

The southern coastal reaches of Snowdonia National Park are almost entirely dominated by **Cadair Idris** (2930ft), a five-peaked massif standing defiant in its isolation. Tennyson claimed never to have seen "anything more awful than the great veil of rain drawn straight over Cader Idris", but catch it on a good day, and the views from the top – occasionally stretching as far as Ireland – are phenomenal. During the last Ice Age, the heads of glaciers scalloped out two huge cwms from Cadair Idris' distinctive dome, leaving 1000ft cliffs dropping away on all sides to cool, clear lakes. The largest of these amphitheatres is Cwm Gadair, the **Chair of Idris**, which takes its name from a giant warrior poet of Welsh legend, although some prefer the notion that Idris' Chair refers to a seat-like rock formation on the summit ridge, where anyone spending the night (specifically New Year's Eve, some say) will become a poet, go mad or die.

Cadair Idris' southern limits are lapped by the broad expanse of the Dyfi estuary, which in turn bleeds into the grand, green scenery of the **Dyfi Valley**. The valley's focal point is the engaging town of **Machynlleth**, which lies just south of the renowned **Centre for Alternative Technology**.

4

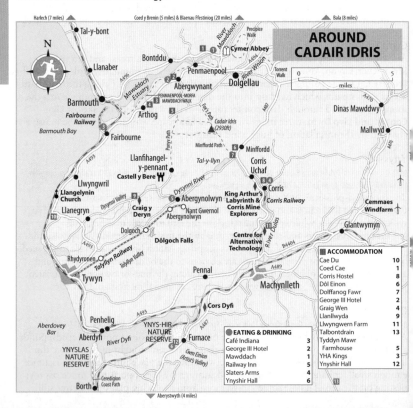

There's pleasure in staying at small-scale coastal resorts such as **Aberdyfi**, a good base for exploring the inland cormorant colony at **Craig yr Aderyn**, the brooding thirteenth-century **Castell-y-Bere** and the quaint narrow-gauge **Talyllyn Railway** which runs seven miles up the **Talyllyn Valley** to **Abergynolwyn** at the foot of Cadair Idris.

Machynlleth and around

MACHYNLLETH (pronounced Mah-hun-cthleth, and referred to locally as Mac) is Wales' "alternative" capital in more ways than one. Shortlisted as a possible capital of Wales in the 1950s and site of Owain Glyndŵr's totemic fifteenth-century Welsh parliament, it retains some handsome architecture, while the town's excellent facilities, lively atmosphere and proximity to the coast make it an ideal jumping-off point for exploring the area. It also boasts a long tradition of progressive and environmentally conscious

OWAIN GLYNDŴR, WELSH HERO

No name is so frequently invoked in Wales as that of **Owain Glyndŵr** (c.1349–1416), a potent figurehead of Welsh nationalism ever since he rose up against the occupying English in the first few years of the fifteenth century.

Little is known about the man described in Shakespeare's *Henry IV, Part I* as "not in the roll of common men". There seems little doubt that the charismatic Owain fulfilled many of the mystical medieval prophecies about the rising up of the red dragon. He was of aristocratic stock – descended from the princes of Powys and Cyfeiliog – and had a conventional upbringing, part of it in England, of all places. He studied in London and became a distinguished soldier of the English king before returning to Wales and marrying a local woman.

Wales in the late fourteenth century was a turbulent place. The brutal savaging a century earlier of Llywelyn the Last and Edward I's stringent policies of subordinating Wales had left a discontented, cowed nation where any signs of rebellion were sure to attract support. Glyndŵr became the focus of the rebellion when his neighbour, the English Lord of Ruthin, seized some of his land. When the courts failed to back him, Glyndŵr took matters into his own hands. With four thousand supporters and a new declaration that he was "Prince of Wales", he attacked Ruthin, and then Denbigh, Rhuddlan, Flint, Hawarden and Oswestry, before encountering an English resistance at Welshpool. As Glyndŵr consolidated his position in north Wales, English king Henry IV imposed punitive laws on Welsh land ownership, even outlawing Welsh-language bards and singers. Glyndŵr's support swelled enough for him to take the castles at Conwy, Harlech and Aberystwyth. By the end of 1403, he controlled most of Wales.

In 1404, Glyndŵr assembled a parliament of four men from every *commot* (community) in Wales at Machynlleth, drawing up mutual recognition treaties with France and Spain. He also had himself crowned ruler of a free Wales. A second parliament in Harlech took place a year later, with Glyndŵr making plans to carve up England and Wales into three as part of an alliance against the English king: Glyndŵr would rule Wales and the Marches of England. He then demanded independence for the Welsh Church from Canterbury and set about securing alliances with English noblemen who had grievances with Henry IV. This last, ambitious move heralded Glyndŵr's downfall.

The English army concentrated with increased vigour on destroying the Welsh uprising, and the Tripartite Indenture was never realized. From then on, Glyndŵr lost battles, ground and castles and was forced into hiding – dying, it is thought, in Herefordshire.

Anti-Welsh laws stayed in place until the accession to the English throne of Henry VII, a Welshman, in 1485. Wales became subsumed into English custom and law, and Glyndŵr's uprising became an increasingly powerful symbol of frustrated Welsh independence. In modern times, the shadowy organization that surfaced in the early 1980s to burn the holiday homes of English people and English estate agents dealing in Welsh property took the name Meibion (the sons of) Glyndŵr.

The figure of Glyndŵr, his trademark double-pointed beard to the fore, can often be seen gracing Welsh pub signs of inns called the Prince of Wales – as distinct from those who, by dint of being the first-born son of the reigning British monarch, have occupied the title ever since.

4

thinking and innovation, long before such concerns became universally fashionable. Organics are strong here: there's even an eco home-decorating store.

The wide main street is **Heol Maengwyn**, busiest on Wednesdays, when a lively **market** swings into action. Heol Maengwyn comes to an end at a fanciful **clock tower**, built in 1873 by local landowner, the Marquess of Londonderry, to commemorate his son and heir's coming of age.

Owain Glyndŵr Centre

Heol Maengwyn • Mid-June to Aug daily 10am–5pm; March to mid-June & Sept Tues–Sat 10am–5pm; Oct–Dec Tues–Sat 11am–4pm • £2.50 • ☎ 01654 702932, ⓦ canolfanglyndwr.org

Glyndŵr's partly fifteenth-century **Parliament House** is a modest-looking black-and-white-fronted building concealing a large interior. Displays chart the course of Glyndŵr's life, his military campaigns, his downfall, and the 1404 parliament in the town, when he controlled almost all of what is now known as Wales and even negotiated international recognition of the sovereign state. The sorriest tales are from 1405 onwards, when tactical errors and the sheer brute force of the English forced an ignominious end to the great Welsh uprising.

Plas Machynlleth

Opposite the Parliament House, a path leads into the landscaped grounds of **Plas**

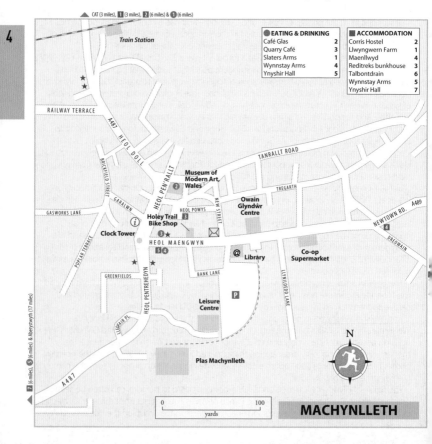

Machynlleth, the elegant seventeenth-century mansion of the Marquess of Londonderry. Its solitude is entirely intentional: in the 1840s the Marquess bought up all the surrounding buildings and had them demolished, and rerouted the main road away from his grounds. It now hosts events and contains a café.

Museum of Modern Art, Wales

Heol Penrallt, towards the station • Mon–Sat 10am–4pm • Free • ☎ 01654 703355 • ⓦ www.momawales.org.uk

The **Museum of Modern Art, Wales** (MOMA Cymru) is housed in Y Tabernacl, a beautifully serene old chapel that hosts an ongoing programme of temporary exhibitions, including some from its own growing collection. It is also the place to go for theatre, comedy, concerts, good coffee and the August Gŵyl Machynlleth festival (last week in August), which combines classical and some folk music with theatre and debate.

Centre for Alternative Technology

A487, 3 miles north of Machynlleth • Daily : Easter–Oct 10am–5.30pm; Nov–Easter 10am–5pm • £8.50 summer, £6.50 winter, £1 off for walkers, cyclists and bus users, 50 percent off for train arrivals • ☎ 01654 705952, ⓦ cat.org.uk

After the inception of the **Centre for Alternative Technology** (CAT or *Canolfan y Dechnoleg Amgen*) during the oil crisis of 1974, seven acres of a once-derelict slate quarry were turned into an almost entirely sustainable community. At one stage, eighty percent of the power was generated from wind, sun and water, but this is no back-to-the-land hippie commune. Right from the start, the idea was to embrace technology – much of the on-site equipment was developed and built here, reflecting the centre's achievements in this field. With the general rise of eco-consciousness in the twenty-first century the emphasis has shifted more towards promoting its application in urban situations. With this in mind, they've used low-carbon-footprint techniques – timber construction with lime and hemp cladding etc – in building the Wales Institute for Sustainable Education (WISE), a structure which won all manner of plaudits in 2010. Its 22ft rammed-earth wall is the highest in Britain.

CAT's water-balanced **cliff railway** (Easter–Oct only) whisks visitors 200ft up from the car park to the main site, sensitively landscaped using local slate and wood, and you can easily spend half a day sauntering around. There's plenty for kids to do, including a **children's theatre** (mainly mid-July to Aug), while the wholefood **restaurant** turns out delicious food and the excellent **shop** stocks a wide range of alternative literature, along with crafts and intriguing toys.

Residential volunteer programmes

This is very much a working community which exists more to educate by example than entertain, partly facilitated by the environmental information centre housed in a rammed-earth building. Short-term volunteers are welcome. For £10 per night to cover bed and board, you can get a week-long taster of life and work at the centre between March and September – enquire as far ahead as possible, as placements are limited and in high demand.

Corris

The spirit of CAT extends three miles higher up the valley to **CORRIS**, a small former slate-quarrying settlement in the middle of the Dyfi Forest. Half a mile further up the valley, the **Corris Craft Centre** occupies a former slate mine, and houses a few run-of-the-mill craft shops, a decent café, a good children's playground, and a couple of modest attractions.

Corris Railway and Museum

Corris village • Generally five services on Sundays April–Sept and four days a week in school holidays • £5 • ☎ 01654 761303, ⓦ corris.co.uk

The **Corris Railway** currently shuttles passengers along a half-mile stretch of the 27in-gauge line that linked the slate quarries of the Dulas Valley with the main line at

Machynlleth. There are plans to restore a further two miles, but for the moment you get a short ride and a look around the engine sheds and a small museum.

King Arthur's Labyrinth and The Bard's Quest

A487 • Late March to Oct daily 10am–5pm, call for winter hours • Labyrinth £7.90, Quest £4.30, jointly £9.95 • ☎ 01654 761584, Ⓦ kingarthurslabyrinth.com

King Arthur's Labyrinth is based deep within the flooded tunnels of a former slate mine. Led by a guide dressed as a monk, the boat trip into the heart of the mountain is huge fun, with son et lumière tableaux illustrating various Welsh legends. The **Bard's Quest** outdoor floral maze reveals "mystical stories echoing across the ages" by way of various iconic figures you meet along the way, and is a great way to help ensure these Welsh stories are retained by younger generations.

Corris Mine Explorers

A487 • Tours all year on demand, book ahead • 1hr Taster £10, 2hr Explorer £16, 4hr Expedition £32 • ☎ 01654 761244, Ⓦ corrismineexplorers.co.uk

With **Corris Mine Explorers** you head into different levels of the same old slate mine that houses King Arthur's Labyrinth, though the experience could hardly be more different. Sporting a climbing harness and miner's helmet, you'll ideally spend at least a couple of hours in the cool, dark tunnels that have been barely touched since the miners downed tools for the last time back in 1970. Ancient tallow candles are stuck to the walls, hand drills lie scatted along the passageways and winch flywheels still spin at the slightest touch. There's no production-line feel about these trips: all are tailored to the fitness of the group. You might just hear fascinating stories about the lives of the miners, while adventurous parties could find themselves clipped into safety wires as they sidle along the steeply shelving walls of a vast slate cavern. Wear something warm and prepare to have fun.

ARRIVAL AND DEPARTURE
MACHYNLLETH

By train Trains stop at the station, a 5min walk up Heol Penrallt from the town's central clock tower.

Destinations Aberdyfi (8 daily; 20min); Aberystwyth (9 daily; 30min); Barmouth (8 daily; 55min); Birmingham (7 daily; 2hr 15min); Harlech (8 daily; 1hr 20min); Porthmadog (8 daily; 1hr 50min); Shrewsbury (7 daily; 1hr 20min).

By bus Buses stop close to the town's central clock tower, and many also call at the train station.

Destinations Aberdyfi (8 daily; 20min); Aberystwyth (hourly; 45min); Corris (hourly; 15min); Dolgellau (mostly hourly; 30min); Tywyn (8 daily; 35min).

INFORMATION

Tourist information There is no TIC, but Dyfi Crafts, next to Parliament House on Heol Maengwyn, has leaflets and will help. In Corris, information is available at Corris Craft Centre (Easter–Oct daily 10am–5.30pm; ☎ 01654 761244).

Internet Free at the library, Heol Maengwyn (Mon & Fri 9.30am–1pm & 2–7pm, Tues & Wed 9.30am–1pm & 2–5pm, Sat 9.30am–1pm), and free wi-fi at *Quarry Café* and *Café Glas*.

ACCOMMODATION

HOTELS AND B&BS

Maenllwyd Newtown Rd ☎ 01654 702928, Ⓦ maenllwyd.co.uk. Comfortable eight-room B&B in a former manse. All is clean and well maintained, the family room has a DVD player and there's a large garden plus off-street parking. **£65**

Talbontdrain Near Uwchygarreg, 4 miles south ☎ 01654 702192, Ⓦ talbontdrain.co.uk. You'll need your own transport to get to this welcoming B&B in a former farmhouse, in stunning countryside. Simple but smart rooms, generous dinners (£18) and even packed lunches (£6). **£64**

Wynnstay Arms Heol Maengwyn ☎ 01654 702941, Ⓦ wynnstay-hotel.com. You'll want to shop around as there's considerable variation in the twenty-odd smartened-up rooms at this 1800 former coaching inn. Some have heavy beams, creaky floors and a four-poster, others are relatively modern. The hotel is effectively the heart of the town's social life and there are cosy guest lounges where you can curl up with a book. **£90**

★ **Ynyshir Hall** A487, 6 miles southwest beside the Ynys-hir Nature Reserve ☎ 01654 781209, Ⓦ ynyshir-hall.co.uk. Sublime country-house hotel in

"MAC" MOUNTAIN BIKING

Machynlleth has become something of a mountain biking mecca, with a number of excellent purpose-built tracks in the vicinity. The best place for information and **cycle rental** is The Holey Trail, 31 Heol Maengwyn (☎01654 700411, ⊛theholeytrail.co.uk), who have hardtails for £25 a day. They also operate guided rides (half-day £20, full day £40) and run the *Reditreks* bunkhouse. To go it alone, download ride maps from ⊛reditreks.com and head southwest to Derwenlas for Mach 1 (16km; moderate), then make for Corris and the Cli-machx (15km; difficult to severe).

expansive manicured grounds, this is gracious without being the slightest bit stuffy. The nine large, opulent rooms are furnished with antiques, service is wonderfully discreet and with in-room spa treatments and an outstanding restaurant. Breakfast is included. **£315**

HOSTELS AND CAMPING

★ **Corris Hostel** Old Rd, Corris, 6 miles north ☎01654 761686, ⊛corrishostel.co.uk. There's a strong ethical philosophy and a spiritual tenor to this low-key hostel. Accommodation is in single-sex dorms and family rooms (bedding provided); reasonably priced (and mostly vegetarian) meals and full self-catering facilities. Dorms **£15**

Llwyngwern Farm Pantperthog, 3 miles north near the Centre for Alternative Technology ☎01654 702492. Machynlleth's closest camping in a grassy field beside oaks and the burbling Afon Dulas. Fairly basic toilets and hot showers; one person **£8**, two people **£12**

Reditreks Bunkhouse Off Heol Powys ☎01654 702184, ⊛reditreks.com. Deluxe bunkhouse in the heart of town with dorm beds, camp sites in their grassy yard, a drying room, bike wash, barbecue area and bike storage shed. Bunks **£15**, weekends **£17.50**, camping **£5**

EATING AND DRINKING

Café Glas Inside MOMA Cymru, Heol Penrallt. The antithesis of the *Quarry Café*: delicate cakes and excellent coffee in peaceful, arty surrounds. Mon–Fri 10am–3pm.

Quarry Café Heol Maengwyn ☎01654 702624. This popular, veggie wholefood café run by the Centre for Alternative Technology is like stepping back into the 1980s (maybe 1970s), with its menu of cheesy vegetable bakes and the "Big Mach" burger (with lentil patty, soya mayonnaise and a wholesome salad). The walls come lined with noticeboards listing info about healing workshops and so on. Mon–Sat 9am–4.30pm.

Slaters Arms Corris, 6 miles north ⊛theslatersarms .com. Welcoming old village pub that is Corris's social centre with straightforward bar meals, pool table, dominoes and some fine, locally brewed ales from the Celt Experience. Daily 11am–11pm.

★ **Wynnstay Arms** Heol Maengwyn ☎01654 702941, ⊛wynnstay-hotel.com. For something casual head for the superb pizzeria out the back (closed Sun), or step up to the classic slate-floored restaurant with inventive Welsh dishes like duck with vegetable linguini and truffle gravy (mains £13–17). A fine place for a beer too. Daily noon–2.30pm & 6–11pm.

★ **Ynyshir Hall** A487, 6 miles southwest ☎01654 781209, ⊛ynyshir-hall.co.uk. This elegant restaurant has earned chef Shane Hughes considerable acclaim. The finest local produce is used in sublime Modern British dishes on the six-course à la carte menu (£72.50) and the ten-course tasting menu (£90). Or try Sunday lunch (three courses for £25), or the full afternoon tea (£19.50) served in the grounds or any of the delightful public rooms. Daily noon–2pm, 3–5pm & 7–10pm.

Aberdyfi

The proud maritime heritage of **ABERDYFI** (sometimes anglicized to Aberdovey) has largely been replaced by the life of a well-heeled resort. With its south-facing aspect across the Dyfi estuary backed by lush mountains, Aberdyfi has one of the highest proportions of holiday homes anywhere on this coast (and with some of the highest property prices, too). There's no watercraft rental on the beach, nor much else in the way of activities, but swimming is possible. Tidal currents make it potentially hazardous in town, so head about a mile and a half north to the safer waters of **Cemetery Beach**. It also makes a great base for exploring the delights of the Talyllyn and Dysynni valleys to the north.

In the mid-nineteenth century, the town, with its seamlessly joined eastern neighbour, **Penhelig**, built shallow-draught coastal traders for the inshore fleet, a past remembered in the small historic and **maritime display** in the tourist office.

ARRIVAL AND DEPARTURE   ABERDYFI

By train Aberdyfi is served by two equally inconvenient train stations: the request-only Penhelig, 0.5 mile east (the most convenient for the centre of town); and Aberdyfi, 0.5 mile west of the tourist office. Destinations Barmouth (8 daily; 35min); Machynlleth (8

daily; 20min); Porthmadog (8 daily; 1hr 30min); Tywyn (8 daily; 5min).
By bus The #28 & #X29 stop close to the TIC.
Destinations Machynlleth (8 daily; 20min); Tywyn (8 daily; 10min).

INFORMATION

Tourist information The TIC is in Wharf Gardens (Easter–Oct daily 9.30am–5.30pm; ☎01654 767321, ✉ tic.aberdyfi@eryri-npa.gov.uk).

ACCOMMODATION

Britannia Inn 13 Seaview Terrace ☎01654 767426, ⓦ britannia-aberdovey.co.uk. Three smart modern rooms, one with superb sea views (£105) above the town's best pub. Bathrooms are spacious and breakfast is included. **£95**
Cartref Guest House Penrhos, near Aberdyfi train station ☎01654 767273, ⓦ cartref-aberdovey.co.uk. Quality B&B in a large, recently renovated house just a few steps from Aberdyfi station. The five rooms are all done in muted tones with crisp white linen, and breakfasts are excellent. **£80**
★ **Llety Bodfor** On the seafront ☎01654 767475, ⓦ lletybodfor.co.uk. The fairly typical frontage of this Aberdyfi townhouse does little to suggest that within lies

the town's swankiest accommodation, done in contemporary style. The eight rooms over three floors include a couple of singles, plus doubles and very spacious suites which all have sea views. Its guest lounge is equipped with a piano, games and a stack of old vinyl. Breakfast Is not included but there is a small self-catering kitchen. You can even buy the designer furnishings in your room. **£75**
The Vanner Seaview Terrace ☎01654 767274, ⓦ thevanner.co.uk. This may be one of the cheapest places around but standards are still high. The two quiet rooms (both at the back of the house) share a guest lounge with great sea views. Full breakfast includes home-made bread and jam. **£65**

EATING AND DRINKING

Britannia Inn 13 Seaview Terrace ☎01654 767426, ⓦ britannia-aberdovey.co.uk. There is usually a lively atmosphere at this town-centre pub, especially when the sun comes out and everyone piles onto the deck for the sunset with a pint of real ale. Meals (mostly £10–13) are a significant cut above the usual pub standard and might include Aberdyfi crab. Good desserts too. Mon–Wed 11am–midnight, Thurs–Sat 11am–1am,

Sun noon–midnight.
Y Bwtri Blasus 7 Seaview Terrace ☎01654 767470. Great little deli and café that makes a fine place to hang out over a coffee and a slice of cake, or stock up on picnic essentials. The bread and quiches are freshly made locally and they'll whip up a sandwich with whatever you desire. Daily 9am–5pm.

The Talyllyn and Dysynni valleys and around

Around four miles north of Aberdyfi, two connected valleys spur northeast from the coast towards Cadair Idris. Although a quick tour around the sites won't take more than half a day, the area is monumentally beautiful, and the superb lowland or mountain walking (particularly on Cadair Idris) warrants more time.

The Talyllyn Valley starts at the faded resort town of Tywyn and is initially traced by dinky **Talyllyn Railway**, the first of Wales' restored narrow-gauge lines, and on to the placid waters of Tal-y-Llyn.

The outflow of the lake initially follows the valley southwest then, because of some ancient geological upheaval, cuts northwest to follow the **Dysynni Valley** with its castle ruins at **Castell-y-Bere** and pretty **church** with historic connections.

Llangelynin, a few miles north up the coast, is worth a brief stop for its time-warped church.

FROM TOP CWMYSTWYTH LEAD MINES (P.280); DEVIL'S BRIDGE FROM THE PUNCH BOWL (P.279) >

Talyllyn Railway

Station Rd, Tywyn, 4 miles north or Aberdyfi • April–Oct 2–7 trains daily, plus some winter weekends • £13 unlimited one-day travel, first class additional £2 each way • ☏ 01654 710472, Ⓦ talyllyn.co.uk

An excellent way to experience the lower Talyllyn Valley is aboard the cute 27in-gauge **Talyllyn Railway**, the inspiration for Thomas the Tank Engine. The railway tootles seven miles inland from Tywyn through the delightful wooded valley to the old slate quarries at Nant Gwernol. From 1866 to 1946, the rail line hauled slate to Tywyn Wharf station. Five years after the quarry's closure, rail enthusiasts took over the running of services, making this the world's first volunteer-run railway. The round trip (at a maximum 15mph) takes just over two hours, but you can get on and off as frequently as the schedule allows, taking in some fine broadleaf **forest walks**, best at Dolgoch Falls station. At the end of the line, more woodland walks take you around the site of the old slate quarries. In mid-August each year, the schedule is disrupted by the "Race the Train" event, when runners attempt to beat the train on its fourteen-mile trip to Abergynolwyn and back. Some do. Of the original Talyllyn rolling stock, two steam engines and all five of the oak and mahogany passenger carriages still run up to Nant Gwernol.

Narrow-Gauge Railway Museum

Mid-April to Sept daily 10.30am–4.30pm • Free

Leave half an hour to peruse the **Narrow-Gauge Railway Museum** at Tywyn Wharf station. Along with the history of the railway and a re-created study of Thomas the Tank Engine inventor, the Revd. W. Awdry, the museum holds some fine rolling stock from the Talyllyn and other narrow-gauge lines around the British Isles, including a Guinness shunter.

Church of St Cadfan

High St, Tywyn • Daily 9am–5pm, later in summer

At the east end of Tywyn's long High Street, the Norman nave of the **church of St Cadfan** houses one of the town's few real sights – the 5ft-high **St Cadfan's Stone**, which bears the earliest example of written Welsh, dating back to around 650 AD.

Talyllyn Valley

Northeast of Tywyn, the Talyllyn Valley deserves stops for a stroll at **Dogoch Falls**, a few waterside minutes at **Tal-y-Llyn** Lake, or a serious hike up the **Minffordd Path** to the summit of Cadair Idris.

Dolgoch Falls

5 miles northeast of Tywyn

The B4405 and the Talyllyn Railway both pass **Dolgoch Falls** where there are tearooms, a hotel and some rewarding walks. Three trails (maximum 1hr) lead off through oak woods to the lower, mid and upper cascades. Pied flycatchers and redstarts can often be seen flitting about.

Abergynolywn and Nant Gwernol

Two miles northeast of Dolgoch Falls the Dysynni Valley joins the Talyllyn at the twin valleys' only real settlement, **ABERGYNOLWYN**. Here, a few dozen quarry workers' houses crowd around a small visitor centre, a café, a pub and the Talyllyn Railway station. It is a short stroll up to the Talyllyn Railway's **Nant Gwernol** station, from where you can start the Quarryman's Trail (4 miles; 2–3hr; 800ft ascent), an excellent loop through quarry remains and a couple of waterfalls. It is easy to follow but also features in the *Dyfi Forest Walks* leaflet (free from TICs).

Tal-y-Llyn Lake

The brown trout-stocked **Tal-y-Llyn lake** is owned by the lakeshore *Tŷn y Cornel Hotel*. Stop by for a fishing permit and boat rental if you fancy trying your hand at landing migratory sea trout and salmon.

CADAIR IDRIS: THE MINFFORDD PATH

The OS Explorer 1:25,000 map OL23 "Cadair Idris & Llyn Tegid" is recommended.
The most dramatic ascent of Cadair Idris follows the **Minffordd Path** (6 miles; 5hr; 2900ft ascent), a justifiably popular route which makes a full circuit around the rim of **Cwm Cau**, probably the country's most impressive mountain cirque.

The path starts just west of the *Minffordd Hotel* at the junction of the A487 and the B4405. From the car park, follow the signs along an avenue of horse chestnuts and up through the woods, heading north. At a fork, take the left path, which wheels around the end of Craig Lwyd into Cwm Cau. Before you reach the lake, fork left and climb onto the rim of Cwm Cau, following it round to **Penygadair** (2930ft), the highest point on the massif. Here, there's a circular shelter and a tin-roofed hut originally built for dispensing refreshments to thirsty Victorians, and now affording none-too-comfortable protection from wind and rain.

The shortest descent follows the summit plateau northeast, then down to a grassy ridge before ascending gradually to **Mynydd Moel** (2831ft), from which you get a magnificent view down into a valley containing the waters of Llyn Arran. The descent starts beside the fence which you cross just before the summit – follow the fence south all the way to the fork below Cwm Cau.

A mile or so further on, the B4405 meets the A487 right by the start of the Minffordd Path (see box).

Dysynni Valley

The **Dysynni Valley** meets the A493 near the church at Llanegryn. From there you head upstream past the birds at Craig y Deryn then either turn southeast to join the Talyllyn Valley at Abergynolwyn or continue up the Dysynni to the ruins of Castell-y-Bere and the church of St Michael at Llanfihangel-y-Pennant.

Llanegryn church

Just off A493 · Generally open daytime

Half a mile northwest of the village of Llanegryn, the little hilltop **Llanegryn church** has an unexpectedly beautiful rood screen, probably carved in the fifteenth century, which is said to have been carried overnight from Dolgellau's Cymer Abbey after its dissolution.

Craig y Deryn

Three miles northeast of Llanegryn at **Craig y Deryn** (Birds' Rock), around thirty breeding pairs of cormorants colonize a stunning 760ft-high cliff some four miles from the coast. As the sea has gradually withdrawn from the valley, the birds have remained loyal to their home, making this Europe's only inland cormorant nesting site. It's reachable via a signposted path (2 miles; 1hr; 750ft ascent).

Castell-y-Bere

Llanfihangel-y-Pennant, 5 miles northeast of Llanegryn · Open access · Free · CADW

With large slabs of the main towers still standing, there's plenty of opportunity to poke around at **Castell-y-Bere**, a native Welsh fortress built by Llywelyn ap Iorwerth (Llywelyn the Great) in 1221 to protect the mountain passes. After being besieged twice in the thirteenth century, this – one of the most massive of the Welsh castles – was consigned to seven centuries of obscurity and decay. Castell-y-Bere seems to rise almost imperceptibly out of the rock upon which it was built – a great place just to sit or picnic, with good views to Cadair Idris and Craig y Deryn.

Church of St Michael and Tŷn-y-ddôl

Llanfihangel-y-Pennant, 5 miles northeast of Llanegryn · Generally open

On the dead-end lane a few hundred yards beyond Castle-y-Bere is Llanfihangel-y-Pennant and its stocky little **church of St Michael**, which has a couple of interesting exhibits in its vestry, including a fabulous 3-D map of the valley, some 14ft long and built to a scale of one foot to one mile from patchwork and cloth. There are also some exhibits centred on **Mary Jones** – famed for her 1800 Bible-buying walk to Bala (see p.323) – whose ruined cottage, **Tŷn-y-ddôl**, is just up the lane and marked with a monument.

Llangelynin church

A493, 7 miles north of Tywyn • Generally daily 9am–5pm

Half a mile short of the hamlet of **Llangelynin**, a track descends seawards off the main road to another ancient **church**: a mainly eleventh-century building on the foundations of an eighth-century structure, and bare but for a few basic pews and a bier which was carried by horses. Look out for the ancient board inscribed with the Ten Commandments in Welsh, and the skeletal **figure of death** wall painting with his scythe. Probably painted in the seventeenth century, it was only discovered during plaster removal in 2003. Just outside the porch is the grave of Abram Wood, patriarch of Y Teulu Wood, a clan of Romanies who settled in Wales at the beginning of the eighteenth century.

ARRIVAL AND DEPARTURE   TALYLLYN AND DYSYNNI VALLEYS

Your own vehicle gives maximum flexibility, but it is possible to explore the Talyllyn Valley using the **Talyllyn Railway** and **bus** #30 (4 daily) which runs from Tywyn to Abergynolwyn and continues to Minffordd (where you can catch #32 or #X32 to Dolgellau or Machynlleth). There is no public transport in the Dysynni Valley.

ACCOMMODATION, EATING AND DRINKING

Dolffanog Fawr B4405 at the north end of Tal-y-Llyn lake ☏ 01654 761247, ⓦ dolffanogfawr.co.uk. Relaxed deluxe B&B with just four rooms, most with great views from big windows. A great getaway with a big lounge, outdoor hot tub, inviting grounds, three-course evening meals (£25) and a very good wine selection. £90

Railway Inn B4405 in Abergynolwyn ☏ 01654 782279. Great little pub that serves the best range of real ales for miles, together with some great pub food. There's a cosy interior and outdoor seating with idyllic valley views. Book for dinner and Sunday lunch. Daily 11am–11pm.

CAMPING

Cae Du A493 at Llangelynin, just over 2 miles west of Llanegryn ☏ 01654 711234. Wonderfully dramatic clifftop site that's pretty simple but has hot showers, access down to a beach and allows campfires. The slope means you'll need to pick your site carefully, and it is pretty exposed when the wind gets up. Closed Nov–Feb. Tents £15

Dôl Einion B4405 at Minffordd, just before A487 junction ☏ 01654 761312. Excellent three-acre campsite at the foot of the Minffordd Path up Cadair Idris. There are toilets, showers and electric hookups. Per person £6

Llanllwyda ☏ 01654 782627. Well-equipped caravan and campsite in a grassy field near the start of the path to Craig y Deryn. Pitches £12

Northern Cadair Idris and the Mawddach Estuary

Gouging their way deep into the heart of the mid-Wales mountains, the Mawddach Estuary's broad tidal flats create dramatic backdrops from every angle. With the sun low in the sky and the tide ebbing, the constantly changing course of the river trickles silver through the golden sands. That colour isn't just an illusion: the sands actually do contain gold, albeit in tiny amounts, as the abandoned mines littering the hills around testify. Spasmodic gold fever still occasionally hits the region's main town, **Dolgellau**, but most people come here for excellent walking up Cadair Idris and along the estuary, the mountain biking at Coed-y-Brenin to the north, or to hit the beaches, particularly at **Barmouth**, the area's main resort.

Fairbourne

The blink-and-you'll-miss-it settlement of **FAIRBOURNE**, on the southern side of the Mawddach Estuary, was developed in the late nineteenth century as the country estate of the chairman of the McDougall's flour company. There's a decent beach and sublime views along the coast and across the estuary, but otherwise the only attraction is the steam-hauled railway.

Fairbourne Railway

April–Oct 4–8 trains most days • £8.20 return • ☏ 01341 250362, ⊕ fairbournerailway.com

Travelling between Fairbourne and Barmouth is easy on the mainline train which crosses the Mawddach Rail Bridge. An entertaining train-and-ferry alternative involves the tiny, 12in-gauge **Fairbourne Railway** which only runs a mile. Midway along, a halt on the line boasts the name Gorsafawddacha'idraigodanheddogleddollônpenrhynareurdraeth-ceredigion ("The station on the Mawddach with dragon's teeth on the north Penrhyn Drive on the golden Cardigan sands"). The "dragon's teeth" are, alas, a set of grim concrete defences left over from World War II.

The line ends at Penrhyn Point where there's a connecting passenger ferry (Easter–Sept; £2.50 return) to Barmouth.

EATING   FAIRBOURNE

Café Indiana 3 Beach Rd ☏ 01341 250891, ⊕ indianacuisine.co.uk. There may be a curry restaurant in every British town but few are like this simply decorated place, run by Noorie, the wife of Bollywood superstar Mayur Verma (Raj). North Indian cuisine is all cooked fresh, and the execution of dishes is way above the norm. Mains £7–10. Daily except Tues 6–10pm, plus Sun 1–3pm.

Dolgellau and around

The old county town of Meirionethshire, **DOLGELLAU** still maintains an air of unhurried importance, never more so than when all the area's farmers roll up for market day every Thursday morning. Its dark buildings gleam forebodingly in the frequent downpours, but in fine weather, the lofty crags of Cadair Idris perfectly frame the stone squares and streets.

As the most convenient access point to the southern reaches of the Snowdonia National Park, Dolgellau makes an enjoyable base. The local **walks** are superb, the **Mawddach Trail** offers some of the finest easy cycling around, and nearby Coed-y-Brenin has become a major centre for **mountain bikers**. The town's lodging and restaurants are increasingly geared to the needs of weekend bikers, and the pubs often put on live music on Saturday nights.

Brief history

Dolgellau is a much older town than appearances suggest, lying at the junction of three Roman roads which converged on a now vanished military outpost. It was here that Owain Glyndŵr assembled the last Welsh parliament in 1404, and later signed an alliance with Charles VI of France for providing troops to fight against Henry IV of England. Seventeenth-century Quakers sought freedom from persecution here, and in the 1860s, Dolgellau became the focus of numerous **gold rushes**, drawing waves of prospectors to pan the estuary or blast levels into Clogau shale or mudstone sediment under the Coed-y-Brenin Forest. The quartz veins yielded some gold, but in quantities too small to make much money.

Quaker Exhibition

Eldon Square, above the TIC • Easter–Oct daily 9.30am–5.30pm; Nov–Easter Mon & Thurs–Sun 9.30am–4.30pm • Free

The **Quaker Exhibition** has explanatory panels detailing the local Quakers' (the Society of Friends) well-recorded sufferings before the 1689 Act of Toleration put a stop – legally, at least – to persecution for their pacifist Nonconformist views, non-attendance at church and non-payment of its tithes. At a trial in Bala in 1679, this last sin earned a group of Friends a prison term, a further encouragement to those thinking of following the two thousand Welsh Quakers who had already fled to the United States and started the Pennsylvania towns of Bangor, Bryn Mawr and others.

Tŷ Siamas

Eldon Square • Tues–Fri 10am–4pm, Sat 10am–1pm • £3.95 • ☎ 01341 421800, ⓦ tysiamas.com

The National Centre for Welsh Folk Music is known as Tŷ Siamas, "The house of Siamas", after the local creator of the Welsh triple harp. Modern examples of his invention can be seen alongside traditional instruments such as the *pibgorn*, the *crwth* and the *pibacwd* (see Music in Wales, p.460). Touch screens allow you to try your hand at playing string, woodwind and percussion instruments, all put into perspective by an instructive film. Staff love anyone showing real interest and can point you to all manner of local musical events, some taking place at the centre.

Cymer Abbey

Signposted off A470, 2 miles north of Dolgellau • Open access • Free • CADW

Gold frenzy first hit Dolgellau when the Romans found flecks glinting in the Mawddach silt. Later, the thirteenth-century Cistercian monks based at **Cymer Abbey** were given "the right in digging or carrying away metals and treasures free from all secular exaction". The fine location at the head of the Mawddach Estuary is typical of this austere order, but unfortunately the surrounding caravan site mars the effect of the remaining Gothic slabs. A path beside the abbey makes an alternative approach to the Precipice Walk (see box opposite).

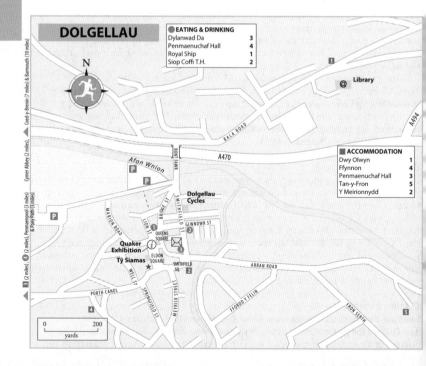

WALKS AND RIDES AROUND DOLGELLAU

Cadair Idris: Pony Path (9 miles; 4–5hr; 2800ft ascent). If the weather is fine, don't miss this classic and enjoyable ascent of Cadair Idris which starts from the car park at Tŷ Nant, 3 miles southwest of Dolgellau along Cadair Road (no buses). Early views to the craggy flanks of the massif are tremendous, but they disappear as you climb steeply to the col, where you turn left on a rocky path to the summit shelter on **Penygadair** (2930ft). Take the 1:25,000 Explorer OL23 map (*"Cadair Idris & Llyn Tegid"*).

Mawddach Trail (10 miles from Dolgellau to Barmouth; flat). Follow this beautiful combined walking and cycle route beside the Mawddach Estuary's broad sands along a disused rail line. Walkers seeking the most interesting section should start from Penmaenpool (catch bus #28), 2 miles west. Highlights include the wooden toll bridge and the George III pub at Penmaenpool, an RSPB wetland walk at Arthog, and the Barmouth bridge.

Precipice Walk (3–4 miles; 2hr; negligible ascent). Though the path is narrow in places and there are some steep banks, there is little precipitous on this easy-going loop with great views to the 1000ft ramparts of Cadair Idris and along the Mawddach Estuary – best in late afternoon or early morning sun. Starts 3 miles north of Dolgellau off the road to Llanfachreth.

Torrent Walk (2 miles; 1hr; 100ft ascent). Attractive lowland stroll following the cascading, bedrock-carved Clywedog River through some gnarled old woodland that drips with antiquity. Starts on the B4416, just off the A470, 3 miles east (bus #32/X32).

Coed-y-Brenin

A470, 7 miles north of Dolgellau. **Forest** open access • Free **Visitor Centre** April–Oct daily 9.30am–5pm; Nov–March Mon–Fri 9.30am–4.30pm, Sat & Sun 9.30am–5pm • Parking £4 all day • ☎ 01341 440747, ⓦ www.forestry.gov.uk/coedybrenin

4

For years, mountain bikers from around Britain and beyond have been flocking to **Coed-y-Brenin** for some of Wales' finest **mountain biking**. With the addition of dedicated forest running and walking trails, a high ropes adventure, orienteering and geocaching courses and a kids' play area, it has developed into one of the most popular spots in southern Snowdonia.

Mountain biking takes place in the evergreens of "The King's Forest", with miles of old trackways, roads and purpose-built trails crisscrossing the hillsides, offering lung-busting uphill rides, and adrenalin-pumping descents – all graded like ski runs: black for experts, red and blue for intermediates and green for family riders. Highlights include the Dragon's Back (20 miles; difficult) and the Beast of Brenin (25 miles; severe), but there's plenty for beginners, families and even trails suitable for adaptive bikes for the disabled.

Start at the **visitor centre** where you can **rent bikes** from Beics Brenin (hardtails £25 per day, full suspension £45; ☎ 01341 440728, ⓦ beicsbrenin.co.uk), buy a pack of trail maps covering Coed-y-Brenin and the Betws-y-Coed's Gwydir Forest (£2.50; also free map downloads from the website), take a shower (£1) and recover in the good café.

Pick up a map to get a taste of **geocaching**, essentially using a GPS (rent for £5 a day) to find your way to one of the four little boxes of treasure hidden in the woods.

Go Ape

At Coed-y-Brenin • March–Nov daily 10am–5pm • Adults £30, 10–18s £20 • ☎ 0845 094 9751, ⓦ goape.co.uk

With complex rope ladders, high wires and swings in the tree tops plus long zipwires back to the ground, **Go Ape** is one of the best of Wales' tree-top ropes courses. After harness-fitting and instruction, you'll be given up to three hours to explore the five separate courses. Adults must supervise under eighteens, and under tens are not allowed.

ARRIVAL AND DEPARTURE	DOLGELLAU

By bus Dolgellau doesn't have a train station, but is well served by buses which all pull into Eldon Square. Most services head north past Coed-y-Brenin. To stick to the coast, pick up the train at Barmouth.

Destinations Bala (hourly; 35min); Barmouth (hourly; 25min); Llangollen (8 daily; 1hr 45min); Machynlleth (mostly hourly; 30min); Porthmadog (6 daily; 50min); Tywyn (6 daily; 55min).

THE BIG SESSION

Dolgellau's Sesiwn Fawr (⊛ sesiwnfawr.co) or "Big Session" was once huge, but has now returned to its smaller Celtic folk roots. It takes place in the meadows west of the river bridge in mid-July and features much of the best of Welsh and wider Celtic folk.

INFORMATION

Tourist information The TIC is on Eldon Square (Easter–Oct daily 9.30am–5.30pm; Nov–Easter Mon & Thurs–Sun 9.30am–4.30pm; ☎ 01341 422888, ⊜ tic.dolgellau @eyri-npa.gov.uk), and it also contains displays concentrating on the southern reaches of Snowdonia. Another handy resource is ⊛ discoverdolgellau.co.uk.

Bike rental Dolgellau Cycles on Smithfield St (☎ 01341

423332, ⊛ dolgellaucycles.co.uk) rent bikes suitable for the Mawddach Trail (£13 a half day, £20 full day).

Internet Free at the library, Ffordd y Bala, on the northeastern edge of town (Mon & Fri 9.30am–7pm, Tues & Thurs 9.30am–5pm, Wed 9.30am–1pm, Sat 9.30am–noon).

ACCOMMODATION

While there's commendable **accommodation** in Dolgellau itself (some catering to the legions of mountain bikers frequenting Coed-y-Brenin), there are more appealing options scattered around the district, some so close to Cadair Idris that you can start your hike at the back door.

HOTELS AND GUESTHOUSES

Coed Cae A496 at Taicynhaeaf, 4 miles west ☎ 01341 430628, ⊛ coedcae.co.uk. Sustainability and appreciation of the outdoors are the watchwords at this three-room B&B handily sited for the Mawddach Trail (bikes rented from £18 a day) and the *George III* pub, just across the toll bridge. There's abundant tea and walking advice, locally sourced meals on request (BYO), and they'll even do you a packed lunch. **£80**

Dwy Olwyn Coed y Fronallt, Llanfachreth Rd ☎ 01341 422822, ⊛ dwyolwyn.co.uk. Homely guesthouse in landscaped gardens with Cadair Idris views. There are just three rooms and a guest lounge with board games; a 10min walk from the centre. **£50**

Ffynnon Love Lane ☎ 01341 421 774, ⊛ ffynnon townhouse.com. The pinnacle of stylish accommodation in the area, this large house has just five rooms, all superbly decorated. All rooms have separate sitting areas, and great views. Pay a little more (say £175 or £200) and everything is taken to the next level. Rates include afternoon tea on arrival, and they will even send you out with a deluxe picnic lunch. **£135**

George III Hotel A493, Penmaenpool, 2 miles west of Dolgellau ☎ 01341 422525, ⊛ georgethethird.co.uk. Superb seventeenth-century hotel with eleven rooms right by the Mawddach Estuary (bus #28). Wood-beamed rooms (some in former train station buildings) have been smartly updated, and the restaurant is outstanding. **£100**

Penmaenuchaf Hall Penmaenpool, 2 miles west of Dolgellau ☎ 01341 422129, ⊛ penhall.co.uk. Grand oak-panelled house, formerly home to a Lancashire cotton magnate and now a classy country hotel, with beautiful decor, a full-size billiard table and free angling for trout and salmon. **£160**

Tan-y-Fron Arran Rd ☎ 01341 422638, ⊛ tanyfron .co.uk. Comfortable B&B with 3 rooms in the house and a couple of separate cottages. All come with a small fridge and a full cooked breakfast, although the family cottage gets breakfast requisites delivered. **£70**

Tyddyn Mawr Farmhouse Islawrdref, 3 miles southwest of Dolgellau ☎ 01341 422331, ⊛ wales -guesthouse.co.uk. Eighteenth-century farmhouse on the slopes of Cadair Idris at the foot of the Pony Path. Very welcoming and great value, with open fireplaces and just two large rooms. Complimentary tea and cakes on arrival. Check ahead for winter closures. **£74**

★ **Y Meirionnydd** Smithfield Square ☎ 01341 422554, ⊛ themeirionnydd.com. This solid stone Georgian townhouse has been re-fashioned as a chic hotel with light tones and blond woods offset by feature cushions and curtains. Along with four well-appointed doubles there's a budget twin, and a wonderfully spacious loft suite. Along with a smart little bar, there's a popular restaurant in the very low-beamed half-basement where a full breakfast is served. **£65**

HOSTELS AND CAMPING

★ **Graig Wen** A493, 5 miles west near Arthog ☎ 01341 250482, ⊛ graigwen.co.uk. Access is steep but the Mawddach Estuary views make it all worthwhile at this wonderfully tranquil caravan and campsite, whose attitude towards sustainability has won them Green awards. In August the lower camping fields are open for a wilder experience: car-free camping, campfires allowed, composting toilets; 3-night minimum. There's easy access to the Mawddach Trail and paths up Cadair Idris. Check the website for details of their two yurts, hire tent, and the *Slate Shed B&B*. Booking essential. Closed Jan & Feb. Discounts for

those arriving without a vehicle. Per person £7
Tan-y-Fron Arran Rd ☎01341 422638, ⊛tanyfron
.co.uk. Well-appointed camping and caravan site handily
sited a 5min walk from town. Countryside views and
spotless facilities, including hot showers. Tents £17
YHA Kings Penmaenpool, 4.5 miles west of Dolgellau
☎0845 371 9327, ✉kings@yha.org.uk. Large country

house a mile up a delightful wooded valley off the #28
Tywyn bus route (last bus around 6pm), with six-bed rooms
and a self-catering kitchen but no TV or even mobile
reception. An ideal base for the Pony Path up Cadair Idris.
Take food with you and check for winter closures. Reception
8–10am & 5–10.30pm. Dorms £15

EATING, DRINKING AND ENTERTAINMENT

Dolgellau and the surrounding area are blessed with some good **eating** options. Evening life focuses on the numerous
pubs, together with odd concerts and performances – see local noticeboards.

★ **Dylanwad Da** 2 Smithfield St ☎01341 422870,
⊛dylanwad.co.uk. Consistently the best restaurant in
town, with creative, affordable dishes – like Thai seafood
soup and cumin-spiced salmon or Moroccan lamb stew
(mains £14–19) – and great desserts served in simple
surroundings. Also open daytimes for good coffee and
cakes. Thurs–Sat 10am–3pm & 7–9pm; closed Feb.
George III A493, Penmaenpool, 2 miles west of
Dolgellau ☎01341 422525, ⊛georgethethird.co.uk.
Superb spot for a cream tea overlooking the Mawddach
Estuary or a sunset drink in the dark-wood bar. Quality pub
meals (mostly £9–12) might include lamb shank, fish and
chips or bacon-wrapped chicken. Daily 11am–10.30pm.
★ **Mawddach** A496, 2 miles northwest ☎01341
424020, ⊛mawddach.com. Dark and slate-floored
downstairs, airy with bare boards and exposed beams
upstairs, this contemporary restaurant occupies a converted
barn with views of Cadair Idris. Quality shines through, with

a short menu of simply prepared and beautifully cooked
dishes (mains mostly £10–15) such as hake with purple
broccoli and caper sauce or butternut squash risotto. Wed–
Sat 12.30–3pm & 6.30–10.30pm; Sun noon–4pm.
Penmaenuchaf Hall Penmaenpool, 2 miles west of
Dolgellau ☎01341 422129, ⊛penhall.co.uk. Superior
Modern British cuisine in a gazebo-style setting. A three-
course set menu costs £40, and there are some superb
vegetarian options. Daily 6.30–10pm.
Royal Ship Queen's Square ☎01341 422209. Large and
cheerful old coaching inn, with good beer, outside seating
and a range of fairly standard bar meals at moderate prices.
Daily 11am–10.30pm.
★ **Siop Coffi T.H.** Glyndŵr St. Great café in a former
ironmonger's, the glassed-in office now a snug where folk
are usually tapping away on laptops (free wi-fi). Baguettes
and panini are all freshly made and there are heaps of
sumptuous cakes. Mon–Sat 9am–5pm, Sun 10am–4pm.

Barmouth and around

Cluttered with shops selling takeaway food, buckets and spades, and pleasure-beach
sideshow attractions, lively **BARMOUTH** (Abermaw) tucks in beneath steep cliffs, lapped
by both estuary and sea. It was popularized by nineteenth-century English Midlands
sea-bathers who mostly arrived over the 2253ft-long **Barmouth Bridge**, which traverses
113 spindly wooden spans across the Mawddach Estuary south of town.

Barmouth was once a shipbuilding centre, and a maritime air lingers around the quay
at the south end of town, departure point for a **passenger ferry** to Fairbourne.

The Last Haul
Corner of The Quay and Church St

The most famous of many shipwrecks along this coast was that of the 700-ton Genoese
galleon known locally as the *Bronze Bell*. It sank in 1709 complete with its cargo of
finest Carrara marble. Forty or so two-ton blocks of marble still lie on the seabed but

---

THREE PEAKS YACHT RACE

In late June each year, the highly competitive **Three Peaks Yacht Race**
(⊛threepeaksyachtrace.co.uk) starts in Barmouth, a two- to three-day amateur monohull
yachting event entailing navigation to Caernarfon, the English Lake District and Fort William in
Scotland, and a run up the highest peak in each country. The current record, set in 2002, is two
days, fourteen hours and four minutes.

4

one piece was raised in the 1980s, and fashioned by local sculptor Frank Cocksey into "**The Last Haul**". Three centuries under the sea have left the surface fabulously pockmarked, though the quality of marble comes through in the carved section which depicts three fishing generations working together to haul in a catch.

Tŷ Gwyn Museum

The Quay • June–Sept daily 1–4.30pm • Free

A medieval tower house where Henry VII's uncle, Jasper Tudor, is said to have plotted Richard III's downfall now houses **Tŷ Gwyn Museum**. The house was thought to have been destroyed until renovations in the 1980s revealed its identity. It now contains explanatory panels on local shipwrecks plus a few artefacts including the 1677 bronze bell that gave the nameless galleon its local moniker.

Tŷ Crwn Roundhouse

The Quay • Daily 10.30am–5pm • Free

Tŷ Crwn Roundhouse acted as a lockup for drunken sailors in the nineteenth century. The circular design was reputedly conceived to prevent the Devil lurking in any corners and further tempting the incarcerated mariners. The male and female cells are now set up as they would have been when in use.

ARRIVAL AND DEPARTURE   BARMOUTH

By train The train station is on Station Rd in the centre of Barmouth.
Destinations Aberdyfi (8 daily; 35min); Harlech (8 daily; 25min); Machynlleth (8 daily; 55min); Porthmadog (8 daily; 50min).

By bus Buses stop on Jubilee Road, near the train station.
Destinations Blaenau Ffestiniog (3 daily; 1hr 10min); Dolgellau (hourly; 25min); Harlech (hourly; 30min).
By ferry There is a passenger ferry to Fairbourne (Easter–Oct; as frequently as custom demands; £2.50 return).

INFORMATION

Tourist information The TIC is on Station Rd (Easter–Oct daily 10am–5pm; Nov–Easter 10am–3.30pm; ☎ 01341 280787, ⟳ barmouth-wales.co.uk) in the train station.
Internet access Free at the library on Talbot Square.

Bike rental Birmingham Garage on Church St (☎ 01341 280644) rent basic machines that are ideal for the Mawddach Trail (£13 a day).

ACCOMMODATION

HOTELS AND GUESTHOUSES

Bae Abermaw Hotel Panorama Hill ☎ 01341 280550, ⟳ baeabermaw.com. Very un-Barmouth, this former Victorian hotel is now contemporary, with minimalist white-on-white rooms, an elegant bare-boards lounge and a pricey but sublime restaurant, almost all with unfurling views over Cardigan Bay. Could do with some refreshing, but still good. **£98**

WALKS FROM BARMOUTH

Barmouth–Fairbourne loop (5 miles; 2–3hr; 300ft ascent). A rewarding low-level coastal circuit, an easily managed walk around Barmouth and Fairbourne gives superb mountain, estuarine and coastal views all the way. You cross the rail bridge (90p return toll; £1.50 with a bike) to Morfa Mawddach station, then follow the lane to the main road, cross it onto a footpath that rises around the back of a small wooded hill to Pant Einion Hall, then follow another lane back to the main road near Fairbourne. Turn north then left down the main street of Fairbourne to the sea; from here you can return to Barmouth either by taking the Fairbourne Railway, or by walking north along the beach and catching the ferry.

Panorama Walk and Dinas Oleu (3 miles; 2hr; 400ft ascent). Bracing walk taking in a fine viewpoint over town and estuary plus Dinas Oleu (Fortress of Light), the cliffs immediately above Barmouth, which became the National Trust's first property in 1895. Essentially the route follows Gloddfa Road off High Street onto the exposed clifftops, where there is a map of the reserve. Go through the metal gate and follow the path past Frenchman's Grave to a road where you turn left to the Panorama Viewpoint. Return by the same route.

★ **Llwyndû Farmhouse Hotel** Llanaber, 2 miles north of Barmouth ☎01341 280144, ⊛llwyndu-farmhouse.co.uk. A gem of a B&B with en-suite rooms either in the seventeenth-century farmhouse building (complete with mullioned windows and inglenook fireplace), in the adjacent converted barn or in the granary. Also wonderful table d'hôte meals (see below). **£90**

Sandpiper 7 Marine Parade ☎01341 280318, ⊛sandpiperguesthouse.co.uk. Well-presented budget B&B just a few steps from the train station, with sea views from some rooms, secure bike storage, good off-season deals and a shared-bath single. **£52**

CAMPING

Hendre Mynach Llanaber Rd, 1 mile north of town ☎01341 280262, ⊛hendremynach.co.uk. Barmouth's closest campsite, well set up, just off the beach and barely afflicted with the fixed caravans that mar most sites in these parts. Closed Jan & Feb. Tents from **£20**

EATING, DRINKING AND ENTERTAINMENT

Bae Abermaw Panorama Hill ☎01341 280550, ⊛baeabermaw.com. Comfy chairs, wooden floors, white walls and a wintertime fire all enhance the best of Modern British cuisine served here – from grilled black bream with cockles and caper butter to seared venison and ginger-and-date pudding for dessert. Mains £15–20. Daily 6.30–10pm.

Last Inn Church St ☎01341 280530, ⊛lastinn-barmouth.co.uk. A cosy bar in a former cobbler's shop where you can also get good pub meals such as Thai red chicken curry and sirloin steak. The outdoor tables catch the afternoon sun. Daily 11am–11pm.

★ **Llwyndû Farmhouse Hotel** Llanaber, 2 miles north of Barmouth ☎01341 280144, ⊛llwyndu-farmhouse.co.uk. Delicious evening meals served in the romantic dining room with candles flickering on the tables. Meals (two courses for £25, three for £28) offer three or four choices per course (one vegetarian) and local ingredients are the order of the day. Mon–Sat 7–10pm.

Ardudwy

4

North of Barmouth, the coast opens out to a narrow coastal plain running a dozen miles towards Snowdonia and flanked by the heather-covered slopes of the Rhinog mountains, five miles inland. This is **Ardudwy**, a fertile land used as a fattening ground for black Welsh cattle on their way to the English markets, and now tamed by caravan sites and golf courses.

No modern road crosses the Rhinogs to the east, but until the early nineteenth-century building of coach roads, the existence of two mountain passes made this a strategic and populous area, as the numerous minor Neolithic burial chambers testify. Further up the coast, the town of **Harlech** was built as one link in Edward I's chain of magnificent fortresses. It is the only real town in the region, followed in importance by **Llanbedr**, from where a road runs west to the dune-backed camping resort on **Shell Island**, and another rises east, splitting into two delightfully remote valleys.

Llanbedr and around

LLANBEDR, seven miles north of Barmouth, isn't much in itself, but is central to a diverse bunch of scattered sites from Neolithic burial chambers and wild dunes to a disused slate quarry and a pair of gorgeous valleys from where hikes lead up into the wild **Rhinog** range.

Morfa Dyffryn National Nature Reserve

Off A496, 2 miles southwest of Llanbedr • Open access • Free

The constantly changing coastal dunes of **Morfa Dyffryn National Nature Reserve** stretch from Llandwyne four miles north to the edge of Shell Island. Notable for its flora, particularly the marsh helleborine, this is a fragile zone and large areas are fenced off, but there's beach access across a boardwalk. Follow the path from Dyffryn Ardudwy station through the caravan parks and the dunes to the splendid, vast **beach**. A section of shore a few hundred yards to the north serves as Wales' only official **naturist beach** (well, when it's warm enough).

Dyffryn Ardudwy Burial Chambers

Signposted behind the school in Dyffryn Ardudwy off A496, 3 miles south • Open access • Free • CADW

Dyffryn Ardudwy Burial Chambers comprise two supported capstones lying among a bed of small boulders, the base stones of a mound thought to have been 100ft long; the site dates from around 3500 BC. Finds from a dig here in the 1960s – including pottery, finely polished stone plaques and bones – are on display at the National Museum in Cardiff.

Shell Island

2 miles west of Llanbedr • Road toll £5 per vehicle; no access at high tide • ⓦ shellisland.co.uk

A lane from Llanbedr snakes its way alongside the babbling Afon Artro, past the train station and redundant airfield to **Shell Island**, or Mochras. A peninsula at anything other than high tide, the island is reached by a tidal causeway and offers the chance to swim, sail, look for wild flowers or scour the beach for some of the two hundred varieties of shell found here. At low tide you can see a line of rocks in the sea leading out towards Ireland, known as Sarn Badrig (St Patrick's Causeway) and traditionally thought to be the road to a flooded land known as the Cantre'r Gwaelod ("The Low Hundreds").

Llyn Cwm Bychan

A narrow road dives six miles northeast of Llanbedr through gorgeous woods as it follows the Afon Artro to the waters of **Llyn Cwm Bychan**, deep in the heather and angular rocks of the Rhinog range. Pay the farmer to park on the property here to take the path up to the **Roman Steps** – most likely a medieval packhorse route, made of flat slabs cutting through the range – onto Rhinog Fawr (see box). Branching off the Cwm Bychan road a mile out of Llanbedr, another delightful road leads to **Cwm Nantcol**, the next valley south. Two hundred yards up the lane, **Capel Salem** is a Baptist chapel immortalized by Sidney Curnow Vosper's 1908 painting of the same name – a copy hangs inside.

Chwarel Hên Slate Caverns

A496 at Llanfair, 1 mile north of Llanbedr • Easter to Sept daily 10am–5pm • Oct daily 11am–4pm • Quarry £5.10; farm £5.30 • ☎ 01766 780247, ⓦ llanfairslatecaverns.co.uk

This small slate quarry is visited on a self-guided underground tour into dark caverns hewn from the rock. It will keep the kids entertained for half an hour, but if they need more, visit the adjacent **Children's Farm Park**.

Llandanwg

Almost two miles north of Llanbedr, a small road branches down to the coastal hamlet of **Llandanwg**, a great place to get out onto the dunes, with a beautiful little church that has to be periodically dug out of the sand by youth scheme workers so that the occasional service can be held.

ARRIVAL AND DEPARTURE   **LLANBEDR**

Bus #38 services the coast from Barmouth to Harlech, then inland to Blaenau Ffestiniog. The Cambrian coast train line covers the same route to Harlech, from where it makes for Porthmadog on the Llŷn.

ACCOMMODATION, EATING AND DRINKING

Nantcol Waterfalls 2 miles east of Llanbedr ☎ 01341 241209, ⓦ nantcolwaterfalls.co.uk. Fairly simple but blissfully secluded tent and caravan site at the base of the Rhinogs and beside a burbling river. There's a good new shower block, while a small shop and ice-cream stand

operate in summer, and campfires are allowed (though you'll need to bring your own firewood or purchase). Per person **£8**

Shell Island campsite ☎ 01341 241453, ⓦ shellisland.co.uk. Massive 300-acre tent and

WALKS ON THE RHINOGS

The northern **Rhinogs** offer some surprisingly tough walking. At under 2500ft, they're hardly giants, but the typically large, rough, gritstone rocks hidden in thick heather make anything but the most well-worn paths hard-going. The rewards for your efforts are long views across Cardigan Bay, a good chance of stumbling across a herd of feral goats and a strong sense of achievement. The two walks described here start at the head of different valleys (see p.300), but share a common summit, that of Rhinog Fawr. Take the OS 1:25,000 Explorer #OL18 "Harlech, Porthmadog & Bala" map.

RHINOG FAWR AND THE ROMAN STEPS FROM CWM BYCHAN

For this walk (5 miles return; 3–4hr; 1900ft ascent), start at the car park in **Cwm Bychan** and follow signs up through a small wood onto the open moor. The **Roman Steps** (most likely a medieval packhorse route) guide you up to a pass, Bwlch Tyddiad, giving views east to Bala and beyond. The terrain then becomes steeper and the path less well-defined. You may have to use your hands to finally reach Rhinog Fawr (2362ft). Return by the same route.

RHINOG FAWR AND RHINOG FACH FROM CWM NANTCOL

This demanding walk (6–7 miles return; 5–6hr; 2900ft ascent) begins by the Maes-y-Garnedd farmhouse at the head of Cwm Nantcol for a fairly rugged circuit over Rhinog Fawr and Rhinog Fach. Follow the track north from the car park to the house, into the fields and over the stile, then turn northeast and walk gradually towards the base of the rocky southwest ridge, following the white marker posts. Eventually, the path turns north to a cairn on the skyline, then east following more cairns up the ridge to the summit trig point of **Rhinog Fawr**.

After an arduous descent into Bwlch Drws Ardudwy (The Pass of the Door of Ardudwy), cross the stone wall and start on a fairly clear line up Rhinog Fach (2236ft). Explore the summit ridge to get the best views of the coast then descend to Cwm Nantcol by first walking to a rocky ledge overlooking Llyn Hywel to the south. From here you should be able to see a scrappy path running very steeply down to the lake on the right-hand edge of the ledge. You'll have to use your hands at times, and there are sections of scree, but you're soon on a clear path that skirts north around the base of Rhinog Fach towards Bwlch Drws Ardudwy and back to Cwm Nantcol.

4

motorhome campsite (no caravans) which spreads along the beach from the harbour down to the vast dunes of Morfa Dyffryn. It is Europe's biggest, and although it can get crowded during the school summer holidays and on long weekends, campers must pitch tents a minimum of 20yd from each other (unless agreed with your neighbours), guaranteeing relative solitude among quite spectacular scenery, with some of the best sunsets in north Wales. No walk-ins; you must have a vehicle. Closed Nov–Feb. Per person £6

Shell Island restaurant and tavern ☎01341 241453, ⓦshellisland.co.uk. People come from miles around for the Sunday lunches here (£15). There are good meals at other times too and the adjacent tavern sells the excellent Purple Moose ales. March–Oct daily noon–10pm.

Victoria Inn Llanbedr ☎01341 241213, ⓦvictoriainnllanbedr.co.uk. Stone-built village pub that's a winner for its beer garden and à la carte meals made from produce from its own market garden. Also five recently redecorated B&B rooms. Bar open Mon–Thurs & Sun 11am–11pm, Fri & Sat 11am–midnight. £80

Harlech

HARLECH, three miles north of Llanbedr, is one of the highlights of the Cambrian coast and makes a dramatic first impression. Its commanding castle clings to a rocky outcrop, while the charming township cloaking the hill behind takes in one of Wales' finest views: over the Morfa Harlech dunes across Cardigan Bay to the Llŷn, and north to the jagged peaks of Snowdonia. There's a handful of inviting places to eat (though relatively few places to stay) in the town's steep and narrow streets, plus wonderful walking country and superb beaches on the doorstep.

HARLECH

4

■ ACCOMMODATION		● EATING	
Castle Cottage	2	Castle Cottage	1
Pen-y-Garth	3	Castle Restaurant & Armoury Bar	2
Tremeifion	1	Cemlyn	3

Harlech Castle

March–June, Sept & Oct daily 9.30am–5pm; July & Aug daily 9.30am–6pm; Nov–Feb Mon–Sat 10am–4pm, Sun 11am–4pm • £3.80 • ☎ 01766 780552 • CADW

Harlech's showpiece is its substantially intact **castle**, rising mightily on its 200ft bluff. Intended as one of Edward I's Iron Ring of monumental fortresses (see box, p.410), construction of Harlech castle began in 1283, just six months after the death of Llywelyn the Last. It was built of a hard Cambrian rock, known as Harlech grit, hewn from the moat. One side of the fortress was originally protected by the sea – the waters have now receded, though, leaving the castle dominating a stretch of duned coastline.

The castle has seen a lot of action in its time: it withheld a siege in 1295, was taken by Owain Glyndŵr in 1404, and the youthful, future Henry VII – the first Welsh king of England and Wales – withstood a seven-year siege at the hands of the Yorkists from 1461 to 1468, until the castle was again taken. It subsequently fell into ruin, but was put back into service for the king during the Civil War, and in March 1647 it became the last Royalist castle to fall.

The first defensive line comprised the three successive pairs of gates and portcullises built between the two massive half-round towers of the **gatehouse**, where an exhibition now outlines the castle's history. Much of the outermost ring has been destroyed, leaving only the 12ft-thick curtain walls rising up 40ft to the exposed battlements, and only the towering gatehouse prevents you walking the full circuit.

The beach

Harlech's **sand dunes** and **beach** are among the finest on this coast and are reached via Beach Road, which shoots off the main road through town, directly below the castle. On the way to the sands, you'll swing by the exclusive **Royal St David's golf course**, venue of many championships.

ARRIVAL AND DEPARTURE
HARLECH

Trains, which stop by the A496 below the castle, serve: Barmouth (8 daily; 25min); Machynlleth (8 daily; 1hr 20min); Porthmadog (8 daily; 20min).

Buses generally call both at the train station and at the southern end of High St. They serve: Barmouth (hourly; 30min); Blaenau Ffestiniog (3 daily; 35min).

INFORMATION

Tourist information The TIC (Easter–Oct daily 9.30am–5.30pm; ☎ 01766 780658, ✉ ticharlech@eryri-npa.gov.uk) is currently on High St in the centre. In 2013 or 2014 it may well move to the former Castle Hotel, opposite the Castle entrance, which is set to become home to a castle interpretive centre.

ACCOMMODATION

★ **Castle Cottage** Pen Llech ☎01766 780479, ⍵castlecottageharlech.co.uk. Established "restaurant with rooms" with a contemporary yet cosily informal feel and great meals. The seven rooms (including 3 fabulous suites) are natural-toned and very well appointed (big TVs, high-flow showers, leather sofa etc) but otherwise totally different, many with massive weathered beams and slate floors. Residents get a discount on dinner and on green fees at the local course. **£126**

Pen-y-Garth Old Llanfair Rd ☎01766 781352, ⍵pen-y-garth.co.uk. High-standard B&B in a former YHA. Some rooms come with sea or castle views. Cyclists, walkers and vegetarians are particularly welcome – they even do packed lunches. **£60**

Tremeifion A496 at Talsarnau, 4 miles north ☎01766 770491 ⍵tremeifionvegetarianhotel.co.uk. Long-standing vegetarian and vegan hotel with three rooms with views across the Dwyryd estuary to Portmeirion. There's no TV but plenty of places to read or play games, and three acres of grounds to explore. Rates include an imaginatively prepared three-course dinner, with many ingredients grown on site. They'll pick up from the train station, a 10min walk away. Including dinner **£180**

EATING, DRINKING AND ENTERTAINMENT

★ **Castle Cottage** Pen Llech ☎01766 780479, ⍵castlecottageharlech.co.uk. People travel from miles around for the wonderful food at this unpretentious Modern British restaurant with Welsh art on the walls. There's just one price (£38) for which you get canapés plus three courses which might include Cardigan Bay dressed crab followed by roasted porcetta and black pudding. Daily 7–10pm.

Castle Restaurant & Armoury Bar Twtil ☎01766 780416, ⍵caribbeancrabharlech.com. Harlech seems an unlikely place to find a restaurant specializing in contemporary Caribbean cuisine, though it makes a welcome change. Many of the dishes (mains £15–18) are Trinidadian in origin so expect spicy concoctions such as lamb shank with allspice and sweet potato, or butternut, chickpea and spinach curry, eaten to calypso or jazz or reggae beats. March–Oct Tues–Thurs 6.30–10.30pm, Fri & Sat 6.30–11pm, Sun 6.30–10pm.

★ **Cemlyn** Stryd Fawr ☎01766 780637, ⍵cemlynrestaurant.co.uk. Upmarket café serving the best loose-leaf teas and espresso coffees around, plus delicious afternoon teas (£6). They serve light lunches and there's even a small terrace with views of Harlech Castle. Mid-March to Nov Wed–Sun 10.30am–5pm.

4

The Dee Valley and around

VALLE CRUCIS

5

The Dee Valley and around

The Dee Valley and its immediate environs is a region with something of a split identity, encompassing both industrialized flatlands that spill over the border from England and attractive folds of green hill country that are as Welsh as anywhere. There's plenty to see here, but few of the region's sights top most people's list, and visitors often travel through with their minds set firmly on the more obvious destinations further west. The two main routes through the region – the Dee Valley and the Vale of Clwyd – both start in the English border country known as the Marches, an area long contested by the Welsh and English. Llangollen is the valley's undoubted highlight, with an international eisteddfod folk music festival each July and a broad selection of ruins, rides and rambles to tempt visitors throughout the rest of the year.

At its heart is the region's largest conurbation, **Wrexham**, where the light industrial hinterland is leavened by the packaged mining and smelting heritage along the **Clywedog Valley**. The only extant Marcher fortress of note is **Chirk Castle**, a potent reminder of the centuries after the Norman conquest of England, when powerful barons fought the Welsh princes for control of these fertile lands. The castle makes a fine introduction to the **Dee Valley**, the umbilical cord which runs between the Welsh borders and the rugged mountains of Snowdonia. The Dee Valley remains more firmly Welsh than the Marches, and three hundred years after the arrival of the Normans, the area was the site of the first big revolt against them. From his base near **Corwen**, Wales' greatest hero, Owain Glyndŵr, attacked the property of a nearby English landowner, sparking a fourteen-year campaign which, at its height, saw Glyndŵr ruling most of Wales. Little remains to commemorate the era, and most people drive through oblivious of its heritage, making straight for **Bala** with its sailing lake and cascading rapids.

The bucolic lands to the north reward a leisurely approach. The historic but dull market town of **Mold** is the gateway to the bald tops of the **Clwydian Range**, easy walking country that overlooks the pastoral **Vale of Clwyd**. Its gentle contours and minor sights take time to appreciate, including the appealing town of **Ruthin** with its fine medieval buildings and jail tour, and **Denbigh**, surmounted by its craggy castle.

GETTING AROUND   THE DEE VALLEY AND AROUND

The region is most easily explored by car, but public transport will get you most places. **Trains** are good for Chirk and Wrexham, but otherwise you'll be reliant on **buses**. Bala and southern Snowdonia are accessed on the X94 from Wrexham to Barmouth via Llangollen, Bala and Dolgellau. There is no easy connection between Llangollen and Betws-y-Coed: if you're making for the immediate vicinity of Snowdon, head along the north coast to Llandudno Junction or Bangor and change there. Check Getting around in Basics for **discount fares** and **passes**.

A short walk from Chirk p.313	Bala in legend p.323
The Llangollen International Eisteddfod p.315	Thomas Charles, Mary Jones and Michael D. Jones p.324
Thomas Telford (1767–1834) p.319	Walks to Foel Fenlli and Moel Famau p.327
Walks from Llangollen p.320	
Rafting and gorge walking p.320	Mountain biking at Llandegla p.329

PONTCYSYLLTE AQUEDUCT AT FRONCYSYLLTE

Highlights

❶ Erddig Amble around the most interesting stately home in Wales, complete with finely preserved servants' quarters, outbuildings and gardens. **See p.311**

❷ Llanarmon Dyffryn Ceiriog Stay to appreciate the great accommodation and food in a tiny village on the edge of bleak moors. **See p.312**

❸ Plas Newydd, Llangollen An elegant monument to romantic friendship, Plas Newydd always inspires. **See p.316**

❹ Castell Dinas Brân, Llangollen Hike up to this ragged ruin of a Welsh castle for a breath of air and great views. **See p.318**

❺ Pontcysyllte Aqueduct, Llangollen Cruise over Thomas Telford's wonderful aqueduct, part of the Llangollen Canal, one of the great late Georgian engineering achievements. **See p.319**

❻ Rug Chapel and Llangar Church, Corwen Buy one ticket to visit two small churches, and a finer pair you couldn't hope to find. **See p.322**

❼ Ruthin Spend time in this compact hilltop town with its cluster of diverting sights and easy access to gentle walks on the Clwydian hills. **See p.327**

HIGHLIGHTS ARE MARKED ON THE MAP ON P.308

5

Wrexham and around

Once a medieval marketplace for the fertile lands all around, Wrexham developed after the discovery of iron ore, coal and lead nearby propelled the town into the industrial age. The legacy of these times is best seen to the south and west of town in the Clywedog Valley and at the splendidly evocative stately home, Erddig.

Wrexham

While not a classically pretty place, **WREXHAM** (Wrecsam), the largest town in North Wales, has a boisterous charm and some fine older buildings amid the identikit chainstores. Having long looked more to the industrial northwest of England than its own Welsh hinterland, Wrexham's Welshness is only flaunted when the Welsh football team plays international matches at the town's Racecourse Ground.

St Giles' Church

Church St • **Church** daily 10am–4pm **Tower** open Thurs at 12.30pm & Sat at 10.30am • £2.50

Topped off with a steeple in the 1520s, the tower's five tiers, rising to four hexagonal pinnacles, are replicated at America's Yale University in homage to the ancestral home of

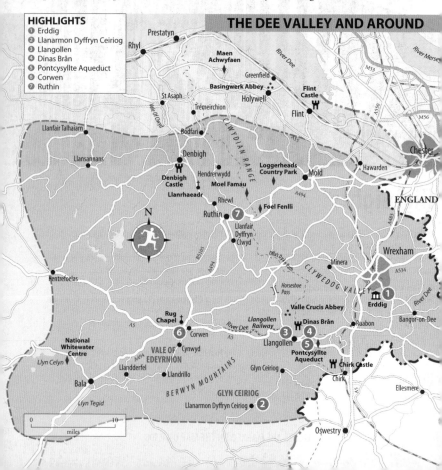

HIGHLIGHTS
- ❶ Erddig
- ❷ Llanarmon Dyffryn Ceiriog
- ❸ Llangollen
- ❹ Dinas Brân
- ❺ Pontcysyllte Aqueduct
- ❻ Corwen
- ❼ Ruthin

THE DEE VALLEY AND AROUND

the college's benefactor, Elihu Yale, whose tomb is here at the base. The engraved stone in the tower wall near his grave came from the university, replacing one that now holds up a replica tower there. The interior boasts the scant remains of a late fifteenth-century mural of *The Last Judgement* above the entrance to the chancel, and an abundance of Victorian and contemporary stained glass. The church is approached through wrought-iron gates installed between 1718 and 1724 by famed Welsh ironworkers Robert and John Davies of Bersham, also responsible for the gates at Chirk Castle and St Peter's church in Ruthin.

Wrexham County Borough Museum

Regent St • Mon–Fri 10am–5pm, Sat 10.30am–3pm • Free • ⓦ wrexham.gov.uk/heritage

The small but engaging **Wrexham County Borough Museum** exhibits a miscellany from the town's nineteenth-century boom years, alongside Roman nuggets and the remarkable remains of the Bronze Age Brymbo Man, who was unearthed from a local sandstone burial cist complete with his pottery beaker and flint knife. Along with the reconstruction of the grave, look out for the coal sculpture commemorating the 266 miners who lost their lives in the 1934 Gresford Mine Disaster not far from here.

ARRIVAL AND DEPARTURE   WREXHAM

By train Trains from Chester, Shrewsbury and Liverpool arrive either at Wrexham Central, incorporated into the Island Green shopping centre, or Wrexham General on Regent Street, a 10min walk northwest.
Destinations Chirk (hourly; 15min); Shotton, for Liverpool (hourly; 30min).

By bus The bus station on King St has assorted local services plus National Express buses from Birmingham, London and Manchester (buy tickets from the TIC).
Destinations Chester (every 15min; 40min); Chirk (roughly hourly; 40min); Llangollen (every 15min; 35min); Mold (every 20min; 40min–1hr).

INFORMATION

Tourist information The TIC is on Lambpit St (April to mid-Oct Mon–Fri 10am–5pm, Sat 9am–4pm; mid-Oct to March Mon–Sat 10am–4pm; ☎01978 292015, ⓦ borderlands.co.uk).

Internet Free at the library on Rhosddu Road (closed Sun), and pay facilities at @rrow CyberWorld (Mon–Sat 9am–6pm) on Vicarage Hill.

ACCOMMODATION

★ **The Lemon Tree** 29 Rhosddu Rd ☎01978 261211, ⓦ lemon-tree-hotel-wrexham.com. Modernized hotel converted from an old Gothic school priory, with small and simple yet tasteful en-suite rooms (some with canopy beds and DVD players), and a good restaurant where breakfast is served. £70

Woodhey 9 Sontley Rd ☎01978 262555, ⓦ woodhey-guesthouse.com. The best of the low-cost central B&Bs, with seven rooms in a Victorian house. Very good value. £55

EATING, DRINKING AND ENTERTAINMENT

Good **places to eat** in Wrexham are hard to find: we've done our best. At weekends, the area around the junction of Brook Street and Vicarage Hill features a handful of lively **nightclubs**. **Male voice choirs** practise in local halls (all year except Aug on Mon, Wed, Thurs & Sun): call the TIC for details.

Anise 1 Smithfield Rd ☎01978 261273, ⓦ anise wrexham.co.uk. Easily the best curry house in these parts, serving all the usual suspects (£9–12) with aplomb. Mon–Thurs & Sun 5.30–10.30pm, Fri & Sat 5.30–11.30pm.

Bwtri At the museum on Regent St. Conservatory café offering the best light lunches in the town centre – panini, jacket potatoes and breakfasts. Mon–Fri 10am–5pm, Sat 10.30am–3pm.

Central Station Hill St ⓦ centralstationvenue.com. The best bet in town for live bands; look out for posters around town advertising events. Thurs–Sun 7pm–2am.

Dao Siam 13 Charles St ☎01978 351071, ⓦ daosiam .co.uk. Good-quality Thai restaurant, with most mains £8–10. Takeaways available. Mon–Sat 5pm–12.30am plus Fri & Sat noon–3.30pm.

The Lemon Tree 29 Rhosddu Rd ☎01978 261211, ⓦ lemon-tree-hotel-wrexham.com. Bustling, brightly decorated Italian restaurant, café and bar with an extensive menu of ciabattas and pasta dishes for lunch (£7–8) and a wider range of vegetarian and meaty dishes for dinner (2/3 courses for £17/21). Save room for tiramisu or chocolate truffle ice cream. Daily 7am–10pm or later.

5

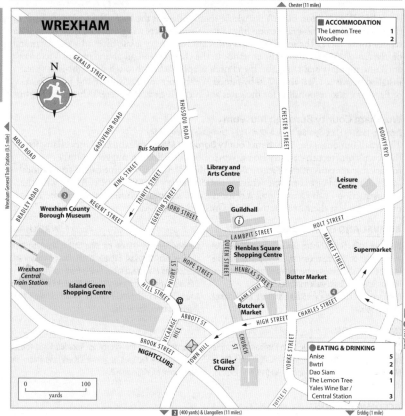

The Clywedog Valley

Forming an arc around the western and southern suburbs of Wrexham, the **Clywedog Valley** was the crucible of industrial achievement in the northern Welsh borders during the eighteenth century. Iron production boomed here, thanks to an abundance of ore deposits and cheap water power harnessed from the River Clywedog. As the Industrial Revolution forged ahead, coal became a more important energy source than water and factories moved away, closer to their raw materials, leaving the valley in peace.

Clywedog Valley Trail

The long-abandoned industrial ruins here – principally a mine, a mill and an ironworks – have been partly restored and are now waypoints on the seven-mile-long **Clywedog Valley Trail**. The area is a bit over-packaged, but no less interesting for that, and you can see everything in one long, varied day.

Minera Lead Mines

Minera, 4 miles west of Wrexham • April to mid-July Sat & Sun noon–5pm; mid-July to Aug daily except Tues & Wed noon–5pm • Free

There isn't a lot to see at the **Minera Lead Mines**, since many of the surface workings are still incompletely excavated. But the engine house and a pithead derrick have been largely rebuilt, together with some ore-processing machinery by the small museum in the former ore house. For a better impression of the mine's layout, walk up onto the

5

hill behind – a heather-clad moor on the fringe of an area called **World's End** – and look back on the valley. In the eighteenth century this was full of mines extracting galena, a silver-and-zinc-rich lead ore, from shafts over 1200ft deep.

Nant Mill

Easter–Sept daily 10.30am–4.30pm; Oct–Easter Sat & Sun 10.30am–4.30pm • Free

You can reach this by taking a path a mile and a half east along the River Clywedog from Minerva Lead Mines. At the child-oriented **Nant Mill** visitor centre you can pick up leaflets for nature trails leading to a very visible section of **Offa's Dyke** in the woods nearby.

Bersham Ironworks

Ironworks April to mid-July Sat & Sun noon–5pm; mid-July to Aug daily except Tues & Wed noon–5pm • Free **Heritage Centre** April–Oct Mon–Fri 10am–5pm, Sat 10.30am–5pm; Sun noon–5pm • Free

The Clywedog Valley Trail runs through woodland to **Bersham Ironworks**, established in the seventeenth century and expanded by Cumbrian ironmaster John "Iron-Mad" Wilkinson who, in 1775, patented his new method for horizontally boring out cylinders. This produced the first truly circular, smooth-bore iron, perfect for highly accurate cannons – hundreds were made here for the American Civil and Napoleonic wars – and the production of fine-tolerance steam-engine cylinders. Engineer James Watt was a big customer, producing steam engines that made water-powered sites unprofitable and eventually put Bersham out of business.

After nearly two centuries of neglect, the ironworks' remains are now being unearthed, revealing a broad area of knee-high foundations around the old foundry. This survived largely intact though it saw service as a corn mill and still retains its huge water wheel.

The Bersham Ironworks foundations really only serve to help you visualize the layout, which is better explained inside the foundry and put in context ten-minutes' walk away at the **Bersham Heritage Centre**, which has a room dedicated to Wilkinson and which is only a mile and a half along the trail to Erddig.

Erddig

2 miles southwest of Wrexham • Mid-March–Oct daily 12.30–4.30pm; Nov & Dec daily 11am–3.30pm • £9.90; outbuildings & gardens only £6.30 • ☎ 01978 355314 • NT

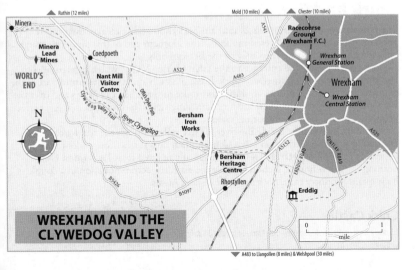

WREXHAM AND THE CLYWEDOG VALLEY

5

Despite the closure of the ironworks, coal continued to be mined around Bersham until 1986. After World War II, coal tunnels were pushed under the local stately home, **Erddig**, adding subsidence to the troubles of an already decaying building. Ever since it was built in the late seventeenth century, its owners – all seemingly called Simon or Philip Yorke – had a hands-off attitude; especially the fourth Simon Yorke, who inherited Erddig in 1922. He failed to install electricity, running water, gas or a phone, and ignored the chronic damp that had the Chinese hand-blocked paper peeling off the walls. The National Trust took charge in 1973, since when it has restored the house to its 1922 appearance and returned the jungle of a garden to its formal eighteenth-century plan.

The servants' quarters

The house itself isn't especially distinguished, but, as nothing was ever thrown away, the collection of fine furniture and portraits – including one by Gainsborough of the first Philip Yorke – is unusually complete. The real interest, however, lies in the servants' quarters, particularly the Servants' Hall, where specially commissioned portraits of eighteenth- and early nineteenth-century staff members are accompanied by personalized dedications in verse written by a Yorke – an extraordinary display of benevolence. You can also see the blacksmith's shop, stables, laundry, the still-used bake house and kitchen.

The walled garden

Reserve an hour for the walled garden, saved from the worst excesses of the eighteenth-century landscaping craze despite the attentions of William Emes, a contemporary of Capability Brown, who worked on the surrounding parkland. Manicured box hedges delineate beds planted with pleached lime trees, the walls support some 150 species of ivy, and apple trees produce fruit celebrated during an annual apple festival in early October.

GETTING AROUND THE CLYWEDOG VALLEY

Aside from Minera and Nant Mill, all the sites lie within a couple of miles of the centre of Wrexham, and can be visited on foot. To take in the whole valley in a day (a total of 9 miles walking), catch a #9 or #10 bus to Minera, walk the full length of the Clywedog Trail to Erddig, then wander the mile and a half back into Wrexham via the *Squire Yorke Inn*.

Chirk and Glyn Ceiriog

The Normans founded **CHIRK** (Y Waun) almost a thousand years ago, their motte remaining as a small tree-covered mound at the southern end of this pleasant enough village with long views up the valley to the Berwyn hills.

Chirk Castle guards the entrance to the Glyn Ceiriog Valley, which runs parallel to, and three miles south of, the Dee Valley. It is a blissfully quiet and beautiful part of the country that was for centuries an important route into the heart of Wales and over the Berwyns into Snowdonia. There are no compelling sights, but the area makes a perfect getaway from the rigours of touring Wales.

The minor B4500 runs beside the river for five miles through the hamlet of Pontfadog to the slightly larger Glyn Ceiriog, then on a further four miles to the appealing **LLANARMON DYFFRYN CEIRIOG** (usually referred to as Llanarmon DC), nothing but a few houses, a church and some excellent **accommodation** in a couple of high-quality country inns, both serving excellent **meals**.

Chirk Castle

0.5 mile west of Chirk • March–June Wed–Sun 10am–5pm; July–Oct daily 10am–5pm; reduced winter hours • £10; garden only £7.20 • ☎ 01691 777701 • NT

5

Roger Mortimer began the construction of massive drum-towered **Chirk Castle** at the behest of Edward I during the thirteenth century, and it eventually fell to the Myddletons who lived here until 2004. Squatting ominously on a rise, this Marcher fortress is guarded by a magnificent Baroque **gatescreen**, the finest work done by the Davies brothers of Bersham, who wrought it between 1712 and 1719. The ebullient floral designs are capped by the Myddleton coat of arms and a red hand, the principal element on the local lairds' coat of arms and the source of all the "Hand" hotels which dot the region. The gates are flanked by a pair of wolves, perhaps a memorial to one of the last wolves in Wales, said to have kept watch over the moat in the 1680s.

From the gates, a mile-and-a-half-long oak-lined avenue leads up to the castle, an austere-looking place softened only by its mullioned windows. The original plan was probably to mimic Beaumaris Castle, started just a couple of months earlier, but Chirk lacks Beaumaris's purity and symmetry. The east and west walls are both incomplete, stopping at the half-round towers midway along the planned length, and the towers have been cut down to wall level, probably after the Civil War when taller towers would have been vulnerable to mortar attack. Internal modifications have been no less extensive, leaving a legacy of sumptuous rooms reflecting sixteenth- to nineteenth-century tastes, many returned to their former states after some Victorian meddling by Pugin in the 1840s. Since the Myddletons' departure, the **east wing** has been opened up, with rooms including one of the last great Welsh family libraries, with volumes dating back to 1535.

The gardens

After touring the house, spend an hour exploring the clipped yew hedges in the beautiful ornamental **gardens** or tracing the section of Offa's Dyke that runs across the front of the house, though it was flattened in 1758 for use as a cart track.

ARRIVAL AND DEPARTURE   **CHIRK**

Trains on the Shrewsbury to Wrexham line stop at Chirk's station on Station Avenue.

Buses run from Chirk to Llanarmon DC (hourly; 30min);

Llangollen (hourly; 20min); Wrexham (roughly hourly; 40min).

ACCOMMODATION, EATING AND DRINKING

Fron Frys Glyn Ceiriog ☏ 01691 718880, ⓦ fronfrys .co.uk. Lovely B&B in converted farm buildings on a smallholding about a mile out of the village towards Oswestry. **£65**

Hand Hotel Llanarmon DC ☏ 01691 600666, ⓦ thehandhotel.co.uk. Converted sixteenth-century farmhouse with a convivial wood-beamed bar and relaxed dining room. Both have the same menu of well-prepared meals from steak and ale pie (£12) to Welsh rib-eye (£20). Try to get one of the older, more atmospheric but less well-appointed rooms (£127) rather than those in the modern

extension. Food served daily noon–2.15pm & 6.30–8.45pm. **£107**

★ **West Arms** Llanarmon DC ☏ 01691 600665, ⓦ thewestarms.co.uk. Ancient farmhouse-turned-inn with stone-flagged floor, a gorgeous inglenook fireplace, snug bar with ancient confessional and a garden out back. There are a couple of cheaper, more modest rooms, but you'll really want one of the older rooms, which have bags of character (£130). Stay for the sumptuous dinners (£33 for three courses) and affordable bar meals. Food served daily noon–2.30pm & 7–9pm. **£70**

A SHORT WALK FROM CHIRK

On the way back from Chirk Castle stop by Chirk train station for a fun short walk (1.5 miles; 30–45min; flat) along the Shropshire Union Canal that takes in a canal tunnel, an aqueduct and the English border. About 50yd west of the station a short track leads down to the entrance to the 459yd Chirk Tunnel. Walk south through the tunnel (torch handy but not absolutely essential), which emerges at the start of Chirk Aqueduct over the River Ceiriog, and a parallel rail viaduct. You can walk to the far end where the canal crosses into England. Return the way you came, or avoid the tunnel using Station Road which runs above it.

5

The Dee Valley

The **Dee Valley** has long been the main transport route from the English Marches to Snowdonia, and it remains the most interesting route west. The course of the River Dee is traced by Thomas Telford's A5 road between London and Holyhead which approaches the region past **Chirk**, with its fine Marcher castle. From Chirk, the bucolic Glyn Ceiriog is a peaceful alternative to the more bustling charms of **Llangollen** with its hilltop castle ruins, broken-down abbey and medieval bridge over the river. Upstream, Owain Glyndŵr's stronghold, **Corwen**, deserves a stop to explore a couple of beautiful small churches.

Llangollen

Clasped tightly in the narrow Dee Valley between the shoulders of the Berwyn and Eglwyseg mountains, **LLANGOLLEN** is the embodiment of a Welsh town in both setting and character. Along the valley's floor, the waters of the River Dee (Afon Dyfrdwy) cut a wide arc around the base of **Dinas Brân**, a conical tor surmounted by the ruins of a native Welsh castle. At the apex of the bend, the Dee licks the angled buttresses of Llangollen's weighty Gothic bridge, which has spanned the river since the fourteenth century. On its south bank, half a dozen streets, their houses harmoniously straggling up the rugged hillsides, are labelled in both Welsh and English, and form the core of the scattered settlement flung out across the low hills. With its wealth of historical sights, canal trips over a fine aqueduct, steam train rides and some highly worthwhile walks, Llangollen is very popular throughout the summer, particularly in early July when the town struggles to cope with the thousands of visitors to Wales' celebration of worldwide folk music, the **Llangollen International Eisteddfod** (see box). This mostly takes place in the 6000-seat, white plastic **Royal International Pavilion**, which was

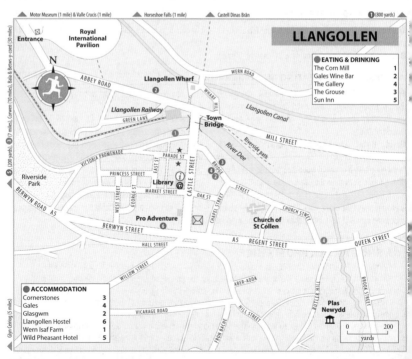

5

THE LLANGOLLEN INTERNATIONAL EISTEDDFOD

Llangollen is heaving in summer, but never more so than during the first or second week of July, when for six days the town explodes into a frenzy of music, dance and poetry. Unlike the very Welsh National Eisteddfod, the **Llangollen International Eisteddfod** (tickets ☎ 01978 862001, ⓦ international-eisteddfod.co.uk) draws around four thousand amateur performers from fifty countries, all competing for prizes in their chosen disciplines. Dances and choral performances take place at Plas Newydd, Valle Crucis and just about anywhere that a group of people can congregate, though competitive performances are concentrated in the main venue, the **Royal International Pavilion**. When the day's competition is over, headlining stars often pack out the pavilion.

The festival has been held in its present form since 1947, when it was started more or less on a whim by one Harold Tudor to soothe the social wounds of World War II. Forty choirs from fourteen countries performed at the first (entirely choral) event, and it expanded, drawing praise quickly from Dylan Thomas, who declared that "the town sang and danced, as though it were right". Today this town of 3000 people is swamped by up to 150,000 visitors, but there is an irresistible *joie de vivre* as brightly costumed dancers walk the streets and fill the restaurants and fish and chip shops.

Tickets for all but the headlining shows can be obtained much closer to the time, often on the day itself. All-day access to the main site, with no guarantee of a seat, costs as little as £10 a day. Accommodation needs to be booked months in advance, so unless you are going specifically for the festivities, avoid trying to stay in Llangollen during the eisteddfod.

The eisteddfod is followed by the less frenetic **Llangollen Fringe** (☎ 0800 145 5779, ⓦ llangollenfringe.co.uk), with a number of more "alternative" acts – music, dance, comedy and so on – performing in the town hall on Castle Street over the third week in July.

designed to evoke the shape of the traditional marquee formerly erected on the eisteddfod site each year, but looks more like some giant armoured reptile.

Brief history

As the only river crossing point for miles, Llangollen was an important town long before the early Romantics arrived at the end of the eighteenth century, when they were cut off from their European Grand Tours by the Napoleonic Wars. Turner came to paint the swollen river and the Cistercian ruin of **Valle Crucis**, a couple of miles up the valley; John Ruskin found the town "entirely lovely in its gentle wildness"; and writer George Borrow made Llangollen his base for the early part of his 1854 tour detailed in *Wild Wales* (see "Books"). The rich and famous came not only for the scenery, but to visit the celebrated **Ladies of Llangollen**, an eccentric couple who became the toast of society from their house, **Plas Newydd**. But by this stage, some of the town's rural charm had been eaten up by the works of one of the century's finest engineers, Thomas Telford (see box), who squeezed both his **London–Holyhead trunk road** and the **Llangollen Canal** alongside the river, spanning the valley with the majestic nineteen-span **Pontcysyllte Aqueduct**.

Town Bridge and Town Falls

Few visitors can resist admiring the view up the valley from the parapet of the **town bridge** which, though widened and strengthened over the years, has spanned the river since the fourteenth century. Below it, the Dee pours through the fingers of shale which make up the unimaginatively dubbed **Town Falls** rapids. The bridge runs onto Castle Street, which heads due south past the TIC.

Church of St Collen

Church St, off Castle St • Late May–Sept Tues–Sat 2–6pm

Llangollen takes its name from the **Church of St Collen**, dedicated to a sixth-century saint. The church features a fine fifteenth-century oak hammerbeam roof, said to have come from Valle Crucis. The graveyard is of equal interest for the triangular, railed-off

5

monument to Mary Carryll erected by her mistresses, the Ladies of Llangollen (see below), who are also buried with her in the churchyard and commemorated on the other two sides of her pillar.

Plas Newydd

0.5 mile up Hill St from the southern end of Castle St • **House** April–Oct Wed–Sun 10am–5pm • £5.50; grounds free • ☎ 01978 862834

For almost fifty years, the two-storeyed mock-Tudor **Plas Newydd** was home to the celebrated **Ladies of Llangollen**. Lady Eleanor Butler and Sarah Ponsonby were a couple of Anglo-Irish aristocrats, who tried to elope together at the end of the eighteenth century. After two botched attempts dressed in men's clothes, they were grudgingly allowed to leave in 1778 with an annual allowance of £280, enough to settle in Llangollen, where they became the country's most celebrated lesbians – though apparently they were affronted by the suggestion that their relationship was anything other than chaste. Regency society was captivated by their "model friendship" in what Simone de Beauvoir called "a peaceful Eden on the edge of the world". Despite their desire for a "life of sweet and delicious retirement", they didn't seem to mind the constant stream of gentry who called on them. They found the Duke of Wellington a "charming young man, hansom, fashioned tall and elegant", and commemorated his visit in typically self-absorbed manner by engraving "E.B & S.P. 1814" over the mantelpiece in the Oak Room. Walter Scott was also well received, though he found them "a couple of hazy or crazy old sailors" in manner, and like "two respectable superannuated clergymen" in their mode of dress. Thomas de Quincey humoured the ladies, if only to bend their favour towards his friend Wordsworth, who had displeased them by referring to their house as "a low roofed cot" in an inelegant poem he had composed in the grounds.

Touring the house

An excellent, self-guided **audio tour** (free) leads you around the half-dozen rooms of the modest black-and-white timbered house. Most of the walls are covered in a riotous frieze of dark wood panelling: a wonderful, if slightly oppressive, effect set off by a mixed bag of furniture in a style similar to that owned by the ladies. As a counterpoint you can also visit the spartan attic room where their loyal housekeeper, Mary Carryll, lived. Outside, take time to wander through the twelve acres of formal **grounds**, including the **knot garden**, which perfectly complements the front of the house.

Llangollen Railway

April–Oct 3–7 services most days; call ahead at other times • £12 return • ☎ 01978 860979, ⊕ llangollen-railway.co.uk

Wherever you are in Llangollen, the hills echo to the shrill cry of steam engines easing along the standard-gauge **Llangollen Railway**. Shoehorned into the north side of the valley, it runs west from Llangollen's time-warped station past Berwyn, near the Horseshoe Falls, as far as Carrog, eight miles up the valley: work has begun on an additional two-mile extension to Corwen which should be operational by mid-2012, though it won't be fully complete for several years. Operating along a restored section of the disused Ruabon–Barmouth line (originally pushed through Llangollen in 1865), belching steam engines (and diesels and railcars) rattle along the river bank, hauling ancient carriages which sport the liveries of their erstwhile owners.

Most visitors simply ride to the end of the line and back (1hr30min), but consider getting off partway along and walking back to town along the Dee Valley Way (see box, p.320), perhaps stopping for a pint in the riverside Grouse pub at Carrog. If you've got kids in tow, look out for the three six-day "Day Out With Thomas" sessions (typically in Feb, Aug & Oct), when Thomas the Tank Engine and his friends ply the tracks. Summer also brings evening trips when you can get on-board for a pie and a pint, and there are occasional driver-experience courses, letting you behind the controls of a steam loco (from £200 for 2hr).

FROM TOP CASTELL DINAS BRÂN (P.318); MYDDLETON ARMS HOTEL, RUTHIN (P.328) >

5

Castell Dinas Brân

Follow signs to Offa's Dyke Path from Llangollen Wharf • Open access • Free

It's the view both ways along the valley which justifies a 45-minute slog up to **Castell Dinas Brân** (Crow's Fortress Castle), perched on a hill 800ft above the town. The lure certainly isn't the few sad but evocative vaulted stumps that stand in poor testament to what was once the district's largest and most important Welsh fortress. Built by the ruler of northern Powys, Prince Madog ap Gruffydd Maelor, in the 1230s, the castle rose on the site of an earlier Iron Age fort. Edward I soon took it as part of his first campaign against Llywelyn ap Gruffydd, and the castle was left to decay, John Leland, Henry VIII's antiquarian, finding it "all in ruin" in 1540.

Although not much to look at, it's a great place to be when the sun is setting, imagining George Borrow sitting up here translating seventeenth-century bard Roger Cyffyn:

Gone, gone are thy gates, Dinas Brân on the height!
Thy warders are blood-crows and ravens, I trow;
Now no-one will wend from the field of the fight
To the fortress on high, save the raven and the crow.

Llangollen Motor Museum

A542, 1 mile west of Llangollen • March–Oct Tues–Sun 11am–5pm • £3.50 • ☎ 01970 860324, ⊛ llangollenmotormuseum.co.uk

An easy walk from Llangollen along the canal towpath is the **Llangollen Motor Museum**, a former slate-dressing shed that now smells evocatively of engine oil and old leather. Two dozen restored cars and three dozen British bikes from the glory years should please any vintage vehicle nut. You'll usually find a couple in here reminiscing over vehicles they've owned and the hours they've spent keeping them running. Check out the 1957 three-wheeler "bubble car" and what is claimed to be Britain's oldest caravan, a tiny wooden affair.

Valle Crucis Abbey

A542, 2 miles west of Llangollen • April–Oct daily 10am–5pm, £2.80 • Nov–March open access, free • ☎ 01978 860326 • CADW

The gaunt remains of **Valle Crucis Abbey** stand in Glyn y Groes, the "Valley of the Cross". In 1201, Madog ap Gruffydd Maelor of Dinas Brân chose this majestic pastoral setting for one of the last Cistercian foundations in Wales, as well as the first Gothic abbey in Britain. Despite a devastating fire in its first century, and a complement of far from pious monks, it survived until the Dissolution in 1535. The church fell into disrepair, after which the monastic buildings, in particular the monks' dormitory, were employed as farm buildings. Later, Turner painted the abbey, imaginatively shifting the perspective so that Dinas Brân sits immediately above the abbey.

Valle Crucis greets you with its best side, the largely intact west wall of the church pierced by the frame of a rose window. Head through the mostly ruined cloister and past the weighty vaulting of the chapterhouse to reach the Monks' Dormitory, where a set of gravestones includes one which is said to be that of Owain Glyndŵr's resident bard, Iolo Goch. There are also displays on monastic life, and the small white cottage out the back contains an excellent exhibit conjuring up life as it would have been at the abbey around 1400.

Eliseg's Pillar

Beside A542, 400yd north of Valley Crucis Abbey • Open access • Free • CADW

The cross that gave Valley Crucis its name is the 8ft-tall **Eliseg's Pillar**, built atop a Bronze Age cairn. It was erected to a Prince of Powys in the ninth century by his great-grandson, and originally stood over 20ft high but was smashed during the Civil War in the 1640s. The stump remains, but you can now only see half of the full 31 lines glorifying the lineage of the Princes of Powys, which Celtic scholar Edward Llwyd translated from the remaining pieces in 1696.

5

The Llangollen Canal

When it was built in 1806, the **Llangollen Canal** was one of Britain's finest feats of canal engineering, designed both to transport slates from the quarries on the Horseshoe Pass and as a water supply for the Shropshire Union Canal. It starts at **Horseshoe Falls**, a crescent-shaped weir which diverts water from the River Dee into the canal, and avoids locks for the first fourteen miles. This was partly achieved by means of the thousand-foot-long **Pontcysyllte Aqueduct**, which spans the Dee Valley at a maximum 127ft above the river. Telford employed long cast-iron troughs supported by nineteen great stone piers – a bold move for its time.

In recognition its significance, and its almost entirely intact state, the canal from Horseshoe Falls across the Pontcysyllte Aqueduct and the Chirk Aqueduct (see box, p.313) to the English border became a UNESCO World Heritage Site in 2009 (Ⓦpontcysyllte-worldheritage.co.uk).

Narrowboat trips from Llangollen Wharf

Across the road from Llangollen train station • Easter–Oct daily • ☎ 01978 860702, Ⓦ horsedrawnboats.co.uk

Llangollen Wharf is the starting point for narrowboat trips along the Llangollen Canal. The Horse Drawn Boat Centre offers taster rides in a horse-drawn narrowboat (45min; £6), horse-drawn trips to Horseshoe Falls (2hr; £10) and motorized trips four miles down to and across the Pontcysyllte Aqueduct (2 daily; 2hr; £12).

Narrowboat trips from Pontcysyllte Aqueduct

At Froncysyllte, off A542 4 miles west of Llangollen

You can walk along the towpath to cross the aqueduct, or take a 45-minute narrowboat ride with Jones the Boats (May–Aug daily; April, Sept & Oct Sat & Sun at noon, 1pm, 2pm & 3pm; £4.50; Ⓦcanaltrip.co.uk) across the aqueduct and back.

Another possibility (for groups of up to ten) is to rent a self-steer narrowboat for the day from Anglo Welsh at Froncysyllte (☎0117 304 1122, Ⓦanglowelsh.co.uk; weekdays £99, weekends £120). You can travel west as far as Llangollen and east across the aqueduct to Chirk; there are a couple of good pubs for lunch.

THOMAS TELFORD (1767–1834)

The English poet Robert Southey dubbed **Thomas Telford** the "Colossus of Roads" in recognition of his pre-eminence as the greatest road builder of his day, if not the greatest ever. Throughout the early years of the nineteenth century, he managed some of the most ambitious engineering projects yet attempted, and there was seldom a public work on which his opinion wasn't sought.

Born in Scotland, he was apprenticed to a stonemason in London where he taught himself engineering architecture, eventually earning himself a position working for the Ellesmere Canal Company, which was planning a canal to join the Severn, Dee and Mersey rivers. His reputation was forged on the **Pontcysyllte Aqueduct**, part of the **Llangollen Canal**, which, though one of his earliest major projects, was recognized as innovative even before he had completed it. Though lured away to build the Caledonian Canal in Scotland and St Katherine's Docks in London, he continued to work in Wales.

After the 1800 Act of Union between Britain and Ireland, a good road was needed to hasten mail and to transport the new Irish MPs to and from parliament in London. What is now the A5 was wedged into the same valley as Telford's Llangollen Canal, then driven right through Snowdonia with its gradient never exceeding 1:20. The combination of its near-level route and the high quality of its well-drained surface cut hours off the journey time, but the Dublin ferries left from Holyhead on the island of Anglesey, separated from the mainland by the Menai Strait. Telford's solution and his greatest achievement was the 580ft-long **Menai Suspension Bridge**, strung 100ft above the strait to allow tall ships to pass under. Though the idea wasn't completely novel, the scale and the balance of grace and function won the plaudits of engineers and admiring visitors from around the world.

5

WALKS FROM LLANGOLLEN

Llangollen is a great place to explore on foot, perhaps using a narrowboat or steam train to shorten a loop. The Explorer map 225, "Llangollen & Berwyn", is useful for the following walks, each of which has an excellent free leaflet available from the TIC.

Dee Valley Way This well-marked route along the north side of the Dee Valley between Llangollen and Corwen is 15 miles long, but can be broken into smaller sections, or shortened by taking the Llangollen Railway to Glyndyfrdwy or Carrog then walking back. A free booklet pinpoints pubs and discusses points of interest along the way, and you can lunch well in *The Grouse* at Carrog (see p.321).

Llangollen History Trail An easy-to-follow loop (6 miles; 3–6hr; 500ft ascent), initially tracing the canal towpath to Horseshoe Falls, then visiting Valle Crucis Abbey and Eliseg's Pillar before returning to town via Dinas Brân.

North Berwyn Way A wilder option running between Llangollen and Corwen flanking the south side of the Dee Valley along the wild moorland tops of the Berwyn hills and past an old slate quarry. The full walk is 15 miles, but shorter versions are explained in the leaflet and you can create a loop using parts of the Dee Valley Way.

ARRIVAL AND DEPARTURE — LLANGOLLEN

With your own vehicle, the most spectacular way to approach Llangollen is over the 1350ft Horseshoe Pass (A542) from Ruthin. Using public transport it is difficult to access central Snowdonia from Llangollen: go via the north coast.

By train Trains stop five miles away at Ruabon, reached by frequent buses on the Llangollen–Wrexham run.

By bus Buses stop on Parade St, including the daily National Express coach on the Wrexham–Llangollen–Birmingham–London run : tickets from the TIC.

Destinations Bala (8 daily; 1hr); Chirk (hourly; 20min); Corwen (8 daily; 20min); Dolgellau (8 daily; 1hr 45min); Glyn Ceiriog (hourly; 35min); Llanarmon DC (6 daily; 50min); Wrexham (every 15min; 35min).

INFORMATION

Tourist information The TIC (Easter–Oct daily 9.30am–5.30pm; Nov–Easter daily 9.30am–5pm; T 01978 860828, E llangollen@nwtic.com, W llangollen.org.uk) is in Y Capel on Castle St.

Books There's a cavernous secondhand bookshop above *Maxine's* café on Castle St.

Internet Free at the library, in the same building as the TIC (closed Sat afternoon and all day Thurs & Sun).

GETTING AROUND

Buses in the immediate locality are fairly infrequent, but you can easily walk most places: even Valle Crucis, the most distant sight, is only a mile and a half along the towpath.

Bike rental Sadly there is no bike rental in town, but you can rent mountain bikes at Llandegla (see box, p.329).

ACCOMMODATION

Llangollen is a fine place to **stay**, with a hostel, handy campsite and an abundance of comfortable B&Bs. For luxury options consider staying over Horseshoe Pass in Ruthin or Denbigh; for upscale **country retreats** make a beeline for Llanarmon DC and the Vale of Edeyrnion. Finding rooms can be a chore in the middle of summer, especially during the eisteddfod (the week beginning the first or second Tuesday of July), though this is alleviated by people letting out one or two bedrooms in the peak period: booking through the TIC.

RAFTING AND GORGE WALKING

ProAdventure 36 Castle St (T 01978 860605, W proadvenure.co.uk) run all sorts of adventure activities and courses including gorge walking, canoeing/kayaking and rock climbing (each £45 a half-day); book in advance.

Whitewater Active (T 01978 860763, W whitewateractive.co.uk) also run modest whitewater rafting trips (£50 for 2hr session) at Mile End Mill, a mile upstream from Llangollen along Berwyn Road. You get several runs down a half-mile bouncy but less than menacing section of the Dee.

HOTELS AND B&BS

Cornerstones 15–19 Bridge St ☎01978 861569, ⊕cornerstones-guesthouse.co.uk. The over-the-top exuberance of this luxury B&B can easily be excused when you see the river views from three of the five rooms spread across three adjacent houses, one dating back to the sixteenth century. **£70**

Gales 18 Bridge St ☎01978 860089, ⊕galesofllangollen.co.uk. Large rooms in a very comfortable and central guesthouse above the restaurant of the same name (or in the house next door), some with brass beds and oak beams. **£70**

★ **Glasgwm** Abbey Rd ☎01978 861975, ⊕glasgwm-llangollen.co.uk. Very relaxed B&B where the relatively modest facilities (no TVs in rooms) are compensated by engaging hosts whose tastes are reflected in the decor of the doubles, twin and single (which has its own deep bath). There are plenty of books, a piano, and they do Offa's Dyke Path pickups and dropoffs as well as packed lunches and dinners. **£55**

Wild Pheasant Hotel Berwyn Rd, A5 0.5 mile west ☎01978 860629, ⊕wildpheasanthotel.co.uk. Venerable hotel with an older wing of standard rooms and a luxurious, tastefully decorated new wing, plus spacious suites. Guests have free use of the modern spa pool, steam room and sauna (£10 day pass for non-guests). Check website for frequent deals. **£70**

HOSTEL AND CAMPING

★ **Llangollen Hostel** Berwyn St. ☎01978 861773, ⊕llangollenhostel.co.uk. Neat bunks in modernized rooms (mostly en suite with 4–6 bunks) in a Victorian townhouse plus a well-equipped kitchen, comfy lounge and free wi-fi – all the ingredients for an excellent town-centre hostel. Bunks **£18**, room **£40**, en suite **£45**

Wern Isaf Farm ☎01978 860632, ⊕wernisaf.co.uk. Simple but idyllic farmhouse campsite on the flanks of Dinas Brân just under a mile steeply up Wern Road (turn right over the canal on Wharf Hill). Some hookups. Closed Nov–March. Pitches **£14**

EATING AND DRINKING

Bailey's Delicatessen Castle St, next to the TIC. Come here for your picnic ingredients – pies, pasties, cold meats, cakes etc. Mon–Sat 9am–6pm.

★ **The Corn Mill** Dee Lane ☎01978 869555, ⊕brunningandprice.co.uk/cornmill. Superb conversion of a town-centre mill, with riverside decking that catches the afternoon sun. Good all day for coffee and well-prepared café-bar food such as beef and horseradish sandwiches (£6) and mains (£10–16) like almond crusted trout and braised beef with mushrooms and mash. The real ales are well kept. Mon–Sat noon–11pm, Sun noon–10.30pm.

★ **Gales Wine Bar** 18 Bridge St ☎01978 860089, ⊕galesofllangollen.co.uk. Old church pews, wooden floors, a blackboard menu of delicious, bistro-style food (mains £9–13) and a good selection of wines from around

the world make this long-standing, chilled-out place a Llangollen favourite. Mon–Sat noon–2pm & 6–10pm, Sun 11am–3pm.

The Gallery 15 Chapel St ☎01978 860076. Friendly evening-only restaurant serving a good range of medium-priced pizza and pasta dishes. Tues–Sun 6–10pm.

The Grouse Carrog, just off A5, 8 miles west of Llangollen. Smart, modernized country pub with freshly-cooked meals and outdoor seating overlooking the River Dee, just a 5min walk from the Carrog station on the Llangollen Railway. Daily noon–10pm.

Sun Inn Regent St. Convivial slate-floored late-closing locals' pub with basic meals for a fiver, a wide range of beers and live bands (of just about any stripe) every Fri & Sat night. Wednesday is open mic night. Daily noon–10pm or later.

ENTERTAINMENT

Outside the eisteddfod and its fringe, there's not a great deal of **nightlife**, but local bands (and occasionally bigger acts) do play from time to time.

Acrefair School Hall Côr Meibion Froncysyllte, one of Wales' most exalted male voice choirs, rehearse here (Mon & Thurs 7–9pm; ⊕fronchoir.com), just off the A539, 5 miles east: directions are on their website.

Royal International Pavilion Abbey Rd ☎01978 860111, ⊕llangollenpavilion.co.uk. The eisteddfod site serves as a year-round venue for anything from choral and classical concerts to comedy and rock gigs.

Corwen and around

In the early fifteenth century, Welsh rebel, local landowner and scourge of Henry IV, Owain Glyndŵr, set out from **CORWEN**, ten miles west of Llangollen, to wrest back all Wales from the English barons. In Glyndŵr's time cattle-droving routes from Anglesey and from Harlech met at Corwen for the final push to the English markets.

Subsequently a major rail junction, it went into steady decline once the line closed. With the imminent extension of the Llangollen Railway to Corwen, this may be reversed, as Corwen could make a handy base for visiting parking-challenged Llangollen.

More enticingly, Corwen has two fine ancient **churches** and the bucolic charms of the **Vale of Edeyrnion** on its doorstep.

Owain Glyndŵr's likeness atop a modern equestrian **statue** in the centre of town looks set to terrorize his persecutors once again, and he is further recalled in the ill-cared-for south porch of the thirteenth-century church of St Mael and St Julien, where the shape of a dagger incised into a grey stone lintel is known as **Glyndŵr's Sword**. He is said to have cast the "sword" in anger at the townspeople from atop the hill behind, though it actually predates him by half a millennium.

Rug Chapel

A494, 1 mile west of Corwen • April–Oct Wed–Sun 10am–5pm • £3.80 (includes Llangar Old Parish Church) • ☎ 01490 412025 • CADW

Taking its name from the Welsh word for heather, **Rug Chapel** is one of Wales' best examples of an unaltered seventeenth-century church. It gives a charming insight into worship almost four hundred years ago, when Mass was a private clerical devotion, with the congregation kept behind the rood screen.

Much here is as it was built in 1637 by the former privateer and collaborator on William Morgan's Welsh Bible (see box, p.400), William Salusbury. The plain exterior design gives no hint of the richly decorated interior: wooden angels support a roof patterned with stars and amoebic swirls, and a painting of a skeleton said to represent the transient nature of life and the inevitability of death. Informative displays in the ticket office give more details of the building's use.

Llangar Old Parish Church

Just off B4401, 1 mile south of Rug Chapel • April–Oct Wed–Sun 12.30–2.30pm • Obtain ticket first at Rug Chapel

This little-changed church dates back to the fourteenth century. Parish boundary changes in 1853 made this church redundant, saving its extensive fifteenth-century wall paintings and seventeenth-century figure of death from obliteration. The interior woodwork is wonderful, from the beamed roof and minstrel's gallery down to the eighteenth-century box pews.

The Vale of Edeyrnion

South of Corwen, the B4401 heads towards Bala through the **Vale of Edeyrnion** past a couple of the best country hotels in the area. None of the vale's peaceful villages (Cynwyd, Llandrillo and Llandderfel) is particularly interesting, but all make convenient bases for hikes on the largely undiscovered Berwyn Range to the east, where you can walk all day without seeing a soul.

ARRIVAL AND DEPARTURE   CORWEN

By bus Buses on the Llangollen–Bala route pass through Corwen.

Destinations Bala (8 daily; 40min); Llandrillo (8 daily;

15min); Llangollen (8 daily; 20min); Ruthin (hourly; 25min).

ACCOMMODATION AND EATING

Bron-y-Graig A5, on the east edge of Corwen ☎ 01490 413007, ☻ north-wales-hotel.co.uk. Comfortable, authentically renovated Victorian rooms in a house built for the Sheriff of Denbigh. Most rooms have a sofa and either river or forest views, and there's a reasonable restaurant. Assorted dinner, B&B and multi-night deals plus self-catering cottages. **£60**

Palé Hall Off B4402, 8 miles southwest of Corwen ☎ 01678 530285, ☻ palehall.co.uk. For sheer grandeur, and the opportunity to stay in a house once frequented by Queen Victoria, you can't beat *Palé Hall*'s hand-painted and intricately carved nineteenth-century interiors located in peacock-inhabited grounds beside a trout stream available for guests' use. Great meals (£35 for three courses) are also served to non-residents: forest mushroom risotto and fillet of duck might be followed by vanilla panna cotta. £125

★ **Tyddyn Llan Country House** B4401 at Llandrillo, 6 miles southwest of Corwen ☎01490 440264, ⓦ tyddynllan.co.uk. Luxuriate in the elegant Georgian surroundings of this superb "restaurant with rooms" (thirteen of them), where a sense of calm descends as you drive through the gate. The rooms are as comfortable as you need, but the emphasis is on Bryan Webb's (Michelin-starred) Modern British food (2 courses for £42, 3 for £50). The restaurant is open to non-guests for dinner and for

lunch on Fri & Sat (£28/35) and Sunday (£35, including roast Welsh beef). £75

Tyn-y-Fron Llandderfel, B4401, 7 miles southwest of Corwen ☎01490 440346, ⓦ tynyfrontipi.co.uk. Beautiful, never crowded camping spot over looking the bucolic Vale of Edeyrnion with dispersed tent sites and a couple of tepees (both April–Sept only) fitted with a double and two single futons (bring a sleeping bag), a warming chiminea, gas cooking hob and exterior fire pits. Also a couple of attractive self-catering cottages (open all year, weekly lets only in summer). Tepees for up to four £60, camping pitches £10, cottages per night £60

Bala

The little town of **BALA** (Y Bala) sits at the northern end of Wales' largest natural lake, **Llyn Tegid** (Bala Lake). The four-mile-long body of water is perfect for **windsurfing**, with steady winds whipping from the coast up the Talyllyn Valley and between the Aran and Arenig mountains that flank the lake.

Bala's second lake, **Llyn Celyn**, five miles northwest of town, is very much an artificial affair created amid huge controversy in the 1960s, to supply Liverpool, in England, with its drinking water. A modern chapel on the shore commemorates the valley-bottom village of Capel Celyn, which was flooded to create the reservoir.

Tomen-y-Bala
Generally open 9am–dusk • Free

Bala has a role in Welsh history that far outweighs its current, modest status. The Romans built a fort at the southern end of the lake (not open to the public), then the Normans erected a motte. This tree-covered **Tomen-y-Bala**, on Heol y Domen off the northern end of the High Street, gives a panoramic view over the rooftops.

Bala Adventure and Watersports Centre
A494, by the shores of Llyn Tegid • ☎01678 521059, ⓦ balawatersports.com

On a warm breezy day head straight for the lakeshore to this watersports centre that runs numerous aquatic courses and rents kayaks (£12 for 2hr), canoes (£35), windsurfers (£25) and more.

Bala Lake Railway
The Station, Llanuwchllyn • April–Sept 4 trains most days • £9.50 return, £6.50 single • ☎01678 540666, ⓦ bala-lake-railway.co.uk

The 24-in-gauge **Bala Lake Railway** follows the level, lakeside course along five miles off the former Ruabon–Barmouth standard-gauge line, which closed in 1963. Renovated north Wales slate quarry trains are put to use for a pretty, if hardly thrilling, run. Either walk from the TIC around the head of the lake to the northeastern end of the line

---

BALA IN LEGEND

Bala sits slightly back from the edge of Llyn Tegid, perhaps to avoid the legendary catastrophe that drowned the old town, which stood where the lake now is. The story tells of the prince Tegid Foel, who was warned by a voice that because of his cruelty to his people "Vengeance will come". On the birth of his son, he held a banquet at which a hired harpist heard a voice saying "Vengeance has come". A bird led him away onto a hill where he slept, waking to find the town submerged beneath the lake which took the prince's name.

The lake also has a legendary beast lurking in its waters, but thankfully the tourist hype about "Teggy", hasn't done to Bala what the Nessie industry has done in Scotland.

5

THOMAS CHARLES, MARY JONES AND MICHAEL D. JONES

During the seventeenth and eighteenth centuries, the religious needs of the Welsh were being poorly met by the established Church. None of the bishops was Welsh, few were resident, and most regarded their positions as stepping stones to higher appointments. This engendered the rise of the newly emerging Nonconformists – Quakers, Baptists and, later, Calvinist and Wesleyan Methodists. Itinerant religious teachers improved literacy and the strident sermons of native Welsh-speakers fired their enthusiasm. **Thomas Charles**, the chief protagonist of Methodism in Wales, gave the movement a massive boost by founding the British and Foreign Bible Society, a group committed to distributing local-language Bibles worldwide. His statue stands outside the Presbyterian church on Tegid Street.

Charles had already reprinted Bishop Morgan's 1588 original Welsh translation, but was down to his last copy when 16-year-old **Mary Jones**, the daughter of a poor weaver from Llanfihangel-y-Pennant, on the other side of Cadair Idris, arrived on his doorstep. She had saved money for six years to buy a Bible from Thomas Charles and, in 1800, walked the 25 miles to Bala, barefoot some of the way, prompting Charles to found the society.

Many of the more pious converts sought greater religious freedom, and in 1865, reformist preacher **Michael D. Jones** recruited around Bala for the 153 Welsh settlers who established Y Wladfa, "The Colony", in Argentine Patagonia. The remains can still be found in the Chubut Valley. Jones stayed in Wales, setting up the Bala-Bangor Theological College and leading campaigns for Welsh causes, and many now regard him as "the father of modern Welsh nationalism".

(10min), or drive six miles southwest to the main terminus at Llanuwchllyn where you can combine your train trip with a visit to the *Eagles Inn*.

The National White Water Centre

A4212, 4 miles west of Bala · Dec to mid-Oct daily 9am–dusk · Free; parking £3 · ☏ 01678 521083, ⓦ ukrafting.co.uk

The only real **whitewater-rafting** trips in Wales take place on the Afon Tryweryn at the **National White Water Centre**. Water is released on around two hundred days a year, crashing down a mile and a half of Grade III rapids where frequent competitions take place on summer weekends. If you're into watersports it is interesting enough to stop in and watch what's going on, with occasional visits to the centre's café. Proficient **kayakers** with their own gear can take to the water free of charge, and **canyoning** trips (£45 for half a day) are also on offer.

Rafting

There are all sorts of rafting options including the Taster (40–60min; £32) involving two runs down the course: wetsuit hire extra. The two-hour session (£60) typically gives you four runs, or you can step up a notch to the Orca Adventure (half-day; £82), involving two runs down in a normal raft followed by a chance to tackle the rapids in a more challenging two-person inflatable.

ARRIVAL AND DEPARTURE   BALA

With your own vehicle, the best approach is the A4212 from south of Blaenau Ffestiniog over the wild open moorlands between the twin peaks of Arenig Fawr and Arenig Fach. Unfortunately, this can't be done by public transport.

By bus Bala's only bus, the #X94, stops on High St. It runs from Chester through the Vale of Edeyrnion to Barmouth.

Destinations Llangollen (8 daily; 1hr); Corwen (8 daily; 40min); Llandrillo (8 daily; 25min); Dolgellau (hourly; 35min).

INFORMATION

Tourist information The TIC is on the A494, half a mile south along High St (April–Sept daily except Wed & Thurs 10am–5pm; ☏ 01678 521021, ✉ bala.tic@gwynedd .gov.uk).

Bike rental is available from R.H. Roberts at 7 High St (☏ 01678 520252; £13 a day).

Internet Free at the library, at Ysgol Y Berwyn on Heol Ffrydan.

ACCOMMODATION

B&BS AND GUESTHOUSES

★ **Abercelyn** A494, 1 mile south of Bala ☎01678 521109, ⓦabercelyn.co.uk. The pick of the local mid-range places, this fine country house occupies an eighteenth-century former rectory. Rooms (two with bathtub) are stylishly understated, and there are also three self-catering cottages. One-night stays attract a £10–14 supplement. **£80**

Bryniau Golau Llangower, off B4403 ☎01678 521782, ⓦbryniau-golau.co.uk. B&B in extensive grounds around the other side of the lake from the town. There are three very spacious rooms richly decorated in antique country style and an elegant guest lounge; walkers and cyclists are very welcome. **£80**

Bryn Tegid Llanycil, A494 1.5 miles south ☎01678 521645, ⓦbryntegid.co.uk. Attractive country house surrounded by lovely grounds and woodland with two of the three spacious rooms overlooking Llyn Tegid. **£80**

Monfa A494 at south end of town ☎01678 521388. The cheapest B&B in town still maintains high standards with one double and one twin room each with private (but not en-suite) bathroom. You get bathrobes, free wi-fi and good single rates (£35). **£55**

HOSTEL, BUNKHOUSE AND CAMPING

Bala Backpackers 32 Tegid St ☎01678 521700, ⓦbala-backpackers.co.uk. Extensively renovated hostel in a central Bala house offering beds (£15–17.50) in both small dorms and larger ones partitioned into smaller areas. There are also private twins (some en suite), most in an adjacent house. Cook for yourself or order breakfast in advance (£3.50). Open May–Sept and winter weekends. Rooms **£45**, en suite **£55**

Bala Bunk House A494 at Tomen-y-Castell, 1.5 miles north ☎01678 520738, ⓦbalabunkhouse.co.uk. Self-catering bunkhouse with small dorms, one self-contained unit sleeping six, and communal lounge and cooking areas. Duvets can be rented (£2) if you haven't brought a sleeping bag, plus there's an inviting barbecue area in the woods round the back. Dorms **£16**

Pen-y-Bont B4319, 1 mile southeast ☎01678 520549, ⓦwww.penybont-bala.co.uk. Well-tended campsite that's the nearest to town, by the outlet of the lake. Along with tent and caravan sites they have a spacious and fully equipped rent-a-tent sleeping 4: bring your own bedding. Closed Nov to mid-March. Rent-a-tent **£50**; own tent, pitches **£15**

Tyn Cornel A4212 4 miles west ☎01678 520759, ⓦtyncornel.co.uk. Camping and caravan park next to the National Watersports Centre; usually packed with paddlers at weekends. Closed Nov–Feb. Per person **£7**

EATING AND DRINKING

Caffi'r Cyfnod High St. A legend in Bala, this café was founded in 1885 and is still going strong for breakfasts, sandwiches and cheap lunches. Daily 9am–5pm.

Eagles Inn 5 miles southwest at Llanuwchllyn, ☎01678 540278, ⓦtheeagleinn-bala.co.uk. Cosy local half a mile from the Lake Railway station, which serves Purple Moose beers and excellent bar meals in hearty portions (mostly £7–11) with several vegetarian options and a kids' menu. Also handy for the male voice choir rehearsals which take place in the village hall at 7.30pm on Thurs. Book at weekends. Daily noon–3pm & 6.30–10pm.

Plas-yn-Dre 29 High St ☎01678 521256. Spacious and airy bistro popular with locals for dishes such as chicken penne with mushrooms and asparagus (£11.50) or pan-fried rib-eye (£15). There's decent espresso at its café next door. Daily noon–10pm.

Mold and the Vale of Clwyd

One of the least-travelled paths through northwest Wales leaves the English Marches at the market town of **Mold**, crosses the soft contours of the **Clwydian Range** – along whose tops runs a section of the long-distance **Offa's Dyke Path** – and approaches the north coast through the wide and fertile **Vale of Clwyd**. Nineteenth-century poet Gerard Manley Hopkins eulogized the valley where he studied for the priesthood, celebrating its beauty in some of his best-loved works, *The Windhover, In the Valley of the Elwy* and *Pied Beauty*. Linked by quiet roads through a patchwork of small farms, two attractive towns of warm-hued stone sit on hillocks above the valley. The ancient market town of **Ruthin** is the pick of the two, with its thirteenth-century castle, compact core of medieval buildings, intriguing jail and a host of good places to stay. Four miles northwest is **Denbigh**, best known for its "hollow crown", the high-walled castle ruin that rings the hilltop behind the town.

5

Mold

The slow pace of **MOLD** (Yr Wyddgrug) is only disrupted by its Wednesday and Saturday **markets**, when stalls supplant cars along the High Street. Despite a good deal of interesting history tied to the town, there's not much reason to linger.

Mold was founded during the reign of William Rufus, though only a copse of beeches atop a mound marks the site of the motte-and-bailey fortifications on **Bailey Hill**, at the top of High Street. Its commanding view over the River Alyn (Afon Alun) shows the strategic value of the site which alternated between Welsh and Anglo-Norman control until Edward I's clampdown on the region. In 1465, during the War of the Roses, local lord Rheinallt ap Gruffydd captured the Mayor of Chester, took him back to the Tower in Nercwys and presented him with a pie containing the rope that would be his noose. Henry VII's assumption of the throne, after his victory at the Battle of Bosworth, stamped some stability on the area.

St Mary's church

High St • Usually Wed morning and summer Sat mornings, can also obtain key from J.H. Jones shop at 53 High St • ⓦ moldchurch.org

In gratitude for Henry's victory, his mother, Margaret Beaufort, commissioned the airy Perpendicular **St Mary's church**. The north aisle retains its original oak roof carved with Tudor roses, and there's a quatrefoil and animal frieze beneath the small clerestory windows.

Among the Tudor stained glass, a Victorian window is Mold's meagre memorial to its most famous son (at least to English-speakers) and Wales' greatest painter, the eighteenth-century landscapist **Richard Wilson**, whose grave is by the church's north entrance. Although Wilson co-founded the Royal Academy in 1768 and was later acclaimed by Ruskin, his work was undervalued and he died a pauper.

Mold Museum

Inside the library, Earl Rd • Mon, Tues, Thurs & Fri 9.30am–7pm, Wed 9.30am–5.30pm, Sat 9.30am–3pm • Free • ☎ 01352 754791

Local tailor and late nineteenth-century novelist **Daniel Owen** is commemorated by a statue, outside the library. "Not for the wise and learned have I written, but for the common people" is inscribed below, and it was his bluntly honest accounts of ordinary life that made him so unpopular with the Methodist leaders of the community. Writing only in Welsh, Owen became his country's most prominent writer. A small museum inside contains a small but effective display on the man, and includes a replica of the **Mold Cape**, an almost 4000-year-old beaten gold ceremonial garment discovered nearby in 1833. The original is in the British Museum.

Loggerheads Country Park

A494, 3 miles west of Mold **Park** daily: Easter–Aug 8am–9pm, Sept–Easter 8am–6pm **Visitor Centre** May–Oct daily 10am–5pm; Nov–April Sat & Sun 10am–4pm • ⓦ denbighshire.gov.uk

For peaceful walks beside the trickling River Alyn it is hard to beat the family-oriented **Loggerheads Country Park**, which offers a mile-long nature trail through mixed ash woodland. Except for an old water channel and the supports for a water wheel, you'd barely know this was a busy lead-mining area in the nineteenth century.

ARRIVAL AND DEPARTURE
MOLD

By bus Buses stop behind the cattle market east of High Street.
Destinations Chester (every 30min; 50min); Flint (every 30min; 20min); Ruthin (hourly; 40min); Wrexham (every 20min; 40min–1hr).

INFORMATION

Tourist information The TIC is on Earl Rd (Easter–Oct Mon–Fri 9.30am–5pm, Sat 9.30am–3pm; Nov–Easter Mon–Fri 10am–4pm; ☎ 01352 759331, ✉ mold@nwtic.com), in the same building as the library.

EATING, DRINKING AND ENTERTAINMENT

56 High Street 56 High St ☎01352 759225, ⓦwww.56highst.co.uk. Mold's top restaurant concentrates on fish and seafood (though not exclusively) using fresh, largely local, ingredients. Go for the two-course lunch specials (noon–3pm; £10) or à la carte dinners (mains £15–20) such as snapper with sesame prawns and kaffir lime rice. Tues–Sat noon–3pm & 6–9.30pm (10.30pm on Fri & Sat).

Alexander's 52 High St. The best spot in town for cooked breakfasts, tasty panini, salads and good espresso. Daily 9am–5pm.

Caffi Florence Loggerheads Country Park ☎01352 759225, ⓦcaffiflorence.co.uk. Extensive lawns outside Loggerheads' excellent café make a great spot for salads, sandwiches, hot lunches and afternoon teas, all made on site with love. Coffee is Fair Trade and they are dedicated to sourcing locally. Daily 10am–5pm.

Clwyd Theatr Cymru A494, 1 mile east ☎0845 3303565, ⓦclwyd-theatr-cymru.co.uk. Local arts powerhouse which stages quality theatre and cinema, aided by revenue from its excellent arts bookshop and café.

Glasfryn Raikes Lane, 1 mile north off A5119 ☎01352 750500, ⓦbrunningandprice.co.uk/glasfryn. Proximity to *Clwyd Theatr Cymru* makes this an ideal spot for a pre-theatre meal of high-class pub fare (mains £10–15) or post-movie nightcap, though you might also come for something from their ever-changing range of real ales on the terrace with views over the fields towards Mold. Mon–Sat 11.30am–11pm, Sun noon–10.30pm.

Hulsons 37 Wrexham St. You might well find a queue stretching out the door of this pork butcher and bakers, most intent on securing some of their famed pork pies. Mon–Sat 9am–5pm, Sun 10am–4pm.

Clwydian Range

6 miles west of Mold • ⓦvisitclwydianrange.co.uk & ⓦclwydianrangeaonb.org.uk • Buses #1 & #1a between Mold and Ruthin; from mid-July to Aug a shuttle bus runs several times a day between Loggerheads and Bwlch Penbarras

Mold is separated from the Vale of Clwyd by the wide-open spaces of the **Clwydian Range**, easily accessed west of Loggerheads, whose the B5429 branches right off the A494 following an old turnpike route between Mold and Ruthin. It climbs up to **Bwlch Penbarras**, a shallow pass where the road meets the **Offa's Dyke Path** (though not the Dyke itself), which runs along these bald tops following the line of a Bronze Age trading route, past the remains of six Iron Age hillforts. The highest point is the 1820ft **Moel Famau**, topped by a truncated **Jubilee Tower**. The subject of many a disparaging remark when it was built in 1810 to celebrate George III's fifty-year reign, this Egyptian-style structure was never completed. The planned pyramid was to rise to 150ft but was damaged in a storm in 1860 and only partially repaired in 1970. The ruins may not be much, but on a clear day the views over the Vale of Clwyd as far as Snowdon and Cadair Idris make a walk out here worthwhile (see box). The relatively gentle terrain makes this a popular spot at weekends: stick to weekdays if possible.

Ruthin

With its attractive knot of half-timbered buildings, a handful of sights and some of the finest food and lodgings in the area, **RUTHIN** (Rhuthun), ten miles west of Mold, should not be missed. The town, built on a commanding rise in the Vale of Clwyd, is centred around **St Peter's Square**, the hub of the town's medieval street plan.

WALKS TO FOEL FENLLI AND MOEL FAMAU

From the car park at Bwlch Penbarras (small charge) you can make the steep climb southwards to the most impressive of the Clwydian hillfort sites on 1800ft **Foel Fenlli** (1 mile return; 40min; 500ft ascent). Excavations here have uncovered 35 hut circles within earthworks three-quarters of a mile across. The height from ditch bottom to bank top reaches 35ft in places, with triple defences on the less easily defended eastern flank.

From the same car park, a broad path leads a mile and a half north to **Moel Famau** (3 miles return; 1–2hr; 650ft ascent) and the Jubilee Tower.

For more information, pick up the *Clwydian Range* leaflet from Loggerheads.

5

Myddleton Arms

St Peter's Square

Ruthin's most photographed building is the **Myddleton Arms** pub, built in 1657 in Dutch style and topped by seven dormer windows known as "The Eyes of Ruthin", which overlook the square.

St Peter's church

St Peter's Square • Daily 9am–4pm or thereabouts • Free

St Peter's church is approached via a photogenic pair of iron gates wrought by the Davies Brothers (who also made the gates of St Giles' church in Wrexham and those at Chirk Castle). The ceiling of its north aisle consists of 408 carved black oak panels with Tudor Rose bosses, reputedly donated by Henry VII from Basingwerk Abbey (see p.397) in gratitude to those who helped him take the English throne. Get someone to turn the lights on for you if you can. One of the busts by the altar is of Gabriel Goodman, who, in 1574, while Dean of Westminster, re-founded the **grammar school** that had been closed by Henry VIII forty years earlier; the building still stands behind the church, next to the Christ's Hospital Almshouses, which Goodman built in 1590 as a gift to the town.

Maen Huail

St Peter's Square

Outside Barclays bank (aka Exmewe Hall) sits an unimpressive chunk of limestone known as **Maen Huail**. A less-than-convincing story has King Arthur and Huail, brother of a Welsh chieftain called Gildas, fighting over the attentions of a woman. Huail pierced Arthur's thigh, giving him a permanent limp, but promised never to mention Arthur's loss of face. Inevitably, though, Huail couldn't resist taunting him about it and an incensed Arthur had him beheaded on this stone.

The old courthouse and prison

St Peter's Square

One of the many timber-framed buildings around town is now the NatWest bank. It was built in 1401 as a courthouse and prison and still retains under the eaves the barely visible stump of a **gibbet**, last used in 1679 to hang a Franciscan priest.

Nantclwyd y Dre

Castle St, just off St Peter's Square • April–Sept Fri–Sun 10am–5pm • £3.60 • ☎ 01824 709822, ⓦ nantclwydydre.co.uk

The restored, timber-framed medieval **Nantclwyd y Dre** partly dates back to 1435, making this medieval townhouse the oldest in Wales. Restored from near dereliction using ancient techniques, it's a wonderfully higgledy-piggledy place, with wonky oak floors, interesting nooks and crannies, and a general atmosphere which makes you feel like you're nosing around someone's home. The house has been extended and updated over five centuries, and the major phases of its existence have been re-created in the seven main rooms which include a Jacobean bed chamber, a Stuart study, a Victorian schoolroom and an entrance hall of 1942, which looks much as it did when the last family moved out in 1984. Outside there's a walled garden and a pretty little summerhouse.

Ruthin Gaol

Clwyd St, 300yd west of St Peter's Square • April–Oct Wed–Sun 10am–5pm • £3.50 • ☎ 01824 708274, ⓦ ruthingaol.co.uk

Ruthin Gaol has been a prison site since 1654, but the so-called "Gruelling Experience" focuses on the Victorian era and the four-storey cell block (1866) inspired by London's Pentonville. It was designed to improve living conditions and penal correction, with one prisoner per cell and the requirement to work while incarcerated. Most upper-floor cells are now used as the county archive, but you can poke around elsewhere, following the free audio guide which traces the prison life of a mythical "Will the Poacher". Informative panels in the lower cells and prison kitchen explain daily prison life and

MOUNTAIN BIKING AT LLANDEGLA

Some of the best mountain biking in northeast Wales is in Llandegla Forest (summer Mon–Thurs 9am–9pm, Fri–Sun 9am–6pm; call ☎01978 751656 for winter hours), roughly 9 miles southeast of Ruthin and 9 miles north of Llangollen. Trails range from a gentle, family-friendly loop to technically challenging black runs. There's a visitor centre (summer Tues–Sun 9am–5.30pm) with a café, workshop and bike rental (£22 a half-day, £32 a day).

behind-the-scenes operations along with the real meaning of "screws" and "bobbies" and the source of the expression "money for old rope". One tale tells of John Jones, the "Welsh Houdini", who seemingly spent half his life escaping from prisons. He absconded from Ruthin in 1913 before being shot five days later.

Ruthin Craft Centre

Park Rd, 300yd northeast of St Peter's Square • Daily 10am–5.30pm • Free • ☎01824 704774, ⓦ ruthincraftcentre.org.uk

Devote a little time in the modern **Ruthin Craft Centre**, set up as Wales' centre for the applied arts and occupying a zinc-and-stone building housing three galleries, six artists' studios, workshops, a shop and café. Check out the website for forthcoming events.

Ruthin Castle

Castle St • ☎01824 702664, ⓦ ruthincastle.co.uk

Hidden away in the trees a quarter of a mile south of town lie the restored, red sandstone ruins of **Ruthin Castle**, which now operates as a hotel. The castle was built by Edward I and by the beginning of the thirteenth century was owned by Lord de Grey of Ruthin, a favourite of Henry IV, who used his influence to have local landowner, Owain Glyndŵr, declared a traitor and acquire his land. In response, Glyndŵr crowned himself Prince of Wales and besieged Ruthin, razing the town once he had plundered the goods brought to its fair by the English. The castle went on to resist the Parliamentarians for eleven weeks during the Civil War, eventually falling to General Mytton in 1646, after which it was destroyed. In 1963, it was partially restored as a **hotel**, with Italian and rose gardens landscaped around the ancient moat and crumbling ruins. Strictly speaking, the grounds are open to residents and peacocks only, but you can wander through if attending one of the tacky medieval banquets or drinking in the panelled library bar.

St Dyfnog's church

Just off A525 at Llanrhaeadr, 4 miles north • Daily 10am–4pm or later

St Dyfnog's church seems much too large for this tiny hamlet. In the sixth century St Dyfnog established a hermitage here on the site of a healing well, and donations from pilgrims funded the building of the present church in 1533. Typically for the area it has twin naves and, though heavily restored in 1880, drips with original features, including a glorious carved barrel roof with vine-leaf patterns and outstanding stained glass.

The **Jesse Window**, at the east end of the north aisle, depicts the descent of Jesus through the House of Israel from Jesse, the father of King David. Regarded as one of the finest such Jesse windows in Britain, it draws you in to the Virgin and Child, surrounded by 21 of their bearded, ermine-robed ancestors, whose names are recorded in medieval Latin. The window is believed to be contemporary with the church, though it was removed and stored in an oak chest during the Civil War, which is when its companion in the south aisle is thought to have been destroyed. In the nineteenth century, fragments which may have belonged to it were found nearby and pieced together to form the west window.

ARRIVAL AND INFORMATION
RUTHIN

Buses, which stop on Market St, serve: Corwen (hourly; 25min); Denbigh (hourly; 20min); Mold (hourly; 40min).

Tourist information There's an unstaffed information point at the Ruthin Craft Centre; the staff at Ruthin Gaol give a more personal touch.

Internet Free access at the library on Record St.

5

ACCOMMODATION

★ **Firgrove** B5105, 1 mile southeast ☎01824 702677, ⓦfirgrovecountryhouse.co.uk. A large Georgian house with manicured gardens, offering B&B and one self-catering cottage. Everything is done with an understated elegance, and the three-course dinners (£30) are superb. **£80**

★ **Gorphwysfa B&B** 8a Castle St ☎01824 702529, ⓦruthinguesthouse.co.uk. Comfortable wood-panelled sixteenth-century Tudor townhouse in the heart of town, with three spacious rooms and a very welcoming atmosphere. **£65**

★ **Manorhaus** 10 Well St ☎01824 704830, ⓦmanorhaus.com. Fluffy duvets, bright colours and bold artworks characterize this eight-room boutique hotel in a Georgian house, complete with a small gym, sauna, DVD/CD, book and games library, and excellent restaurant and bar. **£95**

Rhydonnen Llanychan, 1 mile north of Ruthin ☎01824 790258, ⓦrhydonnen.co.uk. A well-appointed B&B in a fifteenth-century black-and-white farmhouse steeped in history. **£70**

CAMPING

Minffordd Campsite ☎01824 707169. Simple, tent-and-campervan-only site two miles north of Ruthin and just east of Rhewl: follow signs for Gellifor then turn right 150yd after a pair of stone bridges. Closed Oct–Easter. Pitches **£6**

EATING AND DRINKING

Leonardo's Deli 4 Well St ☎01824 707161, ⓦleonardosdeli.co.uk. Great little deli, bakery and much more where dedication to quality is paramount. Take away one of their superb stuffed baguettes, a toothsome steak and red wine pie or a delectable tarte tatin. And the shop is loaded with all sorts of other goodies to thrill any foodie. Daily 9am–5pm.

★ **Manorhaus** 10 Well St ☎01824 704830. Stylish decor, subdued lighting and understated service make this a superb place for dinner (£24/30 for 2/3 courses), which might include dishes such as pea and mint risotto or pork and black pudding tournedo. Desserts are delectable; good wine list. Food: Mon–Fri 6.30–9.30pm, Sat & Sun noon–2pm & 6.30–9.30pm.

On the Hill Restaurant 1 Upper Clwyd St ☎01824 707736. This cosy wood-floored restaurant with oak beams is hard to beat for its bistro-style meals (mains £11–14) with personal service. Lunch comes as just a main (£8.50), two courses (£11.50) or three (£14.50), though you should sample something from the well-thought-out wine list (5 by the glass). Dinner mains are around £13 and they do a great pudding sampler. Tues 6.30–9pm, Wed–Sat noon–2pm & 6.30–9pm.

Ruthin Castle ☎01824 702664, ⓦruthincastle .co.uk. Nip into this grand and extensively refurbished baronial castle for a bar meal or a drink in the panelled library bar. They also do ersatz Welsh medieval banquets (£42). Restaurant daily 6.30–9pm.

Ye Olde Cross Keys B5105, 1 mile southeast of Ruthin ☎01824 705281. Welcoming pub serving bar meals well above the normal standard but at modest prices. Daily noon–3pm & 6–10pm.

Denbigh and around

The hilltop castle ruins dominating the Vale of Clwyd eight miles north of Ruthin herald **DENBIGH** (Dinbych), in medieval times a fortified or bastide town, which tumbles down the hill towards its old centre where the Wednesday market takes place.

High Street is surrounded by a pleasing array of colonnaded medieval buildings which, thankfully, haven't been over-restored, helping retain a working town atmosphere. Beside *The Old Vaults* pub on the High Street, Broomhill Lane runs up past the crumbling **Burgess Gate**, the former northern entry to the town, to the vast grassy ward of the ruined **Denbigh Castle**.

Brief history

For a long time, the River Clwyd formed the border of England and Wales, guarded here by a now vanished Welsh castle, which probably gave the town its name, meaning "small fort". The Welsh castle eventually fell to the English, enabling Edward I to fortify Rhuddlan and Ruthin, and entrust Denbigh to Henry de Lacey, Earl of Lincoln, who employed many of the concepts already implemented by Edward's architect, James of St George.

Denbigh Castle

April–Oct daily 10am–5pm; Nov–March daily 10am–4pm • April–Oct £3.20; Nov–March free • ☎ 01745 813385 • CADW

Denbigh Castle's most imposing remnant is the **gatehouse**, with three octagonal towers enclosing an originally vaulted hall, making it one of the finest defensive structures of the era. You enter beneath a weathered statue of Edward I in a niche, flanked on the right by the Prison Tower (stained by five garderobes discharging into a common cesspit) and the Porter's Lodge Tower on the left. From here, you can walk the only remaining section of the wall, extending as far as the Great Kitchen Tower with its two huge fireplaces. On the far side, the Postern Tower was heavily strengthened after 1294, as were the **town walls** that formed the outer ward branching off at the castle walls. Continue along the short section of wall walk (key from the castle office) down to the **Goblin Tower** from where, at the end of a six-month-long siege in 1646, Charles I threw the castle keys onto the heads of the all-conquering Roundheads.

In 1563, Elizabeth I sold the castle to her favourite, Robert Dudley, Earl of Leicester, who in 1579 chose a site just below the castle for the church that he hoped would supplant St Asaph cathedral, four miles to the north. It was never completed, but the shell still stands today as **Leicester's Folly**.

ARRIVAL AND INFORMATION

DENBIGH

By bus Buses stop centrally on High St.
Destinations Rhyl (every 30min; 40min); Ruthin (hourly; 20min); St Asaph (every 30min; 15min).
Information The County Hall contains the library

(Mon–Wed & Fri 9.30am–5pm, Thurs 1–5pm, Sat 9.30am–12.30pm), which has free internet access and a supply of tourist information leaflets. ⓦ visitdenbigh.co.uk is also useful.

ACCOMMODATION

★ **Bach Y Graig** Tremeirchion, four miles northeast along A543 ☎ 01745 730627, ⓦ bachygraig.co.uk. A relaxed and welcoming farmstay in a sixteenth-century house on a working dairy farm. It has its own woodland trail, and there are self-catering cottages (minimum one-week stay in summer). **£75**
Castle House Bull Lane ☎ 01745 816860, ⓦ castlehousebandb.co.uk. Three wonderfully luxurious rooms in one of Denbigh's finest houses – just below the castle and sharing the grounds of Leicester's Folly – plus two separate cottages all with ornate furnishings and long views. Great guests' lounge and lovely grounds. **£140**
Cayo Guesthouse 74 Vale St, a few hundred yards down the main St Asaph road ☎ 01745 812686, ⓔ stay@cayo.co.uk. Long-standing Denbigh favourite in a homely Victorian house with large bedrooms, comfy beds

and a great breakfast. Excellent value. **£60**
Guildhall Tavern Hall Square ☎ 01745 816533, ⓦ guildhalltavernhotel.co.uk. Classy modern reworking of a town-centre hotel with eleven rooms all having chic wallpapers and crisp white sheets while retaining character features. There's a great bar and restaurant downstairs. **£109**

CAMPING

Station House Caravan Park A541, 4 miles northeast ☎ 01745 710372, ⓦ stationhousecaravanpark.co.uk. Denbigh's handiest campsite in a blissful rural setting close to the Offa's Dyke Path. A good range of facilities and a couple of pubs within an easy walk. Reached on bus #14. Closed mid-Oct to mid-March. Pitches **£12**

EATING AND DRINKING

Glass Onion 1 Back Row ☎ 01745 813125, ⓦ glassonioncafe.co.uk. Relaxed café good for inexpensive home-cooked daytime meals (and specials) plus free wi-fi. Mon–Fri 8.30am–5pm, Sat 8.30am–2pm.
★ **Guildhall Tavern** Hall Square ☎ 01745 816533, ⓦ guildhalltavernhotel.co.uk. A cosy but stylish renovation. Excellent ales, a good wine list and a modern take on quality pub fare (mains £10–13). Food available Mon–Fri noon–2.30pm & 6–9pm, Sat & Sun noon–9pm.

★ **White Horse Inn** 5 miles southeast at Hendrerwydd ☎ 01824 790218, ⓦ whitehorse restaurant.co.uk. Superb, cosy country gastropub in a sixteenth-century inn. They really care about their food and drink here, whether it be a pub classic such as fish, chips and peas (£7) or British tapas such as Menai mussels marinière (£5), or pork belly with caramelized apples and black pudding (£6). Monday curry night is excellent value. Mon 6–11pm, Wed–Sat 11am–11pm.

Snowdonia and the Llŷn

PORTH DINLLAEN, LLŶN PENINSULA

Snowdonia and the Llŷn

The mountains of Snowdonia (Yr Eryri) are north Wales' defining feature, not just in their physical form but in the way they have shaped the communities within them. Trapped between the brash north-coast resorts and the thinly inhabited hill tracts of mid-Wales, this mountainous kernel seemed to Henry VIII's antiquarian, John Leland, as "horrible with the sight of bare stones" but is now widely acclaimed as the most dramatic and alluring region in Wales. This is a compact, barren land of tortured ridges dividing glacial valleys where the sheer faces belie the fact that the tallest peaks only just top three thousand feet. Little more than ten miles by ten, this tightly packed bundle of soaring cliff faces, jagged peaks and plunging waterfalls has enough mountain paths to keep even the most jaded walking enthusiast happy for weeks. It is home to Wales' highest mountain, Snowdon (Eryri), where winter snows cling to 3000ft peaks well into April. Further to the west lies the Llŷn, a peninsula which juts into the Celtic Sea at a near right angle to the Cambrian coast. The Welsh castle at Criccieth, and the museum devoted to Lloyd George a couple of miles away, are good reasons to pause before Wales ends in a flourish of small coves around Abersoch and Aberdaron.

Snowdonia

With everything from gentle woodland strolls to tough mountain scrambles, **SNOWDONIA** is fabulous walking country, and the small settlements that dot the valleys make great bases or places to rest. Foremost among these is the Victorian resort town of **Betws-y-Coed**, while the smaller walkers' hamlets of **Capel Curig** and **Pen-y-Pass** have a

Highlights

❶ Tryfan Some of the finest hikes in Snowdonia converge on the craggy summit where a leap between two monoliths crowns the day. **See p.348**

❷ National Slate Museum, Llanberis Learn about the lives and labours of those who worked the massive slate quarries hewn out from Llanberis' hillsides. **See p.354**

❸ Snowdon Scale Wales' highest mountain, the only one with half a dozen hiking paths and a cog railway converging on the summit-top café and bar. **See p.357**

❹ Caernarfon Castle Scramble around the walls of the mightiest link in Edward I's chain of Norman castles. **See p.360**

❺ Blaenau Ffestiniog Wales' slate capital – a tremendously atmospheric town, surrounded by mountains and rich in industrial heritage. **See p.368**

❻ Ffestiniog Railway The finest of Wales' narrow-gauge railways, climbs 13 miles from the coast into the heart of the mountains. **See p.372**

❼ Portmeirion Spend the day at this surreal seaside "village", made from bits of rescued architecture, and the setting for the cult TV series, *The Prisoner*. **See p.375**

❽ Ynys Enlli A point of Christian pilgrimage for centuries, this windswept sea-bird-strewn "Island of the Currents" is the destination for Wales' best offshore day-trip. **See p.387**

HIGHLIGHTS ARE MARKED ON THE MAP ON P.337

suitably robust atmosphere. The clear focus of the region is **Snowdon**, reached by superb hikes and a cog railway from **Llanberis**. Here you're surprisingly close to the coast, specifically the nationalist stronghold of **Caernarfon**, where its mighty castle guards the southern entrance to the Menai Strait.

Close to Snowdon, other mountains are equally dramatic, often far less busy and give unsurpassed views of Snowdon. The **Glyderau** and **Tryfan** are particular favourites and best tackled from the **Ogwen Valley**. Elsewhere, settlements tend to coincide with some enormous mine or quarry; notably **Beddgelert**, where the former copper mines are open to the public, and **Blaenau Ffestiniog**, the "Slate Capital of north Wales", where one of the mines has opened its caverns for underground tours.

West of here, the mountain landscape bleeds gently into the softer coastal contours around the harbour town of **Porthmadog**, linked to Snowdonia by the magnificent, narrow-gauge **Ffestiniog Railway** and famous for its proximity to the Italianate dream village of **Portmeirion**.

Brief history

It was to this mountain fastness that Llywelyn ap Gruffydd, the last true Prince of Wales, retreated in 1277 after his first war with Edward I; it was also here that Owain Glyndŵr held on most tenaciously to his dream of regaining the title for the Welsh. Centuries later, the English came to remove the mountains; slate barons built huge fortunes from Welsh toil and reshaped the patterns of Snowdonian life forever, as men looking for steady work in the quarries fled the hills and became town dwellers.

From the late eighteenth century, Snowdonia became the focus for the first truly structured approach to **geological research**. The last Ice Age left a legacy of peaks ringed by cwms – huge hemispherical bites out of the mountainsides – while the ranges were left separated by steep-sided valleys, a challenge for even the most fly-footed climber. Scoured valley walls, scalloped mountainsides and hanging valleys became the first reliable evidence of the last Ice Age and its retreat ten thousand years ago. These pioneer geologists created the rock-type classifications familiar to any students of the discipline: Cambrian rock takes its name from the Roman name for Wales, Ordovician and Silurian rocks from the Celtic tribes, the Ordovices and the Silures.

Botanists found rare alpine flora, writers produced libraries full of purple prose, and Richard Wilson, Paul Sandby and J.M.W. Turner all came to **paint** the landscape, alerting the leisured classes to the area's beauty. Soon, those with the means began flocking here to marvel at the plunging waterfalls and walk the ever-widening mountain paths of Wales' first and largest national park (see box below).

SNOWDONIA NATIONAL PARK

In recognition of the region's scientific importance, as well as its scenic and recreational appeal, **Snowdonia National Park** (Parc Cenedlaethol Eryri; ⓦ eryri-npa.gov.uk) was set out in 1951, becoming Wales' first, and still largest, national park. Covering 823 square miles of northwest Wales (more than the central part of Snowdonia covered in this chapter) it runs all the way from Conwy to Aberdyfi encompassing the Rhinogs, Cadair Idris and 23 miles of the Cambrian coast. Jagged mountains predominate, but the harsh lines come tempered by broadleaf lowland woods around calm glacial lakes, waterfalls tumbling from hanging valleys and complex coastal dune systems. However, you won't find total wilderness: sheep and cattle farming supports many of the 27,000 people who live in the park (some 65 percent of them Welsh-speakers) and another fourteen million people come here each year to tramp almost 2000 miles of designated paths; most open areas are "access land" where you have freedom to roam anywhere. In apparent contradiction to its name, the national park is 75 percent privately owned by the Forestry Commission and National Trust. However, trespass isn't usually a problem as long as you keep to the ancient rights of way and access areas.

SNOWDONIA & THE LLYN

HIGHLIGHTS
1. Tryfan
2. Llanberis
3. Snowdon
4. Caernarfon Castle
5. Blaenau Ffestiniog
6. Ffestiniog Railway
7. Portmeirion
8. Ynys Enlli

miles

0 — 10

N

Caernarfon Bay

Cardigan Bay

Tremadog Bay

Bardsey Sound

CARNEDD RANGE

GLYDER RANGE

Llangollen

Bala

Bala Lake Railway

Canolfan Tryweryn

Llyn Tegid

Llanuwchllyn

Pentrefoelas

Trefriw

Llanrwst

Llyn Crafnant

Capel Curig

Betws-y-Coed

Penmachno

Llyn Cowlyd

Llyn Ogwen

Bethesda

Tryfan ①

Moel Siabod

Dolwyddelan

Crimea Pass

Blaenau Ffestiniog ⑤

Llan Ffestiniog

Llyn Celyn

Llyn Trawsfynydd

Trawsfynydd

Mountain Bike Park

COED-Y-BRENIN FOREST

SEE CENTRAL SNOWDONIA MAP FOR DETAIL

Llanberis ②

Llanberis Lake Railway

Llyn Padarn

Llyn Peris

Snowdon Mountain Railway

Snowdon ③

Llanberis Pass

Llyn Gwynant

Llyn Dinas

Ffestiniog Railway ⑥

Maentwrog

Llyn Trawsfynydd

Bethel

Waunfawr

Welsh Highland Railway

Rhyd Ddu

Welsh Highland Railway

Beddgelert

Moel Hebog

Trawsfynydd

Harlech

Llanbedr

Caernarfon ④

Dinas

Penygroes

Clynnog Fawr

Dinas Dinlle

Tremadog

Porthmadog

Morfa Bychan

Borth-y-Gest

Portmeirion ⑦

Penrhyndeudraeth

Criccieth

Criccieth Castle

Llanystumdwy

Llangybi

Llanaelhaearn

Tre'r Ceiri

Yr Eifl

Nant Gwrtheyrn

Nefyn

Morfa Nefyn

Porth Dinllaen

Penarth Fawr

Pwllheli

Llanbedrog

Abersoch

Sam Bach

St Tudwal's Islands

Bwlch Tocyn

Llithfaen

Tudweiliog

Sam Meyllteyrn

Llangwnnadl

Porth Colmon

Porth Oer (Whistling Sands)

Aberdaron

Rhiw

Plas-yn-Rhiw

Porth Neigwl (Hell's Mouth)

Llanengan

Ynys Enlli (Bardsey Island) ⑧

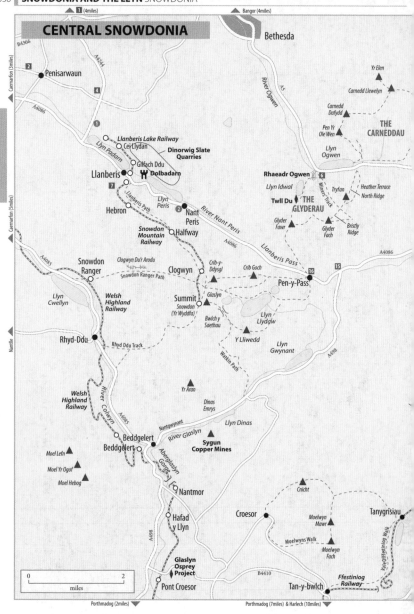

CENTRAL SNOWDONIA

GETTING AROUND

BY TRAIN

Getting to the fringes of Snowdonia from elsewhere in Wales is relatively easy: main-line trains run along the coast to nearby Bangor, while the Conwy Valley line branches at Llandudno Junction, penetrating to

SNOWDONIA AND THE LLŶN

Betws-y-Coed and on to Blaenau Ffestiniog. Here, you can transfer to the useful and highly scenic Ffestiniog Railway for Porthmadog – the latter is also a stop on the Cambrian Coast line, shuffling daily around the coast to Pwllheli on the Llŷn.

6

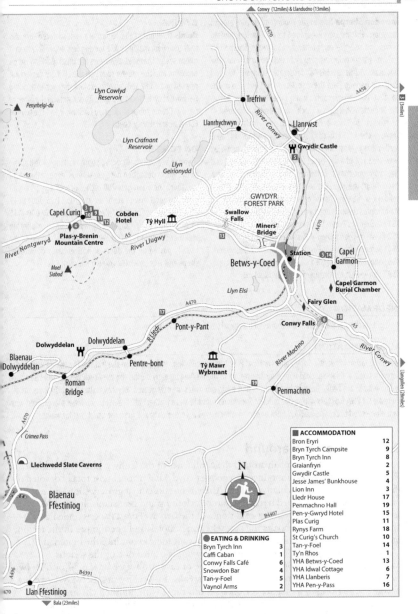

Conwy (12miles) & Llandudno (13miles)

Penyrhelgi-du

Llyn Cowlyd Reservoir

Llyn Crafnant Reservoir

Llyn Geirionydd

• Trefriw

• Llanrhychwyn

River Conwy

• Llanrwst

Gwydir Castle
5

GWYDYR FOREST PARK

Capel Curig
8 9
10 11 12

Cobden Hotel

Tŷ Hyll 🏛

Swallow Falls

Miners' Bridge

Plas-y-Brenin Mountain Centre
4

River Nantgwryd

River Llugwy

13

Station
9 14

Capel Garmon

Betws-y-Coed

Capel Garmon Burial Chamber

Moel Siabod ▲

Llyn Elsi

A470

17

Pont-y-Pant

Fairy Glen

Conwy Falls
6 18

River Machno

River Conwy

Llangollen (28miles)

Dolwyddelan

Dolwyddelan 🏰

R.Lledr

Pentre-bont

Tŷ Mawr Wybrnant 🏛

Blaenau Dolwyddelan

Roman Bridge

19

Penmachno

Crimea Pass

▲ Llechwedd Slate Caverns

Blaenau Ffestiniog

N

B4407

Bala (23miles)

Llan Ffestiniog

B4391

A496

■ ACCOMMODATION	
Bron Eryri	12
Bryn Tyrch Campsite	9
Bryn Tyrch Inn	8
Graianfryn	2
Gwydir Castle	5
Jesse James' Bunkhouse	4
Lion Inn	3
Lledr House	17
Penmachno Hall	19
Pen-y-Gwryd Hotel	15
Plas Curig	11
Rynys Farm	18
St Curig's Church	10
Tan-y-Foel	14
Ty'n Rhos	1
YHA Betws-y-Coed	13
YHA Idwal Cottage	6
YHA Llanberis	7
YHA Pen-y-Pass	16

● EATING & DRINKING	
Bryn Tyrch Inn	3
Caffi Caban	1
Conwy Falls Café	6
Snowdon Bar	4
Tan-y-Foel	5
Vaynol Arms	2

BY BUS

There are frequent bus services from Llandudno Junction (close to Llandudno and Conwy) up the Conwy Valley to Llanrwst (the area's bus hub) and Betws-y-Coed. From there, the Snowdon Sherpa services (see p.340) provide access to Llanberis, Beddgelert, Porthmadog, Bangor and Caernarfon. Pwllheli is the main hub for the Llŷn, with buses to most of the peninsula. Routes and times are all fully detailed on the free *Gwynedd Public Transport Timetables and Information*, available from TICs and bus stations. Check Basics p.30 for discount fares and passes (some of which cover the region's narrow-gauge railways).

6

Snowdon Sherpa bus In the mountainous core around Snowdon, visitors are encouraged to park in surrounding towns and use the comprehensive Snowdon Sherpa bus system (ⓦsnowdoniagreenkey.co.uk) to get into the mountains. This avoids a desperate struggle to find trailhead parking (and the associated fees) but also opens up all sorts of hiking routes using buses to link the paths. The Snowdon Sherpa is a catch-all name for a handful of interconnecting bus services plying the roads between Betws-y-Coed, Bethesda, Llanberis, Caernarfon and Porthmadog. Most meet at Pen-y-Pass. Short one-way fares are £1, and a day ticket (£4; buy from the driver) will give you one day's unlimited travel within this area throughout the day. On summer weekends and school holidays, some services use open-top double-deckers. Major routes through northern Snowdonia are:

#S1 Llanberis to Pen-y-Pass via Nant Peris.

#S2 Betws-y-Coed to Pen-y-Pass via Capel Curig.

#S4 Caernarfon to Pen-y-Pass via Waunfawr and Beddgelert.

#S6 Bangor to Betws-y-Coed via Llyn Ogwen and Capel Curig.

#S97 Pen-y-Pass to Porthmadog via Beddgelert.

BY BIKE

Roads throughout the region are well surfaced but also well travelled, making cycle touring less appealing than it might seem. That said, the views are great, parking isn't a problem, and the quieter roads on the Llŷn are perfect for relaxed pedalling. You can also explore the ever-expanding network of cycle tracks and get off-road among the pines of Coed-y-Brenin south of Blaenau Ffestiniog and the Gwydir Forest near Betws-y-Coed.

ON FOOT

If you're serious about doing some walking – and some of the walks described here *are* serious, especially in bad weather (Snowdon gets 200 inches of rain a year) – you need a good map, such as the OS 1:25,000 OL17 ("Snowdon & Conwy Valley") or the 1:50,000 115 ("Snowdon/Yr Wyddfa"). Always check mountain weather conditions before setting out: latest reports are usually posted on the doors or noticeboards of outdoor shops and TICs, or visit ⓦmetcheck.com.

INFORMATION

Most of this chapter falls within the county of Gwynedd (ⓦdiscovergwynedd.com).

ACCOMMODATION

Accommodation inside the Snowdonia National Park is strictly limited, and most is on the fringes. The main exception is Betws-y-Coed, a village packed with guesthouses, all of them filling up early during the busy summer season. Elsewhere in Snowdonia are B&Bs, hostels, bunkhouses and basic campsites, mostly geared towards walkers and climbers. In all, there are six **YHA hostels** within five miles of Snowdon's summit, and a further half-dozen other budget places. Even with a medium-sized backpack, walking from one to another makes a welcome change from the usual circular walks.

Betws-y-Coed and around

Sprawled out across a flat plain around the confluence of the Conwy, Llugwy and Lledr valleys, **BETWS-Y-COED** (pronounced "betoos-er-coyd") is a place almost totally devoted to the needs of visitors, particularly walkers. There is no substantial grocery shop and no pharmacy but Betws-y-Coed has seven outdoor clothing and gear shops. Its riverside setting, overlooked by the conifer-clad slopes of the **Gwydyr Forest Park**, is undeniably appealing, and the village boasts the best selection of hotels and guesthouses in the region, but after an hour mooching around you'll soon want to head out into the hinterland.

The village is touted as "the gateway to Snowdonia", but none of the serious mountain walks starts from here, just a couple of easy strolls (see box, p.345) to its two main attractions, the **Conwy Falls** and **Swallow Falls**. In recent years, Betws-y-Coed has become something of a magnet for **bikers**, both those with polished chrome hogs parked outside the village's pubs and cafés, and mud-bespattered mountain bikers returning from the pleasures of the Gwydyr Forest.

The quieter valleys in the vicinity can often be a lot more appealing than the village itself. The rail line from the coast comes up the bucolic **Conwy Valley** past **Llanrwst**, five miles north of Betws-y-Coed, a town graced by a fine bridge attributed to Inigo Jones and a couple of beautifully decorated chapels. The train continues south from Betws-y-Coed up the **Lledr Valley**, a wonderfully scenic journey passing the lonely **Dolwyddelan Castle**, on its way to the slate town of Blaenau Ffestiniog. South of

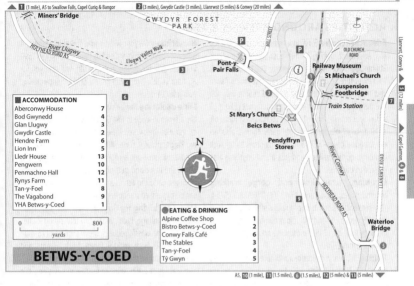

BETWS-Y-COED

A5, **10** (1 mile), **11** (1.5 miles), **6** (1.5 miles), **12** (5 miles) & **13** (5 miles) ▼

Betws-y-Coed, a minor road leads to **Penmachno** and the house of William Morgan, who first translated the Bible into Welsh. Walkers bound for the high hills will be heading west beside the **River Llugwy** to the mountain centre of Capel Curig and beyond to Llanberis and the Ogwen Valley.

Pont-y-Pair Falls

On sunny days the stone slabs around the low cataract of **Pont-y-Pair Falls** are always littered with people relaxing after long walks or too much shopping for outdoor clothing. The waters of the River Llugwy thunder over assorted boulders and funnel under the adjacent **Pont-y-Pair** ("Bridge of the Cauldron").

Conwy Valley Railway Museum

Daily 10am–5pm • £1.50 • ☎ 01690 710568, ⊛ conwyrailwaymuseum.co.uk

Adjoining the train station, the **Conwy Valley Railway Museum** is a fairly dull collection of memorabilia and shiny engines, slightly enlivened by a model of a Welsh slate quarry and the opportunity for kids to take a short ride on a miniature train (£1.50) or tram (£1).

St Michael's church

Old Church Rd • Sun 10am–5pm • Otherwise obtain key from Conwy Valley Railway Museum or TIC

A lych gate and ancient yews frame the fourteenth-century **St Michael's church**, interesting for its whitewashed interior, specifically the thirteenth-century font and a carved effigy of an armoured knight, whose inscription identifies him as Gruffydd ap Dafydd Goch, the grandson of Llywelyn ap Gruffydd's brother, Prince Dafydd.

A BRIEF HISTORY OF BETWS-Y-COED

Betws-y-Coed was founded in the fifth or sixth century, when a monastic cell earned the settlement the moniker of the "oratory in the forest". Apart from some lead mining, it remained a backwater until 1808, when the Irish Mail came this way along Telford's A5 (now the town's High Street) and over the graceful cast-iron **Waterloo Bridge** of 1815, complete with spandrels which use the emblems (rose, thistle, shamrock and leek) of the four countries of the then newly formed United Kingdom.

ACTIVITIES AROUND BETWS-Y-COED

Adventure centre For a dose of vertigo, head for Tree Top Adventure, A470, 1 mile east (daily: May–Sept 10am–5pm, Oct–April 10am–4pm; ☎ 01690 710914, ⓦ ttadventure.co.uk), where you can test your balance and nerve while tethered on a raised course through the treetops (£25). Their Powerfan plummet (£20, £10 with ropes course combo) allows you to safely jump off a 100ft-high platform, if you dare. There's also an orienteering course (£2) and opportunities to try rock climbing, gorge walking and just about anything else offered in the area.

Climbing, scrambling and gorge walking Serenventures, Vicarage Rd (☎ 01690 710754, ⓦ serenventures.com), offer a range of fun activities in the hills nearby. Spend a half-day climbing, scrambling or gorge walking (£45), or combine activities into a full day out (from £80).

Fishing With a rod licence (available from any post office; £3.75 for 1 day, £10 for 8), anglers can try hooking salmon and sea trout on stretches of the Conwy and Llugwy within the village (£18 a day; mid-March to mid-Oct), and brown and American brook trout on Llyn Elsi in the hills just south (£15 a day; late March to late Oct only). For permits, a limited range of tackle and worms visit Pendyffryn Stores, on Holyhead Rd.

Horseriding Gwydyr Riding and Trekking Stables, 4 miles south of Betws-y-Coed in Penmachno (☎ 01690 760248, ⓦ horse-riding-wales.co.uk), will take you for an hour (£22), two hours (£32), or their entertaining pub ride (£45).

Mine exploring Book a day or two in advance and set the afternoon aside to join Go Below (☎ 01690 710108, ⓦ www.go-below.co.uk), exploring magical old mine workings, usually slate. With a harness, helmet and headlamp you'll get a nice balance between learning about the mine and getting active on ziplines, abseils and even paddling across a small lake (though all these can be bypasssed if required). Minimum age 10; £40.

Mountain biking The Gwydyr Forest Park, north and west of the village, is one of the top trail-riding locales in Wales. The classic route is the Marin Trail (78-mile loop; 2–4hr) with mostly forest track ascents and numerous single-track descents of varying difficulty. The scenery is great, with mountain views along the higher sections. Bike rental is available from Planet Fear, Holyhead Rd (hardtails £17 a half day, £25 a full day; full suspension £27/35; ☎ 01690 710888, ⓦ planetfear.co.uk), and Beics Betws (☎ 01690 710766, ⓦ bikewales.co.uk), in the street up behind the post office, who offer hardtails (£26 a day).

Fairy Glen

A mile or so southeast of the village, after negotiating a continuous series of tortuous rapids, the churning waters of the Conwy negotiate a staircase of drops and enter **Fairy Glen**, a cleft in a small wood which takes its name from the Welsh fairies, the Tylwyth Teg, who are said to be seen hereabouts. Take the A470 towards Blaenau Ffestiniog and turn up the lane beside the *Fairy Glen Hotel*. From the car park here (£1) a short path (30min loop; 50p) leads to the glen.

Conwy Falls

Just southeast of Fairy Glen, the River Conwy plunges 50ft over the **Conwy Falls** into a deep pool. After slotting £1 into the turnstile beside the *Conwy Falls Café* (reached by the #64 bus 8 times daily), you can view the falls on the right and a series of rock steps to the left, cut in 1863 as a kind of primitive fish ladder, which is now superseded by a tunnel through the rock on the far side.

Tŷ Mawr Wybrnant

Penmachno, 5 miles south of Betws-y-Coed • Late March–Oct Thurs–Sun noon–5pm • £3 • ☎ 01690 760213 • NT

Just above Conwy Falls is the river's confluence with the River Machno, which drains the hills around the small village of **Penmachno**, a couple of miles upstream. Some two and a half miles beyond Penmachno stands the isolated cottage of **Tŷ Mawr Wybrnant**. Here, Bishop William Morgan, the man who first translated the Bible into Welsh (see p.400), was born in 1545 and lived until his teenage years, when he decamped to Gwydyr Castle to pursue his education. The original cottage has been restored to something like its sixteenth-century appearance: all bare stone and beams, with a gaping fireplace supporting a huge, sagging beam dating back to the thirteenth century. Its star attraction is the collection of Bibles and prayer books, including a Morgan original.

Capel Garmon Burial Chamber

0.5 mile south of Capel Garmon, 2 miles southeast of Betws-y-Coed • Open access • Free • CADW

Neolithic dwellers left their mark at the **Capel Garmon Burial Chamber**, a heavily reconstructed, multi-chambered burial site built between 2500 and 1900 BC. It's an atmospheric spot, comprising some rough stones lining a series of linked pits, with a central chamber covered by an enormous capstone. The site is a five-minute signposted walk across farmland from the road.

Swallow Falls

A5, 2 miles west of Betws-y-Coed • Open all times • £1.50

Easy access makes **Swallow Falls** (a mistranslation of *Rhaeadr Ewynnol*, or "foaming cataract") one of the region's most-visited sights, but it's really no more than a straightforward, pretty waterfall with the occasional mad kayaker scraping down the precipitous rock. A path leads you down from a turnstile to a series of viewing platforms.

Tŷ Hyll

A5, 3 miles west of Betws-y-Coed • Generally mid-July to mid-Sept 10am–5pm and whenever volunteers are available • £1 •
Ⓦ snowdonia-society.org.uk

As the A5 crosses the Llugwy you can't miss **Tŷ Hyll**, known as the "Ugly House" for its chunky appearance. Decked out with period furniture and surrounded by a cottage garden, wildlife pond, and forest full of easy paths, it is also the headquarters of the Snowdonia Society, an environmental campaigning group which lobbies to preserve the region's ecological and social integrity.

ARRIVAL AND DEPARTURE   BETWS-Y-COED

Trains on the scenic Conwy Valley Railway (see box, p.344) arrive at the central train station serving: Blaenau Ffestiniog (6 daily; 30min), Llandudno Junction (6 daily; 30min), Llandudno (6 daily; 50min) and Llanrwst (6 daily; 5min).

Buses (including the Snowdon Sherpa) fan out from near the train station to: Blaenau Ffestiniog (9 daily; 20min); Capel Curig (hourly; 10min); Idwal Cottage (5 daily; 20min); Llandudno (9 daily; 50min); Llanberis (7 daily; 30min); Llanrwst (every 30min; 10min); Penmachno (8 daily; 10min); Pen-y-Pass (6 daily; 15min).

INFORMATION

Tourist information The TIC is in Royal Oak Stables (daily: Easter to mid-Oct 9.30am–5.30pm; mid-Oct to Easter 9.30am–4.30pm; ☎01690 710426, ⊜tic.byc @eryri-npa.gov.uk), and has displays and a film giving a

quick overview of Snowdonia.
Internet access Free wi-fi at several cafés around the village; free wi-fi and internet at the library in Llanrwst.

ACCOMMODATION

Betws-y-Coed has plenty of **accommodation**, but has to cope with large numbers of visitors pushing prices up in the summer. Expect to pay a few pounds more than in other towns in Snowdonia, and don't be surprised to find the places listed below full if you arrive late in the day.

B&BS AND HOTELS

Aberconwy House Lôn Muriau, Llanrwst Rd ☎01690 710202, Ⓦaberconwy-house.co.uk. A friendly and well-appointed Victorian guesthouse, with doubles, twins and family rooms to suit most needs: four rooms enjoy superb views over Betws-y-Coed and the Llugwy Valley and one comes with a four-poster bed. To get there on foot, cross the suspension bridge behind the train station; by car, take

the A470 towards Llanrwst. **£70**

★ **Bod Gwynedd** A5, 0.5 mile towards Capel Curig ☎01690 710717, Ⓦbodgwynedd.com. Welcoming B&B in a Victorian house on the edge of the village with uncluttered rooms, crisp, white linen, powerful showers and excellent breakfasts. One room with a four-poster. **£70**
Glan Llugwy A5 towards Capel Curig, 300yd beyond Pont-y-Pair ☎01690 710592, Ⓦglanllugwy.co.uk. One

CONWY VALLEY RAILWAY

If you love train journeys, don't miss riding the **Conwy Valley Railway** (ⓦ conwy.gov.uk/cvr), one of the more beautiful sections of the National Rail network. It is a gorgeous run from Llandudno Junction (near Conwy) through the pastures of the Conwy Valley to Betws-y-Coed, then through the twisting Lledr Valley. Deciduous and pine forests give way to the smooth, grassy slopes of the Moel Siabod before the route bores through over two miles of slate – the longest rail tunnel in Wales – to Blaenau Ffestiniog.

6

of the cheapest B&Bs around, with one en suite. Helpful owners and good breakfasts. **£62**

★ **Gwydir Castle** B5106, 3 miles north ☎ 01492 641687, ⓦ gwydir-castle.co.uk. One of Wales' best opportunities to stay in an authentic castle that still maintains the air of a family home. Two splendid bedrooms have been fitted out in baronial style with four-poster beds, deep baths and elegantly eclectic decor. There's no TV but you can relax in the oak-panelled parlour, where a hearty breakfast is served. **£85**

Lion Inn B5384 at Gwytherin, 11 miles northeast ☎ 01745 860123, ⓦ thelion-inn.co.uk. For peace and relaxation (no TV, no internet, no mobile coverage) stay at this renovated pub in a tiny village in a fold of rolling hills. A couple of the tastefully upgraded rooms come with bathtub, and there's an extensive DVD library if a few pints in the pub doesn't suit. Breakfast and excellent meals (mains £11–15) are served in the bar or restaurant. **£88**

★ **Pengwern** Allt Dinas, 1.5 miles east on A5 ☎ 01690 710480, ⓦ snowdoniaaccommodation.co.uk. Beautiful, welcoming and tastefully decorated country house set in two acres of woods with guest lounge and just three rooms, two with valley views and one with a four-poster. All have a shower above a bath. There's also a separate self-catering cottage to let from around £360 a week in summer. **£78**

Penmachno Hall B4406 in Penmachno, 5 miles south ☎ 01690 760410, ⓦ penmachnohall.co.uk. There's a secluded feeling to this wonderfully hospitable country house in an 1862 former rectory set among two acres of grounds. All three bedrooms are very spacious, plus there's a sunny lounge (with log fire in winter), an honesty bar and breakfasts cooked to order. To save you having to drive into town they serve a 2-course supper (Tues–Fri; £17.50) but the real event is the inventive 5-course dinner (Sat only £37.50). **£85**

Tan-y-Foel Capel Garmon (A470 towards Llanrwst, then turn right after 2 miles) ☎ 01690 710507, ⓦ tyfhotel.co.uk. Ultramodern public spaces and stylish, luxurious rooms in a sixteenth-century farmhouse make this one of the best small country hotels in the district, with

sweeping views across eight acres of grounds to the Conwy Valley, and outstanding three-course dinners (£49). **£115**

HOSTELS AND CAMPING

Hendre Farm Holyhead Rd, 0.5 mile towards Capel Curig ☎ 07879 437778. The closest tent site to the village with basic facilities including coin-op showers. Per person **£8**

Lledr House A470, 5 miles southwest ☎ 01690 750202, ⓦ ukyh.com. For a real rural experience go for this independent hostel (a former YHA) that makes an ideal starting point for a walk up Moel Siabod. It has beds in double, twin and family rooms with self-catering facilities (bedding included). There's Sky TV, free wi-fi and it's a 10min walk from Pont-y-Pant train station. Dorms **£13.50**

★ **Rynys Farm** A5, 2 miles southeast near the Conwy Falls ☎ 01690 710218, ⓦ rynys-camping.co.uk. Charming and very clean farm campsite and caravan park on undulating terrain with plenty of flat sites tucked behind trees or against dry-stone walls. It's wonderfully peaceful with great valley views and good facilities (hook-ups £3). Also an on-site caravan for two adults and two kids (£40), and handy for the Conwy Falls Café. Per person **£7**

★ **The Vagabond** Craiglan Rd ☎ 01690 710850, ⓦ thevagabond.co.uk. Excellent and central independent hostel with 36 bunks (with sheets) in 4- to 8-bunk dorms, and good facilities including free internet and wi-fi, secure bike lockup and off-street parking. There's a self-catering kitchen but they also serve good breakfasts (£5), evening meals (£7) and have an inexpensive bar with seating on the patio. Bookings recommended at weekends when B&B is obligatory. Bunks **£17**

YHA Betws-y-Coed A5, 2 miles west of Betws-y-Coed ☎ 01690 710796, ⓦ swallowfallshotel.co.uk. Pleasant, modern hostel with dorms, and rooms (including a double and two twins), plus breakfasts and packed lunches available (both £5). It's next door to the Swallow Falls Hotel (which has a bar, restaurant and £3 sauna), and a nice campsite (£6 per person). Dorms **£16**, rooms **£40**

EATING AND DRINKING

Many of the more visible cafés and restaurants along Betws-y-Coed main road are quite mediocre, but better options do exist, both in the village and close by in Llanrwst and Capel Curig. **Entertainment** doesn't usually stretch much further than a beer in one of the pubs, though a couple of **male-voice choirs** give performances during summer: a different choir performs each week in St Mary's church (Sun at 8pm; £5), and there's a free performance every second Friday (8.30–10pm) at The Stables. Also check the website of Cantorion Colin Jones (ⓦ cantorioncolinjones.co.uk) for local performances and rehearsals.

Alpine Coffee Shop Betws-y-Coed train station ☎01690 710747. Bright daytime café with art on the walls and an appealing range of sandwiches, wraps and vegetarian dishes, as well as 45 speciality teas, and espresso. Mon–Fri 8.30am–5.30pm, Sat & Sun 8am–5.30pm.

Bistro Betws-y-Coed Holyhead Rd ☎01690 710328. Casual, wood-floored restaurant with a strong Welsh bias and an emphasis on local produce. Lunch may just be sandwiches (£7–9) or Glamorgan sausage with a basil and tomato sauce (£9), but everything is well presented. Dinners might stretch to breasts of local wood pigeon with a chilli-spiced plum jam (£5) followed by Menai Strait sea bass with a garlic, leek and chorizo stir-fry (£15). Daily noon–10pm.

★ **Conwy Falls Café** A5, 2 miles south ☎01690 710696, ⓦconwyfalls.com. The owners are passionate about the quality of the food, enormous range of teas and the superb coffee at this relaxed café in a Clough Williams-Ellis-designed building by the path to Conwy Falls. Expect the likes of beef lasagne, spinach and mushroom burger and Ploughman's lunches, plus free wi-fi and a good stack of books to browse. They also open Fri & Sat evenings all year for great build-your-own pizza and occasionally host music events: check the website. Easter to mid-Oct Mon–Thurs & Sun 9am–4pm, Fri & Sat 9am–9pm; mid-Oct–Easter Fri & Sat 9am–9pm, Sun 9am–4pm.

The Stables Royal Oak Hotel, High St ☎01690 710219. The village's liveliest bar, with good beer, stacks of outdoor seating, sports TV, jazz on summer Thurs, and a good range of bar food, pizzas and grills at reasonable prices. Their signature haddock, chips and mushy peas is good value at £8. Daily 11am–11pm.

Tan-y-Foel Capel Garmon (A470 towards Llanrwst, then turn right after 2 miles) ☎01690 710507, ⓦtyfhotel.co.uk. The Modern British cuisine (£49 for three courses) is the highlight of any stay here. The restaurant only seats ten, and everything is carefully cooked to order. Expect the likes of duck breast with spiced pearl barley and pear chutney followed by wild turbot, Conwy crab and squid ink risotto. Guests have priority for reservations and smart dress is required. Daily 7–11pm.

★ **Tŷ Gwyn** A5, 0.5 mile southeast ☎01690 710383, ⓦtygwynhotel.co.uk. Superb wood-beamed former coaching inn with excellent meals served either in the wonderfully intimate low-roofed bar or the slightly more formal restaurant. There are both bar meals (£10) and a separate à la carte menu (mains around £15) but, except at busy times, both menus are available in both rooms. Expect anything from wild mushroom stroganoff to lamb Wellington. Daily 11am–11pm.

6

WALKS AROUND BETWS-Y-COED

These two lowland walks explore the valleys and waterfalls on the outskirts of the village. Neither is circular, so unless you plan to hitch back, consult bus timetables first to avoid a long wait for the infrequent services.

Conwy Gorge walk (3 miles; 1hr 15min; descent only). An easy walk which links two of the district's best-known natural attractions, Fairy Glen and the Conwy Falls (see p.342), by way of a cool green lane (once the main road into Betws-y-Coed) giving glimpses of the river through the beech woods. Catch the #64 bus (8 daily) to the *Conwy Falls Café*, then after having a look at the falls, walk 150yd back along the road towards Betws-y-Coed and follow a traffic-free lane (the original road into the village) parallel to the river through the trees. After about half an hour, you'll see the gate to Fairy Glen on your left. Returning to the main path, continue to the *Fairy Glen Hotel*, where you can cross the river by Beaver Bridge, turn right and follow a minor road a mile back to the village.

Llugwy Valley walk (6 miles; 2hr 30min; 600ft ascent). The car park on the north side of the Pont-y-Pair bridge marks the beginning of a forested path following the twisting and plunging river upstream to Capel Curig. With the A5 running parallel to the river all the way, there are several opportunities to cut short the walk and wait for the bus back to Betws-y-Coed. Less than a mile from Pont-y-Pair, you first reach a ford where the Roman road Sarn Helen crossed the river, then pass the steeply sloping Miners' Bridge, which linked miners' homes at Pentre Du on the south side of the river to the lead mines in the Gwydyr Forest. With its plunge pools and rocky diving platforms this is a wonderfully refreshing place to take a dip. The path follows the river on your left for another mile to a slightly obscured view of Swallow Falls. Detailed maps available from the tourist office in Betws-y-Coed show numerous routes back through the Gwydyr Forest, or you can continue half a mile to the road bridge by Tŷ Hyll and follow the right bank to Capel Curig, passing the scant remains of the Caer Llugwy, a Roman fort, and a couple more treacherous rapids: The Mincer and Cobden's Falls.

Llanrwst and around

The Conwy River heads north from Betws-y-Coed along its broad pastoral corridor to the sea. Five miles along the Conwy Valley lies **LLANRWST**, once the largest wool market in north Wales. It had a spell as a centre for harp manufacture in the eighteenth century, and is still the most economically important town in the valley, retaining Wednesday and Friday livestock **markets**, and a general one each Tuesday on the central Ancaster Square.

6

Llanrwst Almshouse Museum

1 Church St • Tues–Fri 10.30am–3.30pm, Sat & Sun noon–3.30pm • £2 • ☏ 01492 642550, ⓦ llanrwstalmshouses.org.uk

Llanrwst Almshouse Museum occupies a set of almshouses which date back to 1610 and were still in use until 1976. Two rooms are done in period style (1610 and 1850), while exhibits in others cover the town's history and detail the lives of some of the residents.

St Gwrst Church

Church St • **Church** free **South transept** • £1 donation requested

St Gwrst Church contains an intricately carved rood screen thought to have come from Maenan Abbey, a few miles downstream, after it was dissolved by Henry VIII in 1536. In the south transept (entered through a separate door) lies the thirteenth-century carved stone coffin (minus its lid) of Llywelyn the Great.

Tu Hwnt i'r Bont and Pont Fawr

It sometimes seem like half of Llanrwst's visitors are photographing **Tu Hwnt i'r Bont**, a tearoom in a fifteenth-century former courthouse entirely smothered in Virginia creeper. It is approached over the beautifully proportioned, humpback **Pont Fawr** (Big Bridge), and was at least designed by the great seventeenth-century architect, Inigo Jones, who is said to have spent his early years in Llanrwst. In summer, its single lane struggles to cope with the traffic across it.

Gwydir Castle

B5106, 0.5 mile west of Llanrwst • March–Oct daily except Mon & Sat 10am–4pm • £4 • ☏ 01492 641687, ⓦ gwydir-castle.co.uk

Most of the land around Betws-y-Coed and along the Conwy Valley was once part of the Gwydyr Estate owned by the Wynn family. Descended from the kings of Gwynedd, they were the most powerful dynasty in the region until the male line died out in 1678; several place names are reminders of the family's might. Foremost of these is **Gwydir Castle**, actually a low-slung manor house begun around 1490 on the site of a fortified house a century older. Despite additions in the sixteenth and nineteenth centuries, with parts plundered from the post-dissolution Maenan Abbey, the ivy- and wisteria-covered building is a fabulous model of early Tudor architecture.

Its core is a three-storey solar tower, whose windows relieve the gloom of the great halls, each with enormous fireplaces and stone-flagged or heavy timber floors. Most of the original fittings and Tudor furniture were sold in 1921, and much of the rest of the house was ruined in a fire a few months later. The subsequent restoration was kept simple – tapestries cover the solid stone walls, a few tables and chairs are scattered about and there's some fine painted glass. Some of the original furnishings have been tracked down, including the heavily carved oak panels, Baroque door-case and fireplace, and abundant gilded Spanish leather of the magnificent **Dining Room**. This was initially installed by Richard Wynn around 1642, and is attributed to Inigo Jones. The complete set was bought during the 1921 sell-off by American newspaper magnate William Randolph Hearst and shipped across the Atlantic. New York's Metropolitan Museum acquired it in 1956 and kept it boxed up for forty years until it was sold back to the castle in 1996 and re-installed.

Outside, the main attraction is the **Dutch Garden**, with its fountain, peacocks and cedars of Lebanon dating back to 1625. There's also excellent accommodation (see p.344).

Trefriw Woollen Mills

B5106 in Trefriw, 2 miles northwest of Llanrwst **Mill** Easter–Sept Mon–Fri 10am–1pm & 2–5pm **Shop** daily: April–Oct 9.30am–5.30pm, Nov–March 10am–5pm • Free • ☎ 01492 640462, ⊕ t-w-m.co.uk

The small village of Trefriw is home to the **Trefriw Woollen Mills**, where rugs, throws and bedspreads are made to traditional Welsh geometric designs using late nineteenth-century weaving methods, all driven by the power of Afon Crafnant which flows right by the mill. The full fleece-to-fabric process is explained and you can often see old looms weaving away. Naturally, there's a big shop: double bedspreads start around £200 but there are cheaper goods.

6

Llyn Crafnant

A road close to the woollen mills is signposted two miles southwest to **Llyn Crafnant**, a calm lake beautifully hemmed in by low crags. It is a gorgeous spot for an **easy stroll** around the lake (3-mile loop; 2hr; almost flat): park at the obvious Forestry Commission car park. The walk passes the simple *Lakeside Café* with tables on the lawn right beside the lake. Here you can also buy a permit for **trout fishing** (⊕ crafnantfishing.co.uk) in the stocked lake.

Trains on the Conwy Valley line and many of the region's **buses** stop close to Ancaster Square.

INFORMATION

Internet access Free at the library (Mon, Wed & Fri 10am–5.30pm, Wed 10am–7pm, Sat 10am–1pm) on Station Rd just north of town.

EATING AND DRINKING

★ **The Tannery** Willow St ☎ 01492 641655. Locally born chef, Gerwyn Williams, brings a Modern Welsh sensibility to this delightful loft bistro with a short menu of inventive and nicely presented à la carte evening meals (most mains around £16) in a relaxed setting. Vegetarians are well catered for and they do fine Sunday lunches. Wed & Sun 10am–4pm, Thurs–Sat 10am–4pm & 6–9.30pm.

Tu Hwnt i'r Bont B5106 ☎ 01492 642322, ⊕ tuhwntirbont.co.uk. Classic, low-beamed tearoom "beyond the bridge" (as it translates from Welsh) that's great for soup and fresh sandwiches but essential for the excellent cream teas (with sultana scones, good jam and leaf tea). Head to the small gallery upstairs if only to experience the ancient stone stairway. Mid-March to mid-June, Sept & Oct Tues–Sun 10.30am–5pm; mid-June to Aug daily 10.30am–5pm; Nov–Christmas Sat & Sun 10.30am–5pm.

Capel Curig

Following the A5 and the River Llugwy west from Betws-y-Coed, you soon pass Swallow Falls and Tŷ Hyll, then continue upstream past a number of roadside cataracts – most notably opposite *Cobden's Hotel*. Tantalizing glimpses of Wales' highest

HIKING MOEL SIABOD FROM CAPEL CURIG

5 miles; 4hr; 2200ft. OS maps: Landranger 115 or Explorer OL17.
Despite Capel Curig's popularity among hikers, the only major **walk** from here is up the grassy-backed **Moel Siabod** (2861ft), a challenging ridge walk with views of the Snowdon Horseshoe. Start opposite the *Plas Curig* hostel, cross the concrete bridge and follow the right bank downstream past the falls by *Cobden's Hotel* to the Pont Cyfyng road bridge (30min), an alternative starting point for the walk. Take the road south and turn right on the second path signposted to Moel Siabod. You pass a disused slate quarry before the long scramble up the east ridge which weaves around outcrops where a moment's inattention could be disastrous. Once you've admired the summit view of the Snowdon Horseshoe, turn northeast and follow the craggy summit ridge, which drops across grass to the moors below, soon rejoining your ascent route for the hike back to Pont Cyfyng.

mountains flash through the forested banks as you climb to **Capel Curig**. There's scarcely a building in this tiny, walker-frequented village that isn't of some use to hikers, making it a perfect base for the walk up Moel Siabod (see box below) and for the two valleys that plunge westwards deep into the mountains. The A4086 follows Nant Gwryd southwest to the Snowdon massif, while the A5 prises apart the Carneddau and Glyder ranges to the northwest, forging through the Ogwen Valley.

6

Plas y Brenin: The National Mountain Centre

A4086, 400yd south of the centre **Climbing wall** daily 10am–11pm • £5 **Dry ski slope** daily 10am–4pm • £8/hr including ski rental, £30/hr for instruction; call for availability • ☎ 01690 720214, ⓦ www.pyb.co.uk

Built around a former coaching inn and hotel, **Plas y Brenin** runs internationally renowned residential courses in hiking, mountaineering, kayaking, skiing and rock climbing (see p.54). If you're just passing through and don't have your own equipment, the two-hour indoor climbing, lake canoeing and dry-slope skiing sessions held during August and other school holidays (£15) may be of interest. Kids who want a full-day taster of canoeing, skiing and abseiling can be left on the "3 in a Day" adventure session (£35), where adults are welcome too. There is also a climbing wall, a dry ski slope and bar. Plas-y-Brenin also rents out all kinds of hiking, camping and mountaineering gear at reasonable prices, and posts daily mountain weather forecasts at reception.

WALKS FROM THE OGWEN VALLEY

Use the OS 1:25,000 OL17 ("Snowdon & Conwy Valley") or the 1:50,000 115 ("Snowdon/Yr Wyddfa") map. For a general layout see our Snowdonia map.

Tourists hike up Snowdon, but mountain connoisseurs almost invariably prefer the sharply angled peaks of the **Glyderau**, with their challenging terrain, an entertaining high-level jump at the summit of **Tryfan**, cantilevered rocks and fantastic views back to Snowdon. We've outlined three walks on Tryfan and one on the Glyderau, but with a map you can plan all manner of more complex variations.

The appearance of the **Carneddau**, on the other side of the Ogwen Valley, could hardly be in greater contrast. These peaceful giants, which present the longest stretch of ground over three thousand feet in Wales, form a rounded plateau stretching to the cliffs of Penmaenmawr on the north coast. The sound of a raven in the neighbouring mist-filled cwms, and the occasional wild pony, can often be your only company on inclement days, but in fine weather the easy walking and roof-of-the-world views make for a satisfying day out.

TRYFAN

Miners' Track (5 miles; 4–6hr; 2000ft ascent). The standard route up Tryfan, from the car park at Idwal Cottage. Take the path to Cwm Idwal then, as it bears sharply to the right, keep straight ahead and make for Bwlch Tryfan, the gap on the horizon between Tryfan and Glyder Fach. From there, the **South Ridge of Tryfan** climbs past the Far South Peak to the summit: this last section is an easy scramble, so you'll need to use your hands. Anyone who has seen pictures of people jumping the 5ft gap between **Adam and Eve**, the two chunks of rhyolitic lava which crown this regal mountain, will wonder what the fuss is about until they get up there and see the mountain dropping away on all sides. In theory the leap is trivial, but the consequences of overshooting would be disastrous. Return the way you came.

Tryfan via Heather Terrace (4 miles; 4–6hr; 2000ft ascent). You'll need a reasonable sense of adventure to enjoy the ascent via Heather Terrace, which follows a fault in the rock running diagonally across the east face. The route starts in the lay-by at the head of Idwal Lake and goes left across rising ground before finding your way onto the exposed "terrace". This ends at the col between South and the Far South peaks, where a right turn then starts your scramble for the summit. Descend the way you came or by the Miners' Track.

North Ridge of Tryfan (3–4 miles; 4hr–6hr; 2000ft ascent). If you've got the head for it this is one of the most rewarding scrambles in the country. It's not as precarious as Snowdon's Crib Goch, but you get a genuine mountaineering feel as the valley floor drops rapidly away and

ARRIVAL AND DEPARTURE

CAPEL CURIG

Buses Snowdon Sherpa buses (see p.340) serve Betws-y-Coed (hourly; 10min), Idwal Cottage (5 daily; 10min), Llanberis (7 daily; 30min) and Pen-y-Pass (6 daily; 10min).

ACCOMMODATION

Bron Eryri A5, 1 mile outside the village towards Betws-y-Coed ☎01690 720240, ⓦwww.eryriguesthouse.fsnet.co.uk. Four comfortable bedrooms and a cosy residents' lounge, plus breakfast served with a view of Moel Siabod. Two-night minimum at summer weekends. **£60**

Bryn Tyrch Campsite A5, 600yd towards Betws-y-Coed ☎01690 720414. Basic grassy site with token showers and very simple bunkhouses (bring everything). Bunks **£7**, camping per person **£4**

Bryn Tyrch Inn A5, 500yd towards Betws-y-Coed ☎01690 720223, ⓦbryntyrchinn.co.uk. Modernized twelve-room inn offering simple but tasteful rooms with well-appointed bathrooms and TV. Also has four-bunk rooms (£25 per person B&B, minimum 3 in one room).

Two-night minimum stay at weekends; midweek and off-season discounts often available. **£85**

Plas Curig A5, 500yd towards Betws-y-Coed ☎01690 720225, ⓦsnowdoniahostel.co.uk. Family-run deluxe backpackers in a revamped former YHA that was yet to open in its new guise when we visited. It offers bunk rooms (with privacy curtains, bed lights and lockable storage), doubles, twins and family rooms (no en suites). Residents can come and go all day, but must check in between 6pm and 10pm. Closed Dec & Jan. Bunks **£20**, rooms **£50**

★ **St Curig's church** A5, by the junction in the heart of the village ☎01690 720469, ⓦstcurigschurch.com. Great B&B fashioned from a former church which comes complete with a domed gilded mosaic of Christ in the pool

the views stretch further and further along it. The route starts in the lay-by at the head of Idwal Lake and goes left across rising ground, until you strike a path heading straight up following the crest of the ridge to the 3010ft summit. Return via Heather Terrace or the Miners' Track.

THE GLYDERAU

Glyder Traverse (6 miles; 5–8hr; 2500ft ascent). This excellent day out is a fairly rugged undertaking (with some moderate scrambling) but very rewarding. From Idwal Cottage, follow Tryfan's Miners' Track to Bwlch Tryfan where (by adding an extra hour) you can also tick off the summit of Tryfan. From Bwlch Tryfan, scramble up Bristly Ridge which runs steeply south past some daunting-looking towers of rock. In good conditions it isn't so difficult, but it should be avoided in winter unless you're suitably skilled and equipped. The ridge ends at the summit of **Glyder Fach** (3260ft), a chaotic jumble of huge grey slabs that many people don't bother climbing up, preferring to be photographed on a massive **cantilevered rock** a few yards away.

From Glyder Fach, it is an easy enough stroll to **Glyder Fawr** (3280ft), reached by skirting round the tortured rock formations of **Castell y Gwynt** (the Castle of the Winds), then following a cairn-marked path to the dramatic summit of frost-shattered slabs angled like ancient headstones. The descent initially follows loose scree down to Llyn Cwn where you turn north, zigzagging down Twll Du (The Devil's Kitchen) to Llyn Idwal and back to Idwal Cottage.

THE CARNEDDAU

Carnedd Loop (9 miles; 5hr; 3500ft ascent). This fine day out, taking in the range's four mighty southern peaks, has less objective danger than the walks on Tryfan and the Glyderau but is just as exhausting. Start from the lay-by at the head of the lake near Tal y Llyn Ogwen farm and head right of the farm towards a small lake, Ffynnon Lloer, before turning left up the east ridge of **Pen yr Ole Wen** (3212ft), with its magnificent view down into Nant Ffrancon and back to Tryfan. In clear weather, you can see your route running north past **Carnedd Fach**, and what looks to be a huge artificial mound, to **Carnedd Dafydd** (3425ft). After a short easterly descent, the path skirts the steep Ysgolion Duon cliffs, then climbs over stones to the broad, arched top of **Carnedd Llywelyn** (3491ft), the highest of the Carneddau.

Descend towards Craig yr Ysfa, a sheer cliff which drops away into the vast amphitheatre of Cwm Eigiau to the north. Continuing with care, skirt around the north of Ffynnon Llugwy reservoir and climb to the grassy top of **Penyrhelgi-du** (2733ft), from where there's a steady broad-ridged descent to the road near Helyg. The mile-long trek back west to the starting point is best done on the old packhorse route running parallel to the A5, and linked to it occasionally by footpaths.

and TV room. There are six very comfortable rooms, two four-poster doubles, two twins, and two (one with Snowdon view) which share the family's bathroom (complete with deep bath). A recess off the lounge has bunks for four, and everyone has access to a hot tub with views of the stars and mountains. Dorms including breakfast **£20**, rooms **£70**

EATING AND DRINKING

★ **Bryn Tyrch Inn** A5, 0.3 miles towards Betws-y-Coed ☎01690 720223, ⓦbryntyrchinn.co.uk. A warm and lively restaurant and bar with real ales, garden seating and a wonderful view of Snowdon. Quality bar meals (mains mostly £12–17) might include chargrilled lamb burger or haddock and salmon fishcakes, plus there are lots of vegetarian choices. You might need a hard day in the hills to justify one of their delectable desserts. Food available daily noon–2.30pm & 6–9pm.

Snowdon Bar Plas y Brenin ☎01690 720214. Outdoor enthusiasts' bar with a couple of its own brews, including the excellent *Bootliquor*. As well as serving good-value bar meals (daily noon–2pm & 7–9pm) it hosts talks and slide shows of recent international expeditions (usually Mon, Wed & Sat at 8pm; free), has cheap internet access and free wi-fi. Meals served daily noon–2pm & 7–9pm.

The Ogwen Valley

Northwest of Capel Curig the gentle **Ogwen Valley** follows the Ogwen River towards the tatty village of Bethesda, home to one of Wales' last operational slate quarries. The frequently mist-shrouded and rounded Carnedd range to the north glowers across at the spiky Glyder range and its triple-peaked **Tryfan**, arguably Snowdonia's most demanding mountain. This forms a fractured spur out from the main range and blocks your view down the valley, the twin monoliths of Adam and Eve that crown Tryfan's summit picked out on the skyline. The courageous (or foolhardy) make the jump between them as a point of honour at the end of every ascent. West of Tryfan, the road follows a perfect example of a U-shaped valley, carved and smoothed by rocks frozen into the undersides of the glaciers that creaked down **Nant Ffrancon** ten thousand years ago.

In the middle of the valley is **Llyn Ogwen**, a post-glacial lake formed behind time-compacted moraine left by the retreating ice. At its western end stands **IDWAL COTTAGE**, the only settlement in the valley and so small it isn't named on most maps, comprising just a mountain rescue centre, a snack bar and a YHA hostel clustered around a car park. The main reason to come here is to tackle some of Wales' most challenging and rewarding hikes, or start the easier twenty-minute walk to the magnificent, classically formed cirque, Cwm Idwal.

Cwm Idwal

Accessed from Idwal Cottage • NT

The Idwal Cottage car park is the starting point of an easy well-groomed path to **Cwm Idwal** (1.5 miles return; 1hr; 200ft ascent), a shallow mountain bowl which in 1954 became Wales' first **National Nature Reserve**. The evidence of glacial scouring is so clear here that you wonder why it took geologists so long to work out the process that created these hollowed faces and scored rocks. In 1842, Darwin recalled his visit with the geologist Adam Sedgewick eleven years earlier, noting "Neither of us saw a trace of the wonderful glacial phenomena all around us". The cwm's scalloped floor traps the beautifully limpid **Llyn Idwal**, which reflects the precipitous grey cliffs behind. The rowan, bilberry and heather in a small but luxuriant fenced-off control area show how the area might look in a few decades' time if the authorities succeed in keeping sheep out of the cwm, though this is proving problematic. Tackling the paths right around the lake can turn this into a half-day outing.

Twll Du

The back of Cwm Idwal is marked by a dark chasm known as **Twll Du**, literally "black cleft" but dubbed the Devil's Kitchen by Victorian visitors. Down this channel, a fine watery haze runs off the flanks of **Glyder Fawr**, soaking the crevices where early botanists found rare arctic-alpine plants (see Contexts, p.455). This is one of the few places where you can see the downfolded strata of what is known as the Snowdon syncline, evidence that the existing mountains sat between two much larger ranges some 300 million years ago. To their left, the smooth inclines of the **Idwal Slabs** act as nursery slopes for budding rock climbers.

Rhaeadr Ogwen

A five-minute walk down the valley from the Idwal Cottage car park, the road crosses a bridge over the top of **Rhaeadr Ogwen** (Ogwen Falls), which cascades down this step in the valley floor. Before you put your camera away, look under the road bridge, where you'll see the simple mortarless arch of a bridge, part of the original packhorse route that followed the valley before Telford pushed the Holyhead road through.

6

ARRIVAL AND DEPARTURE   **OGWEN VALLEY**

By bus Five buses a day run along the valley between Bethesda and Capel Curig, with connections to Betws-y-Coed and Bangor.

On foot A footpath covers the length of the valley from Capel Curig to Idwal Cottage, following a five-mile packhorse route which runs parallel to the fast and fairly busy road.

ACCOMMODATION, EATING AND DRINKING

★ **Gwern Gôf Uchaf** A5, 4 miles west of Capel Curig ☎ 01690 720294, ⓦ tryfanwales.co.uk. Superbly sited campsite right at the base of Tryfan with a modern shower block, and a good fourteen-berth bunkhouse with a fully equipped kitchen and a drying room: bring a sleeping bag and food. Per person £5, bunkhouse £10

Ogwen Falls Snack Bar ☎ 01248 600683. Sandwiches, crisps and chocolate bars to take away; the only food available between Capel Curig and Bethesda. Daily

8.30am–5pm, later at summer weekends.

YHA Idwal Cottage A5, 5 miles west of Capel Curig ☎ 0845 371 9744, ⓔ idwal@yha.org.uk. Perfectly sited for walkers, this recently refurbished but traditional YHA in a former quarry manager's house has mostly four-bunk dorms, a double, a single, family rooms and an alcohol licence, but no meals. Opens 5pm. Closed all of Jan and weekdays in Nov, Dec & Feb. Dorms £18.40, rooms £48, camping £9.50

Llanberis and Snowdon

To any mountain enthusiasts, **LLANBERIS**, ten miles west of Capel Curig, is inextricably linked with **Snowdon**, not least because of the five-mile umbilical cord of the **Snowdon Mountain Railway**, which bonds the town to the summit. Llanberis is the nearest you'll get in Wales to an alpine climbing village, its single main street thronged with weather-beaten walkers and climbers decked out in Gore-Tex – high fashion for what is otherwise a dowdy town.

At the same time, Llanberis is very much a Welsh rural community, albeit a depleted one now that slate is no longer being torn from the flanks of Elidir Fawr. For the best part of two centuries, the **quarries** employed up to three thousand men to chisel out the precious slabs. They closed in 1969, leaving a vast staircase of 60ft-high terraced platforms and tiers of blue-grey rubble covering the mountainside as a testament to their labours. Yet it's an oddly compelling scene, especially when low cloud shrouds the workings and the hilltop **Dolbadarn Castle** looms from the murk like a lonely sentinel.

Soon after the quarries closed, proposals were tabled for a power station to be built over the former quarry sites on the fringes of the national park. Environmentalists were incensed, but the people of Llanberis, reeling from the closure of the quarries, had no such qualms. In the end both parties were pacified: the project went ahead underground as the **Dinorwig Power Station**.

When the sun breaks out, hiking competes with a choice of two **narrow-gauge railways** and myriad activities – from playing around in boats on the lake to scrambling, mountain biking and even scuba diving.

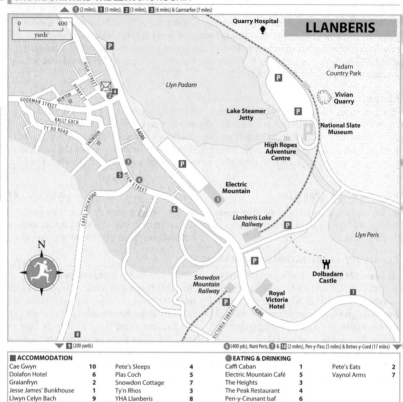

Snowdon Mountain Railway

A4086, opposite the Royal Victoria Hotel • Mid-March to Oct 6–25 trains daily • Summit return £25, one-way £18; phone booking fee £3.50; £6 discount if reserving for 9am train by phone a day in advance • ☎ 0870 720 0033, ⓦ www.snowdonrailway.co.uk

The **Snowdon Mountain Railway** is Britain's only rack-and-pinion railway, completed in 1896. Trains (sometimes pushed by seventy-year-old steam locos) still climb to the summit in just under an hour along the most heavily maintained track in the country. The rails follow the shallowest approach to the top of Snowdon, struggling for five miles and three thousand feet up a mostly one-in-eight gradient.

Times and type of locomotive vary with demand and season, but whether steam or diesel, the full round trip takes two and a half hours, with half an hour on top. From mid-March to mid-May (and during high winds), services terminate three-quarters of the way up at **Clogwyn Station**, thirty minutes' walk from the summit. In summer (especially July, Aug and weekends in June and Sept) trains are often full, so book a day or so in advance. If you walk up by one of the routes detailed on p.358, you can still hope for a stand-by spot on a train down: round-trip passengers get preference and you can't book.

Summit café

Open mid-May to Oct

From Llanberis the railway climbs past the summertime swimming hole at Bishop's Falls and across the mountain's bald slopes to the new *Hafod Eryri* **summit café**. Inside is a bar and a post office where, for a few pence, you can buy a "Railway Stamp" to affix to your letter – along with the Royal Mail one – thereby entitling you to enchant your friends with a "Summit of Snowdon – Copa'r Wyddfa" postmark.

Dinorwig Power Station and Electric Mountain

A4086 **Dinorwig Power Station underground tour** Easter–Oct daily, plus selected winter days • £7.75 • Book on ☎ 01286 870636, ⓦ electricmountain.co.uk **Electric Mountain** June–Aug daily 9.30am–5.30pm; Sept–May daily 10am–4.30pm • Free

Views north from Llanberis are dominated by the entrance to the **Dinorwig Pumped Storage Power Station**, hollowed out of the ground in the mid-1970s starting just five years after the quarries closed. The power station actually consumes more electricity than it produces, but benefits the national grid by being able to supply electricity instantly to cope with the early evening surge in demand. Within sixteen seconds it can attain 1300 megawatts, by letting the contents of the Marchlyn Mawr reservoir rapidly empty through its turbines into Llyn Peris; then, when the demand lessens, pumping it up again.

Visit the innards of the mountain on an hour-long **bus tour** through its rock-hewn tunnels to the powerhouse below. A film about the scheme's construction plays in the viewing gallery overlooking the turbine hall. This is one of Snowdonia's more popular rainy-day activities, so book ahead if the weather turns foul.

Underground tours of Dinorwig Power Station start from **Electric Mountain**, a building beside Llyn Padarn which contains a good café, a panel explaining Snowdon's microclimate (complete with a summit webcam) and an interesting little **boat display** featuring a twelfth-century wooden craft discovered near the lake in the 1970s.

Dolbadarn Castle

Open access • Free • CADW

Perched on a rock between the twin lakes of Llyn Padarn and Llyn Peris, where it once guarded the mouth of the Llanberis Pass, a single dramatic tower and some scattered masonry are all that remain of **Dolbadarn Castle**. Built in the thirteenth century, its construction is usually attributed to Llywelyn ap Iorwerth ("the Great"), even if its circular keep is more redolent of a Norman Marcher fort than a native Welsh castle. Close up, there's not a lot to look at, but, viewed across Llyn Padarn and framed by the grey crags of the Pass behind, it is easy to see why both Richard Wilson and Turner came to paint it.

Llanberis Lake Railway

July & Aug 4–10 services daily; mid-March to June, Sept & Oct 3–5 services daily • £7.40 return • ☎ 01286 870549, ⓦ lake-railway.co.uk

From 1843 to 1961, the original Padarn Railway transported slate and workers between the Dinorwig quarries and Port Dinorwig on the Menai Strait. When it closed it was sold for scrap, but enthusiasts subsequently relaid a two-mile stretch along the scenic shores of Lake Padarn as the family-oriented **Llanberis Lake Railway**. Plucky tank engines which once pulled slate around the quarries now take an hour for the sedate round trip, which includes a stop halfway back at **Cei Llydan** station where there is an idyllic picnic spot by the lake, a play area for kids and plenty of woodland walks up the slopes behind the rail tracks.

Padarn Country Park

Open access • Free

At **Padarn Country Park** lakeside oak woods are gradually recolonizing the discarded workings of the defunct **Dinorwig Slate Quarries**, formerly one of the largest slate quarries in the world. Equipment and engines that once hauled materials up inclined tramways have been partly restored and punctuate the paths which link the levels chiselled out of the hillside. One of the most interesting spots is right near the parking area, where you can walk through a rock arch to the flooded **Vivian Quarry**, a dramatic spot and a popular destination for **scuba divers**.

National Slate Museum

Easter–Oct daily 10am–5pm; Nov–Easter daily except Sat 10am–4pm • Free • ☎ 01286 870630, ⓦ museumwales.ac.uk

The fort-like former quarry's maintenance workshops now house Wales' **National Slate Museum** where a 50ft-diameter water wheel that once powered cutting machines through a cat's cradle of lineshafts and flapping belts still turns. Though most of the equipment dates back to the early part of the twentieth century, it was still in use until the quarries closed and is familiar to the former quarry workers who demonstrate their skills at turning an inch-thick slab of slate into six, even eight, perfectly smooth slivers. The slate was delivered to the slate-dressing sheds by means of a maze of tramways, cranes and rope lifts, all kept in good order in the fitting and repair shops. As you pass through, look out for the scales used to calculate the price each rock cutter would be paid for his work, before the typical deductions for the amount of rope and gunpowder he used to extract the diverse types of slate. Some of these are displayed nearby and range from mottled burgundy and bottle green to every shade of grey. Look out, too, for the set of slate workers' cottages furnished in the style of 1861, 1901 and 1969. To keep everything in working order, the craftsmen here operate a foundry, producing pieces for the scattered branches of the National Museum of Wales, as well as repairing the rolling stock that plies the adjacent **Llanberis Lake Railway**.

Quarry Hospital

500yd north of the Slate Museum • Easter & late May–Sept daily 11am–4.45pm; April and early May Sat & Sun 11am–4.45pm • Free

Leaflets outlining the various colour-coded and **waymarked walking trails** are available for a few pence from a small kiosk near the slate museum, or you can just set off meandering around the old slate workings and through the ancient woodlands of Coed Dinorwig. At some point, direct yourself to the period-furnished **Quarry Hospital**, where the resident surgeon patched up gruesome injuries from gunpowder blasts and falling rock.

ARRIVAL AND DEPARTURE   LLANBERIS

Buses, which stop along High St, serve; Bangor (hourly; 45min); Betws-y-Coed (6 daily; 30min); Caernarfon (every 30min; 25min); Capel Curig (7 daily; 30min); Nant Peris (hourly or better; 10min); Pen-y-Pass (hourly or better; 15min).

INFORMATION

Tourist information The TIC (Easter–Oct daily except Thurs & Fri 9.30am–4.30pm; ☎ 01286 870765, ✉ llanberis .tic@gwynedd.gov.uk) is in the process of moving. Look for signs on arrival.

Internet Free wi-fi at both *Pete's Eats* and *Caffi Caban*.

ACCOMMODATION

There's a wealth of low-cost **accommodation** and **campsites** in or close to town, as well as up at Pen-y-Pass (see p.360). Luxurious places are harder to find, so if you have your own transport and don't mind being a few miles further from the mountain, you might prefer to stay in places listed under Caernarfon, Bangor or even Betws-y-Coed.

HOTELS AND GUESTHOUSES

Dolafon Hotel High St ☎ 01286 870993, ⓦ dolafon .com. Appealing, well-priced B&B in a solid granite three-storey house in its own grounds. Rooms are spacious and comfortable, and breakfast often includes eggs from their own hens. **£60**

Graianfryn Penisarwaun, 3 miles northwest of Llanberis ☎ 01286 871007, ⓦ fastasleep.me.uk. An exclusively vegetarian and vegan wholefood B&B in a Victorian farmhouse. Home-grown vegetables are used in the three-course evening meals (£19). **£60**

★ **Plas Coch** High St ☎ 01286 872122, ⓦ plas-coch .co.uk. A recent refurb has transformed this B&B with seven en-suite rooms plus an extra bathroom with a tub for post-hike soaks. New owners are going the extra mile, even offering packed lunches to hikers. **£55**

Snowdon Cottage A4086, 0.5 miles southeast of central Llanberis ☎ 01286 872015. B&B in a renovated eighteenth-century cottage with three shared-bath rooms, a cosy guest lounge and open fire that's perfect after a blustery day in the hills. Run by a walker who's always keen to help get you on the trail. Also a cute little

ACTIVITIES

By far the most popular activities around Llanberis are hiking (particularly on Snowdon) and rock climbing (on the crags of Llanberis Pass and elsewhere), but there's an abundance of other things to do.

Guided climbing and scrambling High Trek Snowdonia, Tal y Waen, Deiniolen (☎ 01286 871232, ⓦ climbing-wales.co.uk). If you're not equipped or confident enough to get out on the rock by yourself, engage the services of High Trek, who guide everything from straightforward hillwalking to scrambling, rock climbing (all abilities), navigation and winter climbing.

Cruises A diminutive lake steamer, the *Snowdon Star*, operates 40min narrated cruises on Llyn Padarn (May–Oct daily 11am–5pm; £6) from a small jetty near the slate museum.

High Ropes Adventure Centre, by the slate museum, ☎ 01286 872310, ⓦ ropesandladders.co.uk. Spend a couple of hours with an instructor helping you push your boundaries on a course constructed from wooden poles. Adults £24, kids £18.50.

Mountain biking As well as being one of the most popular walking routes up Snowdon, the Llanberis Path (see box, p.358) is designated a bridleway, making it, the Snowdon Ranger Path and the Pitt's Head Track to Rhyd-Ddu accessible to cyclists. A voluntary agreement bans bike access to and from the summit tracks between 10am and 5pm from May to September, but otherwise these paths are open to cyclists. There are loads of other much easier rides in the area: ask at Llanberis Bike Hire, 34 High St (☎ 01286 872787), who rent machines for £22 a day or £15 a half-day.

Scuba diving Vivian Diving Centre, Padarn Country Park (Mon–Fri 10am–5pm; ☎ 01286 870889, ⓦ divevivian.com) offer dives in the fascinating 60ft, 18m-deep Vivian Quarry. The visibility is surprisingly good in the gently flowing waters, and in summer the temperatures aren't too bad. It costs £12 to enter plus £40 all day for a full set of gear.

two-bunk cabin in the garden rented in summer for £40. **£56**

Ty'n Rhos Seion, nr Llanddeiniolen, 6 miles northwest of Llanberis ☎ 01248 670489, ⓦ tynrhos .co.uk. The plushly furnished rooms (some with mountain views) in this peaceful country house are little havens, but the cosy lounge and airy conservatory will lure you out, as should the superb house restaurant (3 courses for £34). **£100**

HOSTELS, BUNKHOUSES AND CAMPING

Cae Gwyn Nant Peris, 2 miles southeast of Llanberis ☎ 01286 870718. Grassy field campsite and primitive bunkhouse (bring everything) with £1 coin-op showers, almost opposite the *Vaynol Arms* pub and very handy for the Pen-y-Pass park-and-ride. Budget-minded climbers and mountain bikers make up the bulk of the clientele. Camping per person **£6**, bunkhouse **£11**

Jesse James' Bunkhouse Buarth y Clytiau, Penisarwaun ☎ 01286 870521, ⓦ jessejames bunkhouse.co.uk. The original bunkhouse, large, rambling, clean and efficiently run since 1970 by a former mountain guide. Accommodation is in dorm beds for £12–15 a night (sleeping bag and towel required) or separate, slightly comfier self-contained rooms. Take the A4086 two miles towards Caernarfon, turn right onto the A4244 and continue for a mile. No credit cards; phone ahead. Dorms **£12**, rooms **£50**

Llwyn Celyn Bach 900yd uphill from town along Capel Coch Rd ☎ 01286 870923. Pick your plot with care on this lovely sloping site spread over several fields with views over town to the slate quarries. £1 coin showers. Per person **£6**

Pete's Sleeps 40 High St ☎ 01286 872135, ⓦ petes-eats.co.uk. Fairly basic dorms above *Pete's Eats* café, plus a couple of twin rooms (breakfast not included), all with access to self-catering facilities. Dorms **£15**, rooms **£35**

YHA Llanberis 700yd uphill from town along Capel Goch Rd ☎ 0845 371 9645, ✉ llanberis@yha.org.uk. Well-appointed but not especially atmospheric YHA hostel with dorms, twin-bunk rooms and a couple of en-suite doubles plus meals (mains £8). Closed Dec & Jan. **£18.40**

EATING, DRINKING AND ENTERTAINMENT

★ **Caffi Caban** Yr Hen Ysgol, Brynrefail, 2.3 miles northwest of Llanberis ☎ 01286 685500, ⓦ caban -cyf.org. Relaxed, licensed daytime café, with big windows overlooking the woods and outdoor seating. Predominantly organic, local or fair-trade ingredients go into their breakfasts (£4–7), sandwiches, baguettes, mains such as bean burritos (£5.25) and a range of blackboard specials. And with free wi-fi it is a great place to hang out on a wet day. Daily 9am–4pm.

Electric Mountain Café Electric Mountain ☎ 01286 873024. Good spacious café with outdoor seating and a range of espresso coffees, jumbo rolls and baguettes, Welsh rarebit, daily specials (£6) and rich ice cream by Conwy's Parisella's. Daily 10am–4pm.

The Heights 74 High St ☎01286 871179, ⓦheightshotelsnowdon.com. Stripped boards and bare surfaces have transformed this long-time favourite into a smart (for Llanberis) café/bar with a short menu of pub favourites, plus real ales. New owners promise great things, so this is one to watch. Daily 11am–11pm.

The Peak Restaurant 86 High St ☎01286 872777, ⓦpeakrestaurant.co.uk. This unflashy open-kitchen restaurant serves easily the best food in Llanberis. Try the toasted haloumi with roast vegetable couscous and mint salad (£6), perhaps followed by their signature bouillabaisse with fresh prawns, salmon and halibut (£17) and a chocolate tart. Booking advised. Wed–Sun 7–10pm.

Pen-y-Ceunant Isaf Snowdon Path ☎01286 872606, ⓦsnowdoncafe.com. Snug, slate-floored eighteenth-century cottage, 400-yd steeply uphill along the Llanberis Path, serving hikers and all comers with Welsh teas, coffee and snacks until 6pm daily (and until 10pm April–Oct). There are no meals but buy a tea and you can eat your sandwiches here. Visit if only to see the cottage, decorated with paintings and prints by Kyffin Williams and other Welsh artists. Daily: April–Oct 9am–10pm; Nov–March 10am–6pm.

★ **Pete's Eats** 40 High St ☎01286 870117. Hikers, climbers and bikers fortify themselves on Pete's large portions of top-value caff food and a few more delicate dishes. Free jukebox, heaps of magazines and maps to browse, free wi-fi and even laptops you can rent (£3/hr). When the weather turns bad, everyone just orders another huge mug of tea. Daily 8am–8pm or later.

Vaynol Arms Nant Peris, 2 miles east of Llanberis ☎01286 872672. Slate-floored pub with good beer, hearty bar meals (£8) and plastered with mountain and slate-mining photos. Always alive with locals midweek, and with climbers and campers at weekends. Daily 11am–3pm & 6–11pm.

Snowdon

The highest British mountain south of the Scottish Grampians, the **Snowdon** massif (3560ft) forms a star of shattered ridges with three major peaks – Crib Goch, Crib-y-ddysgl and Y Lliwedd – and the summit, **Yr Wyddfa**, crowning the lot. If height were its only quality, it would be popular, but Snowdon also sports some of the finest walking and scrambling in Wales. Its Welsh name, Eryri, is derived from either *eryr* (land of eagles) or *eira* (land of snow); since the eagles have long gone, the latter is more appropriate, with winter snows lingering well into April.

Some hardened outdoor enthusiasts dismiss Snowdon as overused, and it certainly can be crowded. A thousand visitors a day press into the postbox-red carriages of the Snowdon Mountain Railway (see p.352), while another fifteen hundred pound the well-maintained paths to make this Britain's most-climbed mountain. Opprobrium is chiefly levelled at the train for its mere existence, and at the brand-new **Hafod Eryri** ("dwelling place atop Snowdon"), café and bar on the summit for selling the country's highest pint of beer. But at least there's a warm place for walkers to rest, and those unable to walk up have the chance (the notoriously fickle weather permitting) of seeing the **view** over most of north Wales – and even across to Ireland on exceptionally clear days.

Brief history

There is no longer a tumulus on the top of Snowdon, but the Welsh for the highest point, Yr Wyddfa, means "The Burial Place" – near proof that people have been climbing the mountain for millennia. More recently, early ascents were for botanical or geological reasons – 500-million-year-old fossil shells can be found near the summit from when Snowdon was on the sea bottom – but the Welsh naturalist Thomas Pennant came up here mainly for pleasure, and in 1773 his description of the dawn view from the summit in his *Journey to Snowdon* encouraged many to follow. Some were guided by the Snowdon Ranger, Evan Roberts, from his house on the south side (now a YHA hostel), but the rapidly improving facilities in Llanberis soon shifted the balance in favour of the easier Llanberis Path, a route later followed by the railway. This remains one of the most popular routes, though many prefer the three shorter and steeper ones from the Pen-y-Pass car park at the top of the Llanberis Pass. By far the

6

WALKS UP SNOWDON

All the following paths are easy to follow in good weather, but the 1:25,000 OS Explorer OL17 map ("Snowdon & Conwy Valley") is still recommended. There's also a series of leaflets (40p each, available from visitor centres) detailing the individual routes up the mountain.

LLANBERIS PATH

The easiest and longest route up Snowdon, the **Llanberis Path** (5 miles to summit; 3hr; 3200ft ascent), following the rail line, is widely scorned by the sort of serious hiker who wouldn't use the railway or deign to visit the summit café. Victoria Terrace runs off the A4086 opposite the *Royal Victoria Hotel* and becomes a path which soon passes the *Pen-y-Ceunant* tearoom (see p.357). The summit gradually comes into view as you rise towards the midway point and the *Halfway House Café* (generally June–Sept daily 10am–5pm; Easter–June & Sept–Dec weekends only). From here there are views of Clogwyn Du'r Arddu (The Black Cliff, or "Cloggy" to its friends), an ominous sheet of rock which frames a small lake. The path next passes Clogwyn station, from where you get a great view down onto the Llanberis Pass. This soon disappears as the path gets steeper, passing the low remains of stables where mule trains used to rest. Bwlch Glas (Green Pass) is marked by the "Finger Stone" where the Snowdon Ranger Path (see opposite) and three routes coming up from Pen-y-Pass join the Llanberis Path for the final ascent to Yr Wyddfa. Llanberis Path is the route used by the annual Snowdon Race (see p.40).

THE MINERS' TRACK

The **Miners' Track** (4 miles to summit; 2hr 30min; 2400ft ascent) is the easiest of the three routes up from Pen-y-Pass. Leaving the car park, a broad track leads south then west to the former copper mines in Cwm Dyli. Dilapidated remains of the crushing mill perch on the shores of Llyn Llydaw, a tarn-turned-reservoir with one of the worst eyesores in the national park, an overground pipeline slicing across Snowdon's east face to the power station in Nantgwynant. Skirting around the right of the lake, the path climbs more steeply to the lake-filled Cwm Glaslyn, then again to Upper Glaslyn, from where the measured steps of those ahead warn of the impending switchback ascent to the junction with the Llanberis Path.

PIG TRACK

The stonier **Pig Track** (3.5 miles to summit; 2hr 30min; 2400ft ascent) is really just a shorter and steeper variation on the Miners' Track, leaving from the western end of the Pen-y-Pass car park and climbing up to Bwlch y Moch (the Pass of the Pigs), which gives the route its name. Ignore the scramble up to Crib Goch (part of the Snowdon Horseshoe) and traverse below the rocky ridge looking down on Llyn Llydaw and those pacing the Miners' Track, content that you're already 500ft up on them. They'll soon catch up, as the two tracks meet just before the zigzag up to the Llanberis Path. The path is also known as the PYG track, supposedly after the nearby *Pen Y Gwryd Hotel*: no one seems able to settle the argument.

SNOWDON HORSESHOE

Some claim that the **Snowdon Horseshoe** (8 miles round; 5–7hr; 3200ft ascent) is one of the finest ridge walks in Europe. The route makes a full anticlockwise circuit around the three glacier-graven cwms of Upper Glaslyn, Glaslyn and Llydaw. Not to be taken lightly, it

most dramatic, if also the most dangerous, is the wonderful Snowdon Horseshoe, which calls at all four of the high peaks.

The Llanberis Pass and Pen-y-Pass

The steady Llanberis Path, which grinds up Snowdon's gentlest ascent, may be the most popular single route up the mountain, but more walkers start from the lofty saddle at the top of the **Llanberis Pass**, the deepest, narrowest and craggiest of Snowdonia's passes, running five miles east from Llanberis itself. This is the Welsh home of **rock climbing**, and if you stop and look for a while you'll almost always see the dots of climbers inching their way up the various crags.

includes the knife-edge traverse of Crib Goch. Every summer's day, dozens of people find themselves straddling the lip, empty space on either side, and wishing they weren't there. In winter conditions, an ice axe and crampons are the minimum requirement. The path follows the Pig Track to Bwlch y Moch, then pitches right for the moderate scramble up to **Crib Goch**. If you baulk at any of this, turn back. If not, wait your turn, then painstakingly pick your way along the sensational ridge to Crib-y-ddysgl (3494ft), from where it's an easy descent to Bwlch Glas and on to Yr Wyddfa. Having ticked off Wales' two highest peaks, turn southwest for a couple of hundred yards to a marker stone where the Watkin Path (see below) drops away to the east. Follow it down to the stretched saddle of Bwlch-y-Saethau (Pass of the Arrows), then on to the cairn at Bwlch Ciliau from where the Watkin Path descends to Nantgwynant. Ignore that route, continuing straight on up the cliff-lined northwest ridge of Y Lliwedd (2930ft), then descend to where you see the scrappy but safe path down to Llyn Llydaw and the Miners' Track.

SNOWDON RANGER PATH

Many of the earliest Snowdon climbers engaged the services of the Snowdon Ranger, who led them up the comparatively long and dull but easy **Snowdon Ranger Path** (4 miles to summit; 3hr; 3100ft ascent), on the now unfashionable south side of the mountain. The path starts from the *YHA Snowdon Ranger Hostel* (see p.368) on the shores of Llyn Cwellyn, five miles northwest of Beddgelert. To the left of the path, a path leads up a track then ascends steeply, flattening out to cross sometimes boggy grass and eventually skirting to the right of the impressive Clogwyn Du'r Arddu cliffs (see Llanberis Path, opposite). Another steep ascent eventually brings you to the Llanberis Path at Bwlch Glas.

RHYD DDU TRACK

The **Rhyd Ddu Track** (4 miles to summit; 3hr; 2900ft ascent) has two branches, one starting from Pitt's Head Rock, two and a half miles northwest of Beddgelert, the other from the national park car park in Rhyd Ddu, a mile beyond that. They join up after less than a mile's walk across stony, walled grazing land, and after crossing a kissing gate continue to the northwest up to the stunning final section along the rim of Cwm Clogwyn and the south ridge of Yr Wyddfa. Use the Welsh Highland Railway or the #S4 bus to turn this and the Snowdon Ranger Path into a loop.

WATKIN PATH

The most spectacular of the southern routes up Snowdon, the **Watkin Path** (4 miles to summit; 3hr; 3350ft ascent), is also the one with the greatest height gain. From Bethania Bridge, three miles northeast of Beddgelert in Nantgwynant, the path starts on a broad track through oaks opening up to long views of a series of cataracts. Ascend beside these to a disused inclined tramway where the track narrows before reaching the natural amphitheatre of Cwm Llan. The ruins of the South Snowdon Slate Works only briefly distract you from Gladstone Rock, at which, in 1892, the 83-year-old Liberal statesman, then in his fourth term as British prime minister, officially opened the route. A narrower path wheels left around the base of Craig Ddu, then starts the steep ascent past Carnedd Arthur to Bwlch Ciliau, the saddle between Y Lliwedd (see Snowdon Horseshoe opposite) and the true summit (Yr Wyddfa), then turning left for the final climb to the top.

At the head of the pass is the YHA hostel, café and car park that make up **PEN-Y-PASS**, the base for the Miners' Track, the Pig Track and the demanding Snowdon Horseshoe (see box above), which all leave from the car park.

ARRIVAL AND DEPARTURE   PEN-Y-PASS

By bus The often-packed car park at Pen-y-Pass costs £5 for up to 4hr and £10 all day so consider using the bus. Park at the park-and-ride at the bottom of the pass close to the *Vaynol Arms* (£2 for up to 4hr and £4 all day) then ride the frequent #S1 & #S2 Snowdon Sherpa buses (7 daily; 10min) to Pen-y-Pass for £1.

Destinations Beddgelert (5 daily; 20min); Betws-y-Coed (6 daily; 15min); Capel Curig (6 daily; 10min); Llanberis (hourly or better; 15min); Porthmadog (4 daily; 45min).

6

KING ARTHUR AND SNOWDON

From the departure of the Romans until the tenth century, Welsh history is pervaded by **legends** of King Arthur (see p.76), Gwrtheyrn (Vortigern) and Myrddin (Merlin; see p.147). Arthur's British (as opposed to Anglo-Saxon) blood gives him a firm place in Welsh hearts, and while Caerleon in southeast Wales lays a powerful claim to being the site of Arthur's court, Snowdon is often held to be his home.

It was atop Dinas Emrys, the seat of Gwrtheyrn's realm near Beddgelert, that the most potent symbol of Welsh independence, the Red Dragon, earned its colours. The Celtic king, Gwrtheyrn, was trying to build a fortress to protect himself from the Saxons, but each night the earth swallowed the masonry. Myrddin divined this to be caused by two dragons sleeping underground: one white, the other red. When woken, they fought unendingly, symbolizing the Red Dragon of Wales' perpetual battle with the White Dragon of the Saxons.

Arthur's domain was higher up the mountain. Llyn Llydaw aspires to being the lake into which Bedivere cast Arthur's sword, Excalibur, after Arthur was mortally wounded by an arrow while on the point of vanquishing his nephew Modred at Bwlch-y-Saethau (The Pass of the Arrows), thirteen hundred feet above the lake.

ACCOMMODATION, EATING AND DRINKING

★**Pen-y-Gwryd Hotel** 1 mile east of Pen-y-Pass ☎01286 870211, ⓦ pyg.co.uk. This wonderfully rustic place comes with ageing furniture, magnificent Edwardian bathrooms, an outdoor sauna, and a lot of muddy boots in the bar. Among others, the first successful expedition up Mount Everest in 1953 stayed at the hotel while doing final equipment testing, and signed the ceiling: Edmund Hillary, Chris Bonington, Doug Scott and Portmeirion designer Clough Williams-Ellis are all there. The Everest team also brought back pieces of the mountain, which now sits in pride of place in the nicely panelled "Smoke Room". Rooms (some en suite) are priced per person, and are good value for singles. Expect lots of plain home cooking (£25 for a 3-course meal, £30 for 5) and a congenial though somewhat regimented atmosphere (they bang a Nepali gong for the single breakfast and dinner sittings). Two-night minimum at weekends; closed Nov & Dec, open weekends only Jan & Feb. **£80**

YHA Pen-y-Pass ☎0845 371 9534, ⓔ penypass@yha .org.uk. The only accommodation at Pen-y-Pass is this fine hostel usually full of walkers. There's 24hr access, limited free parking, a few two-bunk rooms, a bar licence and good meals. Open all year. **£18.40**

Caernarfon and around

Caernarfon, superbly set at the southern entrance to the Menai Strait, has a lot going for it. Its distinctive polygonal-towered **castle** is an undoubted highlight, the **Welsh Highland Railway** now connects the town with the slopes of Snowdon and Porthmadog, and the modern marina development adds **Galeri Caernarfon**, a modest but interesting arts centre. There's also the sheer pleasure of simply meandering among the seventeenth- and eighteenth-century buildings in the knot of streets wedged between the **town walls**. But somehow, the whole is less than the sum of its parts. The quayside below the castle is a car park and the town walls (as complete as those at Conwy) are so boxed-in by modern buildings that they're far less striking, and there's currently no way to get onto them. That said, there's some great accommodation nearby, making Caernarfon a great, central base for exploring both sides of Snowdon, the Llŷn and even Anglesey.

Caernarfon is a town where ardent support for **Plaid Cymru** guarantees the party a seat in Westminster, and the local **dialect** is barely intelligible even to other Welsh-speakers. It is also the county town of Gwynedd, and one of the oldest continuously occupied settlements in Wales, once the site of the Romans' most westerly legion post.

Caernarfon Castle

July & Aug daily 9.30am–6pm; April–June, Sept & Oct daily 9.30am–5pm; Nov–Feb Mon–Sat 10am–4pm, Sun 11am–4pm • £5.25 • ☎01286 677617 • CADW

In 1283, Edward I started work on **Caernarfon Castle**, the strongest link in his Iron Ring (see p.410) and the decisive hammerblow to any Welsh aspirations of autonomy.

Until Beaumaris Castle was built to guard the other end of the Menai Strait, Caernarfon was the ultimate symbol of Anglo-Norman military might and political wrangling. With the Welsh already smarting from the loss of their Prince of Wales, Edward reputedly rubbed salt in their wounds by justifying his own infant son's claim to the title, having promised them "a prince born in Wales who could speak never a word of English", and subsequently presenting them with the newborn baby that had arrived after his pregnant wife had been forced to take up residence in the castle. The story is almost certainly apocryphal, since Edward's son, though born at Caernarfon, wasn't invested until seven years later.

However, Edward attempted to woo the Welsh with gestures to certain local legends. The Welsh had long associated their town with the eastern capital of the Roman Empire: Caernarfon's old Roman name, Caer Cystennin ("Fort of Constantine"), alludes to the emperor after whom Constantinople was named, and there are even some dreamers who claim that Constantine himself was born here. Edward's architect, James of St George, exploited this connection in the distinctive limestone and sandstone banding and polygonal towers, both reminiscent of the Theodosian walls still standing in present-day Istanbul.

The castle is in an excellent state of repair, thanks largely to Anthony Salvin's nineteenth-century reconstruction, carried out after Richard Wilson and J.M.W. Turner had painted their Romantic images of it.

The King's Gate

As you enter the **King's Gate**, the castle's strength is immediately apparent. Indeed, as a military monument of its time, the castle is supreme, and it still has a brooding, imperious presence. Seized only once, before it was finished, it then withstood two sieges by Owain Glyndŵr with a complement of only 28 men-at-arms.

Between the octagonal towers, embrasures and murder-holes cover no fewer than five gates and six portcullises once you've crossed the moat. Inside, the huge lawn gives a misleading impression, since both the wall dividing the two original wards crumbled away and all the wooden buildings that filled the wards disappeared long ago.

The Eagle Tower

The walls and towers are in a much better state, linked by such a honeycomb of wall-walks and tunnels that a tour can be exhausting. The Eagle Tower at the western end is the loftiest and most striking, its three slender turrets adorned with heavily

---

WHAT PRINCE OF WALES?

It was in Caernarfon in 1969 that Charles, the current heir to the throne, was theatrically invested as Prince of Wales, a ceremony that reaffirmed English sovereignty over Wales in the midst of one of the most nationalist of Welsh-speaking regions. Since 1282, when the English defeated Llywelyn ap Gruffydd, the last Welsh Prince of Wales, the title has been bestowed on heirs to the English throne, usually in a ceremony held either at Windsor Castle or in Westminster Abbey in London. However, in 1911, the machinations of Lloyd George – MP for Caernarfon, Welsh cabinet minister and future prime minister – ensured that the investiture of the future King Edward VIII would take place in the centre of his constituency: a paradoxical move for a nationalist, but one that undoubtedly helped to advance Lloyd George's career.

By the time it was Charles' turn, nationalism was on the rise and two extremist members of the Free Wales Army blew themselves up trying to blow up the Prince's train. In many ways, such acts had a detrimental effect on the nationalist cause, wrongly linking extremism with the more moderate and constitutional methods of the party. Charles' 25-year commemorative return visit in 1994 was a far more low-key affair, remembered, if at all, for the local constabulary ruling that the local joke shop risked committing a public-order offence by selling "wingnut" ears and Prince Charles masks.

6

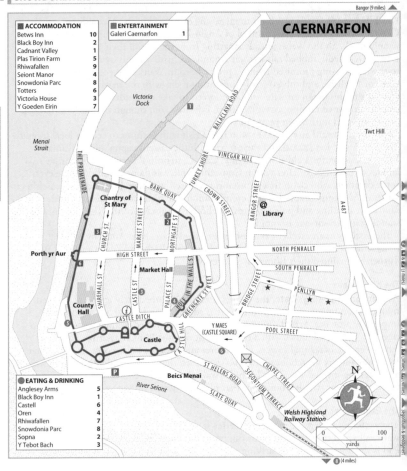

Bangor (9 miles)

CAERNARFON

■ ACCOMMODATION
Betws Inn	10
Black Boy Inn	2
Cadnant Valley	1
Plas Tirion Farm	5
Rhiwafallen	9
Seiont Manor	4
Snowdonia Parc	8
Totters	6
Victoria House	3
Y Goeden Eirin	7

■ ENTERTAINMENT
Galeri Caernarfon	1

● EATING & DRINKING
Anglesey Arms	5
Black Boy Inn	1
Castell	6
Oren	4
Rhiwafallen	7
Snowdonia Parc	8
Sopna	2
Y Tebot Bach	3

eroded eagle sculptures affording superb views of the town. On the lower floors, displays and a short film outline the castle's history and its importance in the context of Edward I's Iron Ring.

The Queen and Northeast towers

The Queen's Tower is entirely taken up by the numbingly thorough **Museum of the Royal Welch Fusiliers** detailing the victories of Wales' oldest regiment through collections of medals, uniforms and a brass howitzer captured from the Russians at the Battle of the Alma in the Crimea in 1854. Crossing the upper ward, you pass the slate dais used for the investiture of the Prince of Wales, a pageant expanded on in the **Prince of Wales Exhibition** in the Northeast Tower.

Segontium Roman Fort

A4085, 0.3 miles east towards Beddgelert • Daily except Mon 12.30–4.30pm • Free • CADW

The western end of the Roman road from Chester terminated at **Segontium Roman Fort**, a five-acre hilltop site which the Romans occupied for three centuries from around 78 AD, though most of the remains are from the final rebuilding after 364 AD.

This was the base of Maximus, the Spanish-born pretender to the imperial throne who was declared Emperor by his British troops in 383 AD, and made a failed march on Rome. The remains of Segontium are about as impressive as his march, seldom more than shin-high and somewhat baffling. Sadly the explanatory museum is closed, but it may reopen in summer 2012.

Greenwood Forest Park

B4366, 3 miles northeast of Caernarfon, just west of the village of Bethel • Mid-March to Aug daily 10am–5.30pm; Sept & Oct daily 11am–5pm • £10.85; reduced off-peak prices • ☎ 01248 670076, ⓦ greenwoodforestpark.co.uk

6

If you don't have kids, borrow some and spend the day at **Greenwood Forest Park**, a fun park on the fringe of a copse of managed woodland with zipwires, slides, longbow shooting, extensive tree houses, adventure playgrounds and the like. There's an underlying desire to educate about woodlands and conservation in general, but they never lose sight of having a whole load of fun. Almost everything is human powered. On the slides you carry your sled back to the top, boats are hand hauled and there's even a roller coaster powered by the energy you expend walking to the start. Follow the temperate forest boardwalk, attempt the maze, and pull off your socks for the Barefoot Trail through leaves, sand, straw, pebbles and water.

There are a couple of **cafés** and if the weather's a bit iffy you can head into the large barn built using ancient methods and forty tons of green Welsh and English oak trees, its gargantuan beams held together with pine struts and wooden pegs. Displays explore tree and forest ecology.

Inigo Jones Slateworks

Groeslon, A487 6 miles south of Caernarfon • Daily 9am–5pm • £5 • ☎ 01286 830242, ⓦ www.inigojones.co.uk

The Lôn Eifion bike path runs south from Caernarfon right by the **Inigo Jones Slateworks**, where slate has been fashioned in roadside sheds since 1861. The factory was started by one Inigo Jones, a local man apparently unrelated to the seventeenth-century architect. Many of the inscribed slate plaques adorning public buildings around north Wales were cut here, ample excuse for an interesting calligraphy exhibition that forms part of the 45-minute self-guided audio tour. You can even try your hand at chiselling out a few random chips of slate to appreciate the skill of the carvers here.

Parc Glynllifon

Off A499, 6 miles south of Caernarfon • Daily 10am–5pm • Craft workshops and café free; grounds £4 • ☎ 01286 830222

Parc Glynllifon occupies the grounds of the sombre nineteenth-century Glynllifon Hall (not open to the public), once home of Lord Newborough. Easy trails weave through a pleasant woodland garden complete with arboretum, but time is equally well spent at the former workshops, now given over to well-respected craftspeople including one of Wales' top artistic blacksmiths, Ann Catrin Evans.

EXPLORING BY THE WELSH HIGHLAND RAILWAY

We've covered the **Welsh Highland Railway** in detail under Porthmadog. Steam- or diesel-hauled trains run from the small station on St Helen's Road, some of them going the full 25 miles to Porthmadog. The following are good ways to explore the railway and the wonderful scenery hereabouts.

Train to Waunfawr (35min) and visit the *Snowdonia Parc* pub and a pleasant campsite.

Train to Snowdon Ranger (1hr), hike up the Snowdon Ranger path (p.359) then stay at the YHA hostel (see p.368).

Train to Rhyd Ddu and hike the Rhyd Ddu track to Snowdon's summit: peak season timetables give you up to 7hr for the hike.

Catch the train to Dinas then walk the three miles back along Lôn Eifion.

6

Dinas Dinlle
7 miles south of Caernarfon, 1 mile west of A499 • Open access • Free • NT

The sea is doing its best to erode the still substantial remains of **Dinas Dinlle**, a 150yd diameter **Iron Age hillfort** built 2500 years ago. The Romans also occupied this now-grassy site and presumably would have enjoyed the same wonderful views along the Llŷn and back to Snowdonia.

ARRIVAL AND DEPARTURE   CAERNARFON

By bus National Express and local buses stop on Penllyn, just a few steps from the central Y Maes (Castle Square). Destinations Bangor (every 10min; 25min); Beddgelert (8 daily; 30min); Llanberis (every 30min; 25min); Porthmadog (7 daily; 40min); Pwllheli (roughly hourly; 45min).

INFORMATION

Tourist office The TIC is on Castle St (Easter–Oct daily 9.30am–4.30pm; Nov–Easter Mon–Sat 10am–4pm; ☎ 01286 672232, ✉ caernarfon.tic@gwynedd.gov.uk).
Internet Free at the library on Bangor St (Mon, Tues, Thurs & Fri 9.30am–7pm, Wed 9.30am–1pm, Sat 9.30am–1pm),

and free wi-fi at the *Anglesey Arms*.
Bike rental Beics Menai, 1 Slate Quay (☎ 01286 676804). All sorts of bikes (at £15 for 2hr up to £22 for 8hr plus tandems for a little more).

ACCOMMODATION

HOTELS AND GUESTHOUSES

★ **Betws Inn** Betws Garmon, A4085, 5 miles southeast ☎ 01286 650324, ⊛ betws-inn.co.uk. A low-beamed former drovers' inn (some parts from 1620) with stylish modern touches. Guests share a cosy lounge with huge inglenook fireplace (lit in winter), and there are excellent three-course dinners (£18–25) by arrangement. **£80**

Black Boy Inn Northgate St ☎ 01286 673604, ⊛ black-boy-inn.com. Characterful low-beamed rooms in what is said to be the town's oldest building (bar the castle), plus newer rooms adjacent, all including a hearty breakfast and free parking. **£90**

Plas Tirion Farm Llanrug, A4086, 3 miles east of Caernarfon ☎ 01286 673190, ⊛ plas-tirion.co.uk. Welcoming and traditional B&B in a stone farmhouse furnished with antiques and with some choice rural views. **£65**

Rhiwafallen Llandwrog, A499 4.5 miles south ☎ 01286 830172, ⊛ www.rhiwafallen.co.uk. Delightful restaurant-with-rooms, five of them, all with wooden floors and modern furnishings, and most with white-painted fireplaces and deep double-ended baths. There's a warm and welcoming feel though, which carries through to the elegant lounge and excellent restaurant. **£100**

Seiont Manor A4086, 3 miles east of Caernarfon towards Llanberis ☎ 0845 072 7550, ⊛ handpicked .co.uk. Rustic edifice converted into a fairly grand hotel, complete with indoor pool, good restaurant, sauna and even fishing within the hotel grounds. **£130**

★ **Victoria House** 13 Church St ☎ 01286 678263, ⊛ thevictoriahouse.co.uk. Very comfortable and good-value B&B within the town walls. Decor is Victorian-styled in rooms (all doubles, no twins) that

come with flatscreen TV/DVD, free wi-fi, complimentary drinks. **£70**

★ **Y Goeden Eirin** Dolydd, 4 miles south of Caernarfon ☎ 01286 830942, ⊛ ygoedeneirin.co.uk. An effortless and very personal style pervades this classy B&B where the warmth and hospitality of a Welsh farmhouse meshes with an appreciation of art, literature and poetry. And there's no doubting the eco credentials; everything is turned off at the wall when not in use. But there's nothing austere about the effortlessly tasteful decor, either in the spacious loft or rooms converted from outbuildings. Dinner (£25 for 4 courses) is a relaxed affair. There's also a self-catering beach cottage sleeping five a few miles away (£300–550 a week). **£80**

HOSTEL AND CAMPING

Cadnant Valley ☎ 01286 673196, ⊛ cwmcadnantvalley.co.uk. Pleasant wooded campsite 10min walk east of town near the start of the A4086 to Llanberis. Closed Nov–Feb. Pitches from **£11**

Snowdonia Parc Waunfawr ☎ 01286 650409, ⊛ snowdonia-park.co.uk. Attractive year-round campsite four miles southeast on the A4085, right by a station on the Welsh Highland Railway and a good brewpub; free showers. Pitches **£18**

★ **Totters** Plas Porth Yr Aur, 2 High St ☎ 01286 672963, ⊛ totters.co.uk. Caernarfon's only backpacker hostel is one of the best in Wales. Centrally located, with clean dorms (rates include continental breakfast) and some inviting communal spaces, including a fourteenth-century cellar kitchen. There's also a great attic en-suite double with sea views and *Over the Road*, a separate self-contained house sleeping six. Dorms **£16**, *Over the Road* per person from **£20**, room **£50**

ACTIVITIES AROUND CAERNARFON

Boat trips About the only way to experience the beauty of the Menai Strait from the water is with RibRide (☎0333 1234 303, ☻ribride.co.uk) who use an eleven-seater, 250-horsepower rigid inflatable to charge up and down the strait. A one-hour trip costs £20: book ahead.

Climbing wall Beacon Climbing Centre, Cibyn Industrial Estate, off the A4086, 0.5 miles east (Mon–Fri 11am–10pm, Sat & Sun 10am–10pm; ☎0845 450 8222, ☻beaconclimbing.com; £7). When inclement weather forces climbers off the crags, the keen ones head straight to this huge indoor climbing wall. They offer taster sessions (£65 total for 1–3 people; 90min).

Cycling One of the most enjoyable ways to get out into the area around Caernarfon is to follow either of two walking and bike paths along the route of a disused railway: **Lôn Las Menai** runs four miles north from Victoria Dock to Y Felinheri (Port Dinorwig) and thence via lanes to Bangor. **Lôn Eifion** heads 12 miles south alongside the Welsh Highland Railway to Bryncir, and then via lanes to Criccieth. For bike rental see p.364.

Scenic flights Caernarfon's tiny airport, eight miles south of town at Dinas Dinlle (☎01286 830800, ☻caernarfonairport.co.uk), offers spectacular flights over Snowdonia and Anglesey. Fixed-wing flights start at £39 per person for 20min, and £59 will get you over Snowdon. Chopper flights are a bit more expensive.

6

EATING, DRINKING AND ENTERTAINMENT

Anglesey Arms The Promenade ☎01286 672158. The sea wall outside makes this the best pub for soaking up the afternoon sun, and it also has good real ales, and live music on Fridays. Daily 11am–11pm.

Black Boy Inn Northgate St ☎01286 673604, ☻black-boy-inn.com. The closest Caernarfon comes to an old-fashioned British pub, with a choice of two wonderfully characterful low-beamed bars and the best bar meals in town. Daily 11am–11pm.

Castell The Square ☎01286 677970, ☻castellcaernarfon.co.uk. For classy bistro food in the relaxed surroundings of a revamped town-square pub you can't go wrong at Castell. Expect the likes of pork belly with wild mushrooms and Madeira (£15), or hake and chips with caper mayonnaise (£12). Meals daily noon–3pm & 6–9.15pm.

Galeri Caernarfon Victoria Dock ☎01286 685222, ☻galericaernarfon.com. Modern arts and entertainment complex which puts on a wide range of plays, shows mainstream and more arty films (mainly Wed evenings) and includes gallery space and a café/bar.

Oren 26 Hole in the Wall St ☎01286 674343. Step away from the ordinary at this delightful wood-floored little restaurant run by a Welsh-speaking Dutchman. There's a set menu (very limited choice of food or wine) which changes weekly, typically with a theme – Mexican, Buddhist vegetarian, Greek/Turkish. Everything is casual and crockery doesn't match, but there's no faulting the

quality of the local produce or the verve, and for £15 you can't go far wrong. Thurs–Sat noon–2.30pm & 6.30–10pm.

Rhiwafallen Llandwrog, A499, 4.5 miles south of Caernarfon ☎01286 830172, ☻rhiwafallen.co.uk. Classy little conservatory restaurant with rural views and a short menu (three courses for £35; Sun lunch £20) on which local produce features prominently. Expect the likes of pea and mint soup with buffalo mozzarella toasts followed by beef sirloin with shitake mushrooms and a watercress and blue cheese salad. Tues–Sat 7–9pm, Sun noon–2.30pm.

Snowdonia Park Waunfawr ☎01286 650409, ☻snowdonia-park.co.uk. Rural pub four miles southeast of town by Waunfaur station on the Welsh Highland line, with beer brewed on site and decent pub meals. Bus #S4 to Beddgelert goes right by. Daily 11am–11pm.

Sopna Felin Wen, Pontrug, A4086, 2 miles east ☎01286 675222, ☻sopna.co.uk. Quality Bangladeshi tandoori restaurant that regularly wins awards for its wide range of spicy balti dishes and delicately flavoured vegetable sides. Mains mostly around £9; £7 to take away. Daily 11.30am–11pm.

Y Tebot Bach 13 Castle St ☎01286 678444. Modern food with old-fashioned attention to detail in this chip-free tearoom that's good for sandwiches, salads, home-baked cakes and cream teas throughout the day. Daily 10am–4.30pm.

MOUNTAIN BIKING

There's good family-oriented off-road riding in the Beddgelert Forest a mile out on the Caernarfon road and a mile uphill from the *Beddgelert Forest Campsite* (see below). Spend half a day pootling around the trails including a six-mile signposted loop.

Beddgelert and around

At the confluence of the Glaslyn and Colwyn rivers on the south flank of Snowdon sits the picture-postcard village of **BEDDGELERT**. Though little more than a few dozen hard grey houses, it is curiously enchanting, its window boxes bursting with flowers, and lots of spots to mooch, eat and drink. It is often thronged with tourists on sunny summer days and parking can be tricky, so consider visiting from Caernarfon or Porthmadog on the newly reopened Welsh Highland Railway.

6

Gelert's Grave

Though the story is more interesting than the site, visitors all dutifully stroll 400yd south, along the right bank of the Glaslyn, to the spot that gives the village its name, **Gelert's Grave** (*bedd* means "burial place"). A railed-off enclosure in a field marks the final resting place of Prince Llywelyn ap Iorwerth's faithful dog, Gelert, who was left in charge of the prince's infant son while he went hunting. On his return, the child was gone and the hound's muzzle was soaked in blood. Jumping to conclusions, the impetuous Llywelyn slew the dog, only to find the child safely asleep beneath its cot and a dead wolf beside him. Llywelyn hurried to his dog, which licked his hand as it died. In fact, the story is an eighteenth-century invention by a local publican, though it's succeeded in luring punters ever since. The real source of the name is probably the grave of Celert, a sixth-century British saint who supposedly lived hereabouts.

Sygun Copper Mine

Almost 1 mile north on A498 · Daily: March–Oct 9.30am–5pm; Nov–Feb 10am–4pm · £8.95 · ☎ 01766 890595, ⓦ syguncoppermine.co.uk

A red-brown stain on the hillside identifies the family-oriented **Sygun Copper Mine**, whose ore drew first the Romans, then nineteenth-century prospectors. The dilapidated remains of what was once the valley's prime source of income have now been restored and made safe for the cool (9°C) 45-minute self-guided **tour** up through the multiple levels of tunnels and galleries. At stations along the way the disembodied voice of a miner describes his working life. Afterwards, you're free to potter around the ore-crushing and separation equipment, or go gold panning.

ARRIVAL AND DEPARTURE   BEDDGELERT

By bus Beddgelert is on two bus routes: the #S4 Snowdon Sherpa from Caernarfon and the #S97 between Pen-y-Pass and Porthmadog. Services stop on the main street from Caernarfon (8 daily; 30min), Pen-y-Pass (5 daily; 20min) and Porthmadog (8 daily; 25min).

INFORMATION

Tourist information The TIC is on the A498 in the village centre (Easter–Oct daily 9.30am–5.30pm; Nov–Easter Fri, Sat & Sun 9.30am–4.30pm; ☎01766 890615, ⓦ beddgelerttourism.com).

EXPLORING BY THE WELSH HIGHLAND RAILWAY

Since 2011 Beddgelert has been linked to both Caernarfon and Porthmadog by the Welsh Highland Railway, which we've detailed more fully under Porthmadog. Here are a few ways to explore the line.

Rent a bike in Beddgelert, catch the train to Rhyd Ddu (3.5 miles) or Waunfaur (9 miles) then ride back along the A4085 (best at quieter times).

Ride the train to Rhyd Ddu (1hr round trip) climbing the steepest part of the route. Trains pass at Rhyd Ddu so there is almost always a train waiting on the other side of the platform for the return trip.

Train through the tunnels of the Aberglaslyn Gorge to Pont Croesor (seasonal osprey viewing) then return on a later train. £14.50 return.

Train to Nantmor (£3.50 one-way) then walk back to Beddgelert along the Fisherman's Path (1hr).

6

WALKS FROM BEDDGELERT

Two fine hikes up Snowdon start near Beddgelert, and there are a couple of good ones closer to town: all are covered by the OS 1:25,000 OL17 ("Snowdon & Conwy Valley") and 1:50,000 115 ("Snowdon/Yr Wyddfa") maps.

ABERGLASLYN GORGE

(3 miles return; 2hr; 100ft ascent.) This fairly easy walk follows the Glaslyn as it tumbles and cascades through the madly picturesque Aberglaslyn Gorge. Cross a footbridge over the Glaslyn River in the village and follow the left bank downstream until you meet the Welsh Highland Railway. Continue between the railway and the river on the **Fisherman's Track** as the train line ducks through two tunnels. The path meets the road at Pont Aberglaslyn – the tidal limit before The Cob was built at Porthmadog – from where you can retrace your steps.

MOEL HEBOG RIDGE

(8-mile loop; 5hr; 2800ft ascent.) West of Beddgelert the lumpish **Moel Hebog** (Bald Hill of the Hawk; 2569ft) is the highest point on a fine panoramic ridge walk which also takes in the lesser peaks of **Moel Lefn**, and **Moel yr Ogof** (Hill of the Cave), named after a refuge used by Owain Glyndŵr when fleeing the English in 1404, after his failed attempt to take Caernarfon Castle. The final forest section can be a bit disorientating, even in good weather, so be sure you have a compass.

Start half a mile northwest of the centre of Beddgelert on the A4085, where Pont Alyn crosses the river to Cwm Cloch Isaf Farm. Follow the signs to a green lane, which soon leads up onto the broad northeast ridge, all the time keeping left of the Y Diffwys cliffs. The summit cairn is joined by two walls, the one to the northwest leading down a steep grassy slope to Bwlch Meillionen, from where you can ascend over rocky ground to Moel yr Ogof. From the top of Moel yr Ogof, it's a clear route north to Moel Lefn, then down to a cairn from where you can plan your descent. The easiest line is to Bwlch Cwm-trwsgl, near the highest point of the Beddgelert Forest, then through the forest to the A4085 and back to Beddgelert.

Bike rental Available from Beddgelert Bikes (☎01766 890434, ⓦ beddgelertbikes.co.uk; £12 for 2hr, £25 for 8hr, less for kids' bikes), located right by the WHR train station In Beddgelert.

ACCOMMODATION

Accommodation is limited and quite expensive. If you're wanting to make an early start on the Snowdon walks you'll find the hostels better sited.

HOTELS AND GUESTHOUSES

Colwyn A498 ☎01766 890276, ⓦ beddgelert guesthouse.co.uk. Central 300-year-old cottage guesthouse with comfortable (if small), renovated rooms, a beamed lounge and an open fire. There's a two-night minimum at weekends. __£70__

Plas Tan y Graig Stryd Smith ☎01766 890310, ⓦ plas-tanygraig.co.uk. Central and well managed guesthouse that's been largely refurbished in recent years. The eight B&B rooms all have a small fridge and flatscreen TV and family rooms also have a DVD player. Walkers will appreciate the drying room, packed lunches (on request) and free flask refills of tea, coffee and hot chocolate. __£82__

★ **Sygun Fawr** 0.7 miles northeast off A498 ☎01766 890258, ⓦ sygunfawr.co.uk. This partly seventeenth-century country house in its own grounds is the pick of the local hotels. Some of its comfy rooms have views of Snowdon, and there are two- and three-night deals which include dinner at the superb restaurant (see p.368). __£82__

HOSTELS AND CAMPING

Beddgelert Caravan & Campsite A498, 1 mile northwest ☎01766 890288, ⓦ forestholidays.co.uk. Excellent, forest campsite with kids' play area, laundry and a host of other facilities including its own (request) stop on the Welsh Highland Line. __£15__

Cae Du Camping 10min walk towards Capel Curig on A498 ☎01766 890345, ⓦ caeducampsite.co.uk. Spacious and peaceful site with hot showers, some streamside tent spots, power sites (extra £3) and a small shop. Closed Oct–Feb. Pitches __£16__

Hafod y Llan Nantgwynant, A498, 4 miles north ☎01766 510129. Tent-only site on a farm purchased by the National Trust and managed to enhance the landscape and for nature conservation. Campfires are permitted. Closed Nov–March. Per person __£6.50__

Llyn Gwynant Campsite A498, 5 miles northeast ☎ 01766 890853, ⓦ gwynant.com. Large, wonderful and often very busy lakeside site in a gorgeous valley hemmed in by mountains. There's a maximum of ten caravans at any one time but there can be over 400 tents. You can access Snowdon's Watkin Path directly from the site, rent kayaks and canoes (June–Sept), and there are free hot showers. Radios are banned, mobile phones don't work and bookings are not required. Closed Nov to mid-March. Per person £9

YHA Bryn Gwynant A498, 4 miles northeast ☎ 0845 371 9108, ⓔ bryngwynant@yha.org.uk. Beautifully sited in a former mansion in Nantgwynant, near the start of the Watkin Path, with dorm beds and private rooms. Meals are available and the hostel is licensed. Closed Nov to early Feb. Dorms £18.40, rooms sleeping four £80

YHA Snowdon Ranger Rhyd Ddu, 5 miles northwest on A498 ☎ 0845 371 9659, ⓔ snowdon@yha.org.uk. A former inn, at the foot of the Snowdon Ranger Path. Bunks are mostly in two- and four-bed rooms, meals are available and the place is licensed. Open April–Aug; call for other times. Dorms £16.40; rooms £41

EATING AND DRINKING

Beddgelert Bistro & Antiques By the bridge ☎ 01766 890543, ⓦ beddgelert-bistro.co.uk. Scones with clotted cream by day; duck breast in cherry and brandy sauce, beef and ale pie or vegetable and pine nut risotto (£12–15) by night. There's a cosy cellar bar, too. Everything is cooked to order, so book ahead for dinner. Daily 10am–10pm.

Glaslyn Ices/Cafe Glyndŵr On the south side of the river bridge ☎ 01766 890339, ⓦ glaslynices.co.uk. Great ice-cream shop with three dozen flavours to take away, plus a family-style restaurant tucked in behind that's well above the usual standard. Baguettes and their varied fillings are all super fresh and they do great pizzas and evening specials. Daily 10am–8pm or later.

Lyn's Café ☎ 01766 890374. Other places are better for meals, but on a fine day the outside seating is *the* place in the village for a clotted cream tea. Feb–Oct daily 10am–4pm or later.

★ **Sygun Fawr** 0.7 miles northeast off A498 ☎ 01766 890258, ⓦ sygunfawr.co.uk. Open to non-residents, with beautifully prepared four-course evening meals (£26) served in a snug dining room. Also à la carte dining with mains £11–15. Bookings recommended. Tues–Sun 7–10pm.

Tanronnen Inn ☎ 01766 890347, ⓦ tanronnen.co.uk. The cosy bar at this old inn feels like a friend's front room; well, a friend who has loads of beers on tap and a row of upside-down spirits. Daily 11am–11pm.

Blaenau Ffestiniog and around

Snowdonia's most southerly major settlement, **BLAENAU FFESTINIOG**, cowers at the foot of stark thousand-foot mountains strewn with heaps of splintered slate. The town attracts some of Snowdonia's worst weather, and when clouds hunker low in the great cwm and rain lashes the grey roofs, walls and paving slabs it looks terrifically gloomy. Fortunately, on days when every tourist office in north Wales is packed with wet visitors wondering what to do, Blaenau Ffestiniog is at its most dramatic, and besides, its slate mine will keep you dry.

Thousands of tons of slate a year were once hewn from the labyrinth of caverns beneath the town, and exported worldwide. They made the first part of their journey on the **Ffestiniog Railway** which took the dressed and packed product down to the ships at Porthmadog, thirteen miles away. Now, only two mines manage to keep ticking over (one of them aided by earnings from tours) and the town's population has dropped to less than half its 1910 peak of 12,000. Its benighted economy now leans on tourism, generated by its mine tour and the fact that it's at the junction of two of the finest train journeys in Wales: the narrow-gauge **Ffestiniog Railway** and the Conwy Valley Railway (see box, p.344).

Brief history

When Snowdonia National Park was created in 1951, it formed a massive doughnut around Blaenau Ffestiniog. The town's heaps of waste slate were deemed incompatible with the values of the national park despite the fact that the now-defunct Trawsfynydd nuclear power station was soon to be built within the park boundary just seven miles to the south. For years, Blaenau Ffestiniog has been in sad decline and as part of a push to make it more of a tourist destination there is now a movement to have the town brought into the park. This needs the approval of the Countryside Council for Wales and then a referendum of locals, so it is likely to be a long process.

Llechwedd Slate Caverns

A470, 1 mile north of town • Daily: April–Sept 10am–6pm; Oct–March 10am–5pm; last tour 45min before closing • Single tour £10, both tours £16.30 • ☎ 01766 830306, ⦿ llechwedd-slate-caverns.co.uk

It's hard to get a real feeling of what slate means to Blaenau Ffestiniog without a visit to **Llechwedd Slate Caverns**, which presents entertaining and informative insights into the rigours of a miner's life. There's no charge to walk around the reconstructed Victorian mining village (April–Sept only) and to watch slate being split, shaped and engraved, though you'll want to change money into old-style pennies and farthings at the Old

6

THE WELSH SLATE INDUSTRY

Slate is as much a symbol of north Wales as coal is of the south: it too peaked around the beginning of the twentieth century and shaped society throughout the period of British mass industrialization, drawing thousands from the impoverished hills to the relative wealth of the new towns which sprang up around the quarries.

Slate derives its name from the Old French word *esclater*, meaning "to split" – a perfect description of its most highly valued quality. Six hundred million years ago, what is now north Wales lay under the sea, gradually accumulating a thousand-foot-thick layer of fine-grained mud which metamorphosed into the purplish Cambrian slates of the Penrhyn and Dinorwig quarries and the blue-grey Ordovician slates of Ffestiniog.

The Romans used it as a cheap and durable **roofing material** for the houses of Segontium in Caernarfon, while Edward I used it extensively in his Iron Ring of castles around Snowdonia. Demand really took off with urbanization during the Industrial Revolution, and during the nineteenth and early twentieth centuries millions of tons of slate were shipped around the globe. Hamburg was re-roofed with Welsh slate after its fire of 1842, and it is the same material that still gives that rainy-day sheen to interminable rows of English mill-town houses.

By 1898, Welsh quarries – run by the English, like the coal and steel industries of the south – were producing half a million tons of dressed slate a year (and ten times as much slate waste), almost all of it from Snowdonia. At Penrhyn and Dinorwig, mountains were hacked away in terraces, with teams of **workers** negotiating with the foreman for the choicest piece of rock and the selling price for what they produced. They often slept through the week in damp dormitories on the mountain, and tuberculosis was common, exacerbated by slate dust. At Blaenau Ffestiniog, the seams required mining underground, with miners having to buy their own candles. Few workers were allowed to join the Quarrymen's Union, and in 1900, the workers in Lord Penrhyn's quarry at Bethesda went out on **strike**. For three years they stayed out – one of Britain's longest-ever industrial disputes – but failed to win any concessions. Those who got their jobs back were forced to work for even less money as a recession took hold, and although the two world wars heralded mini-booms as bombed houses were replaced, the industry never recovered its nineteenth-century prosperity, and most quarries and mines closed in the 1950s.

Welsh slate was firmly established as the finest in the world at the 1862 London Exhibition, where one skilled craftsman produced a sheet 10ft long, 1ft wide and a sixteenth of an inch thick – so thin it could be flexed. Slate is now produced worldwide, and although none beats the quality of north Wales' product, half-priced Spanish slate is imported while Welsh slate lies in the ground and unemployed quarrymen kick their heels. The remaining quarries produce relatively small quantities, much of it used for floor tiling, road aggregate or an astonishing array of ashtrays and coasters etched with mountainscapes.

More memorable are the roadside fences made from lines of broken, wafer-thin slabs, the beautifully carved slate fire surrounds and mantelpieces occasionally found in pubs and houses, as well as Westminster Abbey's memorial to Dylan Thomas, which is made entirely of Penrhyn slate.

6

EXPLORING WITH THE FFESTINIOG RAILWAY

We've covered the Ffestiniog Railway in detail under Porthmadog. Here are a couple of suggested trips.

Do the whole return trip to Porthmadog with a couple of hours to explore the town.
Ride the train to Minffordd, walk the mile or so to visit Portmeirion then get the train back.
Drive to Tan-y-Bwlch and do our Vale of Ffestiniog walk (see box).

Bank to buy something from the old-style sweet shop or buy a drink at the *Miners' Arms* pub.

To visit some of the 25 miles of tunnels and sixteen working levels, however, you need to take one of two fairly pricey 25-minute tours.

Miners' Tramway

Using a small train, the **Miners' Tramway** tour takes you a third of a mile along one of the oldest levels, cut in 1846, disembarking to admire the enormous Cathedral Cave and the open-air Chough's Cavern – both tilted at 30° to follow the slate's bedding plane – as you are plied with facts on slate mining. The scale of the place is awe-inspiring even without the unconvincing tableaux of Victorian miners at work chained high up in the tops of the caverns.

Deep Mine

On the wilder **Deep Mine** tour you're bundled onto special carriages and lowered to one of the deepest parts of the mine down a precipitous 1-in-1.8 incline. After donning waterproofs and headgear, you head off into the tunnels, guided by the disembodied voice of a "Victorian miner" who does a good job of explaining the working and social life of the miners who never saw daylight in winter, taking their breaks in a dank underground shelter known as a *caban*. The long caverns angling back into the gloom become increasingly impressive, culminating in one filled by a softly lit, limpid pool. The site was the setting for the first ever Welsh-language film, *Y Chwarelwr* (The Quarrymen), in 1935.

Dolwyddelan Castle

A470, 6 miles north of Blaenau Ffestiniog • April–Sept Mon–Sat 10am–5pm, Sun 11.30am–4pm; Oct–March Mon–Sat 10am–4pm, Sun 11.30am–4pm • £2.80 • ☎ 01690 750366 • CADW

The lonely **Dolwyddelan Castle** commands the head of the Lledr Valley, over the Crimea Pass from Blaenau Ffestiniog. Llywelyn ap Iorwerth ("the Great"; see p.440) may well have been born here, since his father was reputedly responsible for its construction at the end of the twelfth century. The strategic site, on the important route from Aberconwy to the north and Ardudwy to the south, was soon turned against him when Edward I took the castle, refortified it and used it to further subdue the Welsh. By the end of the fifteenth century, it had become redundant and lay abandoned until the Wynns of Gwydyr treated it to a suitably Victorian reconstruction,

---

THE CURSE OF THE RHODODENDRON

It is against the pervasive greyness of Blaenau Ffestiniog that Snowdonia's **rhododendron** (specifically *Rhododendron ponticum*) invasion is most evident. Come in May or June and many of Snowdonia's valleys are a riot of lilac and purple blooms. There's no doubting their aesthetic appeal, but these Turkish natives are high on ecologists' hate lists. The dense canopy cuts out so much sunlight that nothing can grow underneath – a major threat to native birds and insects which thrive in more open scrub. Volunteer action groups periodically target particular areas, blitzing a valley by digging out all the plants, but the rhododendron is proving difficult to contain.

A WALK DOWN THE VALE OF FFESTINIOG

Vale of Ffestiniog 4–5 miles; 2–3hr; descent only; 1:25,000 OS Explorer map OL18 ("Harlech, Porthmadog & Y Bala"). This gentle walk follows a gorgeous section of the Vale of Ffestiniog and completes the loop using the Ffestiniog Railway. Start at Tan-y-Bwlch station and take the train up to Tanygrisiau to start the walk. Turn right out of the station then take the second left – not the road beside the reservoir but the next one following the footpath signs. Cross the train line and pass a car park on your left before turning left down a track and skirting behind the powerhouse. The path then sticks closely to the railway tracks (occasionally crossing them), following the train line to its 360° loop, through sessile oak woods and past several cascades all the way to Tan-y-Bwlch, offering some great views south to the Rhinogs and west to the Glaslyn estuary en route. Even when there are several paths, you can't go far wrong if you keep the train lines in sight. Recover at the *Oakeley Arms* pub near Tan-y-Bwlch station.

6

---

complete with fanciful battlements and a new roof. Today, it shelters only a small exhibition on native Welsh castles, but gives a panoramic view of Snowdonia from between its castellations.

Vale of Ffestiniog

Slate waste surrounds Blaenau Ffestiniog on three sides, but the fourth drops away into the bucolic **Vale of Ffestiniog**, best explored using the Ffestiniog Railway, or on the walk described in the box. Activity is focused on the railway's Tan-y-Bwlch station (5 miles southwest of Blaenau Ffestiniog) where there is a café and woodland play area. Nearby you'll find Snowdonia National Park's study centre, **Plas Tan y Bwlch**, which runs numerous courses throughout the year (see Basics, p.54), and the *Oakeley Arms* pub.

ARRIVAL AND DEPARTURE

BLAENAU FFESTINIOG

By train The central train station serves both the Ffestiniog Railway, and mainline services to Betws-y-Coed (6 daily; 30min), Llandudno Junction (6 daily; 1hr) and Llandudno (6 daily; 1hr 20min).

By bus Buses stop outside the train station or along High St. The main services are to Barmouth (3 daily; 1hr 10min); Betws-y-Coed (9 daily; 20min); Harlech (3 daily; 40min); Llandudno (9

daily; 1hr 10min); and Porthmadog (hourly; 30min).

By car Blaenau Ffestiniog is most dramatically approached from the north via the Lledr Valley (A470), past Dolwyddelan Castle then climbing over the Crimea Pass, between the Manod and Moelwyn mountains, and plunging down into the town's shattered landscape.

ACCOMMODATION

Bryn Elltyd 1 mile from Blaenau in Tanygrisiau ☎01766 831356, ⓦaccommodation-snowdonia.com. A very popular, environmentally friendly option overlooking Llyn Ystradau and beside the Ffestiniog Railway, run by a mountain leader. Excellent evening meals (from £14) are available. **£70**

Bryn Tirion Farm A470, 6 miles north ☎01690 750366. The Dolwyddelan Castle custodian runs this adjacent and very hospitable farm B&B, a campsite (closed Nov–Feb) and a comfortable, self-catering bunkhouse (open all year), with bedding supplied. Camping per person **£5**, bunkhouse per person **£13**, double **£70**

Cae Du A470, 1.5 miles south ☎01766 830847, ⓦcaedu.co.uk. A comfy, sixteenth-century beamed

farmhouse with four guest rooms, beautifully situated in open country at the end of a long drive. Guided walks are available. **£60**

★ **Cae'r Blaidd** A470, 3 miles south ☎01766 762765, ⓦwww.caerblaidd.fsnet.co.uk. Wonderfully spacious Victorian country house set in four acres of woodland with just three rooms, two with fabulous views of the Moelwyn mountains. Sustaining breakfasts and professionally served table d'hôte dinners (£20 for 3 courses) are very good and the hosts run an extensive array of guided hiking, climbing and scrambling trips. **£80**

Isallt Guest House Church St ☎01766 832488, ⓦisallt.com. Bargain B&B in a solid Victorian house right by the train station with six rooms – double, family, twin and single – and a DVD library. **£56**

EATING, DRINKING AND ENTERTAINMENT

CeLL B Park Square ☎ 01766 832001, ⊛ cellb.org. Fledgling arts centre in a former police station with gigs, occasional cinema nights (featuring a different country each month) and a spruce café/bar with mountain views, good coffee and free wi-fi. Hours very flexible.

Cor Y Brythoniaid ☎ 01766 830435, ⊛ corybrythoniaid.com. The area's best male voice choir practises (usually Thurs at 7.30pm) at Ysgol Y Moelwyn school on the A470 at the south end of town.

6 Porthmadog and around

In a region stuffed with wonderful views, **PORTHMADOG**, at the crook of the Cambrian Coast and the Llŷn, has some of the finest – up the Vale of Ffestiniog and across the estuary of the Glaslyn River to the mountains of Snowdonia. The bustling town itself makes little of its wonderful position, but the legacy of its one-time status as north Wales' busiest slate port makes this a great base for exploring.

Wales' heritage railway obsession reaches its apogee here. As well as the standard-gauge Cambrian Coast line, Porthmadog has three tourist-oriented narrow-gauge railways. The most established is the peerless **Ffestiniog Railway** that originally carried down slates from Blaenau Ffestiniog. Its Harbour Station is also the terminus for the stunning **Welsh Highland Railway** which connects Porthmadog via Beddgelert and the Aberglaslyn Pass to Caernarfon. Confusingly, there's also the family-oriented **Welsh Highland Heritage Railway**, at the northern end of town.

If steam trains don't blow your whistle, spend at least half a day at the strange but wonderful Italianate folly of **Portmeirion**, walk beside the estuary to pretty **Borth y Gest**, have a **swim** at Morfa Bychan or spy on **ospreys** at Glaslyn.

Brief history

Porthmadog would never have existed without the entrepreneurial ventures of Lincolnshire MP, **William Alexander Madocks**. He named the town and its elder brother Tremadog, a mile to the north, after both himself and the Welsh Prince Madog, who some say sailed from the nearby Ynys Fadog (Madog's Island) to North America in 1170. In 1805, Madocks fancied he could get himself some good grazing land by draining a thousand acres of estuarine mud flats here; he bought Ynys Fadog, built an earth embankment, then started on Tremadog. The town prospered and, buoyed by its success, Madocks embarked on a project to enclose a further 7000 acres by sealing off the Glaslyn estuary with a mile-long embankment known as **The Cob**, southeast of present-day Porthmadog. Madocks died before the project came to fruition, but the Glaslyn River was rerouted and soon scoured out a deep watercourse close to the north bank, ideal for a slate wharf. This was the first of several which, boosted by the completion of the Ffestiniog Railway in 1836, spread along a waterfront thick with orderly heaps of slate and the masts of merchant ships. The slate traffic ceased by the middle of the twentieth century, and today only a few dozen yachts grace the harbour.

Ffestiniog Railway

April–Oct 4–8 services daily; Nov–March services several days a week • Return to Blaenau Ffestiniog £19; return to Tan-y-Bwlch £11.80; £15.40 saver fare on 8.45am and 6.30pm trains; under 16s travel free with an adult, and single fares are two-thirds of a return • ☎ 01766 516000, ⊛ festrail.co.uk

The 2ft-gauge **Ffestiniog Railway** is Wales' finest narrow-gauge rail line, twisting and looping up 650ft from Porthmadog to the slate mining town of Blaenau Ffestiniog, thirteen miles away. The gutsy little engines make light of the steep gradients and chug through stunning scenery, from broad estuarine expanses to the deep greens of the Vale of Ffestiniog, only fading to grey on the final approaches to the slate-bound upper terminus at Blaenau Ffestiniog.

When the line opened in 1836, it carried slates from the mines down to the port with the help of gravity, horses riding with the goods before hauling the empty carriages back up again. Steam had to be introduced to cope with the 100,000 tons of slate that Blaenau Ffestiniog was churning out each year in the late nineteenth century, but after the slate-roofing market collapsed in the 1920s, passengers were carried instead until the line was finally abandoned in 1946. Most of the tracks and sleepers had disappeared by 1954, when, encouraged by the success of the Talyllyn Railway, a bunch of dedicated volunteers began to reconstruct the line, only completing the entire route in 1982.

Leaving Porthmadog, trains cross The Cob then stop at Minffordd, an interchange point for the Cambrian Coast main line and the mile-long walk to Portmeirion. Short

6

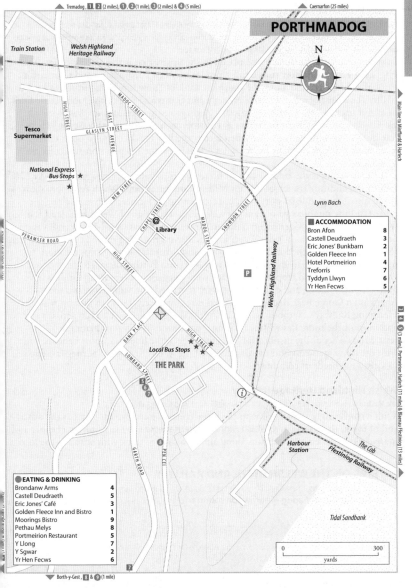

▲ Tremadog, **1**, **2** (2 miles), **1**, **2** (1 mile), **3** (2 miles) & **4** (5 miles)   ▲ Caernarfon (25 miles)

PORTHMADOG

N

Train Station

Welsh Highland Heritage Railway

Tesco Supermarket

National Express Bus Stops ★
★

HIGH STREET
MADOC STREET
EAST AVENUE
GLASLYN STREET
NEW STREET
CHAPEL STREET
MADOC STREET
SNOWDON STREET
PENAMSER ROAD
HIGH STREET

@ Library

Lynn Bach

Welsh Highland Railway

P

ACCOMMODATION	
Bron Afon	8
Castell Deudraeth	3
Eric Jones' Bunkbarn	2
Golden Fleece Inn	1
Hotel Portmeirion	4
Treforris	7
Tyddyn Llwyn	6
Yr Hen Fecws	5

BANK PLACE
HIGH STREET
Local Bus Stops ★ ★
★ ★
THE PARK
LOMBARD STREET
5
6
7

GARTH ROAD
PEN CEI
8

ⓘ

Harbour Station

The Cob

Ffestiniog Railway

Tidal Sandbank

EATING & DRINKING	
Brondanw Arms	4
Castell Deudraeth	5
Eric Jones' Café	3
Golden Fleece Inn and Bistro	1
Moorings Bistro	9
Pethau Melys	8
Portmeirion Restaurant	5
Y Llong	7
Y Sgwar	2
Yr Hen Fecws	6

7

0   300
yards

► Main line to Minffordd & Harlech

► **3**, **4**, **5** (3 miles), Portmeirion, Harlech (11 miles) & Blaenau Ffestiniog (13 miles)

▼ Borth-y-Gest, **8** & **9** (1 mile)

nature trails spur off from Tan-y-Bwlch (the fourth station), as does the longer Vale of Ffestiniog walk (see box, p.371), which passes Dduallt station by the spiral on its way to Tanygrisiau. The full round trip to Blaenau Ffestiniog takes almost three hours, but you can get on and off as frequently as the timetable allows, and the journey is included in some rail passes (see p.30). It costs £2.50 each way for **bikes**, but call first to confirm that there's space. Sit on the right of the carriage going up to get the best view of the scenery; for more legroom or to sit in the observation carriage you'll need to pay £5 each way for a **first-class** upgrade.

Welsh Highland Railway

Late March to Oct 2–4 trains daily • £7 return to Pont Croesor; £17.50 to Beddgelert; £32 to Caernarfon; first-class tickets cost an additional £8 each way between Porthmadog and Caernarfon with lower costs for shorter journeys; under 16s travel free with an adult, and single fares are two-thirds of a return • ☎ 01766 516000, ⓦ festrail.co.uk

In spring 2011 the final piece was placed in the jigsaw that is the narrow-gauge Welsh Highland Railway. It now runs a full 25 miles between Porthmadog and Caernarfon, through Beddgelert and along the southern flank of Snowdon, rising from sea level to 650ft. The statistics are impressive enough, but this is also one of the most scenic lines in a land packed with charming railways. A gorgeous river estuary gives way to oak woods which crowd in on the tracks as you approach the **Aberglaslyn Gorge**, where the line hugs the tumbling river. After Beddgelert the line breaks out into open terrain maintaining a 1:40 gradient for six miles – making it the steepest non-funicular track in Britain.

The re-opening is the culmination of fifteen years of volunteer struggle and over £28 million expenditure, much of it from Millennium lottery and Welsh Assembly sources. It was also a tangled legal story with hurdles put up by farmers with land along the route (and the ramblers who regularly walked it). The original Welsh Highland Railway from Porthmadog to Caernarfon only ran for fourteen years (until 1937) and was pulled up decades ago, but the Welsh love affair with restoring railways as steam-driven tourist attractions kicked in and two organizations began running trips on short sections of track, one from Caernarfon and one from Porthmadog. The feats of engineering needed to reopen the old line were staggering: over twenty bridges have been rebuilt; walking and cycling paths were re-routed; four tunnels down the Aberglaslyn Gorge near Beddgelert needed extensive safety work; to link up with the Ffestiniog Railway's Harbour Station at Porthmadog, trains have to run across a street; and most of the route lies within a national park, with its rigorous planning restrictions. Part of the justification has always been the line's transport benefits, but with the steep gradients and twisting route of the WHR, it's not a journey fast enough to satisfy the needs of commuters.

Welsh Highland Heritage Railway

Late March to Oct 5–6 services daily • £6 ticket valid all day • ☎ 01766 513402, ⓦ whr.co.uk

With a confusingly similar name to the more epic rail journey that starts at the other end of town, the 24in-gauge **Welsh Highland Heritage Railway** is a shorter, cheaper and more child-oriented affair. It runs along almost a mile of track with a stop at the loco

---

TRIPS ON THE WELSH HIGHLAND RAILWAY

Timetables will affect how much you can do in one day, but here are a few suggestions:
Do the full Porthmadog–Caernarfon round trip: a full five hours on the train but only an hour in Caernarfon.
Drive to Pont Croesor (where most trains currently start and there's free parking) and ride to Beddgelert from there.
Ride to Beddgelert then walk down the Aberglaslyn Pass to Nantmor (1hr) and catch the train back to Porthmadog from there.

> ### EASY WALKS AROUND PORTHMADOG
>
> **The Cob** (2 miles return; 1hr; flat). If the weather is fine, and particularly towards sunset, you can't go far wrong wandering around the harbour then strolling along The Cob, with the occasional steam-hauled Ffestiniog Railway service adding atmosphere to views up the estuary towards Snowdon.
>
> **Borth-y-Gest** (2 miles return; 1hr; flat). This easy walk beside the Glaslyn Estuary makes a particularly nice summer evening stroll and a good way to get to your booking at the *Moorings Bistro*. Follow Pen Cei south from Porthmadog below the cliffs of Moel-y-Gest.

6

sheds where you get to see how a steam engine works. Fans over 18 can ride the footplate (£10 extra) or take a driver experience session (3hr; £75) where you take the helm.

Glaslyn Osprey Project

Pont Croesor on B4410, 4 miles northeast of Porthmadog • Late March to Aug • Free • ⓦ rspb.org.uk/datewithnature

When there are **ospreys** on the nest, this small centre opens up with displays on these fine fish-eating eagles, replica nests and excellent archive footage of the birds. There are hopes of establishing a significant population in the area but currently there is just one breeding pair. Telescopes allow you to see the distant nest, but most will appreciate the live CCTV link from a camera just 3ft above the nest. Depending on the time of year, you may see the adults tending the eggs, watch the eggs hatch or see the chicks learning to fly.

Tremadog

William Madocks' original village, founded in 1805, lies just a mile north of Porthmadog. Though really just the intersection of three streets, it is a barely-altered example of early town planning with a central square overlooked by an attractive (though currently empty) town hall.

Borth-y-Gest

The small former boat-building village of Borth-y-Gest envelops a picturesque harbour a mile south of Porthmadog with a semicircle of Victorian houses lining the beach. There's nothing to do here but enjoy the estuary views from one of the waterfront cafés, maybe stay at *Bron Afon* and eat at the delectable *Moorings Bistro* (see p.378). The #99 bus (hourly) runs here from Porthmadog.

Morfa Bychan

If all the sand and water around Porthmadog leaves you hankering for a swim, **Black Rock Sands**, almost three miles southwest of Porthmadog at **Morfa Bychan**, is the best beach: a two-mile swath of golden sands with sublime views down to Harlech and up to the peaks of Snowdonia. At low tide you can explore the rock pool and even some caves.

Portmeirion

Daily 9.30am–7.30pm • £9; free afternoon entry if you pre-book a meal at the Portmeirion Hotel, or have lunch at Castell Deudraeth; free entry Nov–March with downloaded voucher; half-price entry after 3.30pm; free 20min guided tours daily 10.30am–3.30pm • ☎ 01766 770000, ⓦ www.portmeirion-village.com

Don't miss the unique Italianate private village of **Portmeirion**, set on a small rocky peninsula in Tremadog Bay, three miles east near Minffordd. You can walk there in an hour from Porthmadog, or catch the #1b bus, main-line or Ffestiniog trains to Minffordd, from where it's a signposted 25-minute walk.

Portmeirion was the brainchild of eccentric architect **Clough Williams-Ellis** whose dream was to build an ideal village to enhance rather than blend in with its surroundings, using a "gay, light-opera sort of approach". The result is certainly theatrical: a stage set with a lucky dip of unwanted buildings arranged to distort perspectives and reveal tantalizing

6

glimpses of the sea or the expansive sands behind. Portmeirion is perhaps best known as "The Village" in the 1960s British cult TV series *The Prisoner*.

In the 1920s, Williams-Ellis began scouring Britain for a suitable island – he believed only an island could provide the seclusion for his project – but having found nothing he could afford, he was gratified to be offered a piece of wilderness four miles from his home, Plâs Brondanw, at Garreg (see below). A Victorian house already on the site was turned into a hotel, the income from which provided funds for Williams-Ellis's "Home for Fallen Buildings". Endangered buildings from all over Britain and abroad were broken down, transported and rebuilt, every conceivable style being plundered: a neoclassical colonnade from Bristol; Siamese figures on Ionic columns; a Jacobean town hall; a Buddha; and the Italianate touches, a campanile and a pantheon. Williams-Ellis designed his village around a Mediterranean piazza, piecing together a scaled-down nest of loggias, grand porticoes and tiny terracotta-roofed houses, and painting them in pastels: turquoise, ochre and buff yellows. Continually surprising, with hidden entrances and cherubs popping out of crevices, the ensemble is wildly eclectic, yet never quite inappropriate.

More than three thousand visitors a day come to ogle in summer, when it can be a delight; fewer appear in winter, when it's just plain bizarre. Much of your time will be spent outside wandering around the buildings or popping into the shops selling *Prisoner* memorabilia or florally embellished Portmeirion pottery. Guests and visitors can eat at the expensive hotel-restaurant (see p.379), but most will be content with one of several cafés – better still, bring a picnic and find a spot on the paths that wind through the exotic forest which backs Portmeirion.

Hotel Portmeirion

Sometimes dismissed as the grandest folly of all and a symbol of Britain's fascination with eccentrics, Portmeirion at least supports Williams-Ellis's guiding principle that natural beauty and profitable development needn't be mutually exclusive. Architectural idealism aside, it was always intended to be self-sustaining, much of the finance coming from the lovely waterside *Hotel Portmeirion* (see p.378), which also utilizes many of the cottages in the village. In the evening, when the village is closed to the public, guests see the place at its best: peaceful, even ghostly.

The Prisoner convention

For one weekend in April, Portmeirion hosts *The Prisoner* convention (ⓦ portmeiricon .com) when fans book the place out to re-enact scenes as best they can – though, as much of the series was shot in the studio, the juxtaposition of Portmeirion's buildings doesn't match that of *The Village*.

Plâs Brondanw

Signed off A4085 just north of Garreg • Daily 9.30am–5.30pm • £3.50 • ⓦ brondanw.org

Clough Williams-Ellis's talents are also in evidence four miles northeast of Portmeirion at his ancestral home **Plâs Brondanw**, where whimsical topiary creates a formal, yet not quite manicured, setting for a solid Welsh stone house. The house is closed to the public, leaving only the gardens and some of the grounds, visited by following the "To the Tower" sign opposite the entrance. A ten-minute woodland walk brings you to the outlook tower, with expansive views of Porthmadog and the Moelwyns.

ARRIVAL AND DEPARTURE	**PORTHMADOG**

BY TRAIN

The mainline train station and the Welsh Highland Heritage Railway station are at the north end of the High St, near the Tesco supermarket. The Ffestiniog and Welsh Highland railways' station is located down by the harbour, about half a mile to the south. The following exclude Ffestiniog and Welsh Highland services.

Destinations Aberdyfi (7 daily; 1hr 30min); Barmouth (7 daily; 50min); Criccieth (8 daily; 10min); Harlech (8 daily; 20min); Machynlleth (7 daily; 1hr 50min); Pwllheli (8 daily; 25min).

BY BUS

Pwllheli-bound National Express buses from London, Manchester and Liverpool stop outside Tesco: get tickets from the TIC. Note that Dolgellau buses go inland through Coed-y-Brenin: take the train if you want to stick to the coast.

Destinations Beddgelert (8 daily; 25min); Blaenau Ffestiniog (hourly; 30min); Caernarfon (7 daily; 40min); Criccieth (every 15–30min; 15min); Dolgellau (6 daily; 50min); Pen-y-Pass (4 daily; 45min); Pwllheli (every 30min; 40min).

INFORMATION

Tourist information The TIC is at the southern end of the High St (Easter–Oct daily 9.30am–5pm; Nov–Easter Mon–Sat 10am–3.30pm; ☏01766 512981,

ⓦ visitsnowdonia.info).
Internet Free at the library at 29 Chapel St and at Porthmadog Computers, 156 High St.

ACCOMMODATION

HOTELS, GUESTHOUSES AND SELF-CATERING

Bron Afon Borth-y-Gest, 1 mile southwest of Porthmadog ☏01766 513918, ⓦ bronafon.co.uk. Spacious and attractive B&B rooms in this pretty village with fabulous views across the bay to the mountains. Also offers separate self-catering accommodation. **£60**

★ **Castell Deudraeth** Portmeirion ☏01766 772400, ⓦ portmeirion-village.com. Chic designer hotel in a remodelled Victorian "castle" decorated in muted tones with the finest fittings, including widescreen TVs with episodes of *The Prisoner* on DVD. Only a 10min walk from Portmeirion village, where you're free to roam and use the outdoor heated pool. So classy you'll want to stay a week. **£215**

Golden Fleece Inn Tremadog, 1 mile north of Porthmadog ☏01766 512421, ⓦ goldenfleeceinn .com. The best bet for pub accommodation, with stylish, simply furnished rooms above an excellent bar. Breakfast included. **£75**

★ **Hotel Portmeirion** Portmeirion ☏01766 770000, ⓦ portmeirion-village.com. Though it has been stylishly upgraded with feature wallpapers and modern amenities, the spirit of Clough Williams-Ellis shines through. Quirky architectural and decorative elements remain both in the main waterside hotel and in the cottages throughout

Portmeirion village. Every room is different and many come with views over the village or the sands; book well ahead and check for off-season web specials. The hotel also lets luxurious self-catering cottages by the week (or half-week from Nov–March). The cottages sleep three (£670–1050 a week) up to eight people (£1100–1800). **£215**

Treforris Garth Rd ☏01766 512853. Pleasant B&B in a large house overlooking the harbour to the west. Rooms share bathrooms. Bank Place off High St then left onto Garth Rd – a 15min walk in all. **£48**

Yr Hen Fecws 16 Lombard St ☏01766 514625, ⓦ henfecws.com. Relaxed, pleasant B&B with comfy, uncluttered rooms, many with exposed stone walls. Breakfast is served in the owners' café next door. **£70**

BUNKHOUSE AND CAMPING

Eric Jones' Bunkbarn Tremadog, A498 to Beddgelert 2 miles north of Porthmadog, opposite Eric Jones' Café ☏01766 512199, ⓦ ericjones-tremadog.co.uk. Rock climbers' bunkhouse. Mattresses **£5**, camping pitches per person **£4**

Tyddyn Llwyn Black Rock Rd ☏01766 512205, ⓦ tyddynllwyn.com. A superior family campsite on a grassy hillside, with all facilities and a bar, a 15min walk along the road to Morfa Bychan following Bank Place southwest off High St. Closed Nov–Feb. Pitches **£14**

EATING, DRINKING AND ENTERTAINMENT

Brondanw Arms Garreg, 5 miles northwest of Porthmadog ☏01766 770555. This slate-floored traditional inn, known locally as *Y Ring*, has real ales, a beer garden, kids' play area, decent bar meals (mostly under £10), occasional live music and a great atmosphere. Daily 11am–11pm.

Castell Deudraeth Portmeirion ☏01766 770400. Conservatory brasserie overlooking a walled garden – much younger and hipper than the nearby *Portmeirion Restaurant*. Sip a cocktail in the panelled bar then dine on Modern British dishes (mostly £14 at lunch, £15–20 for dinner), helped down with something from the excellent wine list (several by the glass). They also do an excellent Sunday lunch. Daily noon–3pm & 6–10.30pm.

Eric Jones' Café A498, 1 mile east of Tremadog ☏01766 512199. Good, solid food, wolfed down by climbers of the Tremadog crags across the road. There's a good noticeboard, a small stock of climbing gear and guidebooks for sale. Daily 9am–5pm or later.

Golden Fleece Inn and Bistro Tremadog ☏01766 512421. An ancient coaching inn on Tremadog's main square, with a cramped "cave bar" serving meals (£9–10) and excellent ales around the fire or in the courtyard. There's also a swish bistro out the back (generally Thurs–Sat) where you might expect beef fillet with celeriac rosti and wild mushrooms (most mains £16–23). Tuesday is acoustic jam night. Mon–Fri noon–3pm & 6–10pm; Sat & Sun noon–10pm.

Moorings Bistro 4 Ivy Terrace, Borth-y-Gest, 1 mile south of Porthmadog ☎01766 513500, ⓦmooringsbistroborthygest.com. Great little spot specializing in local seafood, and also serving a great Sunday roast lunch (£10) and local ales. Mid-Feb to Dec Wed–Sat 6–10pm, Sun noon–2.30pm.

Pethau Melys 10 Pen Cei ⓦpethaumelys.co.uk, ☎07881 806960. The name means "sweet things" and that's what they serve at this cute little café with seating inside and out by the quay. Come for Welsh cakes, bara brith and coffee (soy milk available) and to check out the owners' pottery and textiles. Daily 10am–6pm.

Portmeirion Restaurant Hotel Portmeirion ☎01766 770480. Delightful, slightly formal hotel restaurant with views across the Traeth Bach sands serving inventive modern cuisine; lamb shoulder with braised potato, wild garlic and aubergine: mains mostly £24–28. Alternatively just come for lunch on the terrace or afternoon tea (£25 for 2, £30 with bubbles). Reserve for dinner and dress up. Daily noon–3pm & 6.30–9.30pm.

Y Llong (The Ship) 14 Lombard St ☎01766 512990. Cosy pub with a stock of real ales and a lively atmosphere. Daily 11.30am–11pm.

★**Y Sgwar** The Square, Tremadog ☎01766 515451. Well-prepared and presented meals at this simple but stylish restaurant – good for a steak-and-ale pie at lunch (£9), or dinner starting with Chinese duck pancakes (£16 for 2) then lamb shank with leeks (£16). The 3-course early-bird special (Mon–Fri 6–7pm) is excellent value at £18. Mon–Sat noon–3pm & 6–10pm.

Yr Hen Fecws 16 Lombard St ☎01766 514625. Cosy licensed daytime café that's all stone walls, wooden floors and sofas. Come for eggs Benedict, goats' cheese tart or just coffee and cake. Daily 8am–5pm.

The Llŷn

An undulating spur from Snowdonia's mountainous heart, the **Llŷn** takes its name from an Irish word for "peninsula", an apt description for this most westerly part of north Wales, which, until the fifth century, had a significant Irish population and which still maintains an atmosphere reminiscent of parts of western Ireland. Nowhere in Wales feels more remote than the tip of the Llŷn or is more staunchly Welsh. In most local shops you'll only hear Welsh spoken, and Stryd Fawr is used instead of High Street.

The Llŷn is approached through either Porthmadog or Caernarfon, towns linked by the A487 which forms an effective boundary between Snowdonia proper and this cliff-and-cove-lined finger of land that juts out south and west, separating Cardigan and Caernarfon bays.

It's the beaches that lure most people to the Llŷn, specifically to the south-coast family resorts of **Criccieth**, **Pwllheli** and **Abersoch**. Unless you want to rent windsurfers or canoes, it's preferable to push on along the narrow roads that dawdle down towards tiny **Aberdaron**, from where ancient pilgrims once sailed for the burial grounds of **Ynys Enlli** (**Bardsey Island**). Alternatively, make for the quiet coves punctuating the north

---

MAINTAINING TRADITIONS ON THE LLŶN

During the 1980s, north and west Wales witnessed a spate of **arson attacks** conducted by the shadowy **Meibion Glyndŵr**, or "Sons of Glyndŵr". Though their campaign against selling homes to wealthy English weekenders petered out by the 1990s, nationalists are very keen to preserve Welsh ways and maintain the vigour of the Welsh language. **Incomers** are encouraged to learn *Cymraeg*, thanks partly to groups like Cymuned (literally "Community"; ⓦcymuned.org), a pressure group formed in 2000. It advocates a minimum ten-year residency clause for home buyers; planning permission to turn a permanent dwelling into a second home; investment in schemes to help residents buy property locally; and a Welsh-learning requirement for residents. Some argue that communities might do better embracing incomers, exploiting any economic spin-off and using that to help preserve the culture and language.

Much of the peninsula falls within the **Llŷn Area of Outstanding Natural Beauty** (AONB) whose managers are endeavouring to improve the physical appearance of the landscape. Excessive road signage is being removed, traditional iron waymarkers are replacing modern ones, and old-style kissing gates and field gates have been fashioned by a local blacksmith.

6

GIRALDUS CAMBRENSIS AND HIS JOURNEY THROUGH WALES

Through his books *The Journey Through Wales* and *The Description of Wales*, Norman-Welsh **Giraldus Cambrensis** (Gerald of Wales, or Gerallt Cymro) has left us with a vivid picture of life in Wales in the twelfth century. Gerald worked his way up the ecclesiastical hierarchy, but failed to achieve his lifelong goal, the bishopric of St Davids, mainly because of his reformist ideals.

Gerald's influence in Wales made him the first choice when Baldwin, the Archbishop of Canterbury, needed someone to accompany him on his 51-day tour around Wales in 1188, preaching the Cross and recruiting for a third Crusade, designed to dislodge the Muslim leader Saladin from Jerusalem. During the tour, Gerald amassed much of the material for his books, where he sensitively portrayed the landscape and its people, judging that "Welsh generosity and hospitality are the greatest of all virtues", but warning "If they come to a house where there is any sign of affluence and they are in a position to take what they want, there is no limit to their demands". But on the whole, he shows sympathy for the Welsh, coming up with a conclusion that has an oddly contemporary ring: "if only Wales could find the place it deserves in the heart of its rulers, or at least if those put in charge locally would stop behaving so vindictively and submitting the Welsh to such shameful ill-treatment".

coast, notably gorgeous **Porth Oer** and the waterside pub at **Porth Dinllaen**. Ancestors of those last Irish inhabitants may have been responsible for the numerous hillforts and cromlechs found on the Llŷn, particularly the hut circles of the **Tre'r Ceiri** hillfort, high above the Welsh Language Centre at **Nant Gwrtheyrn**.

ARRIVAL AND DEPARTURE   THE LLŶN

Trains and National Express buses serve both Criccieth and Pwllheli, leaving an extensive network of infrequent buses to cover the rest. Better still, bring your bike and explore the peninsula's quiet narrow lanes and rolling pastures.

Criccieth and around

CRICCIETH, five miles west of Porthmadog, clusters around its castle, magnificently sited on a small hillock commanding the bay. The castle is firmly Welsh but much of the rest of the town has long been dependent on the English: it's still smarter and more anglicized than its neighbouring towns. When sea-bathing became the Victorian fashion, English families descended on Criccieth's sweeping sand-and-shingle beach and built long terraces of guesthouses (many now retirement homes). These days, beach-bound holiday-makers go further west, leaving a quietly amiable resort that makes a convenient touring base for the peninsula and Porthmadog. The **best view** in town is from the hill behind Marine Terrace, from where you see the hulking castle set against the backdrop of the Cambrian Coast and the Rhinog mountains.

At **Llanystumdwy**, a mile west, a small museum is dedicated to the intriguing life of native son and British prime minister, **David Lloyd George**.

Criccieth Castle

April–Oct daily 10am–5pm; Nov–March Fri & Sat 9.30am–4pm, Sun 11am–4pm, £3.20 • Nov–March Mon–Thurs & Sun 10am–4pm, Free • ☎ 01766 522227 • CADW

Criccieth's only real sight is the battle-worn **Criccieth Castle**, dominating the coastline with what remains of its twin, D-shape towered gatehouse. The castle was started by Llywelyn ap Iorwerth in 1230, but strengthened and finished by Edward I, who took it in 1283. During his 1404 rebellion, Owain Glyndŵr grabbed it back, only to raze it and leave little remaining besides an outline of broken walls and the gatehouse. Nowadays, it's a great spot to sit and look over Cardigan Bay to Harlech or down the ripples of the Llŷn coast in the late afternoon, but leave time for the workaday exhibition on Welsh castles and a wonderful animated cartoon based on the twelfth-century Cambrian travels of Giraldus Cambrensis (see box, p.380) in the ticket office.

Lloyd George Museum

Llanystumdwy, 1.5 miles west of Criccieth • Easter & May Mon–Fri 10.30am–5pm; June Mon–Sat 10.30am–5pm; July–Sept daily 10.30am–5pm; Oct Mon–Fri 11am–4pm • £4 • ☎ 01766 522071

6

Though born in Manchester, the Welsh nationalist, Liberal statesman, social reformer and British prime minister David Lloyd George (1864–1945) lived in his mother's home village until 1880, when he was sixteen. He grew up in Highgate House, the home of his uncle, the village cobbler, which is now part of the **Lloyd George Museum**. It kicks off with an informative thirty-minute film on the life of this witty and powerful orator described by Churchill as "a man of action, resource and creative energy, [who] stood, when at his zenith, without a rival". An extensive collection of gifts and awards attests to the great man's popularity, and the displays are full of anecdotes and little-known facts about him. Read between the lines to get a sense of the betrayal felt by many Welsh nationalists as his interest turned from the politics of Wales to those of Westminster.

Rustic late nineteenth-century beds and dressers furnish Lloyd George's wooden-floored two-up, two-down house, in a garden laid out much as it would have been in Lloyd George's day. Before ambling through the garden, walk down the path towards the River Dwyfor, beside which Lloyd George is buried under a memorial – a boulder and two simple plaques designed by Portmeirion's creator Clough Williams-Ellis.

Penarth Fawr

Off A497, 5.5 miles west of Criccieth • Easter–Sept daily 10am–5pm • Free • NT

Signposts point off the A497 down a tiny lane half a mile inland towards **Penarth Fawr**, a compact fifteenth-century hallhouse built to a common standard for the Welsh gentry. Constructed in 1416, the rare aisle truss hall was originally heated by a huge central hearth, replaced in the seventeenth century by the large fireplace you see today. Alterations at that time included the insertion of an upper floor – a dismantled beam from this work is on display, bearing the date 1656.

ARRIVAL AND DEPARTURE CRICCIETH

By train Trains serve: Porthmadog (8 daily; 10min); Pwllheli (8 daily; 15min).

By bus Both National Express buses from the north Wales coast and local buses stop at Y Maes and serve: Llanystumdwy (every 30min; 5min); Porthmadog (every 15–30min; 15min); Pwllheli (every 30min; 25min).

INFORMATION

Tourist information The nearest TICs are at Porthmadog and Pwllheli.

ACCOMMODATION

Glyn y Coed Porthmadog Rd, 100yd along A497 ☎ 01766 522870, ⓦ glynycoedhotel.co.uk. Refurbished small hotel with ten pretty rooms (some with sea views) and tasty breakfasts using locally sourced bacon. **£80**

Mynydd Du A497, 1 mile east ☎ 01766 522294, ⓦ mynydddu.co.uk. Camp in a slightly sloping, grassy field with fine Snowdonia and sea views. Clean modern shower block. Pitches **£16**

THE CRICCIETH FESTIVAL

The annual **Criccieth Festival** (ⓦ cricciethfestival.co.uk) takes place over the third week of June in venues all over town, and features jazz and classical music, lectures, art shows and plenty for kids.

Mynydd Ednyfed Caernarfon Rd, 1 mile north on B4411 ☎01766 523269, ⓦcriccieth.net. Some rooms in this elegant, renovated country house come with four-poster beds, and you can stroll the attractive grounds before dining at the very good restaurant. Outbuildings are used for all sorts of holistic treatments and massage. **£100**

Tyddyn Morthwyl Farm and Caravan Park On the Caernarfon Rd, 1.5 miles north of Criccieth ☎01766 522115. Not the closest but the nicest campsite, and has hot showers. There's a spacious bunkhouse in converted farm buildings. Book ahead and bring a sleeping bag. Bunkhouse **£8**, pitches **£12**

EATING AND DRINKING

Cadwalader's Castle St ☎01766 523665. Founding outlet of this regional ice-cream empire, now with a spacious airy café and great sea views. Come for coffee, smoothies, tasty pies or one of their rich ice creams. Daily: winter 10am–5pm; summer 10am–10pm.

The Feathers Llanystumdwy, 1.5 miles west ☎01766 523276, ⓦtafarnyplu.com. Classic and very Welsh local pub with a snug bar, hearty, home-cooked meals using local produce (around £8), a changing roster of Welsh ales and a garden bar. Meals daily 6–9pm.

Mynydd Ednyfed Caernarfon Rd, B4411, 1 mile north

☎01766 523269, ⓦcriccieth.net. Upscale cuisine served in a candlelit conservatory with mains (£13–17) such as chargrilled salmon fillet with crispy duck in a red wine and hoi sin sauce; extensive wine list. Daily 6.30–10pm.

★ **Tir A Môr** 1–3 Mona Terrace ☎01766 523084, ⓦtiramor-criccieth.co.uk. Delightful understated restaurant with some of Criccieth's best meals prepared with care. Eat à la carte (mains around £14) or on weekdays go for the set menu (2 courses for £18.50, 3 for £20.50; Tues–Thurs only), served with a glass of one of five house wines. Booking strongly advised. Tues–Sat 6–9.30pm.

Pwllheli and around

The undoubted "capital" of the Llŷn, **PWLLHELI** (pronounced something like "Poothl-heli") is a strange place: not quite a seaside resort, nor a town that exploits its illustrious history. Although the town appears largely Victorian, Pwllheli's market charter dates back to 1355: the Wednesday **market** takes place on Y Maes. It was also here at the *Maesgwyn Temperance Hotel* (now a pet shop marked with a plaque) in August 1925 that six people met to form Plaid Cymru. Even in the height of summer, you'll hear far more Welsh spoken here than English.

The Marina and the West End

From Y Maes, Ffordd-y-Cob leads south, past the spruce **marina**, packed with yachts, to Pwllheli's **West End**, a Victorian seaside development of pastel-shaded villas that seem ripe for renovation. The marina is lively all summer, with **boat trips** to Bardsey Island. The *Shearwater* (Easter–Oct only; ☎01758 613000) runs a morning cruise (2hr; £26) along an impressive section of coast, an afternoon cruise (3hr; £37) that includes a non-landing circuit of Bardsey Island, and an evening cruise (2hr; £32).

ARRIVAL AND DEPARTURE   PWLLHELI

By train The central train station serves: Criccieth (8 daily; 15min), Porthmadog (8 daily; 25min) and on down the Cambrian Coast line.

By bus National Express and local buses pull in at Y Maes.

Destinations include Aberdaron (6 daily; 40min); Abersoch (11 daily; 20–30min); Caernarfon (roughly hourly; 45min); Criccieth (every 30min; 25min); Nefyn (roughly hourly; 15min); Porthmadog (every 30min; 40min).

INFORMATION

Tourist information The TIC is on Station Square (April–Sept daily except Fri & Sun 9.30am–5pm; ☎01758

613000, ⓔpwllheli.tic@gwynedd.gov.uk).

Internet Free at the library on Penlan St.

ACCOMMODATION, EATING AND DRINKING

Bank Place 29 Stryd Fawr ☎01758 612103. Three rooms share two bathrooms at this simple but well-maintained B&B. Cooked breakfasts are served. **£50**

The Old Rectory A497 at Boduan, 4 miles northwest

☎01758 721519, ⓦtheoldirectory.net. Lovely country house in a wonderfully relaxed setting with elegant rooms and a great breakfast. Well positioned for exploring the tip of the peninsula. **£85**

WAKESTOCK

Activity peaks in Pwllheli in early July for **Wakestock** (ⓦ wakestock.co.uk), when 20,000 spectators arrive for a celebration of wakeboarding, skateboarding, BMX and music: Ellie Goulding and Biffy Clyro headlined in 2011.

Penlan Fawr 3 Penlan St ☎ 01758 612864. For a bite or something to drink, head to this four-hundred-year-old slate-floored pub that's been tastefully updated, including sofas around a snug fireplace. There's a good range of burgers, grills and veggie meals (mostly £5–10) and it morphs into the liveliest place in town at weekends. Daily 11am–11pm.

★ **Plas Bodegroes** Efailnewydd, A497, 2 miles north of Pwllheli; ☎ 01758 612363, ⓦ bodegroes.co.uk. The emphasis is very much on the food, but this is still probably the nicest place to stay on the Llŷn, set in a very swish Georgian country house surrounded by wonderful parkland. The rooms are comfortable yet understated, the service attentive but relaxed. The restaurant offers sumptuous dining that has ranked among Wales' finest for 25 years. Modern interpretations of traditional dishes are presented for lunch and dinner (£45 for three courses), the wine list is superb and Sunday lunch costs a modest £20. Hotel closed Sun & Mon; restaurant Tues–Sat 7–10pm, Sun noon–3pm. **£130**

Taro Deg A497 near the train station ☎ 01758 701271, ⓦ tarodeg.com. Comfortable daytime café serving freshly prepared sandwiches and Welsh rarebit plus cake and coffee. Free wi-fi. Daily 9am–5pm.

Llanbedrog

LLANBEDROG, four miles southwest of Pwllheli, is a delightful village worth visiting for its wonderful beach with its nicely sited café and for one of Wales' oldest public art galleries.

Oriel Plas Glyn-y-Weddw

Mid-July to early Sept daily 10am–5pm; mid-Sept to early July daily except Tues 10am–5pm • Free • ☎ 01758 740763, ⓦ oriel.org.uk

Solomon Andrews, the Cardiff entrepreneur who built Pwllheli's West End, bought the Victorian Gothic **Plas Glyn-y-Weddw** in 1896 and turned it into a genteel centre for the arts, with pleasure gardens and legendary tea dances. All rooms peel off a spectacular galleried hallway under a huge stained-glass window and a gorgeous hammerbeam oak roof, topped with a lantern. The exhibitions combine pieces from the gallery's permanent collection with touring works, often with a Welsh theme. There's also a very pleasant conservatory **café** in which to sit and gaze out to the distant sea.

Traeth Llanbedrog

Open access • Free • NT

It's a short stroll from the village down to **Traeth Llanbedrog**, a charming, sheltered strand lined with restored, primary-hued beach huts. From the southern end of the beach, a steep, fairly rough **path** climbs through a wooded glen onto a towering headland known as Mynydd Tir-y-Cwmwd, where the sweeping views are shared by the **Iron Man**, a modern wrought-iron sculpture designed and built locally to replace an 8ft ship's figurehead erected there in 1919.

Abersoch and around

After the distinctly Welsh feel of Pwllheli, **ABERSOCH**, seven miles southwest, comes as a surprise. This former fishing village, pitched in the middle of two golden bays, is a largely anglicized resort, catering to affluent boat-owners and holidaying families. At high tide the harbour is an attractive spot to stroll.

The beaches

It is only five minutes' walk to the closest beach, **Abersoch Bay**, a long, clean strand lined by several dozen colourful beach huts. It's barely visible under beach towels at busy times, although a short walk along the shore shakes off most of the crowds.

WATERSPORTS IN ABERSOCH

Abersoch Sailing School (March–Oct; ☎01758 712963, ⓦabersochsailingschool.com) runs lessons and rents lasers, catamarans and other craft on the town's main beach (from £45 for 2hr).

Offaxis right in the centre of town (☎01758 713407, ⓦoffaxis.co.uk). Open throughout summer. Offaxis runs a wakeboarding and surfing academy (£30 per lesson) and rents gear.

West Coast Surf Lôn Pen Cei (☎01758 713067, ⓦwww.westcoastsurf.co.uk), rents surfing gear (boards £10, wetsuits £8) and offers lessons (£30 for 2hr).

There's more space a mile north at **The Warren**, a fine stretch of beach backed by a holiday park. Surfers make for **Porth Neigwl** (Hell's Mouth), two miles to the southwest, which is one of the finest **surf** beaches in Wales – though beware of the undertow if you're swimming.

ARRIVAL AND DEPARTURE
ABERSOCH

By bus Buses from Pwllheli (11 daily; 20–30min) loop through the middle of Abersoch, stopping on Lôn Pen Cei. To continue to Aberdaron by bus, you must take a Pwllheli-bound service as far as Llanbedrog, then change onto the #17.

INFORMATION

Tourist office The TIC (June–Sept daily 10.30am–3.30pm; Oct–May Sat & Sun 11am–2pm; ☎01758 712929, ⓦabersochtouristinfo.co.uk) is in The Vestry on Lôn Engan.

ACCOMMODATION

There are lots of places to stay in and around Abersoch, but **accommodation** can be tight over summer and at weekends during spring and autumn. Almost all the **campsites** in villages around Abersoch are family-oriented places, so groups need to look reputable to be admitted.

Angorfa Lôn Sarn Bach ☎01758 712967, ⓦangorfa .com. Bare boards and white linen characterize this superior budget B&B. The two attic rooms have the best view, and breakfast is served in the daytime café downstairs. **£70**

★ **Goslings at the Carisbrooke** Lôn Sarn Bach ☎01758 712526, ⓦgoslingsabersoch.co.uk. Friendly, central a/c restaurant (The Dining Room; see below) with rooms, including en-suite doubles, family rooms with DVD players and a couple of self-catering flats nearby. **£85**

Porth Tocyn 2.5 miles south of Abersoch, on the road through Sarn Bach and Bwlchtocyn ☎01758 713303, ⓦporthtocynhotel.co.uk. Comfortable yet relaxed country-house hotel that is unusual in that it caters (magnificently) for families. Several rooms are interconnecting and there's a play room for kids while parents dine, plus an outdoor heated pool, excellent restaurant and great views of Cardigan Bay. There is no shortage of nooks and crannies to curl up with a book. Prices include continental breakfast. Closed early Nov to early April. **£135**

Rhydolion Llangian, 1 mile northwest of Abersoch ☎01758 712342, ⓦrhydolion.co.uk. Small, welcoming tent and caravan site which accepts groups, 15min walk from Porth Neigwl beach. It also has 4 very well-appointed, self-contained units. Closed Nov–Feb. Pitches **£16**

Sgobor Unnos Tanrallt Farm, Llangian, 2 miles west of Abersoch ☎01758 713527, ⓦtanrallt.com. Self-catering bunkhouse/hostel located in Llangian (bus #18 from Pwllheli or Abersoch; 4 daily). Bunks (including continental breakfast) **£17**; camping per person **£7**

Venetia Lôn Sarn Bach ☎01758 713354, ⓦvenetiawales.com. Apart from the view from a couple of rooms, you barely know you're at the seaside at this urban chic boutique hotel with five individually styled rooms, plush bathrooms and an excellent restaurant and bar. **£108**

EATING AND DRINKING

Abersoch Café Lôn Pen Cei ☎01758 713456. Good café serving panini, jacket potatoes and daily specials (£6–9), plus espresso. Daily 9.30am–5pm.

Brig In the Harbour Hotel on Lôn Sarn Bach ☎01758 712406. About the best spot in town for a few pints. Daily 11am–11pm.

Coconut Kitchen Lôn Pont Morgan ☎01758 712250. The best Thai place for miles, with dishes served from an open kitchen. Go for classics like beef Massaman or green chicken curry (around £11), or their exquisite Songkla

ABERSOCH JAZZ FESTIVAL

The varied Abersoch Jazz Festival (ⓦabersochjazzfestival.com) is held annually in several local venues over the second weekend in June.

dishes from south Thailand. (£15). Takeaways available. Daily 5.30–10pm.

The Dining Room Lôn Sarn Bach ☎01758 740709, ⓦthediningroomabersoch.co.uk. Casual wood-floored dinner-only bistro (plus some outside seating) with a short menu plus daily specials, all simply cooked from fresh ingredients. Mains (mostly £14–17) might include sea trout with laver-bread cakes or ribeye with brandy and black pepper sauce. Fish specials on Friday. Daily 7–10pm; closed Mon–Wed in winter.

Porth Tocyn 2.5 miles south of Abersoch, on the road through Sarn Bach and Bwlchtocyn ☎01758 713303, ⓦporthtocynhotel.co.uk. This has been one of Abersoch's best restaurants for half a century, and still welcomes non-residents to its panoramic dining room for superb meals

(£35 for two courses, £42 for four) and Sunday buffet lunch (£25). Closed early Nov to early April.

★ Venetia Lôn Sarn Bach ☎01758 713354, ⓦvenetiawales.com. Marco's Italian heritage influences the menu at this smart modern restaurant, which is usually strong on the fruits of the sea (often straight from local boats). Sip a pre-dinner cocktail in the bar as you select from the seasonal Modern British menu. Everything is superbly presented, and served by attentive but unobtrusive staff. Most mains £14–17. Wed–Sun 6.30–10pm.

Zinc Lôn Pen Cei ☎01758 712880. Cool bar with a relaxed ambience and a wonderful terrace overlooking the inner harbour. Hours vary seasonally; generally evenings only.

Aberdaron and around

At the lime-washed fishing hamlet of **ABERDARON**, two miles short of the tip of the Llŷn, you really feel you're at the end of Wales. For the best part of a thousand years up to the sixteenth century the inn and church here were the last stops on a pilgrim trail to Ynys Enlli or Bardsey Island, around the headland.

St Hywyn's church

Daily: Easter–Oct 10am–6pm; Nov–Easter 10am–4pm

The twelfth-century **church of St Hywyn** on the cliffs behind the stony beach still serves its original purpose, and was ministered by one of Wales' greatest modern poets, R.S. Thomas (see box, p.386). Displays on Thomas have pride of place in the twin-naved interior, beside material on Enlli and its pilgrims, and a pair of Latin-inscribed sixth-century gravestones – among the earliest Christian artefacts in Wales.

Plas yn Rhiw

B4413, 5 miles east of Aberdaron • Late March to April Thurs–Sun noon–5pm; May–Aug daily except Tues noon–5pm; Sept daily except Tues & Wed noon–5pm; Oct Thurs–Sun noon–4pm • £5 • ☎01758 780219 • NT

In the early years of his retirement, R.S. Thomas lived in a cottage in the grounds of **Plas yn Rhiw**, a Regency manor house on Tudor foundations at the western end of Porth Neigwl. The house was derelict in 1938 when it was bought by Thomas' moneyed friends, the Keating sisters, who restored it with the help of Portmeirion architect Clough Williams-Ellis, whose offbeat touch is evident in the flattened arches and a Gothic doorway rescued from a demolished castle. This is a manageable and relaxed place, filled with rustic furniture like a 1920s oil stove used by Honora Keating until her death in 1981, and her accomplished watercolours. The upstairs sitting room is notable for its 6ft-thick wall containing a fireplace, a spiral staircase and a window nook overlooking gorgeous gardens, all clipped box hedges, fuchsias, hydrangeas, roses and wild flowers. The Pwllheli to Aberdaron bus #17b (2 daily) passes the gate.

6

R.S. THOMAS

The reclusive, Cardiff-born poet **R.S. (Ronald Stuart) Thomas** (1913–2000) was something of a Welsh anti-hero. He worked as a minister in rural parishes throughout Wales, most famously in Aberdaron where he spent his last couple of working decades and much of his retirement. It was Thomas' fourth volume of poetry, published in 1955, that brought him lasting recognition, something consolidated with his best-known collections – *The Bread of Truth* (1963) and *Not that he brought Flowers* (1968).

R.S. Thomas's poetry is dark and spartan, illuminated with shafts of vision and clarity. Common themes include religion (Christianity in particular), rural and pastoral strands and the eternal poetic topic of love in human relationships. However, it's in his Welsh-themed work that Thomas most savagely and thrillingly hits the mark. *Selected Poems*, published by Bloodaxe, is a good starter anthology of his work.

I never wanted the drab rôle
Life assigned me, an actor playing
To the past's audience upon a stage
Of earth and stone; the absurd label
Of birth, of race hanging askew
About my shoulders. I was in prison
Until you came; your voice was a key
Turning in the enormous lock
Of hopelessness. Did the door open
To let me out or yourselves in?

Mynydd Mawr

2 miles southwest • Open access • Free • NT

Having made your way out as far as Aberdaron, it's worth using the village as a base for exploring the narrow lanes at the end of the peninsula, leading to **Mynydd Mawr**, the hill overlooking Bardsey Sound. Just as the road begins to climb up the hill, stop at **Braich-y-Pwll**, a headland from where a short path heads down the cliffs to the ruins of St Mary's church, the crossing point at the end of the Pilgrim's Way. The road continues from here to the top of Mynydd Mawr, from where the medieval patchwork of ancient fields which make up the tip of the Llŷn is clearly visible.

Porth Oer

2 miles north of Abersoch • Open access • Free; parking £1.50 • NT

The best beach hereabouts is **Porth Oer**, known as "Whistling Sands" for the white sands which squeak as you walk on them. It is a memorable spot hemmed in by rocky promontories with easy walks either way along the coast. The only facilities are toilets and a small beach shop that's only open in mid-summer.

ARRIVAL AND DEPARTURE   ABERDARON

By bus The #17 bus comes here from Pwllheli (6 daily; 40min).

ACCOMMODATION AND EATING

Mynydd Mawr Llanllawen Fawr, 2 miles southwest ☏ 01758 760223. A couple of peaceful grassy fields right by the entrance to Mynydd Mawr and with views across to Ynys Enlli. Hot showers and electricity hookup available. Closed Nov–Feb. Pitches **£10**

The Ship ☏ 01758 760204, ⓦ theshiphotelaberdaron .co.uk. The cheaper of the village's two hotels, but an excellent array of ales and the better restaurant serving the likes of local crab starter (£8) and a range of meat and vegetarian mains (£10–14). Daily noon–2pm & 6.30–9pm. **£89**

Tŷ Newydd ☏ 01758 760207, ⓦ gwesty-tynewydd .co.uk. Modernized seafront hotel with some sea-view rooms and a good restaurant overlooking the beach for bar snacks and full meals. **£105**

BIRDWATCHING ON YNYS ENLLI

Interesting though the abbey ruins and later buildings are, most visitors come to watch **birds**. Among the dozen or so species of nesting sea birds are Manx shearwaters, fulmars and guillemots, and an amazing number of vagrants turn up after being blown off course by storms. There are hides dotted around the island and **seals** slathered all over the rocks at low tide.

Y Gegin Fawr ☎01758 760359. The fourteenth-century stone " Big Kitchen" once served as the pilgrims' final gathering place before the treacherous crossing to Ynys Enlli. It now operates as a simple café serving clotted cream teas on the raised terrace with glimpses of the sea. Summer daily 11am–4pm.

6

Ynys Enlli (Bardsey Island)

Bardsey Island or **Ynys Enlli** (The Island of the Currents) rises out of the ocean two miles off the tip of the Llŷn, separated from it by a strait of churning, unpredictable water. This national nature reserve has been an important pilgrimage site since the sixth century, when St Cadfan set up the first monastery here: three visits were proclaimed equivalent to one pilgrimage to Rome. Legend claims Ynys Enlli as "The Isle of Twenty Thousand Saints", most likely remembering the huge numbers of pilgrims who came to die at this holy spot. By the twelfth century, Giraldus Cambrensis was already claiming that "no one dies there except in extreme old age, for disease is almost unheard of". Numerous other stories tell of the burial place of Myrddin (Merlin) and the former Bishop of Bangor, St Deiniol, but the only hard evidence is the crumbling **bell tower** of the thirteenth-century Augustinian Abbey of St Mary and a few Celtic crosses scattered around it. After the dissolution of the monasteries in 1536, piracy became the focus of the island's economy for over a century, gradually giving way to agriculture and fishing.

Apart from a dozen seasonal researchers, the island now has just one resident farming family who sell tea, coffee and snacks (11am–1pm). Bring your lunch.

ARRIVAL AND DEPARTURE · YNYS ENLLI

Boats to Ynys Enlli are dependent on sea conditions and a viable load of passengers: be as flexible as possible. The cheapest crossings are with Bardsey Boat Trips (£30 return; ☎07971 769895, ⬁bardseyboattrips.com) who flash across from Porth Meudwy, a tiny cove a mile south of Aberdaron, in around 15min. Enlli Charters (☎0845 811 3655, ⬁enllicharter.co.uk) run from Pwllheli (£35), and take an hour seeing more of the coast. Both trips give around four hours on Enlli.

ACCOMMODATION

Bardsey Island Trust ☎0845 811 2233, ⬁bardsey .org. The island's owners rent eight spartan but substantial electricity-free houses out by the week (mid-April to mid-Oct only; Saturday to Saturday), mostly to birders, but also for yoga retreats, photography workshops or just to get away. Per week from **£210**

The north Llŷn coast

Sprinkled with small coves and sweeping beaches between rocky bluffs, the **north Llŷn coast** is a dramatic contrast to the busier south. It has few settlements of any size and lots of quiet little beaches. The most popular (though seldom thronged) is **Porth Dinllaen** with its pub gorgeously sited beside the sand. A rockier coastline is accessible from the Welsh language school at Nant Gwrtheyrn, which is overlooked by the heights of **Tre'r Ceiri** with its prehistoric hillfort remains. The road northeast from Tre'r Ceiri towards Caernarfon now bypasses one of north Wales' finest churches, the austere church of St Beuno at **Clynnog Fawr**.

Even at the best of times, bus services are infrequent and badly timed, so you're far better off with your own car or bike. Amenities are also thinly scattered hereabouts – a few campsites dotted around, and the odd shop and pub in a village.

6

Nefyn and Porth Dinllaen

There isn't much to recommend **NEFYN**, the largest of the peninsula's northern communities, but neighbouring **MORFA NEFYN**, a mile to the west, and the adjacent shoreline hamlet of **PORTH DINLLAEN**, both benefit from having lost the 1839 battle to become the terminus for ferries to Ireland. Now owned by the National Trust, Porth Dinllaen is just a pristine sweeping bay backed by a handful of houses and the popular waterside *Tŷ Coch Inn*. Easiest access is to walk half a mile along the beach from the National Trust's Porth Dinllaen car park in Morfa Nefyn.

ACCOMMODATION, EATING AND DRINKING   NEFYN AND PORTH DINLLAEN

Penrallt Coastal Campsite Tudweiliog, 6 miles southeast of Morfa Nefyn ☎01758 770654. ⓦpenrallt .co.uk. One of the best north Llŷn campsites, peacefully perched just back from the clifftops with separate fields for families and small tents. There's direct access to the coast path (and nearby beaches), a two-mile walk to the *Lion Inn* in Tudweiliog, and facilities which include hot showers, freezer and laundry. They're also making great strides towards making the place as sustainable as possible.

Closed Oct–Easter. Pitches £11

Tŷ Coch Inn Porth Dinllaen ☎01758 720498. The uninspiring bar meals (jacket spuds, sandwiches and panini) are overpriced but that's not why you come to this village pub hung with tankards and miners' lanterns. Pick a warm day, grab a pint and sit outside at tables or on the sea wall squirming your toes in the sand and watching the boats come and go. Perfect.

Nant Gwrtheyrn

Northeast of Nefyn the mountains of Yr Eifl rise steeply only to plunge into the sea along **Nant Gwrtheyrn** (Vortigern's Valley), an impressively steep cleft in the hills, its edges chewed away by granite quarries. This is supposed to be the final resting place of the Celtic chieftain Vortigern, who was responsible for inviting the Saxons to Britain after his magician, Myrddin (Merlin), had seen the struggle of the two dragons – the red of the ancient Britons and the white of the Saxons.

Nant Gwrtheyrn: The Welsh Language and Heritage Centre

1.5 miles north of Llithfaen, 3 miles northeast of Nefyn • Daily 9.30am–4.30pm • Free • ☎01758 750334, ⓦnantgwrtheyrn.org

Vortigern should be pleased to know that his valley is now doing its best to atone for his error, by keeping the ancient British language alive at **Nant Gwrtheyrn: The Welsh Language and Heritage Centre**, at the foot of the valley. A precipitously steep road corkscrews down to the centre, set in rows of converted cottages built in the late nineteenth century when the valley had three granite quarries. Though primarily for residential courses entirely in Welsh, the valley is also a beautiful spot to spend a couple of hours **exploring**, either along the Llŷn Coastal Path, or around the old mine workings and piles of rock waste that are gradually being colonized by bracken. A free leaflet outlines a 3-mile **walk**.

To put it all into context, visit the **Heritage Centre** in the original chapel, and the **Quarryman's Cottages**, two rooms set up to look as it might have been in 1910 with dresser, needlework sampler and Bible all in pride of place around the hearth.

A good licensed **café** provides sustenance, and there's even self-catering **accommodation** in the cottages (three-night minimum).

Tre'r Ceiri

Open access • Free

Yr Eifl is a trio of mountains which top out at 1850ft. The second highest is crowned by **Tre'r Ceiri** or "Town of the Giants" hillfort, easily the finest prehistoric remains on the Llŷn. A massive tumble of rocks is mostly formed into the waist-high walls of about 150 dry-stone hut circles surrounded by a rampart 12ft high in places. The site is Bronze Age, but the huts are probably only a couple of thousand years old. Locals refer to them as *Cytiau Gwddelod* or "Irishmen's Huts", possibly recalling the Irish immigrant population on the Llŷn in the first few centuries AD, when five hundred people lived on this inhospitable site. Today, the ruins command a stunning **view** over the whole peninsula.

The summit is reached by a steep **path** (4km return; 2hr; 800ft ascent) which starts at a lay-by half a mile southwest of Llanaelhaearn.

Church of St Beuno

Clynnog Fawr, just off A499, 4 miles northeast of Llanaelhaearn • Easter–Oct daily 10am–5pm

Light streams in through the clear windows of the large and airy, early sixteenth-century **church of St Beuno**, built on foundations laid by Saint Beuno in the sixth century. This monastic settlement is rich in ancient spiritual connections and would have been an important stop for pilgrims bound for Ynys Enlli, ensuring a hefty income that probably financed this impressive church. The interior combines spartan whitewash and limestone flags with wealthier flourishes like the fine hammerbeam roof with ornamental bosses, fine choir stalls and imposing chancel.

The road to Caernarfon passes a turn-off to Dinas Dinlle, the gates of Parc Glynllifon, and close by the Inigo Jones Slateworks (see p.363).

6

The north coast and Anglesey

BRITANNIA BRIDGE AND MENAI BRIDGE, MENAI STRAIT

The north coast and Anglesey

Wales' North Coast and its natural extension, Anglesey, encompass both the geographical and social extremities of the country. In the brash towns of the northeast, street signs are the only indication that you are in Wales: further west, there are places where English is seldom spoken other than to visitors. Two major forces shaped the region. The might of thirteenth-century English king Edward I crushed the Welsh princes by means of dramatically situated castles. Then, in the nineteenth century English mill-town factory workers began holidaying here by the trainload. The setup isn't so different today, but cars have largely taken over from the train, caravans are as popular as guesthouses, and amusement arcades rule.

7

Wales' northern seaboard elicits strong reactions. Many return annually to the inexpensive holiday resorts at its eastern end, while others sneer as they pass them by en route to the more highbrow attractions further west. Either way, the initial strip of the **north coast** proper is the ugliest in Wales, a compressed array of caravan parks packed each year with fun-seekers from much of northern England. The amusements scattered along the promenades and beachfronts seem designed to keep you off the beaches: wise counsel, since the sea here is none too clean.

The fast A55 highway largely bypasses **Deeside**, a wedge of former mining communities set between the salt marshes of the Dee estuary and the Clwydian Range. Divert to visit **Flint Castle**, the first link in Edward I's Iron Ring of castles; and understated **Holywell**, whose quiet attractions include St Winefride's Well, a pilgrimage site of varied fortunes during the last 1300 years.

Uninspiring **Prestatyn** is notable mainly as the starting, or finishing, point of the Offa's Dyke Path. Loud and tacky **Rhyl** offers good budget accommodation and is close to several inland attractions, specifically the nuggety castle at **Rhuddlan**, the Victorian portrait gallery at **Bodelwyddan**, and **St Asaph**, home to Britain's smallest cathedral. **Colwyn Bay** is smarter than Rhyl, but pales next to its western neighbours, Llandudno and Conwy.

Victorian **Llandudno** was always a posher resort and remains a cut above the rest. This queen of the north Wales coast with its four-storey terraced beachfront hunkers below the massive limestone hummock of the **Great Orme**, climbed by cable car and tram, and ringed by the scenic Marine Drive. With no real beach, **Conwy** is a different proposition, packing more sights than the rest of the coast put together within the girdle of 700-year-old town walls which spur off from the mighty castle.

The A55 expressway is held tightly to the coast by the northern fringes of Snowdonia's Carneddau range for the final fifteen miles to **Bangor**, home to north Wales' only university, and consequently its liveliest town.

Highlights

❶ Llandudno The town's classy gentility is nicely offset by the ruggedness of the neighbouring limestone hummock of the Great Orme reached by San Francisco-style tram. **See p.403**

❷ Conwy The pick of north Wales' towns with its imposing castle and intact ring of medieval walls enclosing a fascinating centre. **See p.408**

❸ Menai Strait Look back from Anglesey across the swirling tidal races of the Menai Strait, with the great bridges framing long views of Snowdonia. **See p.422**

❹ Beaumaris Another impressive castle and Georgian townscape make this a fine base for

exploring Anglesey's beaches and Neolithic remains. **See p.423**

❺ Penmon Priory Lovely twelfth-century church containing ancient stonework, hidden in an almost forgotten corner of Anglesey. **See p.425**

❻ Newborough Warren Easy strolls through ecologically important dune systems to the remote-feeling peninsula known as Llanddwyn Island. **See p.429**

❼ South Stack Wheeling sea birds, stunning sea cliffs, a picturesque lighthouse on a small island and some great coastal walking. **See p.432**

HIGHLIGHTS ARE MARKED ON THE MAP ON P.394

If it's beaches you're after, head across the treacherous channel of the **Menai Strait** to the island of **Anglesey**, a patchwork of rural communities dotted with burial chambers, standing stones and Wales' greatest concentration of Neolithic remains. There's yet another stupendous castle at **Beaumaris**, built to a highly advanced concentric design.

The southwestern resorts of **Rhosneigr**, **Rhoscolyn** and **Trearddur Bay** are the favoured spots for swimming and watersports, but in scenic terms there's much to be said for the extensive dune system of **Newborough** and the sea cliffs around **South Stack**, both great for birdwatching. Lastly, the ferries from **Holyhead**, at the western end of the island, provide the fastest route to Dublin and Dun Laoghaire in Ireland.

GETTING AROUND   THE NORTH COAST AND ANGLESEY

By train The train is a great way to see the north coast. It links the coastal resorts all the way to Bangor, then across to Anglesey for the run to Holyhead.

By bus With the exception of National Express bus services from Manchester, Liverpool and other English cities to Bangor and Holyhead, bus travel is much more piecemeal, although services are fairly frequent and come listed in

excellent timetable booklets available free at tourist offices. Check Getting around in Basics for discount fares and passes.

By car The A55 dual carriageway allows you to drive from the Welsh border just south of Liverpool through Anglesey to Holyhead in little over an hour, bypassing all the coastal towns and skirting the northern reaches of Snowdonia.

Deeside

The industrial hinterland that spreads over the English border from Chester can best be avoided by heading directly for **Deeside**, a narrow littoral flanking the River Dee

THE NORTH COAST & ANGLESEY

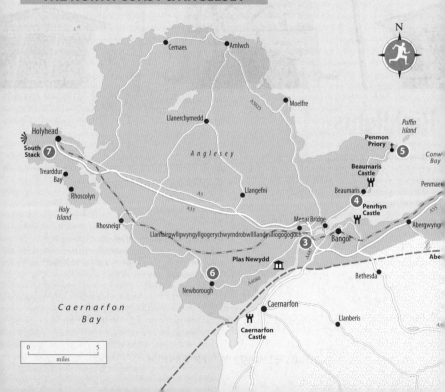

estuary. A short detour off the A55 onto the A548 is rewarded by a few modest sights – castle ruins at Flint, the healing waters of **Holywell**, a minor collection of historic industrial buildings in the **Greenfield Valley Heritage Park** and the gorgeous carved Celtic cross of **Maen Achwyfaen**.

Flint Castle

Open access • Free • CADW

If you're travelling on the North Coast train line, take one of the regional services which stop at **FLINT** (Y Fflint), and spend the hour between trains exploring the buff sandstone ruins of **Flint Castle**. Started in 1277, this was the first of Edward I's Iron Ring of fortresses (see p.410), standing sentinel over once-important shipping lanes into Chester. The 10ft-thick pockmarked walls form a square with drum towers at all except the southeast corner, where a small moat and drawbridge separate the castle from the well-preserved Great Tower, or Donjon. Uniquely in Britain, this was intended as the castle's main accommodation and last place of retreat, and came equipped with its own well. Together with its large grassy outer ward and the adjoining town, the castle formed a unified enclave known as a "bastide".

During the Civil War, Flint remained Royalist until taken in 1647 by General Mytton, who so effectively dismantled the castle that only six years later it was practically buried in its own ruins. It was in this condition when Celia Fiennes found it on the brief – and generally displeasing – Welsh leg of her journeys around Britain between 1698 and 1712.

7

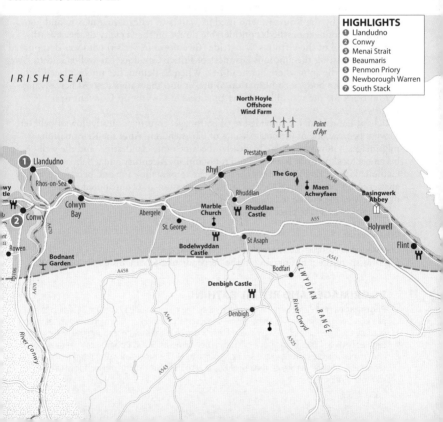

HIGHLIGHTS
❶ Llandudno
❷ Conwy
❸ Menai Strait
❹ Beaumaris
❺ Penmon Priory
❻ Newborough Warren
❼ South Stack

FLINT IN SHAKESPEARE

Flint's greatest hour came in 1399 when Richard II was lured here from the safety of Conwy Castle and captured by Henry Bolingbroke, the Duke of Lancaster and future Henry IV. Shakespeare dramatized the event in *Richard II*, when in response to Bolingbroke's, "My gracious Lord, I come but for mine own", the defeated king replies, "Your own is yours, and I am yours, and all". Even Richard's favourite greyhound is said to have deserted him at this point.

ARRIVAL AND DEPARTURE   FLINT

By train Trains pass every 30min running to: Chester (15min); Prestatyn (15min); and Llandudno Junction (40min).
By bus Buses, from outside the train station, serve: Chester

(every 30min; 50min); Mold (every 30min; 20min); Prestatyn (every 30min; 50min); and Rhyl (every 30min; 1hr).

Holywell and around

A place of pilgrimage for thirteen hundred years, **HOLYWELL** (Treffynnon), just off the A55 four miles northwest of Flint, is fancifully billed as "The Lourdes of Wales", though without the tacky souvenir stalls selling Virgin Mary lighters. Instead, Holywell is a quiet little town that modestly plays down its ancient appeal.

St Winefride's Well

Greenfield Rd • Daily: April–Sept 9am–5.30pm; Oct–March 10am–4pm • 80p • ☎ 01352 713054, ⓦ saintwinefrideswell.com

The source of all the fuss is **St Winefride's Well**, a sacred and ancient spring that was first recorded by the Romans, who used its waters to relieve rheumatism and gout. The Roman connection sheds considerable doubt on the veracity of the seventh-century legend of the virtuous Winefride (**Gwenfrewi** in Welsh) who was decapitated here after resisting the amorous advances of Prince Caradoc. The well is said to have sprung up at the spot where her head fell. When St Beuno, her uncle, placed her head beside the body, a combination of prayer and the waters revived her, setting her on track for the rest of her life as an abbess at Gwytherin Convent near Llanrwst.

Richard I and Henry V provided regal patronage, ensuring a steady flow of believers to what became one of the great shrines of Christendom. After the Reformation, pilgrimages – now punishable by death – became more clandestine, and the well became a focal point of resistance to Protestantism. A century and a half later, the Catholic king of England, James II, came here to pray for a son and heir; the eventual answer to his prayers threatened a Catholic succession and contributed to the overthrow of the House of Stuart.

Pilgrimages still take place (see box).

St Winefride's Chapel

Chapel Key from the ticket office • **Museum** April–Sept Wed, Sat & Sun noon–4pm • CADW

Pilgrims spent the night praying in the Perpendicular **St Winefride's Chapel**, built

PILGRIMAGES AND RITUAL BATHING

Pilgrimages mainly focus on St Winefride's Day, the nearest Sunday to June 22, when over five hundred pilgrims are led through the streets by the Bishop of Wrexham. The procession ends by the open side of the crypt where a few dozen faithful wade through the waters of a calm pool three times in the hope of curing their ailments. Sadly, a pump now fills the pool after mine working disrupted the spring's source in 1917. Immersion isn't limited to the procession: anyone, whatever their beliefs, can take the cure, though most choose to go in the summer "Curing Season".

> ## GREENFIELD VALLEY HERITAGE PARK STROLL
>
> St Winefride's Well and Basingwerk Abbey are just a mile apart, linked by a woodland trail along the trackbed of an old pilgrims' train line. Paths weave past five mill ponds, a series of water races and the preserved remains of copper works and cotton mills that form **Greenfield Valley Heritage Park**. About 200yd down the Greenfield Road from the Well, take the footpath behind the factory and then follow whichever paths take your fancy.

around 1500 to enclose three sides of the well. Henry VII's mother, Margaret Beaufort, paid for the construction and earned herself a likeness among the roof bosses that depict the life of St Winefride in the ornate, Gothic fan-vaulted crypt that surrounds the well. With the gloom only cut by light from votive candles, she's not that easy to see now.

A small **exhibition** features ancient boards inscribed with major donations, a collection of cast-off crutches, and banners once carried on pilgrimages. The former custodian's house contains a small **museum** with more painted banners and a beautiful silver reliquary designed to display Holywell's relic – part of Winefride's thumb bone – which is the subject of daily **veneration**.

Basingwerk Abbey
Greenfield Valley • Daily 10am–4pm • Free • CADW

Vaulted slabs of stonework and a few domestic building foundations are all that survive of **Basingwerk Abbey**. Still, it was obviously a grand place for the Cistercian abbot and dozen or so monks that lived and prayed here.

Greenfield Valley Farm and Museum
April–Oct daily 10am–4.30pm • Visitor centre free, museum: £4.20 • ☎ 01352 714172, ⓦ greenfieldvalley.com

A small **visitor centre** contains historical material on Basingwerk Abbey and serves as the entrance to the family-oriented **Greenfield Valley Farm and Museum**, a collection of reconstructed buildings from around north Wales, many saved from demolition. Particularly interesting are the Victorian school and the agricultural buildings, the latter preserved as a working farm where you can feed the animals.

Maen Achwyfaen
4 miles west of Holywell • Open access • Free • CADW

If you've got your own transport, head four miles west from Holywell to the impressive **Maen Achwyfaen** or "Stone of Lamentation", Britain's tallest **Celtic cross**. Though the shaft, incised with interwoven latticework, is over 10ft high and crowned with a wheel cross, this thousand-year-old monument is little celebrated and stands alone in a field. To get there, take the A5026 almost three miles northwest from Holywell, turn right onto the A5151, after almost a mile take the third exit at the first roundabout and follow signs to Trelogan for a little over a mile.

ARRIVAL AND DEPARTURE HOLYWELL

By bus Buses along the coast call frequently at the bus station at the southern end of High St. They serve Flint (every 30min; 15min) and Rhyl (every 30min; 1hr).

ACCOMMODATION, EATING AND DRINKING

Blue Bell Inn B5123 in Halkyn, 4 miles southeast ☎ 01352 780309, ⓦ bluebell.uk.eu.org. Fine rural pub with an ever-changing range of superb real ales, excellent ciders and perries, great views over the Dee Estuary, simple but well-prepared pub meals (around £7) and a huge range of events such as games evenings, Welsh classes and gigs. Mon–Fri 5–11pm, Sat & Sun noon–11pm.

Glan-yr-Afon Inn Dolphin, Milwr ☎ 01752 710052, ⓦ glanyrafoninn.co.uk. Sixteenth-century country pub that feels a world away from Holywell. They have eight rooms, along with excellent bar meals and real ales served

7

in the tastefully modernized interior or out in the beer garden. Follow the A5026 southwest of town then onto Milwr Rd; 1.2 miles in all. Meals served daily noon–2.30pm & 6–9pm. £65

Greenhill Farm Bryn Celyn ☎01352 713270, ⓦgreenhillfarm.co.uk. A partly sixteenth-century oak-beamed farmhouse on a farm where corgis are used to herd cattle. Four rooms all have en-suite or private bathrooms. Head a few yards northeast from Winefride's Well on B5121 and then take the second left opposite the *Royal Oak* pub. £50

The Mill on the Hill Greenfield Rd ☎01352 711004. Decent daytime tearoom right by St Winefride's Well. The sandwiches, Welsh rarebit and cream teas are nothing fancy but are well made and cheap, and there's free wi-fi. Tues–Sat 10am–5pm, Sun 10am–4pm.

Prestatyn to Colwyn Bay

Almost all the vituperative comments aimed at the north Wales coast are aimed squarely at this heavily populated twenty-mile stretch of amusement arcades, bingo halls, caravan sites and negligible beach. Of the resorts, the best known is **Rhyl** – big, brash and ballsy but with more gentle attractions nearby including the cathedral at tiny **St Asaph**, one of Edward I's castles at **Rhuddlan** and the collection of Victorian portraits and furniture at **Bodelwyddan Castle**. There's little to keep you in **Prestatyn**, although it is the starting point for the Offa's Dyke long-distance path, and close to the Neolithic mound of the **Gop**. The more architecturally coherent, if hardly exciting, **Colwyn Bay** is marginally the nicest of the main resorts.

Offshore in Liverpool Bay, several dozen huge white **wind turbines** go about their business out of earshot.

Prestatyn and around

PRESTATYN is a likeable enough town, though it's really only of interest as the northern terminus of the 177-mile Offa's Dyke Path, which runs from here to Chepstow (see box, p.240). The more committed traditionally start at least ankle-deep in the water, then cross the beach beside the gleaming "Dechrau a Diwedd" ("Beginning and End") sculpture. They then head up the High Street to the **Cross Foxes** pub, from where acorn-marked signs guide you up to the hills behind. You won't come across any of the Offa's Dyke earthworks until the path gets south of the River Dee, since the route planners rightly preferred to send hikers across the Clwydian Range rather than to the scrappy industrial towns on the dyke's route. On a good day, though, the view from atop the Clwydian Range is tremendous – east to Liverpool, west to Snowdonia, and north past the offshore windfarm to Blackpool.

The Gop

Trelawnyd, 4 miles southeast of Prestatyn • Open access • Free

If you've got your own transport, visit the **Gop**, a neglected piece of ancient history that is Britain's second-largest artificial Neolithic mound after Silbury Hill in Wiltshire. The Gop was constructed on top of an existing hill, crowning an already splendid viewpoint with a mysterious mound – prehistoric remains have been found both in the mound itself and in the caves directly below the hill. The superb **views** over the Clwydian hills from the top are accessed via a path from above the village of **Trelawnyd**, on the A5151. In Trelawnyd, park about 200yd up High Street and walk along a narrow gravel lane on the left following the discreet discs to the Gop – about fifteen minutes' walk in all.

ARRIVAL AND DEPARTURE | | PRESTATYN

By train North coastline trains stop in the centre of town, serving: Flint (every 30–60min; 15min); Llandudno Junction (every 30–60min; 25min).

By bus Buses stop close to the train station with services to: Holywell (every 30min; 40min); Rhyl (every 30min; 20min).

ACCOMMODATION

Beaches Hotel Beach Rd East ⊕01745 853072, ⓦthebeacheshotel.com. Upgraded waterfront hotel with comfy rooms, its own restaurant, a bar with outside seating, and an indoor pool. **£86**

Nant Mill Gronant Rd ⊕01745 852360, ⓦnantmilltouring.co.uk. Simple, grassy, family-oriented campsite a mile east along the A548. Closed mid-Oct to mid-March. Pitches **£14**

Plas Ifan 17 Ffordlas, near the Cross Foxes pub ⊕01745 887883, ⓦplasifan.com. Comfortable B&B that's popular with Offa's Dyke walkers. Three en-suite rooms, spacious grounds, packed lunches on request and camping for walkers and cyclists. **£60**

Rhyl and Rhuddlan

For raw and raucous seaside shenanigans, **RHYL** (Y Rhyl), three miles west of Prestatyn, is probably your best bet. The two-mile-long Promenade is a powerful assault on the senses, all pulsing lights, whooping arcade games and the ever-present smell of candyfloss and vinegar on chips. While no one would claim that run-down Rhyl is a sophisticated tourist destination, it's a decent place for a cheap, cheerful holiday blowout, especially if you're with kids.

RHUDDLAN, three miles to the south, and essentially a suburb of Rhyl, is home to **Rhuddlan Castle** on the banks of a tidal reach of the Clwyd River (Afon Clywedog).

Sun Centre

Eastern end of the Promenade • Mid-March to mid-Sept Wed–Sun plus Mon & Tues during school holidays 10.30 or 11.30am–5.30pm • £8.95 • ⊕01745 344433, ⓦrhylsuncentre.co.uk

On a wet day the **Sun Centre** is one of the biggest draws in north Wales, with slides, a surfing-wave pool with overhead monorail, chutes and slides and a relaxing sun terrace.

SeaQuarium

East Parade • Daily: March–Oct 10am–5pm; Nov–Feb 10am–4pm • £8.25 • ⊕01745 344660, ⓦseaquarium.co.uk

Experience an assortment of coastal environments –beach, tropical reef (complete with deadly lionfish), and even a shipwreck zone – at the **SeaQuarium**, an entertaining aquatic zoo which includes a shark tunnel where dogfish, basking sharks and various eels drift leisurely around you until the day's highlight: feeding time. Seals are fed at noon, and don't miss the sea-lion cove where you can watch fifteen-minute shows (at 1pm & 3pm).

Rhuddlan Castle

Rhuddlan, 3 miles south • April–Oct daily 10am–5pm • £3.20 • ⊕01745 590777 • CADW

Rhuddlan Castle, now an impressive hollow ruin, was constructed between 1277 and 1282 by Edward I during his first phase of castle-building. It was designed as both a garrison and royal residence, commanding a canalized section of the then strategic river that allowed boats to service the castle and provided water for the huge stone-lined moat. **Gillot's Tower**, by the dock gate, provided protection for the supply ships. The massive towers behind were the work of James of St George, who was responsible for the concentric plan that allowed archers on both outer and inner walls to fire simultaneously. This had become irrelevant by 1648, when Parliament forces took the castle during the Civil War and demolished it. Stairs now give access to the top of the East Gatehouse.

ARRIVAL AND DEPARTURE   RHYL

The **train and bus stations** are adjacent, near the intersection of the A548 (Russell/Wellington roads) and Bodfor/ Queen streets, which run to the sea.

By train Trains serve: Bangor (25 daily; 40min); Holyhead (23 daily; 1hr 10min–1hr 30min); Llandudno Junction (every 20–30min; 20min).

By bus Buses serve: Denbigh (every 30min; 40min);

Llandudno (every 10–20min; 1hr 10min); Prestatyn (every 30min; 20min); Rhuddlan (every 15min; 10min); St Asaph (every 30min; 25min).

INFORMATION

Tourist information The TIC is on The Promenade (Easter–Sept daily 9.30am–4.30pm; Oct–Easter Mon–Fri 9.30am–4.30pm; ☎01745 355068, ✉rhyl.tic@denbighshire.gov.uk).

ACCOMMODATION, EATING AND DRINKING

Aysha 47 Wellington Rd ☎01745 353978. Excellent-value curries (most dishes under £6) in a welcoming family-run restaurant. Daily noon–2.30pm & 6–10.30pm.

Barratt's Ty'n Rhyl, 167 Vale Rd ☎01745 344138, ⓦbarrattsoftynrhyl.co.uk. Sumptuously decorated and well-appointed rooms in Rhyl's oldest house. Also the best dining in town, offering modern cuisine made from the finest local ingredients. Sunday lunch at £16 is recommended. Meals available Tues–Sat 6.30–10pm, Sun noon–3pm. £95

Melbourne 8 Beechwood Rd ☎01745 342762, ⓦthe-melbourne.co.uk. Welcoming B&B offering neat rooms and a cooked breakfast. Close to the beach and Sun Centre. £50

St Asaph and around

Because of its cathedral, diminutive **ST ASAPH** (Llanelwy), six miles south of Rhyl, ranks as a city. St Davids in Pembrokeshire is a slightly less populous "city", but St Asaph boasts the country's smallest **cathedral** – a squat-towered edifice no bigger than many village churches.

Cathedral

Daily 9am–6.30pm • Free

The town's Welsh name (meaning "the church on Elwy River") dates back to around 570 when St Asaph succeeded the cathedral's founder, St Kentigern, as abbot, and became its first bishop. Both are commemorated in the easternmost window in the north aisle of the cathedral. In 1282, Edward I's men ravaged the church, leaving the incumbent bishop Anian II (whose effigy is in the south aisle) with the task of building the present structure.

From 1601 until his death in 1604, the bishopric was held by **William Morgan** (see box), whose work is commemorated by an octagonal monument in the churchyard. Morgan's grave under the presbytery has been unmarked since George Gilbert Scott's substantial restoration in the 1870s. Around a thousand Morgan Bibles were printed, of which only nineteen remain, one of them displayed in the south transept along with Elizabeth I's 1549 copy of *The Book of Common Prayer*. There's also a handsome collection of Psalters and prayer books, and across in the north transept you'll see an exquisite sixteenth-century ivory Madonna, said to have come from the Spanish Armada.

The church also contains a Welsh-Greek-Hebrew dictionary compiled by nineteenth-century polyglot Richard Robert Jones (usually known as **Dic Aberdaron**, after the

---

WILLIAM MORGAN AND THE FIRST WELSH BIBLE

Until 1588 only English Bibles had been used in Welsh churches, a fact which rankled Welsh-born preacher **William Morgan**, who insisted: "Religion, if it is not taught in the mother tongue, will lie hidden and unknown". This was the professed reason behind Elizabeth I's demand for a translation, though her subjects' disaffection could be most conveniently controlled through the Church. Four clergymen took up the challenge, but it is Morgan who is remembered: working away in Llanrhaeadr-ym-Mochnant, he so neglected his other duties that he needed an armed guard to get to his services and was said to preach with a pistol at his side.

The eventual translation was so successful that the Privy Council decreed that a copy should be allocated to every Welsh church. Though it was soon replaced by a translation of the Authorized Version, Morgan's Bible differs little in style from the latest edition used in Welsh services today. More than just a basis for sermons, The **Welsh Bible** (Y Beibl) served to codify the language and set a standard for Welsh prose. Without it the language would probably have divided into several dialects or even followed its Brythonic cousin, Cornish, into history.

fishing village where he was born). He lived more or less as a tramp while acquiring command of fifteen languages (along with smatterings of another twenty) and is buried in the parish church at the bottom of the hill.

Marble church

Bodelwyddan, off junction 25 of A55, 2 miles west of St Asaph

At Bodelwyddan, the slender 202ft limestone spire of **Marble church** stands as a beacon over the flat coastal plain. The spire's finely worked Gothic tracery is its most impressive feature, and is continued inside where fourteen types of marble – Italian, Irish, Welsh – gave the church its name.

Bodelwyddan Castle: the National Portrait Gallery

Bodelwyddan, off junction 25 of A55, 2 miles west of St Asaph • Generally open mid-April–Oct Wed–Sun plus Mon & Tues in school holidays 10am–5pm; Nov to mid-April Sat & Sun 11am–4pm • £6 including audio tour • ⓦ bodelwyddan-castle.co.uk

Set amid landscaped grounds, **Bodelwyddan Castle** is essentially a nineteenth-century country mansion, its opulent Victorian interiors re-created during its restoration in the 1980s, as home to Lowther College girls' school. It now houses one of three provincial outposts of the **National Portrait Gallery**, specializing in works contemporary with the castle.

7

The gallery

Most of the hundred paintings are on the ground floor, approached through the "Watts Hall of Fame", a long corridor lined with 26 portraits of eminent Victorians by G.F. Watts, among them Millais, Rossetti, Browning and Walter Crane. In the Dining Room, two portraits highlight the Pre-Raphaelite support for social reform: William Holman Hunt's portrayal of the vociferous opponent of slavery and capital punishment, Stephen Lushington; and Ford Madox Brown's double portrait of Henry Farell, prime mover in the passing of the 1867 Reform Bill, and suffragette Millicent Garrett. Works by John Singer Sargent and Hubert von Herkamer also adorn the room, which, like the others, is furnished with pieces from the Victoria and Albert Museum in London. The table and chairs originally belonged to one Alfred Waterhouse, who designed the superb walnut and boxwood grand piano.

More worthy Victorians line the Library, which leads on to the Ladies' Drawing Room, where a beautiful Biedermeier sofa outshines the paintings of nineteenth-century society ladies. A grand staircase leads up to further examples of nineteenth-century portraiture and an interesting exhibit on the castle's time as Lowther College.

ARRIVAL AND DEPARTURE   ST ASAPH

By bus St Asaph is on the #51 bus route from Rhyl to Denbigh, which also comes within a minutes' walk of the Marble Church and Bodelwyddan Castle. Buses all stop outside the cathedral for Denbigh (every 30min; 15min), Rhuddlan (every 30min; 15min) and Rhyl (every 30min; 25min).

ACCOMMODATION, EATING AND DRINKING

The Bridge Lower St ☎01745 536725. This modernized pub is a great spot for a pint outside overlooking the river. Inside there's a pizza room, a full restaurant (mains £10–13) and a cosy cocktail bar with open fire. Mon–Sat 11.30am–11pm, Sun 11.30am–10pm.

★ **Kinmel Arms** St George, 4 miles west of St Asaph ☎01745 832207, ⓦthekinmelarms.co.uk. The picturesque hamlet of St George is home to this special place to stay – a welcoming seventeenth-century pub with just four chic, modern and gorgeously furnished suites. It is a wonderful spot for a classy brasserie lunch (mains £7–13), fancier à la carte dishes in the evenings (£15–25), and a fine selection of real ales and wines. Hotel closed Sun & Mon. Meals available Tues–Sat noon–2.30pm & 6.30–9.30pm. **£135**

★ **Tan-yr-Onnen** Waen, 2 miles east ☎01745 583821, ⓦnorthwalesbreaks.co.uk. Excellent six-room rural B&B set among the green fields of the Vale of Clwyd just off the Offa's Dyke Path. Rooms are comfortably stylish with thoughtful touches, there's free wi-fi, evening meals and an excellent pub just down the road. **£89**

Colwyn Bay and Rhos-on-Sea

The seamless towns of **COLWYN BAY** (Bae Colwyn) and **RHOS-ON-SEA**, twelve miles west of Rhyl, have marginally more charm than their eastern neighbours, with a hilly setting and architecturally intact Victorian main street.

Welsh Mountain Zoo

Old Highway, 2 miles inland from Colwyn Bay • Daily: April–Oct 9.30am–6pm; Nov–March 9.30am–5pm • £9.95 • ☎ 01492 532938,
ⓦ welshmountainzoo.org

Head steeply uphill to reach the **Welsh Mountain Zoo**, which boasts Californian sea lions, snow leopards and free-flying raptor displays. A free shuttle bus runs every twenty minutes (Easter & May to mid-Sept) between the zoo and the town's train station.

Harlequin Puppet Theatre

The Promenade, Rhos-on-Sea • July, Aug and most school holidays daily 3pm & Wed 8pm • £5.50 • ☎ 01492 548166, ⓦ puppets.uk.com

To catch one of the very few remaining marionette acts in the British tradition visit the ninety-minute daytime shows at the **Harlequin Puppet Theatre** which are pitched firmly at younger kids. Evening performances take a slightly more mature slant.

St Trillo's chapel

Marine Drive, Rhos Point, Rhos-on-Sea • Generally Sun at 11am (check the sign outside)

Half a mile north of the puppet theatre, the minuscule **St Trillo's chapel** has seating for just six worshippers, so may have standing room only during services. The chapel stands over an ancient healing well and was reputedly the launch point of Prince Madoc ap Owain Gwynedd's voyage to America in 1170 – Welshmen and women the world over like to claim that he was the first European to visit the New World, over three hundred years before Christopher Columbus.

ARRIVAL AND DEPARTURE   COLWYN BAY

By train Trains stop centrally on Victoria Ave and serve: Bangor (every 20–30min; 25min); Llandudno Junction (every 20–30min; 5min); Rhyl (every 20–30min; 10min).
By bus Buses stop centrally on Rhos Rd and serve: Llandudno (every 10–20min; 15min); Rhyl (every 10–20min; 45min).

By bike The nicest way to explore town is by heading along the Prestatyn to Rhos-on-Sea cycle path which mostly follows the shoreline – you can rent bikes from West End Cycles, 121 Conwy Rd (£10 a half day, £15 a day; ☎ 01492 530269, ⓦ westendcycles.com; Mon–Sat 9am–5.30pm).

ACCOMMODATION, EATING AND ENTERTAINMENT

★ **Ellingham House** 1 Woodland Park West ☎ 01492 533345, ⓦ ellinghamhouse.com. A considerable amount of care and attention goes into the running of this classy B&B with three very large rooms, plus two smaller rooms on the upper floor, one with great view across the rooftops to the sea. **£80**

★ **Pen-y-Bryn** Pen-y-Bryn Rd ☎ 01492 533360, ⓦ penybryn-colwynbay.co.uk. Classy pub food (most mains £10–14), casual service, a continually changing roster of real ales and a great whisky selection has proved a winning formula for this large pub and beer garden high on the hill behind town. Great views. Follow Kings Drive a mile inland. Mon–Sat 11.30am–11pm, Sun noon–10.30pm.
Theatr Colwyn Abergele Rd ☎ 01492 577888, ⓦ www .theatrcolwyn.co.uk. Check out Wales's oldest theatre and the UK's oldest cinema (screening flicks since 1909), which has recently undergone an expensive revamp. Check the website for films, gigs and shows.

Llandudno and Great Orme

The twin limestone hummocks of the 680ft **Great Orme** and its southern cousin the Little Orme provide a dramatic frame for the gently curving Victorian frontage of **Llandudno**, Wales' most enduring archetype of the genteel British seaside resort. The core of the town occupies a low isthmus between two beachfronts: Llandudno

Bay, where the older set of promenading devotees can be found huddled in the glass frontages of once grand hotels; and the less developed West Shore. Despite the arrival of more rumbustious fun-seekers, Llandudno retains an undeniably dignified air, bolstered by its ever-improving selection of chic hotels and quality restaurants.

Llandudno

LLANDUDNO is a supremely easy place in which to wander: on a sunny day, join the ranks of folk on the pier, which juts out into Llandudno Bay, or head down to the beach, a sand and shingle affair where you might find a few sunbathers and the odd hardy swimmer. From the pier, stroll along The Promenade, with its regal four-storey terraced hotels, or focus on the **Llandudno Town Trail**, a series of panels full of interesting nuggets: pick up a free leaflet from the tourist office.

The pier

Daily: summer 9am–11pm, winter 9am–6pm • Free

Once the embodiment of Llandudno's ornate Victoriana, the **pier**'s neat wooden deck is overrun in summer with kids clamouring to board the modest fairground rides, and deckchair denizens cocking an ear to the taped sounds of some Wurlitzer maestro. Ice cream and candyfloss outlets abound, as a town ordinance bars the sale of such fripperies anywhere else on the waterfront.

7

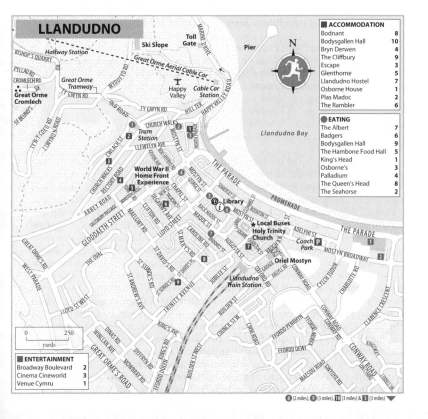

LLANDUDNO

■ **ACCOMMODATION**
Bodnant	8
Bodysgallen Hall	10
Bryn Derwen	4
The Cliffbury	9
Escape	3
Glenthorne	5
Llandudno Hostel	7
Osborne House	1
Plas Madoc	2
The Rambler	6

● **EATING**
The Albert	7
Badgers	6
Bodysgallen Hall	9
The Hambone Food Hall	5
King's Head	1
Osborne's	3
Palladium	4
The Queen's Head	8
The Seahorse	2

■ **ENTERTAINMENT**
Broadway Boulevard	2
Cinema Cineworld	3
Venue Cymru	1

8 (2 miles), 9 (3 miles), 10 (3 miles) & 3 (3 miles) ▼

7

LLANDUDNO'S HISTORY

The town's early history revolves around the Great Orme, where St Tudno, who brought Christianity to the region in the sixth century, built the monastic cell that gives Llandudno its name. When the early Victorian copper mines seemed exhausted, local landowner Edward Mostyn exploited the craze for sea bathing, with a resort for the upper middle classes. As MP for the constituency, with the Bishop of Bangor in his pocket, Mostyn was able to tease through an enclosure act giving him the rights to develop the land.

Within fifty years of its foundation in 1854, Llandudno had become synonymous with the Victorian ideal of a refined resort, drawing music stars such as Adelina Patti and Jules Rivière, the French conductor who sat in a gilded armchair facing the audience as he waved his bejewelled ivory baton. Mostyn Street was said to have some of the finest shops outside London, patronized by the likes of Napoléon III, Gladstone and Queen Elizabeth of Romania, who stayed here for five weeks in 1890 and reputedly gave the town its motto **Hardd**, **haran**, **hedd**, meaning "beautiful haven of peace".

Oriel Mostyn

12 Vaughan St • Daily 10.30am–5pm • Free • ☎ 01492 87921, ⓦ mostyn.org

The elaborate terracotta brick facade gives little clue to the raw interior spaces of the newly refurbished **Oriel Mostyn** gallery – all shards of rough-cast bare concrete. The revamp has breathed new life into the region's premier contemporary art gallery, named after Lady Mostyn, for whom it was originally built in 1901. The gallery has no permanent collection, but its five rooms are almost always showing something of interest, much of it by leading Welsh artists supplemented by an intriguing selection of international touring exhibitions. There's also a good arts shop and the spare *Café Lux*.

World War II Home Front Experience

New St • Mid-March to Oct Mon–Sat 10am–4.30pm, Sun 10am–2pm • £3.25 • ☎ 01492 871032, ⓦ homefrontmuseum.co.uk

The **World War II Home Front Experience** pays a nostalgic visit to early 1940s Britain, with wartime shopfronts, wardens' huts, bomb shelters and the like all packed into one small room, where ration books and children's toys are displayed alongside evocative treatment of the Women's Land Army.

The Great Orme

The views from the top of the **Great Orme** (Y Gogarth) are magical, stretching out over the seascapes all around: east towards Rhyl and the offshore windfarms, west to the shores of Anglesey, and south beyond the sands of the Conwy estuary to the brooding, quarried northern limits of the Carneddau, where Snowdonia plunges into the sea.

Formed 300 million years ago at the bottom of a tropical sea, this huge lump of carboniferous limestone was subsequently veined by mineral-bearing rock. Though there are a few minor Neolithic sites on the hill, it was in the Bronze Age that the settlement really developed, when the people began to smelt the contents of the malachite-rich veins, supplying copper throughout Europe. The Celts further exploited the ore but the Vikings who subsequently visited the area did not. Their legacy is the name: Orme derives from Old Norse meaning "worm" or "sea serpent" – which is just how the Great Orme might have appeared in the mist to those approaching by sea.

Apart from walking, there are three other ways to get up onto the Orme – the **Marine Drive**, the **Great Orme Tramway** and the **cable car**. Once there, head out on foot across the rounded summit to escape from the crowds around the car park. You might spot some of the rare or endangered maritime botanical species – goldilocks aster, spotted cats-ear and spiked speedwell – as you search for somewhere to admire the view as fulmars wheel on the thermals. The feral **cashmere goats** which roam all over the mountain are usually easier to find, especially if you ask the staff at the visitor centre.

Marine Drive

Always open • Free for walkers and cyclists; driving toll (£2.50) applies summer roughly 9am–8pm; winter 9am–4pm

The easiest way to get a feel for the skirts of the Great Orme is along **Marine Drive**, a four-mile loop cut into the rock high above the coast. Make the anticlockwise circuit from near Llandudno's pier with stops at various viewing points and the *Rest & Be Thankful* café. A summit road leads off Marine Drive a quarter of the way around.

Great Orme Tramway

Church Walks • Daily: Easter–Sept 10am–6pm; Oct 10am–5pm • £3.90 single, £5.80 return • ☎ 01492 879306,
Ⓦ greatormetramway.co.uk.

The most atmospheric means of reaching the Great Orme's summit is the vintage, San Francisco-style **Great Orme Tramway**, which creaks along its one-mile route to the top much as it has done since 1902. Tramcars (which leave every 20min) largely follow Old Road to the Halfway Station, where you change to a second tram.

Great Orme Aerial Cable Car

7

Happy Valley • Easter–Oct daily, roughly 10am–5pm, depending on the weather • £6.50

Near the base of the pier and close to the start of Marine Drive, an Italianate colonnade flanks the short road to the **cable car**, which (when it isn't too windy) lifts people up to the summit in open four-seater cabins which swing over the formal gardens of **Happy Valley**.

Great Orme Country Park

Walking paths, roads, the tramway and cable car all converge on the flat summit of the **country park**, where there's a huge car park (small fee), gift shop, a couple of not very inspiring café/bars and a visitor centre. **Walks** are well signposted and easy to piece together using our map: either loop around the walls of the farm park (2-mile loop; 1hr), or head down to St Tudno's church (1 mile return; 30min).

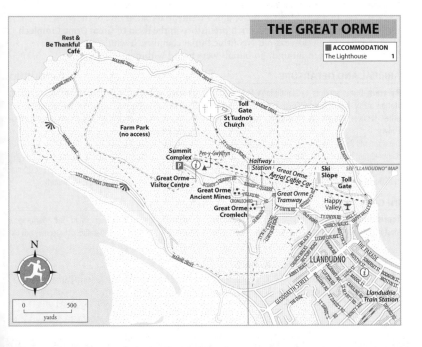

Great Orme Visitor Centre

Easter–Oct daily 10am–5pm • Free

Along with a short orientation film there's a chance to learn something of the birdlife and the lime-loving plants you're likely to see. The huge lighthouse lens on display was once in what is now *The Lighthouse* B&B.

St Tudno's church

April–Oct daily 9am–5pm; Nov–March Sat & Sun 9am–5pm

Small and pretty, **St Tudno's** is the area's original church (after which Llandudno was named) and now stands isolated, though it was once part of a substantial village. The oldest parts are twelfth-century, with later extensions and considerable restoration in the nineteenth century when the church's history appealed to the newly arrived, well-heeled tourists.

Great Orme Ancient Mines

Mid-March to Oct daily 10am–5pm • £6.50 • ☎ 01492 870447, ⓦ greatormemines.info

From the Great Orme Tramway's Halfway Station, it's a five-minute walk to the long-disused **Great Orme Ancient Mines**. The earliest workings here were assumed to be Roman, until excavations in 1987 uncovered 4000-year-old animal bones that had been used as scrapers 200ft down. This is one of the few sites in Britain where mineral veins were accompanied by dolomitization, a rock-softening process which enabled copper to be extracted using the simple tools available in the Bronze Age, and which led to the Great Orme becoming the pre-eminent copper mine in Europe.

After an explanatory film, the **self-guided tour** takes you down through a small portion of the four miles of tunnels so far uncovered – enough to get a feel for the cramped working conditions. Topside, you can see some of the ongoing excavations and get an idea of how the copper ore was smelted to make tools.

Great Orme Cromlech

At end of Cromlech Rd, off St Beuno's Rd, 300yd from Great Orme Tramway Halfway Station • Open access • Free

Tucked away in a small field at the end of a residential road is one of the most impressive remants of the Orme's rich prehistory in the form of **Great Orme Cromlech** (Liety'r Filiast), a 5000-year-old Neolithic burial chamber. It would originally have been within an earth mound; no burials were found within it.

ARRIVAL AND DEPARTURE   LLANDUDNO

By train Direct services to Llandudno's forlorn train station arrive from Betws-y-Coed and Chester; for all other services change at Llandudno Junction, near Conwy.

Destinations Bangor (18 daily; 40min); Betws-y-Coed (4 daily; 40min); Blaenau Ffestiniog (6 daily; 1hr 20min); Chester (roughly hourly; 1hr 10min); Holyhead (18 daily; 1hr 20min); Llandudno Junction (every 30min; 10min).

By bus Local buses stop on either Mostyn St or Gloddaeth St, while National Express buses from Chester, Bangor and Pwllheli (bookings at the TIC) stop at the Coach Park on Mostyn Broadway.

Destinations Bangor (every 15min; 1hr); Betws-y-Coed (9 daily; 50min); Blaenau Ffestiniog (9 daily; 1hr 10min); Conwy (every 15min; 20min); Llanrwst (every 30min; 35–50min); Rhyl (every 10–20min; 1hr 10min).

INFORMATION

Tourist information The TIC is in the Library Building, Mostyn St (Easter–Sept Mon–Sat 9am–5pm, Sun 9.30am–4.30pm; Oct–Easter Mon–Sat 9am–5pm; ☎ 01492 577577, ⓔ llandudnotic@conwy.gov.uk,

SKIING AND TOBOGGANING

Llandudno Ski & Snowboard Centre (generally Mon–Fri 10am–10pm, Sat & Sun 10am–6pm ☎ 01492 874707, ⓦ jnlllandudno.co.uk) offers a couple of hours on the dry slopes (including all equipment; £19), or you can make a run down the 700yd-long, snow-free Toboggan Run (£4.50).

ⓦ visitllandudno.org.uk). Stocks a free map of Great Orme footpaths.
Internet There's free access at the library on Mostyn St

(Mon, Tues & Fri 9am–6pm, Wed 10am–5pm, Thurs 9am–7pm, Sat 9.30am–1pm). Also free wi-fi at *Café Lux* in Oriel Mostyn and other cafés around town.

GETTING AROUND

By bike The nearest bike rental is in Colwyn Bay.
By bus Alpine run an open-top double-decker bus looping from Llandudno to Conwy and back (late May to mid-Sept

every 30min 10am–4pm; £7.50; ⓣ 01492 879133), perfect for a half-day visit to Conwy.

ACCOMMODATION

Llandudno has several hundred **hotels**. so finding somewhere to stay isn't usually a problem, though you should book ahead in high summer, especially bank holidays. Competition keeps **prices** low and rates are often cheaper if you stay for two or more nights. The best general areas for inexpensive accommodation are St David's Rd and Deganwy Ave, each of which has almost a dozen guesthouses. The nearest tent **camping** is at Conwy. All the places below are shown on the Llandudno map unless stated.

Bodnant 39 St Mary's Rd ⓣ 01492 876936, ⓦ llandudno-bedandbreakfast.co.uk. Comfortable six-room guesthouse (including two singles for £35) on a tree-lined street. **£60**

Bodysgallen Hall A470, 3 miles south of town ⓣ 01492 584466, ⓦ bodysgallen.com. Grace and tranquillity are watchwords at this National Trust-owned country hotel, in a partly seventeenth-century house surrounded by 200 acres of terraced lawns and wooded parkland. There are 31 antique-filled rooms and suites in the manor itself and in cottages in the grounds, all beautifully decorated and festooned with flowers. It has two restaurants (see p.408) and a sophisticated spa in the grounds. **£180**

Bryn Derwen 34 Abbey Rd ⓣ 01492 876804, ⓦ www.bryn-derwen.co.uk. Sumptuous yet informal small hotel at the foot of the Orme, with huge Victorian common areas, off-street parking and home-cooked meals. Licensed. Closed Dec & Jan. **£80**

★ **The Cliffbury** 34 St David's Rd ⓣ 01492 877224, ⓦ thecliffbury.co.uk. Stylish wallpapers, free wi-fi, sparkling white bathrooms and dedicated hosts define this classy B&B on a quiet street with six individually decorated rooms; breakfast ingredients are locally sourced where possible. Superior rooms are bigger and come with DVD player and robes. Generally two-night minimum. **£62**

★ **Escape** 48 Church Walks ⓣ 01492 877776, ⓦ escapebandb.co.uk. Chic, boutique B&B with nine individually designed rooms combining clean-lined modernism with retro or antique touches. Aveda toiletries, wi-fi, classy breakfasts and a guest lounge with honesty bar complete the package. £100

Glenthorne 2 York Rd ⓣ 01492 879591, ⓔ rebrw@aol.com. Very good guesthouse with seven comfy rooms and a welcoming atmosphere, plus good-value three-course evening meals (£13). Single supplement only £5. **£54**

The Lighthouse Marine Drive ⓣ 01492 876819, ⓦ www.lighthouse-llandudno.co.uk; map p.405. Very comfortable B&B in a former lighthouse fabulously sited on cliffs over 300ft above the northern end of the Great Orme. All the rooms are completely different (though all have sea views), and include one where the lamp turned until decommissioning in 1985. **£160**

Llandudno Hostel 14 Charlton St ⓣ 01492 877430, ⓦ www.llandudnohostel.co.uk. Family-run, forty-bed hostel in the centre of town with dorm beds, doubles, a family room and a friendly atmosphere. Sheets, towels and a continental breakfast are supplied, but there's no self-catering kitchen. Often full with school groups during term time, so call ahead. Dorms **£20**

★ **Osborne House** 17 North Parade ⓣ 01492 860330, ⓦ osbornehouse.com. Effortless elegance and pampering (antique beds, marble bathrooms, deep bath and shower) in six enormous suites, some overlooking the Promenade, plus a very good attached restaurant. **£145**

Plas Madoc 60 Church Walks ⓣ 01492 876514, ⓦ plasmadocguesthouse.co.uk. Comfortable guesthouse at the base of the Great Orme with five rooms decorated predominantly in white, and with a superior room with bath and good views over the town. Full breakfasts include the option of soy or rice milk, vegan sausages and the like. Free wi-fi. **£65**

The Rambler 15 Deganwy Ave ⓣ 01492 875618. One of the cheapest B&Bs around, clean and well run, with a mix of rooms with and without en suite. **£55**

EATING AND DRINKING

Llandudno is blessed with the best choice of restaurants in north Wales. Most cluster at the foot of the Great Orme around Mostyn St, where numerous pubs cater to most

tastes. The liveliest bars are along Upper Mostyn St, which can be chaotically crowded at weekends.

7

RESTAURANTS AND CAFÉS

Badgers Victoria Centre, Mostyn St ☎01492 871649, ⓦ badgerstearooms.co.uk. Waitresses in black dresses and white aprons give a genteel feel to this café and lunch spot. Attentive service, good-quality food and a range of five blends of cafetière coffee just about justify the relatively high prices. Mon–Sat 9.30am–5pm, Sun (March–Dec only) 11am–4pm.

★ **Bodysgallen Hall** A470, 3 miles south of town ☎01492 584466, ⓦ bodysgallen.com. Oil paintings, heavy curtains and views across the parterre garden make a perfect setting for some of the finest dining around. Sip a sherry by the fire then embark on a three-course Modern British dinner (£49; smart dress required) or a sumptuous lunch (£10–23). The afternoon teas (£14.50) and Sunday lunches (£27.50) are superb. Alternatively, go for the more contemporary *1620* bistro in the former coach house (Mon–Fri 2-course lunches for £14 if booked in advance). Restaurant Tues–Sun 12.30–1.45pm & 7–9pm; bistro Mon–Sat 12.30–3pm & 5.30–9pm.

The Hambone Food Hall 3 Lloyd St ☎01492 860084. Good deli producing made-to-order sandwiches along with a wide range of meat pies, pâtés and salads to go or eat in. Mon–Sat 9am–5pm, Sun 10am–4pm.

Osborne's 17 North Parade ☎01492 860330. Opulent cream-and-white café and grill lit by candles and chandeliers with modern dishes: go for the three-course deal (£19). Also an excellent spot for a full afternoon tea (£11) or for a splurge, the champagne afternoon tea for two (£45). Mon–Sat 10.30am–10pm, Sun 10.30am–9pm.

The Seahorse 7 Church Walks ☎01492 875315, ⓦ theseahorse.co.uk. Unusual two-in-one dinner-only restaurant with an intimate fine-dining feel upstairs and a sociable cellar brasserie tenor below. But the predominantly fish and seafood menu is the same (£26 for 2 courses, £30 for 3) and the food reliably excellent. Expect the likes of Parma ham wrapped monkfish or seafood linguini. Daily 4.30–10pm.

BARS AND PUBS

The Albert 56 Madoc St ☎01492 877188, ⓦ albertllandudno.co.uk. If all you want is quality pub food in gut-splitting portions then this is your spot. Excellent value with most mains £10–12. Daily 11.30am–10pm or later.

King's Head Old Rd ☎01492 877993, ⓦ kingsheadllandudno.co.uk. Llandudno's oldest pub, serving substantial bar meals, ranging from beef burgers and gourmet pies to lamb shanks (most mains £9–12). Mon–Thurs & Sun noon–11pm, Fri & Sat noon–midnight.

Palladium 7 Gloddaeth St ☎01492 863920. *Wetherspoon* chain pub with the usual combo of low-cost meals and discount-priced beer, set in the fabulous surrounds of an old theatre, still with its stalls and wonderful ceiling. Daily 8am–midnight or later.

The Queen's Head Glanwydden, 2.5 miles southeast ☎01492 546570, ⓦ queensheadglanwydden.co.uk. There's a wonderful country feel to this village pub just a short drive from either Llandudno or Conwy. It is a fine spot for a drink, inside or on the terrace, but excels with the wide-ranging menu which extends from open sandwiches and asparagus and broad-bean risotto to Thai green curry and Anglesey scallops in ginger and coriander. Most mains are £10–14 and you'll need to book for their excellent Sunday lunch (£10). Food served Mon–Fri noon–2pm & 6–9pm, Sat & Sun noon–9pm.

ENTERTAINMENT

Broadway Boulevard Grand Theatre, Mostyn Broadway, on the corner of Ty'n y Ffridd Rd ☎01492 879614. Llandudno's liveliest club, with a host of party nights.

Cineworld 3 miles south in Llandudno Junction ☎0871 200 2000, ⓦ cineworld.co.uk. Cinema with nine screens.

Venue Cymru The Promenade ☎01492 872000, ⓦ venuecymru.co.uk. North Wales' premier live entertainment centre, this modern 1500-seat theatre lures touring companies and occasional international acts.

Conwy

Despite its small size, there's a huge amount to see and do in **CONWY**. Its complete belt of town walls encloses not just a stunning early medieval castle but some fascinating glimpses into the past of north Wales. With its marvellous setting and plentiful accommodation, this is the ideal base for a few days spent exploring the Lower Conwy Valley and the coast around its estuary. It's easy to make a day-trip to Llandudno, and there's a smattering of other attractive diversions within a few miles' radius. Thousands come here specifically to see **Bodnant Garden**, and tiny **Rowen** has a low-key appeal.

Conwy remains one of the highlights of the north coast, its setting on the Conwy estuary, backed by a forested fold of Snowdonia, irresistible to painters and

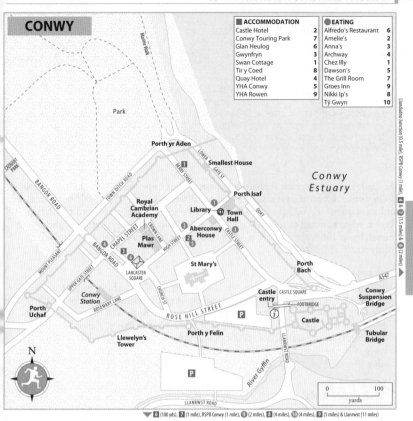

■ ACCOMMODATION		● EATING	
Castle Hotel	2	Alfredo's Restaurant	6
Conwy Touring Park	7	Amelie's	2
Glan Heulog	6	Anna's	3
Gwynfryn	3	Archway	4
Swan Cottage	1	Chez Illy	1
Tir y Coed	8	Dawson's	5
Quay Hotel	4	The Grill Room	7
YHA Conwy	5	Groes Inn	9
YHA Rowen	9	Nikki Ip's	8
		Tŷ Gwyn	10

▼ **6** (100 yds), **7** (1 mile), RSPB Conwy (1 mile), **9** (2 miles), **8** (4 miles), **10** (4 miles), **9** (5 miles) & Llanrwst (11 miles)

photographers ever since Englishman Paul Sandby published his *Views of North Wales* in 1776. And don't let castle-weariness put you off. Nothing within Conwy's core of medieval and Victorian buildings is more than 200yd from the irregular triangle of protective masonry formed by the **town walls**, which makes the town wonderfully easy to potter around. You can easily visit the castle, the Elizabethan townhouse of Plas Mawr, the estuary bridges and cutesy treats like Britain's smallest house in one day, but you might want to stay longer.

Conwy Castle

April–June, Sept & Oct daily 9.30am–5pm; July & Aug 9.30am–6pm; Nov–March Mon–Sat 10am–4pm, Sun 11am–4pm • £4.80; joint ticket with Plas Mawr £7.30 • ☎ 01492 592358 • CADW

Edward I chose a strategic knoll at the mouth of the Conwy River for the site of **Conwy Castle**, built in just five years by James of St George. Overlooked by a low hill, the castle appears less easily defensible than others along the coast, but James constructed eight massive towers in a rectangle around the two wards, the inner one separated from the outer by a drawbridge and portcullis, and further protected by turrets atop the four eastern towers.

Barring a brief siege during the Welsh uprising of 1294, the castle saw little action until 1399, when Richard II stayed there on his return from Ireland, until lured from safety by the Earl of Northumberland, Bolingbroke's vassal. Northumberland swore in

A BRIEF HISTORY OF CONWY

For centuries the Conwy estuary provided a good living for the families who had held mussel-gathering rights on the sands. Spiritual needs were met by the Cistercian monastery of Aberconwy, established in 1172 on the present site of the parish church of St Mary and All Saints. A century later the monastery was moved eight miles upriver to Maenan, near Llanrwst, to make way for the doughtiest links in Edward I's chain of fortresses.

During their incursions along Wales' north coast, Edward I's Anglo-Norman ancestors had all but destroyed the Welsh castle at Deganwy, near Llandudno, but maintaining a bridgehead west of the Conwy River had always eluded them. Accordingly, once over the river in 1283, Edward set about establishing another of his bastide towns, from which the Welsh were mostly excluded for well over a century.

the castle's chapel to grant Richard safe passage, but imprisoned him at Flint, enabling Bolingbroke to become Henry IV. From the fifteenth century, the castle fell into disuse, and was bought in 1627 for £100 by Charles I's Secretary of State, Lord Conway of Ragley, who then had to refortify it for the Civil War. At the restoration of the monarchy in 1665, the castle was stripped of all its iron, wood and lead, and left substantially as it is today.

The interior

Strolling along the ramparts, you can look down onto something unique among the Iron Ring fortresses, a roofless but largely intact interior. The outer ward's 130ft-long Great Hall and the King's Apartments are both well preserved, but the only part of the castle to have kept its roof is the **Chapel Tower**, named for the small room built into the wall whose semicircular apse still shows some heavily worn carving. On the floor below, there's a small exhibition on religious life in medieval castles.

THE IRON RING

Dotting the north Wales coast, a day's march from each other, Edward I's fearsome **Iron Ring** of castles represents Europe's most ambitious and concentrated medieval building project, designed to prevent the recurrence of two hugely expensive military campaigns (see p.441). After Edward's first successful campaign in 1277, he was able to pin down his adversary, **Llywelyn ap Gruffydd** ("the Last") in Snowdonia and Anglesey, gaining space and time to build the now largely ruined castles at **Flint**, **Rhuddlan**, **Builth Wells** and **Aberystwyth**, and consolidate his grip by confiscating and upgrading several Welsh castles.

Although Llewellyn's second uprising (1282) also ultimately failed, Edward was determined not to have to fight a third time for the same land, and set about extending his Iron Ring in an immensely costly display of English might, which – together with the Treaty of Rhuddlan (1284) – effectively crushed Welsh resistance. **Harlech**, **Caernarfon** and **Conwy** are nearly contemporaneous, yet manifest a unique progression towards the later, highly evolved concentric design of **Beaumaris**. All these castles (and the town walls of Caernarfon and Conwy) were built by **James of St George d'Espéranche** – the master military architect of his age – whose work at Conwy, Caernarfon, Harlech and Beaumaris is now recognized with **UNESCO World Heritage Site** status.

Each castle was integrated with a **bastide town** – an idea borrowed from Gascony in France, where Edward I was duke – the town and castle being mutually reliant on each other for protection and trade. The bastides were always populated with English settlers, and the Welsh were only permitted to enter during the day, but not to trade and certainly not carrying arms. It wasn't until the eighteenth century that the Welsh would have towns they could truly call their own.

Conwy Suspension Bridge

Mid-March to Oct daily 11am–5pm • £1 • ☎ 01492 573282 • NT

Anchored to the castle walls as if it were a drawbridge, Thomas Telford's slender **Conwy Suspension Bridge** was part of the 1826 road improvement scheme, prompted by the need for better communications to Ireland after the Act of Union. Contemporary with his far greater effort spanning the Menai Strait, it mimics the crenellations of the battlements above to compensate for spoiling the view of the castle immortalized by J.M.W. Turner. The bridge was used until 1958, was briefly threatened with demolition, and has now been restored to something like its original state. It serves as a footbridge linking the town to a **tollhouse**, furnished as it would have been circa 1900, complete with period toll charges on a board outside.

The town walls

The 30ft-high **town walls** branch out from the castle into a three-quarter-mile-long circuit, enclosing Conwy's ancient quarter. Inaccessible from the castle they were designed to protect, the walls are punctuated by 21 evenly spaced horseshoe towers, as well as twelve latrines bulging out from the wall-walk. Only half of the distance can be walked, the best section being from Porth Uchaf to Porth yr Aden, with great views over the town to the castle and estuary beyond.

Conwy Quay

River and town walls meet beside the brightly rigged trawlers and mussel boats at the pedestrianized **Conwy Quay**. The place is alive on sunny days with people grabbing a beer outside the *Liverpool Arms* or slurping on wonderful locally made ice cream from the *Parisella's* kiosk – try black cherry and amaretto or triple chocolate.

The smallest house in Great Britain

Conwy Quay • Easter to mid-Oct daily 10am–5pm • £1

There's usually a knot of people photographing a woman in traditional stovepipe-hat-and-waistcoat Welsh costume outside the self-proclaimed **smallest house in Great Britain**. The house was built wedged between two terraces, one of them now demolished. The two tiny rooms combined are only 9ft high and 6ft wide, the door taking up a quarter of the frontage. Most people will have to duck to get in, a problem that vexed the last resident, a 6ft 3in-tall fisherman, until he left around 1900.

Aberconwy House

Castle St • Mid-Feb to Oct daily 11am–5pm • £3.40 • ☎ 01492 592246 • NT

The timber and stone **Aberconwy House** is the oldest house in Conwy and its sole surviving medieval building, dating from about 1300. Built for a wealthy merchant, it saw service as a bakery, antique shop, sea captain's house and temperance hotel, somehow managing to survive numerous fires and Victorian improvements. Its various incarnations are re-created in rooms furnished with a simple yet elegant collection of rural furniture on loan from the Museum of Wales. Tours start with an introductory film in the attic, winding up in a kitchen complete with fireside settle, pewter plates and a few hunks of stale bread.

Plas Mawr

20 High St **House** April–Sept Tues–Sun 9am–5pm; Oct Tues–Sun 9.30am–4pm • £5.20, joint ticket with castle £7.30 **Evening tours** mid-April to Oct Thurs 6pm & 7.30pm • £6 • ☎ 01492 580167 • CADW

Conwy's grandest residence is the splendid **Plas Mawr**, or "great mansion", one of the best-preserved Elizabethan townhouses in Britain. It was built in a Dutch style for

Robert Wynn of Gwydir Castle, who was one of the first native Welsh to live in the town, returning to the area after mixing at European courts. The main part of the house dates from 1576, with features such as the gatehouse added some ten years later to augment the grand effect. In the Great Hall, the impressive plaster overmantel was designed to impress visitors with Wynn's noble credentials – especially his descent from the Princes of Gwynedd – and much of the superb plasterwork throughout the house relates to the Wynn dynasty, except in the Great Chamber, where he demurred, presumably so as not to upstage visiting royalty. The tour – aided by an excellent recorded commentary – concludes with an exhibition about Tudor and Stuart attitudes to disease and cleanliness that's highly informative, compulsively gory and hilariously scatological. Blodwen the Maid leads entertaining hour-long **evening tours**.

Royal Cambrian Academy Art Gallery

Crown Lane • Tues–Sat 11am–5pm, Sun 1–4.30pm • Free • ☎ 01492 593413, Ⓦ rcaconwy.org

For over a century, Plas Mawr was home to the Royal Cambrian Academy, a group aiming to foster art in Wales. The **Royal Cambrian Academy Art Gallery** is now located just behind Plas Mawr in a converted chapel on Crown Lane. At their best during the annual summer exhibition, the airy, well-lit galleries display work by the Academy members, almost all Welsh or working in Wales.

RSPB Conwy

Off A55, 1 mile east of Conwy, near Llandudno Junction • Daily 9.30am–5pm • £2.50 • Free guided walks Sat 11am plus May–Aug Wed 7pm • ☎ 01492 584091, Ⓦ rspb.org.uk/conwy

It is hard to imagine that in the early 1990s the wetland site of **RSPB Conwy** was a 3000-ton heap of silt dumped from the creation of the A55 Expressway tunnel under the Conwy Estuary. With the planting of ten thousand trees and careful management, the RSPB has done a fantastic job of replacing the lost salt marsh with a vibrant and very accessible reserve. What you'll see depends on the season, but you might hope to spot Canada geese, shelducks, bitterns, lapwings, stoats, dragonflies and much more. The lakes are a tidal roost, so there's usually more birdlife when high tide forces birds off the adjacent estuary. Borrow a free pair of binoculars and go for a stroll along the boardwalks, spending quiet time in the hides. Or at least hang out in the café with its big windows overlooking the lake and reed beds and telescopes trained on whatever is interesting that day.

Sychnant Pass

Heading west from Conwy towards Bangor it's worth taking a short detour inland along the Old Conwy Road through the narrow cleft of **Sychnant Pass**, which separates

---

WALKS AROUND CONWY

Conwy Mountain (2 miles return; 1hr; 650ft ascent). One of Conwy's best short walks heads onto the gorse-, bracken- and heather-covered slopes of Conwy Mountain and the 800ft Penmaenbach and Alltwen peaks behind, all giving fantastic views right along the coast. The walk starts at a small car park on Mountain Road, reached by following Cadnant Park off Bangor Road just outside the town walls.

Marine Walk (800yd return; 20min; flat). It is hard to beat a simple stroll along the Conwy Estuary. Start at the northern end of Conwy Quay and simply follow the path to a local nature reserve, Coed Bodlondeb, a peaceful woodland around what was a Victorian mansion surrounded by an unusual array of trees among which you might see nuthatches and jays.

CLOCKWISE FROM TOP LEFT SOUTH STACK LIGHTHOUSE (P.432); STAINED GLASS IN ST WINEFIRDE'S WELL, HOLYWELL (P.396); GREAT ORME TRAMWAY, LLANDUDNO (P.405), CONWY CASTLE (P.409) >

Conwy Mountain from the Carneddau range. The road passes the *YHA Conwy* hostel then crosses the pass before dropping into the hamlet of **CAPELULO**, just over two miles west of Conwy, rejoining the A55 at workaday Penmaenmawr.

Rowen

Five miles south of Conwy on the eastern slopes of the Carneddau range, the tiny mountainside hamlet of **ROWEN** is one of the prettiest in the area, composed of a few cottages, a post office, a chapel and the excellent **Tŷ Gwyn** pub (see above). If you don't mind the short drive into Conwy, **Tir y Coed** and the *YHA Rowen* hostel (see p.415) make a great base for exploring the area.

Bodnant Garden

Tal-y-Cafn, off A470, 8 miles south of Conwy • March–Oct daily 10am–5pm; first two weeks of Nov daily 10am–4pm • £7.70 • ☎ 01492 650460, ⓦ bodnantgarden.co.uk • NT • #25 bus from Llandudno and Llandudno Junction roughly every hour

During May and June, the 160ft laburnum tunnel flourishes and banks of rhododendrons are in glorious bloom all over **Bodnant Garden**, Wales' finest formal garden and one of the loveliest in Britain. Laid out in 1875 around Bodnant Hall (closed to the public) by its then owner, English industrialist Henry Pochin, the garden spreads over eighty acres of the Conwy Valley. Divided into an upper terraced garden and lower Pinetum and Wild Garden, shrubs and plants provide a blaze of colour throughout the opening season, but autumn is a perfect time to be here, with hydrangeas still in bloom and fruit trees shedding their leaves. You'll need a minimum of two hours to fully appreciate the place.

ARRIVAL AND DEPARTURE   CONWY

By train Llandudno Junction, less than a mile across the river to the east, serves as the main train station for services from Chester to Holyhead, as well as for trains heading south to Betws-y-Coed and Blaenau Ffestiniog. Only slow, regional services stop in Conwy itself (on request).
Destinations Bangor (11 daily; 20min); Holyhead (11 daily; 1hr); Llandudno Junction (11 daily; 4min).

By bus Local buses stop either on Lancaster Square or outside the town walls on Town Ditch Rd. Head to Llandudno to pick up National Express coaches.
Destinations Bangor (every 15min; 45min); Llandudno (every 15min; 20min); Llanrwst (hourly; 35min); Rowen (10 daily; 15min).

GETTING AROUND

By bike The nearest bike rental is in Colwyn Bay.
By bus Alpine (☎ 01492 879133) run an open-top double-decker bus looping from Conwy to Llandudno and back (late May to mid-Sept every 30min, 10am–4pm; £7.50) perfect for a day visit to Llandudno.

INFORMATION

Tourist information The TIC is in the same building and has the same hours as the castle ticket office (April–Oct daily 9am–5pm; Nov–March Mon–Sat 9.30am–4pm, Sun 11am–4pm; ☎ 01492 592248, ⓔ conwytic@conwy.gov.uk).
Internet At the library, Castle St (Mon, Thurs & Fri 10am–5.30pm, Tues 10am–7pm, Sat 10am–1pm).

ACCOMMODATION

HOTELS AND GUESTHOUSES

Castle Hotel 5 High St ☎ 01492 582800, ⓦ castlewales .co.uk. Former coaching inn in the heart of town, restored to the exalted standard it deserves. All 28 rooms come with contemporary styling touches without abandoning the hotel's heritage. Relax in the house bar and dine in the very good *Dawson's* restaurant, where substantial breakfasts are served. **£75**

Glan Heulog Llanrwst Rd ☎ 01492 593845, ⓦ snowdoniabandb.co.uk. One of Conwy's best small guesthouses, half a mile out on the B5106 Trefriw road in a Victorian house with seven mostly en-suite rooms. **£58**

Gwynfryn 4 York Place ☎ 01492 576733, ⓦ gwynfrynbandb.co.uk. B&B with five tastefully decorated rooms, each boasting a small fridge and DVD player, and access to a film library and free wi-fi.

The "superior" rooms have more space, views and bathtubs. **£68**

★ **Quay Hotel** 2 miles north, off A546 at Deganwy ☎01492 564100, ⊛quayhotel.co.uk. This is about as good as business hotels get, superbly sited on the shores of Conwy Estuary with castle views. Accommodation is smart contemporary, with some premium rooms getting that wonderful view. There's a good pool and gym, and a classy restaurant and bar. Look out for web promotions. **£125**

★ **Swan Cottage** 18 Berry St ☎01492 596840, ⊛swancottage.net. Central B&B with small but attractive en-suite rooms, two with great estuary views, one tucked into the attic overlooking the town walls. **£50**

HOSTELS AND CAMPSITES

Conwy Touring Park ☎01492 592856, ⊛conwytouringpark.com. A fully equipped campsite, just over a mile south along the B5106 (bus #19). It operates a strict "families and couples only" rule, so you'll have to look reasonably respectable to get in. Closed Nov–March. Pitches **£17**.

★ **YHA Conwy** Lark Hill ☎0845 371 9732, ⓔconwy@yha.org.uk. Spacious, modernized hostel a 10min walk from town up the Sychnant Pass Rd with two- and four-bunk rooms, all en suite. The place is open all day, serves good-value meals (including an excellent £5 buffet breakfast), is licensed, and also rents bikes to guests (£8 a half day). Open daily all year. Per person from **£18**

YHA Rowen Rowen, 0.5 mile up a steep hill above the village ☎0845 371 9038. Simple YHA hostel on the flanks of the Carneddau range, with superb views over the Conwy Valley. There's space for two tents. Reached by turning right 200yd past Rowen's pub, and served by bus #19 from Conwy. Open Easter & June–Aug. Dorms **£14.40**

EATING AND DRINKING

For a small town, Conwy has a reasonable range of **restaurants**, though if you want to sample some really great pubs, you've got to get a few miles out into the Conwy Valley. **Drinking** in town is fairly perfunctory, with nightlife being limited to the odd pub gig. People head into Llandudno or Bangor for anything more exciting.

RESTAURANTS AND CAFÉS

Alfredo's Restaurant Lancaster Square ☎01492 592381. Definitely old school, but always a friendly and reliable spot for good-value pizza and pasta dishes (£9–10) and respectable mains (£14–20) among the Chianti bottles. Daily 6–10pm.

Amelie's 10 High St ☎01492 583142. Relaxed café tucked away upstairs in part of what was once a cinema; a cosy spot for soup, a light lunch or just coffee and cake. Evening meals turn on a French accent with the likes of chicken cassoulet (£14) and baked cod on roasted ratatouille (£15). Mon–Wed & Sun 9.30am–4.30pm, Thurs–Sat 9.30am–9.30pm.

Anna's 9 Castle St ☎01492 580908. Old-fashioned tearoom above an outdoors shop, great for Fairtrade coffees, afternoon teas and cakes, but also serves well-prepared dishes such as Welsh rarebit, soup and panini. Daily 9am–4.30pm.

Archway 12 Bangor Rd ☎01492 592458. Quality eat-in and take-out fish and chip restaurant also doing pizza and pies. On a fine evening take your haul to The Quay and wash it down with a pint from the *Liverpool Arms*. Daily 11am–10pm or later.

Chez Illy High St ☎01492 547012. Small café with a limited range of food, but the best coffee in town. Daily 9am–5pm.

Dawson's Castle Hotel, High St ☎01492 582800, ⊛castlewales.co.uk. Smart bar and restaurant that's been recently modernized. The emphasis is on quality ingredients well cooked and served without too much fuss – though there's nothing sloppy here. Come for a pint or pre-dinner cocktail in the bar then something like local haddock and chorizo risotto (£8) followed by tandoori monkfish with vanilla mash (£16). Mon–Thurs & Sun 7.30am–9.30pm, Fri & Sat 7.30am–10pm.

The Grill Room Quay Hotel, 2 miles north off A546 at Deganwy ☎01492 564 100, ⊛quayhotel.co.uk. Sip a wine in the bar with matchless views across the water to Conwy and the mountains, then choose from the intriguing menu designed around their signature steaks (£20–32) and fish dishes (£18–20). There's dockside seating for when the weather behaves. Daily noon–3pm & 6.30–10pm.

Nikki Ip's 57 Station Rd, Deganwy ☎01492 596611, ⊛nikkiips.com. Casual, long-standing mostly Cantonese place across the water from Conwy with a loyal following. Dinner mains (£11) are very good, though the two-course lunch specials (£10) are better value and might include Korean seafood pancakes followed by fish steamed with lemongrass and coriander. Daily noon–3pm & 6.30–10pm.

BARS AND PUBS

Groes Inn Tyn-y-Groes, 2 miles south on B5106 to Llanrwst ☎01492 650545, ⊛groesinn.com. Excellent bar meals (mostly using local produce) and cask ales at an atmospheric fifteenth-century pub which claims to be the oldest licensed house in Wales, dating back to 1573. Most mains £11–15. Food served daily noon–2pm & 6.30–9pm.

Tŷ Gwyn Rowen, 4 miles south of Conwy. Sitting outside on a sunny evening is the perfect way to experience this village pub in an idyllic setting. There's a friendly atmosphere, decent bar meals and a nice garden. Mon–Wed 4–10pm, Thurs 4–11.30pm, Fri 3pm–1am, Sat noon–midnight, Sun noon–11.30pm.

7

Bangor

After a few days travelling through mid-Wales or in the mountains of Snowdonia, **BANGOR** makes a distinct change. It's not big; but as the largest town in Gwynedd and home to the **Bangor University**, whose grandiose buildings dominate the skyline, it passes in these parts for cosmopolitan. With only a trickle of summer visitors the city struggles to keep an active social life going outside term time; and after the construction of a newish shopping centre, the rest of the downtown shops are obviously suffering. In contrast to the largely English-speaking resorts on the north coast, Bangor is overwhelmingly Welsh-speaking.

While the slate industry and road and rail projects brought some urbanization to Bangor in the nineteenth century, for well over a millennium before that the city was noted solely for its bishopric, founded as a monastic settlement by St Deiniol in 525 AD, predating even Canterbury by some seventy years.

7

The cathedral

Daily 11am–5pm • Free

Bangor's **cathedral** boasts the longest continuous use of any cathedral in Britain. A hint of its ancient origins can be gleaned from the blocked-in window dating from the

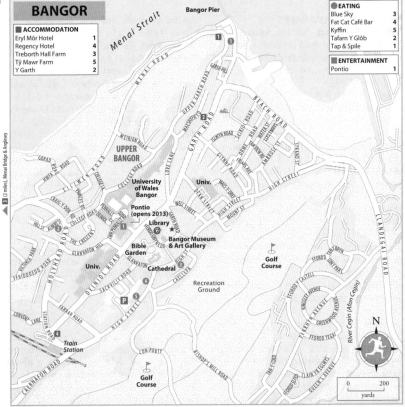

BANGOR

Bangor Pier

Menai Strait

MENAI ROAD

GARTH HILL

UPPER GARTH ROAD

BEACH ROAD

MAESOFFRYN

GARTH ROAD

ISGWYN ROAD

DEINIOL ROAD

GWYNE ROAD

GARNEDD ROAD

FERN AVE

WATERLOO

AMBROSE

STRAND ST

METHON ROAD

UPPER BANGOR

LOVE LANE

GLYNNE ROAD

FRIAR AVE

MAES-TREFOR

HIGH STREET

GORAD ROAD

HWFA ROAD

ST TWROG ROAD

COLLEGE ROAD

Univ.

DEAN STREET

WELL STREET

HIGH STREET

MOUNT ST

CRAIG-Y-DON RD

PENCES RD

PENRALLT

PENDERLAY

RANDALL

College Road

University of Wales Bangor

Pontio (opens 2013)

Library @

Bangor Museum & Art Gallery

HILL ST

ALBERT ST

THE CRESCENT

UPPER DEAN ST

GLANRAFON HILL

GWYNEDD

Bible Garden

Univ.

Cathedral

GLANRAFON ROAD

DEINIOL ROAD

SACKVILLE ROAD

HIGH ST

CAELLEPA

Golf Course

TFORDD TAN-Y-BRYN

LLANDEGAI ROAD

VICTORIA PARK

TFFRIDDOEDD ROAD

HOLYHEAD ROAD

FARRAR ROAD

P

HIGH STREET

Recreation Ground

TFORDD Y CASTELL

KINGSLEY AVENUE

GREENWOOD AVENUE

TFORDD TEGAI

River Cegin (Afon Cegin)

CONVENT LANE

STATION ROAD

Train Station

LÔN-PORTH

BISHOP'S MILL ROAD

Golf Course

TYBERNY AVENUE

QUEEN'S AVENUE

GLAIN-YR-EGLWYS

N

0   200

yards

CAERNARFON ROAD

1 (2 miles), Menai Bridge & Anglesey

5 (5 miles), Caernarfon & Llanddeiniolen (10 miles)

Norman rebuilding of 1071. The rest of the structure is the result of reconstructions after being sacked by King John (1211), Edward I (1277) and Owain Glyndŵr (1402), with final heavy-handed touches by George Gilbert Scott in 1866.

The spacious white-walled interior houses the sixteenth-century wooden **Mostyn Christ**, depicted bound and seated on a rock. Look, too, for the arched tomb in the south transept, said to contain the remains of Owain Gwynedd, though the story goes that after being posthumously excommunicated for incest with his first cousin the Bishop of Bangor was asked to remove his body from the cathedral. It was probably re-interred in the churchyard.

Bangor Museum and Art Gallery

Ffordd Gwynedd • Tues–Fri 12.30–4.30pm, Sat 10.30am–4.30pm • Free • ☎ 01248 353368

The standard regional museum fare at the **Bangor Museum and Art Gallery** is enlivened by a collection of traditional costumes and an archeology room containing the most complete Roman sword found in Wales. The most insightful rooms are those devoted to a complete set of furniture from a moderately wealthy Criccieth farm, covering three hundred years of acquisitions, from brooding Welsh dressers to fine Italian pieces. There's also a detailed model of Telford's Menai bridge and an art gallery concentrating on Welsh contemporary works.

Bangor Pier

Mon–Fri 8.30am–dusk, Sat & Sun 10am–dusk • 50p

North of the centre, there's a fine view of Telford's bridge from Bangor's pristine **Victorian pier**, which juts 1550ft into the Menai Strait – over halfway across to Anglesey. It's just a fifteen-minute walk from the town centre and makes a good place to sit and watch the world drift idly by.

Penrhyn Castle

A5 at Llandygai, 2 miles east of Bangor • Mid-March to June, Sept & Oct daily except Tues noon–5pm; July & Aug daily except Tues 11am–5pm • £9, or £6 for grounds & railway museum only • ☎ 01248 363219 • NT • Buses #5, #6, #67 and #75 run frequently from Bangor to Penrhyn's gates, a mile-long walk from the house

There can hardly be a more vulgar testament to the Anglo-Welsh gentry's oppression of the rural Welsh than the nonetheless compelling **Penrhyn Castle**, which overlooks Port Penrhyn from its acres of isolating parkland. Built on the backs of slate miners, this monstrous nineteenth-century neo-Norman fancy, with over three hundred rooms dripping with luxurious fittings, was funded by the quarry's huge profits.

The responsibility falls ultimately on Caribbean sugar plantation owner, slave trader and vehement anti-abolitionist Richard Pennant, First Baron Penrhyn, who built a port on the northeastern edge of Bangor in order to ship his Bethesda slate to the world. But it was his self-aggrandizing great-great-nephew George Dawkins who inherited the 40,000-acre estate and with the aid of architect Thomas Hopper spent thirteen years from 1827 encasing the neo-Gothic hall in a Norman-style fortress complete with a monumental five-storey keep.

Leave time too for the sumptuous **gardens** and the excellent **café**.

The interior

Overblown though it may be, the decoration is impressive, and fairly true to the Romanesque, with its deeply cut chevrons, billets and double-cone ornamentation. Hopper even looked to Norman architecture for the design of the furniture, but abandoned historical authenticity when it came to installing the central heating system, which piped hot air through ornamental brass ducts at the cost of twenty tons of coal a month.

Everything is on a massive scale and no more so than in the Great Hall with its pair of stained-glass zodiac windows by Thomas Willement. Three-foot-thick oak doors separate subsequent rooms: the Library, with its full-size slate billiard table, and the oppressive Ebony Room, which leads onto the Grand Staircase.

Upstairs, the lightness of the original William Morris wallpaper and drapes around the King's Bed are in marked contrast to the Slate Bed, designed for Queen Victoria but declined by her in favour of the Hopper-designed four-poster in the State Bedroom.

Away from the pomp you can visit the enormous **kitchens**, convincingly laid out as if about to cater for the 1894 visit of the Prince and Princess of Wales.

Painting collection

The family managed to assemble the country's largest private **painting collection**. Much of this remains, especially in the two dining rooms, where there's a Gainsborough landscape, Canaletto's *The Thames at Westminster*, and a Rembrandt portrait. During the Blitz of 1940, some 1800 masterpieces from Britain's National Gallery were sent here for safekeeping, though Lord Penrhyn's drunken clumsiness and demands for rental payments forced the then prime minister, Winston Churchill, to have the treasures moved to a former slate mine at Manod for the rest of the war.

Industrial Railway Museum

Open 1hr before castle • Entry included in castle or grounds tickets

The stable block houses the **Industrial Railway Museum**, packed with gleaming examples of rolling stock once used on the estate's quarry-to-port rail line. Look out for the 1848 *Fire Queen*, a very early loco built for the Padarn Railway in Llanberis, retired in the 1880s and (very unusually) preserved in a shed near what is now the National Slate Museum until the quarries closed in 1969.

ARRIVAL AND DEPARTURE   BANGOR

By train All trains on the north coast line between Chester and Holyhead stop at Bangor's train station on Station Rd, at the south end of Holyhead Rd.
Destinations Chester (21 daily; 1hr); Conwy (11 daily; 20min); Holyhead (22 daily; 30–40min); Llandudno (18 daily; 40min); Rhosneigr (9 daily; 25min); Rhyl (25 daily; 40min).
By bus National Express and local buses stop in the centre of town on a short spur off Garth Rd.
Destinations Beaumaris (every 30min; 20–35min); Caernarfon (every 10min; 25min); Conwy (every 15min; 45min); Holyhead (hourly; 1hr 15min); Llanberis (hourly; 45min); Llandudno (every 15min; 1hr); Llangefni (every 30min; 35min); Llanfairpwll (every 30min; 15min); Menai Bridge (every 30min; 20min).

INFORMATION

Tourist information There is no TIC, but limited tourist information is available from the Bangor Museum.
Internet Free access at the library, Ffordd Gwynedd (Mon, Tues, Thurs & Fri 9.30am–7pm, Wed & Sat 9.30am–1pm), and at *Blue Sky*.

ACCOMMODATION

Bangor doesn't have a huge choice of accommodation, with most of the cheaper options at the northern end of Garth Rd, a 20min walk from the train station.

Eryl Môr Hotel 2 Upper Garth Rd ☎ 01248 353789, ⓦ erylmorhotel.co.uk. Quiet, comfy, fully licensed hotel with its own restaurant. The best rooms overlook Bangor's pier and the Menai Strait. £75
Regency Hotel Holyhead Rd ☎ 01248 370819. Good-value small hotel opposite the train station. Breakfast available from £5. £45

Treborth Hall Farm A487, 1.8 miles southwest of upper Bangor between the two Menai Strait bridges ☎ 01248 364104, ⓦ www.treborthleisure.co.uk. The nearest campsite to town is a relaxed spot partly in an old walled garden. There are coin-op showers (£1) and everything is well kept. #5 buses pass the entrance. Pitches £12

Tŷ Mawr Farm B4366, 5 miles southwest of Bangor (and 0.5 mile east of Llanddeiniolen) ☎01286 670147, ⓦtymawrfarm.co.uk. Cosy B&B on a working farm with views of Snowdonia and very good home-made food. Quality, well-equipped self-catering cottages also available

for short lets outside the school holidays. **£75**
Y Garth Garth Rd ☎01248 362277, ⓦthegarthguesthouse.co.uk. En-suite rooms and full breakfasts in marginally the best in a row of three serviceable B&Bs. **£60**

EATING, DRINKING AND ENTERTAINMENT

Bangor has few really good **restaurants**, though as befits a university town there are lots of inexpensive places to eat. The southern end of High St is the best zone for grazing, with an abundance of cheap cafés, pasta and sandwich joints.

★ **Blue Sky** Rear of 236 High St ☎01248 355444, ⓦblueskybangor.co.uk. Bangor's finest daytime café occupies an airy space with exposed rafters, mismatched wooden tables and free wi-fi. There's a casual feel but everything is done with great flair including delicious breakfasts, soups, sandwiches, burgers and platters, often organic and usually £5–7. The coffee and range of teas are great too, and there are evening gigs and films; check the website. Mon–Sat 9.30am–5.30pm and occasional evenings.
Fat Cat Café Bar 161 High St ☎01248 370445. Breezy modern decor and a moderately priced menu – from massive burgers to salmon-and-broccoli pasta quills – help pack this place out with students and locals. The rear deck gets afternoon sun. Daily 10am–10pm.
Kyffin 129 High St ☎01248 355161. Vegetarian and vegan café with excellent Fairtrade coffee and a warm

atmosphere that makes you want to stick around for their light lunches (mostly under £6). Mon–Sat 9.30am–5pm.
Pontio Deiniol Rd ⓦpontio.co.uk. Bangor's cultural life will be limited until the expected 2013 completion of Pontio, an "Arts and Innovation Centre" with a 450-seat theatre, outdoor amphitheatre and slew of dining areas and bars. It should become the major performance hub for north Wales. The website lists current cultural events.
Tafarn Y Glôb 7 Albert St, Upper Bangor ☎01248 362095. Good bar, popular with both students and locals, with real ales and occasional Welsh bands. Daily 11.30am–10pm or later.
Tap & Spile Garth Rd ☎01248 370835. Popular students' and locals' pub with great views of the pier and Menai Strait, plus meals and real ales at good prices. Tues–Sun noon–11pm.

Anglesey

The island of **Anglesey** (Ynys Môn) is a world apart, its green ripple of fields and farms a far cry from the mountains and hemmed-in settlements of Snowdonia. Seen from the four-lane A55 expressway which speeds across Anglesey towards Holyhead, the island can look dull, but take to the smaller roads, and you'll discover Wales' greatest concentration of pre-Christian sites and some superb coastal scenery.

Anglesey comes billed as **Mam Cymru**, "The Mother of Wales", attesting to the island's former importance as the country's breadbasket. In the twelfth century, Giraldus Cambrensis noted that "When crops have failed in other regions, this island, from its soil and its abundant produce, has been able to supply all Wales". The land remains predominantly agricultural, with small fields, stone walls and white houses reminiscent of parts of Ireland and England. Linguistically and politically, though, Anglesey is intensely Welsh, with over seventy percent of its population using Welsh as their first language – one of the country's highest proportions of native speakers. Most residents will at least understand the lines of one of Anglesey's most famous poets, Goronwy Owen, whose eulogy on his homeland translates as "All hail to Anglesey/ The delight of all regions/ Bountiful as a second Eden/ Or an ancient paradise". Judging by the numbers who flock to the island's necklace of fine sandy coves and rocky headlands, many agree with Owen.

The densest concentration of sights is at **Beaumaris** with its wonderful setting and solid castle. Following the south coast clockwise there's a string of minor sights and lovely beaches until you reach **Holy Island** (Ynys Gybi), an hourglass of land just a few yards off the northwest coast of Anglesey, and connected by road and rail bridges. The more ancient and picturesque approach turns west at Valley, and passes close to the fine beaches at **Rhoscolyn** and **Trearddur Bay** before reaching Holyhead (ferry port for Ireland) and the impressive seabird cliffs around **South Stack**. Most road traffic to

7

7

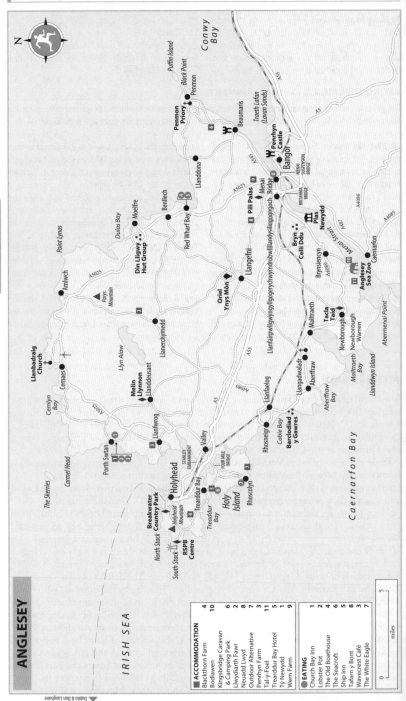

ANGLESEY

N

Conwy Bay

Puffin Island

Black Point
Penmon
Penmon
Priory
Beaumaris
Traeth Lafan
(Lavan Sands)
Penrhyn
Castle
Bangor
Llanddona
Menai
Pili Palas Bridge
Llandegfan
Benllech
Dulas Bay
Moelfre
Red Wharf Bay
Plas
Newydd
Bryn
Celli Ddu
Brynsiencyn
Din Lligwy
Hut Group
Llangefni
Anglesey
Sea Zoo
Caernarfon
Point Lynas
Oriel
Ynys Môn
Amlwch
*Parys
Mountain*
Tacla
Taid
Malltraeth
Newborough
Warren
Abermenai Point
Llanerchymedd
Llanfairpwllgwyngyllgogerychwyrndrobwllllantysiliogogogoch
Llyn Alaw
Mynai Strait
*Malltraeth
Bay*
Llanddwyn Island
Llanbadraig
Church
Melin
Llynnon
Llanddeusant
Llangadwaladr
Aberffraw
Caernarfon Bay
*Cemlyn
Bay*
Cemaes
Llanfwrog
Cable Bay
Barclodiad
y Gawres
*Aberffraw
Bay*
Carmel Head
Llanfaelog
Rhosneigr
The Skerries
Valley
STANLEY
EMBANKMENT
FOUR MILE
BRIDGE
Porth Swtan
Breakwater
Country Park
*Holyhead
Mountain*
Holyhead
Treaddur Bay
Holy
Island
Rhoscolyn
*Treaddur
Bay*
North Stack
South Stack
RSPB
Centre
IRISH SEA

ACCOMMODATION	
Blackthorn Farm	4
Bodlawen	10
Kingsbridge Caravan & Camping Park	6
Llwydiarth Fawr	2
Neuadd Lwyd	8
Outdoor Alternative	3
Penrhyn Farm	11
Tal-y-Foel	5
Treaddur Bay Hotel	1
Tŷ Newydd	9
Wern Farm	7

EATING	
Church Bay Inn	1
Lobster Pot	2
The Old Boathouse	4
The Seacroft	6
Ship Inn	5
Tafarn y Bont	8
Wavecrest Café	3
The White Eagle	7

0   miles   5

Holyhead takes the modern A55 bridge, though rail and the older A5 still follow Thomas Telford's 1200yd **Stanley Embankment**.

The north and west coasts of Anglesey are quieter with just a smattering of minor sights and some highly rewarding stretches of the 125-mile **Anglesey Coast Path**.

Some history

The earliest people on Anglesey were Mesolithic hunters who arrived between 8000 and 4000 BC. Around 2500 BC, a new culture developed among the small farming communities, giving rise to the many henges and stone circles on the island, which held sway until the Celts swept across Europe in the seventh century BC, led by their priestly class, the druids. In the centuries prior to the Roman invasion, Anglesey – well positioned at the apex of Celtic sea traffic – became the most important druidic centre in Europe. The druids were so firmly established that Anglesey was the last place in Wales to fall to the Romans, in 61 AD.

The vacuum left by the Romans' departure in the fifth century was soon filled by the greatest of all Welsh dynasties, the Princes of Gwynedd, who held court at **Aberffraw**. Under Rhodri Mawr, in the ninth century, their influence spread over most of Wales as he defeated the encroaching Vikings, earning thanks from Charlemagne for his efforts. Anglesey again fell to outsiders towards the end of the thirteenth century when Edward I defeated the Welsh princes, sealing the island's fate by forging the final link in his Iron Ring of castles at **Beaumaris**, nowadays by far the most absorbing town on the island.

7

GETTING AROUND ANGLESEY

By train The train line from Bangor crosses the Menai Strait, stopping at the station with the longest name in the world – usually abbreviated to Llanfairpwll – before continuing on to meet the ferries at Holyhead.

By bus Where trains don't go, buses generally do – all detailed in the free Ynys Môn public transport timetable. One of the most useful is #42 which links Bangor, Menai Bridge and Llanfairpwll before looping around the south coast to Aberffraw then inland to Llangefni.

By bike Anglesey is crisscrossed by a spider's web of bike routes: download route maps from Ⓦ visitanglesey .co.uk. Bike rental is available from Llys Llywelyn in Aberffraw near Cable Bay (☎ 01407 840940, Ⓦ llys-llewelyn.com).

On foot Ynys Môn is ringed by the 125-mile Anglesey Coastal Path (Ⓦ angleseycoastalpath.com), covered in detail in *The Rocks and Landscapes of the Anglesey Coastal Footpath* by John Conway.

ACCOMMODATION RURAL ANGLESEY

The island is so compact that, at least if you have your own transport, the choice of accommodation should be based on factors other than solely location. There are some excellent, moderately priced B&Bs and farmhouses, many relatively distant from any recognized sight, but no less appealing for it.

Throughout this section we list accommodation in Beaumaris, Trearddur Bay and Holyhead. The following add to those suggestions and are all marked on our map of Anglesey.

WILLS AND KATE ON ANGLESEY

For an island not noted for its royalist sentiment, Anglesey seems to have taken to Prince William and Kate (the Duke and Duchess of Cambridge) living among them – and frankly the locals love the exposure. William has been an RAF search-and-rescue helicopter pilot based at Valley, near Holyhead, since 2010, and he looks set to continue his stint until late 2013.

As soon as the **Royal Wedding** was announced for 2011, Anglesey hit the world headlines with Kate being papped doing the grocery shopping at Waitrose in Menai Bridge. Though the location of their rented farmhouse remains an enforced secret, the couple are often seen around the island (though never without bodyguards nearby). The White Eagle in Rhoscolyn meets their favour, though possibly not Trearddur Bay's Seacroft, which famously turned away William and a large bunch of his RAF mates when they turned up unannounced on a busy night.

The raised profile has even led to Anglesey getting its own version of Monopoly, which should surely be called Môn-opoly.

Bodlawen Brynsiencyn ☎01248 430379, ⓦangleseyfarms.com. A large modern guesthouse overlooking the Menai Strait and Caernarfon with a relaxed atmosphere and an acclaimed opera-singing owner, Marian Roberts. £65

★ **Llwydiarth Fawr** B5111, 0.5 mile north of Llanerchymedd ☎01248 470321, ⓦangleseyfarms .com. A spacious, agreeable Georgian mansion amid rolling hills on a working farm; self-catering also available. £75

★ **Neuadd Lwyd** off the B5420, 4 miles northwest of Menai Bridge ☎01248 715005, ⓦneuaddlwyd.co.uk. This superb country house exudes informal elegance. Just a few modern touches freshen the early Victorian rectory ambience beautifully. The breakfasts are outstanding, while the immaculate four-course table d'hôte dinner (£42; open

to non-residents) is an integral part of any visit. Closed Mon & Tues. £150

Penrhyn Farm Llanfwrog ☎01407 730134, ⓦangleseyfarms.com. An antique-furnished farmhouse B&B in a wonderful coastal setting with easy access to beach, rockpools and the coastal path. They also have a self-catering cottage. £60

Tal-y-Foel Dwyran, Brynsiencyn ☎01248 430977, ⓦtal-y-foel.co.uk. A particularly nice farmhouse B&B with views across the Menai Strait to Caernarfon, large simply furnished rooms and access to the horseriding school next door. £75

Wern Farm Off A5025, 2 miles north of Menai Bridge ☎01248 712421, ⓦangleseyfarms.com. Book ahead to get a place at this amazingly hospitable B&B in an early seventeenth-century farmhouse with great Snowdonia views. There are spacious grounds and even a tennis court. £75

Menai Bridge

The town of **MENAI BRIDGE** (Porthaethwy) was created during the building of the first of the two bridges across the Menai Strait. It nestles in the shadow of the older crossing, with a few private islands to break the view across the Strait to the mainland.

Thomas Telford Centre

Mona Rd, 200yd from the Anglesey end of the Menai Suspension Bridge • Easter & July–Sept daily except Fri & Sat 10am–4pm • £3, kids free • ☎01248 715046, ⓦmenaibridges.co.uk

The design and history of both the Menai Strait bridges and the men responsible for them are explored at the **Thomas Telford Centre**. Among the architectural bridge drawings, pretty

---

SPANNING THE MENAI STRAIT

Two bridges – both engineering marvels of their time – link Anglesey to the mainland over the **Menai Strait**, a perilous fourteen-mile-long tidal race that in places narrows to 200yd wide, forcing the current up to eight knots as it rushes between Conwy and Caernarfon bays. The **best views** are from the Anglesey shore, where you can look over the rocky mid-channel islets, some adorned with jetties and small houses, and backed by the heartland of Snowdonia: make for the lay-by on the A5, a mile east of Llanfairpwll.

For centuries before the bridges were built, drovers used the Strait's narrow stretches to herd Anglesey-fattened cattle on their way to market in England. Travellers had to wait for low tide to cross Lafan Sands, northeast of Bangor, then find a boat to take them across to Beaumaris, in foggy weather guided only by the sound of church bells. So it's not surprising that Irish MPs, needing transport to Westminster and a faster mail service, pushed for a fixed crossing.

MENAI SUSPENSION BRIDGE

The first permanent link, in 1826, was Telford's graceful **Menai Suspension Bridge**, the world's first large iron suspension bridge, spanning 579ft between piers and 100ft above the water to allow high-masted sailing ships to pass. Almost everything about the project was novel, including the process of lifting the sixteen 23-ton chains into place, which involved a pulley system and 150 men kept in time by a fife band. One man celebrated their achievement by running across the nine-inch-wide chain from Anglesey to the mainland.

BRITANNIA TUBULAR BRIDGE

In 1850, Robert Stephenson also made engineering history with his **Britannia Tubular Bridge**, which carried trains across the Strait in twin wrought-iron tubes. It was severely damaged by fire in 1970, however, leaving only the limestone piers that now support the twin-deck A5/A55 road and rail bridge to Llanfairpwll and Holyhead.

aquatints and explanatory panels you'll find a few intriguing hunks of grey iron – chain links, a huge rivet punch, capstan arms and a 12ft-long spanner – plus the original pulleys used for hauling up the chains. The collection is continually expanding and may, by 2014, move to a new complex on Prince's Pier on the Menai Bridge waterside.

Church of St Tysilio

Open mid-July to Aug daily, and for occasional Sunday services

The fourteenth-century **church of St Tysilio** occupies Church Island, where its patron saint founded his cell around 630 AD. Topped by a Celtic cross war memorial, the island has delightful views along the Strait and to both bridges. It can be reached through the woodland behind the car park on the approach to the Menai Bridge itself, or from the town along a causeway and waterside promenade named **Belgian Walk** (having been built by refugees during World War I).

EATING AND DRINKING	MENAI BRIDGE

Tafarn y Bont Telford Rd ☎ 01248 714864, ⓦ tafarnybont.com. Located right by the Menai Suspension Bridge, this pub and restaurant is rightly popular. With a conservatory, a couple of fireplaces and plenty of afternoon sun out the front there is always somewhere appealing for a pint or to tuck into quality pub meals (lunches £6–9; dinner mains £14–17). Meals served daily noon–2.30pm & 6–9.30pm.

Beaumaris and around

The original inhabitants of **BEAUMARIS** (Biwmares) were evicted by Edward I to make way for the construction of his new castle and bastide town, dubbed "beautiful marsh" in a ploy to attract English settlers. Today the place can still seem like the small English outpost Edward intended, with a grand Georgian terrace (designed by Joseph Hansom, of cab fame) and more plummy English accents than you'll have heard for a while. Many of their owners belong with the flotilla of yachts, an echo of the port's fleet of merchant ships, which disappeared with the completion of the Menai bridges and subsequent growth of Holyhead.

With its attractive setting and plenty of things to do and see, Beaumaris inevitably draws the summer crowds, though evenings are peaceful, with day-trippers gone and overnighters ensconced in their hotel restaurants.

While you can spend an hour or two mooching around Beaumaris' antique shops, enjoying the views across the Strait towards Bangor and along the coast to Llandudno's Great Orme from the stumpy pier, this shouldn't distract you from visiting the main attractions – the castle, court and gaol – each offering its own angle on Welsh subjugation. In good weather, a cruise out around Puffin Island or a wander along the nearby coastline close to Penmon Priory may suit better.

Beaumaris Castle

Castle St · March–June, Sept & Oct daily 9.30am–5pm; July & Aug daily 9.30am–6pm; Nov–March Mon–Sat 10am–4pm, Sun 11am–4pm · £3.80 · ☎ 01248 810361 · CADW

The town's central feature is **Beaumaris Castle**, the most picturesque of Edward's gargantuan fortresses with its water-filled moat and loop-holed ramparts. It was built in response to Madog ap Llywelyn's capture of Caernarfon in 1294, architect James of St George producing a symmetrical octagonal form, his finest and most highly evolved expression of concentric design. Lacking the domineering majesty of Caernarfon, Conwy or Harlech, its low outer walls seem almost welcoming – belying the deadly ingenuity of its design.

Sited on flat land at the edge of town, the castle is approached over a moat and through Moorish-influenced staggered entries at the huge towers of the Gate Next the Sea and the South Gatehouse. The moat originally linked the castle to the sea (now well over a hundred yards away), with a shipping channel allowing boats of up to forty

7

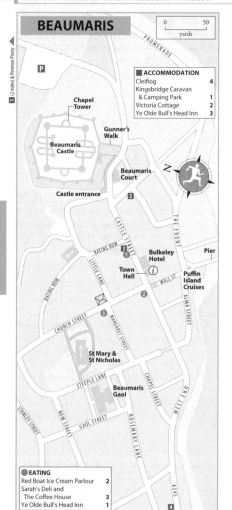

BEAUMARIS

0   50
yards

PROMENADE

Chapel
Tower

Gunner's
Walk

Beaumaris
Castle

Beaumaris
Court

Castle entrance

CASTLE STREET

RATING ROW

LITTLE LANE

RATING ROW

THE FRONT

Bulkeley
Hotel

Town
Hall

Pier

Puffin
Island
Cruises

WALL ST.

ALMA STREET

CHURCH STREET

MARGARET STREET

St Mary &
St Nicholas

STEEPLE LANE

Beaumaris
Gaol

CHAPEL STREET

STANLEY STREET

NEW LANE

GAOL STREET

ROSEMARY LANE

WEST END

A545

■ ACCOMMODATION
Cleifiog	4
Kingsbridge Caravan & Camping Park	1
Victoria Cottage	2
Ye Olde Bull's Head Inn	3

● EATING
Red Boat Ice Cream Parlour	2
Sarah's Deli and The Coffee House	3
Ye Olde Bull's Head Inn	1

tons to tie up at the iron rings hammered into a protective spur of the outer defences, **Gunner's Walk**. Supplies could be brought in, including the corn that was fed into a mill, still visible immediately below.

Around the battlements

Despite over thirty years' work and plans for a lavish palace, the castle was never quite finished, leaving most of the inner ward empty, and the corbels and fireplaces unused. You can explore around half of the inner and outer **wall walks**, from which archers could fire simultaneously from the inner and outer defences. Then wander through miles of internal passages in the walls, finding your way to the first floor of the **Chapel Tower**, whose small but wonderfully resonant lime-washed chapel lies immediately above a modest "Castles of Edward I" exhibition.

When put to the test, the castle failed to withstand Owain Glyndŵr – who took it in 1403 and held it for two years – but during the Civil War, its Royalist defenders held out against General Mytton and 1500 Parliamentarian troops until 1646. After Charles II's accession, the castle was returned to the Bulkeley family, only to be left to fall into ruin before twentieth-century restoration returned some of its glory.

Beaumaris Court

Castle St • April–Sept daily except Fri 10.30am–5pm • £3.50, £7 joint ticket with Gaol • ☎ 01248 811691, Ⓦ visitanglesey.co.uk

Fittingly, the castle overshadows the juridical instruments of English rule, the Jacobean **Beaumaris Court**. From 1614 until 1971, it hosted the quarterly Assize Courts. These were traditionally held in English, giving the jury little chance to follow the proceedings, and Welsh-speaking defendants none against judges notorious for slapping heavy penalties on relatively minor offences. Undoubtedly they sympathized with the sentiments embodied in **The Lawsuit**, a plaque in the main courtroom depicting two farmers pulling the horns and tail of a cow as a lawyer milks it. A good free audio tour fills in the details.

Beaumaris Gaol

Steeple Lane • April–Sept daily except Fri 10.30am–5pm • £4.25; £7 joint ticket with Beaumaris Court • ☎ 01248 810921, Ⓦ visitanglesey.co.uk

Many citizens were transported from the court to the colonies for their felonies; others wound up in **Beaumaris Gaol**. When it opened in 1829, this was considered a model prison, with running water and toilets in each cell and an infirmary. Women prisoners did the cooking and were allowed to rock their babies' cradles in the nursery above by means of a pulley system. Advanced perhaps, but nonetheless this is a gloomy place: witness the windowless punishment cell, the stone-breaking yard and the treadmill water pump. The least fortunate inmates were marched along a first-floor walkway through a door in the outer wall to the gibbet, where they were publicly hanged.

Penmon Priory

4 miles northeast of Beaumaris • Open access • Free; parking £2.50 • CADW • Bangor–Beaumaris bus #57 runs to Penmon, Mon–Sat roughly hourly

Penmon Priory's original wooden buildings were razed by the Danes in the tenth century. Their replacements, the twelfth-century church and the thirteenth-century south range of the cloister, are still standing. Only the **church** is in good repair and still used, the serene, lime-washed nave housing an unusual Norman pillar-piscina – a font gouged from the plinth of a pre-Norman cross still used for Sunday services – and the Penmon Cross, moved here to prevent a thousand years of Welsh weather completely scouring off its plait and fret patterns. There's more patterned stonework in the south transept, approached through a magnificent chevron- and chequerboard-patterned arch. The church's site was chosen for its proximity to the refreshing waters of **St Seiriol's Well**, which now feeds a calm pool and is reached by either the path behind the church, or another opposite the distinctive domed **dovecote**, built around 1600 to house one thousand pairs of birds.

Black Point and Puffin Island

5 miles northwest of Beaumaris

The parking fee for Penmon also covers you for the toll road which runs three-quarters of a mile beyond the dovecote to **Black Point**, the easternmost point of Anglesey. A short strait separates you from **Puffin Island**, known in Welsh as Ynys Seiriol, recalling Penmon's St Seiriol, whose original Augustine community was on the island. It is now home to nesting razorbills, guillemots and puffins, all once permissible food during Lent. Cruises around Puffin Island leave from Beaumaris. A café in an ancient cottage at Black Point provides sustenance between short strolls along the coast.

ARRIVAL AND INFORMATION   BEAUMARIS

By bus There are regular buses (#53, #56, #57 and #58) from Bangor (every 30min; 20–35min), Menai Bridge (every 30min; 15min) and Penmon (11 daily; 15min).

Tourist information A desk in the foyer of the Town Hall on Castle St stocks leaflets and sometimes has volunteers in attendance.

ACCOMMODATION

★ **Cleifiog** Townsend ☎01248 811507, ⓦ cleifiogbandb.co.uk. There are just three rooms (plus a spacious guest lounge) in this large, mostly Georgian townhouse with great views across Menai Strait to Snowdonia. The best room is on the corner with plenty of light, masses of wood panelling and a deep bath. A welcome tray with jars of biscuits and coffee, plus a great breakfast, round out the welcoming hospitality. Two-night minimum at weekends and good rates for singles. **£85**

Kingsbridge Caravan & Camping Park Llanfaes, 2 miles northeast of Beaumaris ☎01248 490636, ⓦ www.kingsbridgecaravanpark.co.uk. Spacious campsite with a shower block, campervan hookups and static caravans (£220–300/week). Pitches **£20**

★ **Victoria Cottage** Victoria Terrace ☎01248 810807, ⓦ victoriacottage.net. A boutique B&B tucked in behind Hansom's grand waterfront terrace, with two spacious en-suite rooms with views and two loft rooms which share a bathroom with a big bath. There's a comfy guest lounge and great breakfasts. **£70**

WHITE AND TAWNY SAINTS

In the sixth century, St Seiriol was head of the Augustine **Penmon Priory** and soon became known as the White Saint, not for his unblemished purity, but because his weekly walk to Llanerchymedd to meet St Cybi involved journeying with his back to the sun in both directions. Cybi, journeying into the sun from present-day Holyhead, was dubbed the Tawny Saint.

Ye Olde Bull's Head Inn 18 Castle St ☎ 01248 810329, ⓦ bullsheadinn.co.uk. The best hotel in Beaumaris, this ancient coaching inn was used as General Mytton's headquarters during the Civil War and, in more peaceful circumstances, by Dr Johnson and Charles Dickens. It has a fantastic restaurant and a decent brasserie and bar. Accommodation is either in antique-styled and very comfortable rooms in the main building or chic modern rooms and suites across the road in *The Townhouse*. All include an excellent breakfast. **£100**

EATING AND DRINKING

Red Boat Ice Cream Parlour 34 Castle St ⓦ redboatgelato.com. Slip into one of the booths in this retro ice-cream parlour with an ever-changing selection of superb gelati and sorbets, all freshly made on the premises. Stick around for panini, Fairtrade coffee, cakes and smoothies. Daily 10am–6pm.

Sarah's Deli and The Coffee House 11 Church St ☎ 01248 811534. This licensed, daytime café and deli has shelves groaning with Anglesey and wider Welsh produce – especially cheeses and relishes. Ham is cooked in-house, as is just about everything on the menu from melt-in-the-mouth cakes to Welsh rarebit (£6.50), tapas and meze platters, meaty or veggie ploughman's (£8), sweet and savoury cream teas (£4) and daily blackboard specials.

Daily except Wed & Sun 9am–5pm.

★ **Ye Olde Bull's Head Inn** 18 Castle St ☎ 01248 810329, ⓦ bullsheadinn.co.uk. Beaumaris' top hotel doesn't disappoint when it comes to eating and drinking. There's a cosy old-fashioned bar but a more modern angle in the bare-boards conservatory brasserie, where you might expect goat's cheese and shiitake filo tart (£6) followed by chorizo meatballs on spaghetti (£12). The superb *Loft* restaurant is more formal, though no less contemporary, serving inventive modern dishes using seasonal produce, much of it from Anglesey (£41 for 3 courses). Loft Tues–Thurs 7–9.30pm, Fri & Sat 6.30–9.30pm; Brasserie daily noon–2pm (Sun 3pm) & 6–9pm.

Llanfairpwllgwyngyllgogerychwyrndrobwllllandysiliogogogoch and the south coast

When Robert Louis Stephenson wrote "to travel hopefully is a better thing than to arrive" he might have been thinking of **LLANFAIRPWLL**, the village with the longest place name in Britain and little else except a wool shop and a small train station (request stop only) bearing the famed sign **Llanfairpwllgwyngyllgogerychwyrndrobwllllandysiliogogogoch**. Sadly, "St Mary's church in the hollow of white hazel near a rapid whirlpool and the Church of St Tysilio near the red cave" is no authentic Welsh tongue twister, but simply the fabrication of a Menai Bridge tailor in the 1880s, who added to the original first five syllables in an attempt to draw tourists – as indeed it has.

You'll very soon want to push on around the south coast stopping at sights along the way: Whistler's mural at **Plas Newydd**; the burial mound of **Bryn Celli Ddu** and **Barclodiad y Gawres**; the **Anglesey Sea Zoo** with its ecological approach to the region's sealife; the wild dunes of **Newborough Warren**; and the pretty beaches and coves around **Rhosneigr**, **Rhoscolyn** and **Trearddur Bay**.

Marquess of Anglesey's Column

A5, 0.5 mile east • Daily 9am–5pm • £1.50

You can hardly miss the bronze figure atop the 91ft-high Doric **Marquess of Anglesey's Column**. The apocryphal story has him declaring to Wellington, on having a leg blown off at Waterloo, "Begod, sir, there goes me leg", to which Wellington dryly replied, "Begod, sir, so it do". There hadn't been much love lost between them since the Marquess ran off with Wellington's sister-in-law some years previously. You can climb the 115 steps up to the Marquess to share his view across the Strait to Snowdonia, and see his replacement leg at Plas Newydd.

INFORMATION   LLANFAIRPWLL

Tourist office The TIC here (April–Oct Mon–Sat 9.30am–5.30pm, Sun 9.30am–4.30pm; Nov–March Mon–Sat 9.30am–5pm, Sun 9.30am–4.30pm; ☎ 01248 713177; ⓦ visitanglesey.co.uk) is effectively the tourist office for the whole island.

Plas Newydd

A4080, 1.5 miles southwest of Llanfairpwll • Mid-March to Oct daily except Thurs & Fri; 11.15am–1pm access by free guided tours only, 1–5pm free flow access • Gardens open an hour earlier • £9.30, garden only £7.30 • ☎ 01248 715272 or 01248 714795 • NT

Plas Newydd is the ancestral home of the marquesses of Anglesey, as it has been since the eighteenth century. A house has stood here, overlooking the Menai Strait, since the sixteenth century, but it was the First Marquess's huge profits from Anglesey's Parys Mountain and other ventures that paid for its transformation by James Wyatt and Joseph Potter into a Gothic mansion in the late eighteenth century. Potter designed the pleasing, castellated stable block that almost upstages the modest-looking three-storey house with incongruous Tudor caps on slender octagonal turrets.

The **Gothic Hall**, with its Potter-designed fan-vaulted ceiling, leads to the finest room in the house, the Music Room, originally the great hall. All available space is covered with oil paintings, including portraits of the First Marquess and Lady Paget, his first wife, both by John Hoppner. There's a transition to the neoclassical on entering the Staircase Hall with its cantilevered staircase and deceptively solid-looking Doric columns, actually just painted wood. The gallery is lined with portraits of monarchs and family members, those of the Sixth Marquess and his sister being the work of Rex Whistler, who spent two years here in the 1930s.

Whistler's masterwork is the magnificent 58ft-long trompe l'oeil **mural** of some imaginary seascape seen from a promenade. At first it seems utterly incongruous, but you are soon drawn into the fantasy, your position seeming to shift by over a mile as you walk along, altering your perspective on the mountains of Snowdonia and a whimsical composite of elements. Portmeirion is there, as are the Round Tower from Windsor Castle and the steeple from St Martin-in-the-Fields in London. Whistler himself appears as a gondolier, and again as a gardener in one of the two right-angled panels at either end, which appear to extend the room further.

The **Cavalry Museum**, a few rooms further on, exhibits the world's first articulated leg, a synthesis of wood, leather and springs, designed for the First Marquess, who lost his leg at Waterloo.

Allow a couple of hours to see the house and visit the Neolithic **cromlech** located in grounds landscaped by Humphrey Repton in the early nineteenth century. Recover in (or on the lawns around) the former milking parlour, now a lovely tiled **tearoom** serving snacks and light meals (open daily year-round).

Bryn Celli Ddu

0.5 mile north of A4080, about 2.5 miles southwest of Llanfairpwll • Open access • Free • CADW

Atmospheric **Bryn Celli Ddu**, the "Mound of the Dark Chamber", is one of Anglesey's most significant prehistoric features, built four thousand years ago on the site of a Neolithic henge. Archeological digs have shown it to be an extensive religious site, but all you can see today is a well-proportioned henge and stone circle, later built over to turn it into a passage grave beneath an earthen mound. The original entrance stone was whisked off to the National Museum in Cardiff, but a replica gives an idea of its carved spiral patterns. In the last chamber you'll find an impressive, smooth monolith under a rather less than impressive supporting concrete beam. The #42 **bus** passes within half a mile; otherwise it's an hour-long walk from Llanfairpwll.

Anglesey Sea Zoo

Brynsiencyn, 7 miles southwest of Llanfairpwll • Feb–Oct daily 10am–5.30pm • £7.50 • ☎ 01248 430411, ⊛ angleseyseazoo.co.uk

Facing Caernarfon across the Menai Strait, the **Anglesey Sea Zoo** is one of the most absorbing attractions on Anglesey. Local marine environments are simulated in wave tanks, and in shallow pools where plaice, turbot and dogfish, camouflaged against the shingle bottom, are barely visible from the catwalks above. They haven't entirely got away from glass-sided tanks, but most are large and the contents chosen to depict specific environments: tidal flats, quayside, wrecks and kelp forest among them.

> ## WORTH ITS SALT?
> With provenance being key in modern foodie circles, **Halen Môn**, who source the sea water for their salts from the Menai Strait beside the sea zoo, is on a roll. Some of the world's top restaurants use it, and their smoked sea salt is an important ingredient in Barack Obama's favourite chocolates. Quality food shops around Wales stock the white stuff along with flavoured varieties such as vanilla and celery.

Windows allow you watch the lab work and food preparation. In keeping with the buildings' previous functions as an oyster hatchery and lobster breeding farm, the zoo uses aquaculture to give the lobsters a much greater chance of survival once released into the wild. Research ecology is a big part of the operation, and the ethics carry through to the good, licensed café where most things are recycled, Fairtrade and/or organic. There's even a chip-free kids' menu.

Newborough Warren

Newborough, 3 miles west of the Sea Zoo • Open access • Free, parking £3 in £1 coins only

The southwestern end of the Menai Strait is marked by Abermenai Point, a huge sand bar backed by the 600-acre **Newborough Warren**, one of the most important dune systems anywhere in Britain. Rabbits are common here, as are the otherwise rare thick-horned **Soay sheep**, Britain's oldest native breed. Since 1948, much of the land has been clad in pines which stabilize the ground and provide habitat for goldcrests, warblers and rare native red squirrels, justifying the Warren's designation as a national nature reserve. From the small town of Newborough (Niwbwrch), head a couple of miles to the main car park.

Llanddwyn Island

From the car park at Newborough Warren, three main trails, all well marked and none more than an hour or two's stroll, weave through the pines to the beach and **Llanddwyn Island**, a glorious peninsula of rocky coves and sandy beaches. On it stands Twr Mawr (the Great Tower), built in 1800 to warn the ships in Caernarfon Bay, later supplanted by the disused lighthouse, built in 1873 in the style of an Anglesey windmill. There's also a row of restored cottages and the ruined thirteenth-century **Church of St Dwynwen**, dedicated to the patron saint of lovers in Wales. In the fifth century, after her abortive affair with Welsh prince Maelon, Dwynwen became a nun at Llanddwyn and requested that hopeful lovers who make a supplication to God in her name should receive divine assistance.

Llangadwaladr church

A4080, 4 miles northwest of Newborough • Usually closed except Sun mornings • ☎ 01407 840282

The area around tiny Llangadwaladr was once the seat of the great ruling dynasty of the Princes of Gwynedd who, from the seventh-century reign of Cadfan until Llywelyn ap Gruffydd's death in 1282, controlled northwest Wales, and often much of the rest of the country. Evidence lies in **Llangadwaladr church**, built in the thirteenth century, with a memorial plaque, carved in Latin about 625, incorporated into an inside wall. It reads "Cadfan the King, wisest and most renowned of all kings".

Barclodiad y Gawres

Scheduled visits Sat & Sun noon–4pm from the Wayside Stores, 1 mile north in Llanfaelog • Free • Call ahead ☎ 01407 810153 • CADW

Cable Bay (Porth Trecastell) was the eastern terminus of the first telegraph cable to Ireland, though it is now better known for its good sandy beach. On the headland to the north, the heavily reconstructed remains of the 5000-year-old **Barclodiad y Gawres** (the Giantess's Apronful) burial chamber are more dramatic than nearby Bryn Celli Ddu, with chevrons and zigzag patterns.

Rhosneigr

The weekday roar of fighter jets from the nearby RAF Valley airfield deafens you long before you reach the otherwise peaceful Edwardian seaside resort of **RHOSNEIGR**, midway along the southwest coast. Rambling over consolidated dunes behind a series of small bays, Rhosneigr remains justifiably popular with English holiday-makers, although space on the beach is these days contested by the dozens of devoted **windsurfers** and **kitesurfers** who flock here when the wind is right. It's the sort of low-key place where you might feel like joining in: rent a board and rig from Funsport, 1 Beach Terrace (£15–25 per day, tuition £35 for 2hr; ☎01407 810899, ⓦbuckys .co.uk), and take to the sea or the small Maelog Lake, safer when the wind is offshore.

Rhoscolyn

At the western extremity of Anglesey is **Holy Island**, though you'll barely notice you've changed island as you cross a small inlet at **Four Mile Bridge**. At the southern tip of the island lanes wander down to the tiny, scattered seaside settlement of **RHOSCOLYN**. With a couple of exquisite sandy beaches, lots of rocky outcrops and coastal walking, this is the ideal place to spend a day or two chilling out.

ACCOMMODATION, EATING AND DRINKING   RHOSCOLYN

Outdoor Alternative ☎01407 860469, ⓦwww .outdooralternative.co.uk. A relaxed, simple campsite a few yards from the beach that mostly caters to activity groups (kayakers, walkers etc). Phone in advance for directions. Kayaks can be rented (£20 a day) and staff can point you to some of the best walks. Camping per person **£5.50**

★ **The White Eagle** ☎01407 860267, ⓦwhite-eagle .co.uk. Excellent gastropub offering some of the best eating on Holy Island, serving modern British cuisine (mains mostly £11–14) and a bunch of excellent cask ales. The huge deck with long views of the indented coastline is a great spot for a pint or two before dinner. Bookings for groups only. Mon–Sat noon–11pm, Sun noon–10.30pm.

Trearddur Bay

At the waist of Holy Island's hourglass shape, the scattered settlement of **TREARDDUR BAY** (Bae Trearddur) shambles across low grassy hills, around a deeply indented bay punctuated by rocky coves. There's no centre to speak of, but it's a much nicer base than Holyhead and has a good, clean swimming beach.

ACCOMMODATION, EATING AND DRINKING   TREARDDUR BAY

Blackthorn Farm 2 miles northwest ☎01407 765262, ⓦblackthornleisure.co.uk. Comfy B&B plus a nicely sited campsite (£10 per pitch) with a new shower block. Camping per person **£10**, rooms **£65**

The Seacroft Ravenspoint Rd ☎01407 860348, ⓦwww.theseacroft.com. Big, modern restaurant and bar with a freshly scrubbed nautical feel usually bustling with people in for a pint or a meal. There are separate bar and dining areas, though the menu works across both

– expect anything from burgers with chunky chips (£10) and pizzas (£8–10) to Thai curry, fajitas and steaks (mostly £10–15). Daily 11.30am–10pm or later.

Trearddur Bay Hotel ☎01407 860301, ⓦtrearddurbayhotel.co.uk. This venerable hotel is the best place to stay hereabouts, with 42 rooms, some overlooking the main bay. It has a heated indoor pool, a good traditional restaurant (mains £19–27) and decent bar meals (around £9). Meals daily noon–2.30pm & 6–9pm. **£155**

Holyhead and South Stack

Drab **HOLYHEAD** (Caergybi; pronounced in English as "holly-head") is Anglesey's largest town and the terminus for ferry routes to Ireland. It isn't somewhere you'll want to spend much time, and reasonably well-integrated train and ferry timetables mean you shouldn't need to. Walking into town from the train and ferry terminals you get to experience the town's latest rejuvenation attempt, a pedestrian steel-arch bridge known as the **Celtic Gateway**, which deposits you on depressing Market Street. All is not lost, though, with some rewarding coastline all about and the cliff-top delights of **South Stack** just over the hill.

Church of St Cybi

June–Sept Mon–Sat 11am–3pm

The town's Welsh name indicates that this was the site of a Roman fort and home of the sixth-century saint Cybi, after whom the island gets its holiness. His hermit's cell was built in the protection of the Roman walls and is now marked by the partly thirteenth-century **church of St Cybi**. Both walls and church have undergone substantial reconstruction, and the addition of the Stanley Chapel with its glass by Edward Burne-Jones and the beautiful "Tree of Life" window by William Morris.

Holyhead Maritime Museum

Beach Rd • Mid-April to Oct daily 10am–4pm • £3.50 • ☎ 01407 769745, ⓦ holyheadmaritimemuseum.co.uk

The **Holyhead Maritime Museum** sits beside the Newry Beach seafront overlooking Britain's longest breakwater (nearly 1.5 miles long). Tucked into Wales' oldest lifeboat station, the museum contains haunting memorabilia of local maritime disasters along with models of lifeboats through the years, and the ferries that have plied the Ireland route over the centuries. There are even some whale's eardrums, which show a passing resemblance to a human head and face. For no apparent reason, two on display here have been carved to portray Mussolini and Hitler.

7

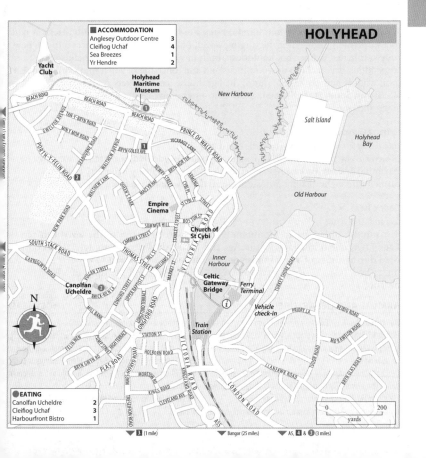

Breakwater Country Park

2 miles west of town along Beach Rd • Daily 9am–dusk • Free

Breakwater Country Park is one of the better ways to pass the time if you miss your boat. An old brickworks marks the starting point for a bracing clifftop **walk** to the foghorn station on North Stack (an hour or so return), or on to South Stack, an hour's walk beyond.

South Stack and around

You really need your own transport to get to **South Stack** (Ynys Lawd), two miles west of Holyhead, where you can watch seabirds, visit a dramatic lighthouse and follow a path (45min) to the top of the 700ft **Holyhead Mountain** (Mynydd Twr).

Ellin's Tower Seabird Centre

Easter–Sept daily 10am–5.30pm • Free • ☎ 01407 762100, ⓦ rspb.org.uk/wales

Views of the cliffs around South Stack are best from the RSPB-run **Ellin's Tower Seabird Centre**, where from April until the end of July, binoculars and closed-circuit TV give an unrivalled opportunity to watch up to 3000 birds – razorbills, guillemots and a few puffins – nesting on the nearby sea cliffs while choughs and peregrines wheel outside the tower's windows.

South Stack Lighthouse

Easter–Sept daily 10.30am–5.30pm • £4

A twisting path with over four hundred steps leads down from the South Stack car park to a suspension bridge over the surging waves, once the keeper's only access to the now fully automated pepper-pot **lighthouse**, built in 1809. Views on to the cliffs are stupendous as you climb down to the island and, once there, you'll find exhibitions on local wildlife and can take a tour of the lighthouse itself. Tickets are issued at the RSPB-run **South Stack Kitchen**, a café-cum-interpretive centre a hundred yards back along the lane.

Cytiau'r Gwyddelod

Across the road from South Stack Kitchen • Open access • Free • CADW

Nineteen low stone circles comprise the **Cytiau'r Gwyddelod** hut circles, probably late Neolithic or early Bronze Age. There seem to have originally been fifty buildings, formed into eight distinct farmsteads separated by ploughed fields.

Caer y Twr

Open access • Free • CADW

The summit of Holyhead Mountain is ringed by the remains of the seventeen-acre **Caer y Twr**, one of the largest Iron Age sites in north Wales. Seemingly, it was only used during times of war, as no signs of permanent occupation have been unearthed, just a 6ft-high dry-stone wall enclosure around the ruins of a Roman beacon.

ARRIVAL AND DEPARTURE   **HOLYHEAD**

By train The A55 Expressway spills you into central Holyhead right by the train station, which has Arriva trains to north Wales destinations and inter-city Virgin trains as far as London.

Destinations Bangor (22 daily; 30–40min); Chester (23 daily; 1hr 30min–2hr); Conwy (11 daily; 1hr); Llandudno (18 daily; 1hr 20min); Llanfairpwll (9 daily; 30min).

By bus Local and National Express bus stops are clustered together by the passenger ferry terminal.

Destinations Amlwch (7 daily; 50min); Bangor (hourly; 1hr 15min); Cemaes (7 daily; 45min); Llanfairpwll (hourly; 1hr); Llangefni (hourly; 45min); Menai Bridge (hourly; 1hr); Rhoscolyn (5 daily; 15min); Trearddur Bay (hourly; 10min).

By ferry For ferries to and from Ireland see Getting there in Basics.

ACCOMMODATION

Anglesey Outdoor Centre Porthdafarch Rd, just over 1 mile southwest ✆ 01407 769351 ⊚ angleseyoutdoors .com. Associate YHA and independent activity centre with abundant camping and bunk accommodation. There are self-catering facilities and bargain meals at the *Paddlers Return* bar, plus all sorts of activities you can join, and gear to rent. Camping per person, weekdays **£5**, weekends **£10**; tepees (for 4) **£70**; yurts (for 4) **£100**; dorms **£12.50**; en-suite twin rooms **£36**

★ **Cleifiog Uchaf** Spenser Rd, Valley, 4 miles southeast ✆ 01407 741888, ⊚ cleifioguchaf.co.uk. Outstanding eight-room hotel in a beautifully restored sixteenth-century farmhouse set in utterly peaceful grounds. There's an almost French country feel to the off-white interiors though the spirit is thoroughly Welsh with wool throws, slate flagstones, a cosy guest library and superb Welsh breakfasts with thick-cut local bacon. **£95**

Sea Breezes 95 Newry St ✆ 01407 765682. One of the more homely and welcoming of several budget places on this street, well used to the needs of late-arriving ferry passengers. **£55**

Yr Hendre Porth-y-Felin Rd ✆ 01407 762929, ⊚ yr-hendre.net. Very comfy B&B with three floral rooms and a generous welcome, set in a charming ex-manse. **£65**

EATING, DRINKING AND ENTERTAINMENT

Canolfan Ucheldre Mill Bank ✆ 01407 763361, ⊚ ucheldre.org. Anglesey's premier centre for the performing arts and exhibitions, fashioned from a former convent chapel. Presents recent films three nights a week and has the *Gegin Ucheldre* daytime café (closed Sun morning) with everything home-made. Meals Mon–Sat noon–2pm.

★ **Cleifiog Uchaf** Spenser Rd, Valley, 4 miles southeast ✆ 01407 741888, ⊚ www.cleifioguchaf .co.uk. It is all very well sourcing major ingredients from within four miles and growing many vegetables on site, but you still need to know what to do with them … and

they really do. There are usually only three choices for each course (including one vegetarian, one Welsh cheese platter). Expect the likes of pan-fried cod with fennel (£17) followed by rhubarb tart with crème anglaise (£6). Tues–Sat 6–9pm.

Harbourfront Bistro Newry Beach ✆ 01407 763433, ⊚ harbourfrontbistro.co.uk. Sandwiches, toasted baguettes, cakes and good coffee plus dishes such as seared tiger prawns (£9) and veggie pasta bake (£8) with good harbour views and some outdoor seating. Wed & Sun 11am–2.30pm, Thurs–Sat 11am–2.30pm & 6–9pm.

Northern, eastern and inland Anglesey

The **northern and eastern sides of Anglesey** are quieter than the south and west; their settlements cluster behind sheltered coves that, with the odd rocky headland, form an appealing (if seldom dramatic) coastline. This is primarily family holiday country, though its thinner spread of caravan sites makes it much less oppressive than the north Welsh coast.

GETTING AROUND   NORTHERN, EASTERN AND INLAND ANGLESEY

Towns are well spaced along (or just off) the A5025, making cycling between them, or walking the coastal path, an ideal way to get around. Relying on **buses** is possible, though less rewarding.

Melin Llynnon

Llanddeusant • Easter–Sept daily 11am–5pm • £3 • ✆ 01407 730797, ⊚ visitanglesey.co.uk

A few miles inland from the A5025, signposts tempt you towards **Melin Llynnon**, Anglesey's sole working, traditional windmill. At one time, fifty-odd mills all over Anglesey ground away to feed all of north Wales; today, over thirty can still be seen, their sail-less stumps either rotting away in field corners or converted into barns and houses. Restored from dereliction under the guidance of Lincolnshire millwrights, Melin Llynnon is now white-painted, canvas-sailed and once again producing flour. Everything in the mill is wind-powered, even the hoists that lift the grain through trapdoors, and almost extinct milling skills have been re-learnt by modern millers, who now demonstrate the process and sell the result – in bag and cake form – from a good café.

This was originally the site of an Iron Age village, something recalled in the two 30ft-diameter, thatched **round houses** built here in 2007.

Porth Swtan

The highlight of the northwest coast is **PORTH SWTAN** (Church Bay), a gently understated settlement gathered around a picturesque sweep of sand backed by yellow rocks dating from the pre-Cambrian era, some 570 million years ago. There's limited free parking.

Swtan

Easter–Oct Fri–Sun noon–4pm • £3 • ☏ 01407 730186, ⓦ swtan.co.uk

Just back from the beach, **Swtan** is the only surviving thatched cottage on Anglesey, the story of its restoration told in a short film. There's always a fire burning in the inglenook fireplace in the tiny stone-flagged kitchen dining room, and the thatch construction can be easily seen in the roof of the hen house.

ACCOMMODATION, EATING AND DRINKING   PORTH SWTAN

Church Bay Inn Church Bay, 0.5 mile back from the beach ☏ 01407 730867. Friendly pub with real ales, and about the only place in these parts with a beer garden looking out towards the setting sun. Daily noon–3pm & 6–10pm or later.

The Lobster Pot Church Bay ☏ 01407 730241, ⓦ lobster-pot.net. Super-fresh lobsters, crabs and Menai Strait oysters are combined with local produce here; you might tuck into lobster salad (£21) or a wonderful fish pie (£14). Tues–Sat noon–2.30pm & 6–9pm.

Tŷ Newydd Church Bay ☏ 01407 730060. Simple, low-key camping on a grassy site opposite the *Lobster Pot*. Mostly tents, hot showers. Per person £5

Wavecrest Café Church Bay ☏ 01407 730650. Great little spot with tables in the conservatory and more on the grass over the road with sea views. Come for the straightforward home-made baguettes and salads (£5–9), but leave space for the best cream-and-strawberry-filled scones (£3.25). Daily except Tues & Wed 10am–4.30pm.

Cemaes

The harbourside village of **CEMAES** is wedged between several dozen **windfarm** towers and the brooding bulk of the **Wylfa Nuclear Power Station** (which will close in 2012). Nonetheless, Cemaes is a charming spot with one of the most attractive harbours on the north coast, occupied by the odd trawler and boatloads of yachties.

Llanbadrig Church

On the headland at the eastern side of Cemaes Bay • May–Sept daily 10am–noon & 2–4pm

The mainly fourteenth-century **Llanbadrig Church** is one of only two Welsh churches dedicated to St Patrick. Its origins date back to the fifth century, when Ireland's patron saint is supposed to have been shipwrecked and made his way to a cave below the site of the present church. The current building was restored in the nineteenth century by Lord Stanley of Alderley, Bertrand Russell's grandfather, a Muslim who used Islamic imagery in the stained glass.

Amlwch and Parys Mountain

AMLWCH, five miles east of Cemaes, would be just another tiny fishing village but for **Parys Mountain** (Mynydd Parys), once the world's largest source of **copper**. Neolithic and Roman miners were followed by industrial production in the eighteenth century when Amlwch boomed. Pollution had become a problem, but people noticed that the iron hulls of ships didn't corrode in the copper-laced harbour waters, fuelling a demand for protective copper sheathing that boosted the market for Parys copper. International competition virtually killed the mines in the early nineteenth century.

Sail Loft Visitor Centre

Easter–Oct daily 10am–5pm; Nov–Easter Sat & Sun 10am–5pm • Free • ☏ 01407 832255, ⓦ copperkingdom.co.uk

The Watch House beside Amlwch's pretty port houses the **Sail Loft Visitor Centre**, full of material on Amlwch's remarkable past, and with a café on the intentionally sloping floor of a former sail loft. The centre distributes a free **Porth Amlwch Heritage Trail** leaflet and can direct you to walks along a rewarding stretch of the Anglesey Coast Path.

Parys Mountain

Visit the ruined pumping mill on top of **Parys Mountain** by a path from the car park on the B5111. A box at the car park has leaflets for the Industrial Heritage Trail which leads around Parys' ravaged moonscape, made all the more bizarre by the derelict remains, multicoloured rocks, coppery pools of water and patches of scrubby heather and gorse.

From Moelfre to Red Wharf Bay

MOELFRE has a reputation for shipwrecks, though wandering around the peaceful grey-pebbled cove on a sunny day it seems unlikely. An anchor behind the beach was salvaged from the **Hindlea**, which went down in October 1959, exactly a century after the 2700-ton **Royal Charter** foundered, with the loss of 400 lives and nearly £400,000-worth of gold.

Din Lligwy Hut Group

1 mile west of Moelfre, off A5025 • Open access • Free • CADW

The late Neolithic **Din Lligwy Hut Group** forms the centrepiece of a site spanning three thousand years of human occupation. A five-sided walled enclosure contains the foundations of several circular and rectangular buildings dated to the second and fourth centuries which, along with the hut group on Holy Island, give the best indication of how these people actually lived, rather than how they buried their dead. To the northeast of the main enclosure stands **Capel Lligwy**, a forlorn-looking twelfth-century church, and a short distance to the south is the **Lligwy Burial Chamber** with its 28-ton capstone.

7

Red Wharf Bay

A few miles south of Moelfre, **Red Wharf Bay** (Traeth Coch) forms a broad, enticing sweep of golden sand which never gets too crowded. Most people head for the northern side where facilities are concentrated.

EATING AND DRINKING   **RED WHARF BAY**

The Old Boathouse Red Wharf Bay ☎ 01248 852731, ⓦ boathouserestaurantanglesey.co.uk. Excellent café and restaurant with a great location overlooking the bay, particularly from the upstairs restaurant section. It is a great spot for a tuna and mozzarella panini (£6), cream teas or a full pub-style meal (around £10). Daily 9am–9pm.

★ **Ship Inn** Red Wharf Bay ☎ 01248 852568, ⓦ shipinnredwharfbay.co.uk. Ancient inn where, on sunny days, the tables outside by the water are invariably packed with people supping real ales and tucking into the excellent meals (£12–16 mains). Daily 11am–10pm.

Llangefni

The main reason to venture inland is to visit **LLANGEFNI**, Anglesey's low-key county town, and the **Oriel Ynys Môn** gallery and café.

Oriel Ynys Môn

0.5 mile north of Llangefni on B5111 • Daily 10.30am–5pm • Free • ☎ 01248 724444, ⓦ visitanglesey.co.uk

The combined museum and art gallery, **Oriel Ynys Môn**, provides an excellent overview of the sheer variety of factors in the island's turbulent history, from pre-Christian sites and the dynastic lines of the Princes of Gwynedd to exhibits about conservation, shipwrecks and the Welsh language. One corner of the gallery is devoted to the life and works of **Charles Tunnicliffe** who spent thirty years from 1947 painting wildlife from his Shorelands home in Malltraeth, near Newborough Warren. A separate room is dedicated to constantly changing works by exalted Llangefni-born landscape painter **Kyffin Williams** (1918–2006), who returned to paint Anglesey in his later years.

ARRIVAL AND DEPARTURE   **LLANGEFNI**

Llangefni is 5 miles west of Llanfairpwll, and on the #4 bus route between Holyhead (hourly; 50min) and Bangor (hourly; 35min).

DYLAN THOMAS

Contexts

History

Before the end of the last Ice Age around ten thousand years ago, Wales and the rest of Britain formed part of the greater European whole, while the early migrant inhabitants eked out a meagre existence on the tundra or a better one amongst the oak, beech and hazel forests in the warmer periods. Most lived in the southeast of Britain, but small groups foraged north and west, leaving 250,000-year-old evidence in the form of a human tooth in a cave near Denbigh in north Wales and a hand axe unearthed near Cardiff.

It wasn't until the early part of the **Upper Paleolithic age** that significant communities settled in Wales, those of the Gower peninsula interring the "Red Lady of Paviland" around 24,000 BC. This civilization remained on Europe's cultural fringe as the melting ice cut Britain off from mainland Europe around 5000 BC. Migrating Mesolithic peoples had already moved north from Central Europe and were followed by **Neolithic colonists**, whose mastery of stone and flint working found its expression in over a hundred and fifty cromlechs (turf-covered chambered tombs) dotted around Wales, primarily Bryn Celli Ddu and Barclodiad y Gawres on Anglesey, and Pentre Ifan in Mynydd Preseli. Skilled in agriculture and animal husbandry, the Neolithic people also began to clear the lush forests covering Wales below 2000 feet, enclosing fields, constructing defensive ditches around their villages and mining for flint.

The earliest stone circles – more extensive meeting places than cromlechs – were built at this time. As the Neolithic period drifted into the **Bronze Age** around 2000 BC with more sophisticated use of metals, social structures became well-organized. The established aristocracy engaged in much tribal warfare, as suggested by large numbers of earthwork forts built around this period – the chief examples being at Holyhead Mountain on Anglesey and the Bulwarks at Chepstow.

The Celts

Celtic invaders spreading from their central European homeland settled in Wales in around 600 BC, imparting a great cultural influence. Familiar with Mediterranean civilization through trading routes, they introduced superior methods of metalworking forging iron into weapons and coins. Gold was used for ornamental works – the first recognizable Welsh art – heavily influenced by the symbolic, patterned **La Tène** style still thought of as quintessentially Celtic.

The Celts are credited with introducing the basis of modern Welsh (see p.469). This highly developed language was emblematic of a sophisticated social hierarchy headed by **druids** (see p.438). Yet the Celts were unable to maintain an organized civic society to match that of their successors, the Romans.

250,000 BC	2000 BC	600 BC	78 AD	80–100
Earliest evidence of human existence in Wales.	Bronze Age settlers arrive from the Iberian peninsula.	Celts reach the British Isles bringing their ritual priests, the druids.	Roman conquest of Wales completed as Agricola kills druids of Anglesey.	Construction of Caerleon amphitheatre completes the trappings of Roman life.

THE DRUIDS

During Celtic times, the **druids** were a ritual priesthood with attendant poets, seers and warriors. Through a deep knowledge of ritual, legend and the mechanics of the heavens, the druids maintained their position between the people and a pantheon of over four thousand gods. Most of these were variations of a handful of chief gods worshipped by the great British tribes: the Silures and Demetae in the south of Wales, the Cornovii in mid-Wales and the Ordovices and Deceangli in the north.

The Romans in Wales

Life in Wales, unlike that in most of England, was never fully Romanized, the region remaining under legionary control throughout its three-hundred-year occupation. **Julius Caesar** made cross-Channel incursions in 55 and 54 BC, kicking off a century-long but low-level infusion of Roman ideas which filtered across to Wales. After the full-scale invasion in 43 AD the Romans swept across southern England to the frontier of south Wales. Expansionism fomented anti-Roman feeling along the frontier between the Lowland Zone (southern and central England) and the Highland Zone (northern England, Scotland and Wales). Traditionally insular Welsh hill tribes united with their Brythonic cousins in northern England to oppose the Romans, who forced a wedge between them. The Roman historian **Tacitus** recorded the submission of the Deceangli near Chester, providing the oldest written mention of a Welsh land. The Romans sent an expeditionary force against the Silures and the toughest nut, the druid stronghold of Anglesey, but were kept at bay until around 75 AD, when legionary forts were built at Deva (Chester, England) and Isca Silurium (Caerleon).

By 78 AD, Wales was under Roman control, its chief fortresses at Deva, Isca Silurium and Segontium (Caernarfon) boasting all the trappings of imperial Roman life: bath houses, temples, mosaics and underfloor heating. Through three centuries of occupation, the Celtic people sustained an independent existence, though elements of Roman life filtered into the Celtic culture: agrarian practices improved, Christianity was partly adopted, the language adopted Latin words (pont for "bridge", ffenestr for "window") and the prevailing La Tène artistic style took on classical Roman elements.

The Roman Empire was already in decline when **Magnus Maximus** (Macsen Wledig) led a campaign to wrest control of the western empire from Emperor Gratian in 383 AD. Maximus' rule was short-lived but Wales was effectively free of direct Roman control by 390.

The age of the saints

Historical orthodoxy views the departure of literate Latin historians, skilled stonemasons and an all-powerful army as heralding the **Dark Ages**. In fact, a civic society probably flourished until a century later, when the collapse of trade routes was hastened by the dramatic spread of Islam around the Mediterranean, and Romanized society gave way to a structured form of **Celtic society**. For the next few centuries, **Teutonic barbarian tribes** struggled for supremacy in the post-Roman power vacuum in southern and eastern England but had little influence in Wales where Irish incursions (see box) took place against a background of increasing religious energy.

early 4thC	5th–6thC	c.589	616	c.784
Roman departure from Wales.	Age of Saints.	Saint David (Dewi Sant) dies after a life of miracles. He later becomes Wales' patron saint.	Battle of Chester – Wales isolated from rest of Britain.	The completion of Offa's Dyke physically separates England from Wales.

KING ARTHUR MUDDIES THE WATERS

The fourth and fifth centuries AD were marked by the establishment of the main dynastic kingdoms that were set to steer Wales through the next seven hundred years. The already sketchy history of this period was further muddied in 1136, when Geoffrey of Monmouth published his *History of the Kings of Britain*, portraying **King Arthur** as a feudal king with his court at Caerleon. Victorian Romantics embellished subsequent histories, making it practically impossible to extract much truth from this period.

Between the fifth and the sixth centuries the **Celtic Saints**, ascetic evangelical missionaries, spread the gospel around Ireland and western Britain, promoting the Middle Eastern eremitical tradition of living a reclusive life. Where their message took root, they founded simple churches within a consecrated enclosure, or llan, which often took the saint's name, hence Llanberis (Saint Peris), Llandeilo (Saint Teilo) and numerous others. In south Wales, **Saint David** (Dewi Sant) was the most popular (and subsequently Wales' patron saint), dying around 589 after a miracle-filled life, during which he established the religious community at St Davids, which had become a place of pilgrimage by the twelfth century.

The Welsh kingdoms

Towards the end of the sixth century the **Angles** and **Saxons** in eastern Britain began to entertain designs on the western lands. The inability of the independent western peoples to unify against this threat left the most powerful kingdom, Gwynedd, as the centre of cultural and political resistance. The weaker groups were unable to hold the invaders, and after the battle at Dyrham, near Gloucester in 577, the Britons in Cornwall were separated from those in Wales, who became similarly cut off from their northern kin in Cumbria after the battle of Chester in 616.

The eighth-century construction of **Offa's Dyke** (Clawdd Offa) – a linear earthwork demarcating, rather than defending, the boundary between Wales and the kingdom of Mercia – gave the Welsh a firm eastern border and allowed them to concentrate on unifying the patchwork of kingdoms as their coasts were being harried by **Norse and Viking invaders**.

Rhodri Mawr (Rhodri the Great) killed the Viking leader off Anglesey, helping the country's rise towards statehood through his unification of most of Wales. By this stage, England had developed into a single powerful kingdom, and though the various branches of Rhodri's line went on to rule most of Wales down to the late thirteenth century, the princedoms were frequently forced to swear fealty to the English kings.

IRELAND INVADES WALES

In the fifth century, the Irish (Gwyddyl), who had a long tradition of migrating to the Llŷn and parts of mid-Wales, attacked the coast and formed distinct colonies, but were soon expelled from the north by Cunedda Wledig, the leader of a Brythonic tribe from near Edinburgh, who went on to found the royal house of Gwynedd, consolidating the Brythonic language and naming regions of his kingdom – the modern Ceredigion and Meirionydd – after his sons. In the southwest, the Irish influence was sustained; the kingdom of Dyfed shows clear Irish origins.

c.900–50	1066	1180–93	1188
Hywel Dda largely reunifies Wales and codifies the Law of Wales.	Normans invade England and set up Lords Marcher to control the Welsh borderlands.	St Davids Cathedral built.	Archbishop Baldwin (accompanied by Giraldus Cambrensis) recruits for the Third Crusade.

Defensive problems were exacerbated by the practice of partible inheritance that left each of Rhodri's sons with an equal part of Wales to control.

Rhodri Mawr's grandson **Hywel Dda** (Hywel the Good) largely reunified the country from southwest Wales. He added Powys and Gwynedd to his domain, but his most valuable legacy is his codification and promulgation of the medieval **Law of Wales** (see box). After Hywel's death in 950, anarchy and internal turmoil reigned until his great-great-grandson, **Gruffydd ap Llywelyn**, seized power in Gwynedd in 1039. He unified all of Wales, taking the coronation of the weak English king, Edward the Confessor, as an opportunity to annex some of the Marches in Mercia. Edward's successor, Harold, wasn't having any of this and killed Gruffydd, heralding a new phase of political fragmentation.

The arrival of the Normans

In 1066, the **Normans** swept across the English Channel and stormed England. Though Wales was unable to present a unified opposition to the invaders, the Norman king, William, didn't attempt to conquer Wales. The **Domesday Book** – commissioned in 1085 to record land ownership as a framework for taxation – indicates that he only nibbled at parts of Powys and Gwynedd. Instead, he installed a huge retinue of barons, the **Lords Marcher**, along the border to bring as much Welsh territory under their own jurisdiction as possible. Despite generations of squabbling, the barons managed to hold onto their privileges until Henry VIII's Act of Union over four hundred years later.

A lack of English commitment or resources allowed the Welsh to claw back their territory through years when distinctions between English, Normans and Welsh were beginning to blur, which helped form three stable political entities: Powys, Deheubarth and Gwynedd. The latter, led by Owain Gwynedd from his capital at Aberffraw on Anglesey, now extended beyond Offa's Dyke and progressively gained hegemony over the other two. Owain Gwynedd's grandson, Llywelyn ap Iorwerth (the Great), incorporated the weaker territories to the south into his kingdom and captured several Norman castles to reach the peak of the Welsh feudal pyramid. After tussling with England's King John, Llywelyn won a degree of Welsh autonomy, though this largely fell apart after his death.

1196–1240	1246–82	1270–1320	1277
Llywelyn ap Iorwerth (the Great) rules as Prince of Gwynedd and later most of Wales.	Llywelyn ap Gruffydd (the Last) intermittently rules large parts of Wales.	Tintern Abbey built.	Llywelyn humiliated. Signs Treaty of Aberconwy at the end of the First War of Welsh Independence.

THE STATUTE OF RHUDDLAN

The **Statute of Rhuddlan** in 1284 set down the terms by which the English monarch was to rule Wales: much of it was given to the Marcher lords who had helped Edward I, the rest was divided into administrative and legal districts similar to those in England. Though the treaty is often seen as a symbol of English subjugation, it respected much of Welsh law and provided a basis for civil rights and privileges. Many Welsh were content to accept and exploit Edward's rule for their own benefit. In 1294, however, a rebellion led by Madog ap Llywelyn gripped Wales and was only halted by Edward's swift and devastating response. Most of the privileges enshrined in the Statute of Rhuddlan were rescinded.

Edward I's conquest

Most of the work of regrouping Wales around one standard fell to Llywelyn the Great's grandson, **Llywelyn ap Gruffydd** (Llewellyn the Last). In the 1250s, he won control of Gwynedd, then pushed the English out of most of Wales. The English king Henry III was forced to ratify the **Treaty of Montgomery** in 1267, thereby recognizing Llywelyn as "Prince of Wales" in return for his homage. The English monarchy's war with the barons allowed Llywelyn time to politically consolidate his lands, which now stretched over all of modern Wales excepting Pembrokeshire and parts of the Marches.

The tables turned when Edward I succeeded Henry III and began a crusade to unify Britain. With effective use of sea power, Edward had little trouble forcing the already weakened Llywelyn back into Snowdonia. Peace was restored with the **Treaty of Aberconwy**, which deprived Llywelyn of almost all his land and stripped him of his financial tributes from the other Welsh princes, but left him with the hollow title of "Prince of Wales".

Edward now set about surrounding Llywelyn's land with castles at Aberystwyth, Builth Wells, Flint and Rhuddlan. After a relatively cordial four-year period, Llywelyn's brother Dafydd rose against Edward, inevitably dragging Llywelyn along with him. Edward didn't hesitate and swept through Gwynedd, crushing the revolt and laying the foundations for the remaining castles in his **Iron Ring**, those at Conwy, Caernarfon, Harlech and Beaumaris. Llywelyn, already battered by Edward's force, was captured and executed at Cilmeri in 1282.

Throughout the fourteenth century, famine and the Black Death plagued Wales. The Marcher lords appropriated the lands of defaulting debtors, while royal officials clawed in all the income they could from towns around the castles. These factors and the pent-up resentment of the English sowed seeds of a rebellion led by the tyrannical but charismatic **Owain Glyndŵr** (see box, p.283).

The Tudors and union with England

During the latter half of the fifteenth century, the succession to the English throne was contested in the **Wars of the Roses** between the houses of York (white rose) and Lancaster (red rose). Welsh allegiance lay broadly with the Lancastrians, who had the support of the ascendant north Welsh Tewdwr (or Tudor) family. Henry Tudor escaped from besieged Harlech Castle to Brittany when Yorkist Richard III took the English throne in 1471. Fourteen years later, Henry returned to Wales, defeating Richard at the Battle of Bosworth Field, so becoming **Henry VII** and sealing the Lancastrian ascendancy.

1277–83	1284	1301	1400–12
Edward I begins Aberystwyth, Flint, Rhuddlan, Caernarfon, Conwy and Harlech castles.	Statute of Rhuddlan signed by Edward I.	Edward I revives title of "Prince of Wales" and bestows it on his son, Edward II.	Owain Glyndŵr's revolt ushers in a third War of Welsh Independence. Glyndŵr dies in hiding in 1416.

ACT OF UNION

Sovereignty was finally fixed in Henry VIII's 1536 **Act of Union** (and a subsequent act of 1543). It's a misleading title, and one that was not used to describe the Act until the twentieth century, for it implies a level of equality between the two nations that did not exist. Unlike the Acts of 1707 and 1800 that brought Scotland and Ireland into the Union – and were the decisions of independent parliaments in Edinburgh, Dublin and London – the 1536 Act was a unilateral decision by Westminster, which had no Welsh representation. It decreed that English was to be the only language of the courts and other official bodies, effectively creating a two-tier Wales of English-speaking lords and masters and a Welsh-speaking proletariat. At the same time the Marches were replaced by shires (the equivalent of modern counties), the Welsh laws codified by Hywel Dda were voided, and partible inheritance (equal among all offspring) gave way to primogeniture, the eldest son becoming the sole heir. This period set in stone the struggles and the injustices that are still playing out nearly five hundred years later.

For the most part Henry lived up to the high Welsh expectations, removing many of the restrictions on land ownership imposed at the start of Glyndŵr's uprising, and promoting many Welshmen to high office. Still, Wales had been largely controlled by the English monarch since the Statute of Rhuddlan.

Just as Henry VIII's decision to convert his kingdom from Catholicism to Protestantism was born more from his desire to divorce his first wife than from any religious conviction, it was his need for money which brought about the **Dissolution of the Monasteries** in 1536 – ultimately resulting in a more studied approach to religion and learning in general. Under the reign of Elizabeth I, Jesus College was founded in Oxford for Welsh scholars, and the Bible was translated into Welsh for the first time by a team led by Bishop **William Morgan** (see p.400).

The Dissolution hastened the emergence of the Anglo-Welsh gentry, a group eager to claim a Welsh pedigree while promoting the English language and the legal system.

The Civil War and the rise of Nonconformism

A direct descendant of the Tudors, **James I** came to the throne in 1603 to general popular approval in Wales. Many privileges granted to the Welsh during the Tudor reign came to an end, but the idea of common citizenship was retained, the Council of Wales remaining as a focus for Welsh nationalism. James, fearful of both Catholicism and the new threat of Puritanism – an extreme form of Protestantism – courted a staunchly Anglican Wales and curried the favour of Welsh ministers in the increasingly powerful Parliament. Though weak in Wales, Puritanism was gaining a foothold, especially in the Welsh borders, where William Wroth and Walter Cradock set up Wales' first dissenting church at Llanfaches in Monmouthshire in 1639.

The monarchy's relations with the Welsh were strained by **Charles I**, who was forced to levy heavy taxes and recruit troops, but the gentry were mostly loyal to the king at the outbreak of the **Civil War**, which saw the Parliamentary forces install **Oliver Cromwell** as the leader of the **Commonwealth**. The Puritan support for Parliament didn't go unnoticed, and after Charles' execution, they were rewarded with the livings of numerous parishes and the roots of Puritan Nonconformism spread in Wales.

1485	1536–38	1536–43	1588
Henry VII ascends the throne after landing from exile at Pembroke and beating Richard III at Bosworth.	Henry VIII suppresses monasteries.	Acts of Union unite Wales and England, conferring equal rights but with government conducted wholly in English.	The complete Bible is translated into Welsh for the first time, chiefly by William Morgan.

As Cromwell's regime became more oppressive, the Anglican majority welcomed the successful return of the exiled **Charles II**, and the monarchy was restored, thereby suppressing Nonconformity. The Baptists, Independents and Quakers who made up the bulk of Nonconformists continued to worship in secret, until **James II** passed the **Toleration Act** in 1689, finally allowing open worship, but still banning the employment of dissenters in municipal government; a limitation which remained in force until 1828.

The rise of Methodism

The propagation of Nonconformism led to a welter of new religious books in Welsh in the late seventeenth century, but with most people still illiterate, religious observance remained an oral tradition. In 1699, the **Society for Promoting Christian Knowledge** established schools where the Bible, along with reading, writing and arithmetic, was taught in Welsh as well as English. This met with considerable success in middle-class anglicized towns, but failed to reach rural areas where children couldn't be spared from farm duties. The next big reformist push came in 1731, when **Griffith Jones** organized reading classes in the evenings and quieter winter season, so farmers and their families could attend. Within thirty years, half the Welsh population could read.

By the middle of the eighteenth century, a receptive and literate populace was ready for what became the **Methodist Revival**, driven by a strong belief in a resurgent Welsh nation. In contrast to the staid Anglican services, the Methodists held evangelical meetings. Meanwhile, improved schooling brought about a literary revolution, and Wales re-established itself as the language for a vast body of literature.

In 1811, the Calvinist Methodists broke from the framework of Anglicanism. As the gentry remained with the Established Church, the chapel became the focus of social life, discouraging folk traditions considered incompatible with puritanical thrift and temperance. Political radicalism was also discouraged and since only property owners were eligible to vote, established dynasties perpetuated.

Wales and the Industrial Revolution

Small-scale mining and smelting had taken place in Wales since the Bronze Age, but agriculture remained the mainstay of an economy centred on meat, wool and butter. The enormous rise in grain prices in the early nineteenth century forced Welsh farmers to diversify and adopt the more advanced English farming practices of crop rotation, fertilizing and stock breeding. Around the same time, acts of Parliament allowed previously common land to be "enclosed", the grazing rights often being assigned solely to the largest landowner in the district. Inevitably, this forced smallholders to migrate to the towns where ever more workers were required to mine the seams and stoke the furnaces, fuelling the **Industrial Revolution**. In the north, **John Wilkinson** started his ironworks at Bersham and developed a new method of boring cylinders for steam engines; while in the south, foundries sprang up in the valleys around Merthyr Tydfil under English ironmasters. Gradually the under-educated, impoverished chapel-going Welsh began to be governed by rich, church-going, English industrial barons.

Improved materials and working methods enabled the exploitation of deeper coal seams, particularly in the south Wales valleys, not just to supply the iron smelters but

1639	1646	1759	1782	1794
First Puritan congregation in Wales convened at Llanfaches, Gwent.	Harlech and Raglan besieged during the Civil War. Harlech, the last Royalist castle, falls in 1647.	Dowlais Ironworks started, followed by Merthyr Tydfil iron industry.	Beginning of north Wales slate industry with the opening of Pennant's Penrhyn slate quarry at Bethesda.	Cardiff to Merthyr canal completed.

for domestic fuel and to power locomotives and steamships. South Wales' rural valleys were ripped apart and quiet hamlets turned into long rows of terraced houses snaking up the valley sides, roofed in north Wales slate. Transportation of huge quantities of coal and steel was crucial for continued economic expansion, initially on the roads and canals built in the early nineteenth century, then by train as the 1850s rail boom took hold.

In mining towns, working conditions were atrocious, with men and women toiling incredibly long hours in dangerous conditions; children as young as six worked alongside them, until this was outlawed by the Mines Act in 1842. Pay was low and often in a currency redeemable only at the poorly stocked, expensive company (Truck) shop. The **Anti-Truck Act** of 1831 improved matters, but a combination of rising population, fluctuating prices and growing need for political change brought calls for reform. The 1832 **Reform Bill** fell far short of the demands for universal suffrage by ballot and the removal of property requirement for voters. This swelled the ranks of the Reformist Chartist movement, and when a petition with over a million signatures was rejected by Parliament, the **Chartist Riots** broke out in northern England and south Wales. The Newport demonstration was disastrous, the marchers walking straight into a trap laid by troops, who killed over twenty men and captured their leader, **John Frost**. Chartism continued in a weakened form for twenty years, buoyed by the **Rebecca Riots** in 1839–43, when guerrilla tactics put an end to tollgates on south Welsh turnpikes.

1850 to World War I

During the latter half of the nineteenth century the radical reformist movement and religion slowly became entwined, with the Nonconformists petitioning for **disestablishment** of the Church in Wales. Eventually, as a consequence of the 1867 Reform Act, industrial workers and small tenant farmers got the vote, giving a long-awaited strong working-class element to the electorate. The following year, **Henry Richard** was elected as Liberal MP for Merthyr Tydfil, becoming the first Welsh member of what soon became the dominant political force and bringing the ideas of Nonconformity – land reform, disestablishment and the preservation of the Welsh language – to Parliament for the first time.

The 1872 Secret Ballot Act and 1884 Reform Act enfranchised farm labourers and further freed up the electoral system, although the Anglican Church was only disestablished in 1920. The Nonconformist Sunday Schools offered primary education for the masses, supplemented by a number of secondary schools, as well as Wales' first major tertiary establishment in Aberystwyth in 1872, followed by colleges at Cardiff (1883) and Bangor (1884). Until they were federated into the University of Wales in 1893, voluntary contributions garnered by Nonconformist chapels supported the colleges. The apotheosis of "Chapel power" came in 1881 with the passing of the Welsh Sunday Closing Act, enshrining Nonconformism's three basic tenets: observance of the Sabbath, sobriety and Welshness.

Industry and the rise of trade unionism

The rise in Welsh consciousness (see box) paralleled the rise in importance of the **trade unions**. The 1850s were a prosperous time in the Welsh coal fields, but by the end of

1839–43	1845–50	1872	1884	1900
Rebecca Riots put an end to tollgates on turnpikes.	Britannia Tubular Bridge built across the Menai Strait.	University College of Wales opens in Aberystwyth, followed by Cardiff (1883) and Bangor (1884).	Reform Act. Farm labourers and small tenant farmers get the vote for the first time.	Britain's first Labour MP, Kier Hardie, elected for Merthyr Tydfil.

RAIL, STEAM AND SPEED

Britain's greatest nineteenth-century **engineers** made their names in Wales: **Thomas Telford** built canal aqueducts and successfully spanned the Menai Strait with one of Britain's earliest suspension bridges; **Isambard Kingdom Brunel** surveyed the Merthyr–Cardiff train line, then pushed his Great Western network almost to Fishguard; and **Robert Stephenson** speeded the passage of trains between London and Holyhead on Anglesey for the Irish ferry connection.

the 1860s the Amalgamated Union of Miners was forced to call a strike (1869–71), which resulted in higher wages.

A second strike in 1875 failed and the miners' agent, **William Abraham** (**Mabon**), ushered in the notorious "sliding scale" which fixed wage levels according to the selling price of coal. This brought considerable hardship to the Valleys, which became insular worlds with strictly ordered social codes and a rich vibrancy born from the essential dichotomy of the chapel and the pub. Meanwhile, annual coal production doubled in twenty years. By 1913, 57 million tons were being extracted each year by a quarter of a million people. Similarly punitive pay schemes were implemented in the north Wales slate quarries where membership of **Undeb Chwarelwyr Gogledd Cymru** (The North Wales Quarrymen's Union) was all but outlawed by the slate barons. Things came to a head in 1900 when the workers at Lord Penrhyn's quarry at Bethesda started one of Britain's longest-ever industrial disputes, lasting three years.

From 1885, the vast majority of Welsh MPs were Liberals who helped end the sliding scale in 1902 and brought in an eight-hour day by 1908. The start of the twentieth century heralded the birth of a new political force when **Keir Hardie** became Britain's first Labour MP, for Merthyr Tydfil.

World Wars I and II

World War I (1914–18) was a watershed for Welsh society. The Welsh identified with the plight of defenceless European nations and rallied to fight alongside the English and Scots. At home, the state increasingly intervened in people's lives: agriculture was controlled by the state, rationing food, and industries, mines and railways were under public control. The need for Welsh food and coal boosted the economy and living standards rose dramatically. Many were proud to be led through the war by Welsh lawyer **David Lloyd George** (see p.381), who rose to the post of Minister of Munitions, then of War, becoming Prime Minister by 1916. By the time conscription was introduced, patriotic fervour had waned. Many miners, reluctant to be slaughtered in the trenches and resentful of massive wartime profits, welcomed the 1917 Bolshevik Revolution, and though Communism never really took hold, the socialist Labour Party caught the postwar fallout.

Similar dramatic changes were taking place in rural areas, where Welsh farming was embracing new machinery and coming out of nearly a century of neglect. High wartime inflation of land prices and the fall in rents forced some landowners to sell off portions of major estates to their tenants in the so-called "green revolution".

After the postwar boom came the Depression. All of Wales' mining and primary production industries suffered, and unemployment reached 27 percent, worse than in England and Scotland. South Wales soon became the **Labour movement**'s stronghold in

1907	1925	1926	1936	1951
Founding of National Museum, Cardiff, and National Library, Aberystwyth.	Plaid Genedlaethol Cymru (Welsh National Party) formed.	Miners' strike and General Strike.	Saunders Lewis and nationalist colleagues burn building materials on the Llŷn.	Minister for Welsh Affairs appointed.

THE RISE IN WELSH CONSCIOUSNESS

Immigration to the coal fields from England meant that English became the language of commerce and the route to advancement, Welsh being reserved for the home and chapel life of seventy percent of the population. Welsh was still being spoken in Nonconformist schools when, in 1846, they were inspected by three English barristers and seven Anglican assistants. The inspectors' report – known as **The Treason of the Blue Books** – declared the standards deplorable, largely due to the use of the Welsh tongue. The public defence of Welsh that ensued failed to prevent the introduction of the notorious "Welsh Not", effectively a ban on speaking Welsh in school.

As the nineteenth-century Romantic movement took hold throughout Britain, the London Welsh looked to their heritage. The ancient tales of *The Mabinogion* were translated into English, the **Welsh Language Society** was founded in 1885, eisteddfodau were reintroduced as part of rural life, and the ancient bardic order, the **Gorsedd**, was reinvented. But disestablishment remained the cause célèbre of Welsh nationalism. Perhaps the greatest advocate of both separatism and Welsh nationalism was **Michael D. Jones** (see box, p.324), who helped establish a Welsh homeland in **Patagonia**.

By 1907 Wales had a national library at Aberystwyth, and a national museum was planned for Cardiff, by now the largest city in Wales.

Britain. This was challenged by Lloyd George's newly resurgent Liberal Party, but his Westminster-centred politics were no longer trusted in Wales and Labour held firm, seeking to improve workers' conditions: the state of housing was still desperate, and health care and welfare services needed boosting. The Labour Party effectively became the hope that had previously been entrusted to the chapels, though nationalists were drawn to a new party, **Plaid Cymru** (see box).

Some relief from the Depression came with re-armament in the lead-up to **World War II**, but by this stage vast numbers had migrated from south Wales to England, leaving the already insular communities banding together in self-reliant groups centred on local co-ops and welfare halls. The demands of the war saw unemployment all but disappear and the Welsh economy gradually restructured, with more people switching from extractive industries to light manufacturing, a process which continues today.

The postwar period

Any hopes for a greater national identity were dashed by the Attlee Labour government from 1945 to 1951, which nationalized transport and utilities with little regard for national boundaries. However, under the direction of Ebbw Vale MP, **Aneurin Bevan**, the postwar Labour government instituted the National Health Service, dramatically improving health care in Wales and the rest of Britain, and providing much-improved council housing.

The nationalized coal industry, now employing less than half the number of twenty years before, was still the most important employer at nationalization, but a gradual process of closing inefficient mines saw the number of pits drop from 212 in 1945 to 11 in 1989, and none today. Sadly, the same commitment wasn't directed at cleaning up the scars of over a century of mining until after 1966, when one of south Wales' most tragic accidents left a school and 116 children buried under a slag heap at **Aberfan**.

1955	1963	1964	1966	1967
Cardiff declared capital of Wales.	Cymdeithas yr Iaith Gymraeg (Welsh Language Society) formed.	James Griffiths, first cabinet-level Secretary of State for Wales, appointed.	Gwynfor Evans, first Plaid Cymru MP, elected for Carmarthen. Aberfan disaster.	Welsh Language Act passed. Limited recognition of Welsh as a formal, legal language.

PLAID CYMRU: THE EARLY YEARS

By 1925, a new sense of nationalism emerged and champions of Welsh autonomy formed **Plaid Genedlaethol Cymru** (the National Party of Wales), often known as Plaid. In September 1936, in one of the first modern separatist protests, its president **Saunders Lewis** joined two other Plaid members (the Rev. Lewis Valentine and D.J. Williams) and set fire to the construction hut of a new aerodrome being built on the Llŷn as part of Britain's build-up to the war. They immediately reported themselves to the nearest police station, attracting huge publicity in the process. Interest in the ensuing trial electrified Wales, causing howls of outrage when the government decided to divert it from sympathetic Caernarfon to the Old Bailey in London. Even recalcitrant nationalist Lloyd George was outspokenly critical of the English decision. The three men were duly imprisoned for nine months, becoming Plaid Cymru's first heroes. Lewis spent the rest of his life immersed in literary criticism, becoming one of Wales' greatest modern writers.

Similar public displays and powerful nationalist rhetoric won over an intellectual majority, but the voting majority continued to fuel the Labour ascendancy in both local and national politics. Plaid Cymru were less enthusiastic about World War II, remaining neutral and expressing unease at the large number of English evacuees potentially weakening the fabric of Welsh communities. However, the war saw the formation of a Welsh elementary school in Aberystwyth and Undeb Cymru Fydd, a committee designed to defend the welfare of Wales.

The Labour Party remained in overwhelming control during the 1960s and 1970s, though the party's reluctance to address nationalist issues allowed Plaid Cymru to become a serious opposition for the first time. Attlee had thrown out the suggestion of a Welsh Secretary of State in 1946, and not until Plaid Cymru fielded numerous candidates in the 1959 election did the Labour manifesto promise a cabinet position for Wales.

The position of **Secretary of State for Wales** was finally created in 1964 by Harold Wilson's Labour government, who also created the **Welsh Development Agency** and moved the Royal Mint to Llantrisant in south Wales. With Plaid Cymru's appeal considered to be restricted to rural areas, Labour was shocked by the 1966 Carmarthen by-election, when **Gwynfor Evans** became the first Plaid MP. It wasn't until 1974 that Plaid also won in the constituencies of Caernarfon and Meirionydd, and suddenly the party was a threat, forcing Labour to address the question of devolution (see box).

Modern Wales

The Conservative government of **Margaret Thatcher** came to power in 1979, achieving an unprecedented 31 percent of Welsh votes. The referendum that year effectively sidelined the home-rule issue and Thatcher was able to implement her free-market policies. With 43 percent of the Welsh workforce as government employees, privatization had a dramatic impact. The number of jobs in the steel industry, manufacturing and construction all plummeted, doubling unemployment in five years. Despite this, the Conservatives increased their tally of MPs at the 1983 election, while Labour saw their lowest percentage since 1918.

The resulting breakdown of traditional Valley communities and successive anti-union measures failed to break the solidarity of south Welsh workers during the year-long **Miners' Strike** (1984–85). Meanwhile, the Welsh continued to turn away from the

1982	1984–85	1992	1997
Welsh-language TV channel S4C begins broadcasting.	Miners' strike.	Welsh Language Bill gives Welsh equal status with English in public bodies.	Referendum on Welsh Assembly. Only half the country votes, of whom 50.3 percent vote yes, a majority of just 6000 nationwide.

NO TO SELF-GOVERNMENT

In 1978 Labour tabled the **Wales Act**, promising the country an elected assembly to act as a voice for Wales, but with no power to legislate or raise revenue. In the subsequent **referendum** in 1979, eighty percent of voters opposed the proposition, with even the nationalist stronghold of Gwynedd voting against.

established religions and the chapel ceased to be the focal point of community life. Something like two-thirds of the country's six thousand chapels have since closed.

During the 1980s, support for Plaid Cymru shifted back to the rural areas, enthusiasm for the Welsh language increased and a steady decline in numbers of Welsh-speakers was reversed. New Welsh-only schools opened even in predominantly English-speaking areas, learners' classes sprouted everywhere and in 1982, S4C, the first **Welsh-language television channel**, began broadcasting.

When Tony Blair and "New" Labour won a huge majority in 1997, one of the central policy proposals was the **devolution** of some degree of power from London to a parliament in Scotland and a **National Assembly for Wales** – the first all-Wales tier of government for six hundred years. The proposal was endorsed by the Welsh people only by the most slender of margins in a referendum. The first of the four-yearly elections to the Assembly took place in 1999, when a huge swing to Plaid Cymru denied the Labour party its assumed overall majority. Labour have remained the largest party ever since, with **Rhodri Morgan**, a committed supporter of Welsh devolution, as First Minister for most of that time. **Carwyn Jones** took over as leader of Labour and First Minister in 2009.

In the 2007 election, after more than 80 years in opposition, **Plaid** helped form the government, but four years later its support dropped dramatically and it recorded its worst showing at an assembly election – so low that the Conservatives became the major opposition.

In 2006 the Government of Wales Act affirmed that the Queen would, for the first time, appoint Welsh Ministers and sign Welsh Orders in Council. As the Assembly moved into a snazzy new building on the waterfront of Cardiff Bay, the Welsh Government really began to enmesh itself into the fabric of Welsh life.

The 2006 Act also made provision for a **referendum** on further devolution of powers. In March, 2011 a "Yes" vote finally allowed the Welsh Government to create primary legislation (i.e. "Welsh laws") without consulting Westminster. Almost two-thirds of voters supported the change, and Monmouthshire was the only county to vote "No".

It's not just in the political arena that the country has grown up: there has been a significant surge of national confidence and self-expression, particularly in the cultural and sporting arenas. That is not to say that everything is rosy: farming lurches along in a state of semi-paralysis, and poverty and ill health still dog many old working-class communities. But these are interesting times in Wales: there is the undeniable feeling that this small country is facing a brighter future than many would have dared predict even one generation ago.

1999	2006	2011
First Welsh Assembly elections. Assembly begins sitting. Wales hosts the Rugby World Cup.	The new Welsh Assembly building (the Senedd) opens on St David's Day. Government of Wales Act gains Royal Assent.	Wales emphatically votes for primary law-making powers.

Modern Welsh nationalism

Plaid Cymru – the Welsh nationalist political party – was formed in 1925, but the political impetus that gave birth to the new movement had been bubbling for decades, if not centuries.

The Welsh identity had always been culturally rich, but was politically expressed only as part of the great Liberal tradition: in the dying years of the nineteenth century, 25 or 30 Welsh Liberal MPs often voted en bloc, making their voice heard. The fiery Welsh patriot **David Lloyd George** (1863–1945; prime minister 1916–22) had embodied many people's nationalist beliefs, although his espousal of greater independence for Wales came unstuck when, ever the expedient politician, he realized the potential difficulty of translating this ideal into hard votes in the industrialized, anglicized south of Wales. During Lloyd George's premiership, the Irish Free State was established, drawing inevitable comparisons with the Home Rule demands being less stridently articulated in Scotland and Wales. But the Liberal Party was in sharp decline, nowhere more markedly than in the industrialized Valleys, which had deserted them in favour of new socialist parties. With the urban slide of Liberalism, Welsh nationalism was gradually honed into the embryonic Plaid Cymru (see box, p.447).

Postwar Wales

Prewar Liberal tradition was still strong in rural Wales, though by the 1951 election this had become just three parliamentary seats out of 36. The **Labour party** was now the establishment in Wales, winning an average of around sixty percent of votes in elections from 1945 to 1966. Two Welsh Labour MPs, Megan Lloyd George, daughter of the great Liberal premier, and S.O. Davies, spearheaded new parliamentary demands for greater Welsh independence, presenting a 1956 petition to parliament demanding a Welsh assembly which was signed by a quarter of a million people. Massive popular protests against the continued flooding of Welsh valleys and villages to provide water for England shook the establishment.

The 1963 formation of the boisterous Cymdeithas yr Iaith Gymraeg – the **Welsh Language Society** – attracted a new youthful breed of cultural and linguistic nationalists. The ruling Conservatives offered the sop of nominating a part-time Welsh Minister, confirming Cardiff as the capital and making the red dragon the official Welsh flag. Meanwhile, the Labour party formed a Welsh Council where Labour MPs, trade unionists and ordinary party members began to articulate the need for greater independence.

In the **general election of 1964**, the party stood on a more nationalistic platform than ever before. As usual, they swept the board in Wales, and finally won throughout the UK as a whole. As promised in their manifesto, the post of **Secretary of State for Wales**, backed by a separate Welsh Office, was created, although with fewer powers than the Scottish equivalent which had existed since just after the war.

Plaid Cymru starts to win

Plaid Cymru scored its first hit when its president, Gwynfor Evans, won a by-election in Carmarthen in July 1966. In the heart of socialist south Wales, Plaid ran the Labour government astonishingly close in two by-elections – in Rhondda West (1967) and Caerphilly (1968) – and the party saw swings of over 25 percent to cut Labour majorities of over twenty thousand to just a couple of thousand. It seemed that Plaid's time had come. Its traditional vote in the north and west was soaring and it appeared that the party had finally overcome its single-issue status around the Welsh language.

Despite amassing 176,000 votes (11 percent of the poll in Wales) in the **1970 general election**, Plaid failed to take any new seats and even lost their place in Carmarthen. Gwynfor Evans was returned in Carmarthen in 1974, but Plaid's earlier success in the industrialized south had evaporated, and they once again became a party of rural Wales.

The new Labour government now set up the **Wales Development Agency**, devolved the huge responsibilities of the Department of Trade and Industry in Wales to the Welsh Office in Cardiff, and even supported a referendum on devolution.

The 1979 referendum and beyond

On St David's Day 1979, the Welsh people made their feelings known, when a four-to-one majority rejected the devolution proposal. People feared being swamped by (toothless) bureaucracy, and a large number of the eighty percent of the country who did not speak Welsh feared that a Welsh assembly would be the preserve of a new "Taffia", a *Cymraeg* elite. Both north and south Walians worried about potential domination by the other.

The shock waves were great. Weeks later, the Labour government fell and **Margaret Thatcher**'s first Conservative administration was ushered in. Political nationalism seemed to have gone off the boil, and Plaid Cymru were back to just two MPs in the northwest. In the early 1980s Britain's manufacturing base collapsed and unemployment rose, particularly in south Wales, where mines and foundries closed. Welsh nationalism was suffering an identity crisis, typified by Plaid Cymru's controversial 1981 rewriting of its own constitution to fight for an avowedly "Welsh socialist state", causing some of its more conservative members to quit the party. Basing itself as a republican, left-wing party would, it was believed, bring greater fruit in the populated south.

Like so many other political affiliations and ideals in the 1980s, Welsh nationalism underwent something of a sea change. Plaid Cymru began to broaden its base with a firmly socialist, **internationalist outlook**. The party matured, developing serious policies on all aspects of Welsh life, from traditional rallying calls of language and media to sophisticated analyses of economic policy, the Welsh legal framework and the country's role in the European Union. But Welsh devolution ceased to be the preserve of Plaid Cymru alone. Both Labour and the Liberal Democrats evolved devolutionary strategies for Wales and Scotland. Even the ruling Conservatives devolved more decision-making out to the Welsh Office in Cardiff. This, ironically, strengthened the nationalist hand. Plaid and the other parties pointed out that a huge swath of government existed in Wales, not overseen by any all-Wales authority. The call for a Welsh assembly to oversee this vast array of public expenditure was consistently supported by huge majorities in opinion polls, and formed the basis of the Labour Party's manifesto for Wales throughout the 1990s.

Labour government and a new referendum

The **1997 general election** changed everything. The Conservatives were spectacularly swept from power, failing to keep any seats whatsoever in Wales. Labour – or "New" Labour as the party was styled under Tony Blair – won hugely, denting any further Plaid progress and keeping the nationalists firm in their northern and western strongholds and on little more than one-tenth of the vote.

Within six months of Blair's election, referenda took place in Wales and Scotland on the devolution proposals. Scotland voted for its parliament; in Wales, the proposals barely scraped through. Although this was potentially the first piece of self-government for Wales in 600 years, many nationalists felt that it fell far short of expectations and was not worth supporting. Plaid Cymru's own stance mirrored this ambivalence: initially unenthusiastic and only coming out for the Assembly in the latter stages of the campaign. Wales itself was split in half by the devolution vote. The border areas and Pembrokeshire, true to their historical anglicization, voted no, while Plaid's west coast strongholds and the "Old" Labour bastions of the industrial Valleys were just enthusiastic enough to swing the ballot.

A CHANNEL FOR WALES

Plaid President and former MP, Gwynfor Evans, was single-handedly responsible for the most high-profile activity of Welsh nationalism in the early 1980s. The Conservative party had fought the 1979 election on a manifesto that included a commitment to a Welsh-language TV channel. When plans for the new UK Channel 4 were drawn up, this promise had been dropped. Evans decided to fast until death, if necessary, as a peaceful protest. The huge publicity quickly force the Thatcher government to make its first U-turn, and **Sianel Pedwar Cymru** (S4C) was born in 1982. Perhaps the Tories realized the political advantage of bringing Welsh nationalism into the legitimate fold, for the Welsh media industry dissipated many angry and impassioned arguments for national self-determination. Certainly, many of the most heartfelt radicals ended up in prominent positions within Wales' media.

The National Assembly for Wales

When it came to voting for the sixty-seat Welsh Assembly, Plaid Cymru achieved spectacular gains, taking Labour strongholds like Rhondda, Islwyn and Llanelli. The Plaid share of the vote was their highest ever, at nearly 30 percent, and it was enough to deny Labour – once the absolute party in Wales – an overall majority. So far, this has proven to be Plaid's high-water mark.

One of Plaid's main drawbacks has been confusion, and disillusion, over its leadership, particularly in the Assembly under the lacklustre Anglesey AM Ieuan Wyn Jones. There is, however, an impressive new generation emerging in Plaid, who, if given half the chance, should be able to restore some status to the party.

Since the arrival of the Assembly, it's hard for even the most ardent of nationalists to argue that Wales' system of government is the most pressing issue facing the nation. With farming in utter crisis, one of the poorest standards of living in the UK, and job opportunities limited to the low-wage old industrial sectors of the south, there are plenty of meatier matters to chew on. If the Assembly can be seen to make a difference to these issues, its reputation will soar.

However, in the early years of the twenty-first century, it's safe to say that the majority of Welsh people are fairly happy with things as they are. Although the percentages of Welsh-speakers have fallen slightly in the language's heartlands according to the 2001 census results, huge rises in the anglicized southeast mean that the number of Welsh-speakers in Wales is at its highest level for forty years, and rising. Language aside, the general sense of Welshness has been much augmented in recent years, as much by sporting achievements and rock music as by any politician. Wales is more and more happily, and very easily, calling itself a nation. The question that still hangs in the air is simply this: to be a nation, does Wales really need to be a state?

NATIONALISM AWAY FROM THE ASSEMBLY

With Plaid Cymru having to play it as a sober democratic party, much of the more interesting aspects of Welsh nationalism are to be found away from party politics. Regular dust-ups over patronizing English attitudes still periodically ignite the media, while debates rage on about English in-migration and the purchase of second homes in the heartlands of the Welsh language and culture. In a journalistic atmosphere that has at times been decidedly febrile and ill-tempered, the first casualty has been proper debate, with everything reduced to hysterical soundbites. Out of this environment has come the pressure group **Cymuned** ("Community"; ⓦ cymuned.org), whose slogan "Dal dy dir!" ("Hold your ground!") is seen daubed all around Wales. Cymuned is slick, modern and thoughtful, and could well prove to be the intellectual driving force for modern Welsh nationalism, especially as Plaid Cymru continues to struggle with its wings clipped for electoral expediency.

Natural history of Wales

Whole bookshelves are devoted to Wales' landscapes, land use, flora and fauna. What follows is a general overview of the effects of geology, human activity and climate on the country's flora, fauna and land management. It must be remembered that nowhere in Wales is untouched, almost every patch of "wilderness" being partially the product of human intervention, thoroughly mapped, mined and farmed. Still, Wales is covered with a wide array of sites deemed to be of national or international importance (see box opposite). Nor is anywhere free from pollution: the conurbations of England are too close, power stations and factories dot the countryside and some of the seas are in a poor state. That said, several clean-air-loving lichen species – found in few other places in Britain – abound in Wales. The country also supports 1100 of Britain's 1600 native plants, with ferns and other moisture-loving species particularly well represented.

Geology

Wales' mountain ranges often provide the best insight into the country's geological history. Between 600 and 400 million years ago, **Snowdonia** was twice submerged for long periods in some primordial ocean where molten rock from undersea volcanoes cooled to form igneous intrusions in the sedimentary ocean-floor layers. Snowdon, Cadair Idris and the Aran and Arenig mountains are the product of these volcanoes, with fossils close to the summit of Snowdon supporting the theory of its formation on the sea floor.

After Silurian rocks had been laid down, immense lateral pressures forced the layers into concertina-like parallel folds with the sedimentary particles being rearranged at right angles to the pressure, giving today's vertically splitting sheets of **slate**, the classic metamorphosed product of these forces. The folded strata that rose above the sea bore no resemblance to today's mountains; the cliff face of Lliwedd on Snowdon shows that the summit was at the bottom of one of these great folds between two much higher mountains.

In the very recent geological past from 80,000–10,000 years ago, these mountains were shaped by the latest series of **Ice Ages**, with glaciers scouring out hemispherical cirques divided by angular ridges, then scraping down the valleys, gouging them into U-shapes, with waterfalls plunging down their sides.

Snowdonia is linked by the long chain of the **Cambrian Mountains** to the dramatic north-facing scarp slope of the **Brecon Beacons**, south Wales' distinctive east–west range at the head of the south Wales coal field. Erosion of the ancient rocks which once covered what is now northern Britain washed down great river systems, depositing beds of old red sandstone from 350–400 million years ago. These **Devonian** rocks lay in a shallow sea where the molluscs and corals decayed to form limestone, which in turn was overlaid by more sediment forming millstone grit. Subsequent layers of shale and sandstone were interleaved with decayed vegetable matter, forming a band known as **coal measures**, from which the mines once extracted their wealth. The whole lot has since been tilted up in the north, giving a north-to-south sequence which runs over a steep sandstone ridge (the Brecon Beacons), then down a gentle sandstone dip-slope arriving at the pearl-grey limestone band where any rivers tend to dive underground into **swallow holes**. They reappear as you reach the gritstone, often tumbling over waterfalls into the coal valleys.

WALES' PROTECTED AREAS

3 National Parks Snowdonia, the Brecon Beacons and the Pembrokeshire Coast comprise almost twenty percent of Wales. All are outstanding, though they do contain towns, accommodation and even industry.

5 Areas of Outstanding Natural Beauty (AONB) The Anglesey coast, the Llŷn coast, the Clwydian Range, the Gower peninsula and the Wye Valley collectively encompass two percent of Wales.

72 National Nature Reserves (NNR) Smaller areas (from a few acres to large chunks of the Cambrian Mountains) with specific habitats such as lowland bogs, sweeping sand dunes or ancient woodlands. They're widely promoted, usually posted with information boards and threaded with easy, well-signed walking trails.

1000 Sites of Special Scientific Interest (SSSI) Generally small areas singled out for special protection. Most are on private land with no right of access.

Land settlement and usage

During the last interglacial period, Wales was warm enough to support hippos and lions, but humans, pressed for space by the expanding ice sheets, killed them off, leaving bears and boars which in turn were dispatched by human persecution.

After the last ice sheet drew back from Wales around 10,000 years ago, the few plant species which had survived on the ice-free peaks were in a strong position to colonize, producing an open grassland community. Over several thousand years, forests of birch, juniper and hazel became mixed deciduous woodland with oak, elm and some pine, and in wetter areas, damp-loving alder and birch.

Early settlement

The Neolithic tribes began to settle on the upland areas, using their flint axes to clear the mountain slopes of their forests. The discovery of bronze and later iron hastened the process, especially since wood charcoal was required for **smelting** iron ore. And so began the spiralling devastation of Wales' native woodlands. As the domestication of sheep and goats put paid to any natural regeneration of saplings, more land became available for arable farming. Thin, acidic mountain soils and a damp climate made **oats** – fodder for cattle and horses – about the only viable cereal crop, except in Anglesey which, by the time the Romans arrived in the first century AD, was already recognized as Wales' most important **wheat**-growing land.

Meanwhile, some of the last beaver lodges in Britain dammed the Teifi in the twelfth century, while half a millennium later, wolves disappeared from the land.

Cattle droving

Until the sixteenth century, Cistercian monasteries kept extensive lands, cleared woods and developed sheep and cattle farms which subsequently became part of the great estates which still take up large tracts of Wales. By contrast, the less privileged were still smallholders living simple lives. In the 1770s the travel writer Thomas Pennant noted in his *Tours in Wales* that the ordinary people's houses on the Llŷn were "very mean, made with clay, thatched and destitute of chimneys". The poor state of housing had much to do with the right to build (Tŷunnos) on common land with common materials.

TOP 5 WILDLIFE VIEWING SPOTS

Skomer, Skokholm and Grassholm Pembrokeshire. Seabirds. See p.180
Ramsey Island Pembrokeshire. Seabirds and dolphins. See p.189
Bwlch Nant-yr-Arian Rheidol Valley. Red kites. See p.278
Newborough Warren Anglesey. Red squirrels, soay sheep. See p.429
South Stack, Holyhead. Seabirds. See p.432

In the eighteenth century, **droving** reached its peak. Welsh black cattle, fattened on Anglesey or the Cambrian coast, were driven to market in England, avoiding the valley-floor toll roads by taking highland routes that can still be traced. Nights were spent with the cattle corralled in a halfpenny field (so called because this was the nightly rate per animal) next to a lonely homestead heralded by three Scots pines, which operated as an inn. It was a hard journey for men and cattle, but tougher still for the geese, whose webbed feet were toughened for the long walk with tar and sand.

At home, women ground the wheat, aided by mills driven by fast-flowing streams which later provided power for textile mills, especially around Ruthin, Denbigh, Newtown, Llandeilo and along the Teifi Valley. The Cistercians had laid the foundations of the **textile industry** for both wool and flannel, but it had generally remained in the cottages, with nearly every smallholding keeping a spinning wheel next to their harp.

The Industrial Revolution

The next major shift in land use came with a wave of **enclosure acts** from 1760 to 1820, which effectively removed smallholders from upland common pasture and granted the land to holders of already large estates. The people were deprived of their livelihood, and access to open country was denied.

The mountain building processes discussed above have left a broad spectrum of minerals under Wales. **Copper** had been mined since the Bronze Age and the Romans dabbled in **gold** extraction, but mining became big business in the latter half of the eighteenth century with the extraction of **slate** (see box, p.369) in north Wales and **coal** (see box, p.110) in the south.

Forests

Until five thousand years ago, birch, juniper, hazel, oak and elm covered the mountainsides, but devastating forest clearances and a wetter climate have left only a few pockets of native woodland in the valleys. **Pengelli Forest** in Pembrokeshire represents one of Wales' largest blocks of ancient woodland, comprising **midland hawthorn** and **sessile oak**, the dominant tree in ancient Welsh forests. Parts of the Severn and lower Wye valleys are well wooded, as is the Teifi Valley, where oak, ash and sycamore predominate. You can still occasionally see evidence of **coppicing** – an important and ancient practice common a century ago – where trees are cut close to the base to produce numerous shoots harvested later as small-diameter timbers. Under the canopy, **bluebells** and **wood sorrel** are common, and in the autumn look out for the dozens of species of **mushroom**, especially the delicious but elusive **chanterelle**, found mainly under beech trees.

It is a delight to wander in relict stands of the ancient oak woodlands, and along the streams where the **dipper** and **kingfishers** flourish. On sheltered water you might also find shelduck, Canada geese and three species of swan.

A far greater area of Wales is smothered in gloomy forests of planted **conifers** (predominantly sitka spruce) which are too shaded and acidic for wildflowers and are forbidding to most birds. But elusive **pine martens** thrive there, where their diet of small rodents is readily available. Both pine martens and the more common **polecats**

THE ROCKS OF WALES

Geologists puzzled over the forces that shaped the Welsh landscape for centuries before early nineteenth-century geologist **Adam Sedgwick** and his collaborator (and later rival) **Roderick Murchison** began to unravel their secrets. They explained the source of the shattered, contorted and eroded rocks that form the ancient peaks of Snowdonia and gave the rock types names associated with the land where their discoveries took place.

Anglesey, the Llŷn and Pembrokeshire all have older **pre-Cambrian** rocks, while those around St Davids are some of the most ancient in the world.

The **Silurian** (400–440 million years ago) period is named after the ancient south Welsh tribe, the Silures, while the Celtic Ordovices who occupied mid- and north Wales gave their name to the **Ordovician** (440–500 million years ago), and the **Cambrian** (500–600 million years ago) is from the Roman name for Wales.

are found in wild corners throughout Wales. **Foxes** are widespread, along with **brown hares**, **stoats** and **weasels**. **Rabbits** seem to be everywhere, and the North American **grey squirrel** has all but dislodged the native red squirrel from its habitat.

Thanks to its protected status, the elusive **badger** is increasingly common. There have been contentious attempts to have an official cull to combat the spread of TB in cattle, though its likely efficacy is still subject to a scientific investigation.

With Welsh red dragons dying out along with King Arthur, much smaller lizards and two species of snake are all that remain of Wales' reptiles. The venomous, triangular-headed **adder** is sometimes spotted sunning itself on dry south-facing rocks, but, except in early spring when it is roused from hibernation, it frequently slithers away unnoticed. The harmless **grass snake** prefers a wetter environment and is equally shy. Easily mistaken for a snake, the **slowworm** is actually a legless lizard and is common throughout Wales, as are **toads** and **frogs** – though the rare **natterjack toad** is only found in a few locations.

Open moorland and mountains

Much of the Welsh high country is grazed, both by farmed sheep and (in Snowdonia) by **goats** which are descended from domesticated escapees. Generally welcomed by farmers, they forage on the precipitous ledges, thereby discouraging sheep from grazing ventures beyond their capabilities. On the Carneddau in Snowdonia and on the Brecon Beacons you might also see shy herds of feral **ponies**.

Grazing makes forest regeneration impossible as animals munch on fresh seedlings. It looks like only grass survives, but open moorlands are also home to **arctic alpines**, which cling to small pockets of soil among the high crags and gullies of Snowdonia and the Brecon Beacons (their southernmost limit in Britain). Their range hasn't changed since they were discovered by seventeenth-century botanists such as Thomas Johnson and Welshman Edward Lhuyd, who found *Lloydia serotina*, a glacial relic more popularly known as the **Snowdon Lily**, actually a spiderwort that looks not unlike a small off-white tulip. In Britain, it is found only around Snowdon and then only rarely seen between late May and early June, when it blooms.

Cwm Idwal in the Ogwen Valley is a great place to spot some of the more common species, in particular the handsome **purple saxifrage**, whose tightly clustered flowers often push through the late winter snows, later followed by the starry and mossy saxifrages and spongy pink pads of **moss campion**. The star-shaped yellow flowers of **tormentil** are typical of high grassy slopes, and you may also find **mountain avens**, distinguished by its glossy oak-like leaves, and, when it blooms in June, by its eight white petals. From June to October, purple heads of **wild thyme** cover the ground, providing food for a small beetle unique to Snowdonia.

Poor acid soils on the igneous uplands foster the growth of lime-shy bracken, bilberry and purple **heather** which combine with decayed **sphagnum moss** in wetter areas to form peat bogs. These support the **bog asphodel**, which produces its brilliant yellow spikes in late summer, often in company with the **spotted orchid** and less frequently the tiny **bog orchid**. Insectivorous plants such as **butterwort** and **sundew** both gain nutrients that their poor surroundings cannot provide by digesting insects trapped on the sticky hairs of their leaves.

The high country supports **red kites** (see box) and large populations of **kestrels**, usually seen hovering motionless before plummeting onto an unsuspecting mouse or vole. Golden-brown **buzzards** gently wheel on the thermals on the lookout for prey which can be as big as a rabbit. Buzzards and peregrine falcons are as happy picking at carrion, but have to compete with sinister black **ravens** that inhabit the highest ridges and display their crazy acrobatics, often banding together to mob the bigger birds.

Acidic heather uplands provide habitats for **grouse**, whose laboured flight is in complete contrast to the darting zigzag of its neighbour, the **snipe**. On softer grassland, expect to find the **ring ouzel**, a blackbird with a white cravat, and the **golden plover**, a bird still common, but being threatened, like many others, by the spread of conifer forests.

Rivers, estuaries and wetlands

Wales' clean, fast-flowing rivers make ideal conditions for the **brown trout**, a fish managed for sport throughout the country. **Salmon** are less common, found mainly in the Wye (where it is important as game fish) and the Usk. Along with **roach**, **perch** and other coarse fish, the depths of Bala Lake (Llyn Tegid) claim the unique silver-white **gwyniad**, an Ice Age relic not dissimilar to a small herring, said never to take a lure.

Otters almost became extinct in Wales some years back, but a concerted effort on the part of the Otter Haven Project has seen their numbers climbing in the Teifi and some of the rivers in Montgomeryshire, though they are seldom seen.

Wales' rivers spawn estuarine "meadows", which in summer are carpeted with bright violet **sea lavender** and mauve **sea aster**. An unusual coastal feature is the dam-formed string of **Bosherston Lakes**, south of Pembroke, where the fresh water supports rafts of **white-water lilies**. Further west, the Pembrokeshire coast is a blaze of colour in early summer, with white-flowered **scurvy grass** and **sea campion**, yellow **kidney vetch** and **celandine**, and blue **spring squill**. Bluebells and **red campion** cloak Pembrokeshire's islands, while the majority of species mentioned can be found in abundance in Newborough on Anglesey.

The mud flats and saltings of Wales' estuaries provide rich pickings for wintering waders. The **Dee estuary**, on the northern border with England, plays host to Europe's largest concentration of **pintail** as well as **oystercatchers**, **knot**, **dunlin**, **redshank** and many others. Numerous terns replace them in the summer months. Commercially viable beds of **cockles** still exist on the north coast of the Gower and families still own rights to musselling the sands of the Conwy estuary.

RED KITE RECOVERY

Like many other raptors, fork-tailed **red kites** were traditionally persecuted by gamekeepers and suffered from the use of pesticides, which caused thinning of eggshells. Before the banning of DDT in the 1960s Welsh red kite numbers were down to a handful of breeding pairs, mostly in the Elan Valley. But with careful management numbers have been on the increase for years and there are now over 600 breeding pairs. Their once narrow range has expanded as far south as Pembrokeshire, and they are now even seen far across the border into parts of England.

Though best observed in their natural environment hunting or simply wheeling on thermals, for a real spectacle, head to one of the **feeding sites**: Bwlch Nant yr Arian, near Aberystwyth (see p.278); Llandeusant Red Kite Feeding Station, in the Brecon Beacons (⦿redkitewales .co.uk); or Gigrin Farm, near Rhayader (see p.234).

The coast

The long Welsh coast is thick with **sea birds**, thanks partly to the profusion of islands and its position on the main north–south migratory route. The islands off the Pembrokeshire coast are incomparable for sea-bird colonies, the granite pinnacle of **Grassholm**, eight miles offshore, hosting the world's third-largest Atlantic gannet colony with 39,000 pairs. Nearby, **Skokholm** and **Skomer** between them support 3500 pairs of **storm petrels** and an internationally significant population of 150,000 pairs of the mainly nocturnal **Manx shearwater**, which spend their winter off the coast of South America. Burrows vacated by rabbits on the islands also provide nests for puffins, while **razorbills**, **guillemots** and **kittiwakes** nest on the cliffs. Since the eradication of the rats that previously deterred burrow-nesting birds, Manx shearwaters are also now colonizing nearby **Ramsey Island**. In the north, make for **Ynys Enlli** (Bardsey Island) off the Llŷn coast, and the wonderful **South Stack Cliffs** on Anglesey which, especially from May to July, are alive with breeding guillemots, razorbills and puffins.

In the water, dolphins can often be seen: the coast of mid-Wales is notable for **bottlenose dolphins**. The same territory has recently also seen occasional visits by **leatherback turtles**, particularly in late summer. Perhaps global warming is attracting new species to Wales just as it threatens others.

Ecology and the future

With smokestack industries now largely absent from Wales, and the Valleys mostly devoid of working coal mines, nature is struggling to claw its way back. A verdure inconceivable forty years ago now cloaks the hillsides, and already the industrial remains are being cherished as cultural heritage; as much a valid part of the "natural" landscape as the mountain backdrops. If you need convincing, climb up to the disused slate workings behind Blaenau Ffestiniog or walk the old ironworks tramways around Blaenafon.

In other areas, much remains to be done to restore the ecological balance. The increasing commercialization of farming has led not just to the damaging application of pesticides and excessive use of nitrogen-rich fertilizers, but to the wholesale removal of **hedgerows** and **dry-stone walls**, ideal habitats for numerous species of flora and fauna. Conservation groups promote the skills needed to lay hedges and build dry-stone walls, but for every success, another chunk of farmland is paved over with a new bypass, or a meadow is turned over to **conifers** which are clear-felled every thirty years or so.

The largest forest owner, the Forestry Commission, is keen to shake off its monoculture image and is bordering its forests with a mix of broad-leaved trees and conifers of different ages. As an extended public relations exercise it also welcomes mountain bikers in some forests.

Far from being areas where nature is allowed to take its course, the **national parks** can be their own worst enemies, attracting thousands of people a day. Some attempt is being made to control the effects of tourism through path management and the promotion of public transport, but this is more than outweighed by the increasingly aggressive promotion of these regions.

Paradoxically, and for all the wrong reasons, **military zones** – Mynydd Eppynt and most of the Castlemartin peninsula, for example – have become wildlife havens away from the worst effects of human intervention.

Environmental groups are also keeping a weather eye on offshore **oil** and **gas** exploration off the west Wales coast, while in south Wales, there has been considerable resistance to developments in Milford Haven where, since 2009, huge liquefied natural gas-carrying ships from Qatar have been offloading their cargo and feeding it into Britain's gas network.

One success in recent years has been the decision not to press ahead with the **Usk Barrage**, which was planned to create a freshwater lake on the outskirts of Newport by damming the estuary, forcing otters and other protected species to abandon the river.

Music in Wales

Dylan Thomas' observation that "We are a musical nation" is as relevant as ever. Despite the near-obliteration of the mining industry, male voice choirs (see box, p.119) remain a feature of Welsh life, with many choirs opening their practice sessions to the public. But Welsh music extends far beyond the dwindling chapels, into the country's village halls, clubs, festival sites and pubs. In quieter venues, harp players repay their musical debt to ancestors who accompanied the ancient bards (traditional poets and storytellers), while modern folk music draws directly from the broader Celtic musical tradition.

Welsh-language rock musicians have traded commercial success for unabashed nationalism, spanning styles from punk to hip-hop. Some bands sing in both English and Welsh, and there is a fast-growing scene in English-language Welsh rock, building on the success of outfits like the Manic Street Preachers. These days, Wales continues to punch above its weight, churning out a huge amount of good music for a country its size.

Folk

The Welsh *gwerin* has a much wider meaning than its English counterpart "folk". At a Welsh *gŵyl werin* (folk festival), you're as likely to encounter the local rock band as the local dance team – with the entire community turning out, too.

Welsh folk song has always remained close to the heart of popular culture, conveying political messages and social protest. After centuries of political and religious suppression, traditional Welsh music and dance have fought back from near-extinction. Unlike their Celtic cousins in Ireland, Scotland and Brittany, many folk musicians in Wales have learnt their tunes from books and manuscripts rather than from older generations of players.

As you travel around, scan posters for the word *twmpath* – the equivalent of a barn dance or ceilidh, and used when Welsh dances are the theme of the night. Calling (dance instructions) could be in Welsh or English, depending on where you are in the country. *A Noson Lawen*, literally "a happy night", usually offers a harpist, perhaps some dancers and a repertoire of Welsh standards.

History

The bardic and **eisteddfod** traditions have played a key role in Welsh culture. Often the **bard**, who held an elevated position in Welsh society, was the non-performing composer, employing a harpist and a *datgeiniad*, whose role was to declaim the bard's words. The first eisteddfod appears to have been held in Cardigan in 1176, with contests between bards and poets and between harpers, pipers and *crwth*-players (see p.460). Henry Vlll's **Act of Union** in 1536 was designed to anglicize the country by stamping out Welsh culture and language, and the eisteddfod tradition degenerated over the next two centuries.

In the eighteenth and nineteenth centuries, the rise of **Nonconformist religion**, with its abhorrence of music, merry-making and dancing, further hammered for Welsh traditions. **Edward Jones**, *Bardd y Brenin* (Bard to the King), observed sorrowfully in the 1780s that Wales, which used to be one of the happiest of countries, "has now become one of the dullest". Folk music only gained some sort of respectability when London-based Welsh people, swept along in a romantic enthusiasm for all things Celtic, revived it at the end of the eighteenth century.

GIGS AND FESTIVALS

VENUES

Listed approximately from south to north Wales.

Newport Folk Club Newport Fugitives Athletic Club, High Cross Rd, Rogerstone, Gwent (☎01633 897923; ⓦnewportfolkclub.co.uk). Sessions Thurs at 8.45pm plus occasional gigs.

Llantrisant Folk Club The Windsor Hotel, Pontyclun (☎01443 226892). International guest list mixed with local sessions centred on Welsh tunes. Wed at 8.30pm.

Castle Folk Club Castle Hotel, Jewel St, Barry. All are welcome to perform. Tues at 8.30pm.

Royal Oak Fishguard. Informal session; Tues.

Pontardawe Acoustic Club Pontardawe Inn, 123 Herbert St, Pontardawe (☎01792 865171). Mainstay of the Welsh folk scene, good for anything from very traditional stuff to modern folk-rock. Wed, plus live music Fri and Sat.

Halfpenny Folk Club The Greyhound, Llanrhidian, Gower (☎01792 850803). Designer clientele rub shoulders with the chunky jumper brigade. Sun.

Gwerin Aber Y Cŵps (Coopers Arms), Llanbadarn Rd, Aberystwyth. Folk session, all instrumentalists welcome. Tues.

Llangollen Folk Club Sun Inn, Regent St, Llangollen. Cheerful session and open mic. Wed 8.30pm.

Conwy Folk Club Royal British Legion, Rosehill St, Conwy (ⓦconwyfolkclub.org.uk). Mon 8pm.

The Nelson Beach Rd, Bangor. Irish sessions Fri 9pm.

FESTIVALS

Listed in chronological order.

Cwlwm Celtaidd Porthcawl, near Bridgend ⓦcwlwmceltaidd.com. Fantastic, increasingly high-profile Celtic festival of pan-Celtic music and partying over a long weekend in early March.

Cadi Ha Holywell. Small traditional dance event. First weekend in May.

Tredegar House Festival Newport, Gwent ⓦtredegarhousefestival.org.uk. A laidback and enjoyable long-weekend at the country house, good for session players and dancers. Mid-May.

Fishguard Folk Festival Pembrokeshire ⓦpembrokeshire-folk-music.co.uk. Small, traditional event with a good spread of international performers and plenty of busking. Late May.

Gower Folk Festival Parkmill, Gower peninsula ⓦgowerfolkfestival.co.uk. Varied line-up in beautiful surroundings. Mid-June.

Gŵyl Ifan Cardiff ⓦwww.gwylifan.org. Wales' biggest and most spectacular folk dance festival, with hundreds of dancers giving displays in Cardiff city centre, the Bay and St Fagans National History Museum. Mid- to late June.

Small Nations Festival near Llandovery ⓦsmallnations.co.uk. Lovely, small camping event on a farm, with global beats from Africa to home. Early July.

Sesiwn Fawr ("Big Session") Dolgellau ⓦsesiwnfawr .co. This once-huge rock-fest returns to its Celtic roots with gigs over a week. Mid-July.

Pontardawe International Festival Pontardawe ⓦwww.pontardawefestival.com. One of Britain's flagship folk events, with an ambitious line-up of international performers heading for the Swansea Valleys town each year. Mid-August.

Green Man Festival Near Crickhowell ⓦgreenman .net. Fantastic mid-sized three-day music festival in the Brecon Beacons – folk, new folk, Americana etc. Mid-August.

FOLK MUSIC RESOURCES

Cob Records ⓦcobrecords.com. Extensive mail-order business.

Cwmni Fflach ⓦfflach.co.uk. Great label, with indie, rock, pop, folk and choral releases.

Cymdeithas Genedlaethol Ddawns Werin Cymru (Welsh National Folk Dance Society; ⓦdawnsio .com/en). A useful source of events information with access to heaps of CDs, DVDs and dance pamphlets.

Sain ⓦsainwales.com. The major Welsh recording company.

St Fagans: National History Museum Near Cardiff. A vibrant museum and a vital centre for research and collecting work.

Taplas ⓦtaplas.co.uk. English-language bimonthly magazine of the folk scene in Wales; a great source for current events, with back editions archived on its website.

Tŷ Siamas Dolgellau ⓦtysiamas.com. The National Centre for Welsh Folk Music.

WEBSITES

ⓦfolkwales.org.uk

ⓦtony-franks.co.uk/northwalesfolk.htm

ⓦwww.welshgigs.com

In the heartland of the Welsh language around mid- and northwest Wales, folk music can be heard in many of the same **venues** that stage rock events. The language is considered more important than musical categories, and the folk club concept is alien to Welsh-speakers, who never saw the need to segregate music that was a natural part of their cultural life. Folk clubs are found in the anglicized areas and only a few of them feature Welsh music.

The harp

Historically the most important instrument in the folk repertoire, the **harp** has been played in Wales since at least the eleventh century, although no instruments survive from the period before the 1700s. The only surviving ancient music is the manuscript of **Robert ap Huw**, written about 1614 in a strange tablature that has intrigued music scholars: five scales were used, but no one has yet defined satisfactorily how they should sound.

The simple early harps were superseded in the seventeenth century by the rich-sounding **triple harp**, with its complicated arrangement of two parallel rows of strings sounding the same note, with a row of accidentals between them. The nineteenth-century swing towards classical concert music saw the invasion of the large **chromatic pedal harps** that dominate today, but the triple, always regarded as the traditional Welsh harp, was kept alive by gypsy musicians who preferred to play something portable. One Welsh harp performance that's well worth catching is the **Cerdd Dant**, where the harpist leads with one tune, accompanying soloists and groups take a counter-tune, and they all end up together on the final note. Wales even has a royal harpist, a position reinstated in 2000 after almost a century and currently held by Hannah Stone from Swansea.

In recent years craftsmen have re-created the *crwth* (a stringed instrument which may have been either plucked or bowed), the *pibgorn* (a reed instrument with a cow's horn for a bell) and the *pibacwd* (a primitive Welsh bagpipe), championed by masters such as Ceri Rhys Matthews.

Folk musicians

The country's foremost triple harpist, **Robin Huw Bowen**, has revived interest in the instrument with appearances throughout Europe and North America, and also makes unpublished manuscripts of Welsh dance music widely available through his own publishing company. The lineage of North Wales triple harpist **Llio Rhydderch** stretches back centuries. For a more contemporary take on the instrument, poet/musician **Twm Morys** blends modern Welsh and Breton influences. One of Wales' most well-known harpists is **Elinor Bennett**, who has accompanied some of Wales' biggest rock acts.

The father of Welsh folk, politician/songwriter **Dafydd Iwan**, remains as hugely popular and prolific as ever with charismatic performances and powerful albums such as 2007's *Man Gwyn* (featuring songs about the early Welsh emigration to Patagonia and North America). Songwriter **Meic Stevens** (often referred to as the "Welsh Bob Dylan") straddles folk and acoustic rock: if you get the chance to see him live, grab it. Singer/harpist **Siân James**, from mid-Wales, has found fame for her spine-tingling voice and exquisite tunes. Other female pacesetters include the Cardiff-born veteran singer **Heather Jones**, and the soulful **Julie Murphy**, born in Essex but now a fluent Welsh-speaker and part of Welsh cultural ambassadors, **Fernhill**.

One to watch is the young, high-energy **Mabon**, a seven-piece line-up of folk talent led by Celtic accordionist Jamie Smith. Likewise, **Elin and the Tribalites** and **Calan** feature a mix of Welsh and Irish traditions with a contemporary edge. Both are playing high-profile festivals and garnering attention nationwide.

English-language Welsh pop

The historic lack of international pop artists to emerge from Wales – long blamed on the music-industry dominance of London-based labels and media – has changed

EISTEDDFOD

The National Eisteddfod Society was formed in the 1860s, and today, three major week-long competitive events are held every year: the **Llangollen International Eisteddfod** (ⓦwww .international-eisteddfod.co.uk) in July; the **National Eisteddfod** (ⓦwww.eisteddfod.org.uk) in the first week of August; and the Urdd Eisteddfod (ⓦurdd.org), Europe's largest youth festival, at the end of May. The National and the Urdd alternate between north and south Wales.

The competitions' rules have meant that eisteddfodau have helped formalize Welsh culture. Such parameter-defining is naturally alien to the free evolution of traditional song and music, but eisteddfodau have played a major role in keeping traditional music, song and dance at the heart of national expression.

utterly in the last couple of decades, at least for English-language groups. It started with the Manic Street Preachers in the early 1990s, who spawned an unprecedented interest in contemporary Welsh rock. London A&R reps descended on Cardiff and Newport in search of the next big thing, accelerating the careers of bands like the Super Furry Animals, Catatonia and the Stereophonics. Their widespread success has meant bands from Wales no longer feel hampered by their provenance, and there is a wealth of fine new talent coming through.

The early years

The most enduring name in English-language Welsh pop is 1960s sex symbol **Tom Jones**, now in his seventies and still pulling crowds around the world. Similarly, Cardiff-born singer **Shirley Bassey** has carved out a hugely successful career since the mid-1950s, particularly with the immortal theme song to the 1964 James Bond film *Goldfinger*, and, in 1972, *Diamonds Are Forever*. In 2007, aged 70, Bassey played to a rapturous Glastonbury crowd, while she still guests on TV shows and performs occasionally.

Cardiff musician-turned-record-producer **Dave Edmunds**, whose first band Love Sculpture scored a UK hit in 1968, has had his hands on many a hit record since then – both as a producer and a solo performer – during the 1970s and 1980s. Classically trained pianist **John Cale** went to America in 1963 and found fame alongside Lou Reed with the **Velvet Underground**, one of the most influential avant-garde rock bands of the 1960s. He has since recorded solo (including collaborative projects with other Welsh artistes).

In the 1980s, Welsh rock music was personified by Rhyl's rabble-rousing rock fundamentalists **The Alarm**, fronted by Mike Peters. Swansea's husky-toned rocker **Bonnie Tyler** (cousin by marriage to actress Catherine Zeta Jones) achieved huge commercial success from the late 1970s onwards, and still tours. Possibly the most surprising Welsh success story of the 1980s was Fifties rock'n'roll impersonator **Shakin' Stevens**, who had a string of massive, nostalgia-driven hits.

The Welsh renaissance

It all changed in the 1990s. South Wales rock nihilists the **Manic Street Preachers** became the most successful Welsh band ever. After the 1995 disappearance, and presumed suicide, of fractured, anorexic guitarist Richey James Edwards, they returned as a three-piece, displacing their bedsit rock/punk for the anthemic album, *Everything Must Go* (1996), their most successful album to date. Their follow-up album, *This Is My Truth, Tell Me Yours* (1998), continued their progress to megastardom, and included their first UK number one single, *If You Tolerate This, Then Your Children Will Be Next*. After several patchy records, the Manics made a triumphant return to form in 2009 with the blistering *Journal for Plague Lovers*, the album featuring lyrics left to the band by Edwards. This was followed a year later by the fine *Postcards from a Young Man*.

The now legendary Welsh bands compilation album, *Dial M for Merthyr* (1995), showcased the Manics alongside many who subsequently became huge, all united by a tendency towards clever, zeitgeist lyrics and Welsh loquaciousness. Most exciting among them are the **Super Furry Animals**, whose fusion of Seventies psychedelia with new millennium clubland quirkiness and techno-geekery has created a niche all of their own. Their nine albums to date range from poignant ballads to thumping raw rock, proving them to be masters of many genres and true innovators. They record in Welsh and English, and their all-Welsh language album, *Mwng* (2000), became the best-selling work ever in Welsh, reaching number eleven in the UK album charts. Frontman Gruff Rhys also performs solo; his most recent release, *Hotel Shampoo* (2011), is a typically off-kilter affair.

In a similar vein, indie-psych band **Gorky's Zygotic Mynci** were responsible for a handful of marvellously quirky records, such as the folksy *Barafundle* (1997) and the gorgeous *The Blue Trees* (2000), before splitting in 2006.

A more mainstream sound came from the likes of the now-defunct **Catatonia**, whose strongly Welsh-accented frontwoman, **Cerys Matthews**, was responsible for some wonderful lyrics; the most memorable of these feature on their best-selling album, *International Velvet* (1998), whose title track contains the chorus "every day, when I wake up, I thank the Lord I'm Welsh" – still something of an unofficial national anthem.

More lyrical dexterity, combined with clean-cut guitar chords, are the hallmarks of Valleys band **Stereophonics**, whose distinctive sound is shaped around singer Kelly Jones' rasping voice. Although not as identifiably Welsh as these acts, mega-group **Feeder** offer a diverse style that encompasses haunting tunes of aching melancholy right through to bombastic rock blow-outs.

The new millennium

While the likes of the Manics and the SFA continue to produce exciting records, there has been a new generation of bands whose influence has come more from the thrashier elements of post-millennial American rock. South Wales has been a particularly fertile breeding ground for this angst-ridden wall of noise, producing some of the genre's most celebrated protagonists: Swansea/Bridgend rockers **Funeral for a Friend** (aka FFAF), their Bridgend counterparts **Bullet for My Valentine** and Rhondda nu-metal screamers **The Lostprophets** whose album *The Betrayed* (2010) is the pick of their releases to date.

Back in the mainstream, the major Welsh success story has been **Duffy** (Aimee Anne Duffy), whose big, soulful voice has seen her storm the charts at home and abroad. Her debut album *Rockferry* (2008) featured the single, *Mercy*, which went straight to number one, making Duffy the first Welsh female to achieve a number one pop single in a quarter of a century, and the first-ever female from the Llŷn peninsula to top the UK music singles charts. Newer bands making waves on the indie-rock and pop front include the ebullient Cardiff collective **Los Campesinos!**, the powerful, guitar-heavy **The Joy Formidable**, and the poppier **Marina and the Diamonds**, who are fronted by the Abergavenny-born singer Marina Diamandis.

There's a thriving **dance music** scene, too, in all its fragmented glory. Tongue-in-cheek Newport rappers **Goldie Lookin' Chain** had a mammoth following for a while. Rural west Wales is the base for dub gurus **Zion Train**, doing spliffed-up remakes of classic new wave tracks. Big beatz'n'breaks come from Cardiff's **Phantom Beats**. **Vandal** is a local hero in the dance music realm, as is James Hannam who operates as **Culprit One**.

ESSENTIAL LISTENING

Catatonia *Way Beyond Blue*
Gorky's Zygotic Mynci *The Blue Trees*
Los Campesinos! *Romance is Boring*
Manic Street Preachers *The Holy Bible* and *Journal for Plague Lovers*
Super Furry Animals *Rings around the World*

Welsh-language rock

While English-language Welsh bands have usually enjoyed success by making their nationality an irrelevance, Welsh-language bands have highlighted their strong national identity, fostering a unique, self-propagating Welsh-language rock scene. Boundaries are now increasingly blurred: many bands choose to sing in both Welsh and English, simply because it's the way most of their members use both languages. Indeed, established English-language artists like the Super Furry Animals' frontman **Gruff Rhys** has raised the profile of Welsh-language music to new heights. But this is only a recent phenomenon and remains largely outside the mainstream.

The roots of this thriving, youthful and innovative scene owe much to the punk explosion of 1976 which kicked over many of rock's statues, partly thanks to the anarchic fervour of London bands like The Clash and the Sex Pistols, but also by virtue of its strong DIY ethic. The home-grown Welsh-language pop scene consolidated when in 1983 Caernarfon punk band **Anhrefn** (Disorder) set up **Recordiau Anhrefn**, churning out what it called "dodgy compilations of up-and-coming left-field weirdo Welsh bands". Throughout the 1980s, any band that couldn't get some sort of record deal would simply press their own vinyl and sell their records at gigs. From this era, perhaps the most enduring legacy is the band **Datblygu**, most often described as a Welsh version of spectacularly misanthropic The Fall. Meanwhile North Walians **Llwybr Llaethog** (Milky Way) were ploughing their anti-establishment furrow.

Such DIY efforts were boosted by Radio One DJ **John Peel** – to many, the standard-bearer for underground pop in the UK. Peel became aware of the growing number of Welsh-language bands and began playing their records on air and inviting them in for sessions. This introduced Welsh music to a Europe-wide audience and proved an important catalyst to new Welsh bands. By the 1990s, Welsh-language pop music had established a solid infrastructure of bands, labels and venues that continues to this day. One of the most prolific, eclectic and innovative of these labels is **Ankstmusik**, releasing Welsh-language pop of varied styles, best seen in some wonderful compilation albums, including *S4C Makes Me Want To Smoke Crack*, which contained tracks by Catatonia and professional Welsh weirdos **Rheinallt H. Rowlands** and **Ectogram**. On the same label, former Tystion rapper Gruff Meredith has metamorphosed to great acclaim into **MC Mabon**.

Other major promoters of Welsh-language pop are the Caernarfon-based **Crai Records**, a subsidiary of the more folk-oriented **Sain Records** and the **Fflach** label in Aberteifi (Cardigan), and their subsidiary **Rasp** for dancier artistes and projects.

The grassroots Welsh **gig circuit** is also healthy, with a lively local pub and club scene. University student unions also regularly put on Welsh bands. Welsh-language pop bands can also be found at the **National Eisteddfod**, and at local bars and clubs.

Film

Wales' wonderful scenery has formed the backdrop to many a film – from low-budget local efforts to *Lawrence of Arabia* and even Bollywood blockbusters. But few of the big films have Welsh themes. Those that do have tended to be at the budget end of the spectrum, often playing on a slightly whimsical view of Wales. The star power of Welsh actors from Richard Burton through to Catherine Zeta Jones, Christian Bale, Rhys Ifans, Ioan Gruffudd and Matthew Rhys hasn't really helped the domestic industry. However, in 2006, the Film Agency for Wales was established with a charter "to ensure that the economic, cultural and educational aspects of film are effectively represented in Wales, the UK and the world".

This commitment to a viable and sustainable Welsh film industry, combined with the output of talent from the International Film School Wales in Caerleon (such as Cannes- and BAFTA-winning writer/director Asif Kapadia), and star-powered films like 2008's *The Edge of Love* may help establish something with legs.

Meanwhile, Wales' biggest current splash on screen – albeit the smaller one – is the revamp of *Doctor Who* and its spin-off *Torchwood*, made to startling effect by BBC Wales and featuring many prominent local landmarks, particularly around Cardiff, Barry and Pontypridd (for a list of locations, visit ⦿www.doctorwholocations.net).

Location seekers should also check out ⦿www.moviemapnorthwales.co.uk and ⦿www.traveltrade.visitwales.com/en/content/cms/itineraries/fact-files/film-tv-locations.

The Edge of Love (2008). Jealously threads this fairly limp exploration of the relationships between Dylan Thomas (Matthew Rhys), his wife (Sienna Miller) and his childhood sweetheart (Keira Knightley). Partly filmed in Thomas's old haunts on the Cambrian coast around New Quay.

The Englishman Who Went Up a Hill and Came Down a Mountain (1995). Bumbling yarn full of cod Welsh stereotypes and Hugh Grant as a similarly one-dimensional Englishman; filmed around Llanrhaeadr-ym-Mochnant and near Cardiff.

First Knight (1995). Sean Connery stars as King Arthur, with Richard Gere as Sir Lancelot, in this patchy action film filmed largely in Snowdonia.

Happy Now (2001). Distinctly oddball thriller, filmed in and around Barmouth, which becomes the mysterious Welsh seaside town Pen-y-Wig.

Hedd Wyn (1993). First Oscar-nominated Welsh-language film, about the north Wales poet who went off to fight in World War I and never returned.

House of America (1997). Dark and depressing tale of secrets and yearning in one family stuck on a mouldering farm in west Wales.

How Green was my Valley (1941). None of it was filmed in Wales, but this Oscar-winning version of the classic Welsh book came to define the world image of Wales for generations.

Human Traffic (1999). Feelgood E-culture film, with a star cameo by Welsh drug-trafficking guru Howard Marks. Filmed in Cardiff.

Inn of the Sixth Happiness (1958). Snowdonia puts in a fine performance as northern China in this Ingrid Bergman-led classic tale of self-discovery.

King Arthur (2004). Big-screen epic, with huge battles and a rather less sensational account of the "real" king of the Britons than had gone before. Ioan Gruffudd shines as Sir Lancelot.

Kyun! Ho Gaya Na Pyaar (2004). Translating as "It has happened – love", this is a big-budget Bollywood production, with former Miss World, Aishwarya Rai, as the love interest. Large sections were filmed in mid-Wales and Snowdonia.

On the Black Hill (1987). Hauntingly beautiful adaptation of the downbeat Bruce Chatwin novel about twin brothers growing up in the Black Mountains.

Patagonia (2011). Romantic road movie starring Matthew Rhys with parallel stories following both a Cardiff couple visiting Welsh Patagonia and two Patagonians travelling through Wales. Not entirely successful, but sumptuously shot and includes an odd cameo by Duffy.

The Prisoner (1971). Big-screen version of the enigmatic cult TV series, also filmed largely at the fantasy village of Portmeirion.

Sleep Furiously (2008). This tender documentary tells about the slow decline of Trefuerig, the tiny Ceredigion farming village where director, Gideon Koppel, grew up after his parents sought refuge from Nazi Germany there.

Solomon a Gaenor (1998). Filmed in both Welsh and English versions, this Oscar-nominated weepie is a *Romeo and Juliet* tale set in the *Valleys in Edwardian times*.

Submarine (2011). Richard Ayoade's quirky, funny and warm-hearted coming-of-age drama is set in 1980s Swansea. Wonderfully offbeat.

Twin Town (1997). Entertaining drug-fuelled romp set in Swansea that introduced Rhys Ifans to the world.

Under Milk Wood (1972). Phantasmagoric take on the classic Dylan Thomas "play for voices", with an all-star cast including Richard Burton and Elizabeth Taylor. Filmed partly in Fishguard.

Very Annie Mary (2001). Offbeat tale of love and singing in the Valleys, with Ioan Gruffudd and Matthew Rhys camping it up to the nines as the only gays in the village.

Books

Some of the books listed here are published by small local presses, and you're unlikely to find them in bookshops outside Wales, though most can be ordered online. The Welsh Books Council website (ⓦwww.gwales.com) sells a huge selection, and you'll often be able to pick up rare and out-of-print titles by scouring the many independent or secondhand bookshops in Wales – Hay-on-Wye is particularly good for the latter.

For information on readings and literary events throughout the year, check out Literature Wales (ⓦliteraturewales.org). Welsh fiction is undergoing something of a renaissance; look out for works by the current leading crop of Welsh wordsmiths, spanning a wide range of styles and subject matters. Ones to watch include English-language writers such as Trezza Azzopardi, Kitti Harri, Rachel Tresize and Dannie Abse, and Welsh-language authors including Tony Bianchi, Gwyn Jenkins, Ceri Wyn Jones and Alan Llwyd.

TRAVEL AND IMPRESSIONS

★ **George Borrow** *Wild Wales*. Highly entertaining and easy-to-read account of the author's walking tour of Wales in 1854.

Giraldus Cambrensis (Gerald of Wales) *The Journey Through Wales* and *The Description of Wales*. Learned ruminations and unreserved opinions form the basis of two witty and frank books in one volume, written in Latin by the quarter-Welsh clergyman after his 1188 tour around Wales recruiting for the Third Crusade. *The Journey* "through our rough, remote and inaccessible countryside" contains anecdotes and ecclesiastical point-scoring, while *The Description* covers rural life.

★ **Gwynfor Evans** *Eternal Wales* (published as *Cymru o Hud* in Welsh). With magnificently moody photography by Marian Delyth, this is a passionate and erudite tour de force through some of Wales' lesser-known corners.

★ **Peter Finch** *Real Cardiff, Real Cardiff Two* and *Real Cardiff Three*. Compelling ambles around the Welsh capital, full of oddball nuggets and with a terrific sense of context and place.

Jeremy Moore and Nigel Jenkins *Wales, The Lie of the Land*. A gorgeous, glossy tome that combines the luscious photography of Jeremy Moore and the musings of poet Nigel Jenkins. Spirited, passionate and a fine souvenir of contemporary Wales.

★ **Jan Morris** *Wales: Epic Views of a Small Country*. Prolific half-Welsh travel writer Jan Morris immerses herself in the country that she evidently loves. Highly partisan and fiercely nationalistic, the book combs over the origins of the Welsh character and describes the people and places of Wales with precision and affection.

H.V. Morton *In Search of Wales*. Learned, lively and typically enthusiastic snapshots of Welsh life in the early 1930s. A companion volume to his *In Search of England*.

★ **Mike Parker** *Neighbours from Hell?* English émigré and original co-author of this Rough Guide, Mike holds few punches as he rips into English attitudes to Wales, the Welsh and all things Cymric. A hugely entertaining romp (rant?) through history, politics, the nature of Welsh tourism, sex and the royal family.

Pamela Petro *Travels in an Old Tongue*. An American woman comes to Wales to study, is bewitched by the place, attempts to learn Welsh and then sets off on a global pursuit of Welsh enclaves and speakers from Japan to Norway, Germany and Patagonia. Funny, informative and extremely perceptive about the language and its wider cultural significance.

Peter Sager *Wales*. A passionate and fabulously detailed 400-page celebratory essay on Wales, and especially its people, by a German convert to the cause of all things Welsh.

Meic Stephens *A Most Peculiar People: Quotations About Wales and the Welsh*. Varied volume of quotations going back to the century before Christ and up to 2000. As a portrait of the nation, with all of its frustrating idiosyncrasies and endearing foibles, it is a superb example.

HISTORY, SOCIETY, ART AND CULTURE

Jane Aaron et al (ed) *Our Sisters' Land: The Changing Identities of Women in Wales*. A series of challenging and well-written essays that delve deep into male-dominated Welsh society, from the home to the political system. Includes personal testimonies and some startling facts about just how entrenched bigotry still is within much of the Welsh establishment.

Richard Booth *My Kingdom of Books*. Typically bullish autobiography by the man who made Hay-on-Wye the world's biggest secondhand bookshop. Some interesting stuff on his tussles with authority and his semi-serious declaration of Hay as an independent country.

Janet Davies *The Welsh Language*. Very readable history and assessment of one of Europe's oldest living languages. Packed full of maps showing the demographic and geographic spread of Welsh over the ages.

★ **John Davies** *A History of Wales*. Exhaustive run through Welsh history and culture from the earliest inhabitants to the 21st century. This is clearly written and very readable, but, at 700 pages, it's hardly concise.

Gwynfor Evans *Land of My Fathers* and *For the Sake of Wales*. Plaid Cymru's late elder statesman first produced the former tome in Welsh, translating it into English for publication forty years ago. It's a thorough and polemical history of the country. The latter work, his autobiography, covers Welsh political and social life from the World War II to the National Assembly. Hugely readable and inspirational.

Geoffrey of Monmouth *History of the Kings of Britain*. First published in 1136, this is the basis of almost all Arthurian legend. Writers throughout Europe and beyond used Geoffrey's unreliable history as the basis of a complex corpus of myth.

Alan Llwyd *Cymru Ddu/Black Wales: a History*. A long and insightful look at the history of multi-racial Wales in both Welsh and English.

Peter Lord *The Visual Culture of Wales*. Lavishly produced and beautifully illustrated three-volume overview of the art and architecture of Wales, from the early industrial society to the present day.

Elizabeth Mavor *The Ladies of Llangollen*. The best of the books on Wales' most celebrated lesbian couple traces the ladies' inauspicious beginnings in Ireland, their spectacular elopement and the way that their Llangollen home, Plas Newydd, became a place of pilgrimage for dozens of influential eighteenth-century visitors.

John Meirion Morris *The Celtic Vision*. Masterful examination by the superb Welsh sculptor of La Tène Celtic art and its religious meaning.

Trefor M. Owen *The Customs and Traditions of Wales*. Pocket guide to everything from outdoor prayer meetings to the curious Mari Lwyd, when men dress as grey mares and snap at all the young girls.

Patrick Thomas *Candle in the Darkness: Celtic Spirituality from Wales*. Tales from the "Age of Saints" in Wales, with particular focus given to the numerous Celtic saints who originated here.

LITERATURE

Enid Blyton *Five Get Into a Fix*. In this, the seventeenth of Blyton's timeless series of kids' adventure novels, Julian, Dick, Anne, George and Timmy the dog unearth secret passageways to rescue an old woman from a sinister tower in the snowy Welsh mountains. Vintage "Famous Five".

Bruce Chatwin *On the Black Hill*. This entertaining and finely wrought novel follows the Jones twins' eighty-year tenure of a farm on the mid-Wales border with England. Chatwin casts his sharp eye for detail over both the minutiae of nature and the universal human condition, providing a gentle angle on Welsh–English antipathy.

★ **Alexander Cordell** *The Fire People*. Set against the backdrop of the Merthyr Tydfil riots of 1831, this is a feisty fictionalization of the life and unjust death of Dic Penderen, the "first Welsh Martyr of the working class". The same author's *Rape of the Fair Country*, *Hosts of Rebecca* and *Song of the Earth* form a dramatic historical trilogy in the bestseller tradition, partly set in the cottages on the site of the Blaenafon ironworks during the lead-up to the Chartist Riots. *This Sweet and Bitter Earth* immortalizes Blaenau Ffestiniog in a lusty slate epic.

Lewis Davies *Work, Sex and Rugby*. Perennially popular novel that tells you all you need to know (and much you don't) about Valleys men.

Richard John Evans *Entertainment*. Scabrous roller-coaster ride through Rhondda living and loving, guaranteed to offend and cause maximum hilarity.

Thomas Firbank *I Bought a Mountain*. One of the few popular books set in north Wales in which Anglo-Canadian Firbank spins an autobiographical yarn of his purchase of most of the Glyder range and subsequent life as a Snowdonian sheep farmer during the 1930s.

Iris Gower *Copper Kingdom; Proud Mary; Spinners' Wharf; Black Gold; Fiddler's Ferry; The Oyster Catchers* – the list goes on. Romantic novels by Wales' most popular author, who died in 2010.

★ **Niall Griffiths** *Grits; Sheepshagger; Kelly + Victor; Stump; Wreckage; Runt*. Arguably the best dissector of darkness, drugs, comradeship and hopelessness in modern Britain, Griffiths' panoply of novels set between Aberystwyth and Liverpool are suffused with a metaphysical sense of culture and landscape.

Emyr Humphreys *The Gift of a Daughter*. The mood and landscape of Anglesey is beautifully evoked by perhaps the greatest living Welsh novelist.

Siân James *Not Singing Exactly*. Dazzling and diverse short-story collection from one of Wales' premier romantic novelists.

Glyn Jones *The Island of Apples*. Set in south Wales and Carmarthen in the early years of the twentieth century, this is an artful portrayal of a sensitive Valleys youth's enthralment in the glamour of the district's new arrival.

Gwyn and Thomas Jones (trans) *The Mabinogion*. Welsh mythology's classic, these eleven orally developed heroic tales were finally transcribed into the *Book of Rhydderch* (around 1300–25) and the *Red Book of Hergest* (1375–1425). Originally translated by Lady Charlotte Guest between 1838 and 1849 at the beginning of the Celtic revival.

Lewis Jones *Cwmardy*. Longtime favourite socialist novel, written in 1937 and portraying life in a Rhondda Valley mining community in the early years of the twentieth century. Followed by its sequel, *We Live*.

Richard Llewellyn *How Green Was My Valley; Up into the Singing Mountain; Down Where the Moon is Small; Green, Green My Valley Now*. Vital tetralogy in eloquent and passionate prose, following the life of Huw Morgan from his youth in a south Wales mining valley through emigration to the Welsh community in Patagonia and back to 1970s Wales. A bestseller during World War II and still the best introduction to the vast canon of "valleys novels", *How Green Was My Valley* captured a longing for a simple, if tough, life, steering clear of cloying sentimentality.

★ **Caradoc Pritchard** *One Moonlit Night*. Dense, swirling tale of a young boy's emotional and sexual awakenings in an isolated north Wales village. Full-blooded Welsh prose at its most charged.

Malcolm Pryce *Aberystwyth Mon Amour*. Surprise bestseller in the shape of this furious, funny black comedy set in an Aberystwyth overlaid with film-noir surrealism

TOP 5 WELSH READS

Jan Morris *Wales: Epic Views of a Small Country*
Mike Parker *Neighbours from Hell?*
Niall Griffiths *Grits*
Caradoc Pritchard *One Moonlit Night*
R.S. Thomas *Selected Poems*

and dastardly twists of plot. Follow-ups *Last Tango in Aberystwyth*, *The Unbearable Lightness of Being in Aberystwyth* and *Don't Cry for me Aberystwyth* are just as entertaining.

Kate Roberts *The Living Sleep* and *Feet in Chains*, among others. Penned by one of the bestselling contemporary Welsh-language writers, these two novels, available in English translation, tell the tales of life in a north Wales slate village.

Ruth Janette Ruck *Hill Farm Story* and *Along Came a Llama*. Evocative stories about a farming area around Beddgelert.

★ **Dylan Thomas** *Collected Stories*. All of Thomas' classic prose pieces: *Quite Early One Morning*, which metamorphosed into *Under Milk Wood*, the magical *A Child's Christmas in Wales* and the compulsive, crackling autobiography of *Portrait of the Artist as a Young Dog*. In all of Thomas' works, the language still burns bright.

★ **Dylan Thomas** *Under Milk Wood*. Thomas' most popular play tells the story of a microcosmic Welsh seaside town (modelled on New Quay) over a 24-hour period. Ideally, obtain a recorded version of the play to absorb its rich poetry (or, as Thomas himself described it, "prose with blood pressure").

Alice Thomas Ellis (ed) *Wales – An Anthology*. A beautiful book, combining poetry, folklore and prose stories rooted in places throughout Wales. All subjects, from rugby and mountain climbing to contemporary descriptions of major events, are included in an enjoyably eclectic mixture of styles. Excellent introduction to Welsh writing.

★ **Charlotte Williams** *Sugar and Slate*. Humorous and unstintingly honest memoir of mixed identity: the author is the daughter of a black Guyanese father who grew up in a Welsh-speaking community.

John Williams *The Cardiff Trilogy*. Omnibus of Williams' contemporary low-life Cardiff crime writing containing: *Five Pubs, Two Bars And A Nightclub*, a very funny short-story collection what inspired the E-culture hit film *Human Traffic*; *Cardiff Dead*, a full-length novel that packs in the Welsh cultural references effortlessly and to great effect; and *Temperance Town*, a novella in the same vein.

Raymond Williams *Border Country*. 1960 novel that perfectly captures the sense of change overwhelming rural Welsh life in that era. A timeless classic.

POETRY

Dannie Abse *Welsh Retrospective* and *Arcadia, One Mile.* Two superb collections from one of Wales' most prolific modern poets, showing his huge range of intellectual interests and warm, beguiling style of writing.

John Barnie *The City* and *The Confirmation.* One of Wales' best contemporary writers, notable mainly for his combination of poetry and prose styles, narration and description. Evocative tales of wartime childhood and stifling parenting, leading to a poignant search for love.

Gillian Clarke *Collected Poems.* A good introduction to the nature-inspired and homely poetry of one of Wales' leading contemporary writers and the current National Poet.

Dafydd Johnston *Iolo Goch: poems.* All of the surviving poems of Owain Glyndŵr's court bard are shown in translation and context. A fascinating insight into courtly medieval Wales at a time of great national resurgence.

Gwyneth Lewis *Keeping Mum.* Wales' first-ever National Poet shows her verbal power and dexterity with this 2003 collection, especially when combing over the irregularities of bilingual existence.

Robert Minhinnick *Selected Poems.* Overview of the early career of one of Wales' finest poets: best when picking over his English-speaking south Walian youth in rich, impassioned imagery.

Meic Stephens (ed) *New Companion to the Literature of Wales.* A customarily thorough volume of Welsh prose, spanning the centuries from the folk tales of *The Mabinogion* to modern-day writings.

Dylan Thomas *Collected Poems.* Though Thomas is renowned for his dense and difficult poems, look out for lighter poems which resound with perfect metre and precise structure. Classics include *Do Not Go Gentle Into That Good Night*, a passionate yet calm elegy to his dying father.

★ **R.S. Thomas** *Selected Poems.* Thomas wrote poetry that tugs at issues such as God (he was an Anglican priest), Wales ("brittle with relics") and the family. His passion shines throughout this book, probably the best overview of his prolific work.

★ **Harri Webb** (ed. Meic Stephens) *Collected Poems.* Fine collection of 350 works by a modern-day patriot and poet of biting satire and eloquent expression.

WILDLIFE AND THE ENVIRONMENT

Douglas Botting *Wild Britain: A Traveller's Guide.* Not much use for species identification but plenty of information on access to the best sites and what to expect when you get there. Excellent photos.

Collins Field Guides Series of thorough, pocket-sized identification guides. Topics include insects, butterflies, wildflowers, mushrooms and toadstools, birds, mammals, reptiles and fossils.

★ **William Condry and Jeremy Moore** *Heart of the Country.* Jeremy Moore's gorgeous photography is the perfect accompaniment to the late William Condry's Country Diary entries from *The Guardian.*

David Saunders *Where to Watch Birds in Wales.* Enthusiasts' guide to Wales' prime birding locations, along with a bird-spotting calendar and a list of English–Welsh–scientific bird names. Not an identification guide.

OUTDOOR PURSUITS

Cicerone Guides *The Ridges of Snowdonia; Hill Walking in Snowdonia; Ascent of Snowdon; Welsh Winter Climbs; Scrambles in Snowdonia* and others, various authors. Clearly written pocket guides to the best aspects of Welsh mountain activities.

Ordnance Survey National Trail Guides Large, paperback editions full of instructive descriptions and additional side-walks from *Offa's Dyke North, Offa's Dyke*

South, Glyndŵr's Way and *Pembrokeshire Coast Path.*

★ **Carl Rodgers** *Mountain and Hill Walking in Snowdonia.* Superb pocket hikers' guide in two volumes, the first covering Snowdon and its environs, the second detailing southern Snowdonia. Beautifully produced with great photos, detailed colour maps, info on the best parking spots and even some of the easier scrambles.

Welsh

The Welsh language, *Cymraeg*, is spoken widely throughout the country and as a first language in many parts of the west and north. Its survival and resurgence is remarkable considering that the heart of English culture and its language – the most expansionist the world has ever seen – lies right next door.

Brief history

The Welsh language can be traced back to the sixth century. Celtic inscriptions on stones, a section of written Welsh in the eighth-century **Lichfield Gospels**, the tenth-century codified laws of Hywel Dda in neat Welsh prose, and the twelfth- and thirteenth-century **Mabinogion** folk tales (believed to have been collated from earlier Welsh writings) show that Welsh was a thriving language for centuries. Moreover, the early language is still identifiable and easily comprehensible for any modern-day Welsh-speaker.

English domination since the Norman era has been mirrored in the fate of the Welsh tongue. The Norman lords were implanted in castles throughout Wales to subjugate the natives, with official business conducted in their native French.

Real linguistic warfare came with the 1536 **Act of Union** (see box, p.442) which legitimized the growing practice of imposing English lords and churchmen on the restless, but effectively cowed, Welsh. It is likely that the language would have died out, but William Morgan's 1588 **translation of the Bible** into Welsh brought Welsh into the everyday public arena, ultimately ensuring its survival. Certainly, new and Nonconformist religious movements from the seventeenth century onwards embraced the language.

In the first half of the nineteenth century, over ninety percent of the country's population spoke Welsh, with English dominant in pockets of Pembrokeshire and along the English border. But as the **Industrial Revolution** progressed, mine owners and

---

THE FALL AND RISE OF CYMRAEG

According to the first British census of 1851, 90 percent of Welsh people spoke Welsh. Every decade thereafter the figures dipped quite spectacularly – 49.9 percent in 1901, 37.1 percent in 1921, 28.9 percent in 1951 and 18.9 percent in 1981. Then, in 1991 and again in 2001, the percentage of Welsh-speakers rose slightly. The proportion still hovered around the one-fifth mark but the most marked increase was among the lower age groups, those most able to ensure its future.

From the sharp decline of the mid-twentieth century, it's a dramatic turnabout and testament to bold policies, particularly in education and mass media. National TV and radio stations broadcast in Welsh, road signs are written in both Welsh and English, official publications, many tourist brochures and even restaurant menus are bilingual, Welsh-medium schools are everywhere, books in Welsh are published at a growing rate of around four hundred every year, and magazines, newspapers and websites in the old language are mushrooming.

WHERE WELSH IS SPOKEN

Over a fifth of the population speak Welsh, but the spread is far from even with a far lower percentage of speakers in the populous and anglicized regions of Gwent and around Cardiff. Although it is unusual to hear Welsh regularly in the border counties, it is commonly understood throughout most of West Glamorgan, Carmarthenshire, the northern half of Pembrokeshire and around Cardigan Bay. The northwestern corner, centred on Snowdonia, Anglesey and the Llŷn, is the real stronghold of Welsh, reflected in these areas' steadfast political affiliation to Welsh nationalism.

capitalists from England came into the rapidly urbanizing southeastern corner of Wales, substantially diluting the language.

In 1854, **George Borrow** undertook his marathon tour of Wales and noted the state of the native tongue throughout. As a natural linguist, he had mastered Welsh and fired questions at people he encountered as to their proficiency in both Welsh and English. The picture he paints is of poorer people tending to be monolingual Welsh-speakers, wealthier people and those near the border bilingual.

Discouragement of Welsh continued in many guises, most notably in it being forbidden in schools in the latter half of the nineteenth and early twentieth centuries. Anyone caught speaking in Welsh had to wear a "**Welsh Not**", a piece of wood on a leather strap that would only be passed on if someone else was heard using the language. At the end of the school day, the child still wearing the Welsh Not was soundly beaten. It is hardly surprising that use of the language plummeted.

The politics of the language

Welsh has survived thanks to those who campaigned to save it, principally the eisteddfod revivalists of the eighteenth century and the political movements of the twentieth century. The formation of **Plaid Cymru**, the Welsh National Party, in 1925 was largely around the issue of language, as indeed its politics have been ever since.

Concerns about the language reached a zenith with the 1962 radio broadcast *Tynged yr iaith* (The Fate of the Language) by the Plaid founder member, Saunders Lewis. This became a rallying cry that resulted in the formation of *Cymdeithas yr Iaith Gymraeg*, the **Welsh Language Society**, the following year. One of the most high-profile early campaigns was the daubing of monoglot English road signs with their Welsh translations. Nearly all signs are now in both languages. A 1967 Welsh Language Act allowed many forms of officialdom to be conducted in either language, stating that Welsh, for the first time in over 400 years, had "equal validity" with English.

Welsh-medium education also blossomed, with bilingual teaching in all primary schools and for at least a year in all secondary schools. In traditionally Welsh-speaking areas students got five years of Welsh, and since 2000 all Welsh schools much teach Welsh up to age 16. Increasing numbers of schools all over the land educate their students in all subjects through the Welsh language. Early objections from some non-Welsh-speaking parents that their children were being "forced" to learn a "dead" language have now largely abated. Welsh-language university courses are also becoming more popular, so, for pretty much the first time in Wales' history, it is possible to be educated in Welsh from nursery to degree level.

The other modern cornerstone for developing Welsh has been **broadcast media**. The BBC Welsh-language Radio Cymru began in the late 1970s, to be joined – after a considerable battle – by the S4C TV station in 1982. Together, they have sponsored and programmed popular Welsh learners' programmes and given the old language greater space than it has ever enjoyed before.

The situation today

Welsh-language classes are now offered right across the country, as well as outside the country in language centres across Britain, and universities in Europe and North America.

The Welsh language is both one of Wales' key strengths and its key drawbacks in the quest for some sort of national emancipation. There is still suspicion towards the Welsh-speaking "elite" who are seen to control the media and local government in the country. Welsh nationalism is so defined by the language that Plaid Cymru has nearly always had great difficulty in appealing to those who speak only English, particularly in the urban southeast. Nonetheless, the Welsh language continues to flourish. The **Welsh Language Board** was formed in 1994, and with the arrival of the **National Assembly** in 1999, with around half of its members proficient in Welsh, the language has gained a number of firm footholds in official life. In 2010 the Welsh Assembly unanimously passed the **Welsh Language Measure**, which puts Welsh on equal footing with English, though some contend it still doesn't make Welsh an official language in all cases. Still, its other provisions should ensure that Welsh continues to flourish. Increasingly, Wales is developing as a model bilingual entity, in which there is room for both languages to thrive together.

Speaking Welsh

Although Welsh words, place names in particular, can appear bewilderingly incomprehensible, the rules of the language are far more strictly adhered to than in English. Thus, mastering the basic constructions and breaking words down into their constituent parts means that pronunciation need not be anywhere near as difficult as first imagined.

The Welsh alphabet

The Welsh **alphabet** is similar to the English, though there are no letters j, k, v, x and z in Welsh, except in occasional words appropriated from other languages. As well as the five English vowels, Welsh has y and w. Most vowels have two sounds, long and short: a is long as in c**a**r, short as in f**a**t; e long as in th**e**re, short as in p**e**t; i long as in s**e**a, short as an t**i**n; o long as in m**o**re, short as in d**o**g; u roughly like a Welsh i; w long as in s**oo**n, short as in l**oo**k; y long as in s**e**a and short as in b**u**n or p**i**n. A circumflex over any vowel lengthens its sound. **Adjoining vowels** are pronounced as the two separate sounds, with the stress generally on the first.

Welsh **consonants** are pronounced in similar ways to English, except c and g are always hard as in **c**at and **g**ut (never soft as in ni**c**e or ra**g**e), and f is always pronounced as v as in **v**ine. Additional consonants are ch, pronounced as in German or as in lo**ch**, dd, pronounced as a hard th as in **th**ose, ff and ph as a soft f as in **f**ive, and si as in **sh**oe. The Welsh consonant that causes most problems is ll, featured in many place names such as L**l**ango**ll**en. This has no direct parallel in English, although the tl sound in Bent**l**ey comes close. The proper way to pronounce it is to place the tongue firmly behind the top row of teeth and breathe through it without consciously making a voiced sound.

Some Welsh words also **mutate**, where a word affects the beginning of a following one,

---

RESOURCES FOR WELSH LEARNERS

Acen ☎ 029 2030 0800, ⓦ www.acen.co.uk. Cardiff-based, S4C-originated company providing a multimedia Welsh course, a Welsh-learners' magazine and copious numbers of useful contacts.

Cymdeithas Madog (Welsh Studies Institute in North America) ⓦ www.madog.org. Runs an annual week-long residential language course somewhere in the US or Canada, plus a directory of resources.

Cymdeithas yr Iaith (Welsh Language Society) ☎ 01970 624501, ⓦ www.cymdeithas.org.

Campaigning and political organization dedicated to improving the status of the Welsh language.

Nant Gwrtheyrn ☎ 01758 750334, ⓦ www.nantgwrtheyrn.org. Residential national language centre on the coast of the Llŷn (see p.388).

National Language Unit of Wales ☎ 029 2026 5000, ⓦ www.wjec.co.uk/nlu. Provides a comprehensive guide to Welsh teaching provision.

Welsh Language Board/Bwrdd yr Iaith Gymraeg ☎ 029 2087 8000, ⓦ www.byig-wlb.org.uk.

principally to ease pronunciation. Prepositions commonly mutate the following word, turning an initial B into F or M, an initial C into G or Ngh, a D into Dd or N, F into B or M, G into Ngh or the initial letter being dropped altogether, Ll into L, M into F, P into B, Mh or Ph, T into Th, D or Nh. Thus, "in Cardiff (Caerdydd)" is "y**ng Ngh**aerdydd" (note that the "yn" also mutates to ease pronunciation) and "from Bangor" is "o **F**angor". Mutated words are extremely common in the component parts of place names.

WELSH VOCABULARY

mouth of a river; confluence of two rivers	Aber	**Welsh**	Cymraeg
		Welshness	Cymreictod
river	Afon	**Wales**	Cymru
Scotland	Alban	**the Welsh people**	Cymry
museum	Amgeuddfa	**good**	Da
son of	Ap (ab)	**south**	De
open	Ar Agor	**Saint David**	Dewi Sant
closed	Ar Gau	**no (as an instruction), nothing**	Dim
for sale	Ar Werth		
slow	Araf	**fort**	Din or dinas
small, lesser	Bach	**thank you**	Diolch
bread	Bara	**end**	Diwedd
good morning	Bore da	**over**	Dros
morning	Bore	**black**	Du
slope of a hill	Bron	**water**	Dŵr
hill	Bryn	**day**	Dydd
mountain pass	Bwlch	**vale**	Dyffryn
table	Bwrdd	**man (men)**	Dyn (-ion)
bus	Bws	**church**	Eglwys
stronghold, chair	Cadair	**festival**	Eisteddfod
fort	Caer	**ridge**	Esgair
song	Cân	**small, lesser**	Fach
centre	Canol	**big, greater**	Fawr
hundred	Cant	**farm**	Fferm
chapel	Capel	**road**	Ffordd
stone	Carreg	**forest**	Fforest
home	Cartref	**garden**	Gardd
castle	Castell	**blue**	Glas
national	Cenedlaethol	**valley**	Glyn
meadow	Clun	**hotel**	Gwesty
gate, perch	Clwyd	**white**	Gwyn
red	Coch	**temporary summer-house**	Hafod
forest, woodland	Coed	**half**	Hanner
rock	Craig	**today**	Heddiw
artificial island on a lake	Crannog	**police**	Heddlu
		old	Hen
craft	Crefft	**road**	Heol
welcome	Croeso	**longing, yearning**	Hiraeth
rood screen	Croglen	**spirit**	Hwyl
literally "curved stone", generally used to refer to megalithic burial chambers	Cromlech	**lower**	Isaf
		language	Iaith
		sacred enclosure, early church	Llan
valley	Cwm	**lodging place, B&B**	Llety
public	Cyhoeddus	**England**	Lloegr
society	Cymdeithas	**path**	Llwybr

book	Llyfr	**The Party of Wales**	Plaid Cymru
lake	Llyn	**hall, mansion**	Plas
place, court	Llys	**bridge**	Pont
stone	Maen	**port, gateway**	Porth
field	Maes	**hill**	Rhiw
market	Marchnad	**English language**	Saesneg
big, greater	Mawr	**Englishman**	Sais
mill	Melin	**saint**	Sant
woman	Menyw	**Parliament**	Senedd
burial place of saint	Merthyr	**hello**	Shwmae
mile	Milltir	**shop**	Siop
bare or rounded mountain	Moel	**county, shire**	Sir
sea	Môr	**street**	Stryd
coastal marsh	Morfa	**how are you?**	Sut ydych chi? (formal)
mountain	Mynydd		or Sut ywt ti? (informal)
valley, stream	Nant	**office**	Swyddfa
hall	Neuadd	**post office**	Swyddfa'r Post
new	Newydd	**pub**	Tafarn
to swim	Nofio	**beach**	Traeth
good night	Nos da	**town**	Tref
good evening	Noswaith dda	**tower**	Twr
please	Os gwelwch chi'n dda	**house**	Tŷ
good afternoon	P'nhawn da	**uppermost, highest**	Uchaf
vale	Pant	**the**	Y, Yr or 'r
park	Parc	**island**	Ynys
football	Pêl-droed	**hospital**	Ysbyty
head, top (as of a valley)	Pen	**school**	Ysgol
village	Pentre(f)		

WELSH NUMBERS

1	un	20	dau-ddeg
2	dau (fem. dwy)	21	dau-ddeg-un
3	tri (fem. tair)	22	dau-ddeg-dau
4	pedwar (fem. pedair)	30	tri-deg
5	pump	40	pedwar-deg
6	chwech	50	pum-deg
7	saith	60	chwe-deg
8	wyth	70	saith-deg
9	naw	80	wyth-deg
10	deg	90	naw-deg
11	un-deg-un	100	cant
12	un-deg-dau	200	dau gant
13	un-deg-tri	1000	mil

Small print and index

A ROUGH GUIDE TO ROUGH GUIDES

Published in 1982, the first Rough Guide – to Greece – was a student scheme that became a publishing phenomenon. Mark Ellingham, a recent graduate in English from Bristol University, had been travelling in Greece the previous summer and couldn't find the right guidebook. With a small group of friends he wrote his own guide, combining a highly contemporary, journalistic style with a thoroughly practical approach to travellers' needs.

The immediate success of the book spawned a series that rapidly covered dozens of destinations. And, in addition to impecunious backpackers, Rough Guides soon acquired a much broader readership that relished the guides' wit and inquisitiveness as much as their enthusiastic, critical approach and value-for-money ethos.

These days, Rough Guides include recommendations from budget to luxury and cover more than 200 destinations around the globe, as well as producing an ever-growing range of eBooks and apps.

Visit **roughguides.com** to see our latest publications.

Rough Guide credits

Editor: Tim Locke
Layout: Pradeep Thapliyal
Cartography: Rajesh Chhibber and Ed Wright
Picture editor: Chloë Roberts
Proofreader: Jan McCann
Managing editor: Alice Park
Assistant editor: Jalpreen Kaur Chhatwal
Production: Rebecca Short
Cover design: Nicole Newman, Pradeep Thapliyal
Photographers: Diana Jarvis and Scott Stickland
Editorial assistant: Eleanor Aldridge

Senior pre-press designer: Dan May
Design director: Scott Stickland
Travel publisher: Joanna Kirby
Digital travel publisher: Peter Buckley
Reference director: Andrew Lockett
Operations coordinator: Becky Doyle
Operations assistant: Johanna Wurm
Publishing director (Travel): Clare Currie
Commercial manager: Gino Magnotta
Managing director: John Duhigg

Publishing information

This seventh edition published March 2012 by
Rough Guides Ltd,
80 Strand, London WC2R 0RL
11, Community Centre, Panchsheel Park,
New Delhi 110017, India
Distributed by the Penguin Group
Penguin Books Ltd,
80 Strand, London WC2R 0RL
Penguin Group (USA)
375 Hudson Street, NY 10014, USA
Penguin Group (Australia)
250 Camberwell Road, Camberwell,
Victoria 3124, Australia
Penguin Group (NZ)
67 Apollo Drive, Mairangi Bay, Auckland 1310,
New Zealand
Rough Guides is represented in Canada by Tourmaline
Editions Inc. 662 King Street West, Suite 304, Toronto,
Ontario M5V 1M7
Printed in Singapore
© Catherine Le Nevez, Mike Parker and Paul Whitfield 2012

Maps © Rough Guides
No part of this book may be reproduced in any form
without permission from the publisher except for the
quotation of brief passages in reviews.
488pp includes index
A catalogue record for this book is available from the
British Library
ISBN: 978-1-40538-981-5
The publishers and authors have done their best to
ensure the accuracy and currency of all the information
in **The Rough Guide to Wales**, however, they can accept
no responsibility for any loss, injury, or inconvenience
sustained by any traveller as a result of information or
advice contained in the guide.
3 5 7 9 8 6 4 2

MIX
Paper from
responsible sources
FSC FSC™ C018179
www.fsc.org

Help us update

We've gone to a lot of effort to ensure that the seventh
edition of **The Rough Guide to Wales** is accurate
and up-to-date. However, things change – places get
"discovered", opening hours are notoriously fickle,
restaurants and rooms raise prices or lower standards. If
you feel we've got it wrong or left something out, we'd like
to know, and if you can remember the address, the price,
the hours, the phone number, so much the better.

Please send your comments with the subject line
"**Rough Guide Wales Update**" to ✉ mail@uk.roughguides
.com. We'll credit all contributions and send a copy of the
next edition (or any other Rough Guide if you prefer) for
the very best emails.

Find more travel information, connect with fellow
travellers and book your trip on ⊛ roughguides.com

ABOUT THE AUTHORS

Paul Whitfield spent childhood holidays secreting plastic toys in the sands of Welsh coastal resorts. In his twenties, he devoted numerous weekends to exploring Snowdonia. Now resident in New Zealand, he still makes frequent return trips to Wales in between other Rough Guide assignments.

Catherine Le Nevez has authored or contributed to well over a dozen guidebooks, after completing her Doctorate of Creative Arts in Writing, Masters of Professional Writing and postgrad qualifications in Editing and Publishing. Wales' Celtic spirit (and its close ties to her Breton heritage), its biblio-paradise of Hay-on-Wye, and its surf continue to lure her back.

Mike Parker became hypnotized by Wales at the age of 12. He has written books on four UK cities; gay guides to Scotland, Ireland and northern England; and a history of the relationship between England and Wales. He lives in the Dulas Valley, writing and presenting TV travelogues.

Acknowledgements

Paul Whitfield: A big *Diolch yn fawr* goes out to all the great people of Wales who provided insights into their land, guided me to good places to eat and generally proved uplifting during long days on the road. Thanks too to the wonderful tourism professionals throughout the land, especially Ceri Jones and Bob Hackett at Visit Wales, who helped make my job so much easier. Cheers to Jim Krawiecki for showing me the Ynys Môn coast from the seat of a kayak, Mike Parker for his always insightful and entertaining conversation (and a fine roast), and Tim and Norm, my co-authors on this edition, who threw themselves so enthusiastically into the project. At Rough Guides, thanks to Tim Locke for fine editing and understanding when deadlines were tight, and to Rajesh and Katie for the great new maps. And lastly, a huge thank you to Marion for holding the fort and putting up with my long absences.

Tim Burford: Thanks above all to Freddie and Robbie in Haverfordwest, and to Ceri Jones and Jane Harris at Visit Wales, Susan Owen at Carmarthenshire Tourism, George and Linda at Glangwili Mansion, Sarah and Tom at Trefloyne, Mike and Jill at the Drovers Inn, Llandovery, and Sylvia at the New White Lion, Llandovery. Also to Katy, Norm, Paul, Tim Locke, Alice Park and all at Rough Guides.

Norm Longley: Thanks to Tim Locke for his diligent and enthusiastic editing, and for guiding us superbly throughout. Very special thanks to Ceri Jones and Jane Harris at Visit Wales for their invaluable assistance, and thanks to my colleagues, Paul and Tim, for their support on this book. Finally, to Christian, Luka, Patrick and Anna.

Readers' letters

Thanks to all the readers who have taken the time to write in with comments and suggestions (and apologies if we've inadvertently omitted or misspelt anyone's name):

Dr Stephen Brigley; Neville Featherstone; Brodie Hayward; Toeja Gerson Lohman; Malcolm Pittman; Antosh Wislocki

Photo credits

All photos © Rough Guides except the following:
(Key: t-top; b-bottom; c-centre; l-left; r-right)

Index

Maps are marked in grey

W

Y

Map symbols

The symbols below are used on maps throughout the book

)(	Bridge	🌸	Country park	⛺	Campsite
⊠	Gate	∴	Ruins	✈	Airport
	Cliff	⅏	Archeological site	★	Bus stop
▲	Mountain peak	♦	Place of interest	P	Parking
⌂	Cave	⊠	Post office	⌂	Abbey
	Waterfall	@	Internet access		Church (regional maps)
	Marshland	ⓘ	Tourist office	⬭	Stadium
	Viewpoint	♟	Museum		Building
	Wind farm	🏛	Monument		Church/cathedral (town maps)
	Lighthouse		Golf course	▭	Park/forest
♜	Castle		Swimming pool	▭	Beach
🏛	Stately home	⊂	Arch	▭	Cemetery
	Gardens	⤳	Pass		

Listings key

- ■ Accommodation
- ● Restaurants, cafés and pubs
- ■ Nightlife & entertainment

MAKE THE MOST OF YOUR CITY BREAK

NEW YORK CITY HONG KONG & MACAU BERLIN MARRAKESH ROME

FREE PULL OUT MAP WITH EVERY SIGHT AND LISTING FROM THE GUIDE

ESSENTIAL ITINERARIES AND RELIABLE RECOMMENDATIONS